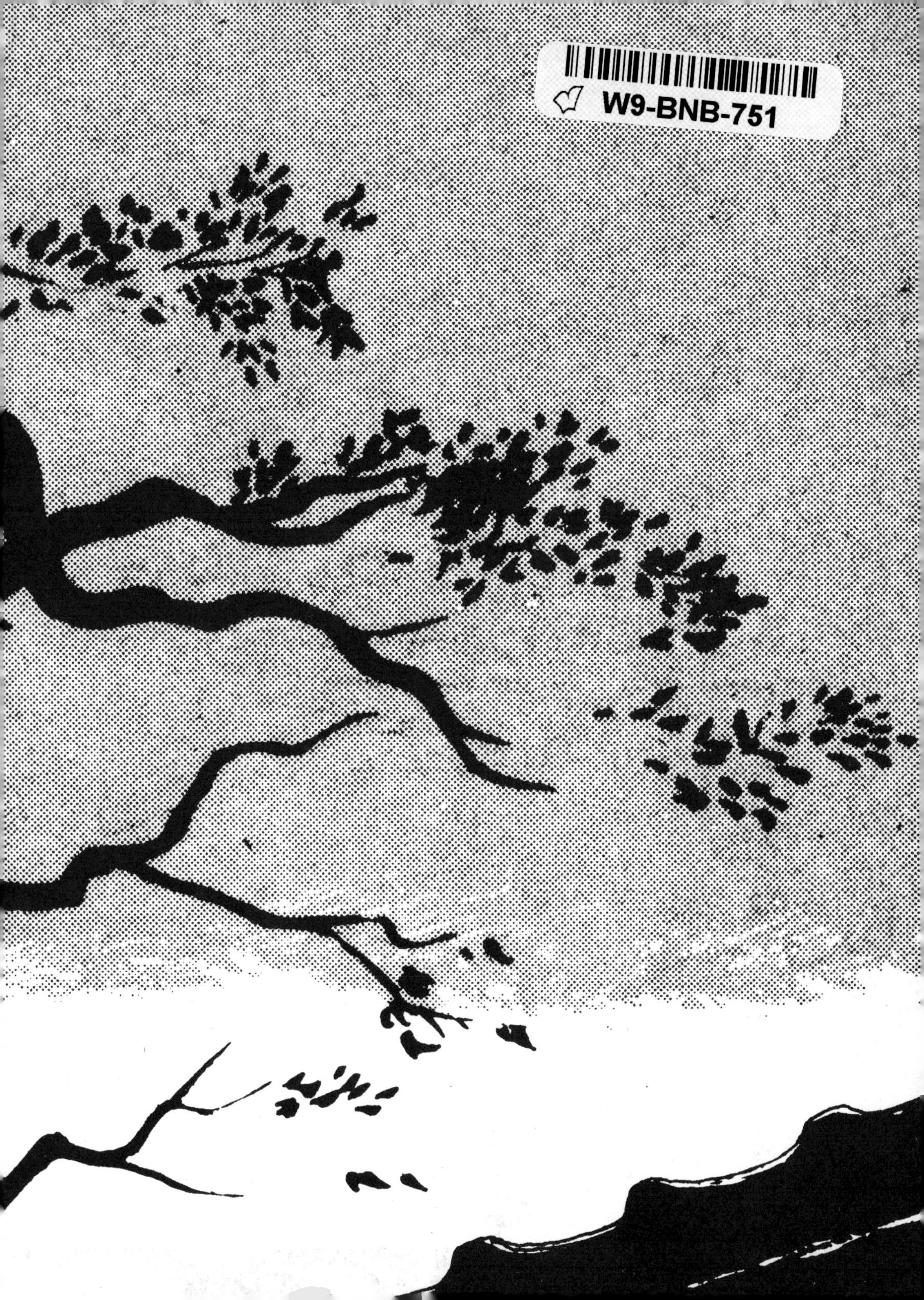

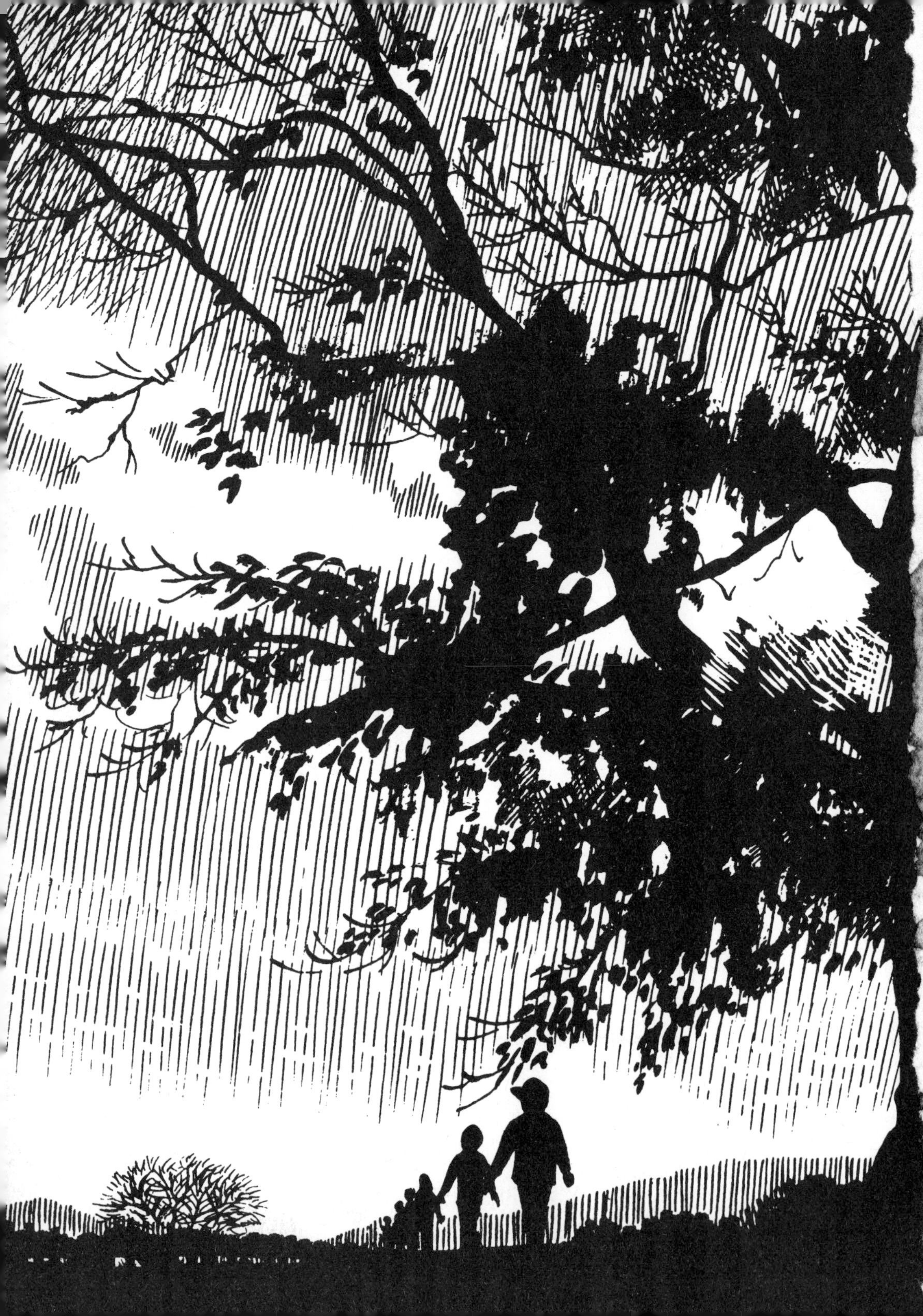

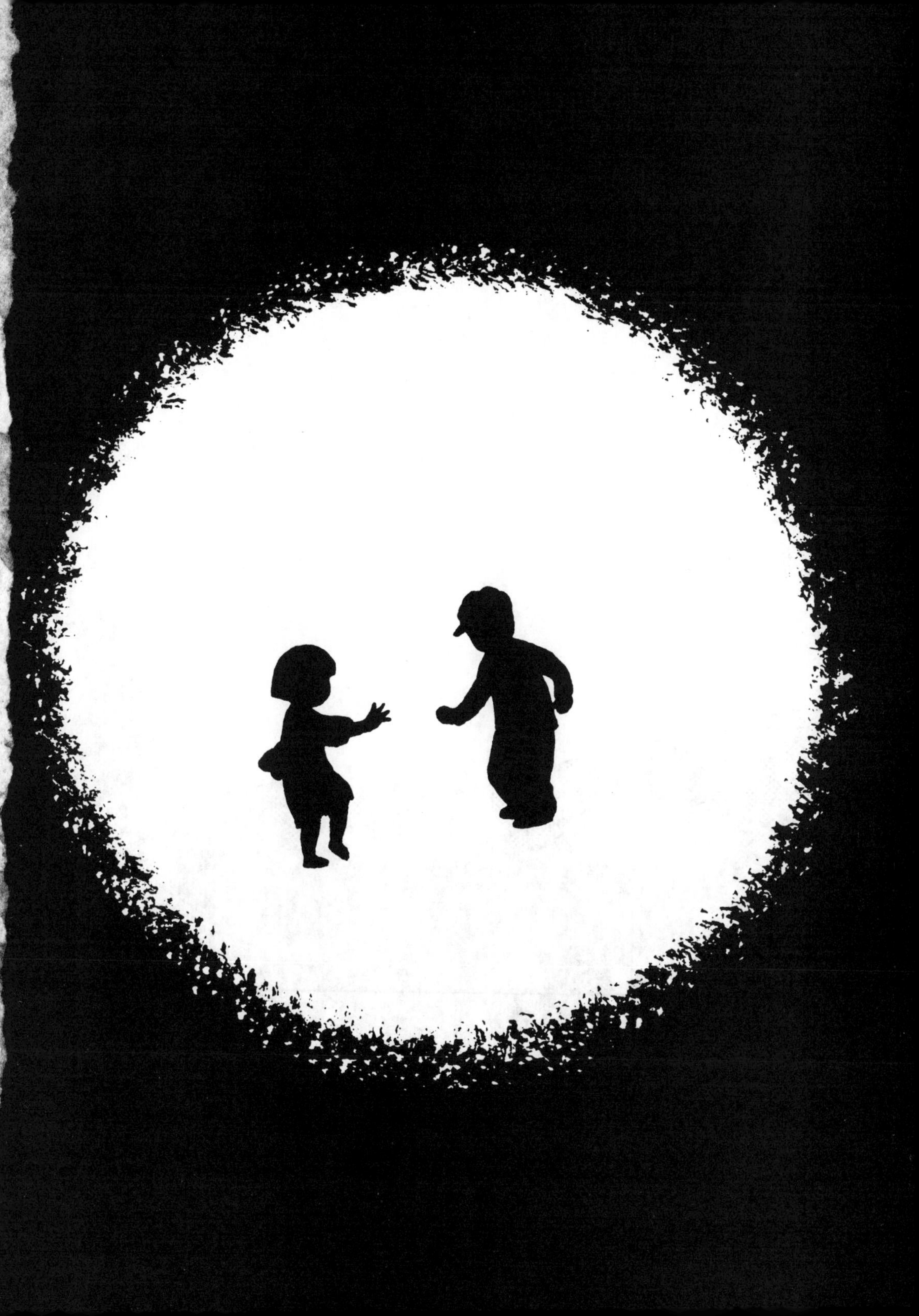

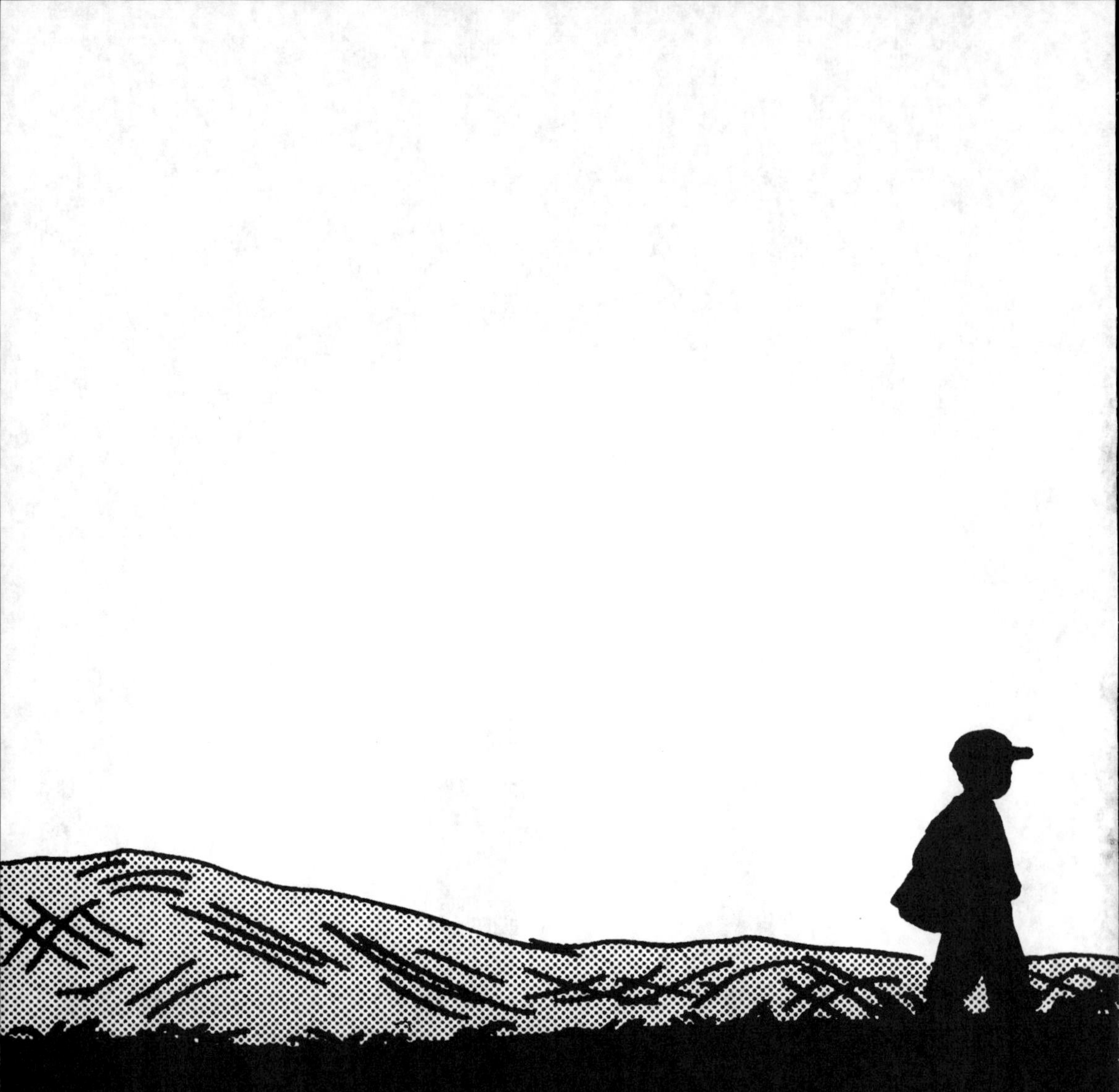

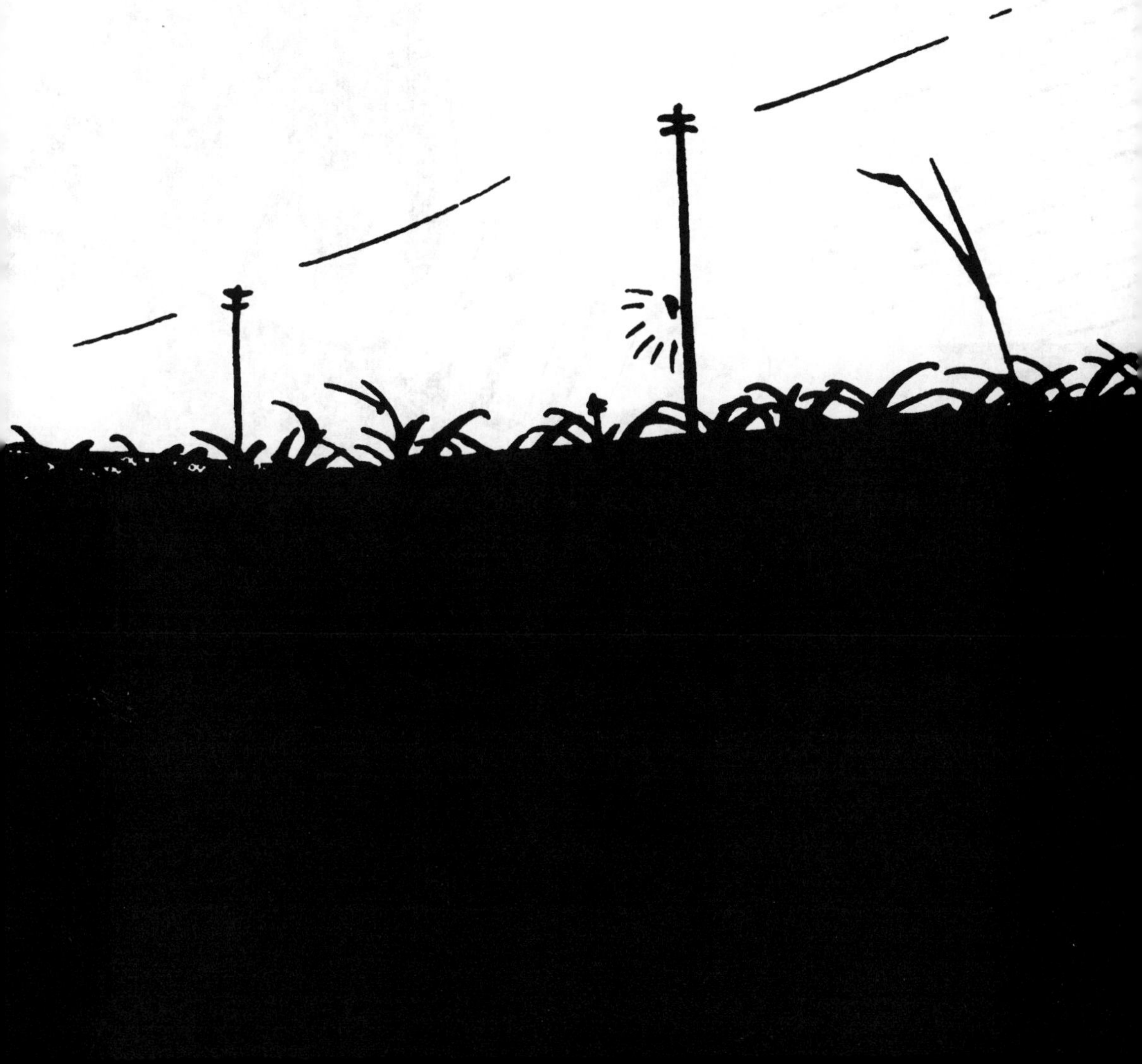

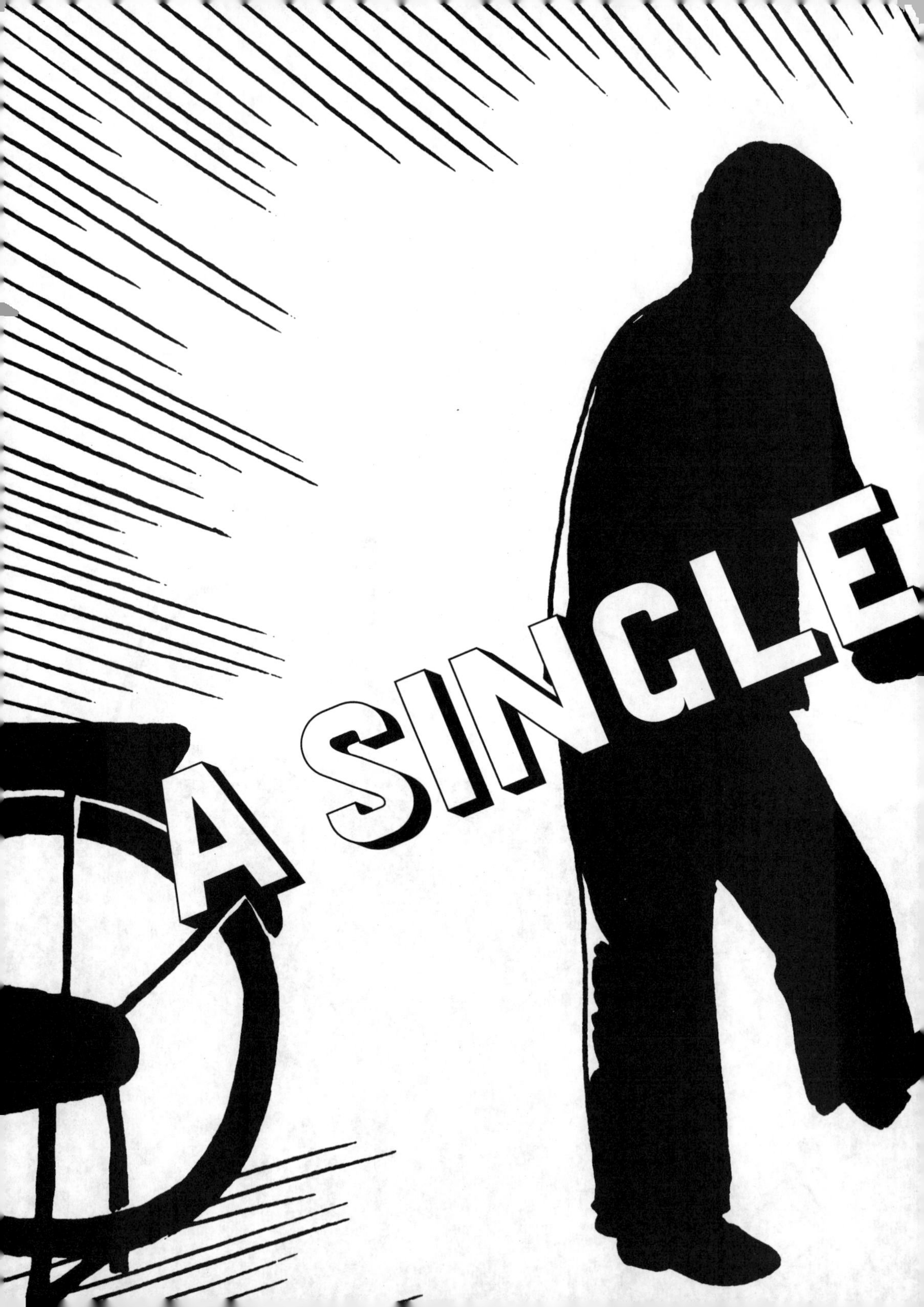
A SINGLE

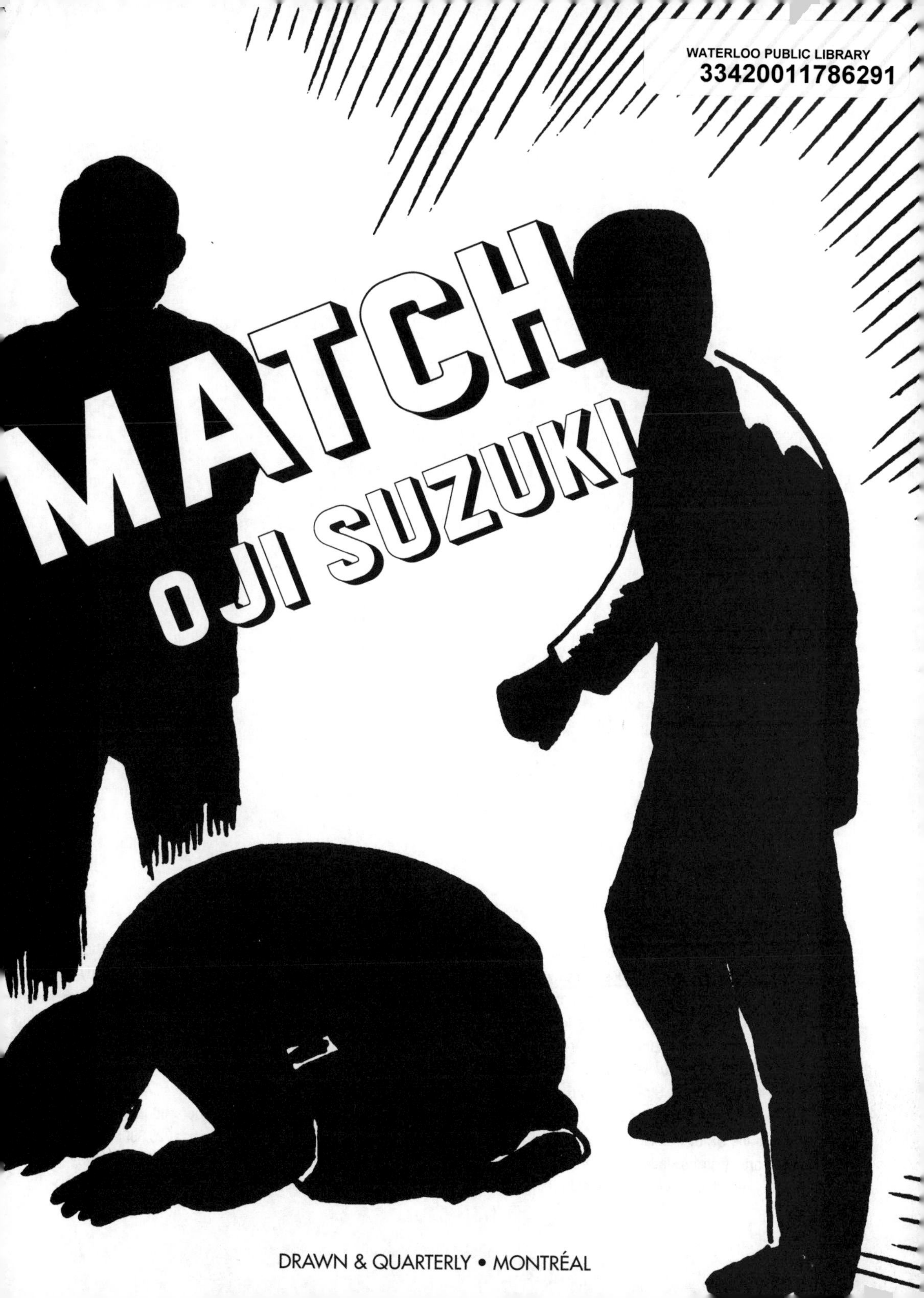
MATCH
OJI SUZUKI

DRAWN & QUARTERLY • MONTRÉAL

Entire contents © copyright 2010 by Oji Suzuki. All rights reserved. No part of this book (except small portions for review purposes) may be reproduced in any form without written permission from Oji Suzuki or Drawn & Quarterly. Translation: Jocelyne Allen. Font design: Matt Forsythe. Drawn & Quarterly, PO Box 48056, Montréal, Quebec, Canada H2V 4S8; www.drawnandquarterly.com; First hardcover edition: October 2010. Printed in Canada. 10 9 8 7 6 5 4 3 2 1. Library and Archives Canada Cataloguing in Publication; Suzuki, Oji, 1949-; A Single Match / Oji Suzuki; ISBN 978-1-77046-009-6; I. Title. PN6790.J33S88 2010   741.5'952   C2010-901618-1; Distributed in the United States by Farrar, Straus & Giroux, 18 West 18th Street, New York, NY 10011; Orders: 888.330.8477 ext. 6540; Distributed in Canada by Raincoast Books, 9050 Shaughnessy Street, Vancouver, BC V6P 6E5; Orders: 800.663.5714; Distributed in the UK by Publishers Group UK, 8 The Arena, Mollison Avenue, Enfield EN3 7NL; Orders: 020.8804.0400. Drawn & Quarterly acknowledges the financial support of the Government of Canada through the Canada Book Fund and the Canada Council for the Arts for our publishing activities and for support of this edition.

A SINGLE MATCH

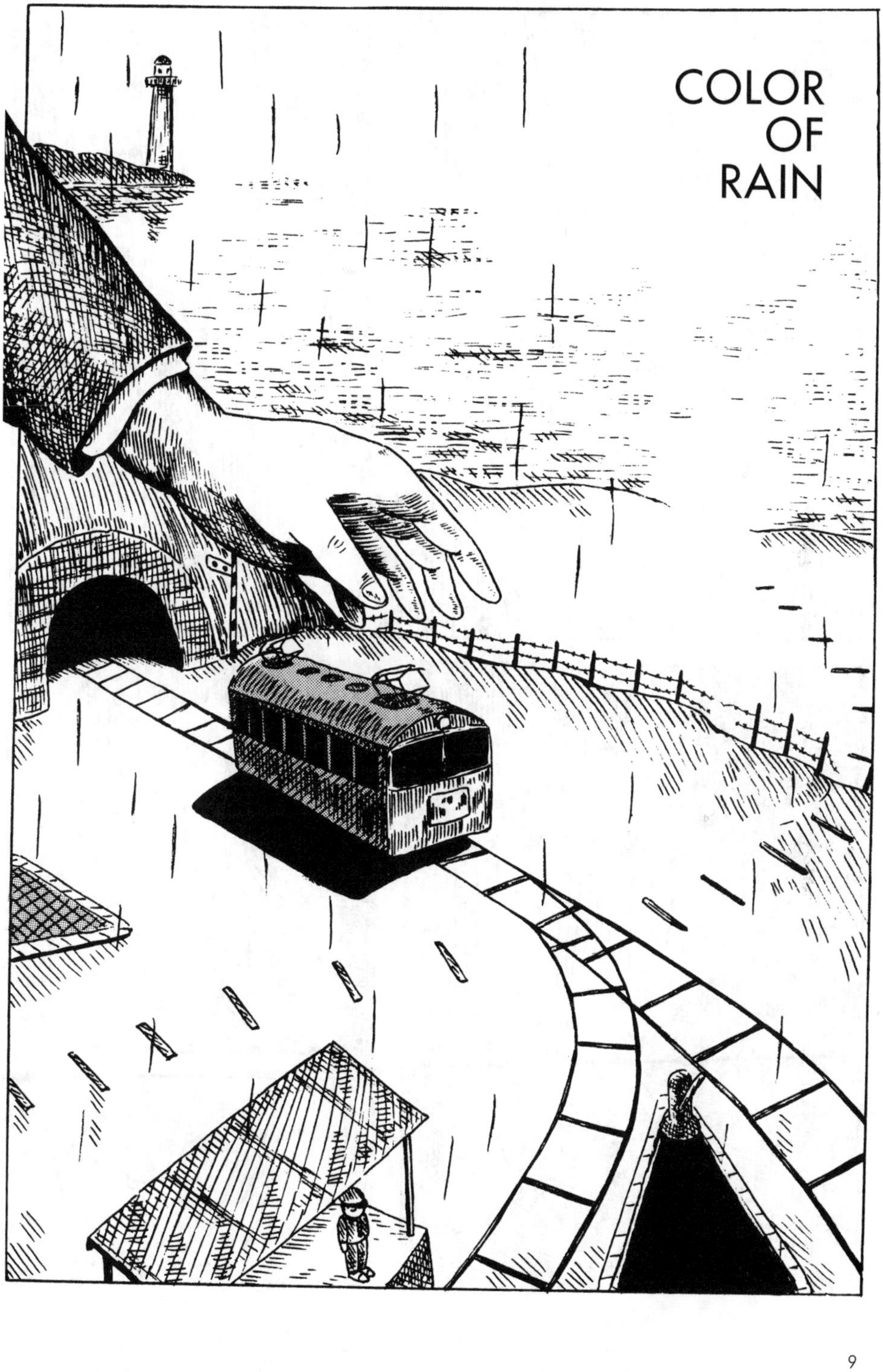
COLOR
OF
RAIN

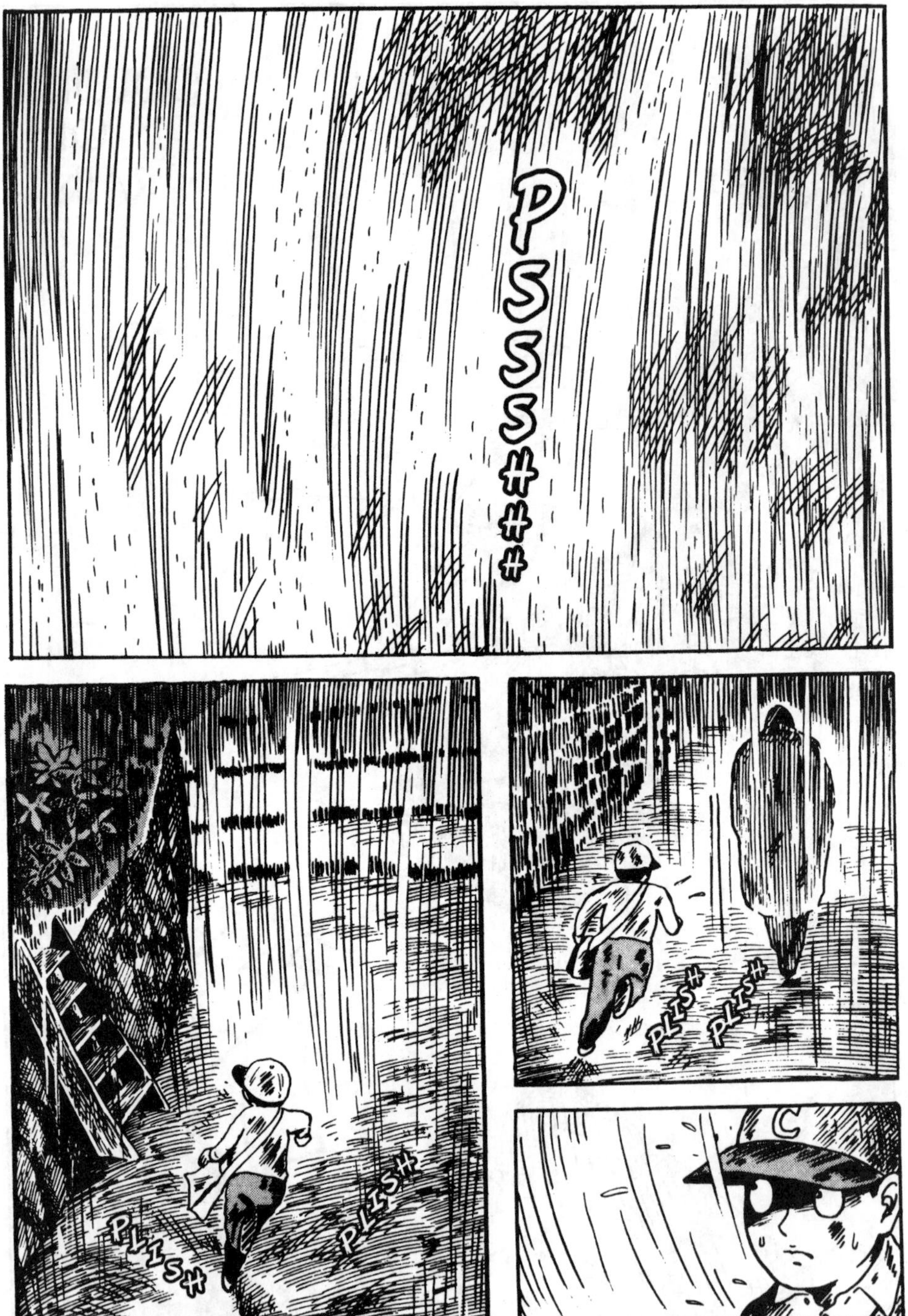
PSSSSHHH
PLISH
PLISH
PLISH
PLISH

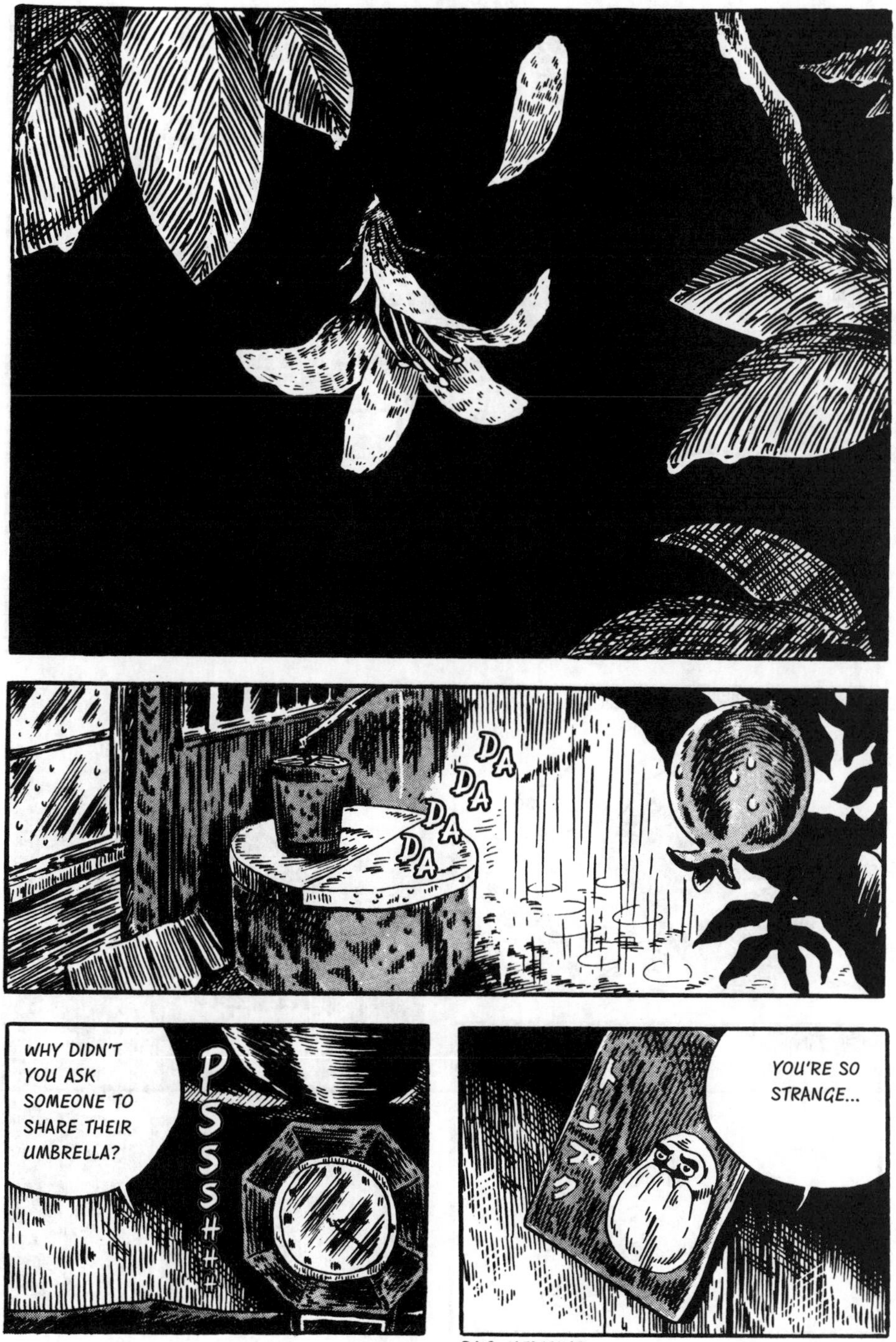
DA
DA
DA
DA
WHY DIDN'T YOU ASK SOMEONE TO SHARE THEIR UMBRELLA?
PSSSHHH
YOU'RE SO STRANGE...

BAG: MEDICINE

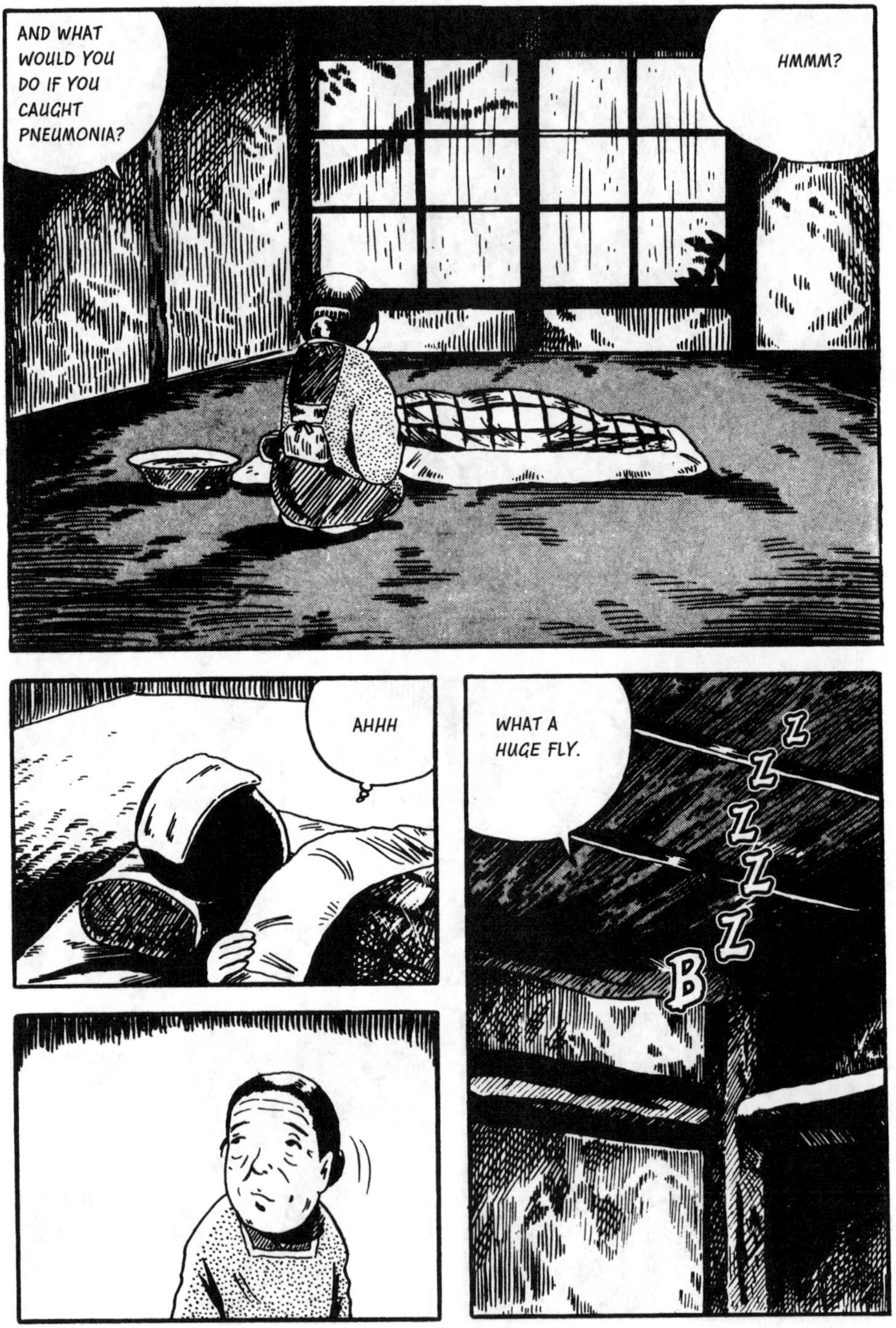
AND WHAT WOULD YOU DO IF YOU CAUGHT PNEUMONIA?
HMMM?
AHHH
WHAT A HUGE FLY.
ZZZZZB

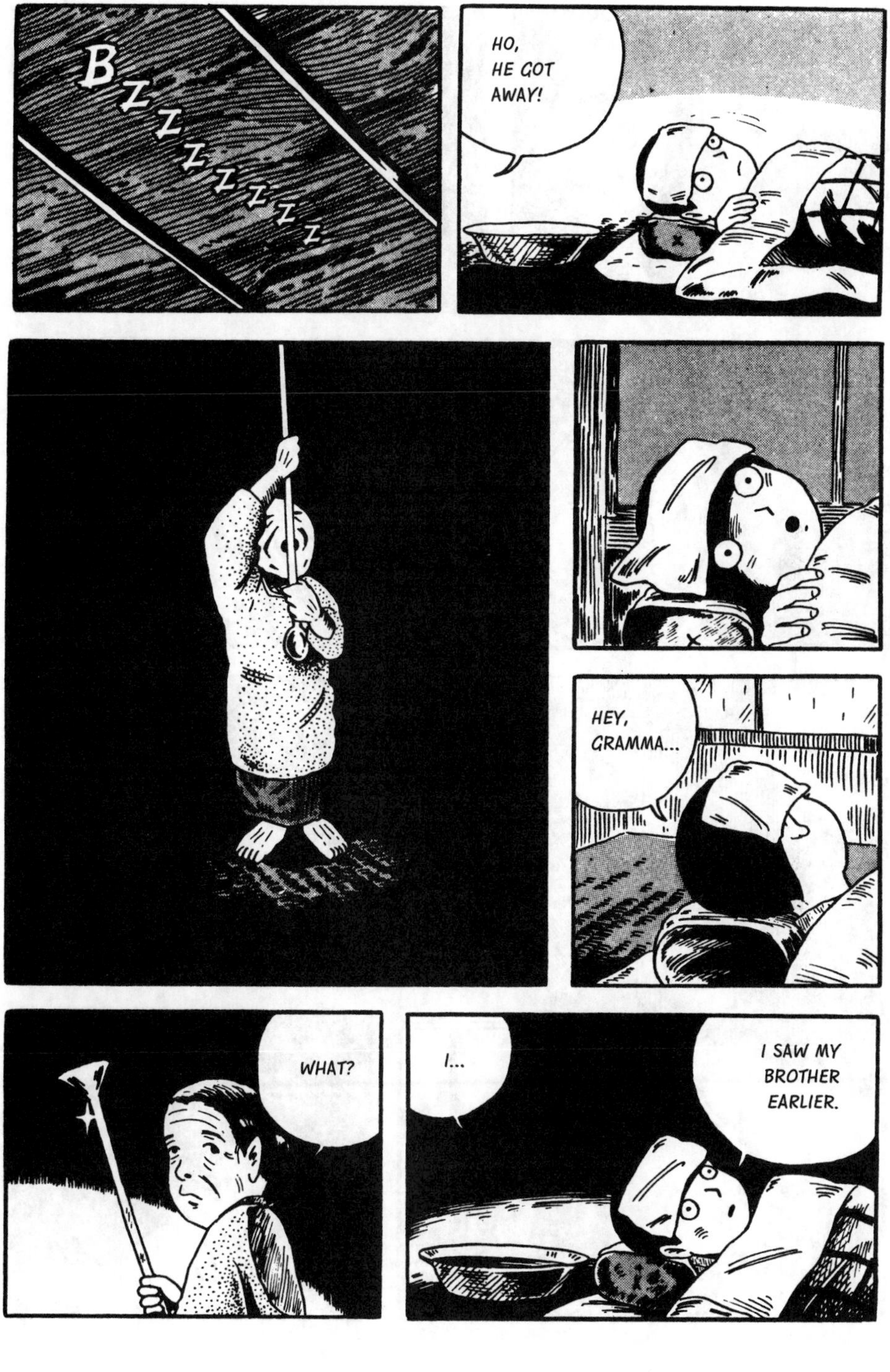
BZZZZZZZ
HO, HE GOT AWAY!
HEY, GRAMMA...
WHAT?
I...
I SAW MY BROTHER EARLIER.

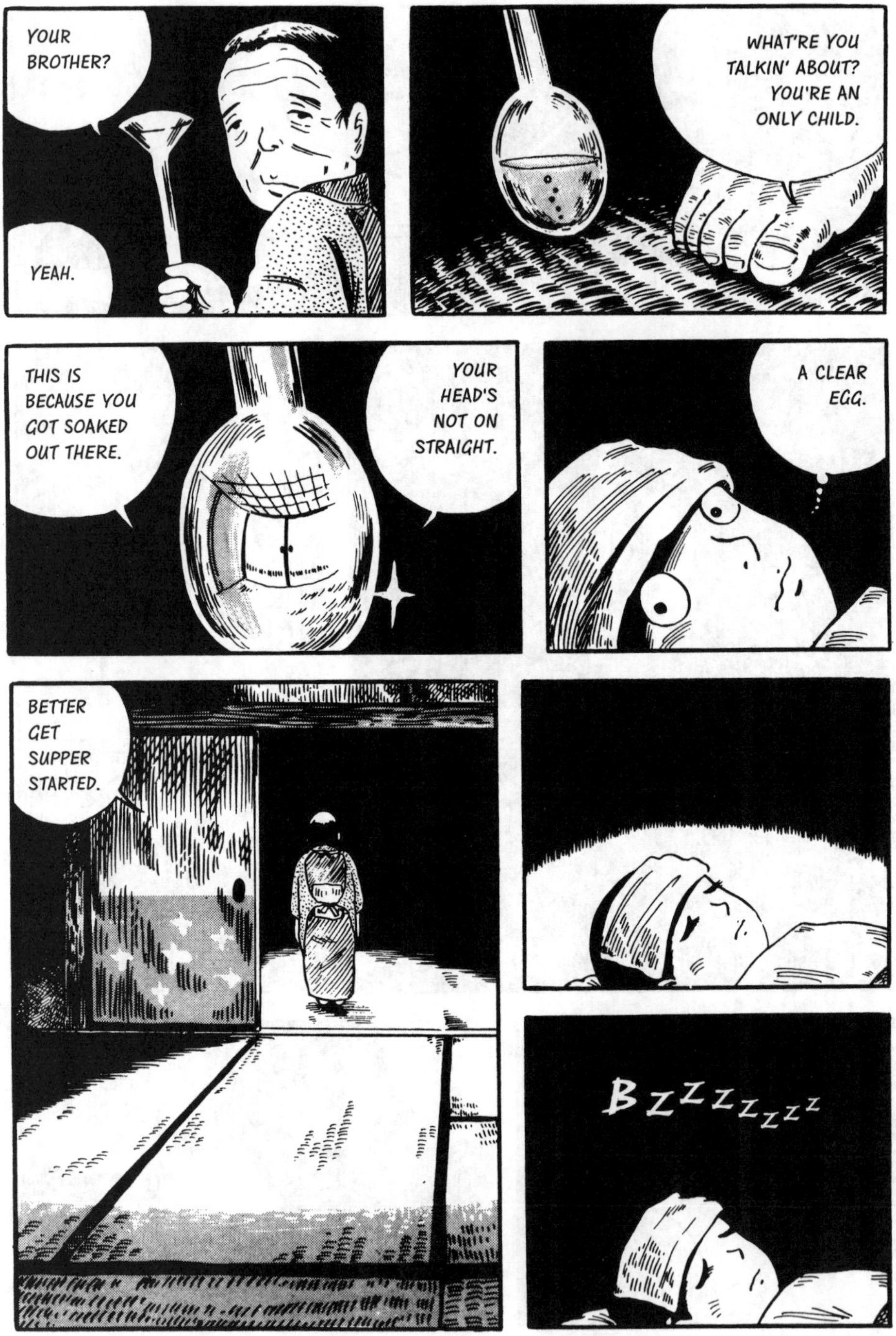

YOUR BROTHER?
YEAH.
WHAT'RE YOU TALKIN' ABOUT? YOU'RE AN ONLY CHILD.
THIS IS BECAUSE YOU GOT SOAKED OUT THERE.
YOUR HEAD'S NOT ON STRAIGHT.
A CLEAR EGG.
BETTER GET SUPPER STARTED.
BZZZZZZZZ

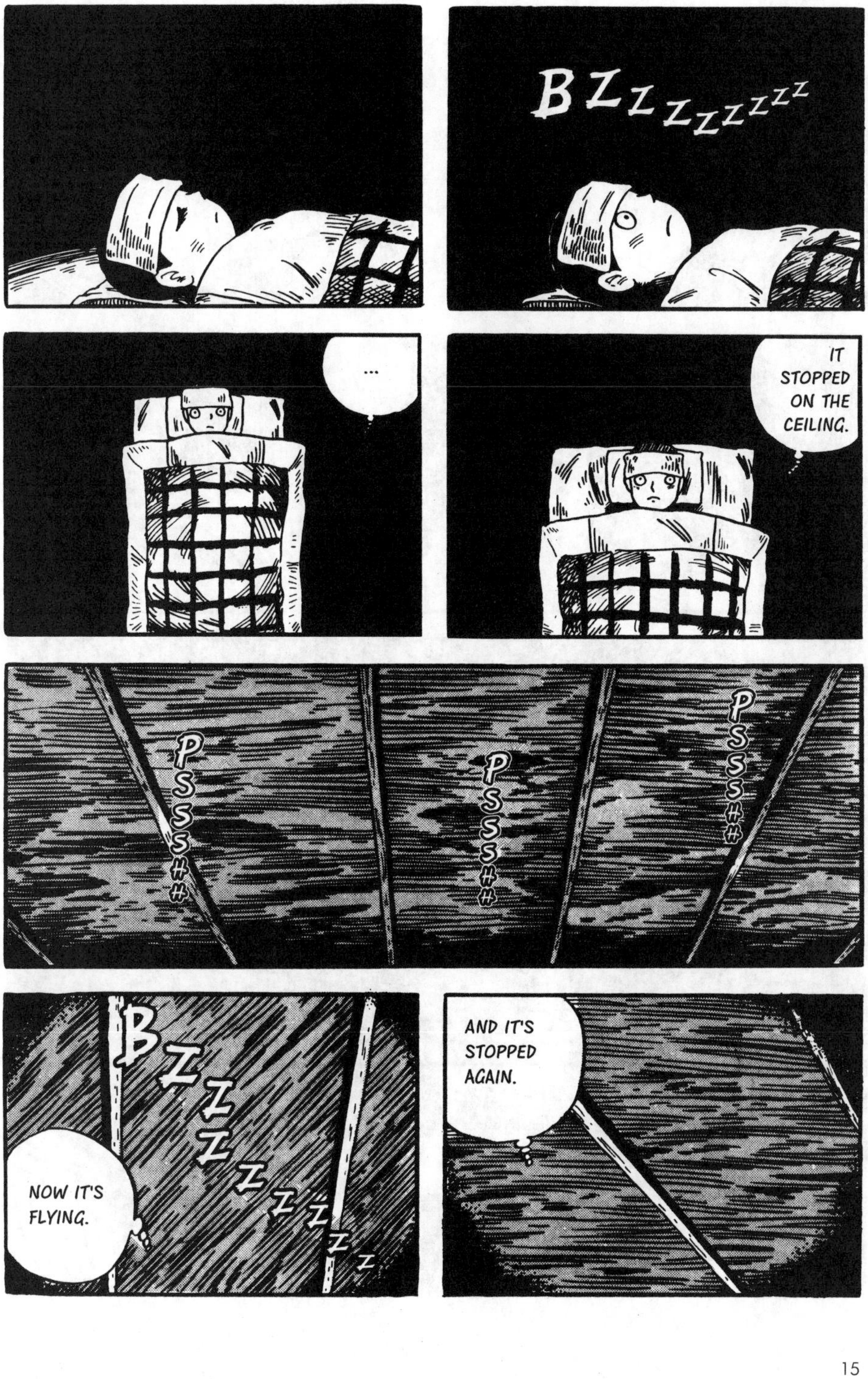
BZZZZZZZZZZ
...
IT STOPPED ON THE CEILING.
PSSSHH
PSSSHH
PSSSHH
BZZZZZZZZZ
NOW IT'S FLYING.
AND IT'S STOPPED AGAIN.

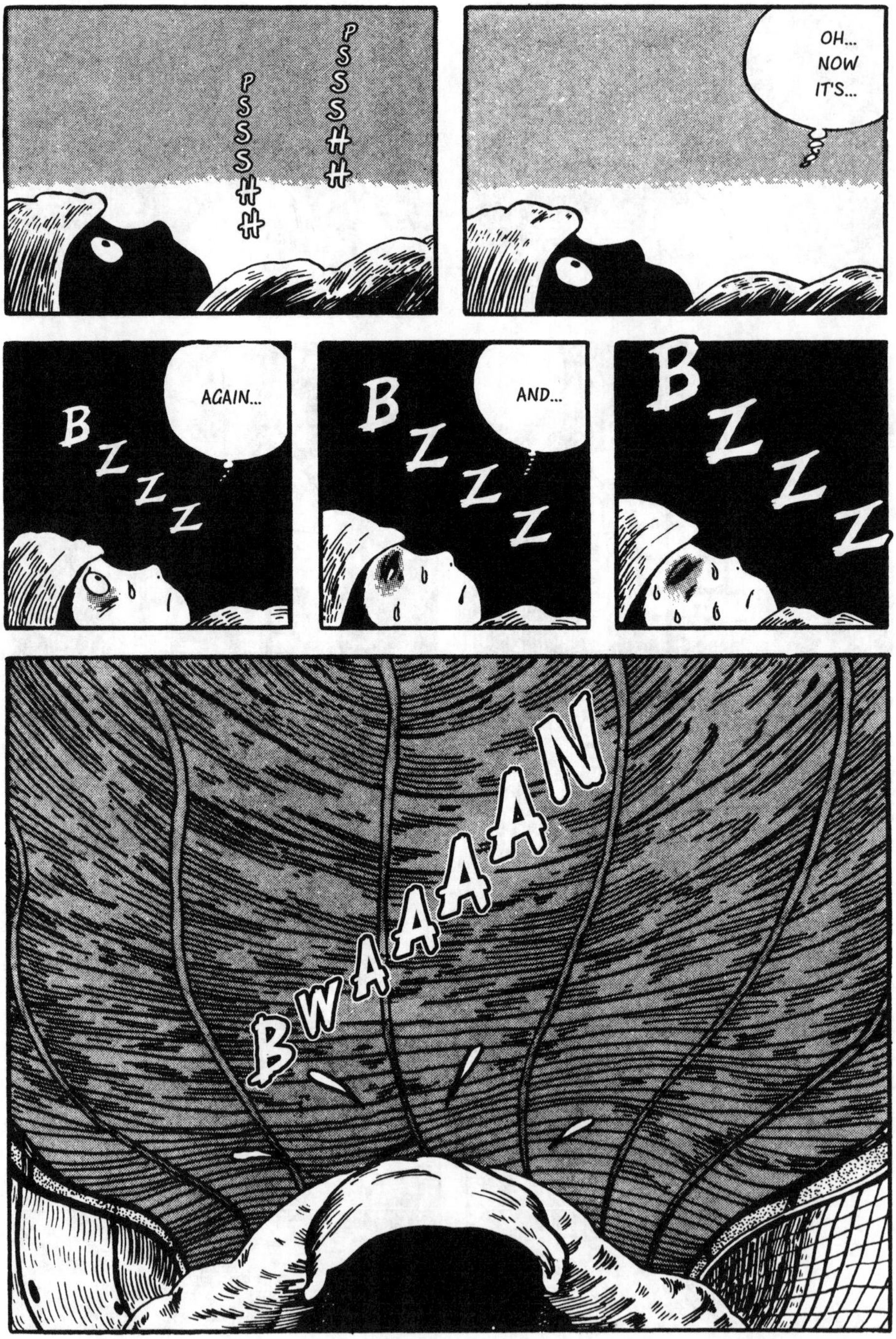
PSSSHH
PSSSHH
OH... NOW IT'S...
AGAIN...
BZZZ
BZZZ
AND...
BZZZ
BWAAAAAN

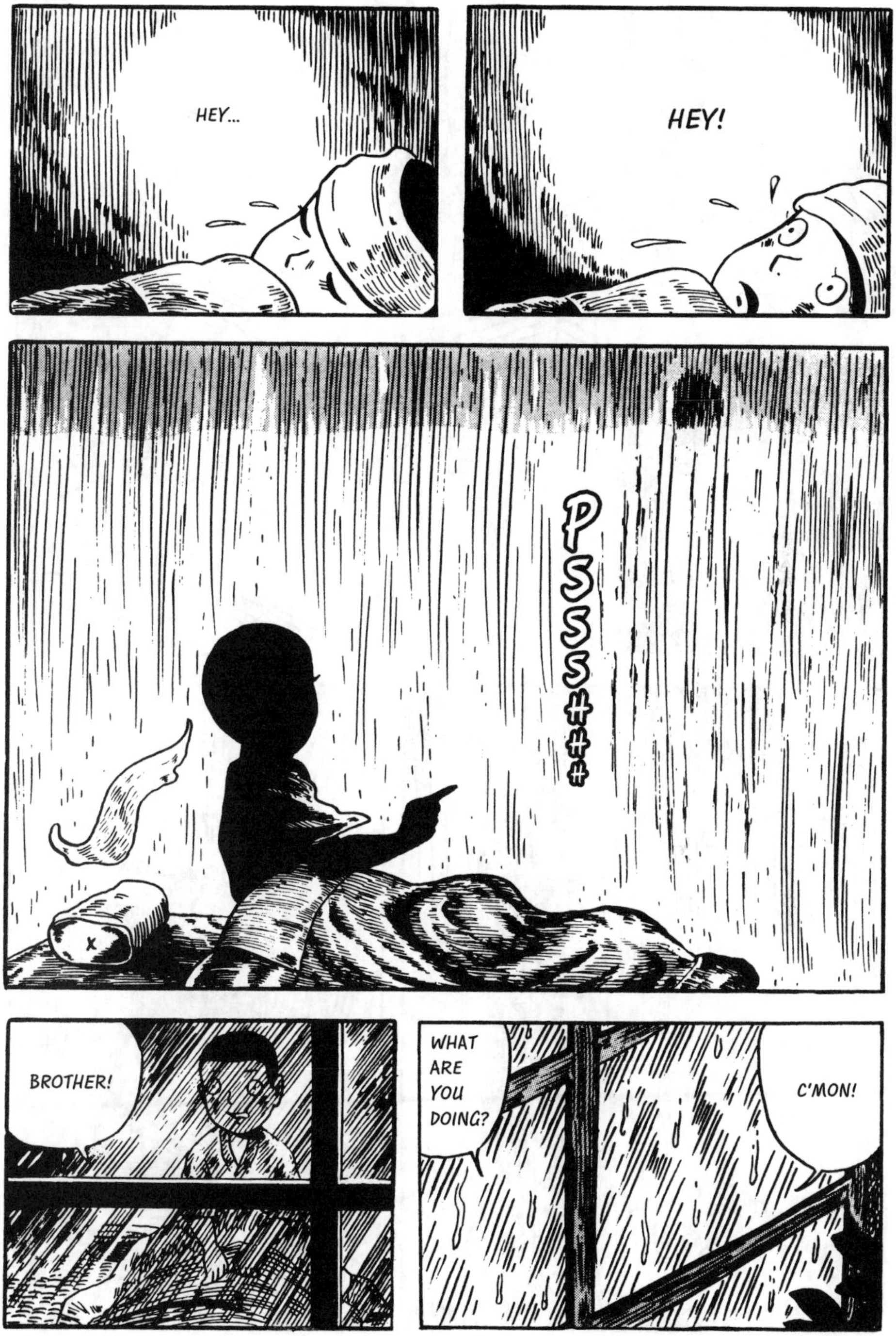
HEY...
HEY!
PSSSSHHH
BROTHER!
WHAT ARE YOU DOING?
C'MON!

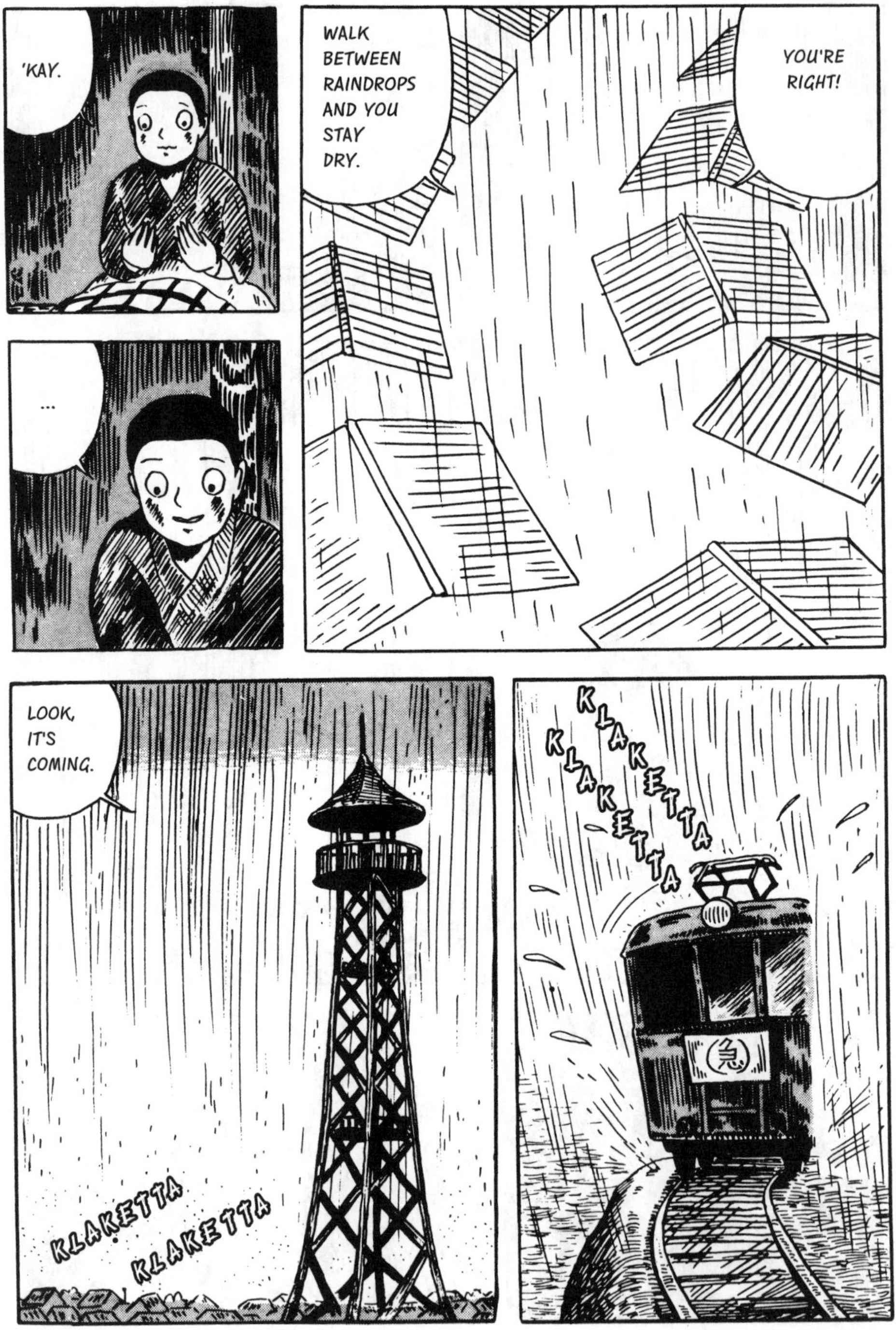

'KAY.
WALK BETWEEN RAINDROPS AND YOU STAY DRY.
YOU'RE RIGHT!
...
LOOK, IT'S COMING.
KLAKETTA KLAKETTA
KLAKETTA KLAKETTA

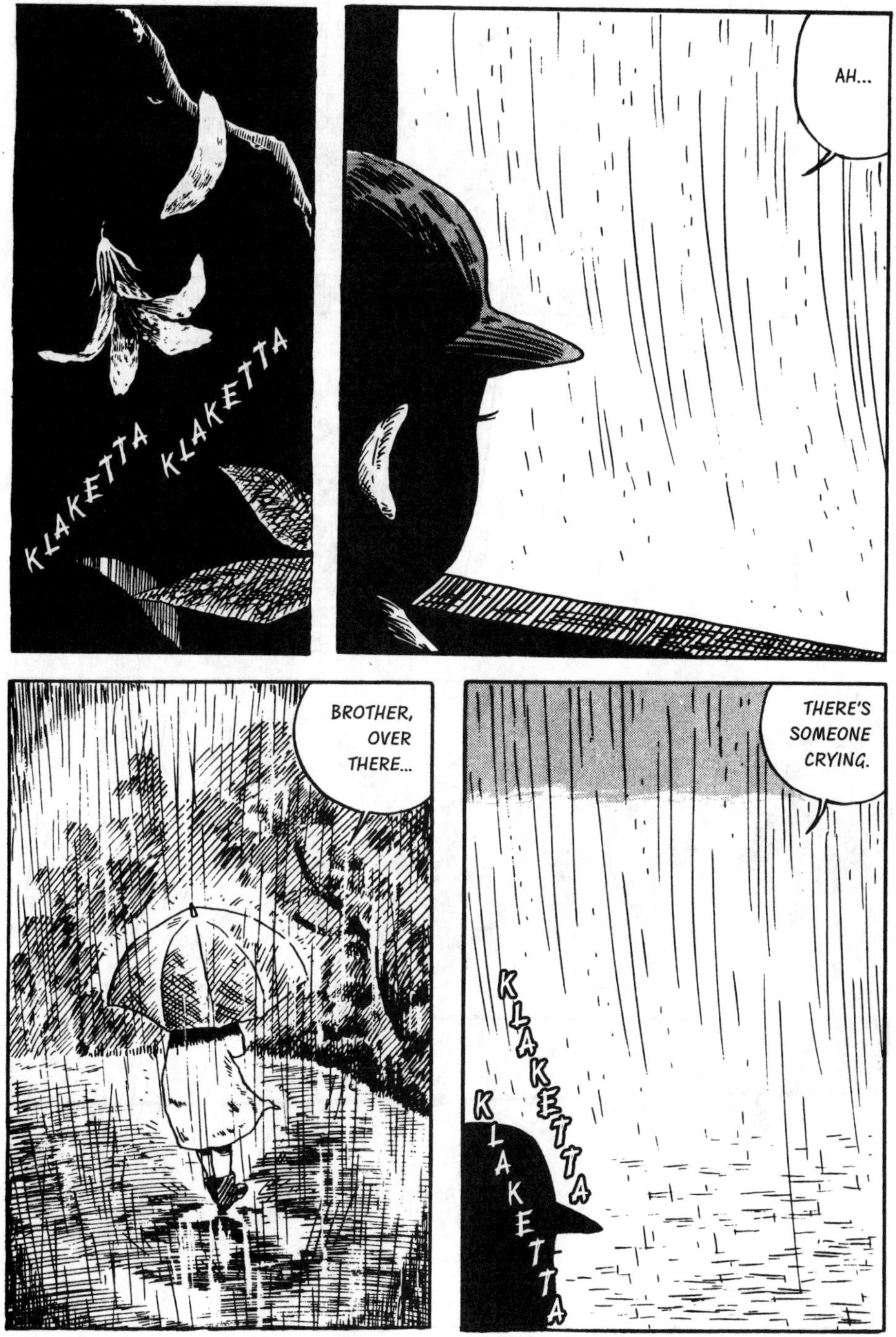
KLAKETTA KLAKETTA
AH...
BROTHER, OVER THERE...
THERE'S SOMEONE CRYING.
KLAKETTA
KLAKETTA

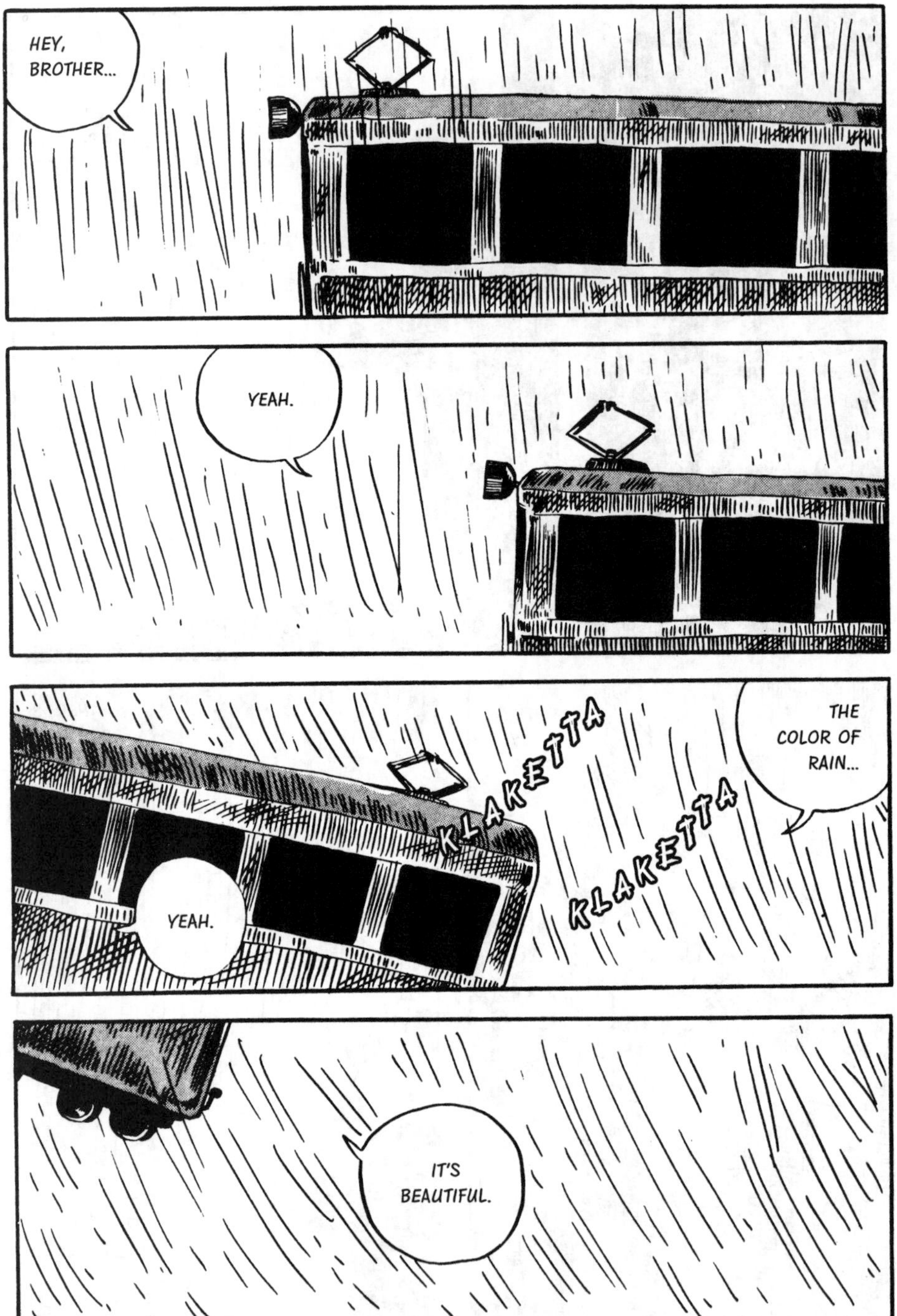
HEY, BROTHER...
YEAH.
YEAH.
KLAKETTA
KLAKETTA
THE COLOR OF RAIN...
IT'S BEAUTIFUL.

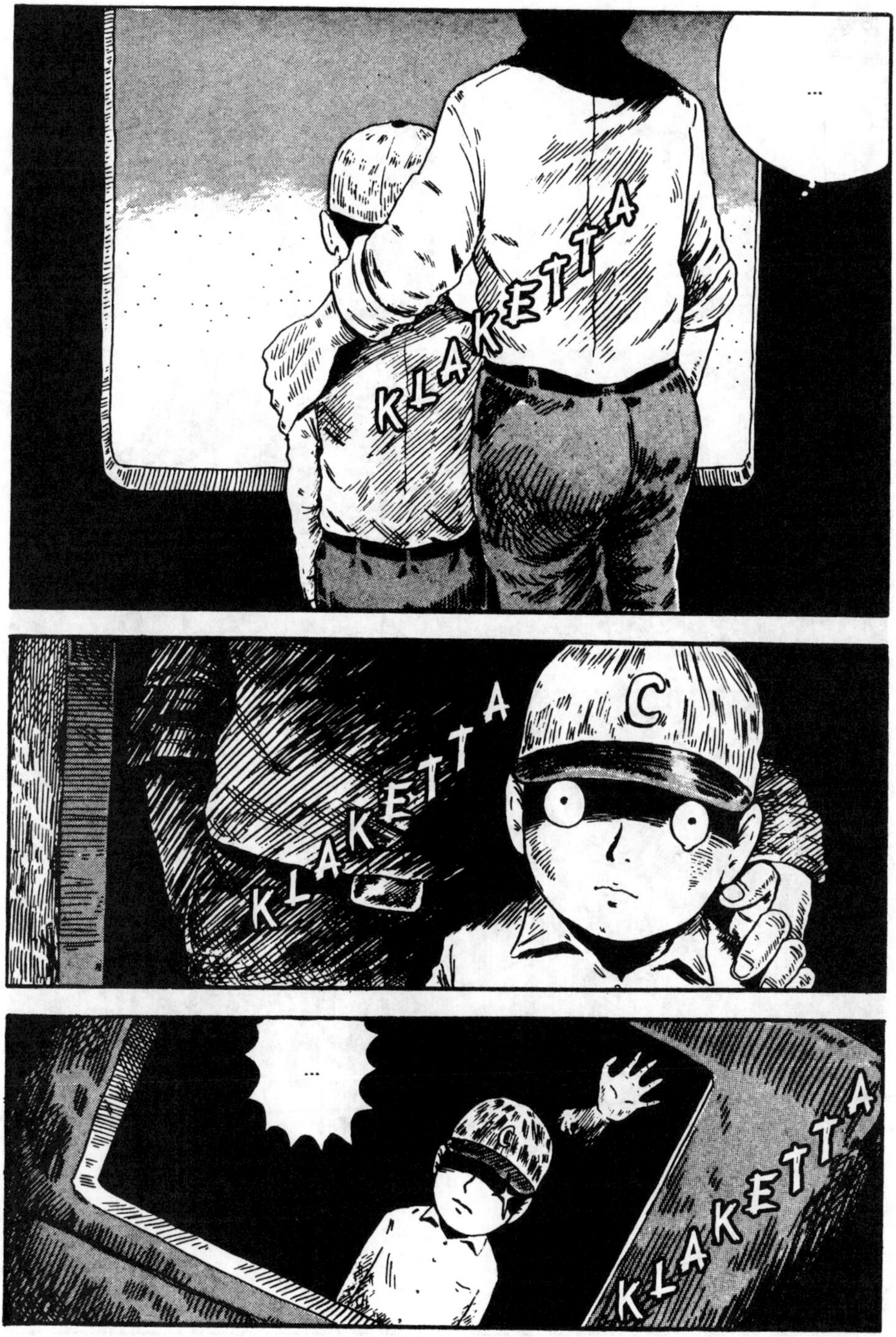
...
KLAKETTA
KLAKETTA
...
KLAKETTA

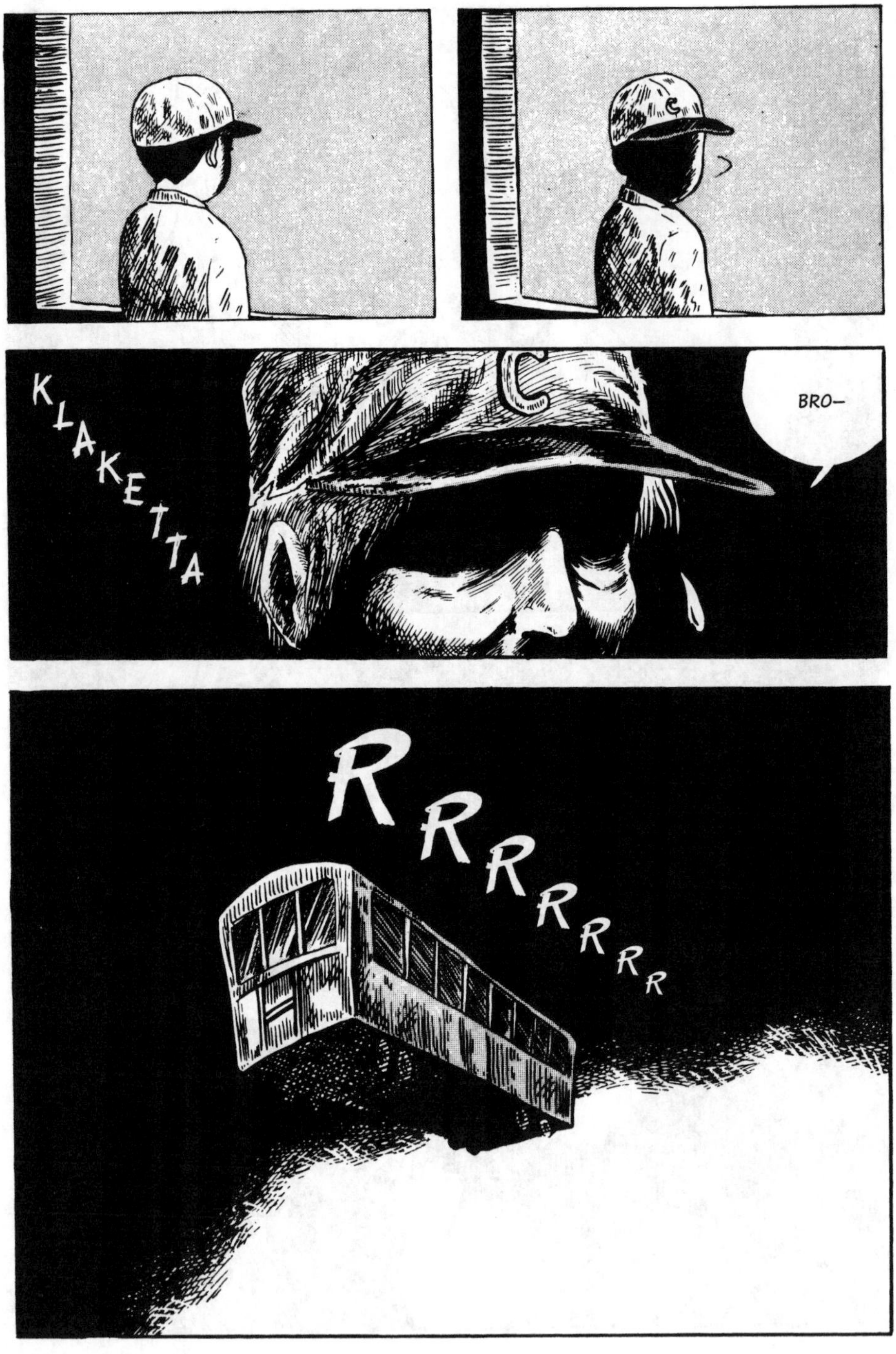
KLAKETTA
BRO—
RRRRRRRR

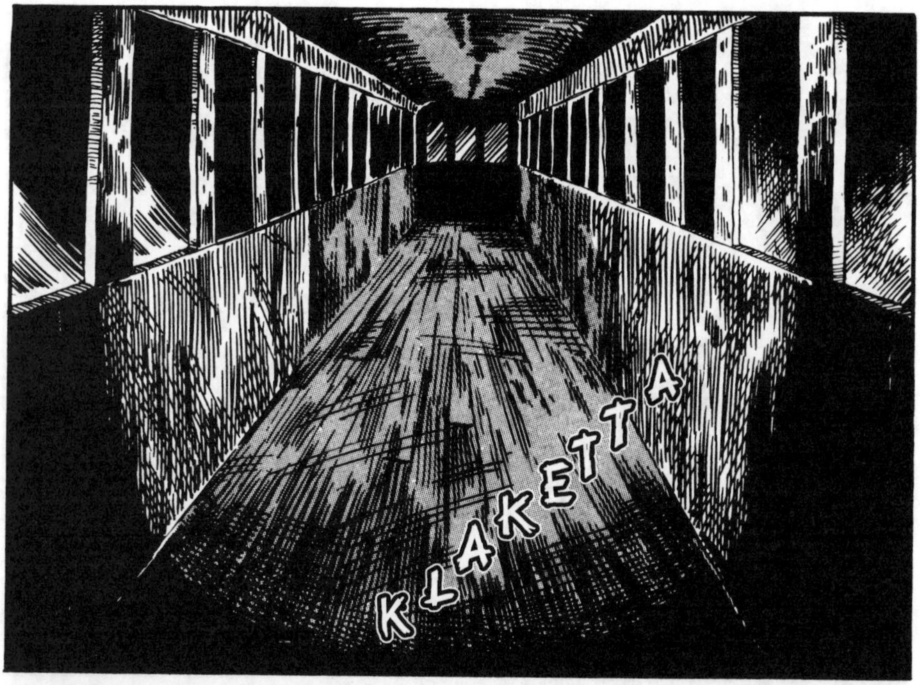
KLAKETTA
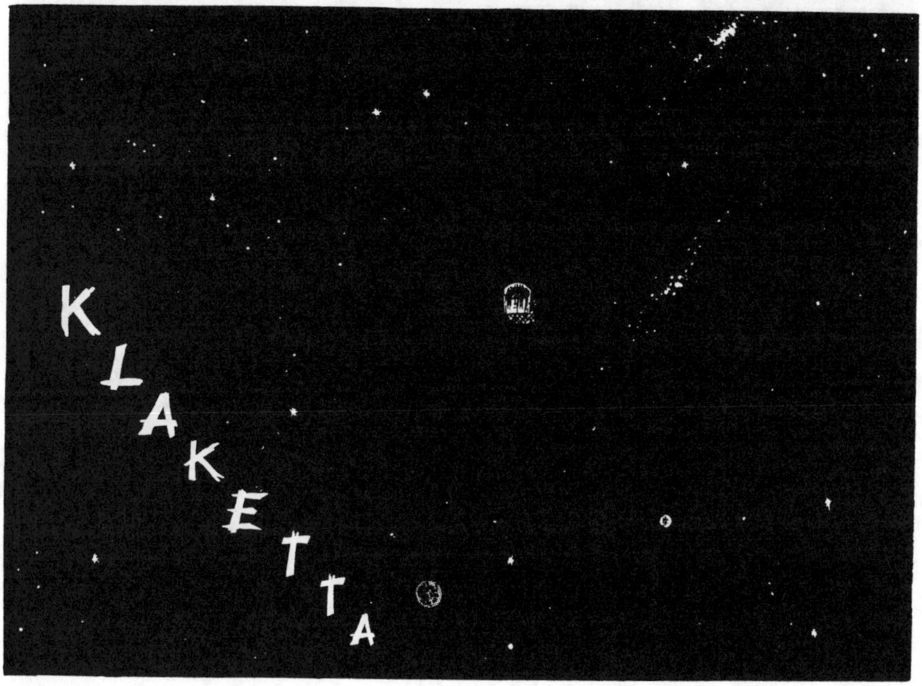
KLAKETTA

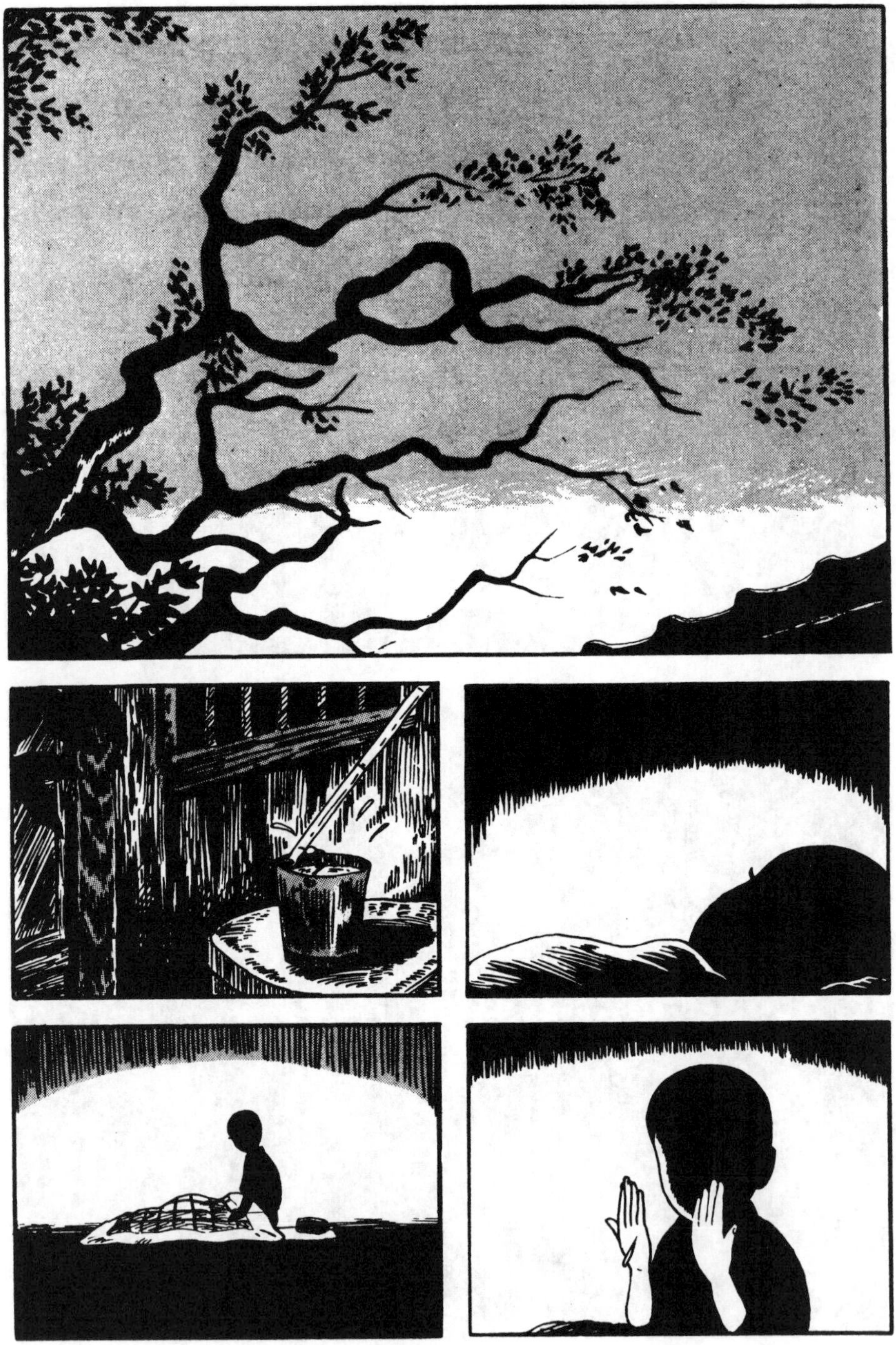

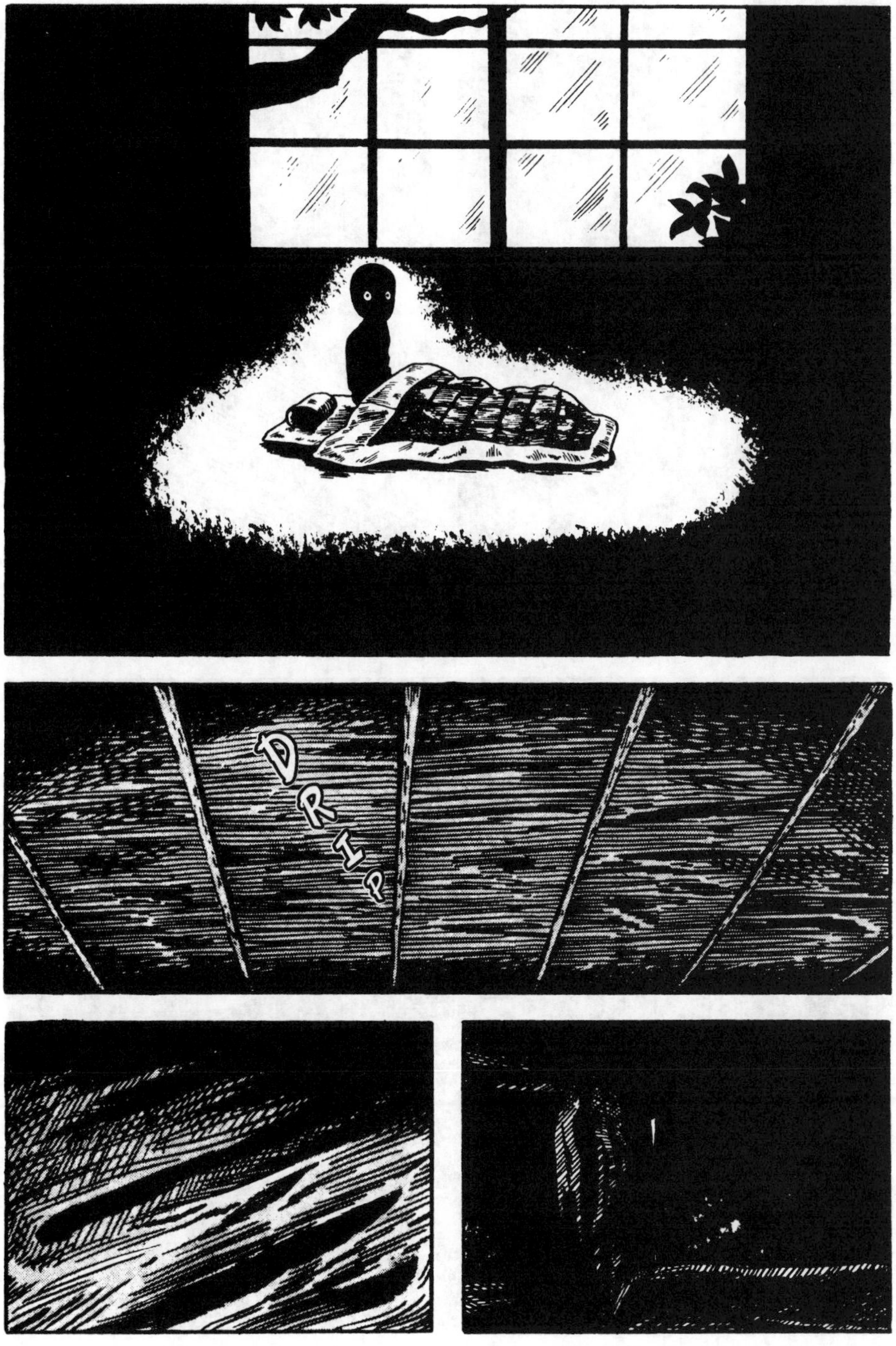
DRIP

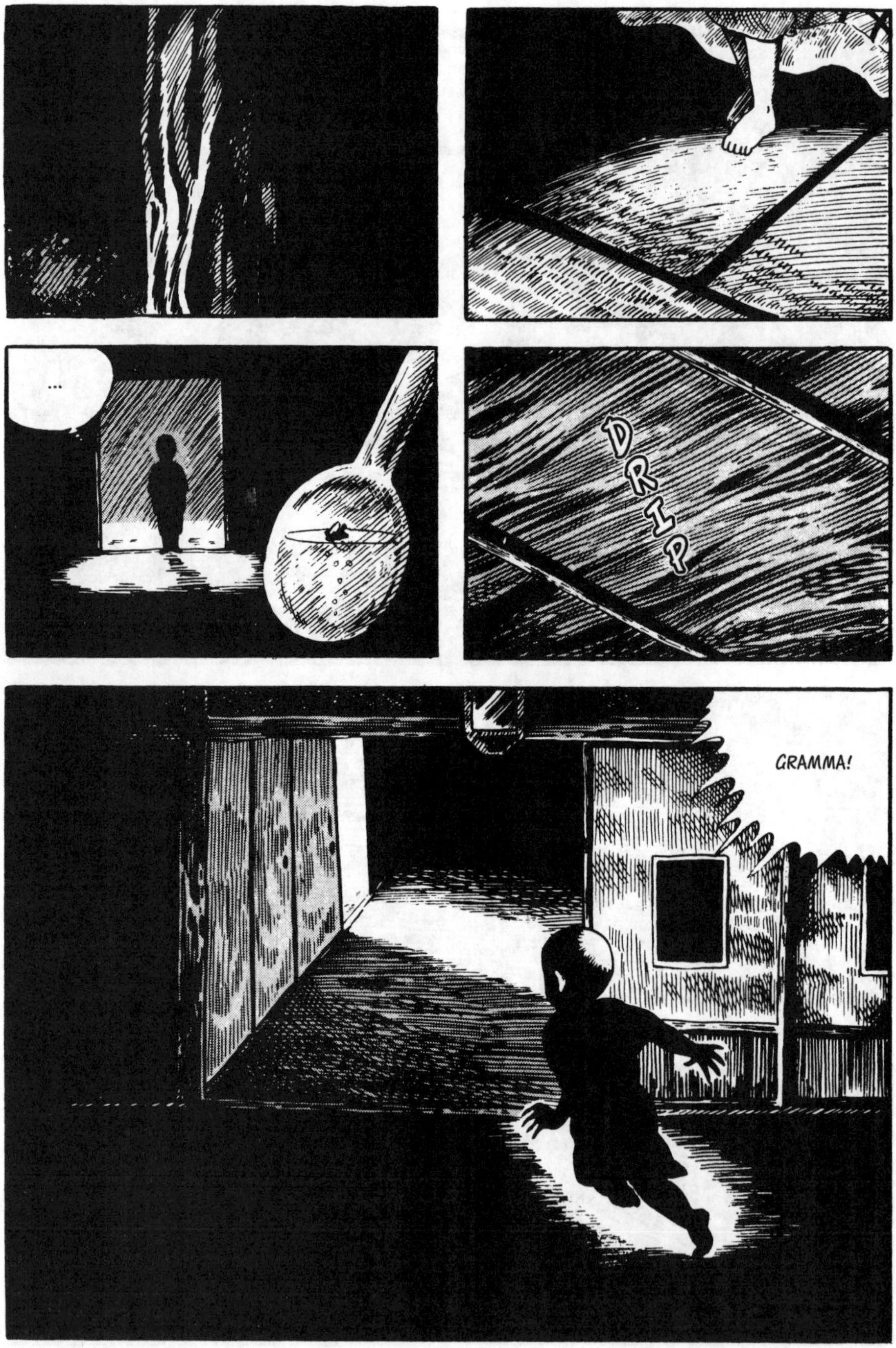
...
DRIP
GRAMMA!

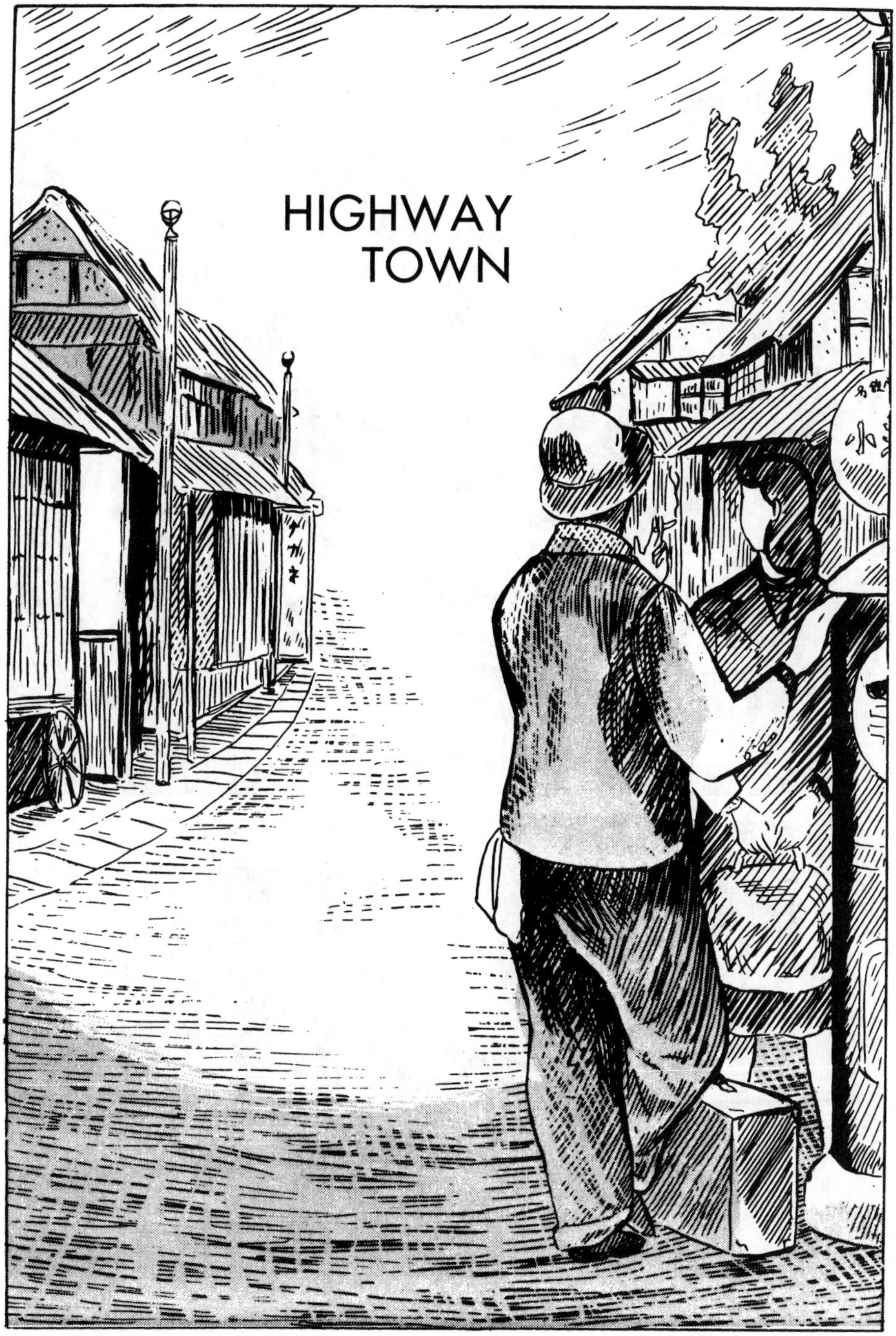
HIGHWAY
TOWN

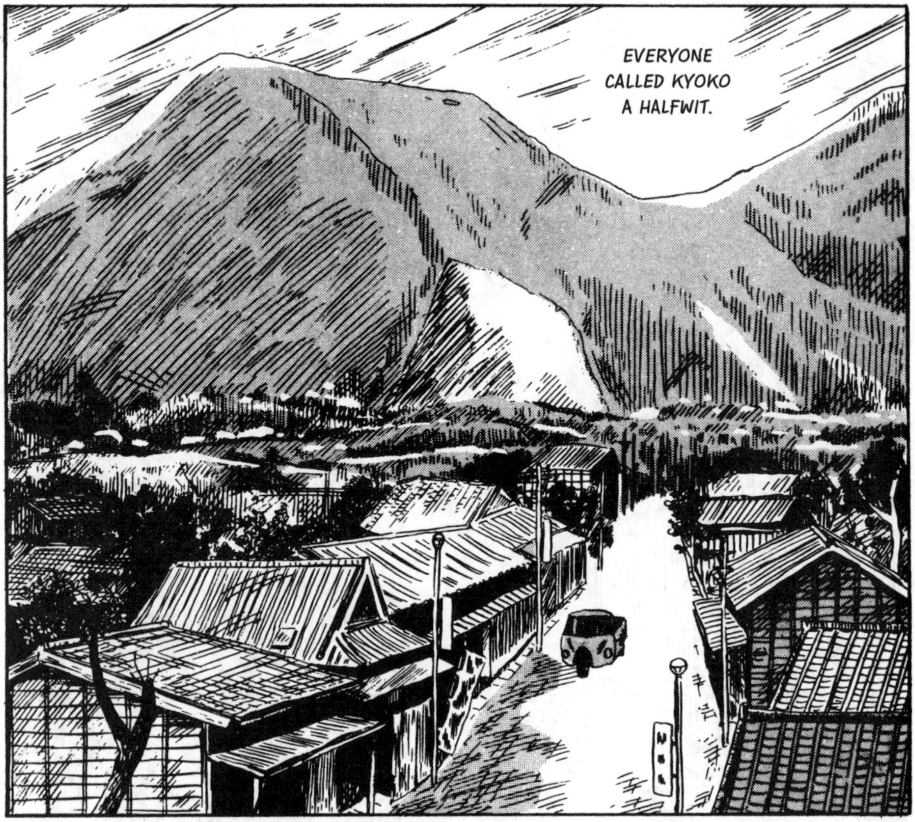
EVERYONE CALLED KYOKO A HALFWIT.

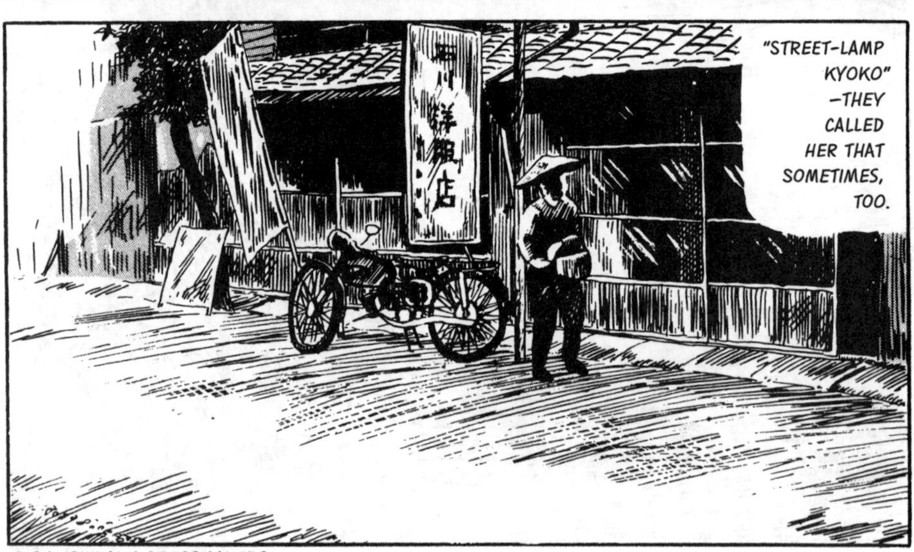
"STREET-LAMP KYOKO" —THEY CALLED HER THAT SOMETIMES, TOO.

SIGN: ISHIKAWA DRESSMAKERS

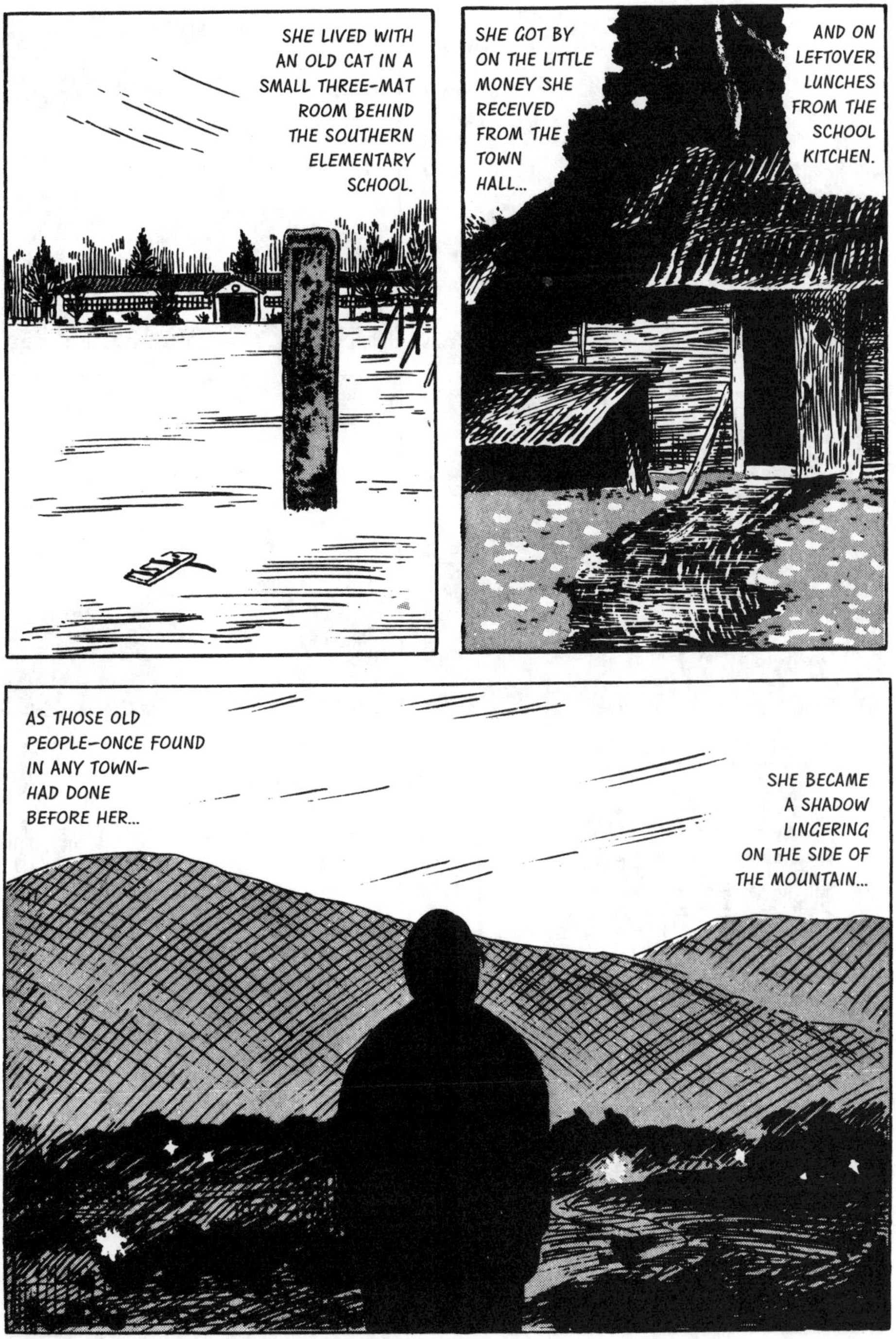
SHE LIVED WITH AN OLD CAT IN A SMALL THREE-MAT ROOM BEHIND THE SOUTHERN ELEMENTARY SCHOOL.
SHE GOT BY ON THE LITTLE MONEY SHE RECEIVED FROM THE TOWN HALL...
AND ON LEFTOVER LUNCHES FROM THE SCHOOL KITCHEN.
AS THOSE OLD PEOPLE—ONCE FOUND IN ANY TOWN—HAD DONE BEFORE HER...
SHE BECAME A SHADOW LINGERING ON THE SIDE OF THE MOUNTAIN...

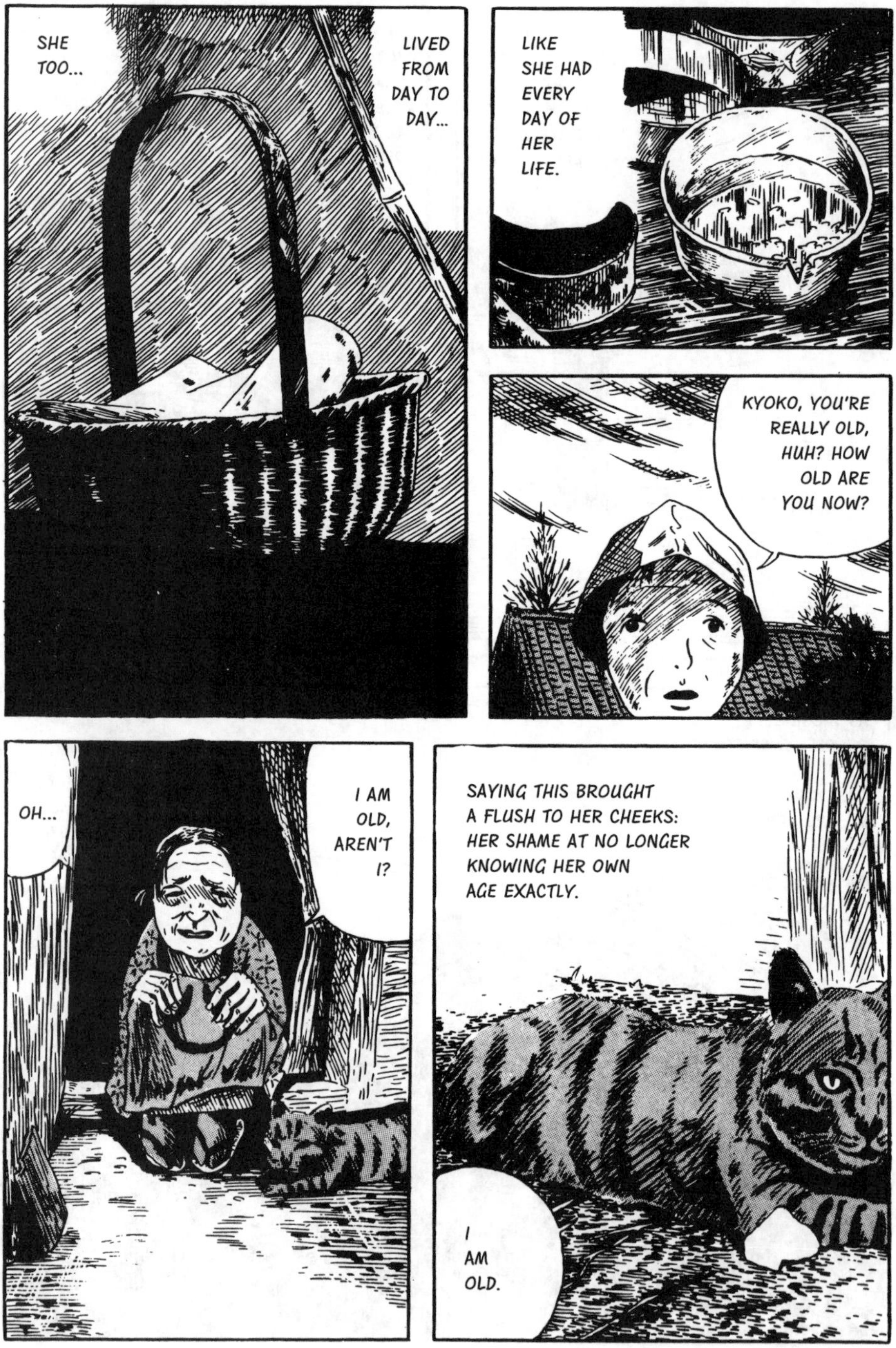
SHE TOO...
LIVED FROM DAY TO DAY...
LIKE SHE HAD EVERY DAY OF HER LIFE.
KYOKO, YOU'RE REALLY OLD, HUH? HOW OLD ARE YOU NOW?
OH...
I AM OLD, AREN'T I?
SAYING THIS BROUGHT A FLUSH TO HER CHEEKS: HER SHAME AT NO LONGER KNOWING HER OWN AGE EXACTLY.
I AM OLD.

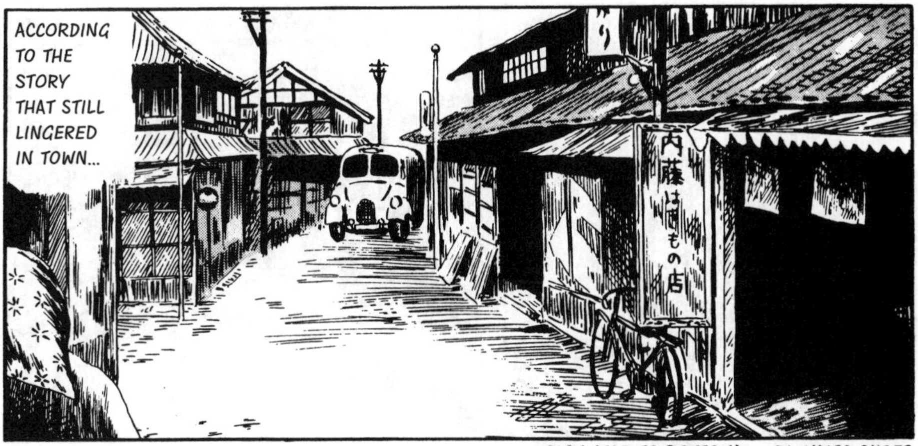
ACCORDING TO THE STORY THAT STILL LINGERED IN TOWN...
SIGN (TOP TO BOTTOM): --RI; NAITO SHOES

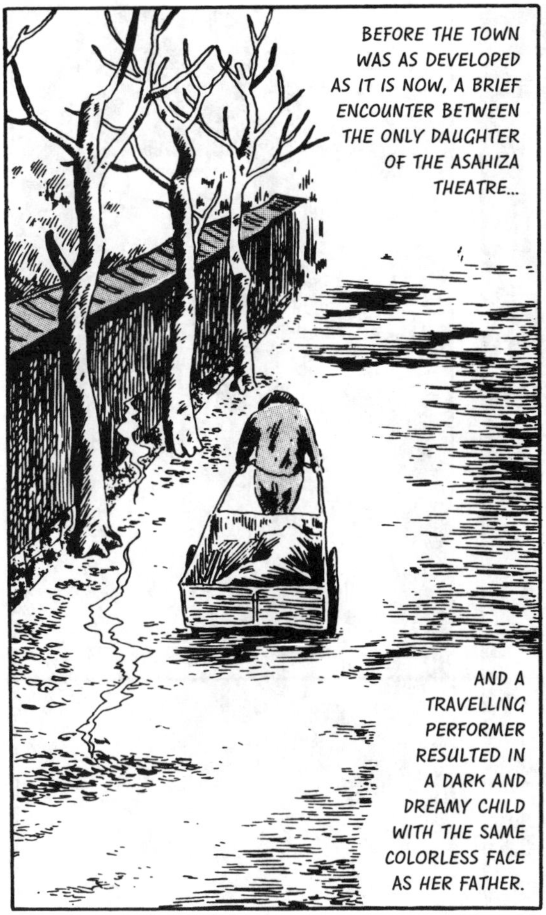
BEFORE THE TOWN WAS AS DEVELOPED AS IT IS NOW, A BRIEF ENCOUNTER BETWEEN THE ONLY DAUGHTER OF THE ASAHIZA THEATRE...
AND A TRAVELLING PERFORMER RESULTED IN A DARK AND DREAMY CHILD WITH THE SAME COLORLESS FACE AS HER FATHER.

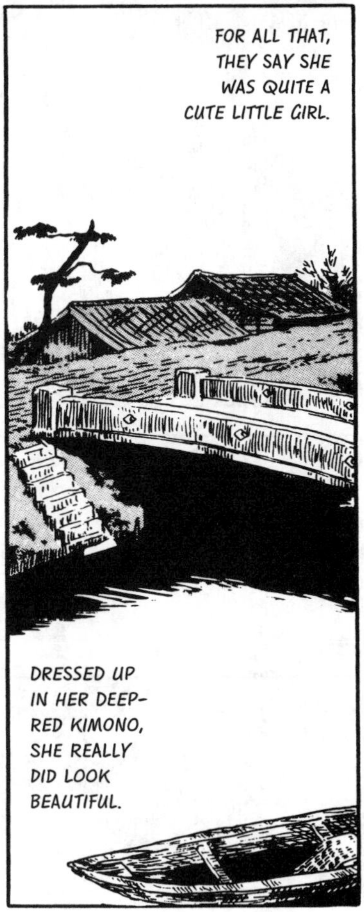
FOR ALL THAT, THEY SAY SHE WAS QUITE A CUTE LITTLE GIRL.
DRESSED UP IN HER DEEP-RED KIMONO, SHE REALLY DID LOOK BEAUTIFUL.

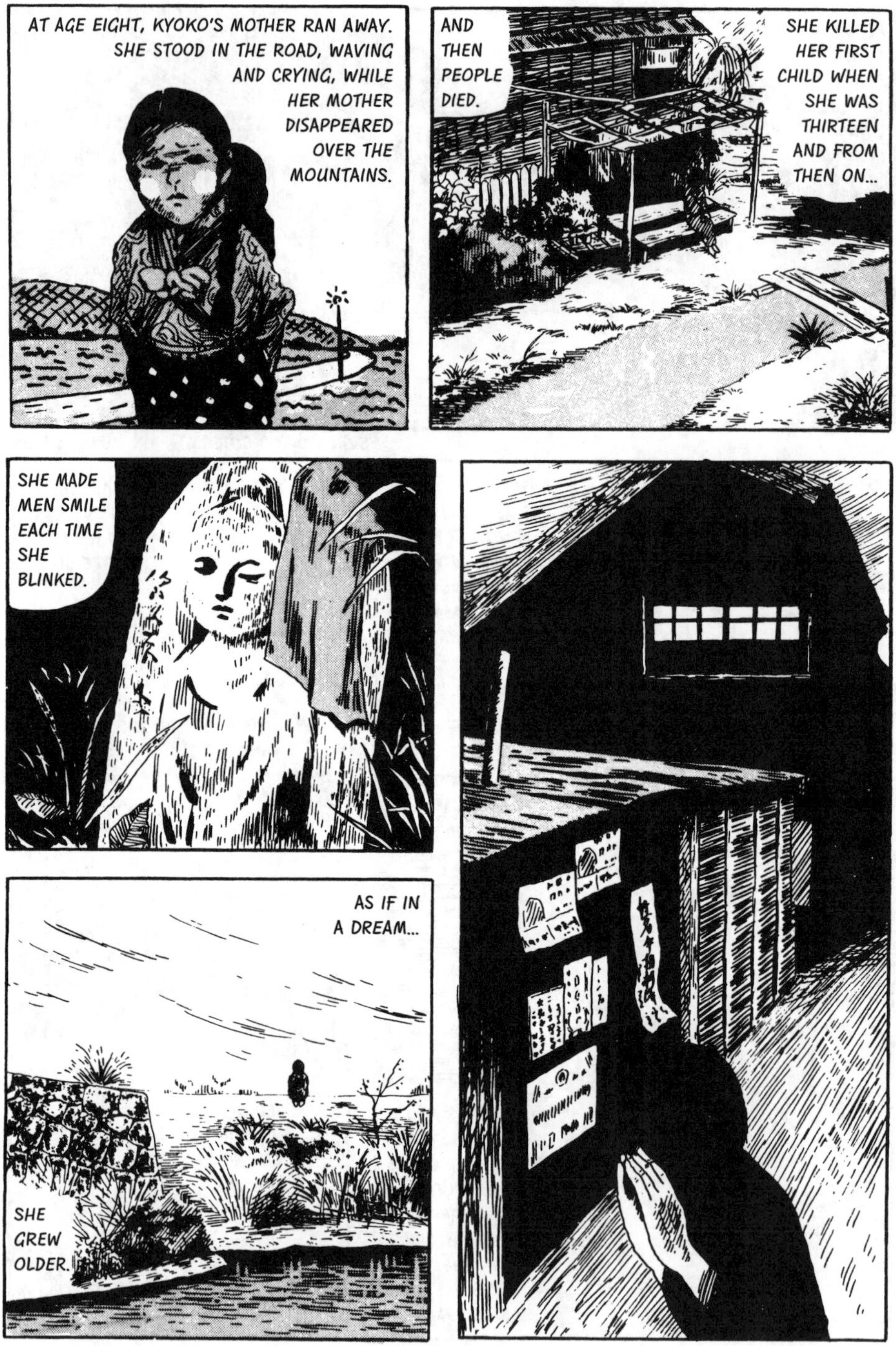
AT AGE EIGHT, KYOKO'S MOTHER RAN AWAY.
SHE STOOD IN THE ROAD, WAVING AND CRYING, WHILE HER MOTHER DISAPPEARED OVER THE MOUNTAINS.
AND THEN PEOPLE DIED.
SHE KILLED HER FIRST CHILD WHEN SHE WAS THIRTEEN AND FROM THEN ON...
SHE MADE MEN SMILE EACH TIME SHE BLINKED.
AS IF IN A DREAM...
SHE GREW OLDER.

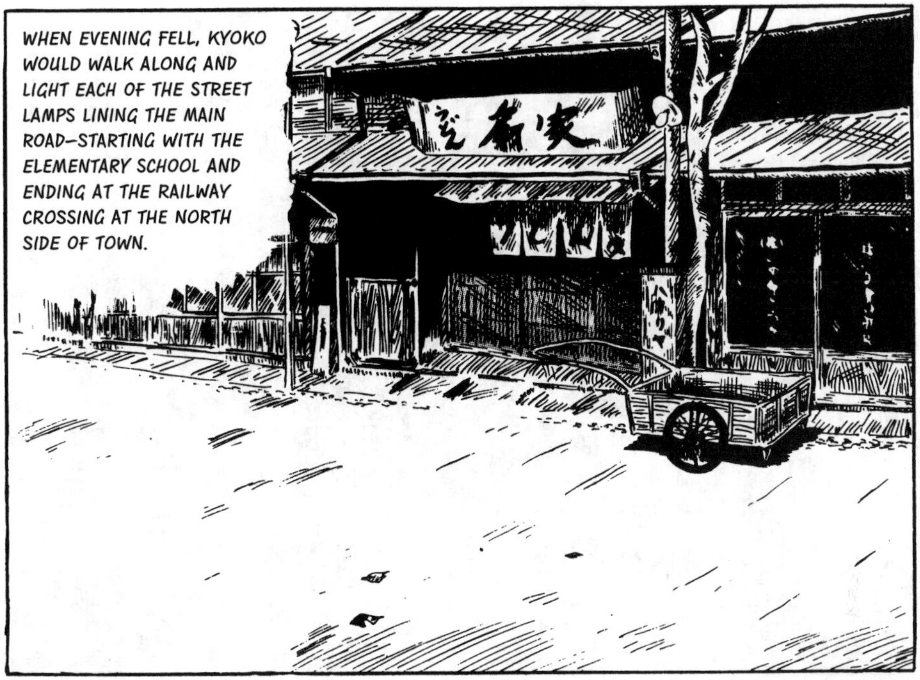
WHEN EVENING FELL, KYOKO WOULD WALK ALONG AND LIGHT EACH OF THE STREET LAMPS LINING THE MAIN ROAD—STARTING WITH THE ELEMENTARY SCHOOL AND ENDING AT THE RAILWAY CROSSING AT THE NORTH SIDE OF TOWN.

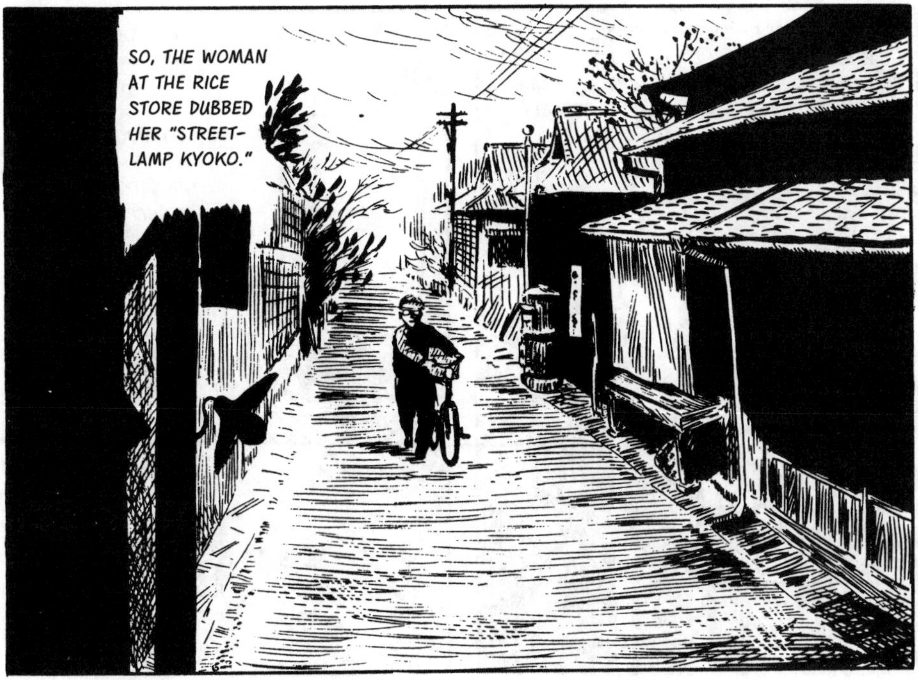
SO, THE WOMAN AT THE RICE STORE DUBBED HER "STREET-LAMP KYOKO."

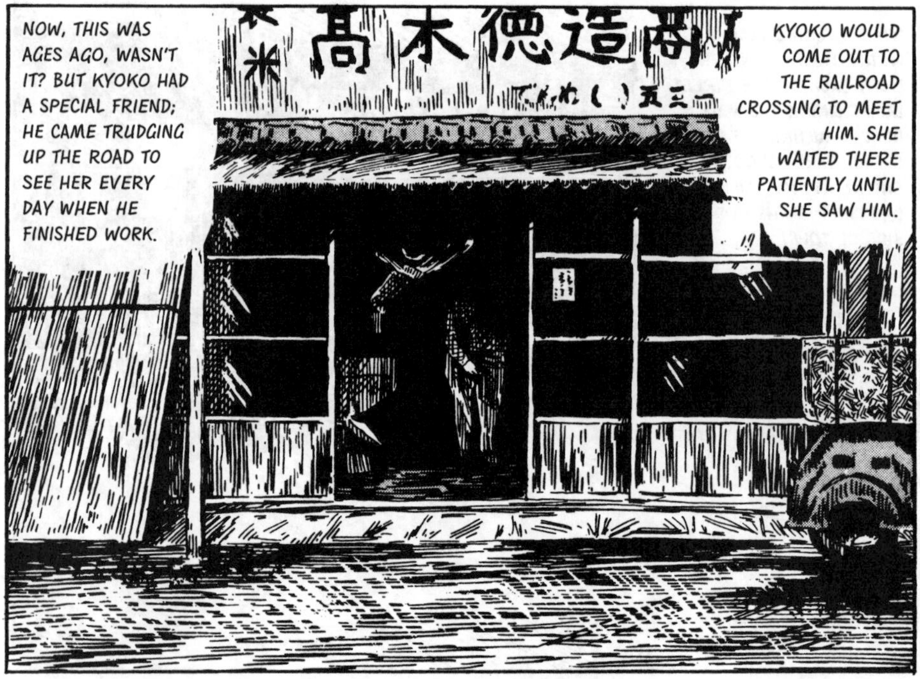
NOW, THIS WAS AGES AGO, WASN'T IT? BUT KYOKO HAD A SPECIAL FRIEND; HE CAME TRUDGING UP THE ROAD TO SEE HER EVERY DAY WHEN HE FINISHED WORK.
高木徳造商
KYOKO WOULD COME OUT TO THE RAILROAD CROSSING TO MEET HIM. SHE WAITED THERE PATIENTLY UNTIL SHE SAW HIM.

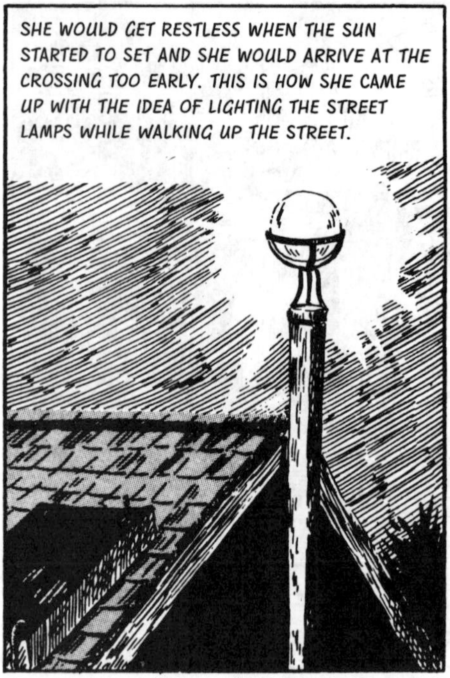
SHE WOULD GET RESTLESS WHEN THE SUN STARTED TO SET AND SHE WOULD ARRIVE AT THE CROSSING TOO EARLY. THIS IS HOW SHE CAME UP WITH THE IDEA OF LIGHTING THE STREET LAMPS WHILE WALKING UP THE STREET.

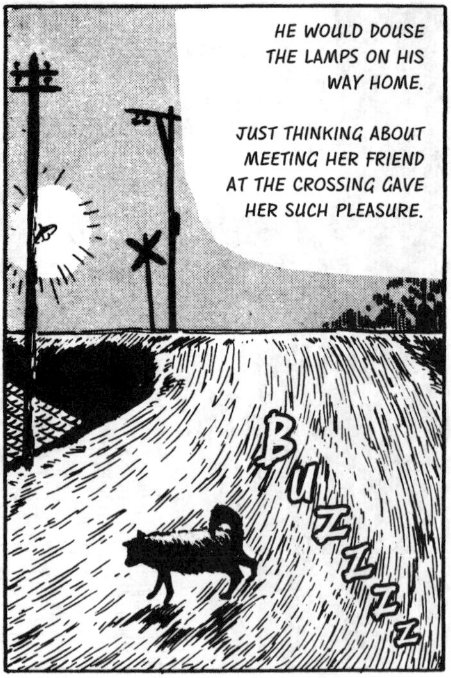
HE WOULD DOUSE THE LAMPS ON HIS WAY HOME.
JUST THINKING ABOUT MEETING HER FRIEND AT THE CROSSING GAVE HER SUCH PLEASURE.
BUZZZZZ

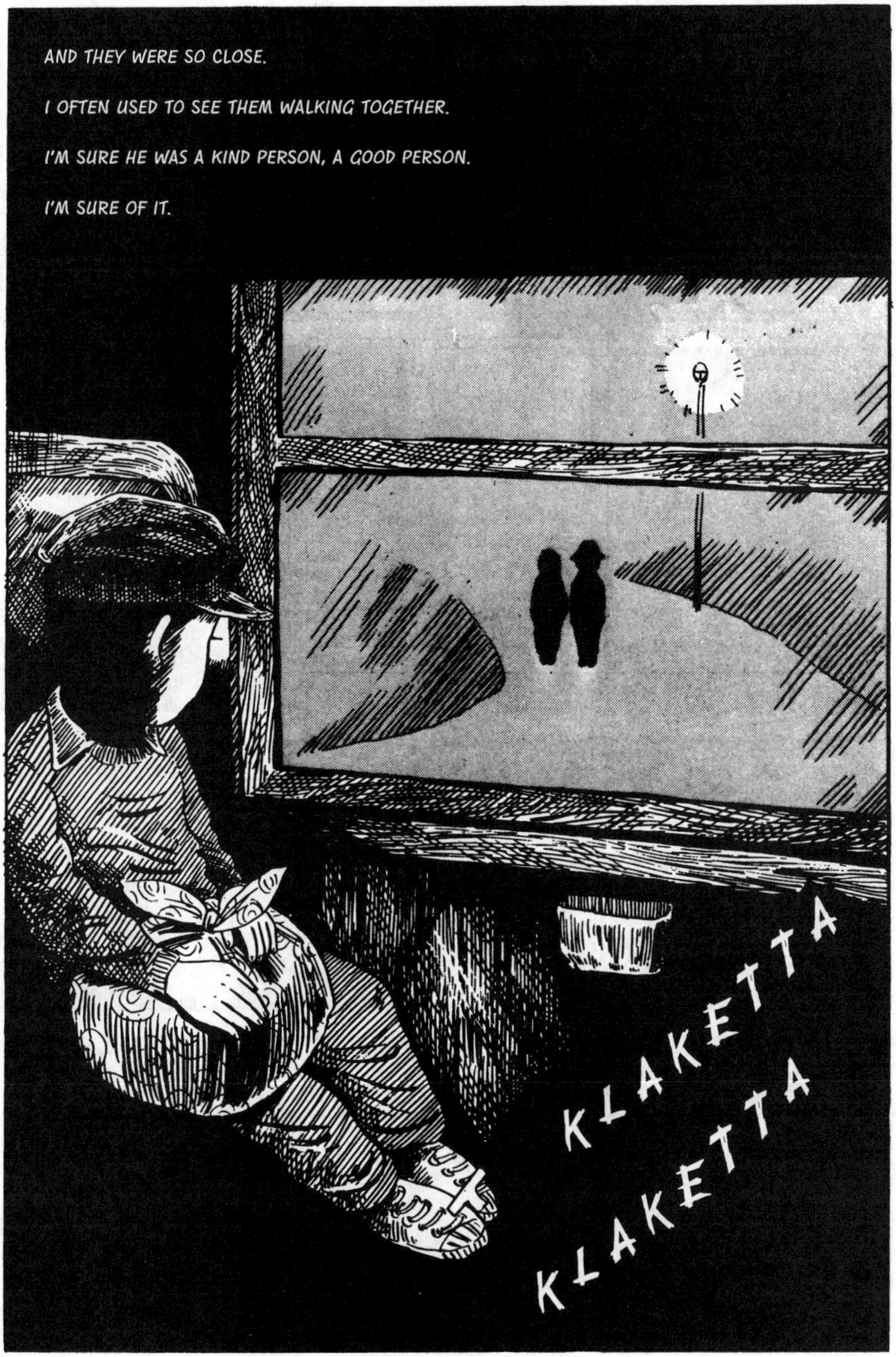
AND THEY WERE SO CLOSE.
I OFTEN USED TO SEE THEM WALKING TOGETHER.
I'M SURE HE WAS A KIND PERSON, A GOOD PERSON.
I'M SURE OF IT.
KLAKETTA
KLAKETTA

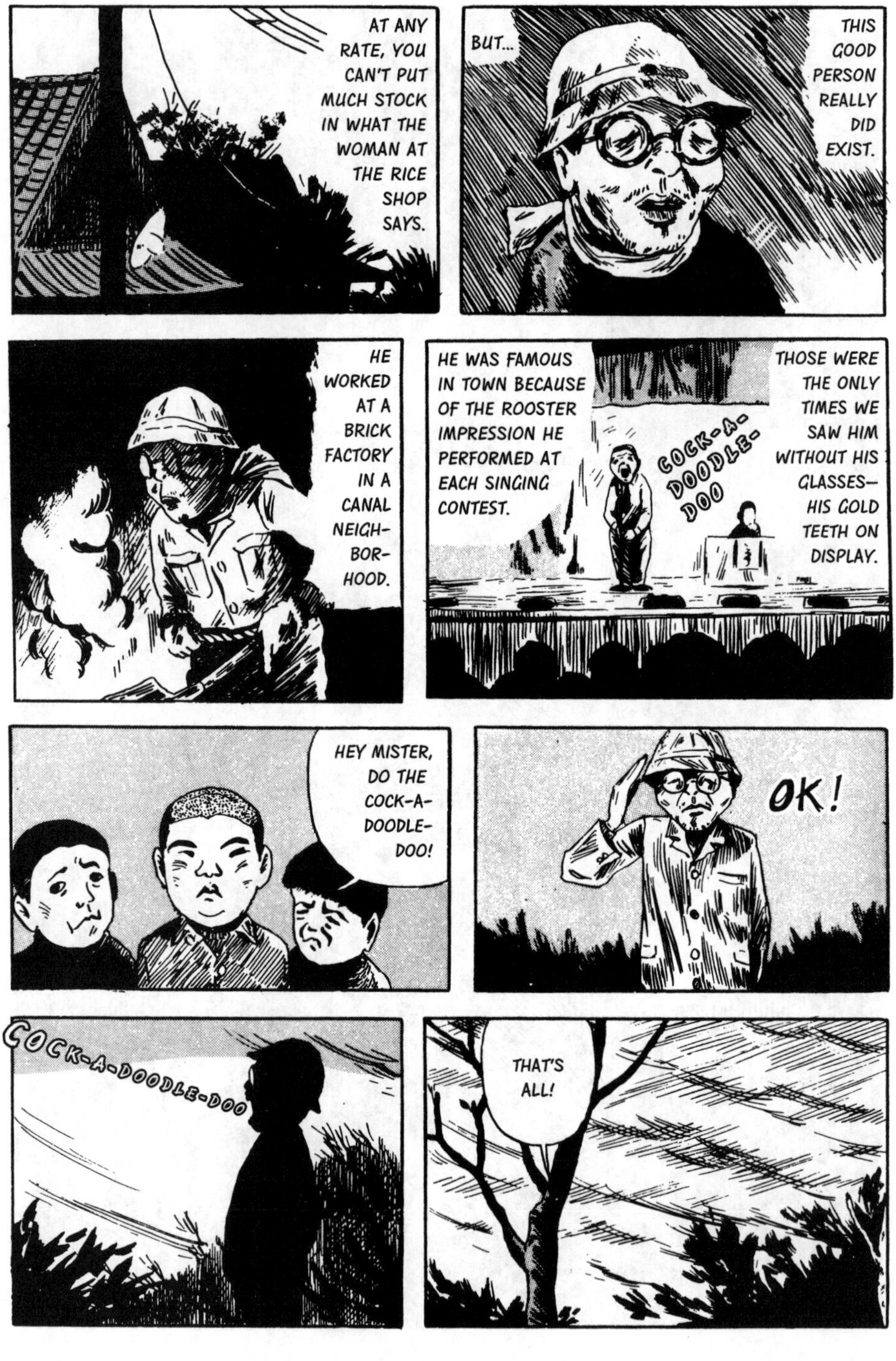
AT ANY RATE, YOU CAN'T PUT MUCH STOCK IN WHAT THE WOMAN AT THE RICE SHOP SAYS.
BUT...
THIS GOOD PERSON REALLY DID EXIST.
HE WORKED AT A BRICK FACTORY IN A CANAL NEIGH-BOR-HOOD.
HE WAS FAMOUS IN TOWN BECAUSE OF THE ROOSTER IMPRESSION HE PERFORMED AT EACH SINGING CONTEST.
COCK-A-DOODLE-DOO
THOSE WERE THE ONLY TIMES WE SAW HIM WITHOUT HIS GLASSES—HIS GOLD TEETH ON DISPLAY.
HEY MISTER, DO THE COCK-A-DOODLE-DOO!
OK!
COCK-A-DOODLE-DOO
THAT'S ALL!

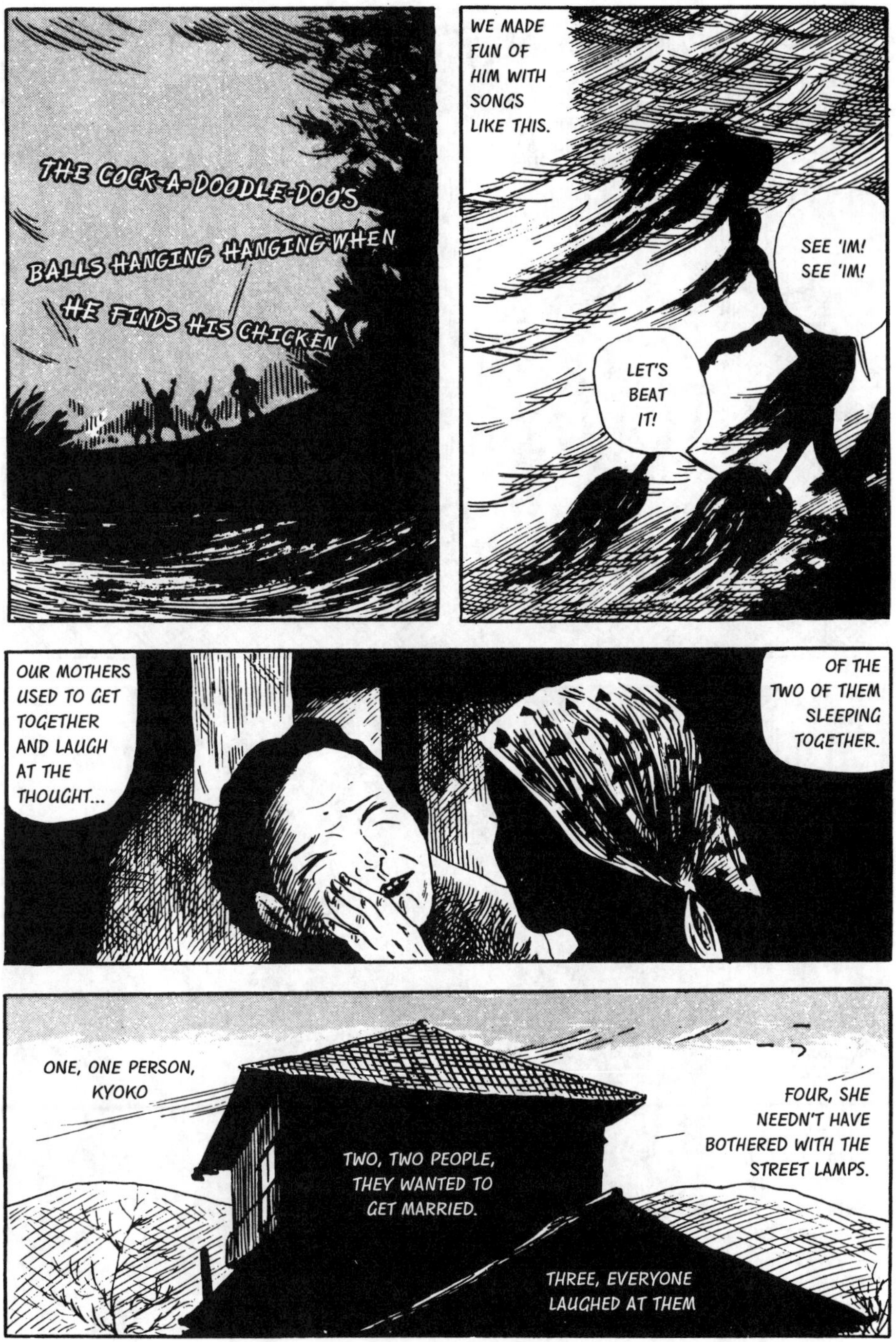
THE COCK-A-DOODLE-DOO'S
BALLS HANGING HANGING WHEN
HE FINDS HIS CHICKEN
WE MADE FUN OF HIM WITH SONGS LIKE THIS.
SEE 'IM! SEE 'IM!
LET'S BEAT IT!
OUR MOTHERS USED TO GET TOGETHER AND LAUGH AT THE THOUGHT...
OF THE TWO OF THEM SLEEPING TOGETHER.
ONE, ONE PERSON, KYOKO
TWO, TWO PEOPLE, THEY WANTED TO GET MARRIED.
THREE, EVERYONE LAUGHED AT THEM
FOUR, SHE NEEDN'T HAVE BOTHERED WITH THE STREET LAMPS.

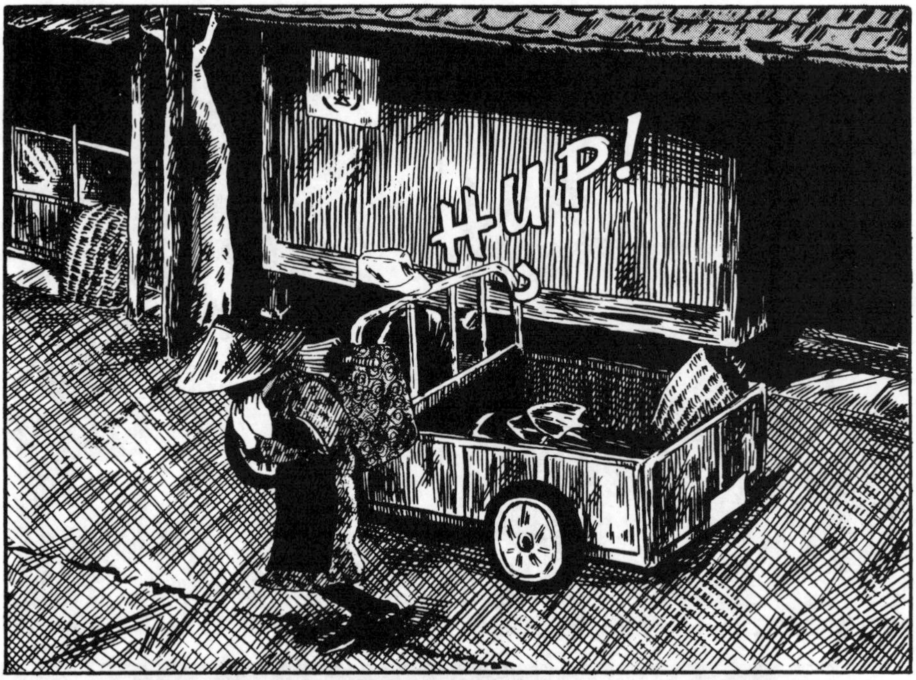
HUP!

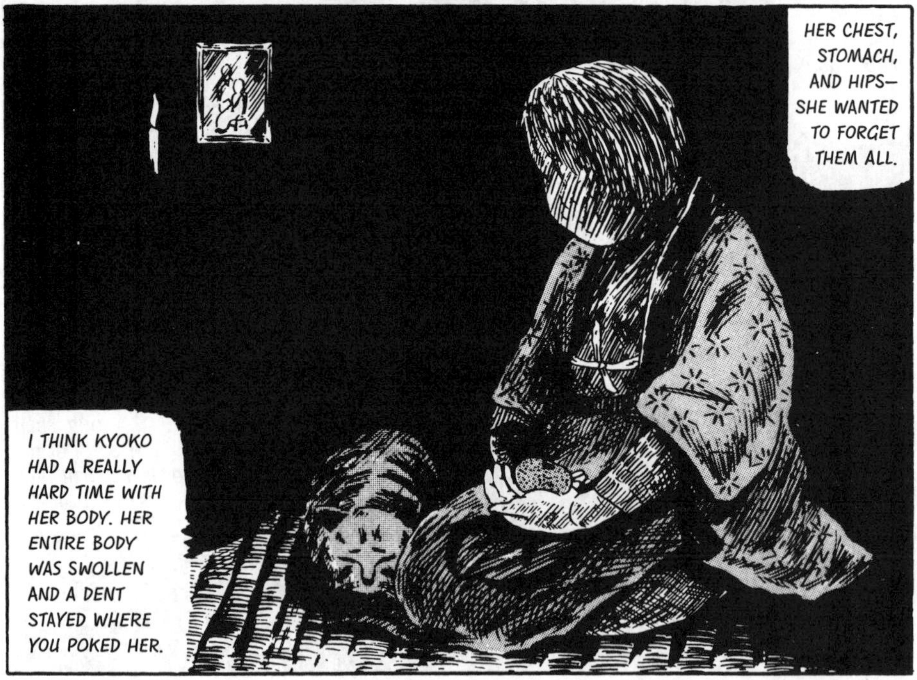
HER CHEST, STOMACH, AND HIPS— SHE WANTED TO FORGET THEM ALL.
I THINK KYOKO HAD A REALLY HARD TIME WITH HER BODY. HER ENTIRE BODY WAS SWOLLEN AND A DENT STAYED WHERE YOU POKED HER.

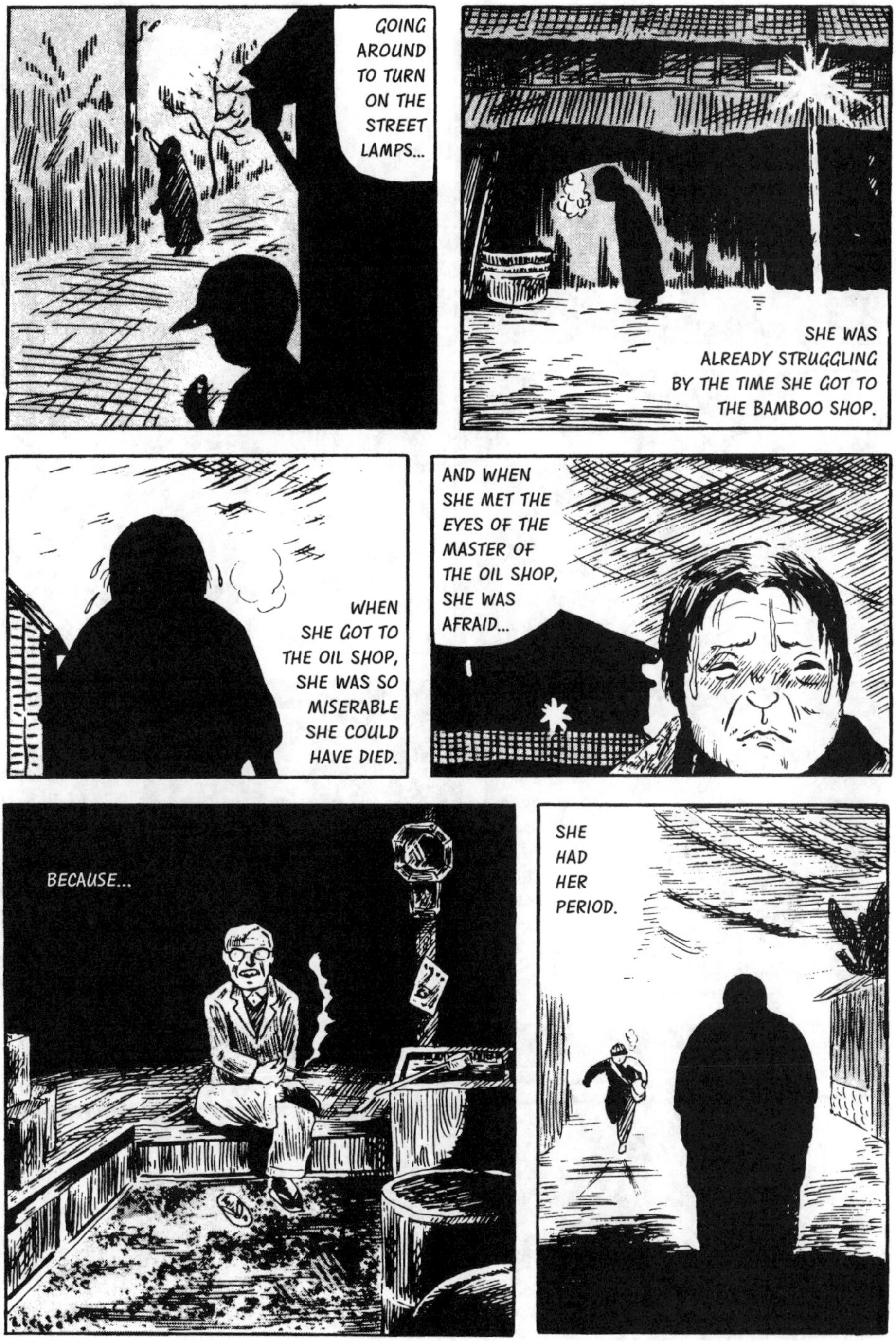
GOING AROUND TO TURN ON THE STREET LAMPS...
SHE WAS ALREADY STRUGGLING BY THE TIME SHE GOT TO THE BAMBOO SHOP.
WHEN SHE GOT TO THE OIL SHOP, SHE WAS SO MISERABLE SHE COULD HAVE DIED.
AND WHEN SHE MET THE EYES OF THE MASTER OF THE OIL SHOP, SHE WAS AFRAID...
BECAUSE...
SHE HAD HER PERIOD.

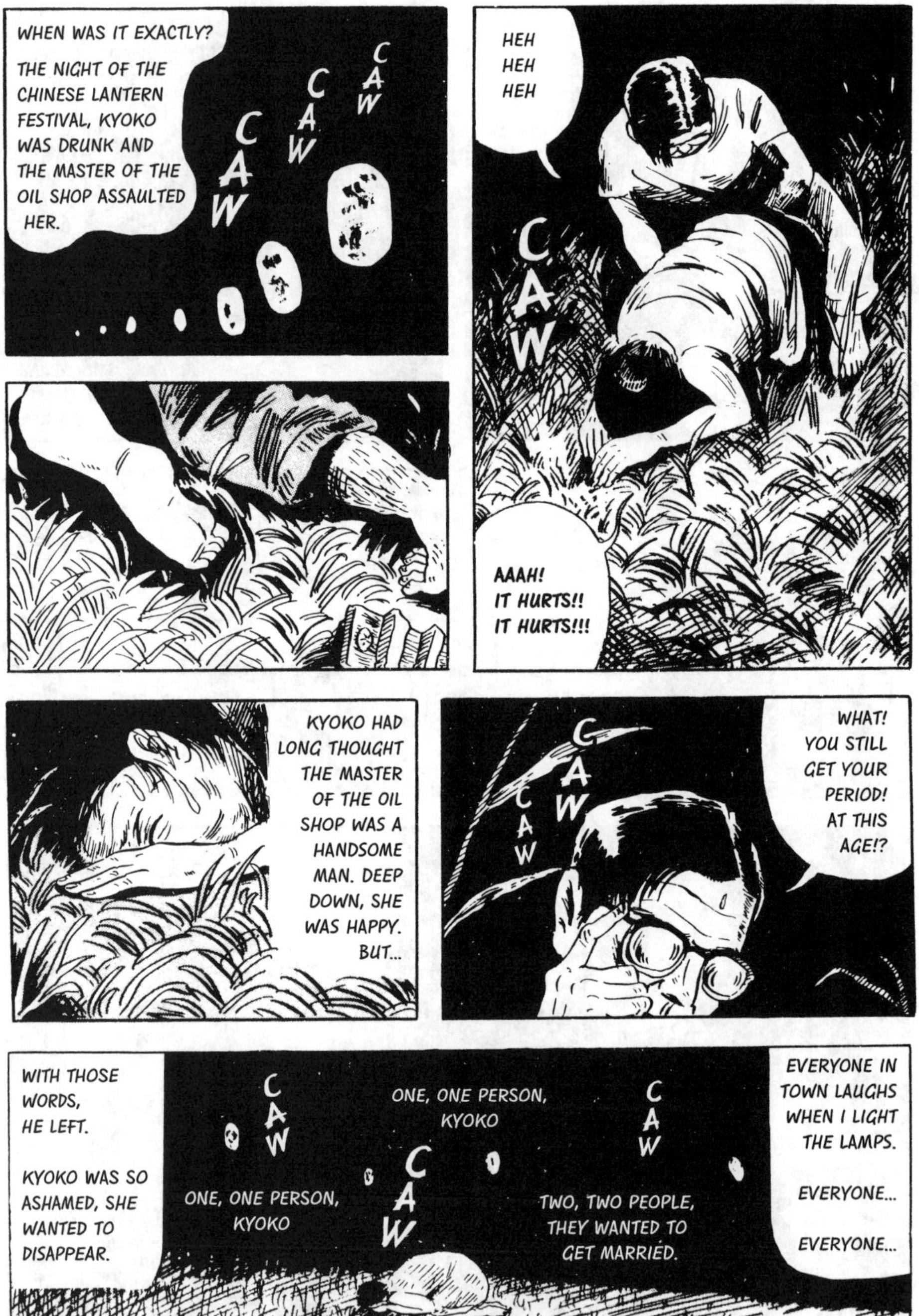
WHEN WAS IT EXACTLY?
THE NIGHT OF THE CHINESE LANTERN FESTIVAL, KYOKO WAS DRUNK AND THE MASTER OF THE OIL SHOP ASSAULTED HER.
CAW
CAW
CAW
HEH HEH HEH
CAW
AAAH! IT HURTS!! IT HURTS!!!
KYOKO HAD LONG THOUGHT THE MASTER OF THE OIL SHOP WAS A HANDSOME MAN. DEEP DOWN, SHE WAS HAPPY. BUT...
CAW
CAW
WHAT! YOU STILL GET YOUR PERIOD! AT THIS AGE!?
WITH THOSE WORDS, HE LEFT.
KYOKO WAS SO ASHAMED, SHE WANTED TO DISAPPEAR.
CAW
ONE, ONE PERSON, KYOKO
ONE, ONE PERSON, KYOKO
CAW
CAW
TWO, TWO PEOPLE, THEY WANTED TO GET MARRIED.
EVERYONE IN TOWN LAUGHS WHEN I LIGHT THE LAMPS.
EVERYONE...
EVERYONE...

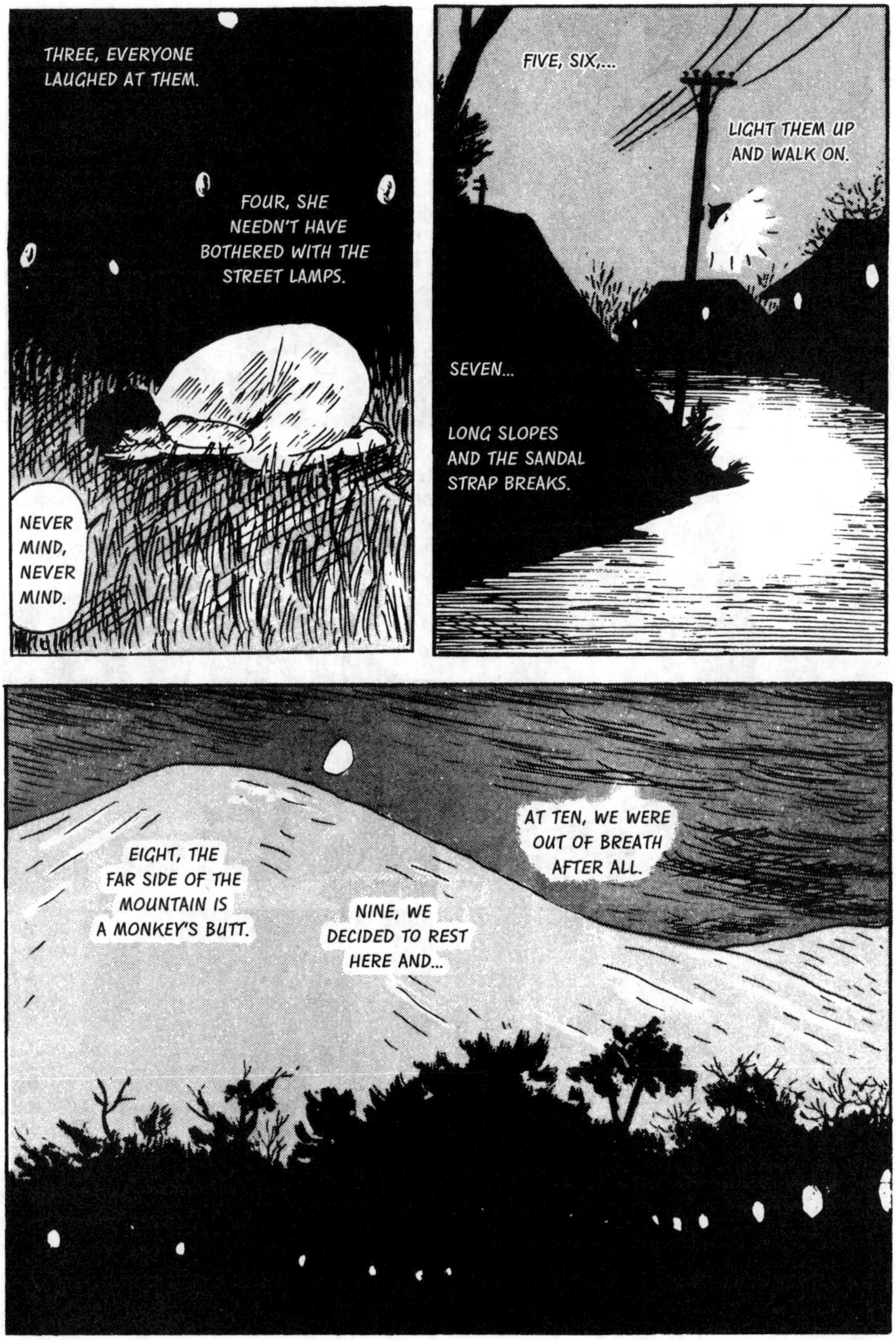
THREE, EVERYONE LAUGHED AT THEM.
FOUR, SHE NEEDN'T HAVE BOTHERED WITH THE STREET LAMPS.
NEVER MIND, NEVER MIND.
FIVE, SIX,...
LIGHT THEM UP AND WALK ON.
SEVEN...
LONG SLOPES AND THE SANDAL STRAP BREAKS.
EIGHT, THE FAR SIDE OF THE MOUNTAIN IS A MONKEY'S BUTT.
NINE, WE DECIDED TO REST HERE AND...
AT TEN, WE WERE OUT OF BREATH AFTER ALL.

PERHAPS KYOKO WAS AT PEACE IN HER HEART THAT NIGHT.

THE POLKA DOT DRESS HANGING ON THE WALL WAS CERTAINLY BEAUTIFUL IN THE LIGHT OF THE BULB.

I WAS SO ASHAMED OF SUCH A SHOWY DRESS. HE...HE SAID IT LOOKED REALLY GOOD ON ME.

I WORE THIS DRESS AND WE HAD OUR PHOTO TAKEN AT THE TOWN'S PHOTO STUDIO.

HE WAS SUCH A KIND PERSON.

I'M A REAL IDIOT... BUT HIM...

KYOKO SUDDENLY REMEM-BERED.

THAT'S RIGHT. HE'S COMING TONIGHT. WHEN HE COMES LATE AFTER WORK-ING OVERTIME, HE OFTEN IMITATES A CRICKET.

AAH, WHAT SHOULD I DO, WHAT SHOULD I DO? I'M ASHAMED OF MY PERIOD. WHAT'LL I DO IF HE LAUGHS AT ME?

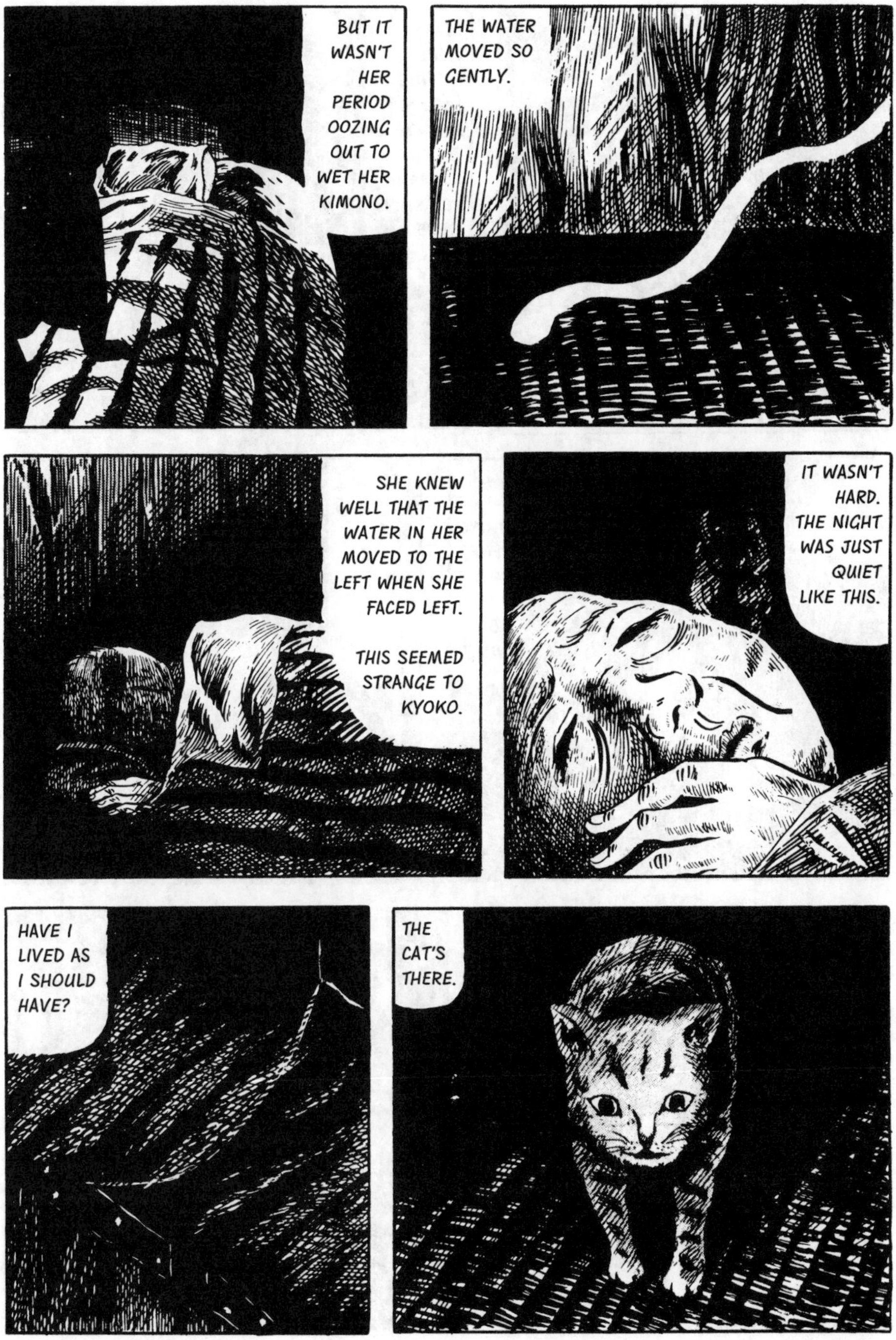
BUT IT WASN'T HER PERIOD OOZING OUT TO WET HER KIMONO.
THE WATER MOVED SO GENTLY.
SHE KNEW WELL THAT THE WATER IN HER MOVED TO THE LEFT WHEN SHE FACED LEFT.
THIS SEEMED STRANGE TO KYOKO.
IT WASN'T HARD. THE NIGHT WAS JUST QUIET LIKE THIS.
HAVE I LIVED AS I SHOULD HAVE?
THE CAT'S THERE.

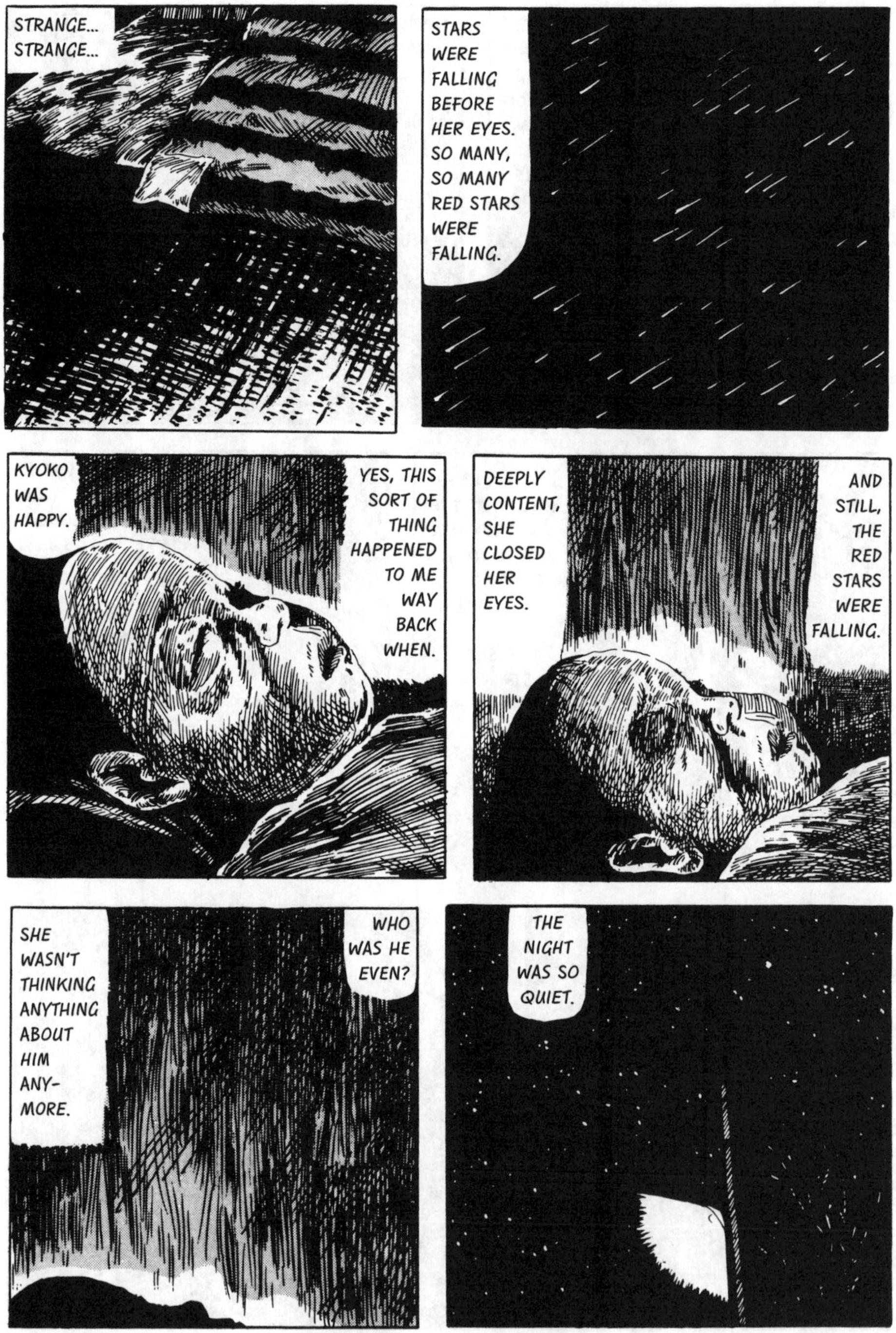
STRANGE... STRANGE...
STARS WERE FALLING BEFORE HER EYES. SO MANY, SO MANY RED STARS WERE FALLING.
KYOKO WAS HAPPY.
YES, THIS SORT OF THING HAPPENED TO ME WAY BACK WHEN.
DEEPLY CONTENT, SHE CLOSED HER EYES.
AND STILL, THE RED STARS WERE FALLING.
SHE WASN'T THINKING ANYTHING ABOUT HIM ANY-MORE.
WHO WAS HE EVEN?
THE NIGHT WAS SO QUIET.

AND THEN, KYOKO TOOK ON HER SISTER'S FEATURES...

AND FELL ASLEEP.

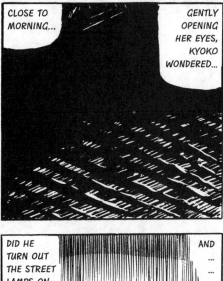

CLOSE TO MORNING...

GENTLY OPENING HER EYES, KYOKO WONDERED...

DID HE TURN OUT THE STREET LAMPS ON HIS WAY HERE?

AND ...
...

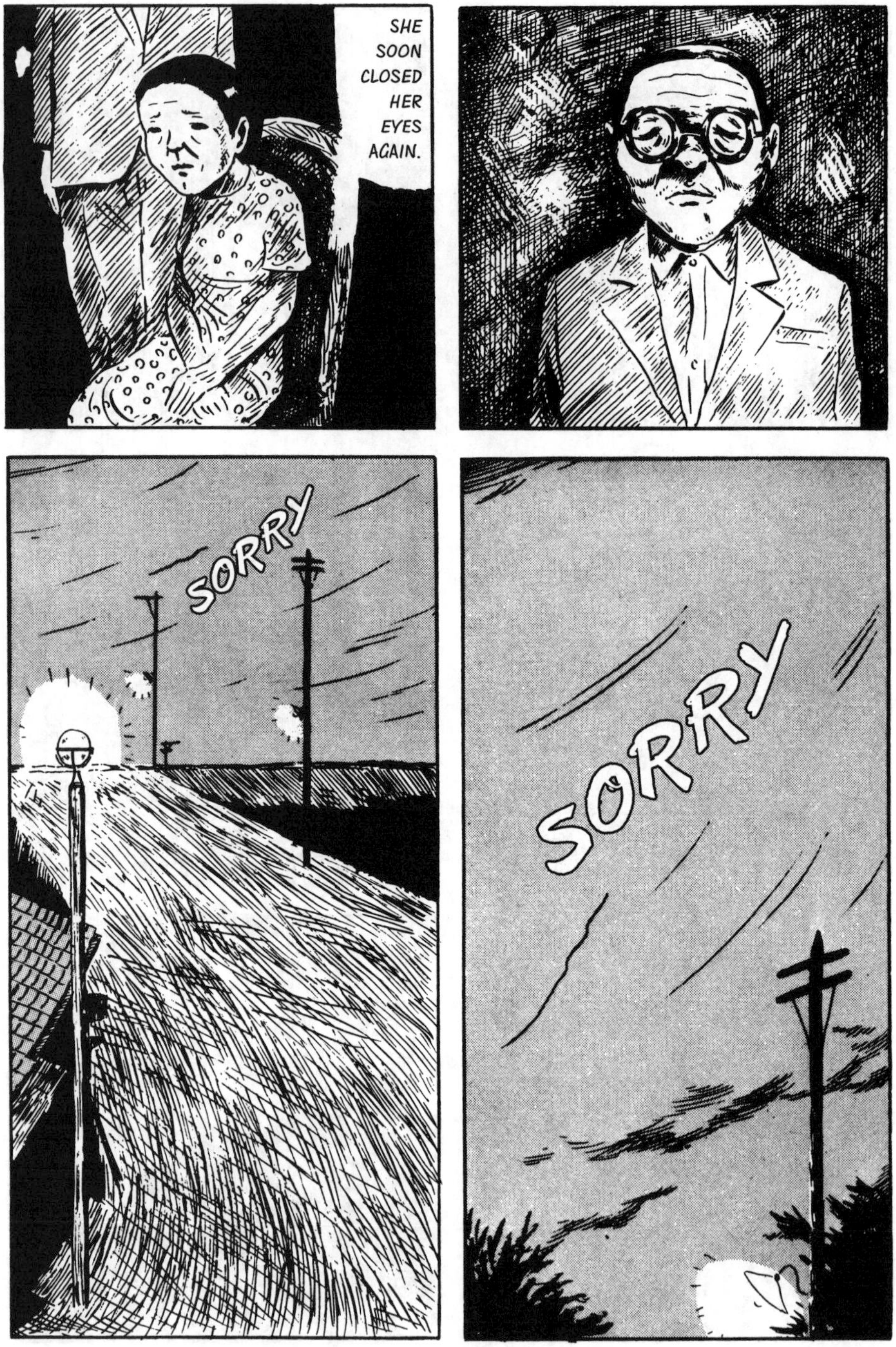
SHE SOON CLOSED HER EYES AGAIN.
SORRY
SORRY

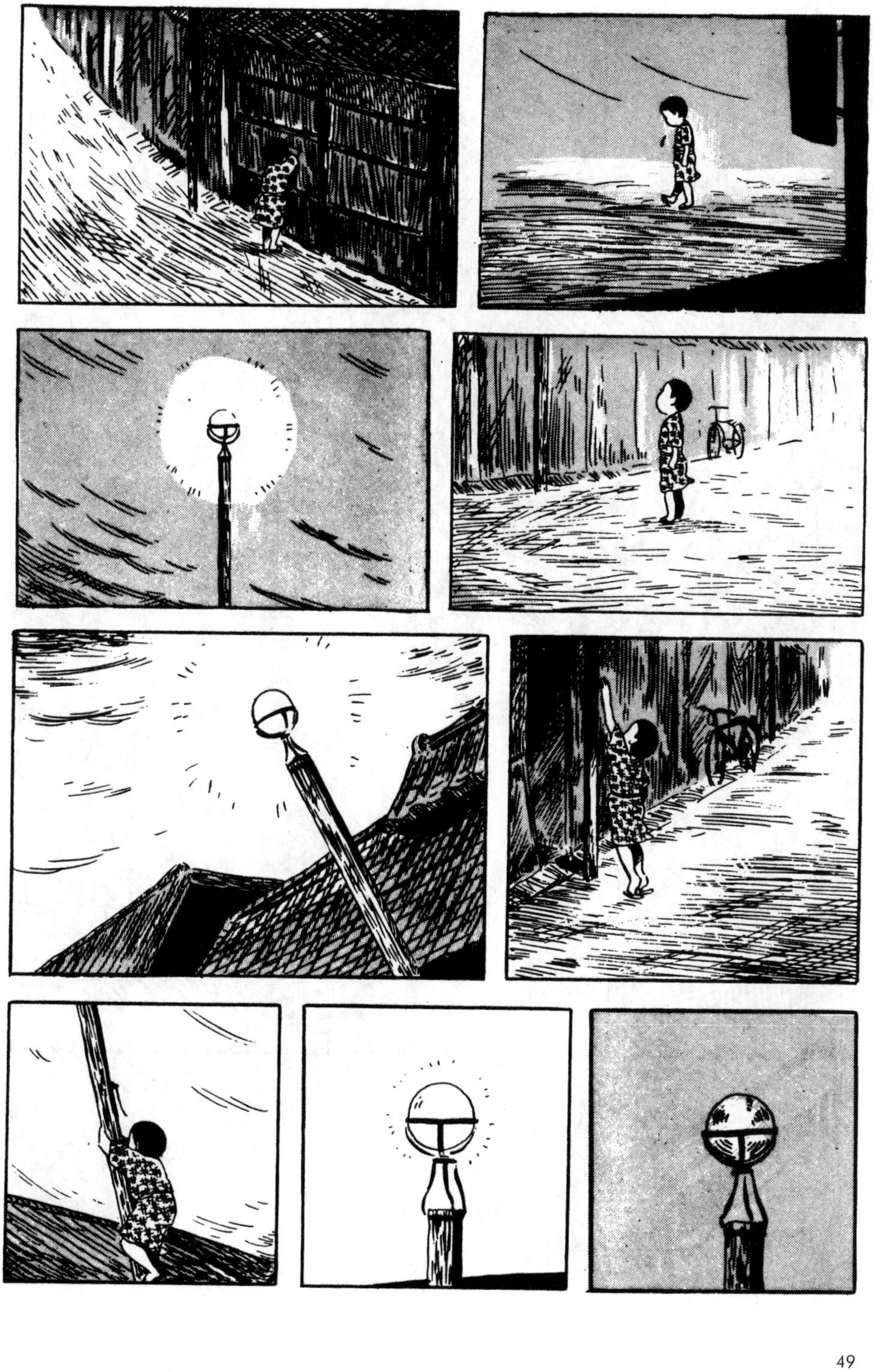

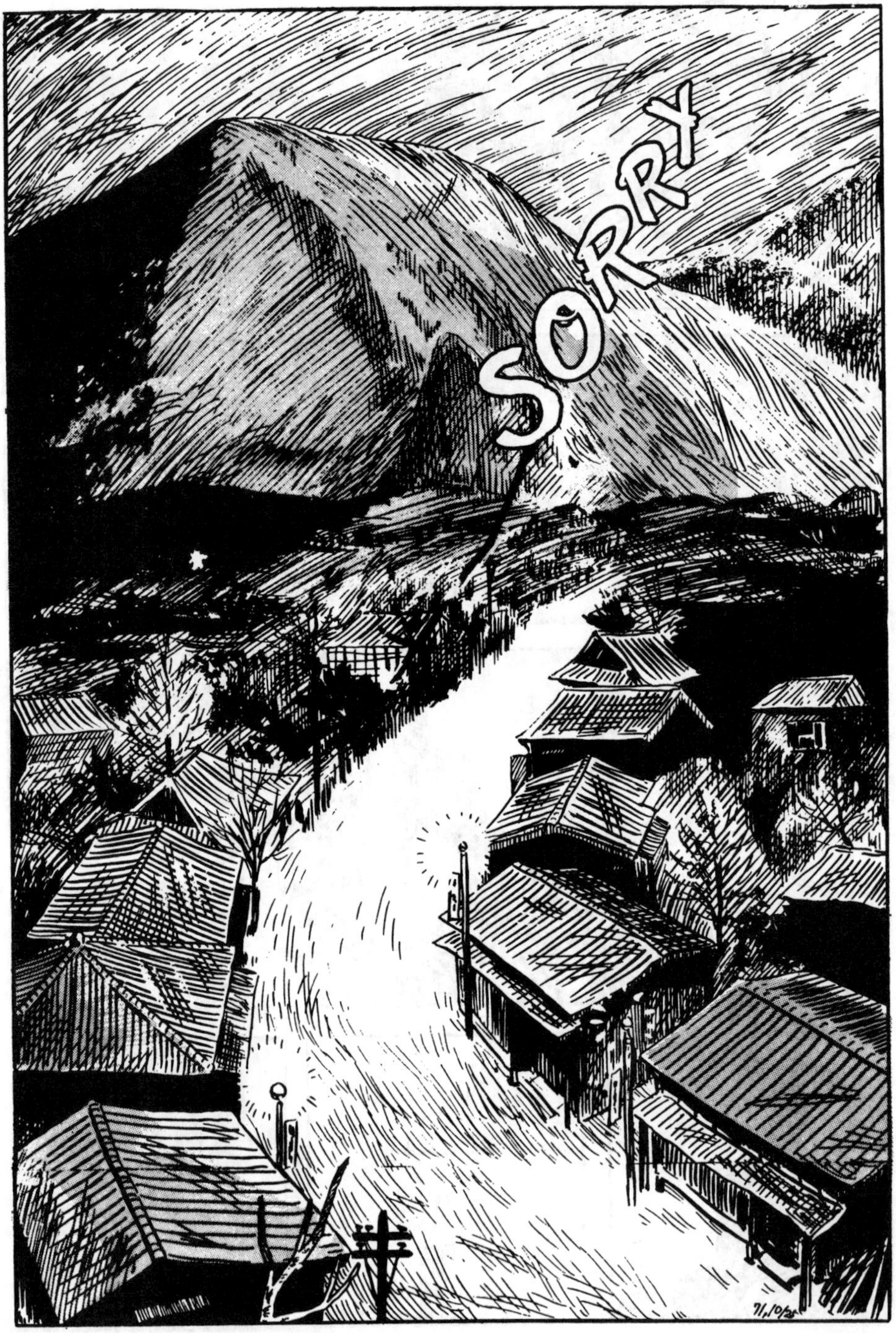
SORRY

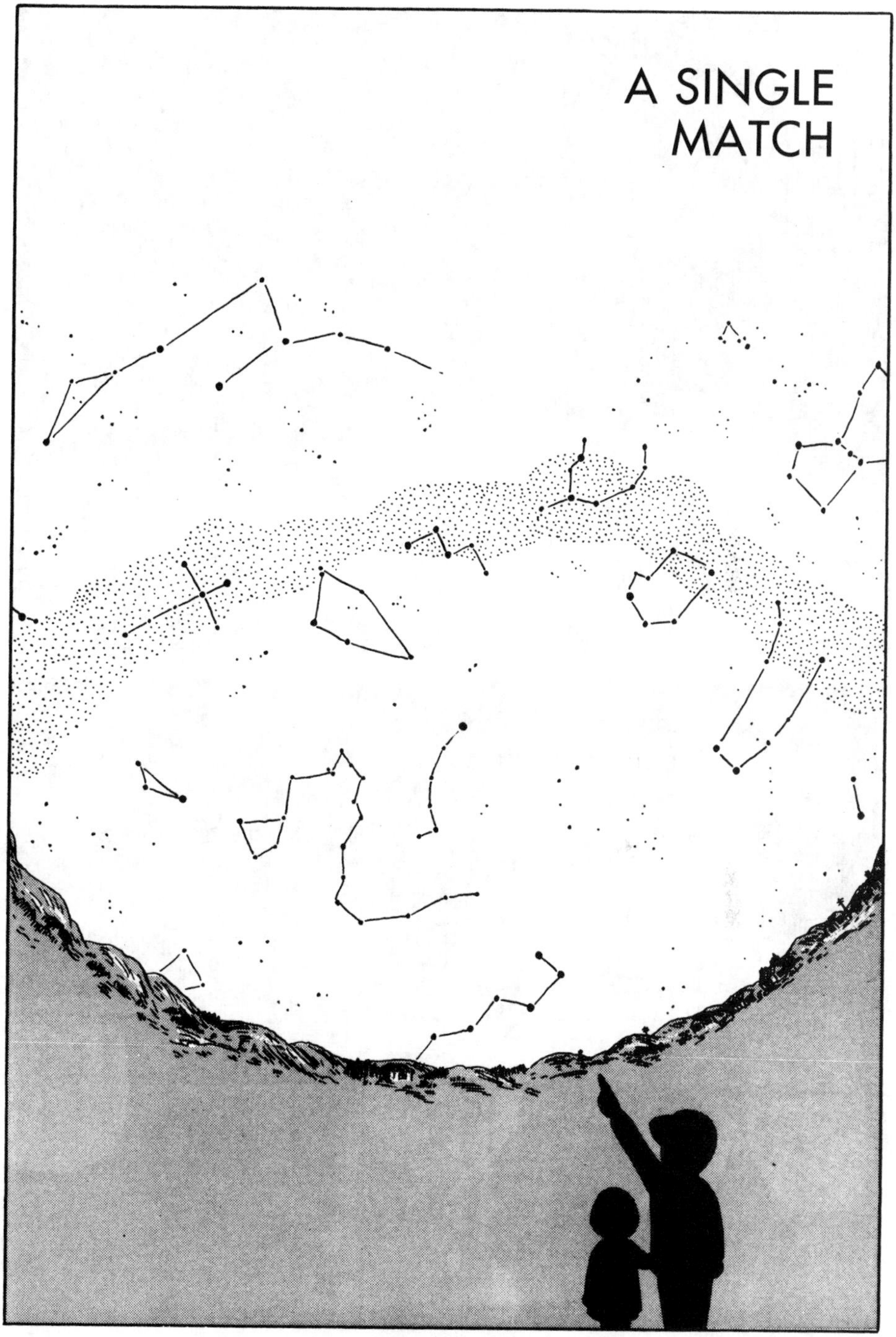
A SINGLE MATCH

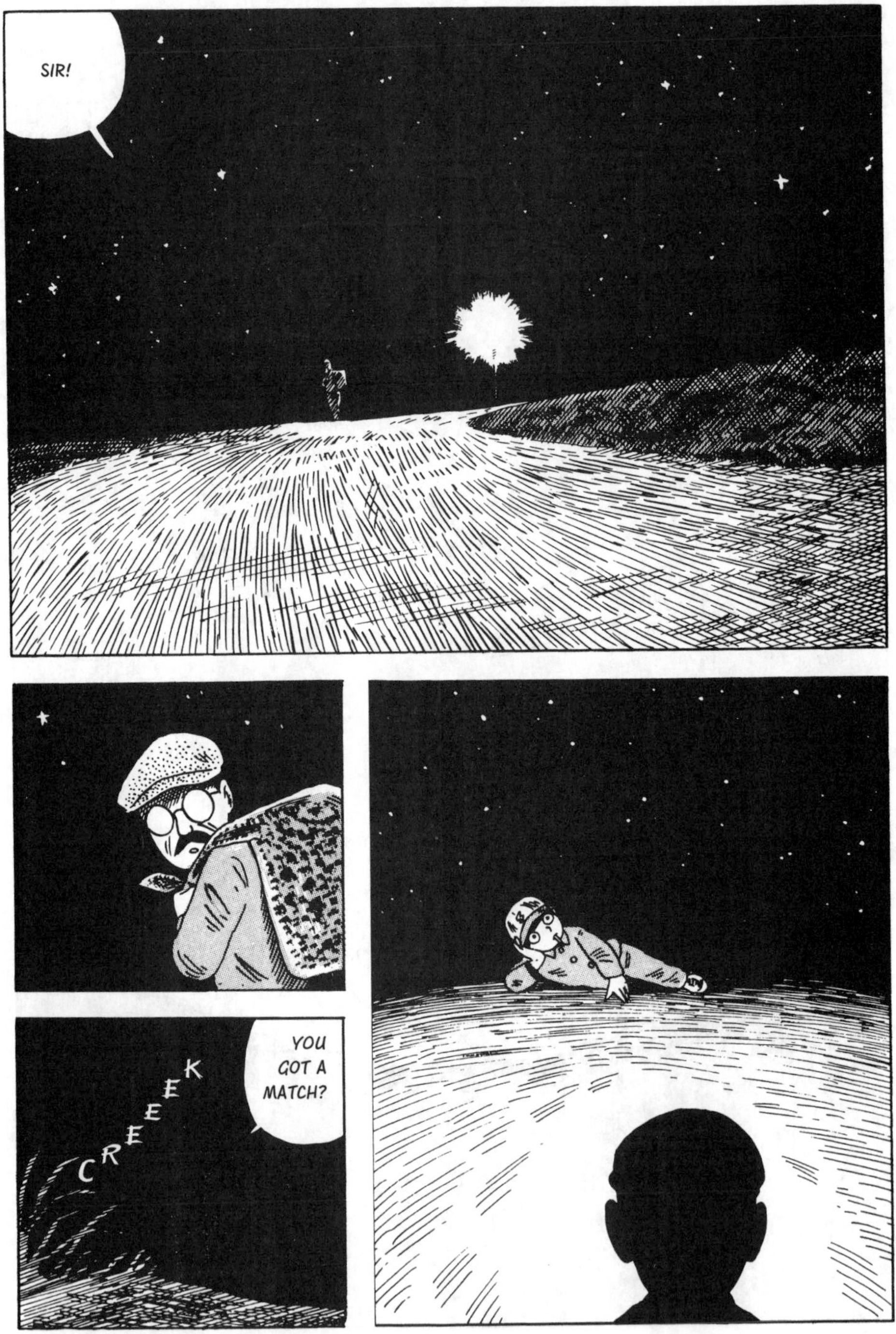
SIR!
CREEEK
YOU GOT A MATCH?

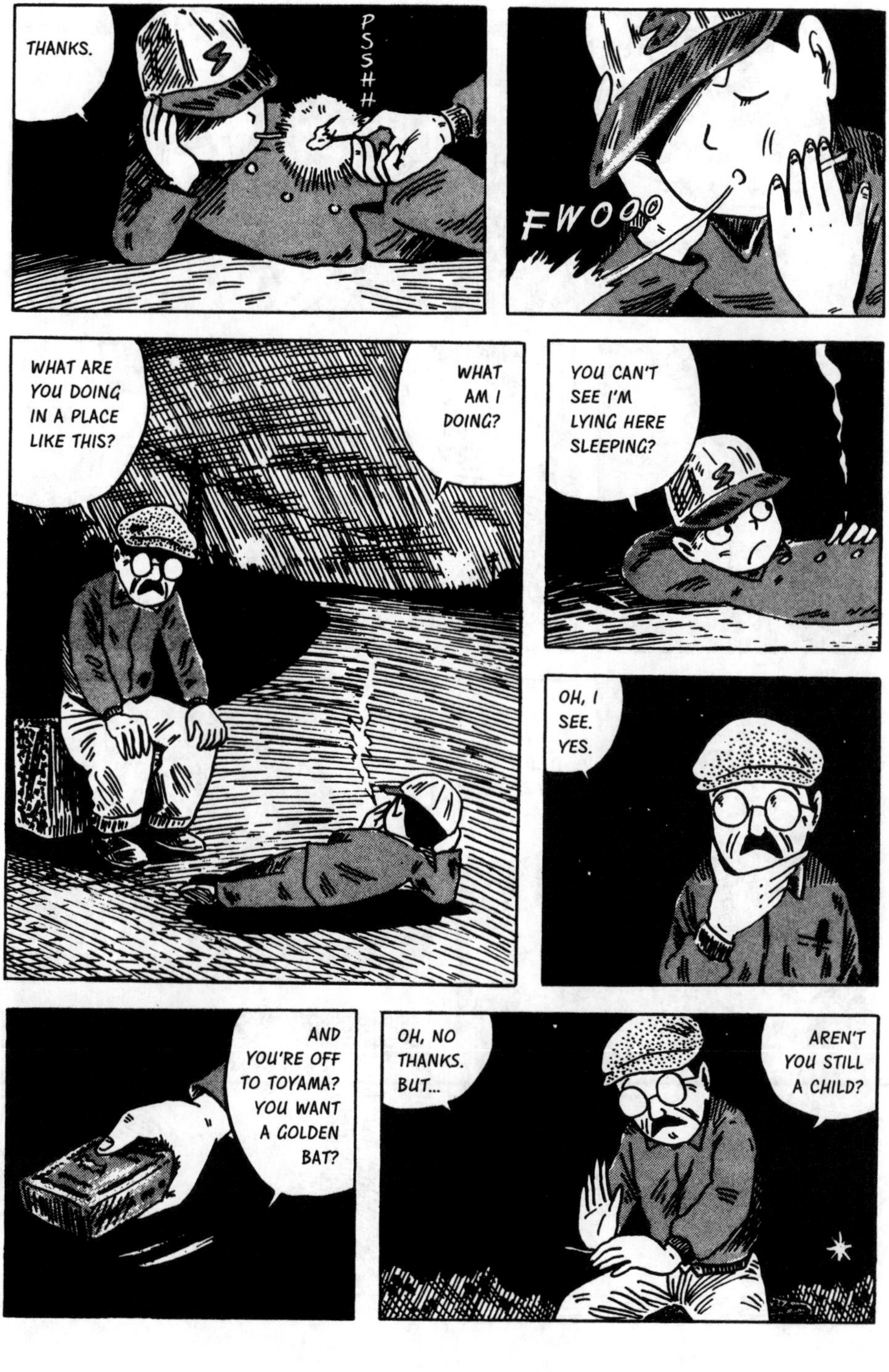
THANKS.
PSSHH
FWOOO
WHAT ARE YOU DOING IN A PLACE LIKE THIS?
WHAT AM I DOING?
YOU CAN'T SEE I'M LYING HERE SLEEPING?
OH, I SEE. YES.
AND YOU'RE OFF TO TOYAMA? YOU WANT A GOLDEN BAT?
OH, NO THANKS. BUT...
AREN'T YOU STILL A CHILD?

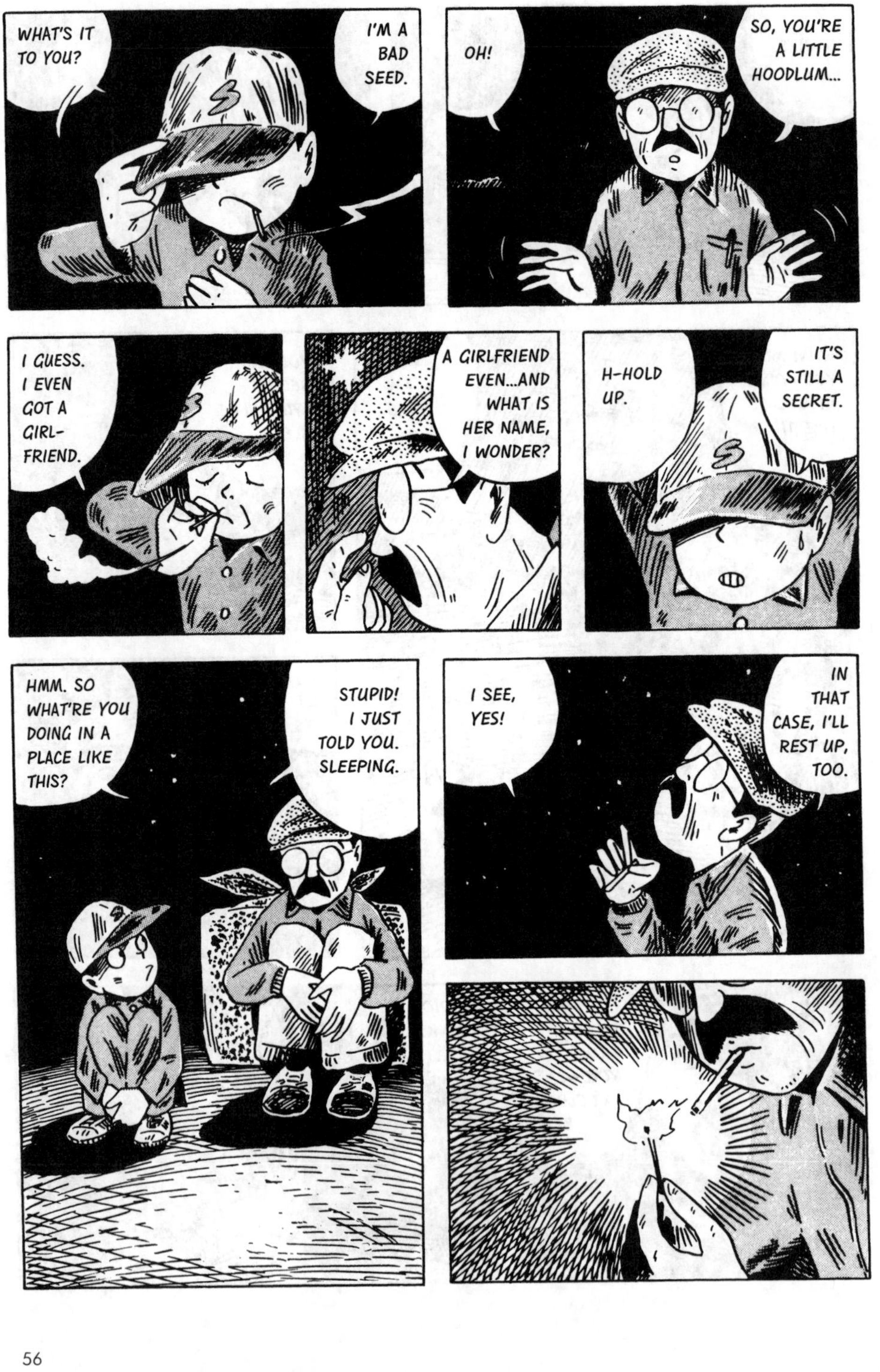
WHAT'S IT TO YOU?
I'M A BAD SEED.
OH!
SO, YOU'RE A LITTLE HOODLUM...
I GUESS. I EVEN GOT A GIRL-FRIEND.
A GIRLFRIEND EVEN...AND WHAT IS HER NAME, I WONDER?
H-HOLD UP.
IT'S STILL A SECRET.
HMM. SO WHAT'RE YOU DOING IN A PLACE LIKE THIS?
STUPID! I JUST TOLD YOU. SLEEPING.
I SEE, YES!
IN THAT CASE, I'LL REST UP, TOO.

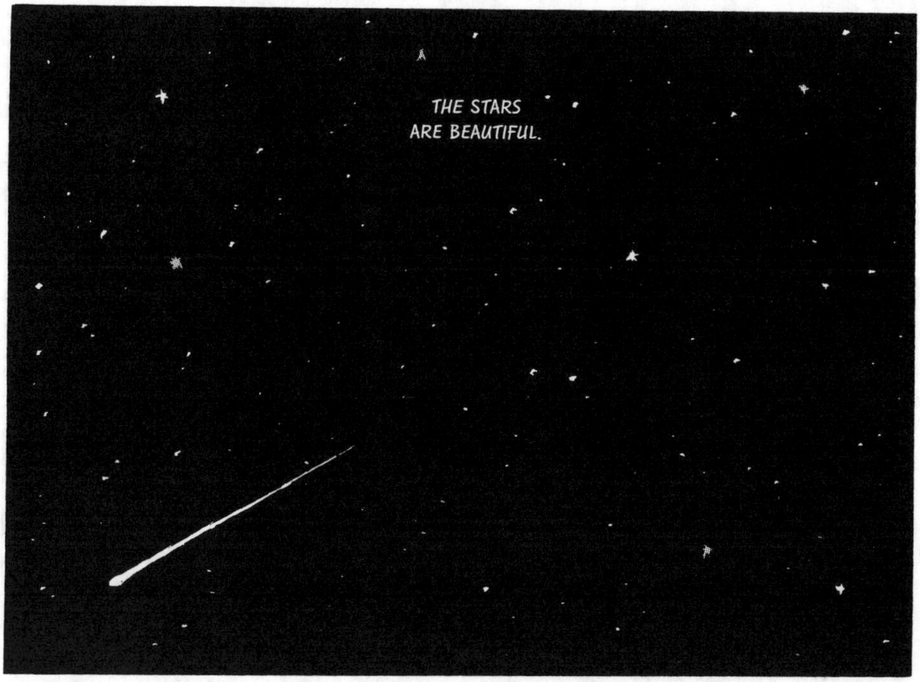
THE STARS
ARE BEAUTIFUL.

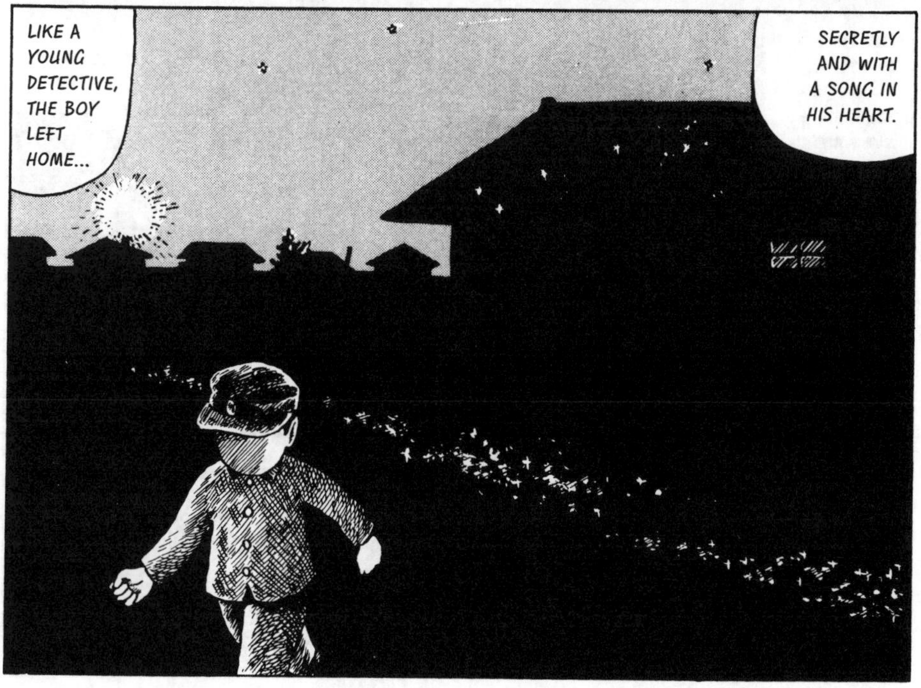
LIKE A YOUNG DETECTIVE, THE BOY LEFT HOME...
SECRETLY AND WITH A SONG IN HIS HEART.

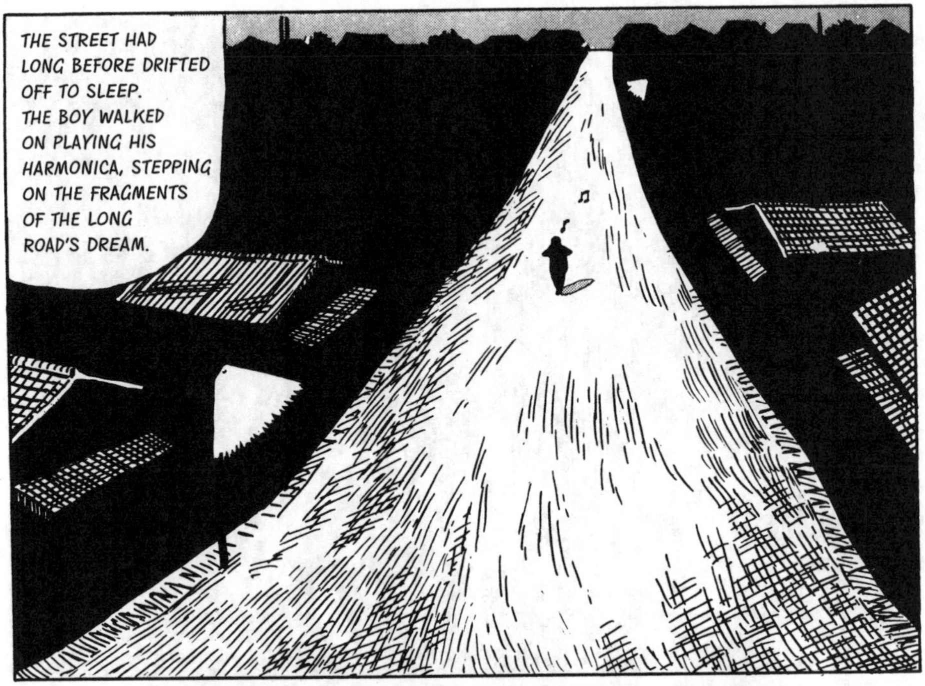
THE STREET HAD LONG BEFORE DRIFTED OFF TO SLEEP. THE BOY WALKED ON PLAYING HIS HARMONICA, STEPPING ON THE FRAGMENTS OF THE LONG ROAD'S DREAM.

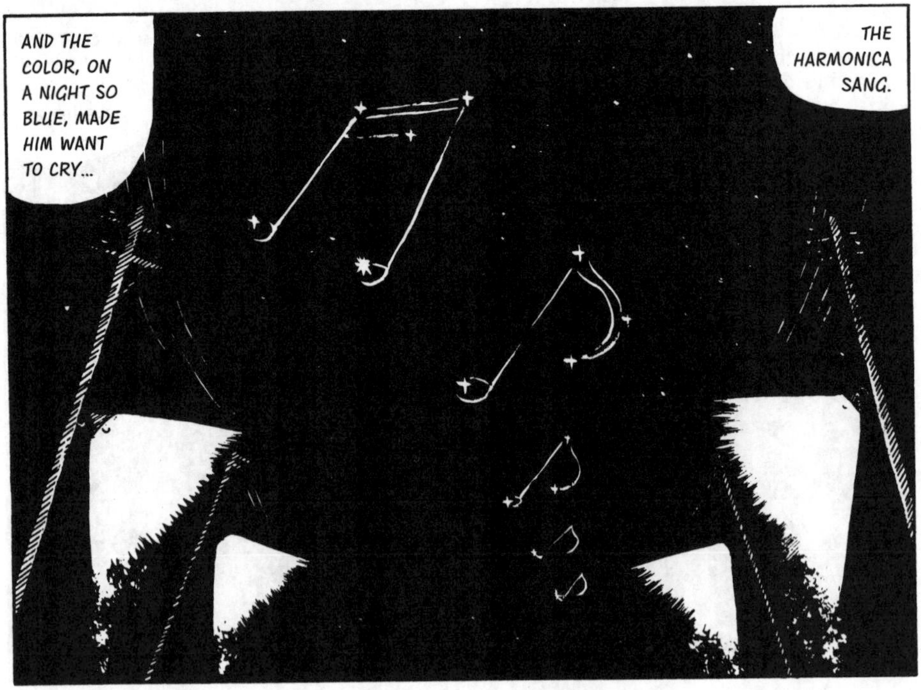
AND THE COLOR, ON A NIGHT SO BLUE, MADE HIM WANT TO CRY...
THE HARMONICA SANG.

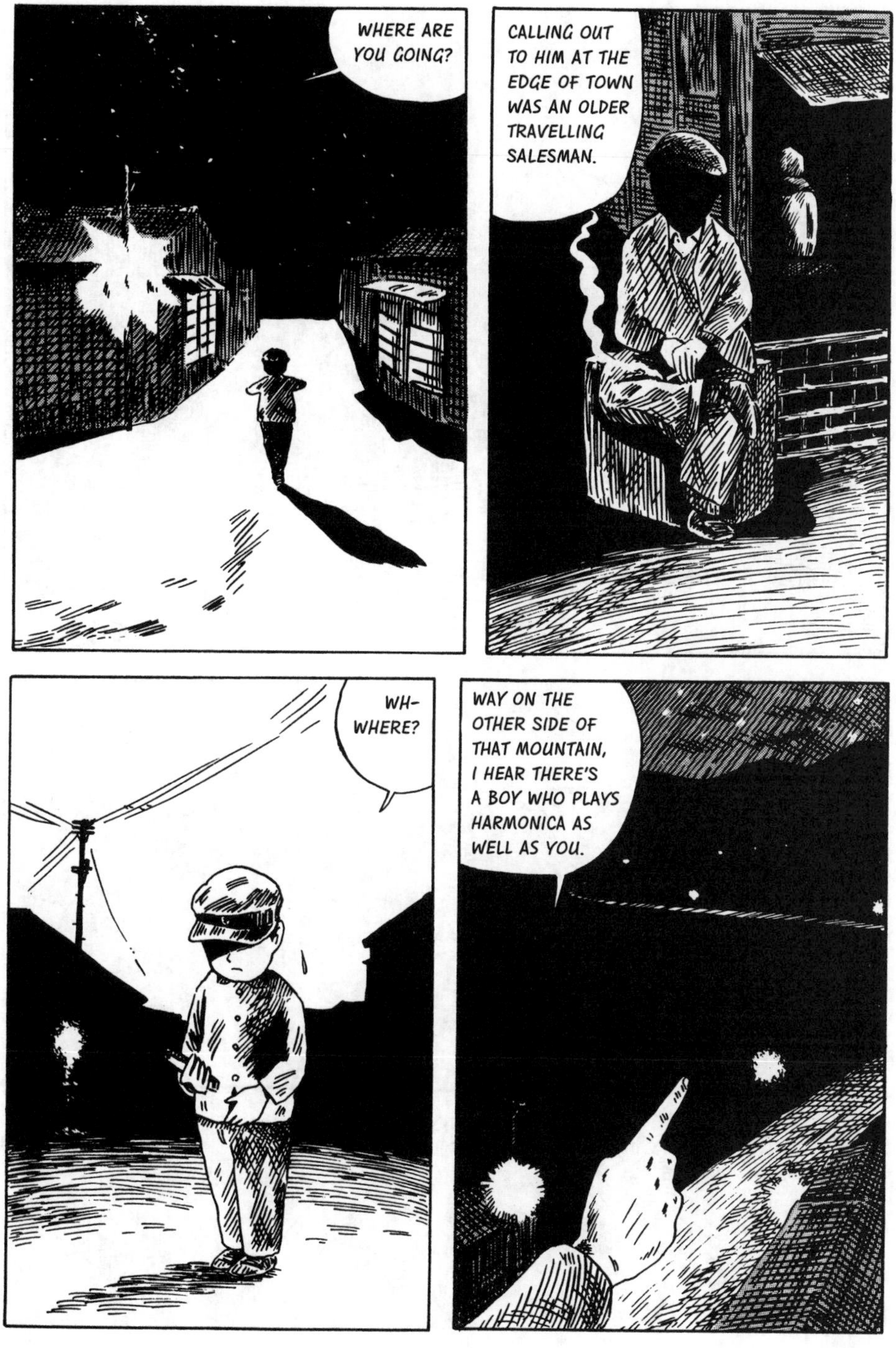
WHERE ARE YOU GOING?
CALLING OUT TO HIM AT THE EDGE OF TOWN WAS AN OLDER TRAVELLING SALESMAN.
WH- WHERE?
WAY ON THE OTHER SIDE OF THAT MOUNTAIN, I HEAR THERE'S A BOY WHO PLAYS HARMONICA AS WELL AS YOU.

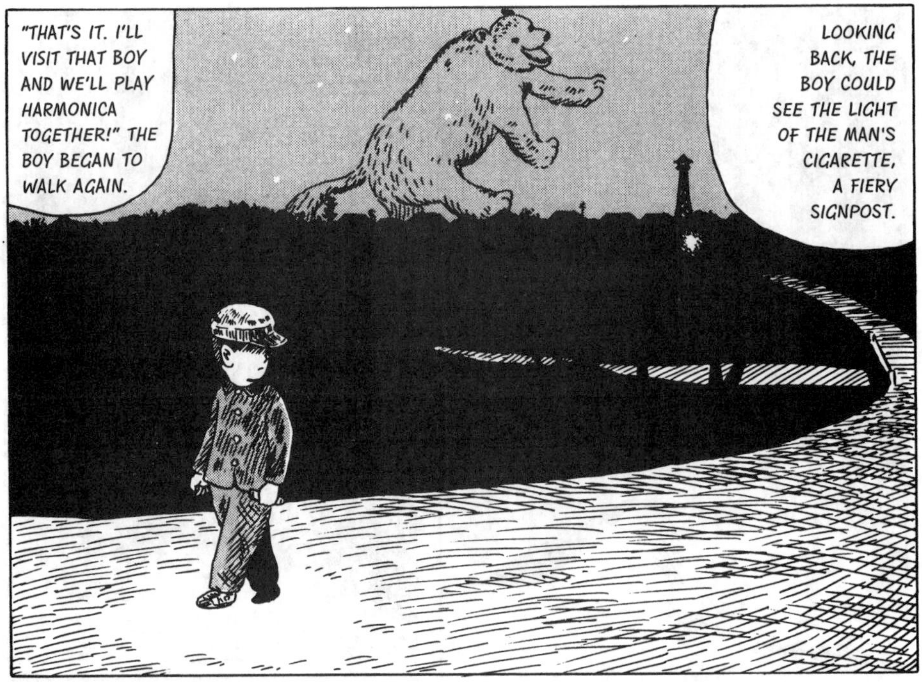
"THAT'S IT. I'LL VISIT THAT BOY AND WE'LL PLAY HARMONICA TOGETHER!" THE BOY BEGAN TO WALK AGAIN.
LOOKING BACK, THE BOY COULD SEE THE LIGHT OF THE MAN'S CIGARETTE, A FIERY SIGNPOST.

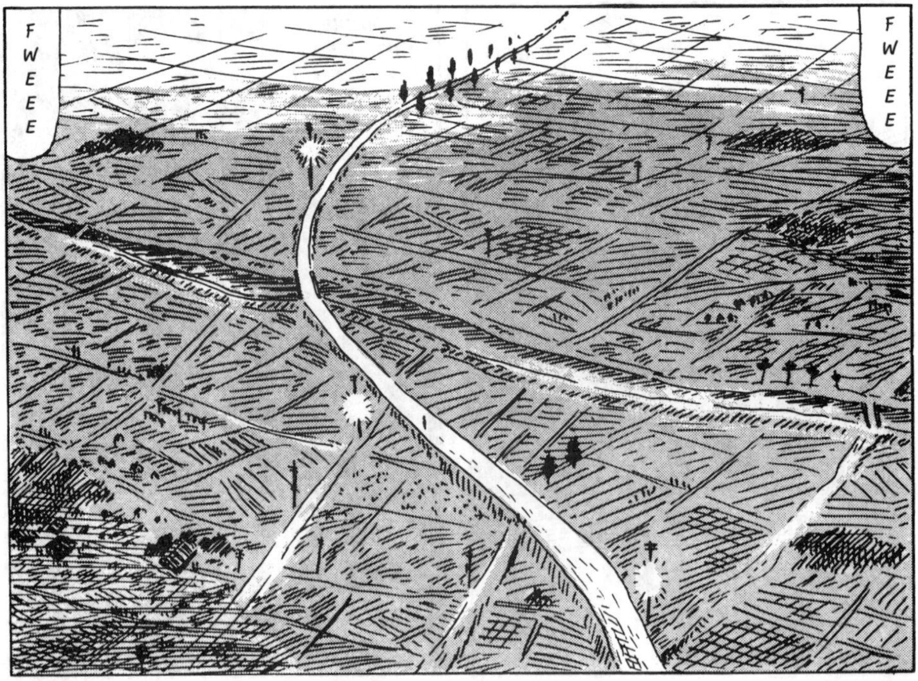
FWEEE
FWEEE

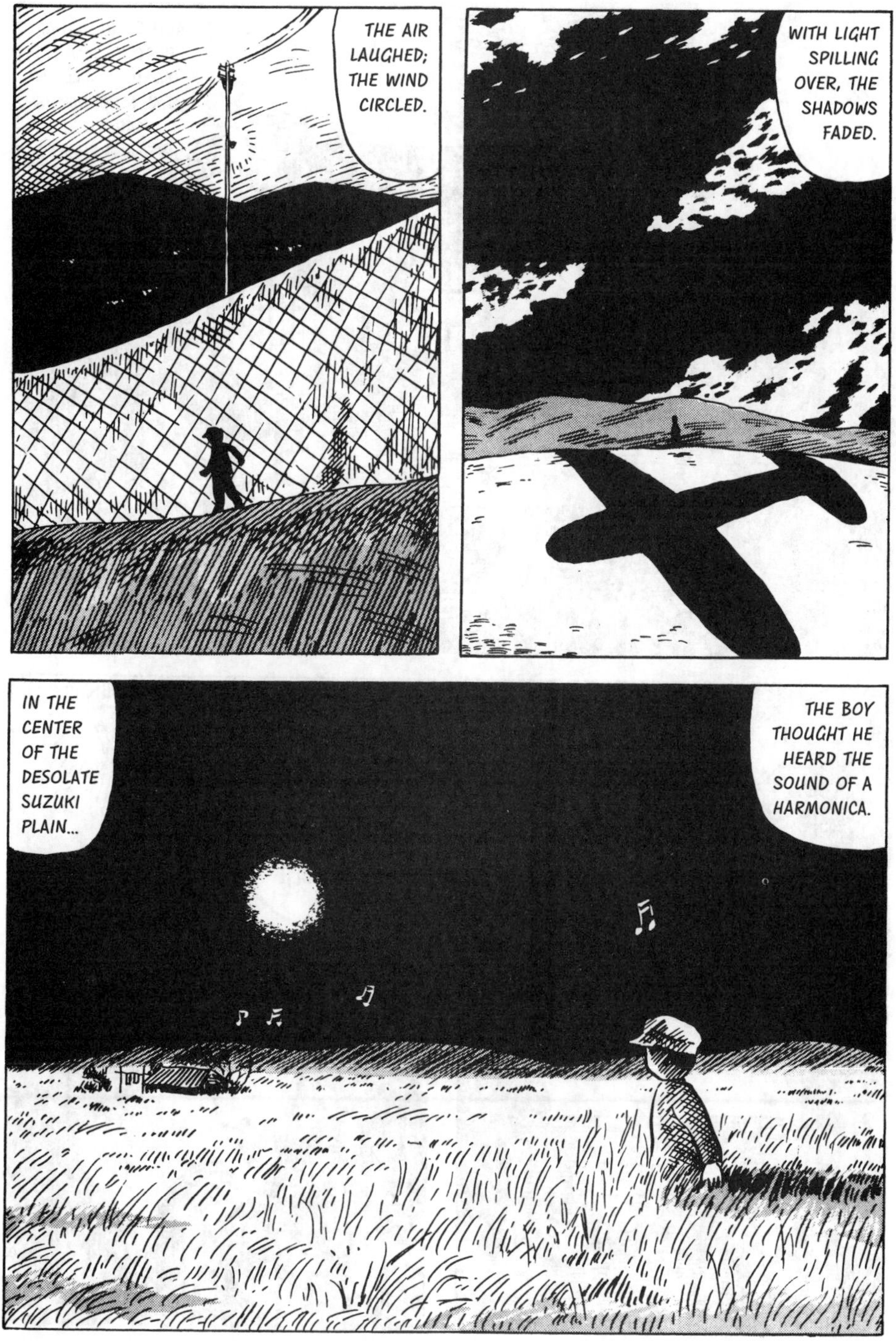
THE AIR LAUGHED; THE WIND CIRCLED.
WITH LIGHT SPILLING OVER, THE SHADOWS FADED.
IN THE CENTER OF THE DESOLATE SUZUKI PLAIN...
THE BOY THOUGHT HE HEARD THE SOUND OF A HARMONICA.

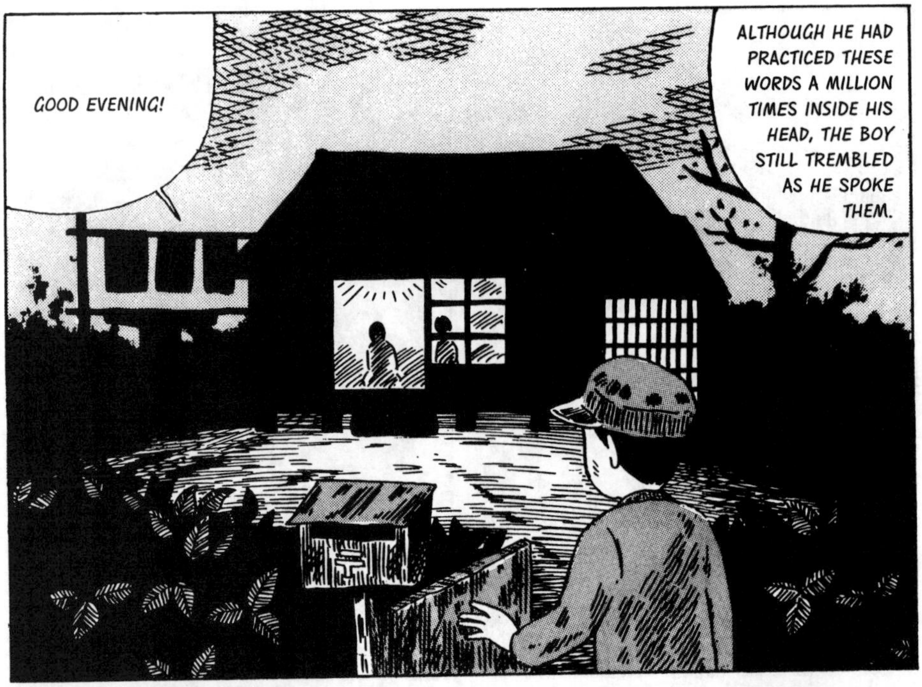
GOOD EVENING!
ALTHOUGH HE HAD PRACTICED THESE WORDS A MILLION TIMES INSIDE HIS HEAD, THE BOY STILL TREMBLED AS HE SPOKE THEM.
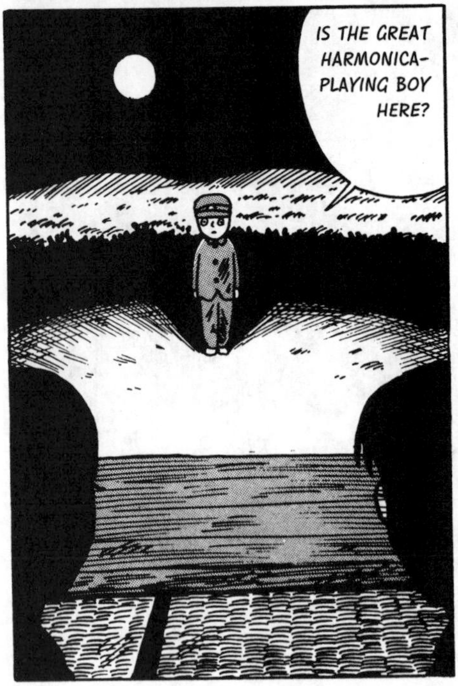
IS THE GREAT HARMONICA-PLAYING BOY HERE?
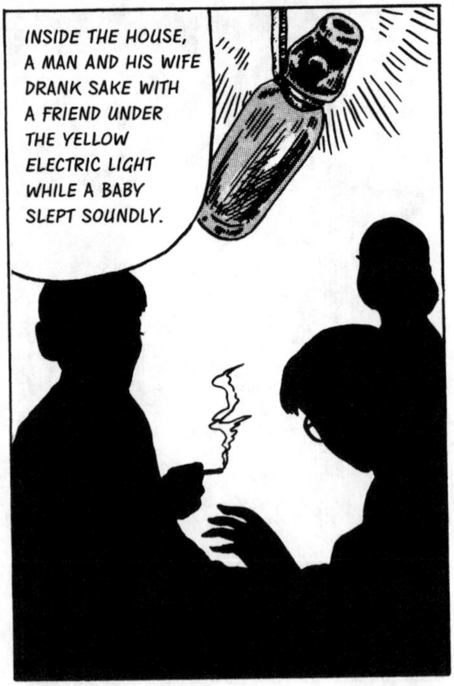
INSIDE THE HOUSE, A MAN AND HIS WIFE DRANK SAKE WITH A FRIEND UNDER THE YELLOW ELECTRIC LIGHT WHILE A BABY SLEPT SOUNDLY.

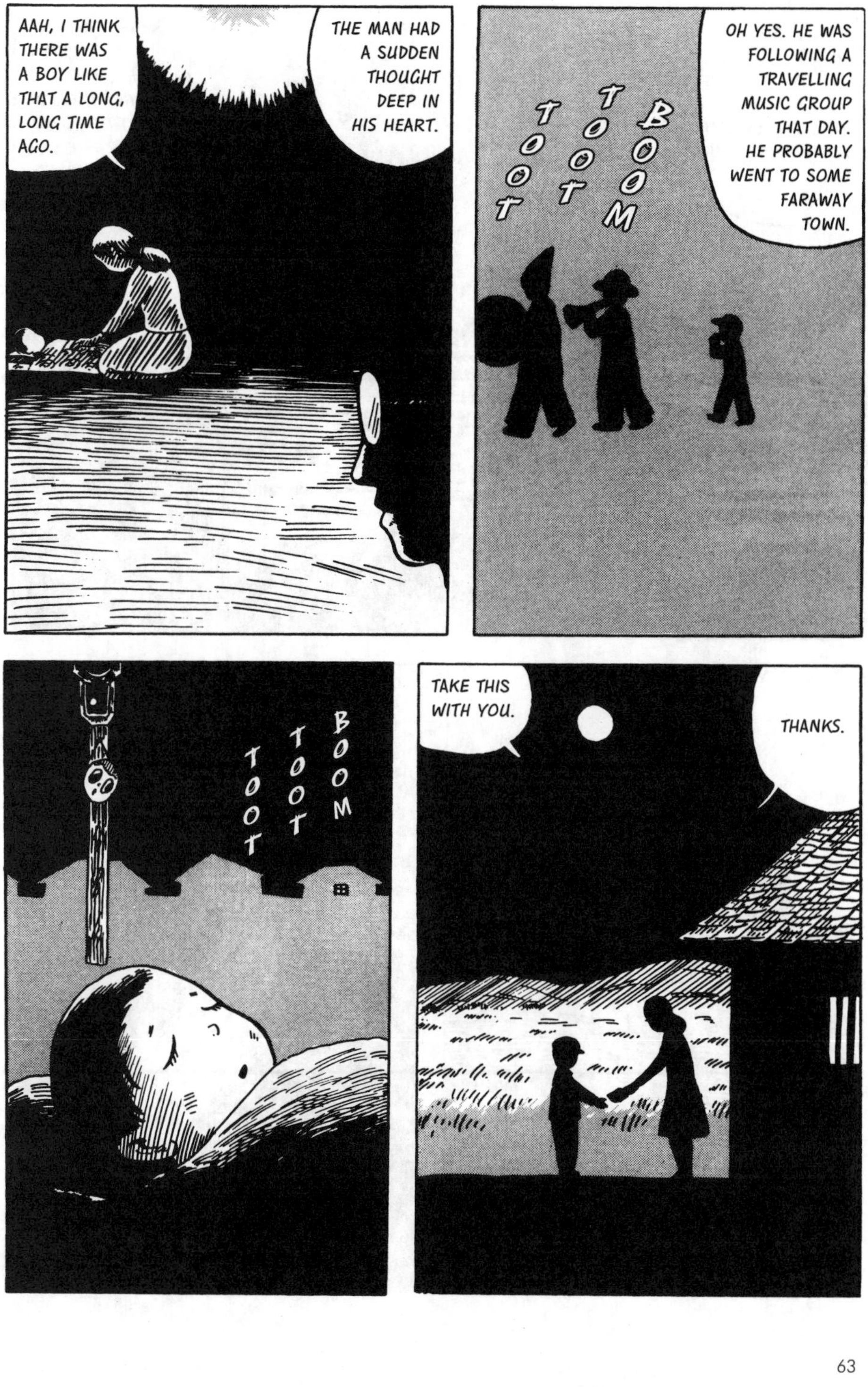
AAH, I THINK THERE WAS A BOY LIKE THAT A LONG, LONG TIME AGO.
THE MAN HAD A SUDDEN THOUGHT DEEP IN HIS HEART.
OH YES. HE WAS FOLLOWING A TRAVELLING MUSIC GROUP THAT DAY. HE PROBABLY WENT TO SOME FARAWAY TOWN.
TOOT
TOOT
BOOM
TOOT
TOOT
BOOM
TAKE THIS WITH YOU.
THANKS.

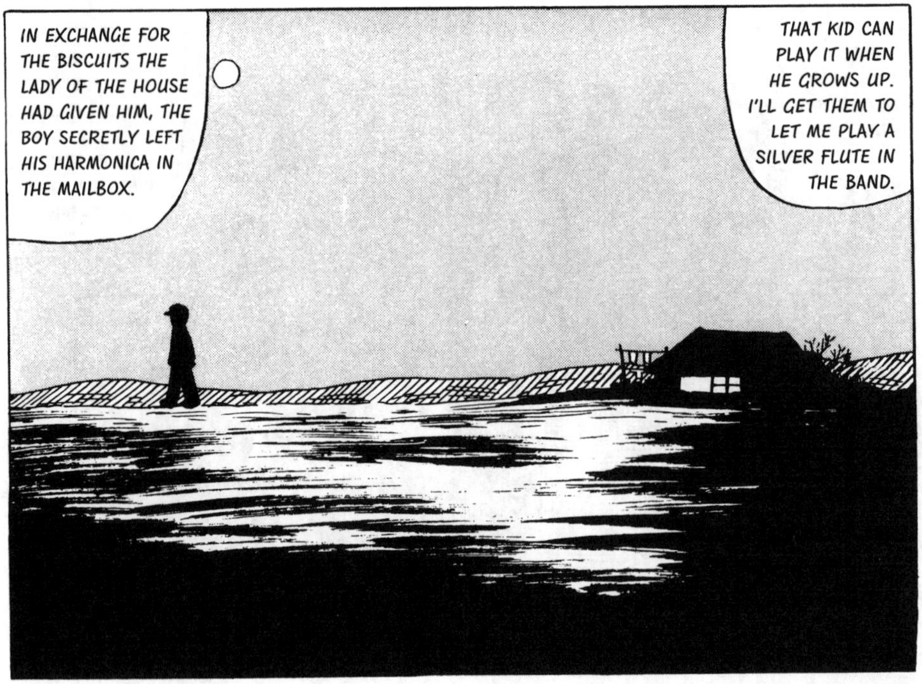
IN EXCHANGE FOR THE BISCUITS THE LADY OF THE HOUSE HAD GIVEN HIM, THE BOY SECRETLY LEFT HIS HARMONICA IN THE MAILBOX.
THAT KID CAN PLAY IT WHEN HE GROWS UP. I'LL GET THEM TO LET ME PLAY A SILVER FLUTE IN THE BAND.

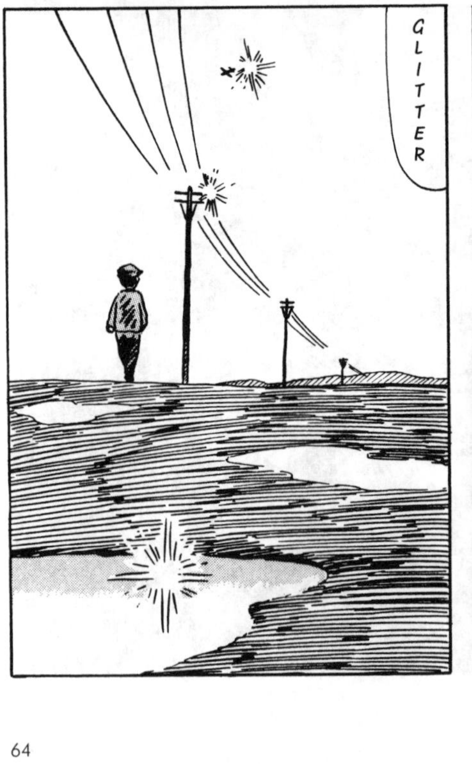
GLITTER

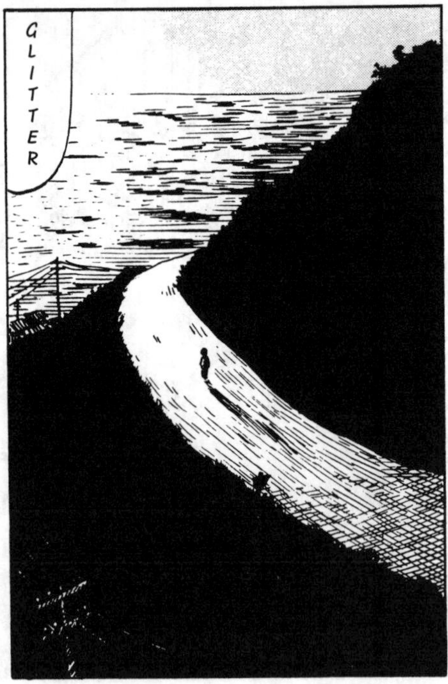
GLITTER

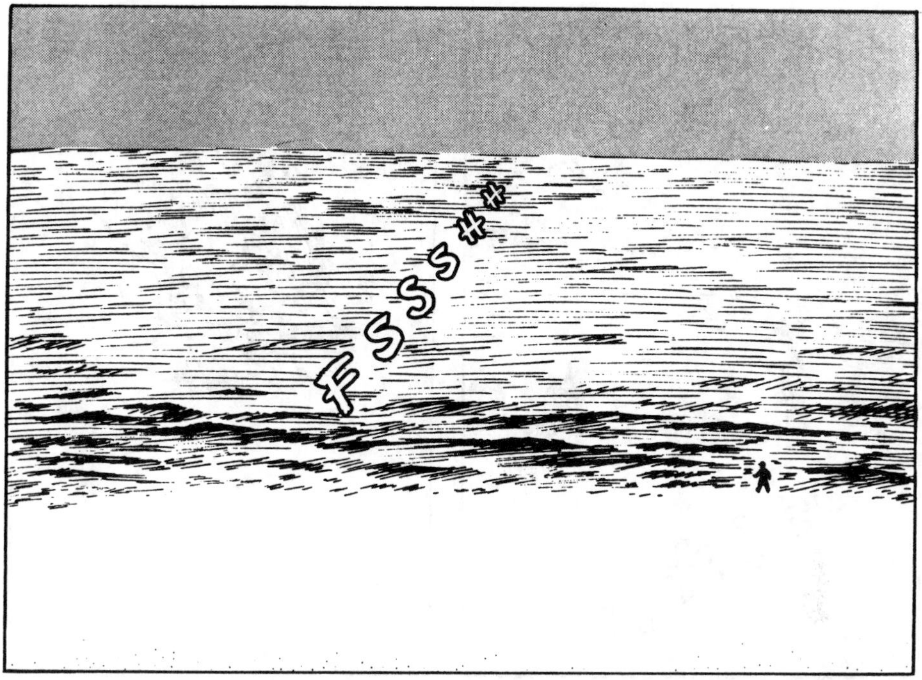
FSSSHH

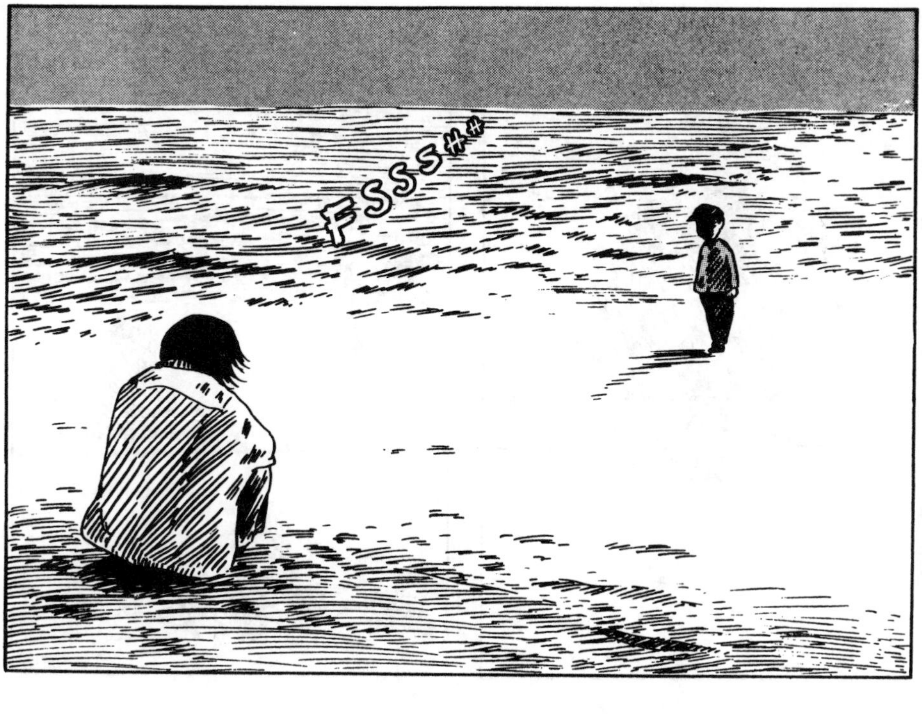
FSSSHH

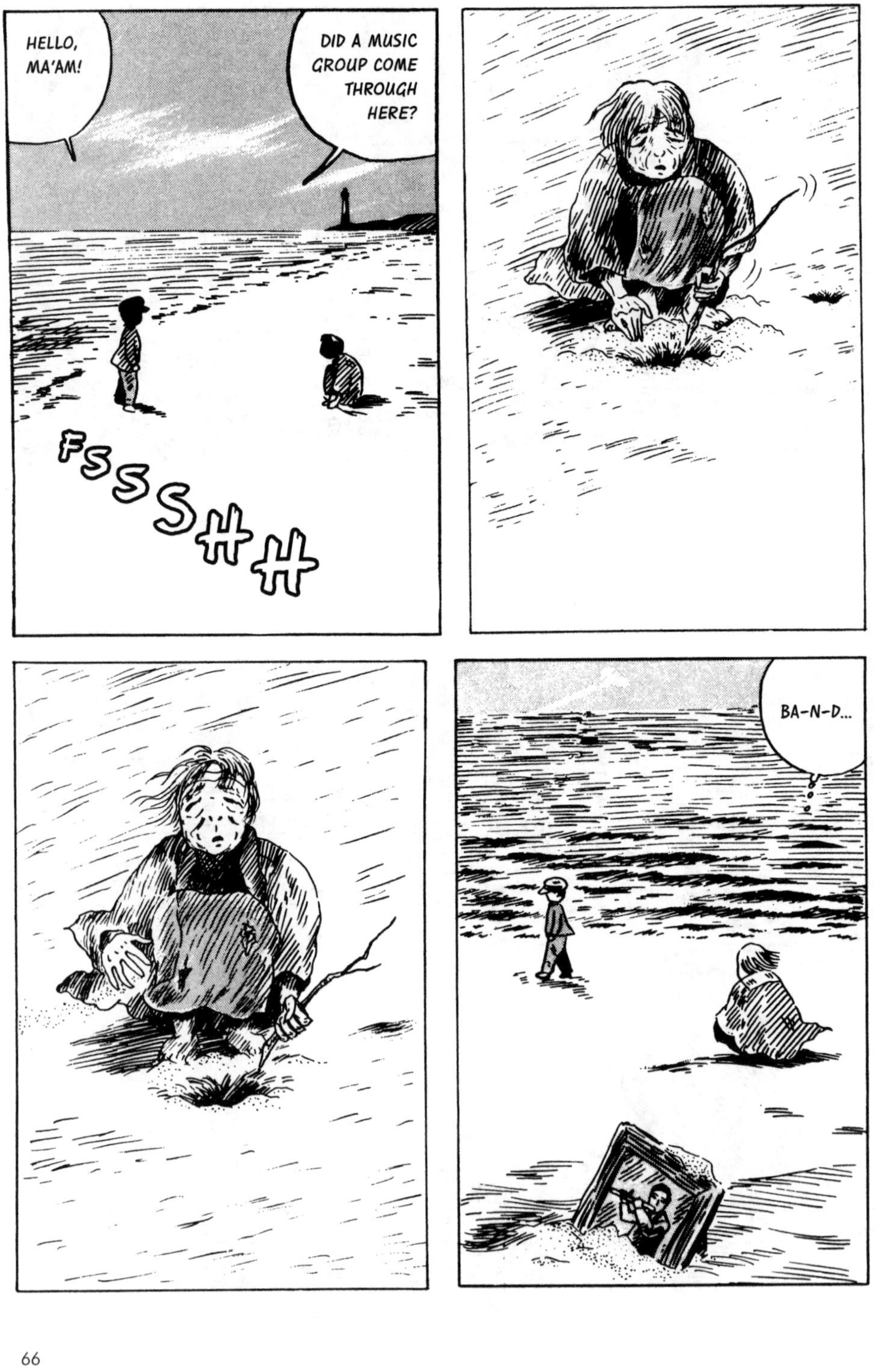
HELLO, MA'AM!
DID A MUSIC GROUP COME THROUGH HERE?
FSSSHH
BA-N-D...

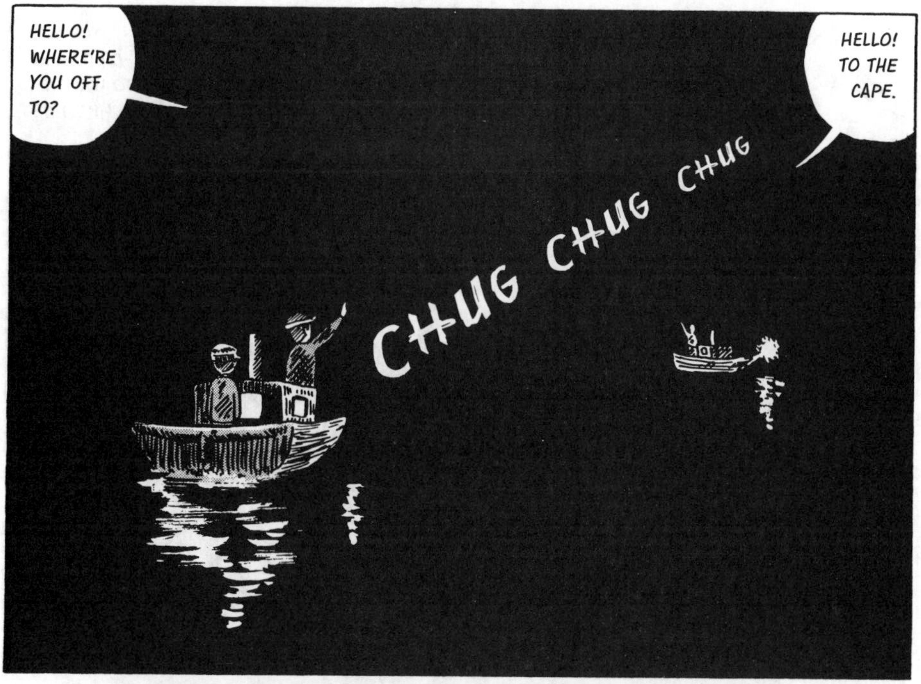
HELLO! WHERE'RE YOU OFF TO?
HELLO! TO THE CAPE.
CHUG CHUG CHUG
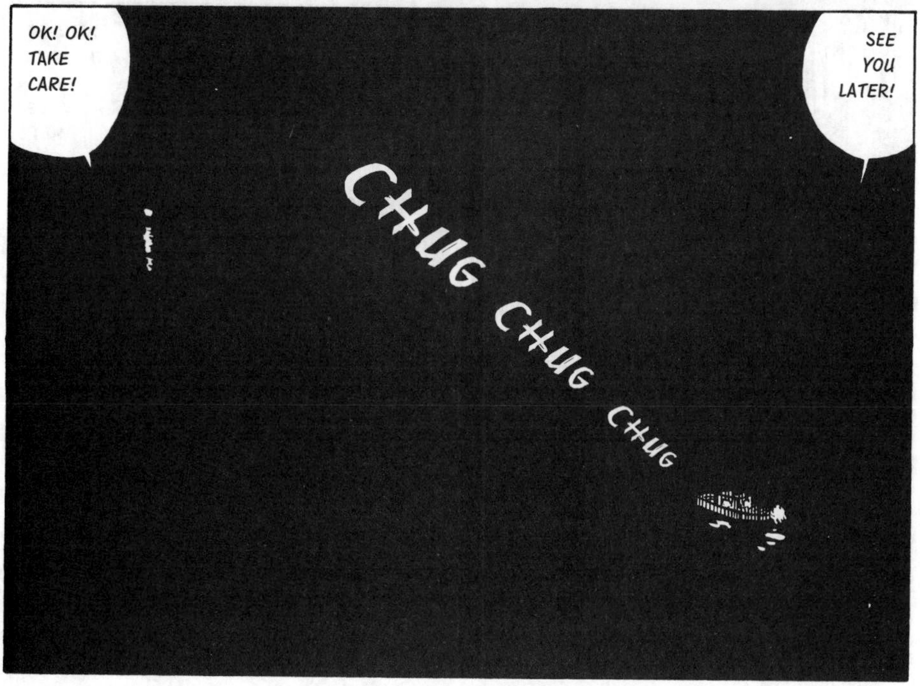
OK! OK! TAKE CARE!
SEE YOU LATER!
CHUG CHUG CHUG

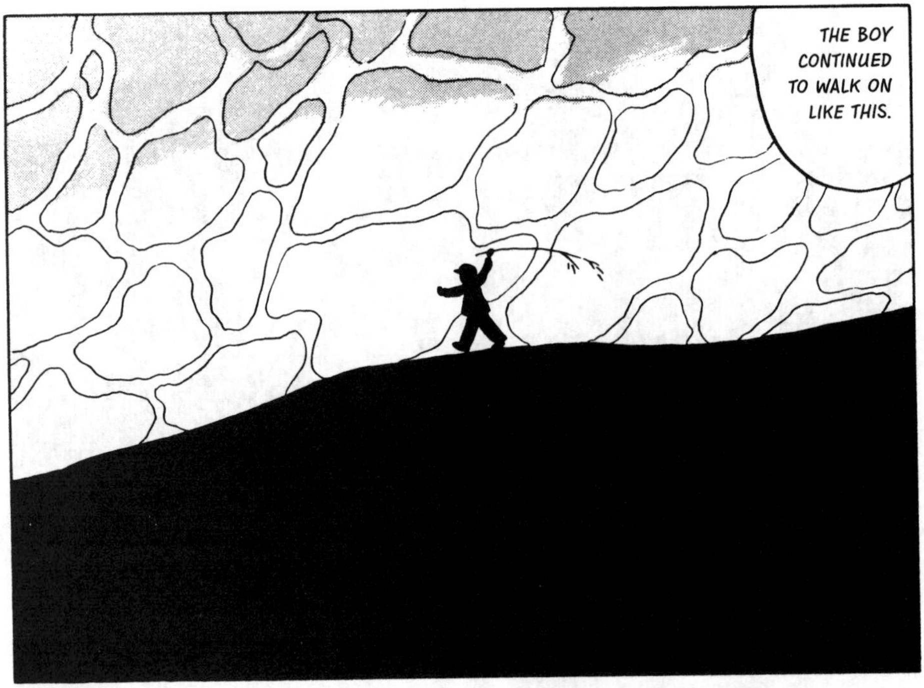
THE BOY CONTINUED TO WALK ON LIKE THIS.

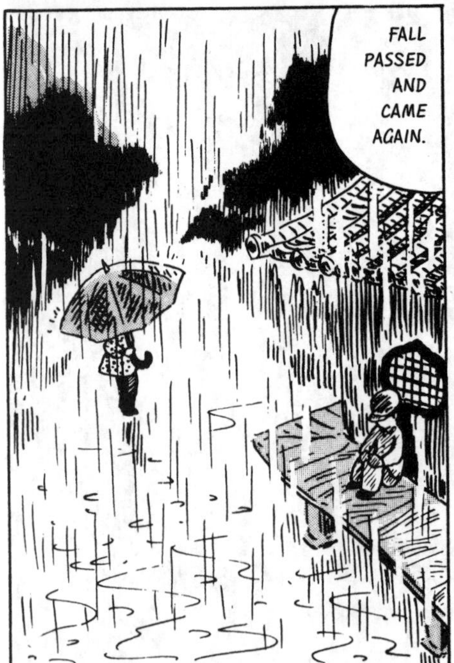
FALL PASSED AND CAME AGAIN.

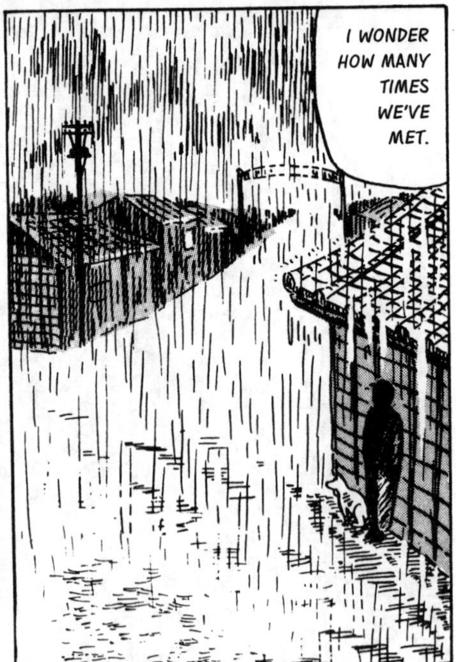
I WONDER HOW MANY TIMES WE'VE MET.

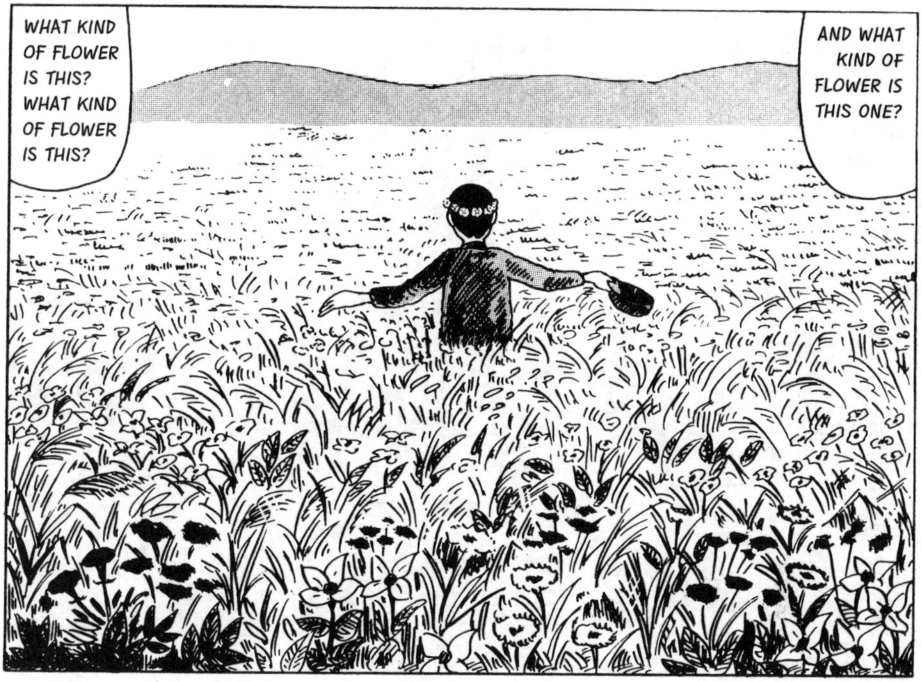
WHAT KIND OF FLOWER IS THIS? WHAT KIND OF FLOWER IS THIS?
AND WHAT KIND OF FLOWER IS THIS ONE?

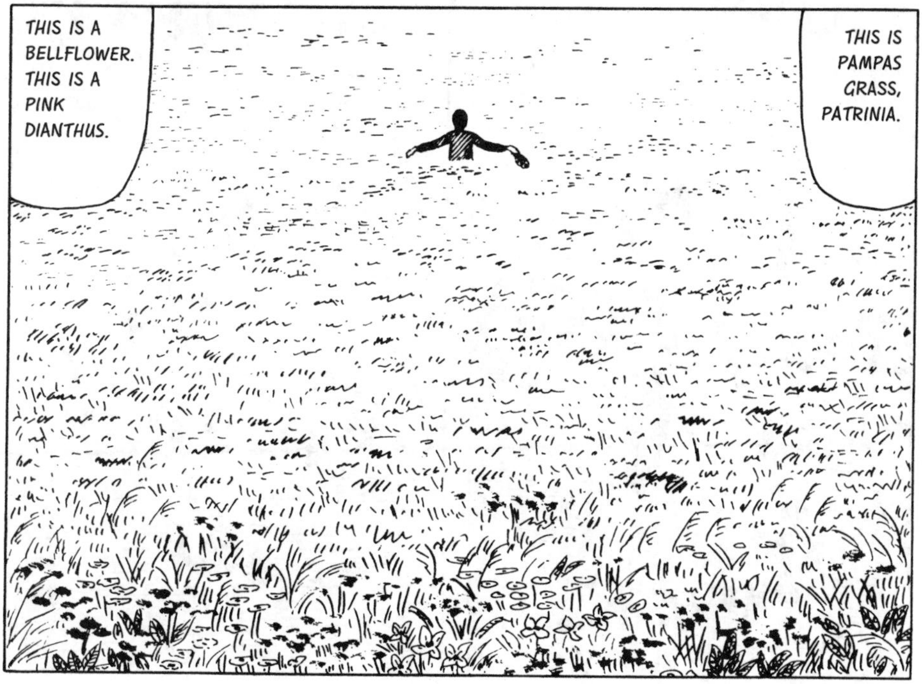
THIS IS A BELLFLOWER. THIS IS A PINK DIANTHUS.
THIS IS PAMPAS GRASS, PATRINIA.

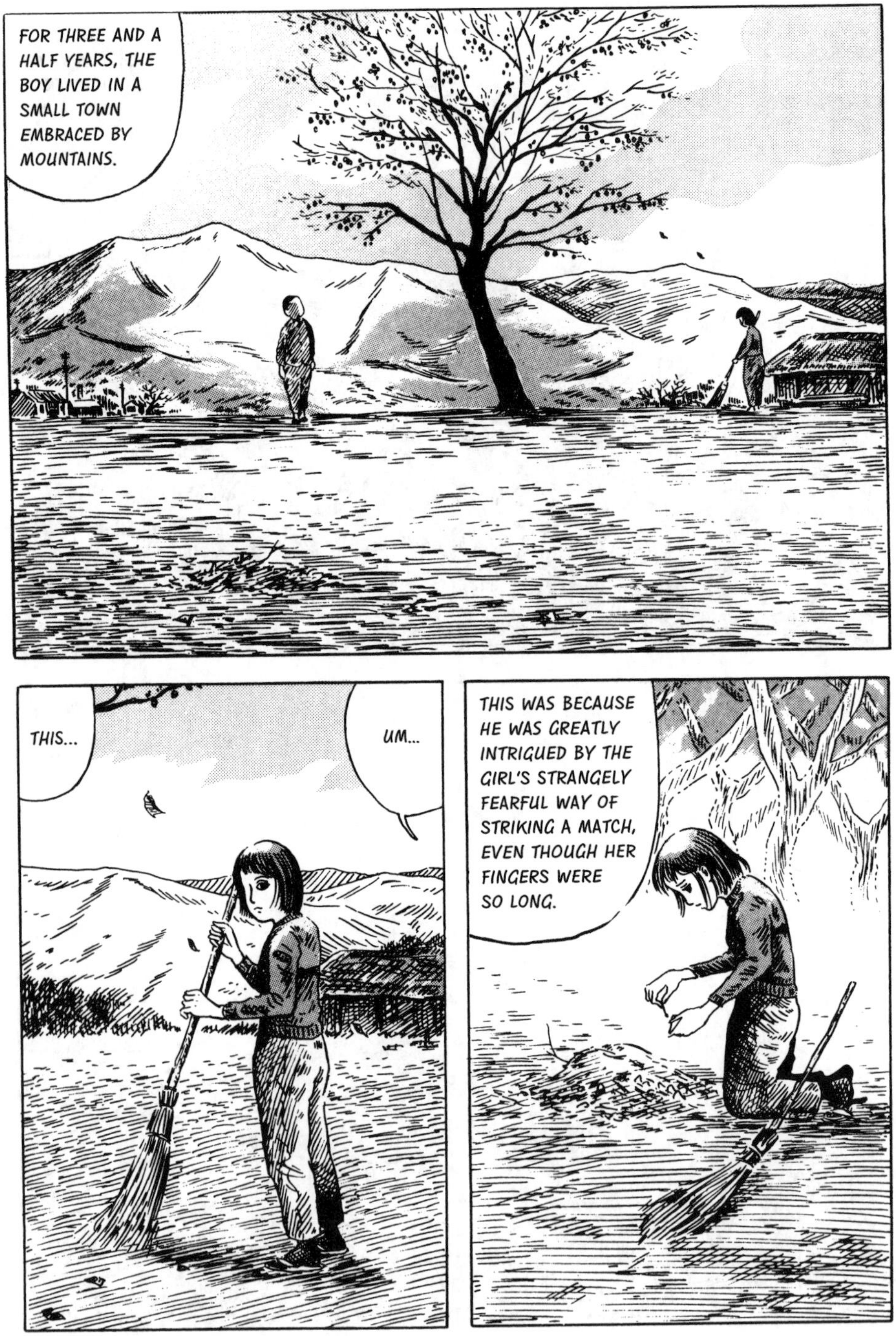
FOR THREE AND A HALF YEARS, THE BOY LIVED IN A SMALL TOWN EMBRACED BY MOUNTAINS.
THIS...
UM...
THIS WAS BECAUSE HE WAS GREATLY INTRIGUED BY THE GIRL'S STRANGELY FEARFUL WAY OF STRIKING A MATCH, EVEN THOUGH HER FINGERS WERE SO LONG.

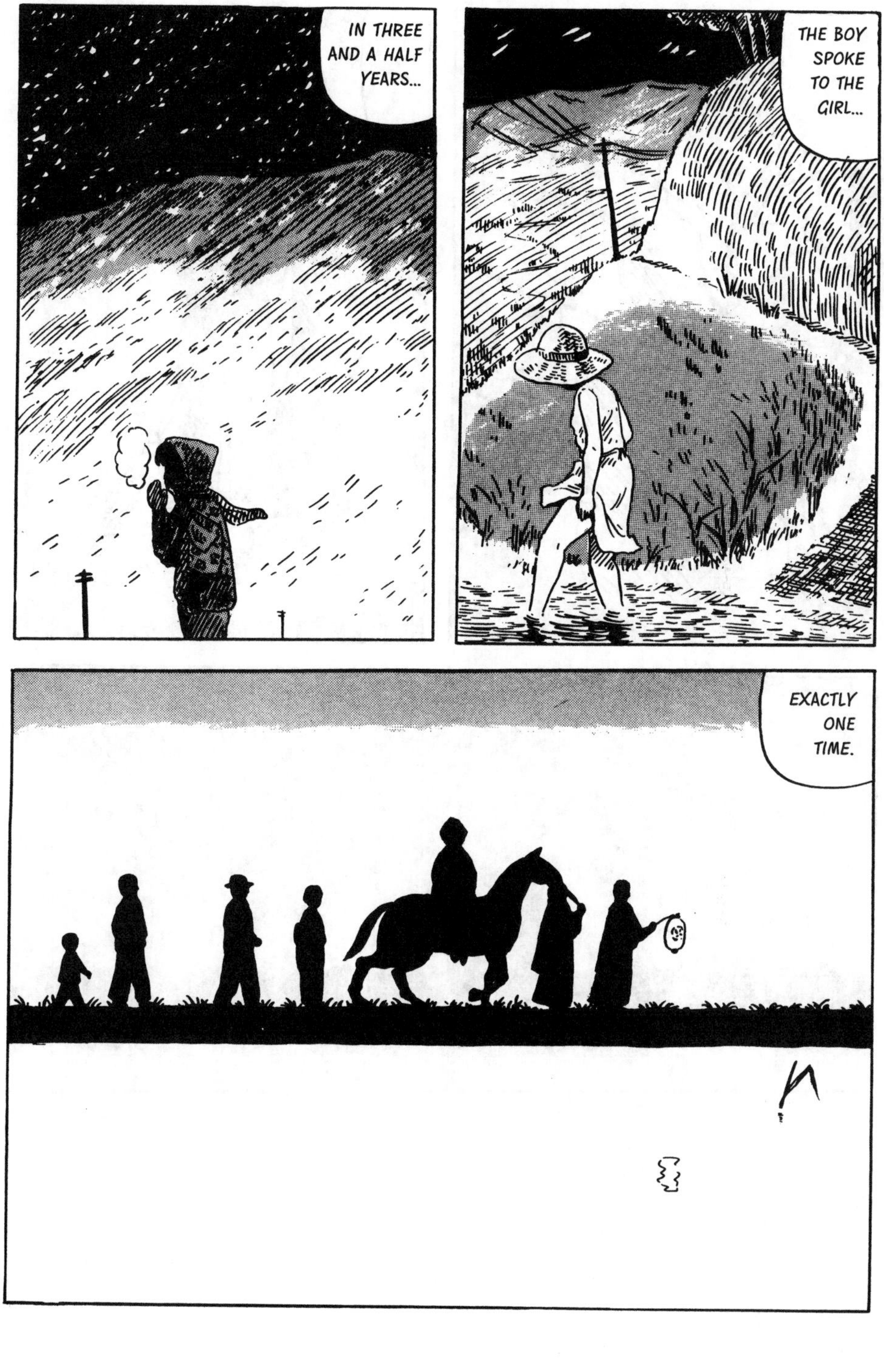
IN THREE AND A HALF YEARS...
THE BOY SPOKE TO THE GIRL...
EXACTLY ONE TIME.

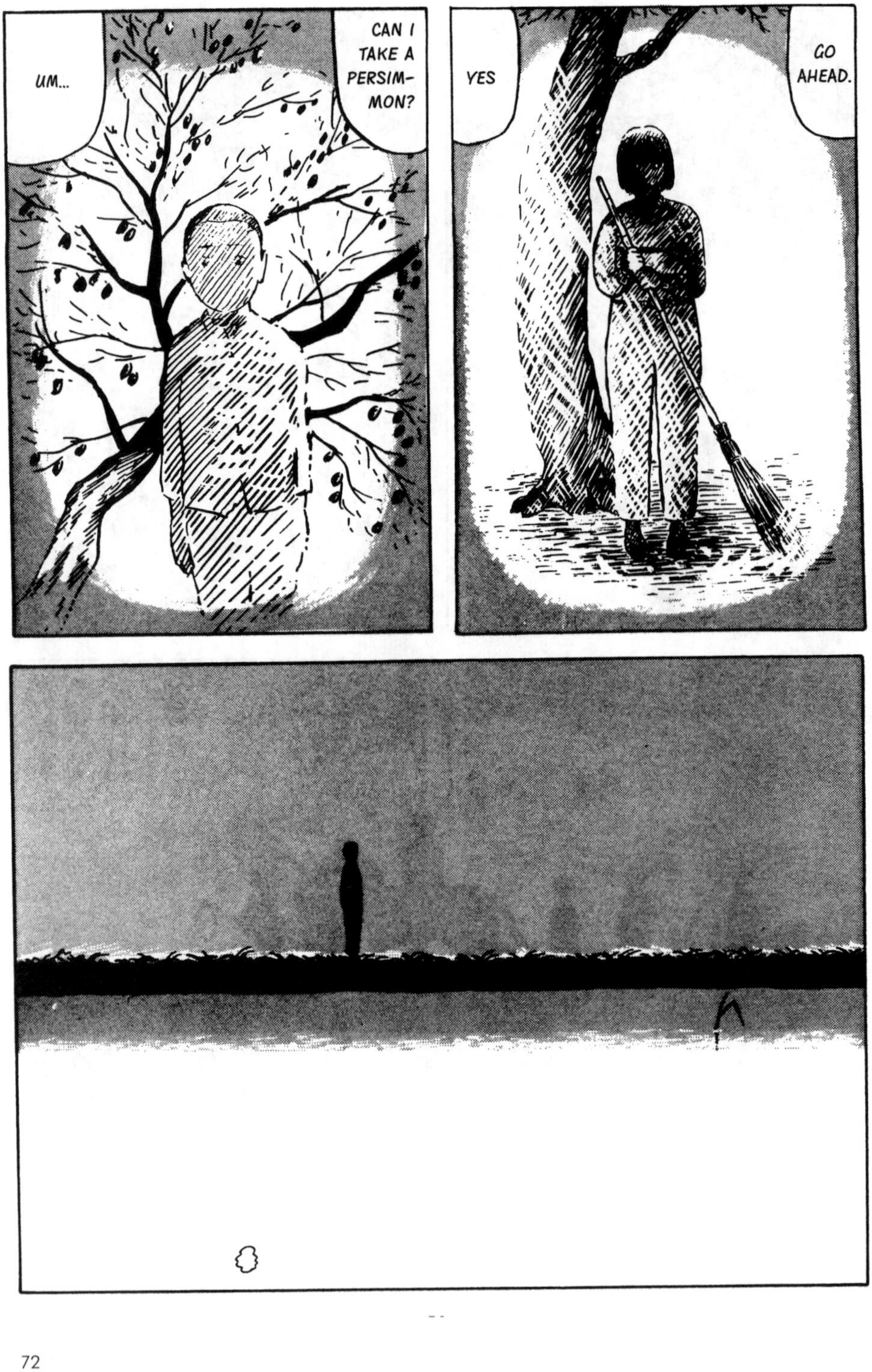
UM...
CAN I TAKE A PERSIM-MON?
YES
GO AHEAD.

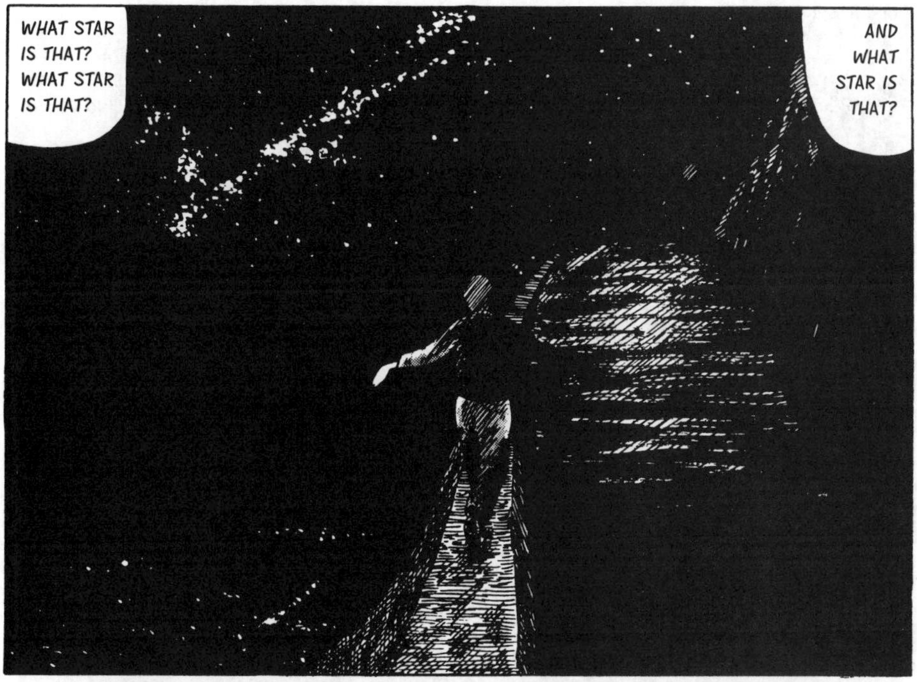
WHAT STAR IS THAT? WHAT STAR IS THAT?
AND WHAT STAR IS THAT?

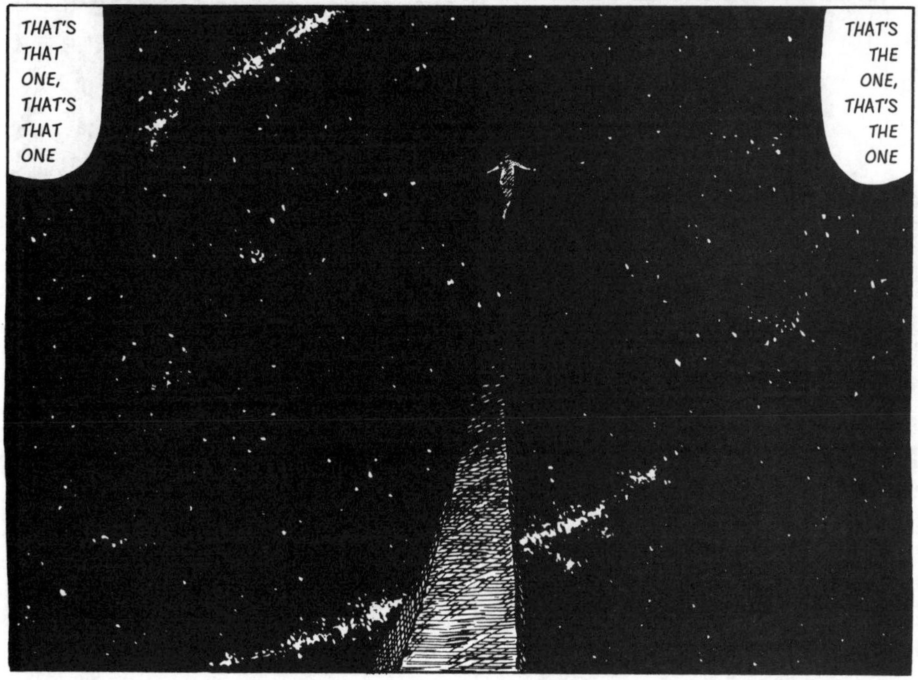
THAT'S THAT ONE, THAT'S THAT ONE
THAT'S THE ONE, THAT'S THE ONE

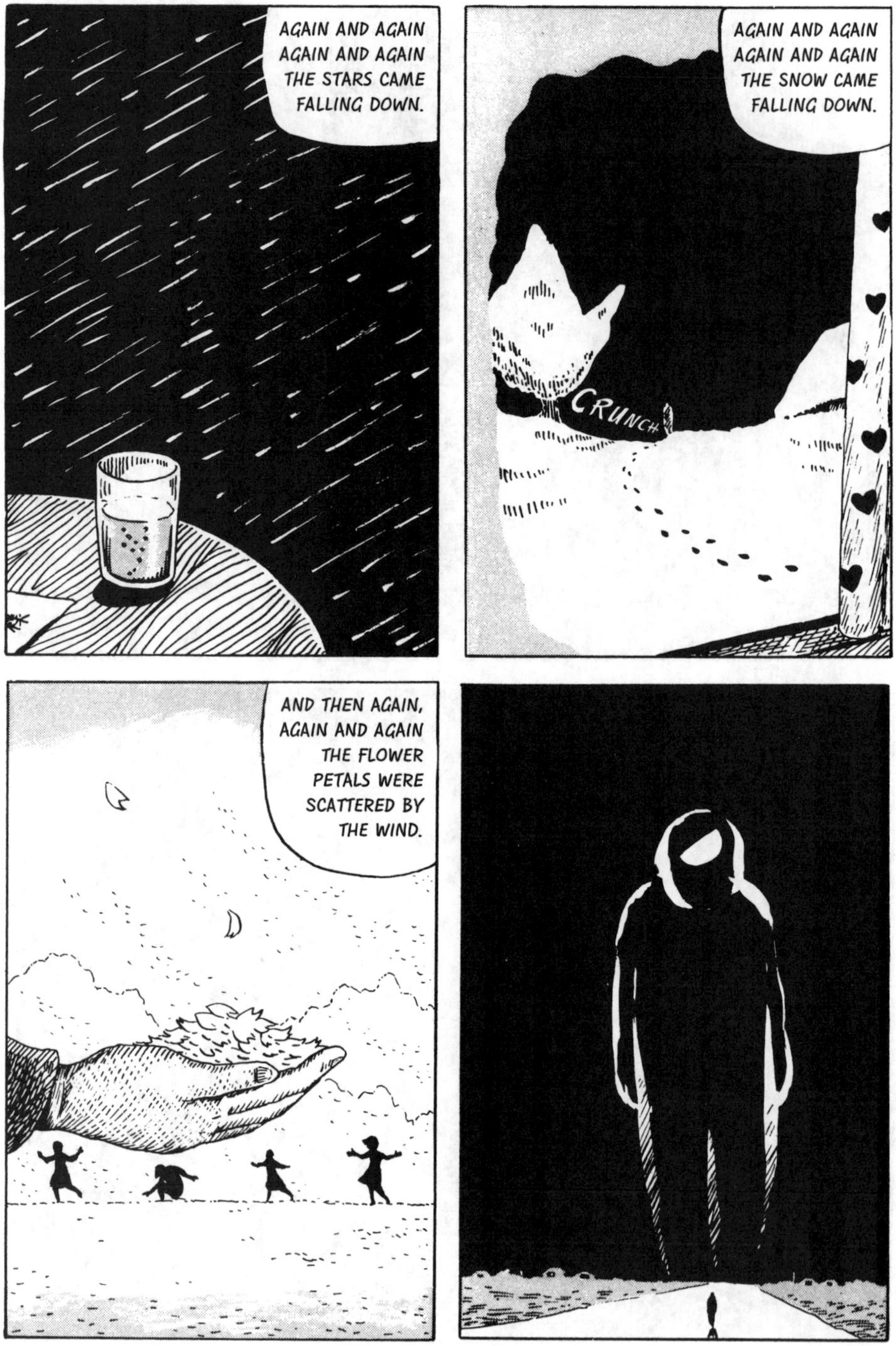
AGAIN AND AGAIN AGAIN AND AGAIN THE STARS CAME FALLING DOWN.
AGAIN AND AGAIN AGAIN AND AGAIN THE SNOW CAME FALLING DOWN.
CRUNCH
AND THEN AGAIN, AGAIN AND AGAIN THE FLOWER PETALS WERE SCATTERED BY THE WIND.

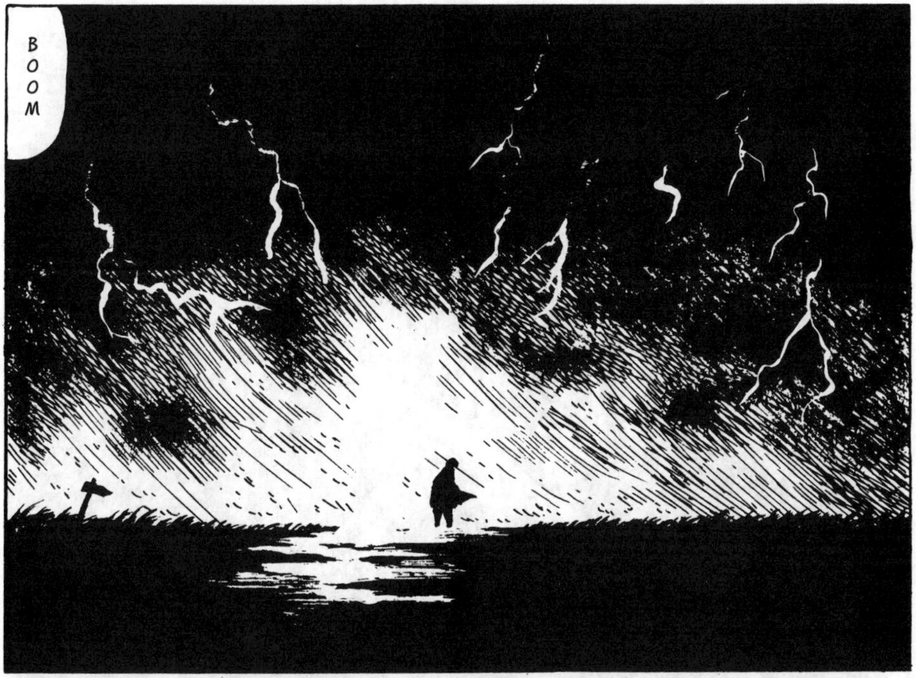
BOOM

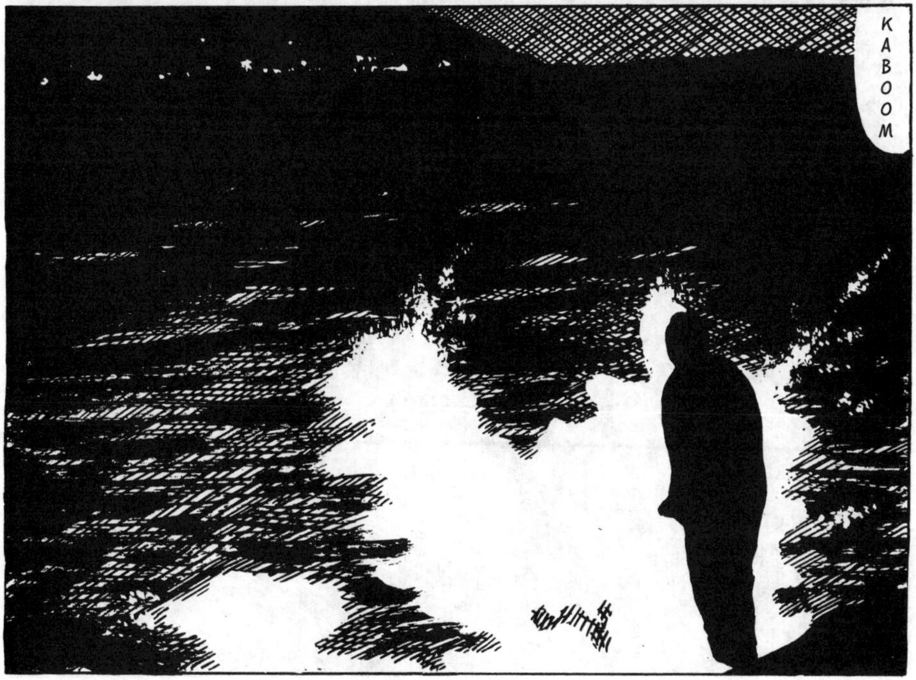
KABOOM

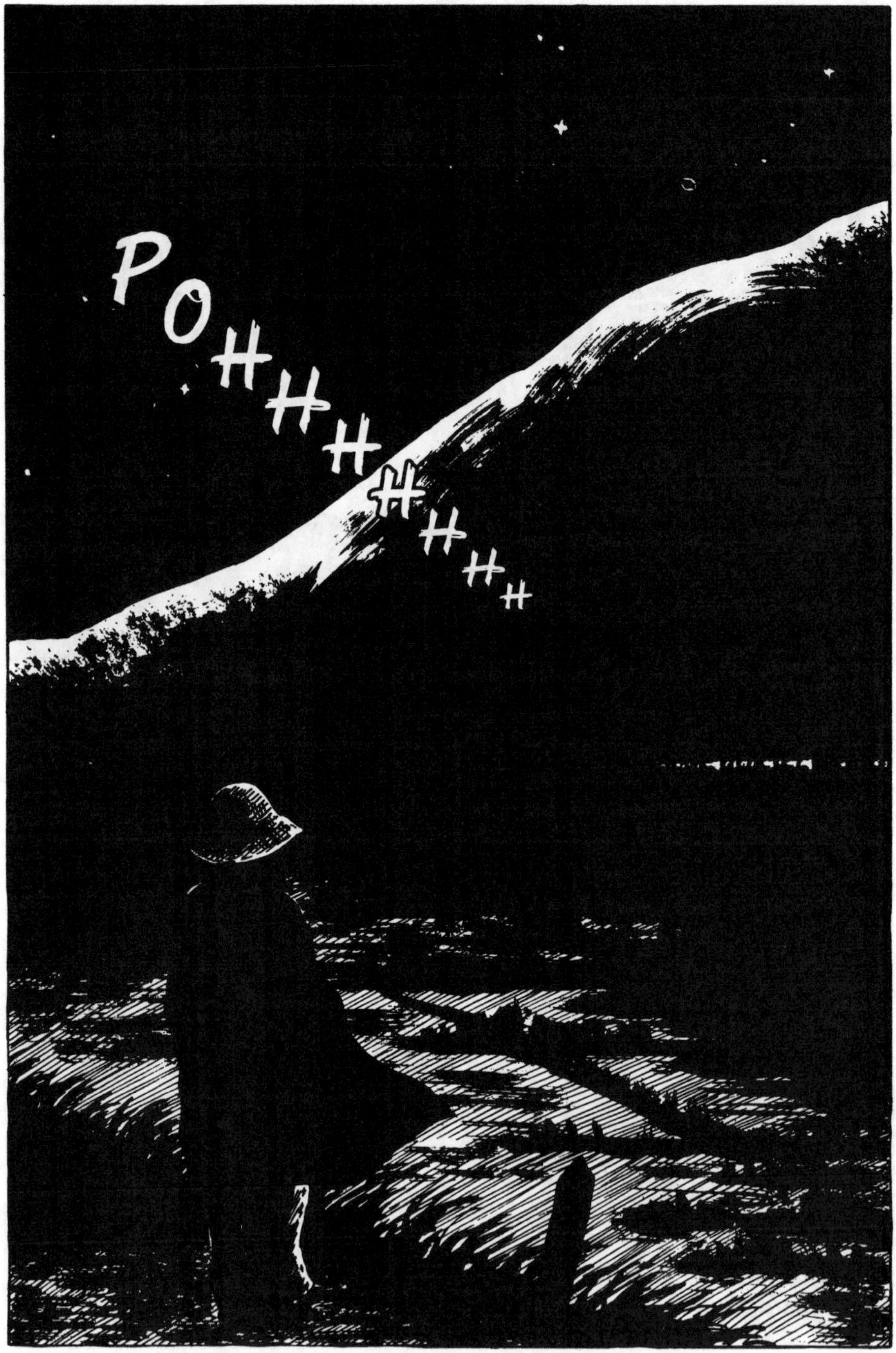
POHHHHHHH

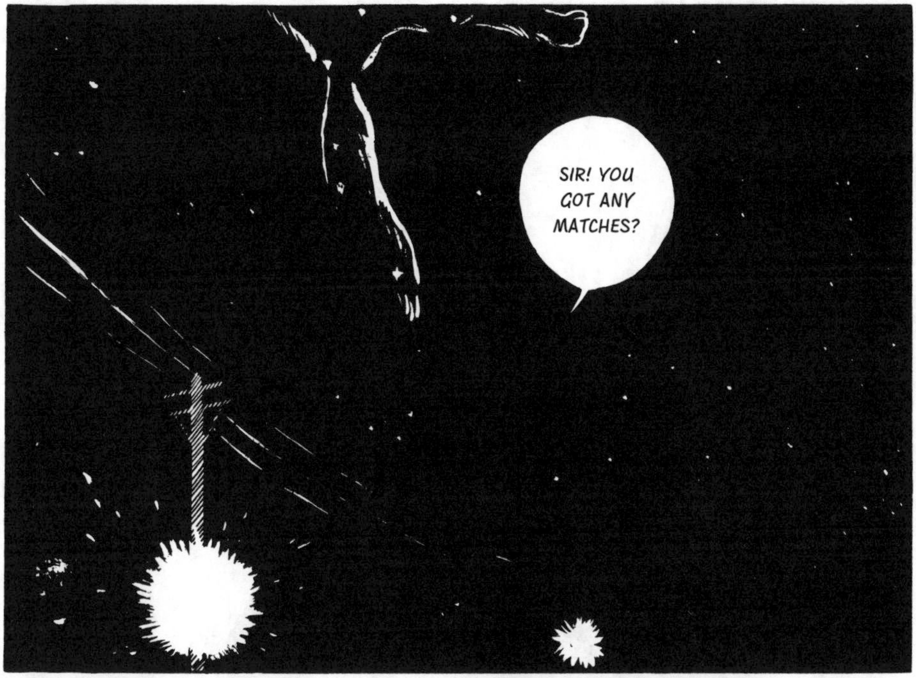
SIR! YOU GOT ANY MATCHES?

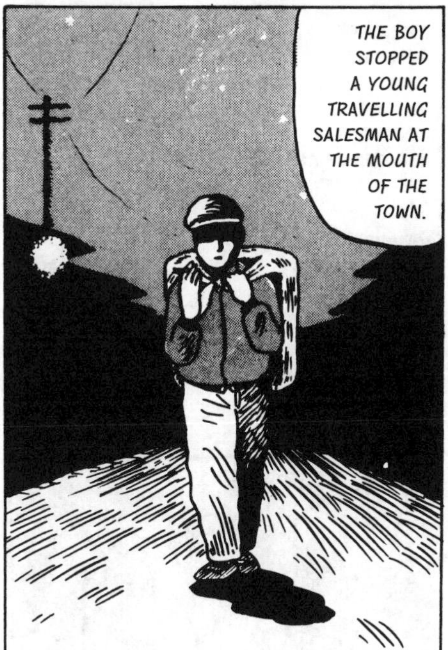
THE BOY STOPPED A YOUNG TRAVELLING SALESMAN AT THE MOUTH OF THE TOWN.

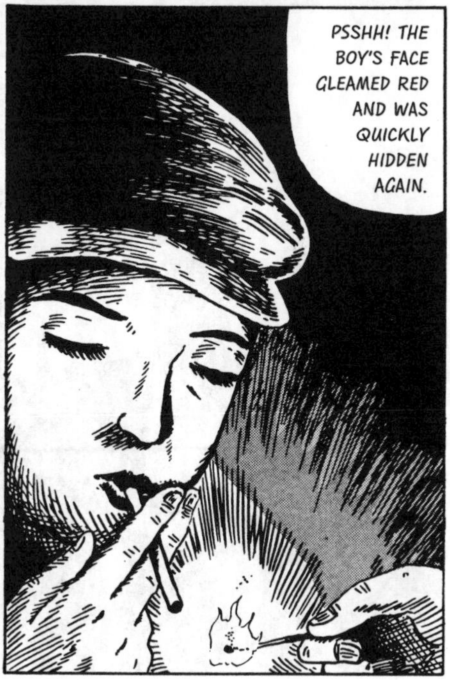
PSSHH! THE BOY'S FACE GLEAMED RED AND WAS QUICKLY HIDDEN AGAIN.

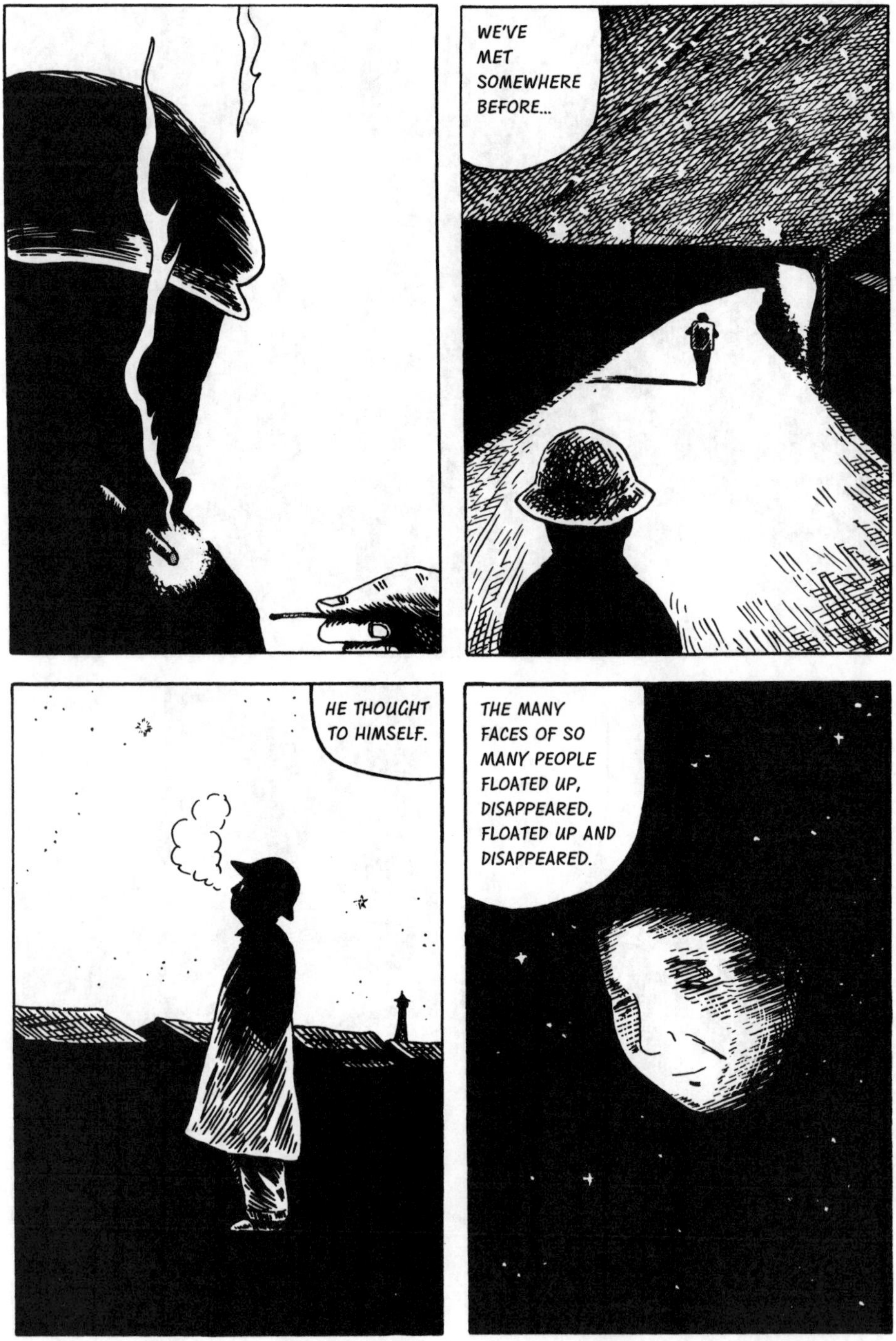
WE'VE MET SOMEWHERE BEFORE...
HE THOUGHT TO HIMSELF.
THE MANY FACES OF SO MANY PEOPLE FLOATED UP, DISAPPEARED, FLOATED UP AND DISAPPEARED.

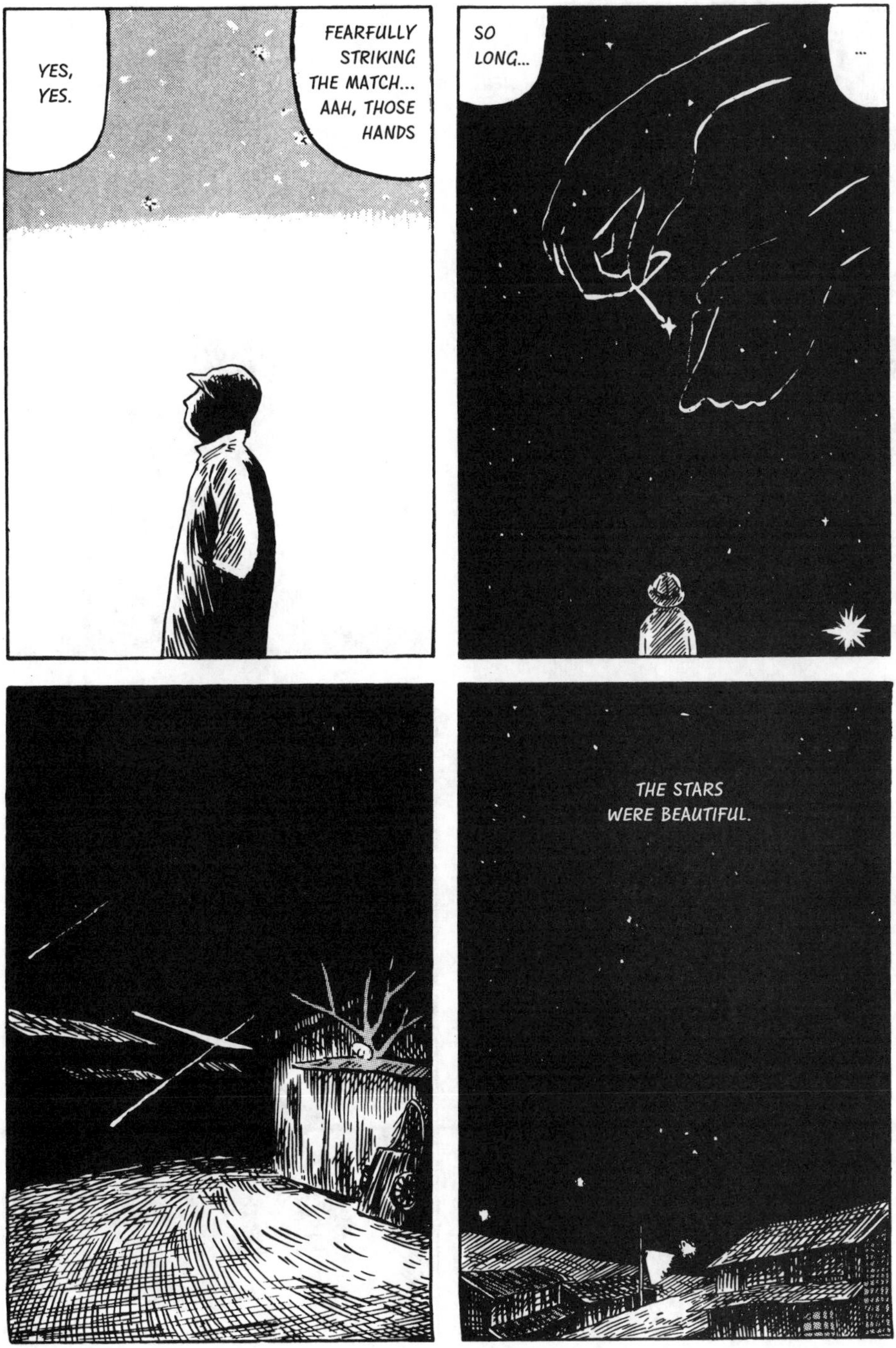
YES,
YES.
FEARFULLY
STRIKING
THE MATCH...
AAH, THOSE
HANDS
SO
LONG...
...
THE STARS
WERE BEAUTIFUL.

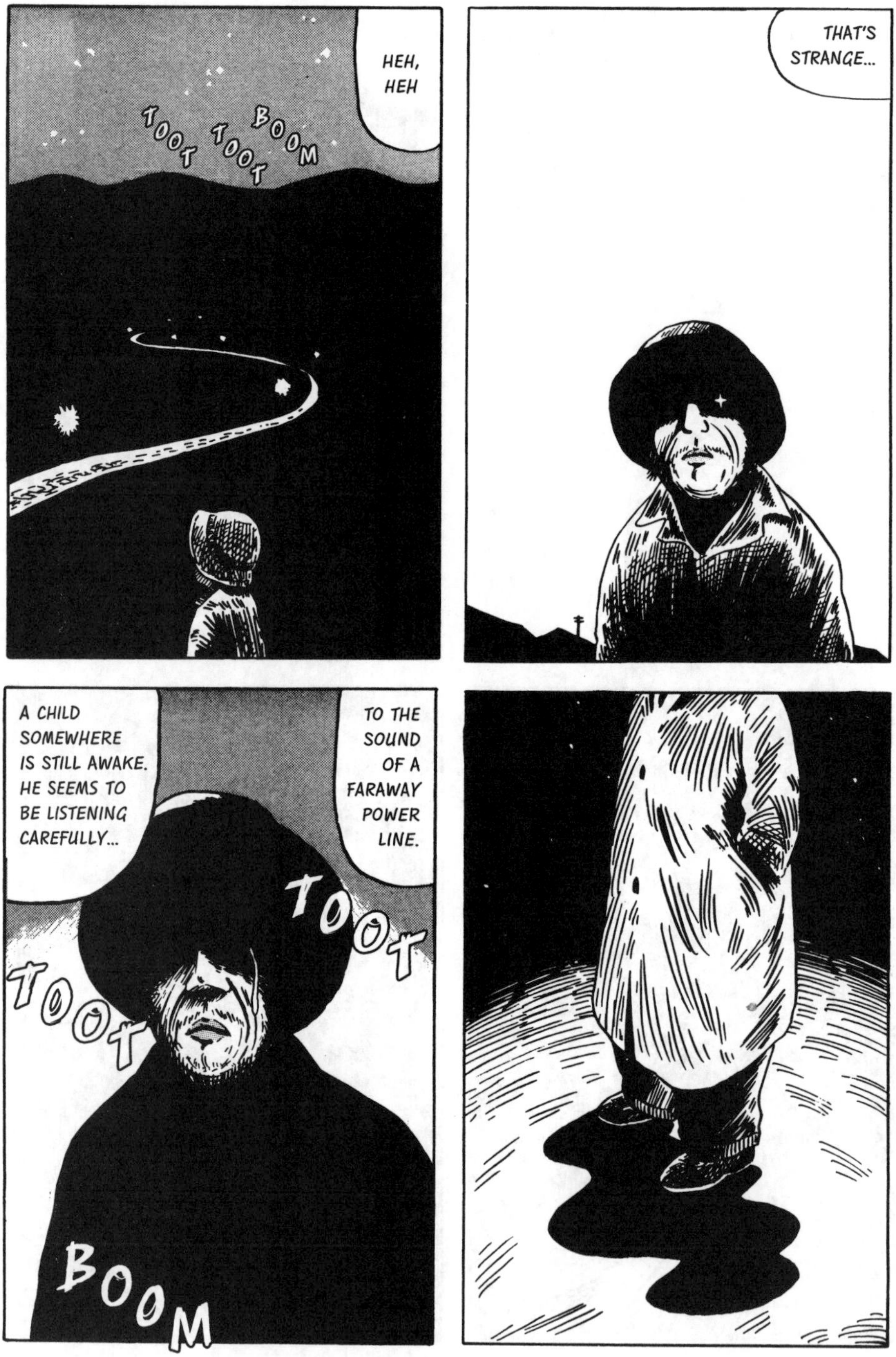
HEH, HEH
TOOT TOOT BOOM
THAT'S STRANGE...
A CHILD SOMEWHERE IS STILL AWAKE. HE SEEMS TO BE LISTENING CAREFULLY...
TO THE SOUND OF A FARAWAY POWER LINE.
TOOT
TOOT
BOOM

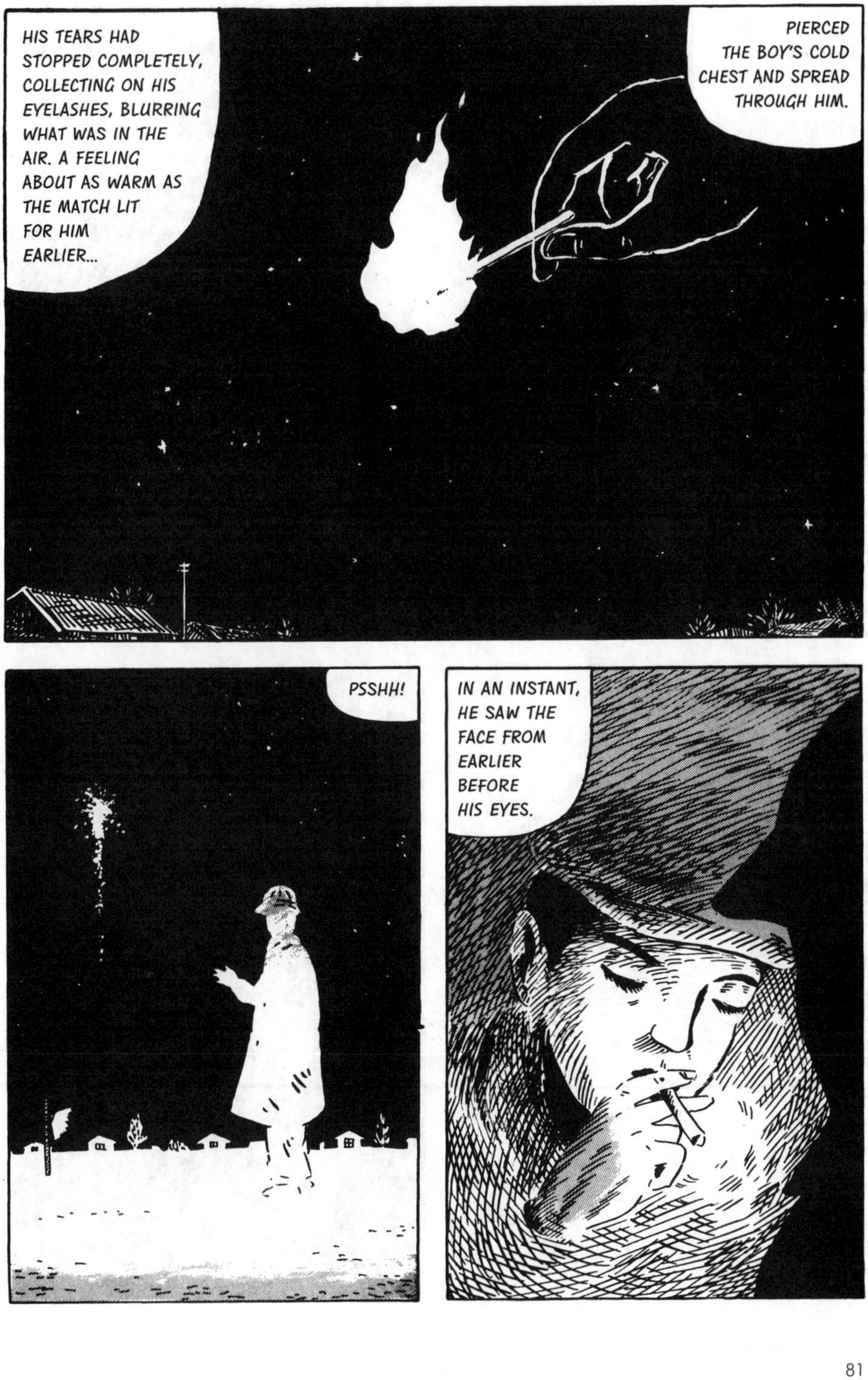
HIS TEARS HAD STOPPED COMPLETELY, COLLECTING ON HIS EYELASHES, BLURRING WHAT WAS IN THE AIR. A FEELING ABOUT AS WARM AS THE MATCH LIT FOR HIM EARLIER...
PIERCED THE BOY'S COLD CHEST AND SPREAD THROUGH HIM.
PSSHH!
IN AN INSTANT, HE SAW THE FACE FROM EARLIER BEFORE HIS EYES.

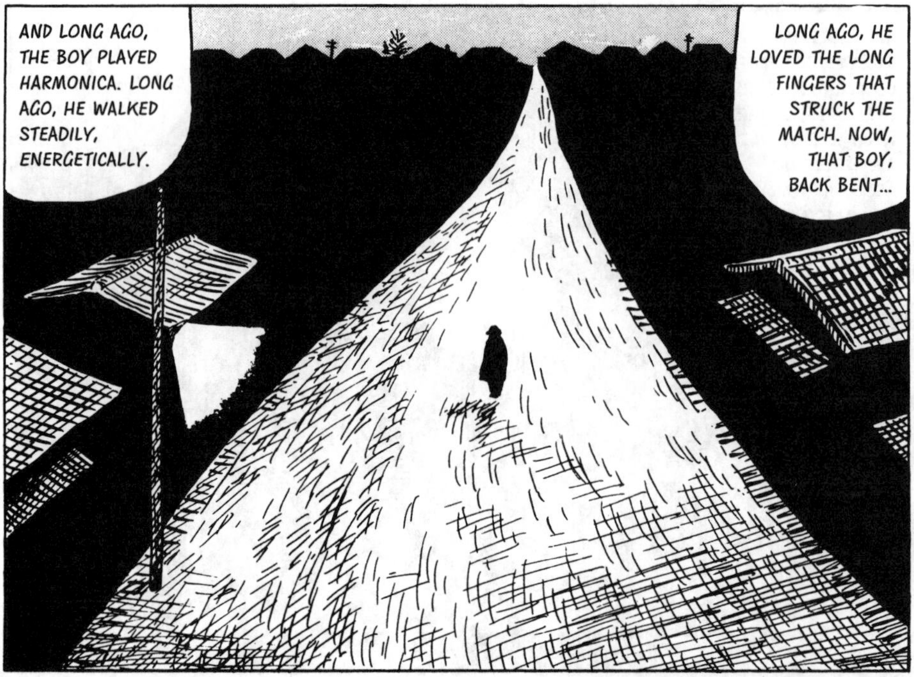
AND LONG AGO, THE BOY PLAYED HARMONICA. LONG AGO, HE WALKED STEADILY, ENERGETICALLY.
LONG AGO, HE LOVED THE LONG FINGERS THAT STRUCK THE MATCH. NOW, THAT BOY, BACK BENT...
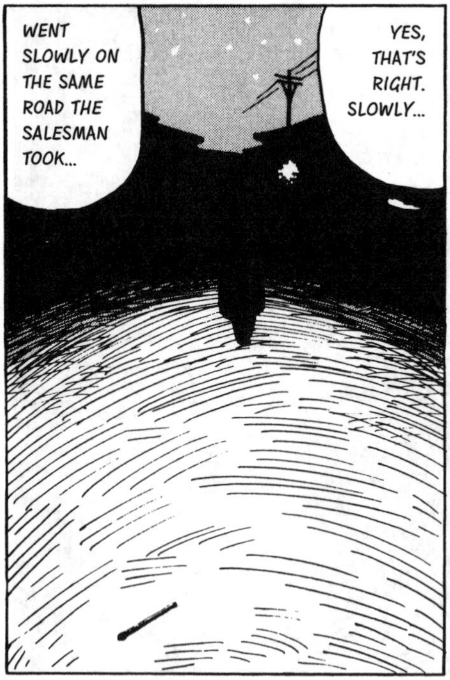
WENT SLOWLY ON THE SAME ROAD THE SALESMAN TOOK...
YES, THAT'S RIGHT. SLOWLY...
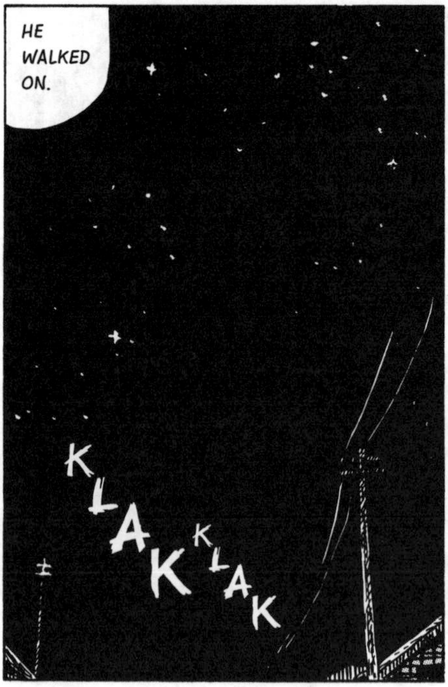
HE WALKED ON.
KLAK
KLAK
KLAK

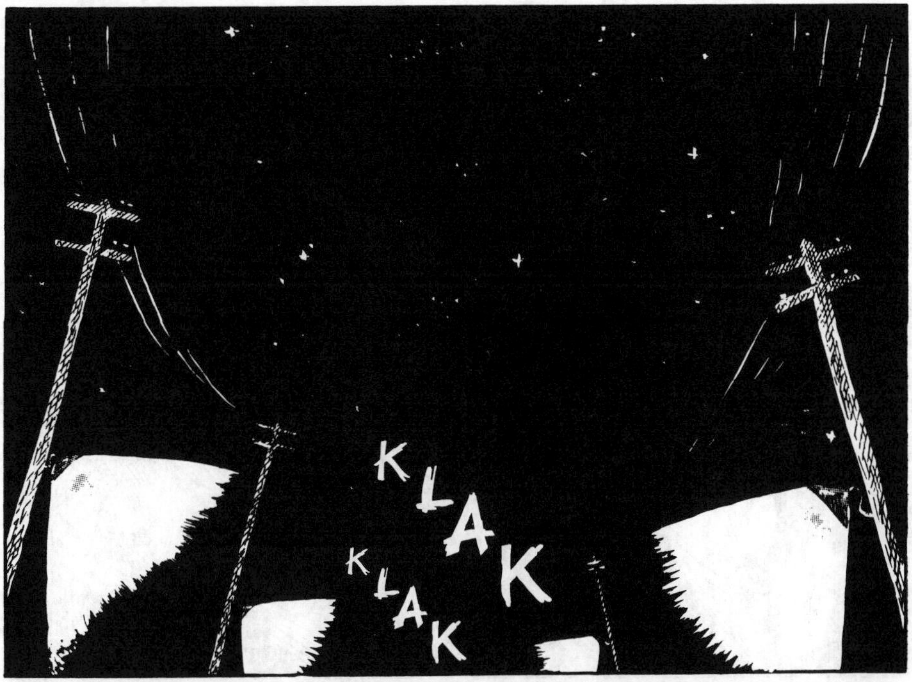
KLAK
KLAK
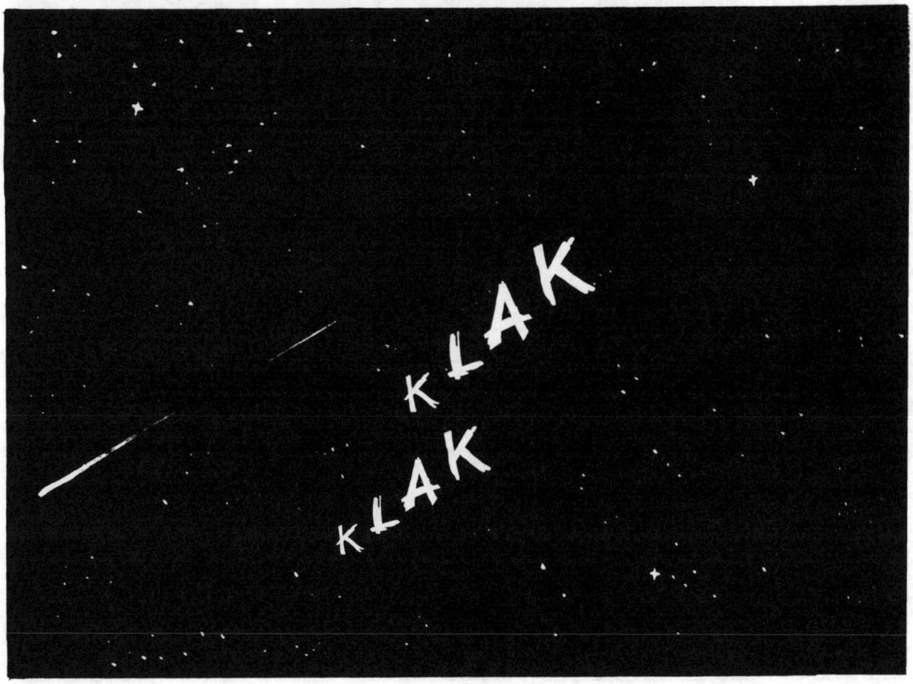
KLAK
KLAK

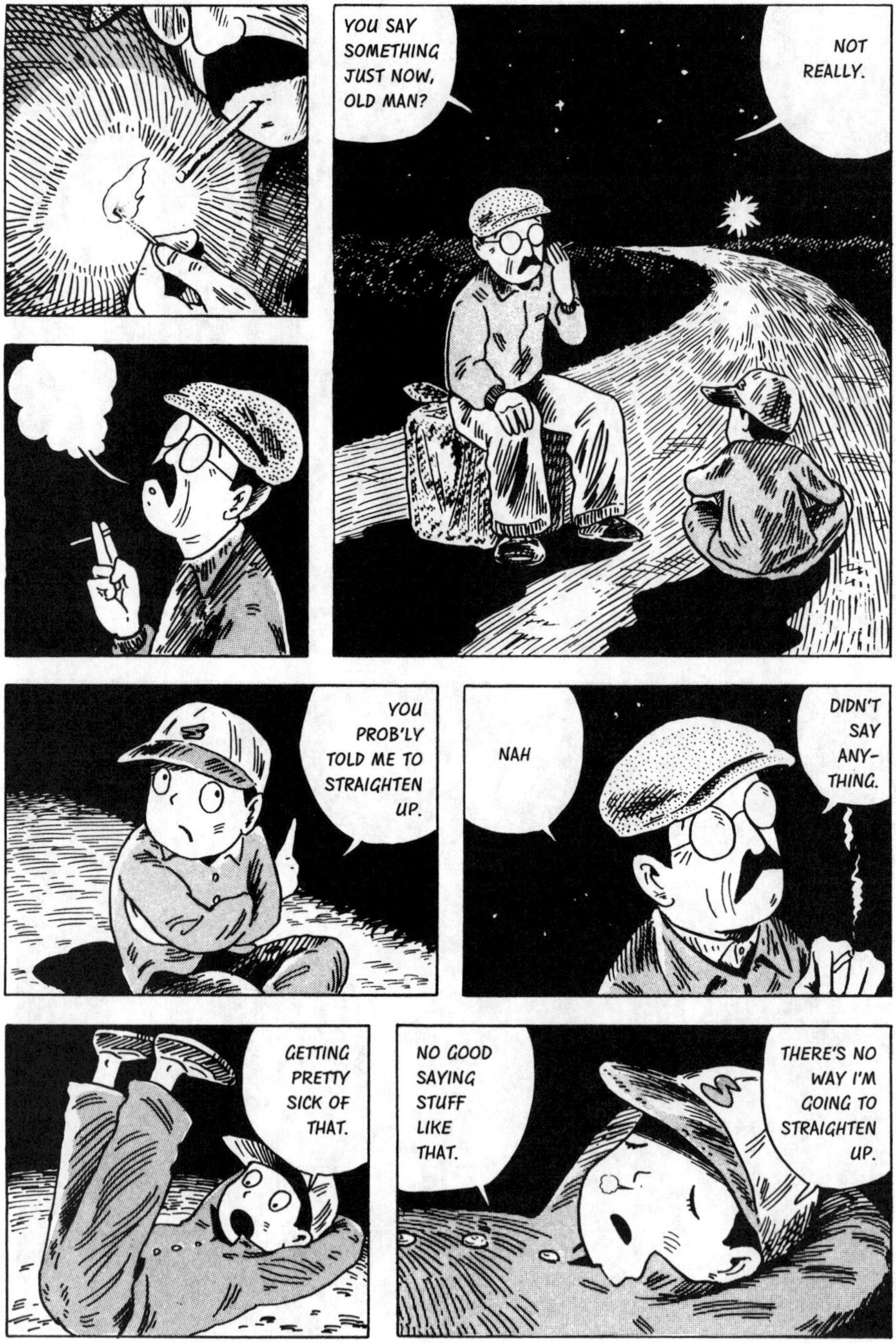

YOU SAY SOMETHING JUST NOW, OLD MAN?
NOT REALLY.
YOU PROB'LY TOLD ME TO STRAIGHTEN UP.
NAH
DIDN'T SAY ANY-THING.
GETTING PRETTY SICK OF THAT.
NO GOOD SAYING STUFF LIKE THAT.
THERE'S NO WAY I'M GOING TO STRAIGHTEN UP.

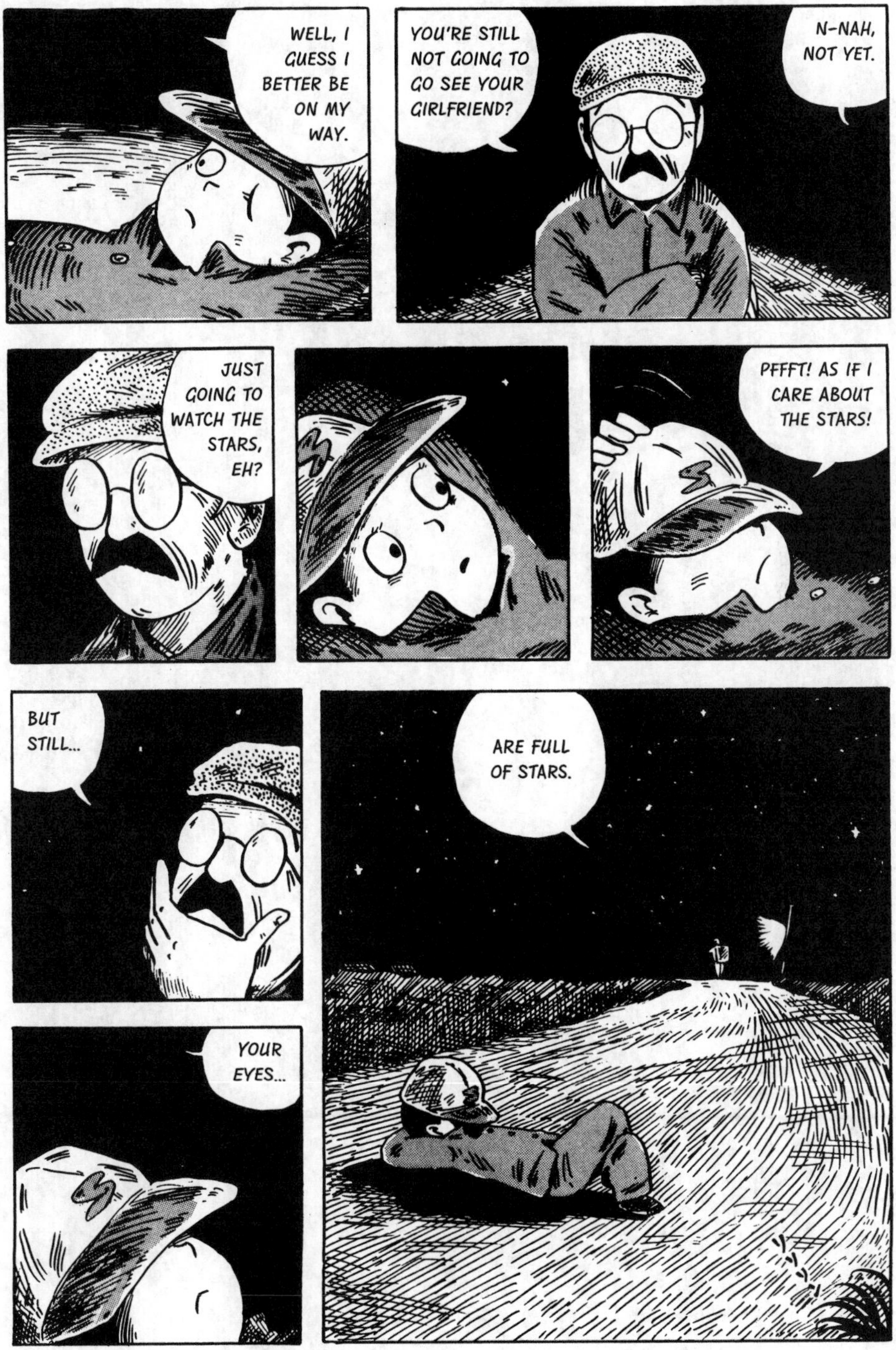
WELL, I GUESS I BETTER BE ON MY WAY.
YOU'RE STILL NOT GOING TO GO SEE YOUR GIRLFRIEND?
N-NAH, NOT YET.
JUST GOING TO WATCH THE STARS, EH?
PFFFT! AS IF I CARE ABOUT THE STARS!
BUT STILL...
YOUR EYES...
ARE FULL OF STARS.

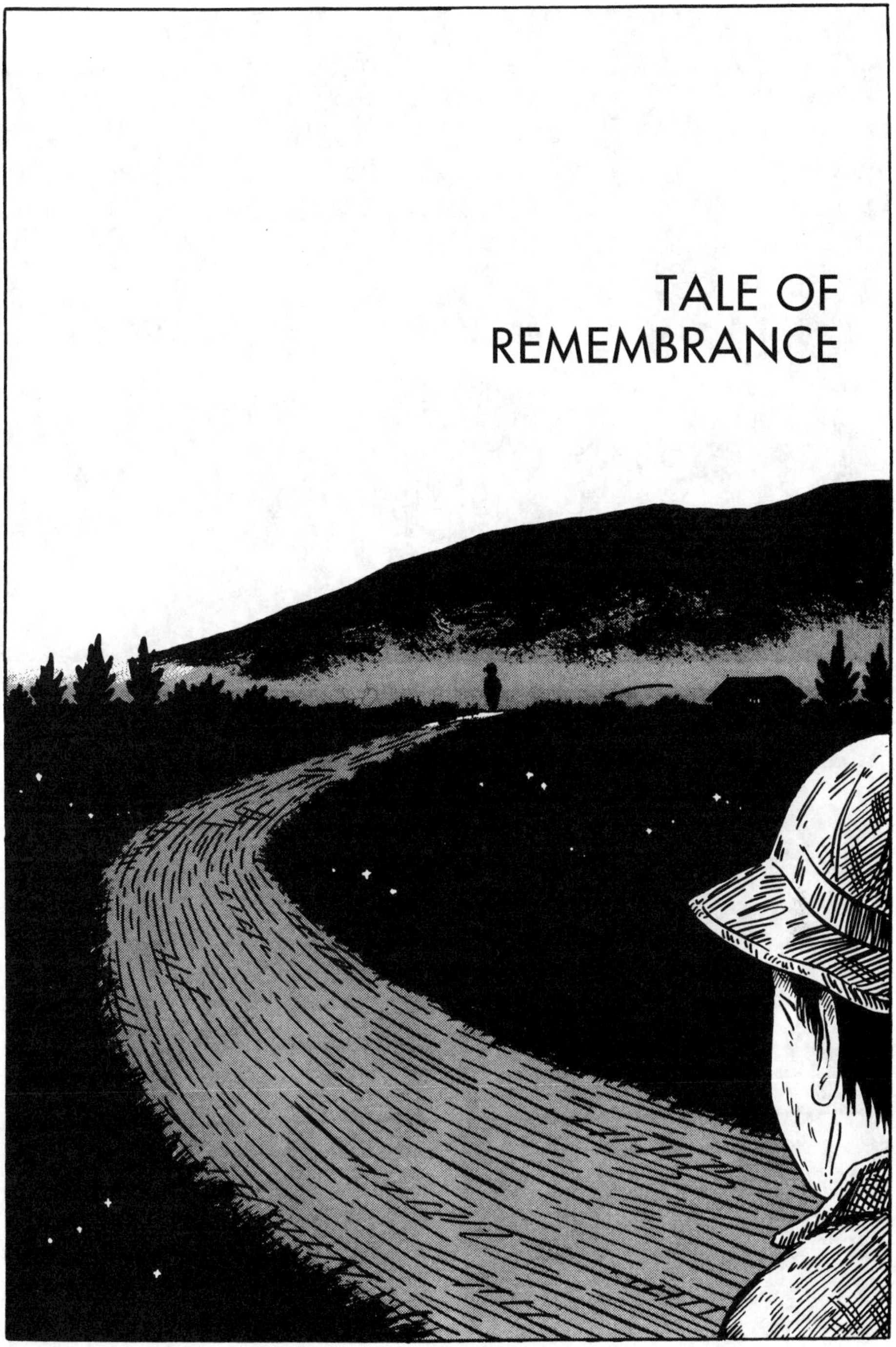
TALE OF
REMEMBRANCE

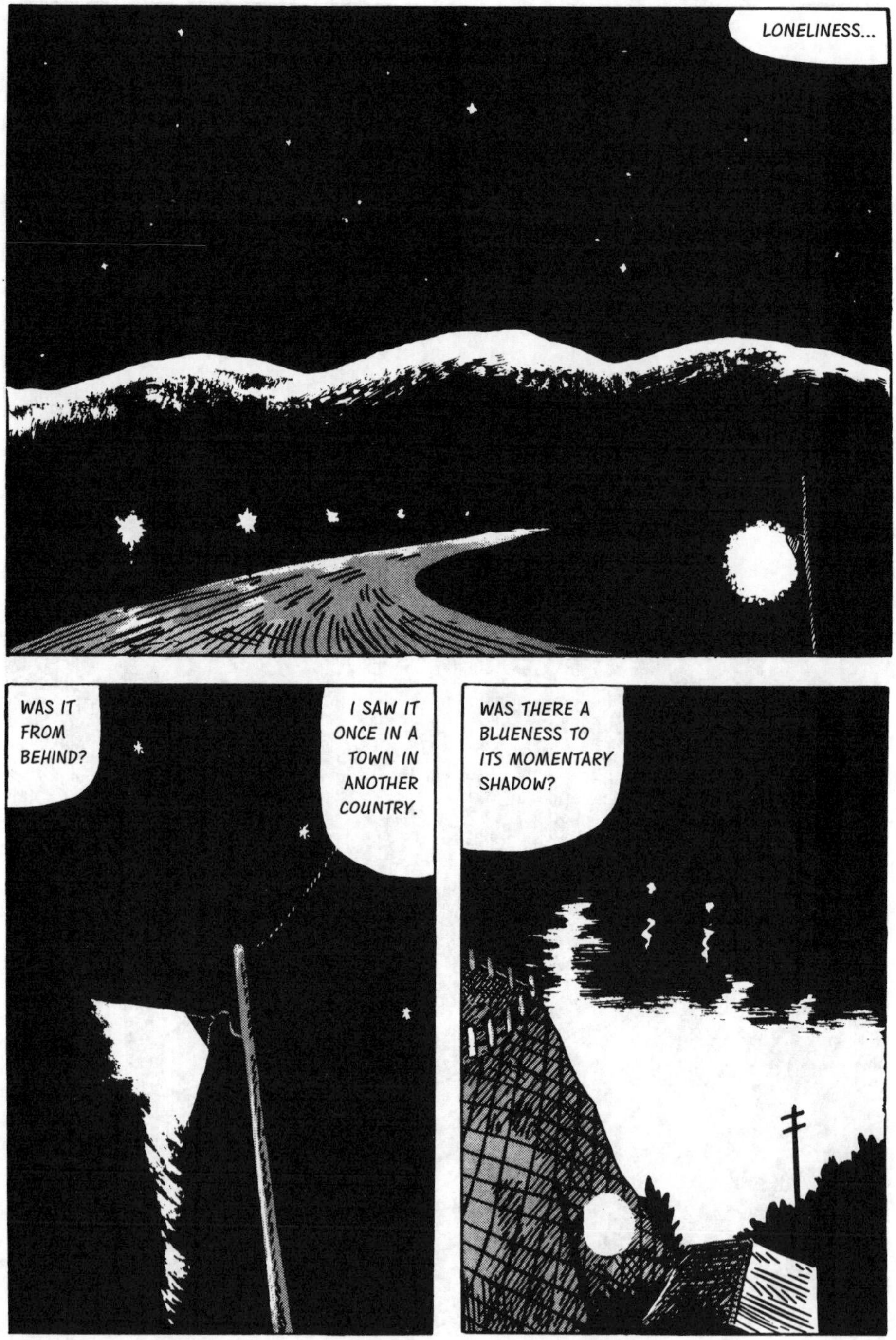
LONELINESS...
WAS IT FROM BEHIND?
I SAW IT ONCE IN A TOWN IN ANOTHER COUNTRY.
WAS THERE A BLUENESS TO ITS MOMENTARY SHADOW?

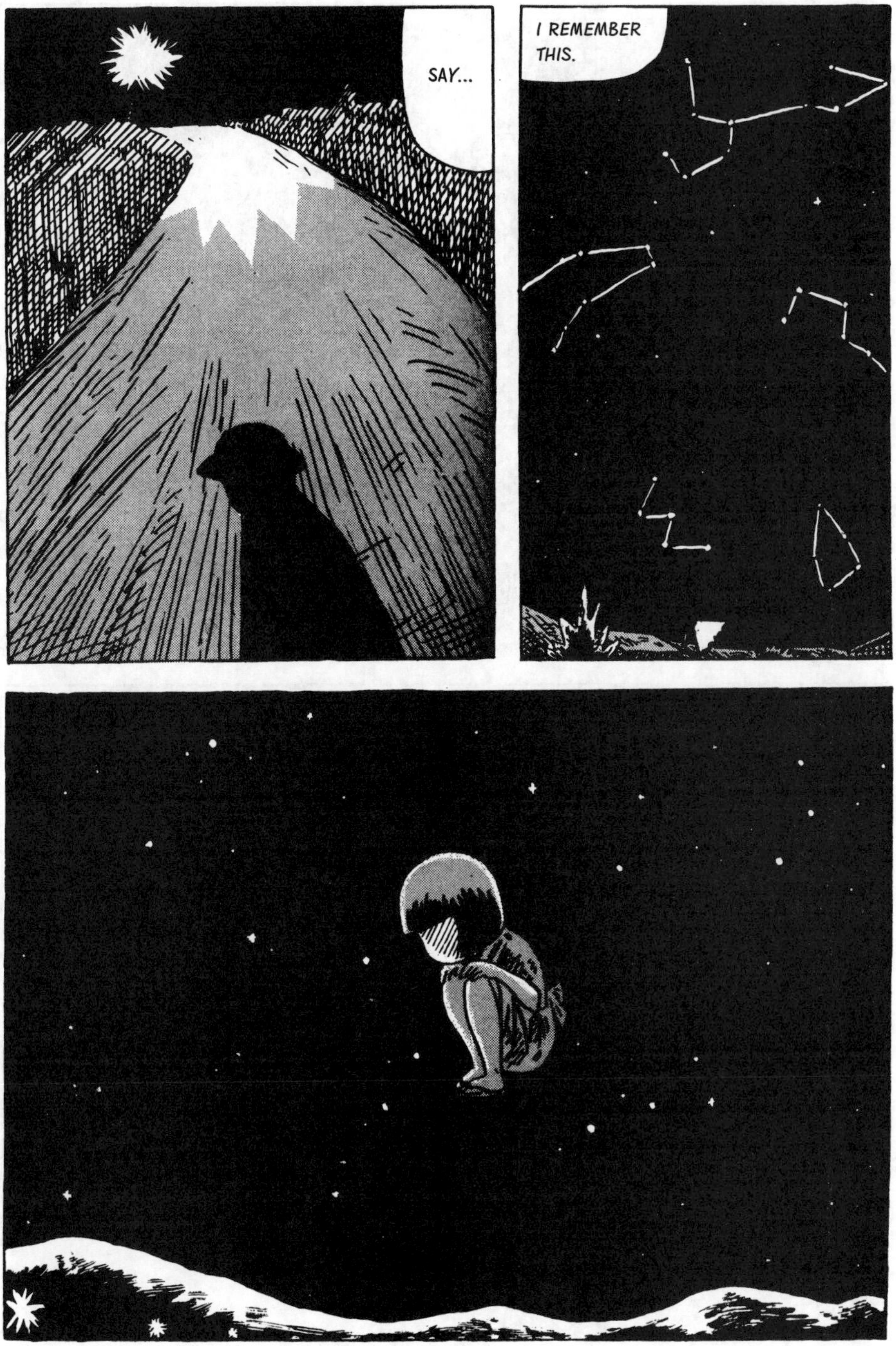
SAY...
I REMEMBER THIS.

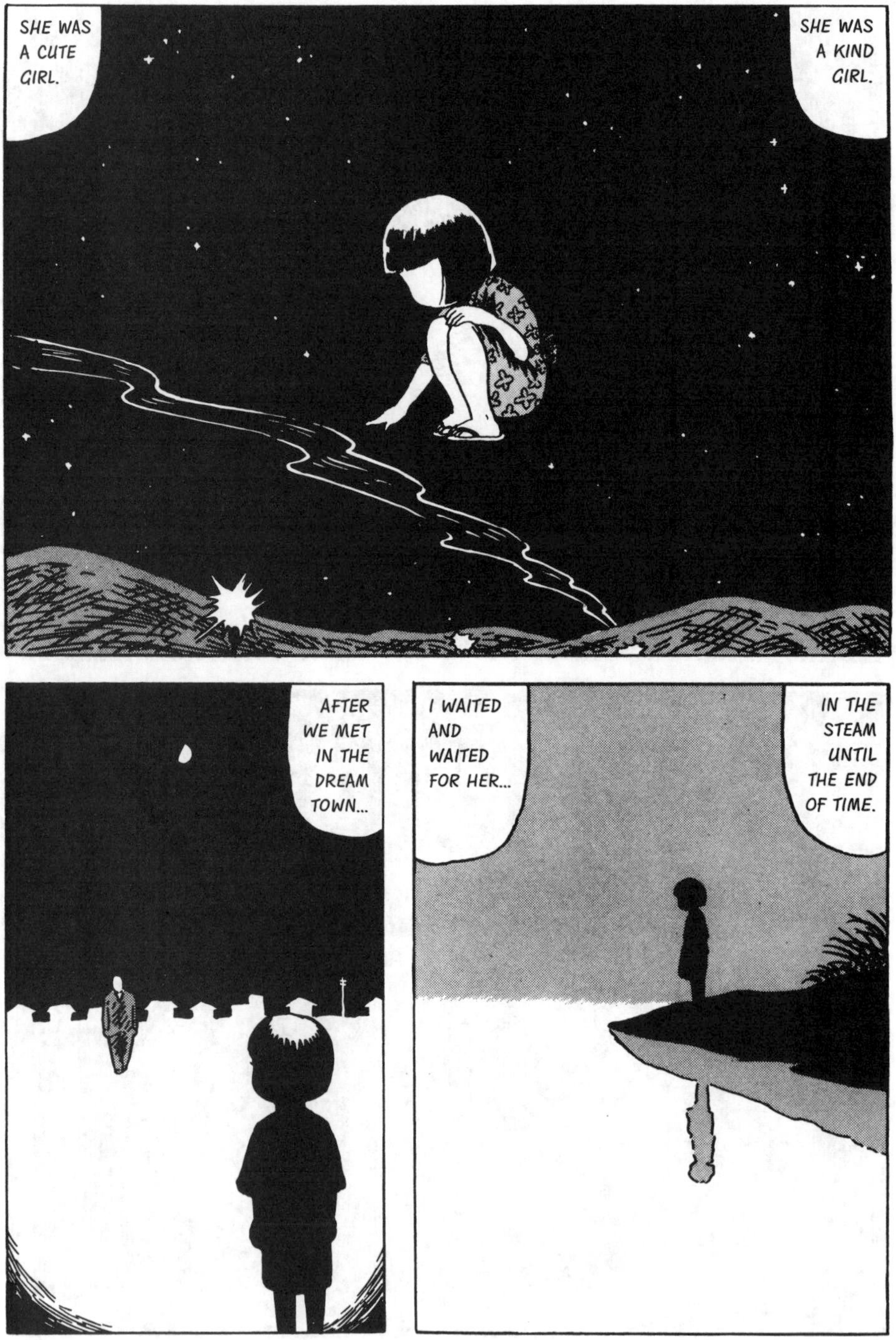
SHE WAS A CUTE GIRL.
SHE WAS A KIND GIRL.
AFTER WE MET IN THE DREAM TOWN...
I WAITED AND WAITED FOR HER...
IN THE STEAM UNTIL THE END OF TIME.

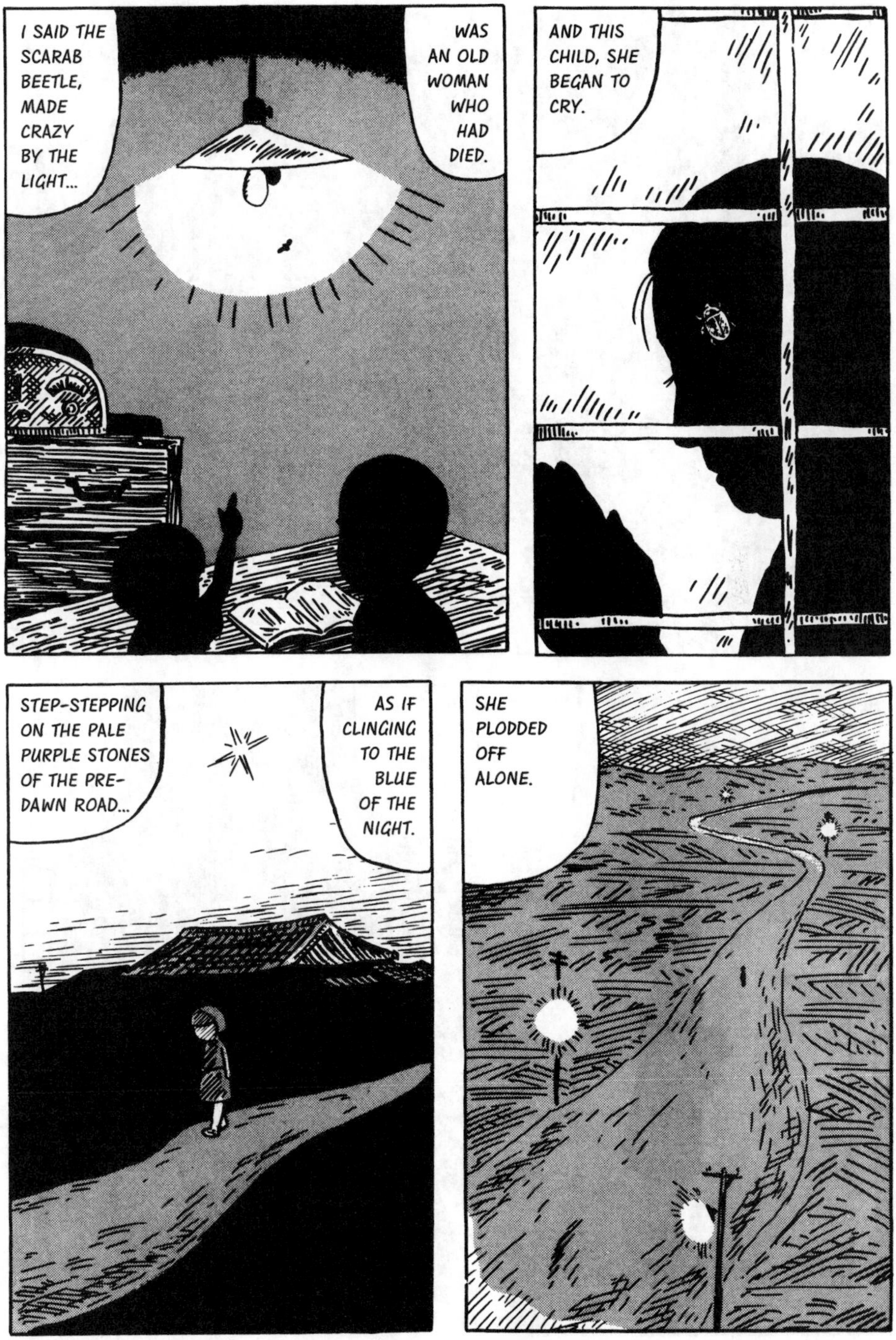
I SAID THE SCARAB BEETLE, MADE CRAZY BY THE LIGHT...
WAS AN OLD WOMAN WHO HAD DIED.
AND THIS CHILD, SHE BEGAN TO CRY.
STEP-STEPPING ON THE PALE PURPLE STONES OF THE PRE-DAWN ROAD...
AS IF CLINGING TO THE BLUE OF THE NIGHT.
SHE PLODDED OFF ALONE.

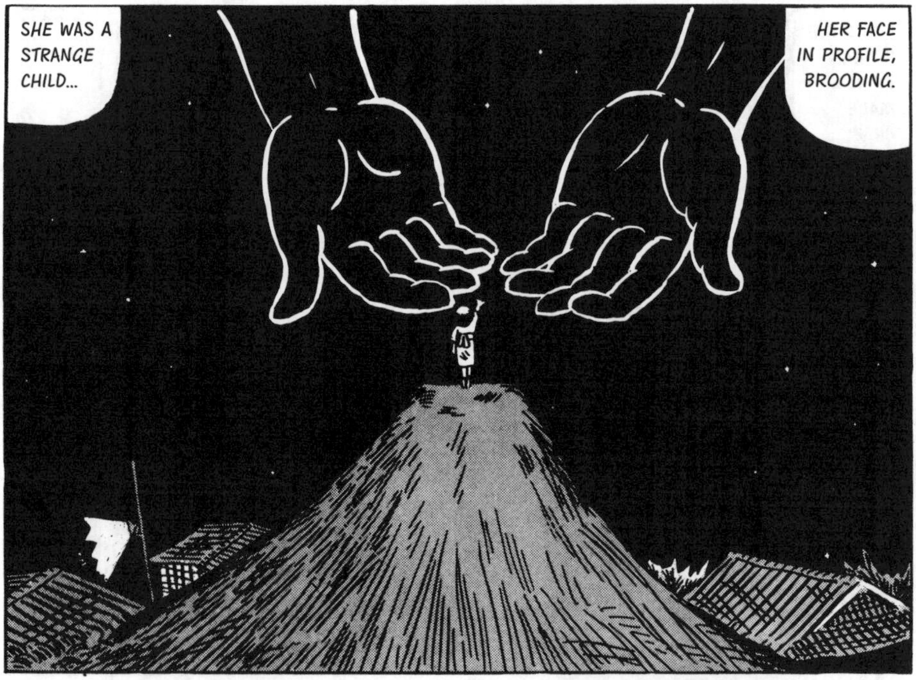
SHE WAS A STRANGE CHILD...
HER FACE IN PROFILE, BROODING.
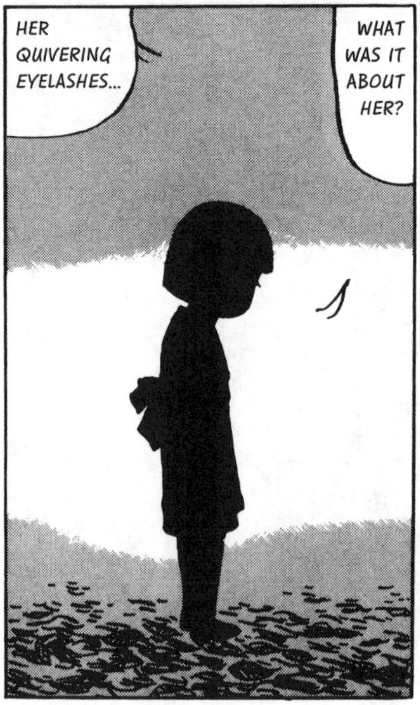
HER QUIVERING EYELASHES...
WHAT WAS IT ABOUT HER?
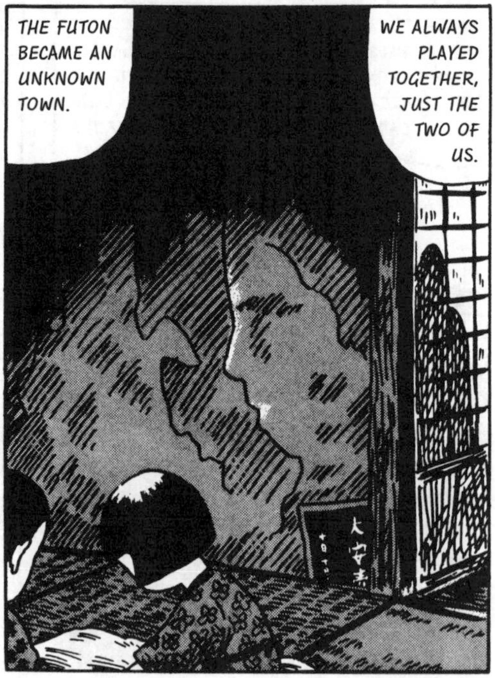
THE FUTON BECAME AN UNKNOWN TOWN.
WE ALWAYS PLAYED TOGETHER, JUST THE TWO OF US.

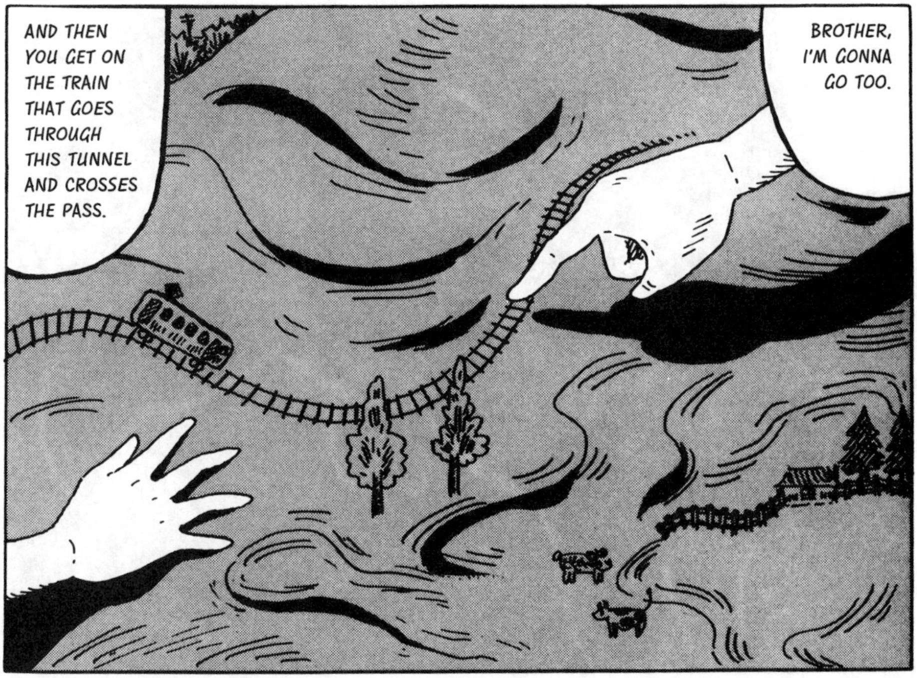
AND THEN YOU GET ON THE TRAIN THAT GOES THROUGH THIS TUNNEL AND CROSSES THE PASS.
BROTHER, I'M GONNA GO TOO.

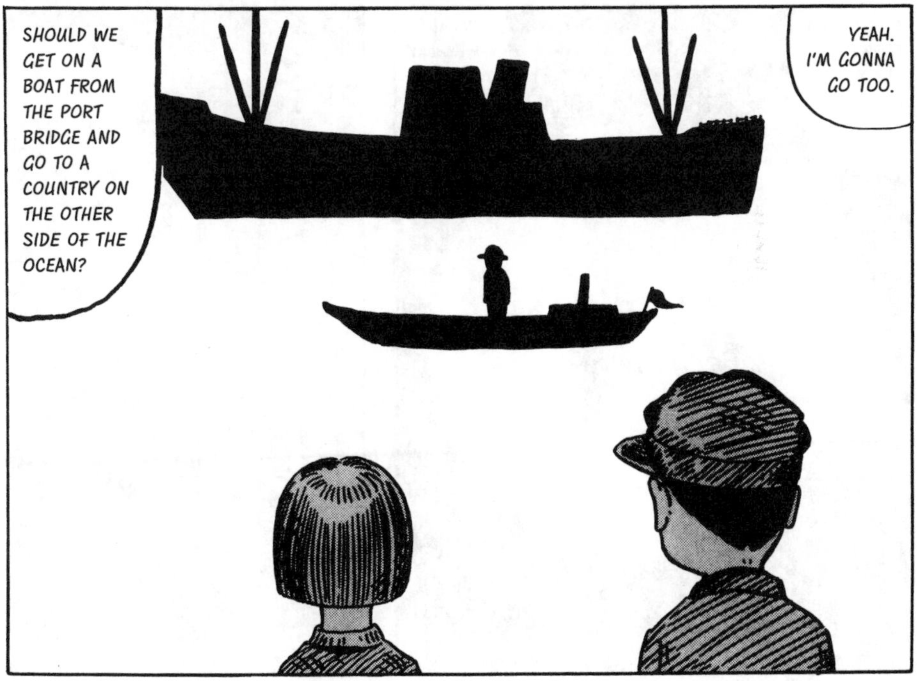
SHOULD WE GET ON A BOAT FROM THE PORT BRIDGE AND GO TO A COUNTRY ON THE OTHER SIDE OF THE OCEAN?
YEAH. I'M GONNA GO TOO.

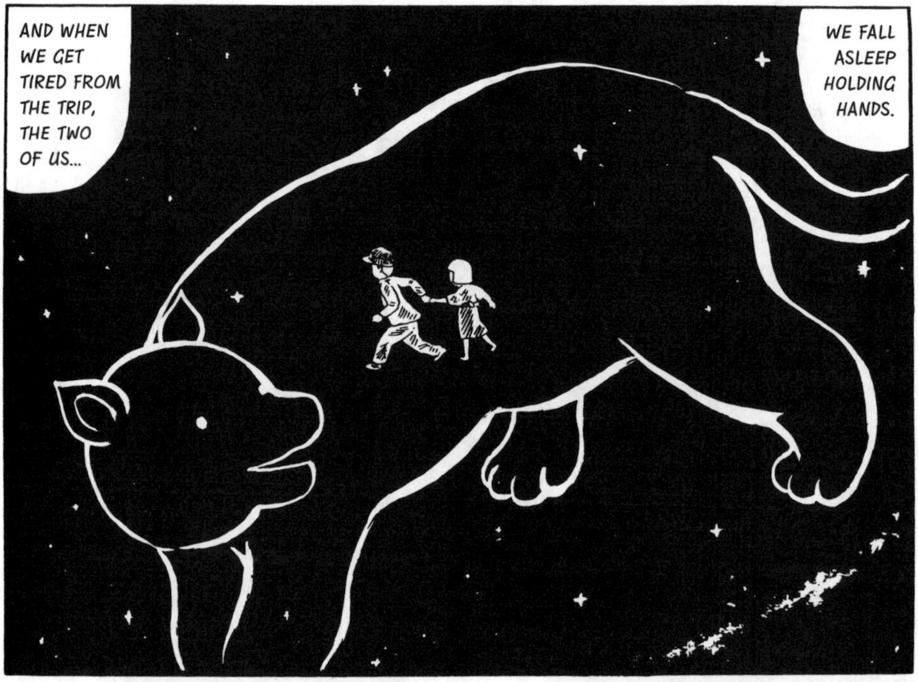
AND WHEN WE GET TIRED FROM THE TRIP, THE TWO OF US...
WE FALL ASLEEP HOLDING HANDS.

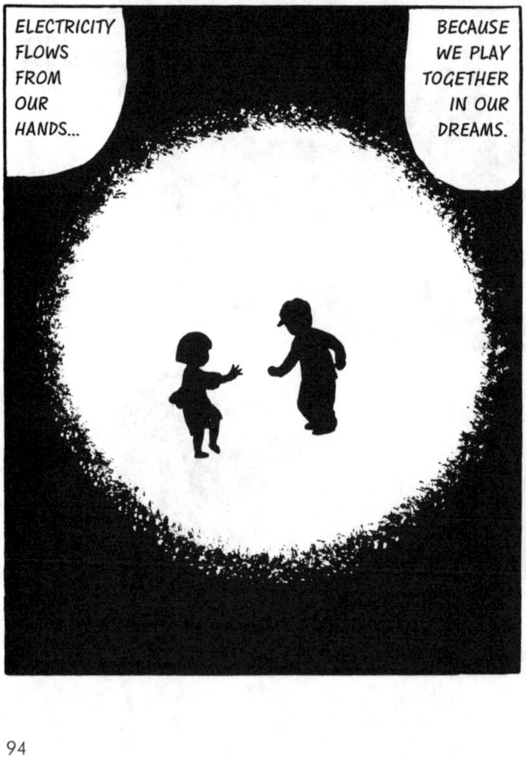
ELECTRICITY FLOWS FROM OUR HANDS...
BECAUSE WE PLAY TOGETHER IN OUR DREAMS.

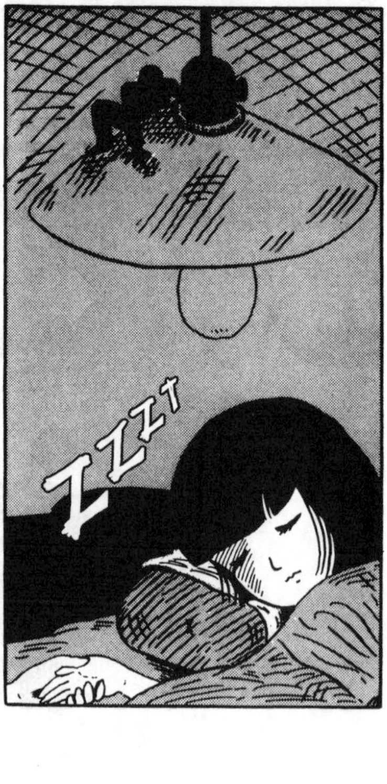
ZZZZ

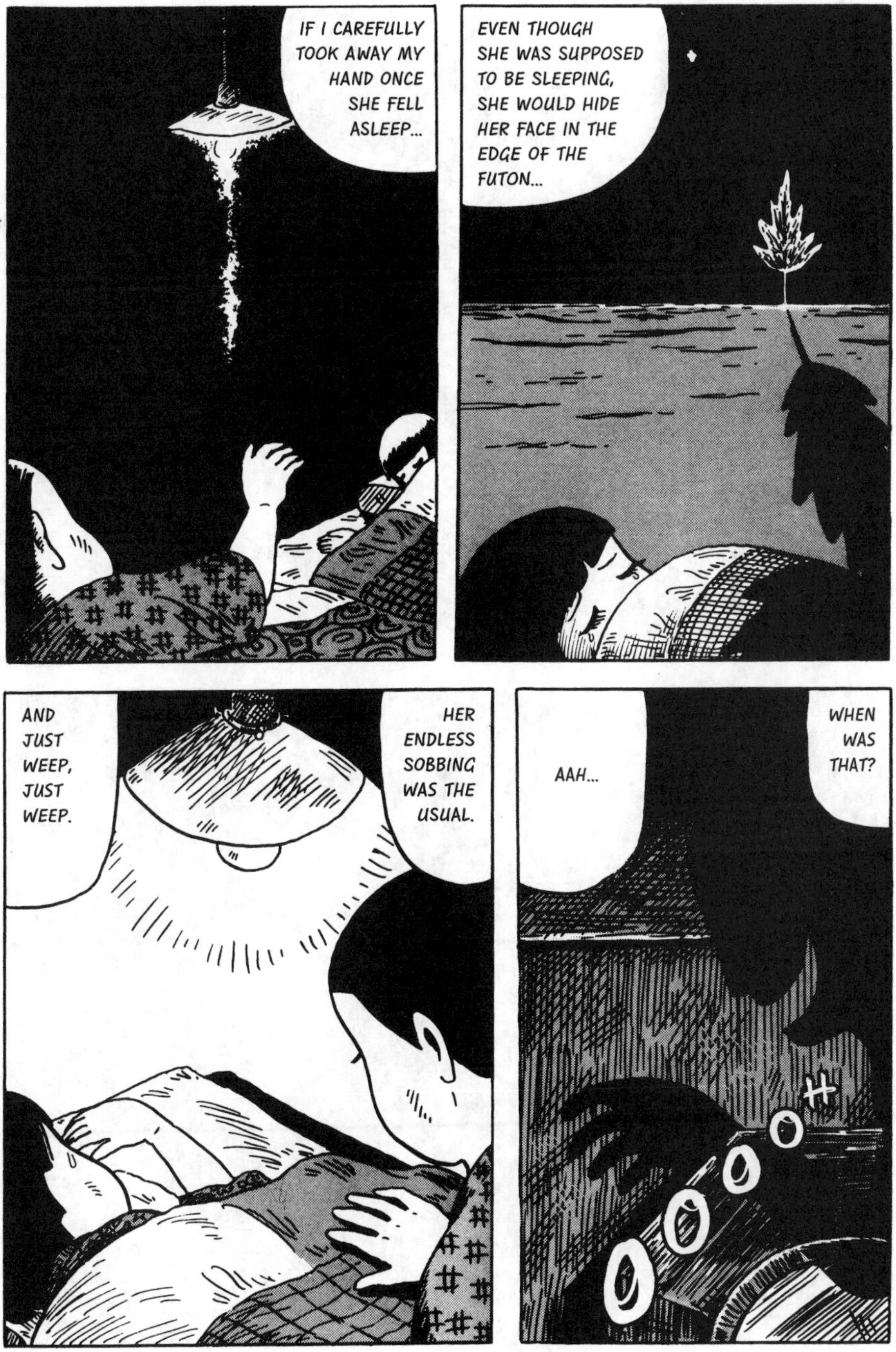
IF I CAREFULLY TOOK AWAY MY HAND ONCE SHE FELL ASLEEP...
EVEN THOUGH SHE WAS SUPPOSED TO BE SLEEPING, SHE WOULD HIDE HER FACE IN THE EDGE OF THE FUTON...
AND JUST WEEP, JUST WEEP.
HER ENDLESS SOBBING WAS THE USUAL.
AAH...
WHEN WAS THAT?

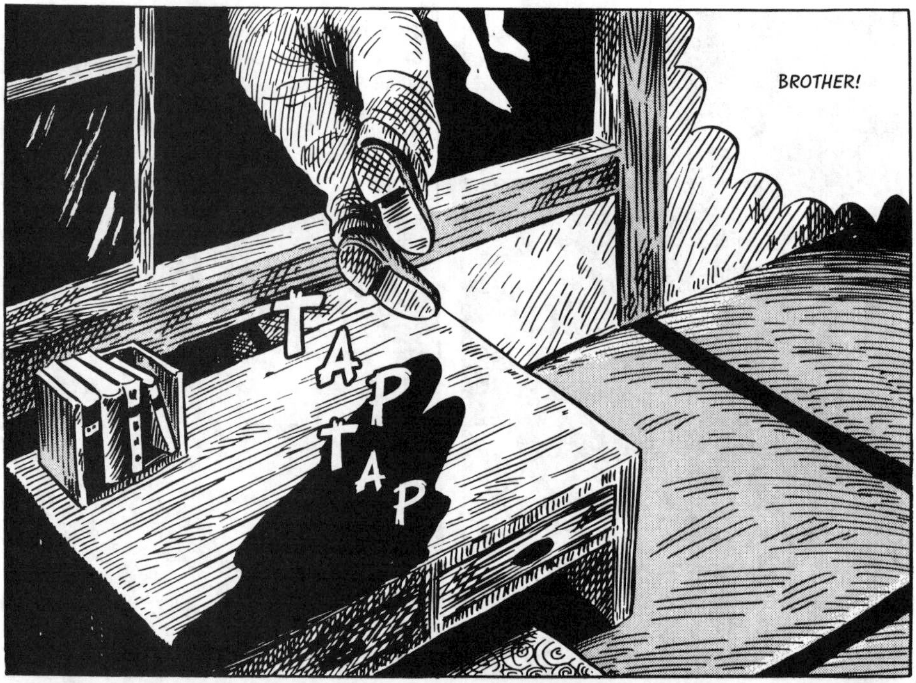
BROTHER!
TAP
TAP

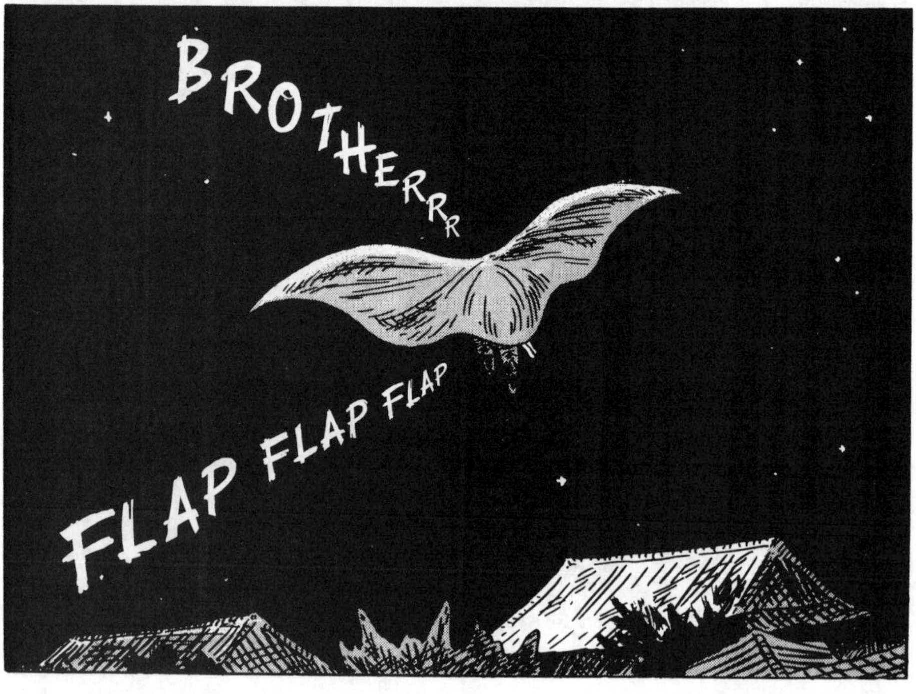
BROTHERRR
FLAP FLAP FLAP

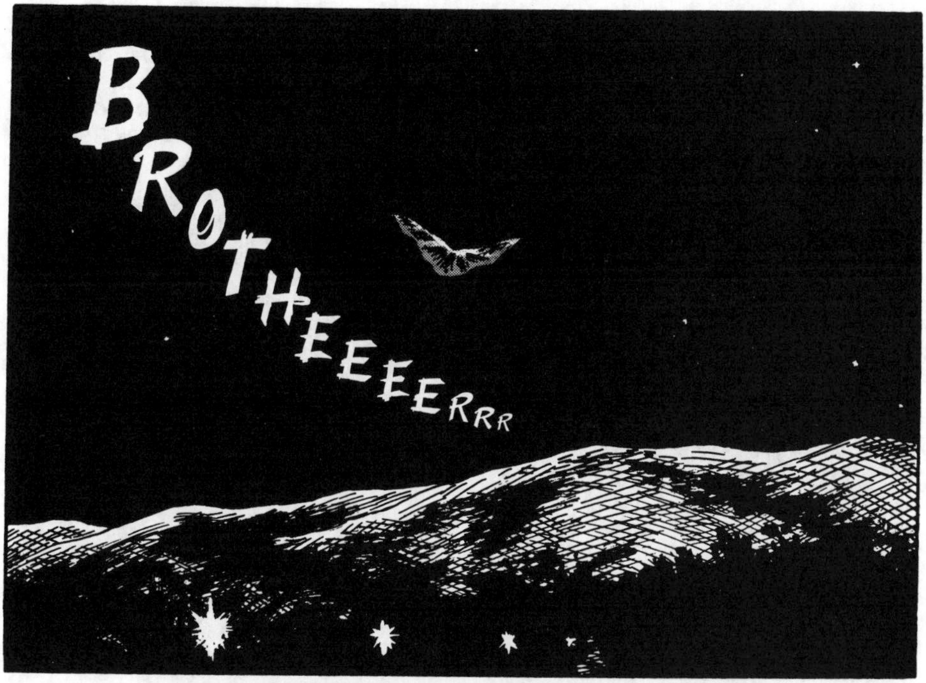
BROTHEEEEERRR

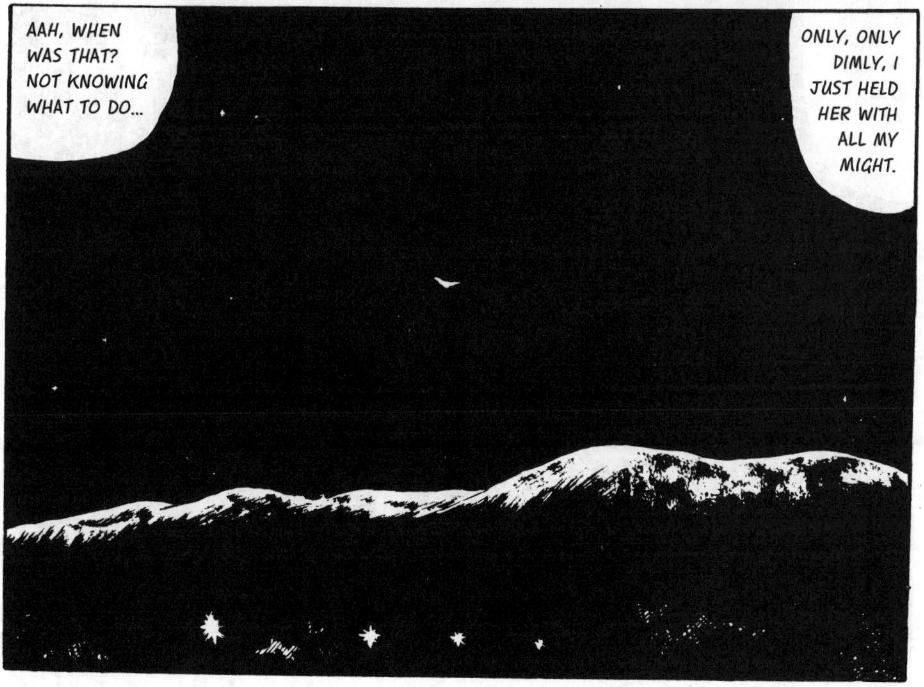
AAH, WHEN WAS THAT? NOT KNOWING WHAT TO DO...
ONLY, ONLY DIMLY, I JUST HELD HER WITH ALL MY MIGHT.

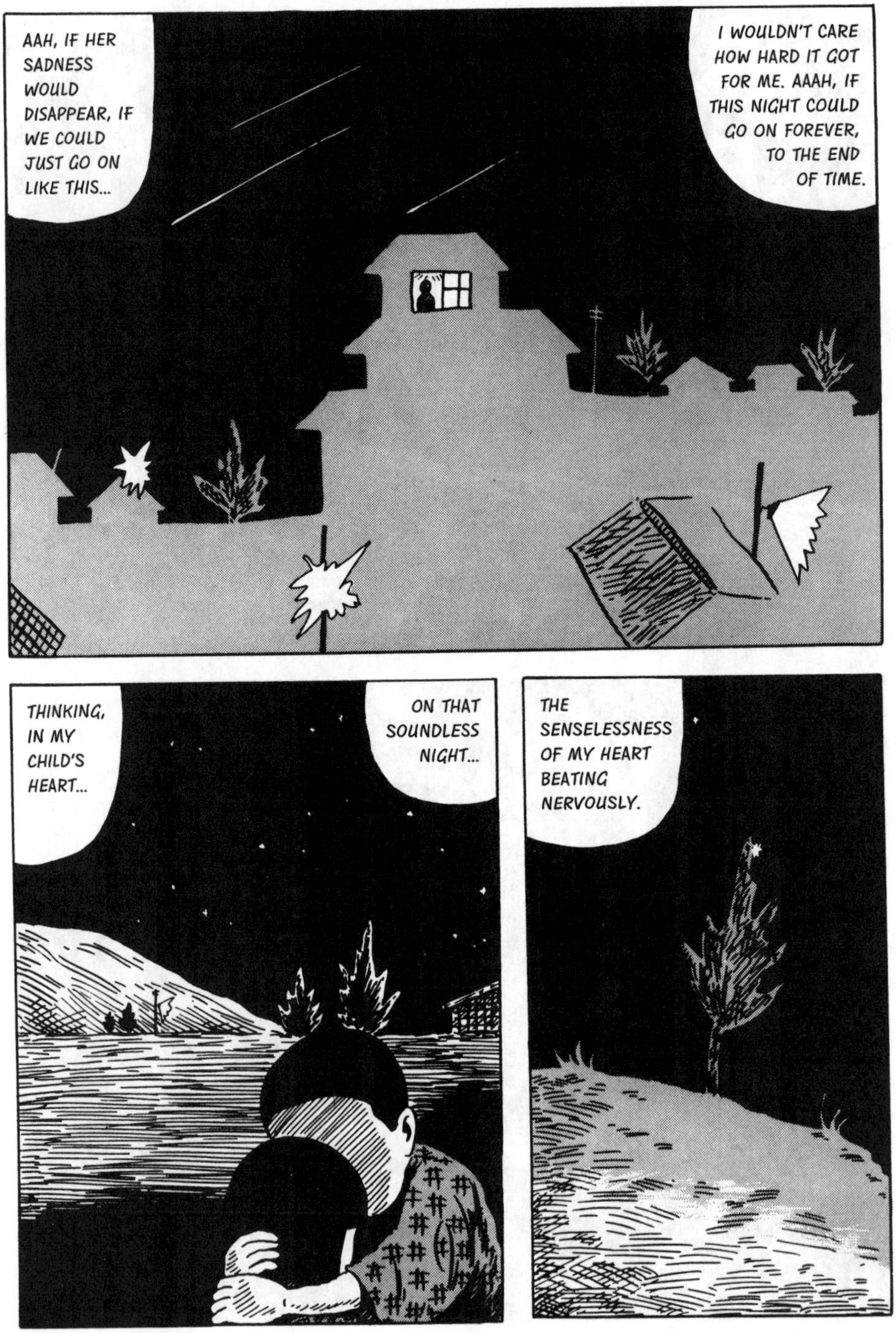
AAH, IF HER SADNESS WOULD DISAPPEAR, IF WE COULD JUST GO ON LIKE THIS...
I WOULDN'T CARE HOW HARD IT GOT FOR ME. AAAH, IF THIS NIGHT COULD GO ON FOREVER, TO THE END OF TIME.
THINKING, IN MY CHILD'S HEART...
ON THAT SOUNDLESS NIGHT...
THE SENSELESSNESS OF MY HEART BEATING NERVOUSLY.

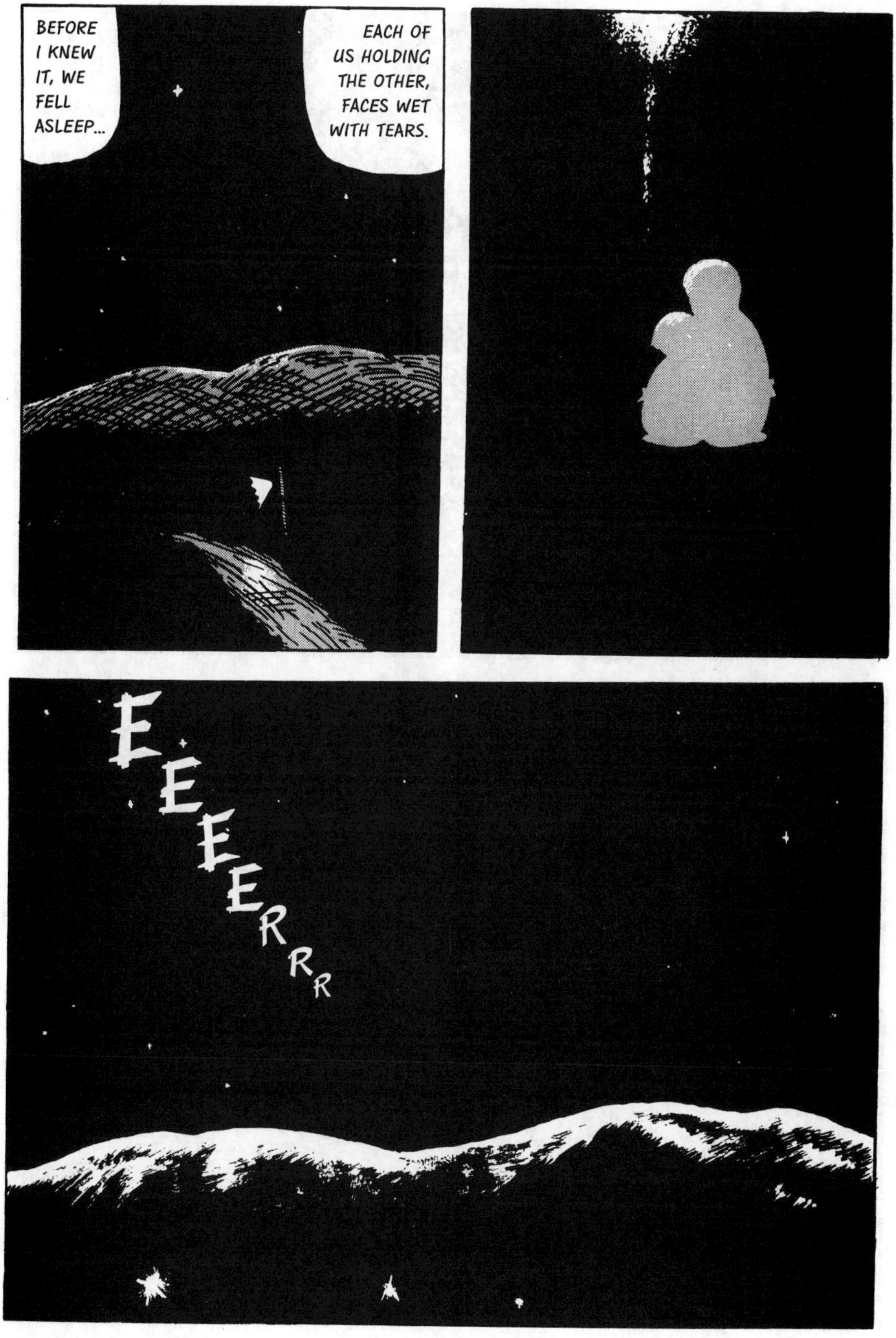
BEFORE I KNEW IT, WE FELL ASLEEP...
EACH OF US HOLDING THE OTHER, FACES WET WITH TEARS.
EEEERRR

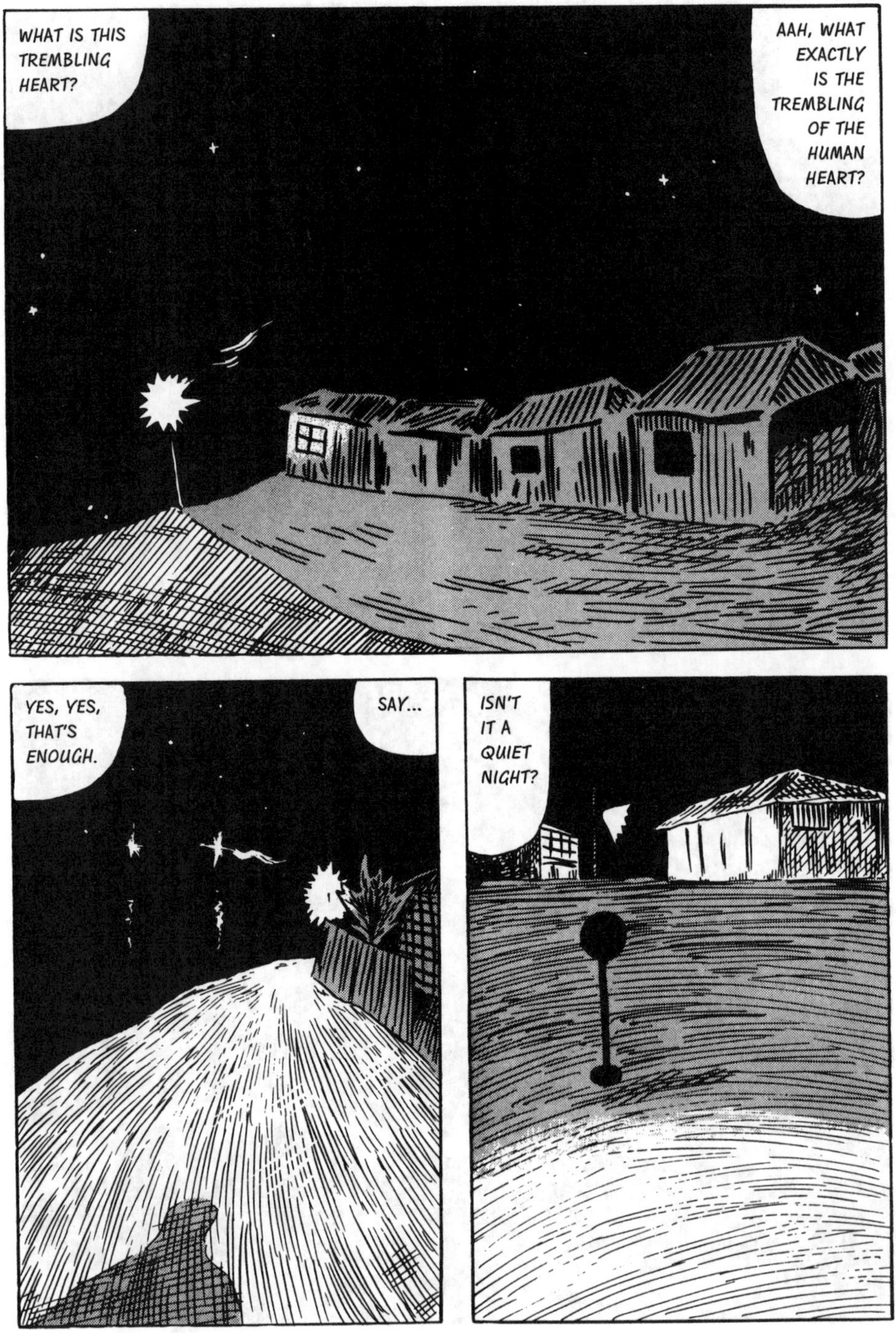
WHAT IS THIS TREMBLING HEART?
AAH, WHAT EXACTLY IS THE TREMBLING OF THE HUMAN HEART?
YES, YES, THAT'S ENOUGH.
SAY...
ISN'T IT A QUIET NIGHT?

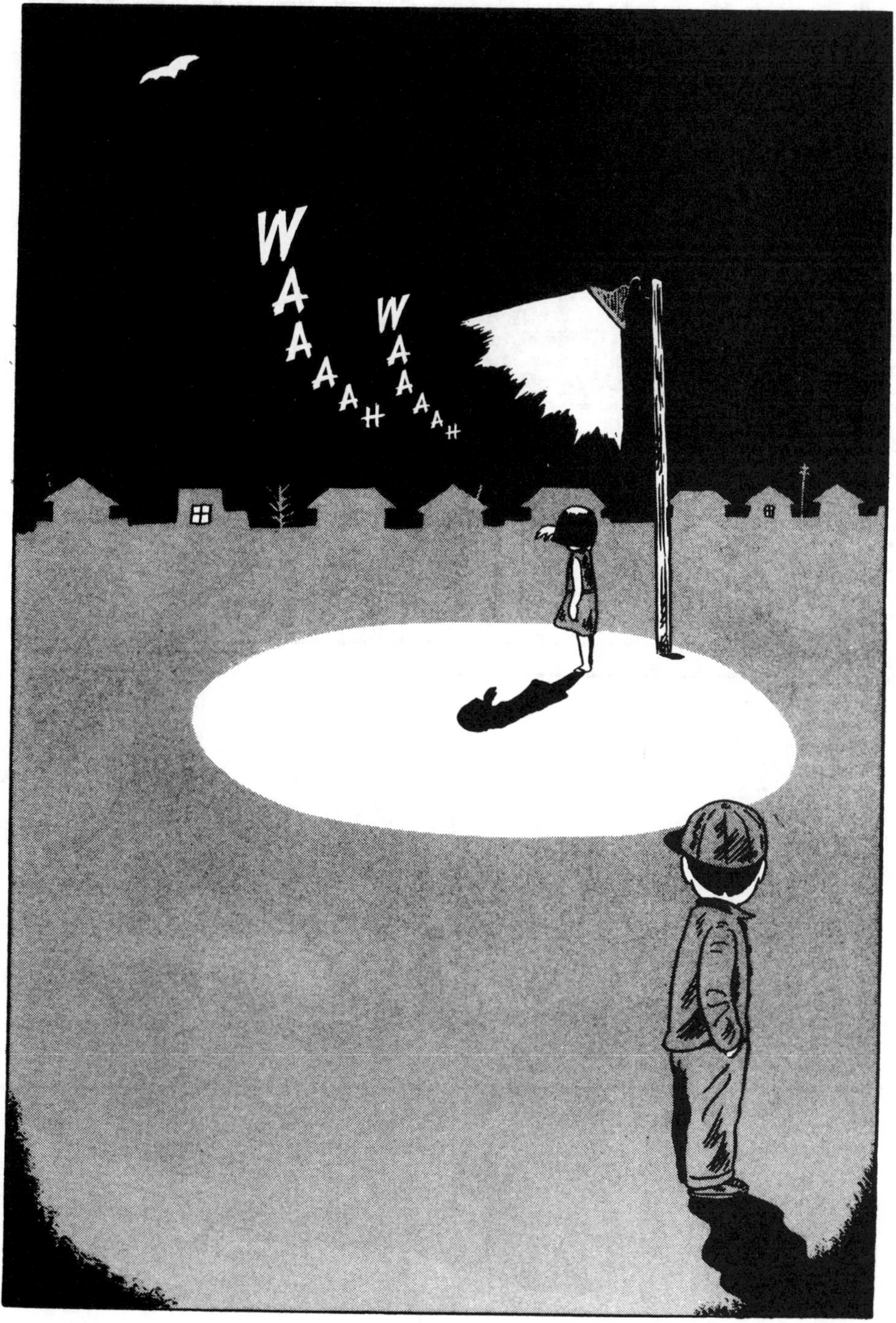
WAAAAH
WAAAAH

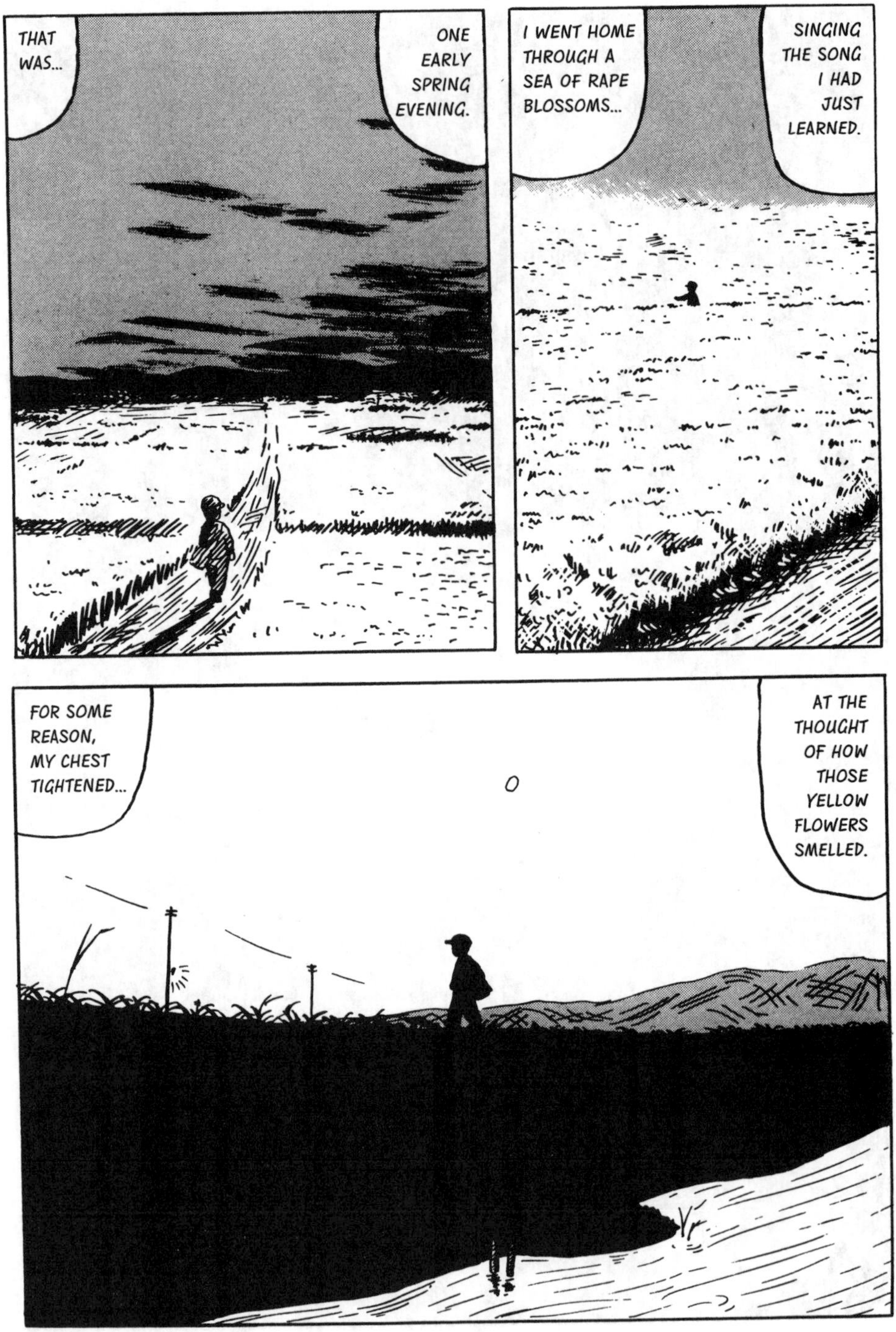
THAT WAS...
ONE EARLY SPRING EVENING.
I WENT HOME THROUGH A SEA OF RAPE BLOSSOMS...
SINGING THE SONG I HAD JUST LEARNED.
FOR SOME REASON, MY CHEST TIGHTENED...
AT THE THOUGHT OF HOW THOSE YELLOW FLOWERS SMELLED.

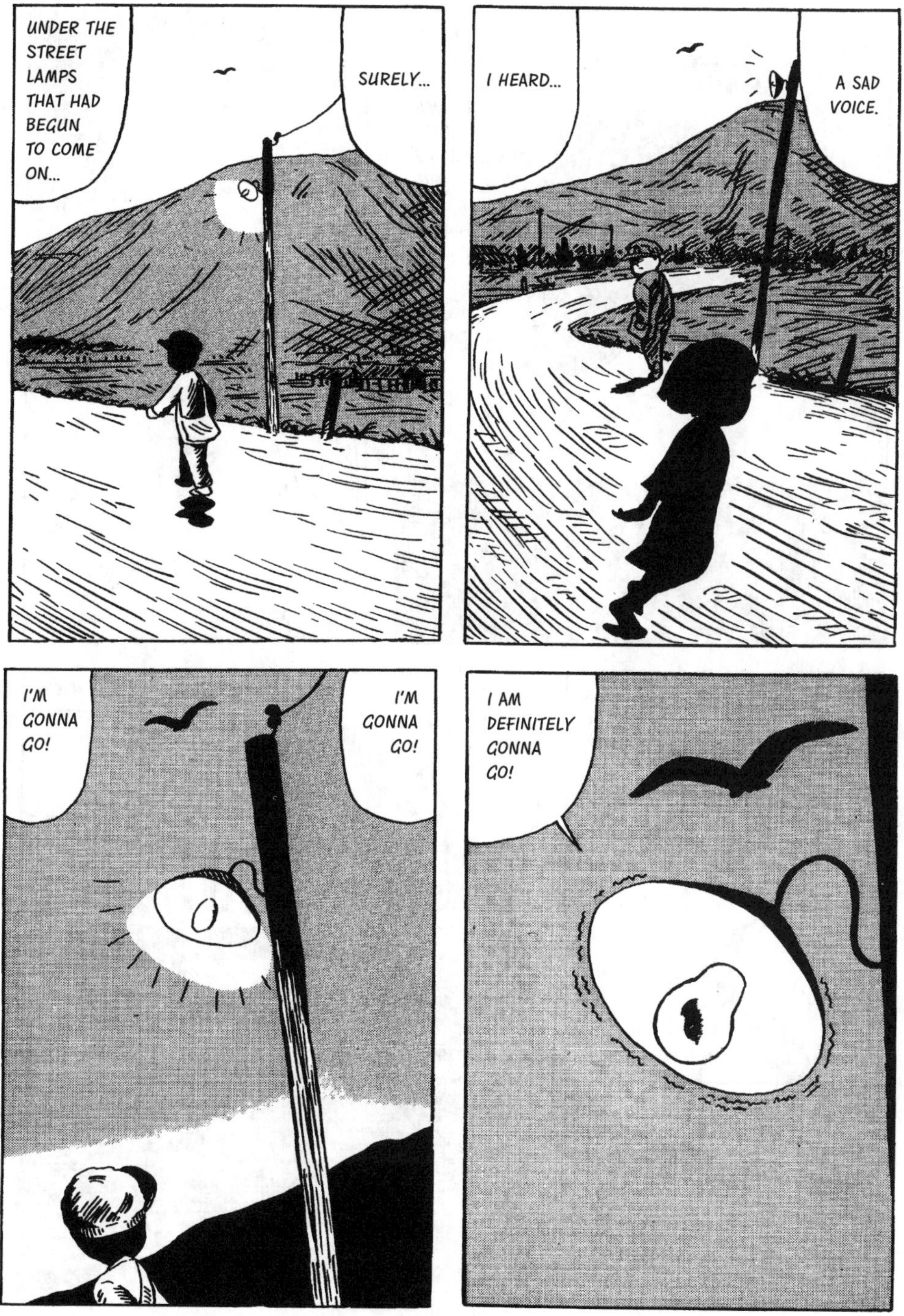
UNDER THE STREET LAMPS THAT HAD BEGUN TO COME ON...
SURELY...
I HEARD...
A SAD VOICE.
I'M GONNA GO!
I'M GONNA GO!
I AM DEFINITELY GONNA GO!

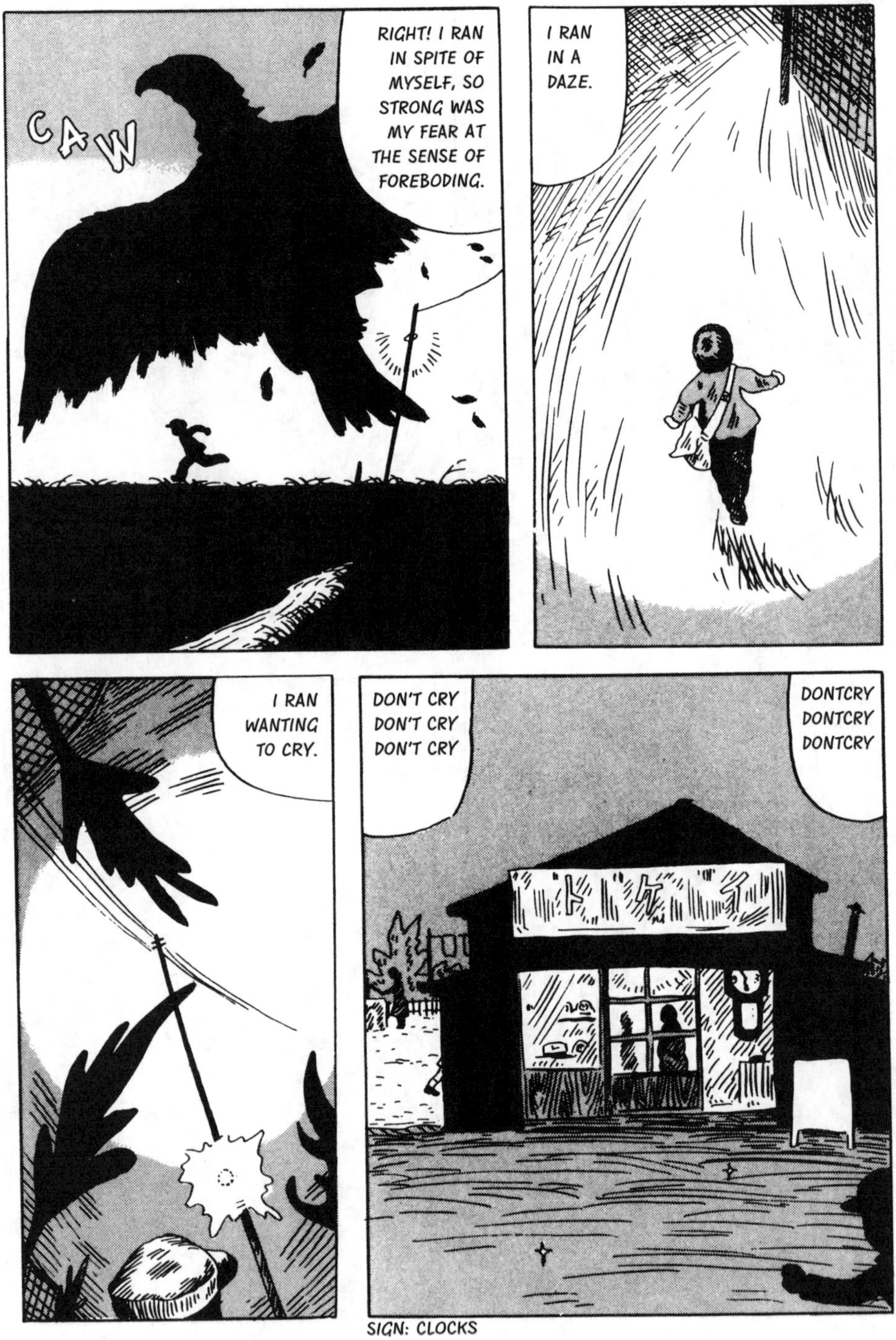
CAW
RIGHT! I RAN IN SPITE OF MYSELF, SO STRONG WAS MY FEAR AT THE SENSE OF FOREBODING.
I RAN IN A DAZE.
I RAN WANTING TO CRY.
DON'T CRY DON'T CRY DON'T CRY
DONTCRY DONTCRY DONTCRY
トケイ

SIGN: CLOCKS

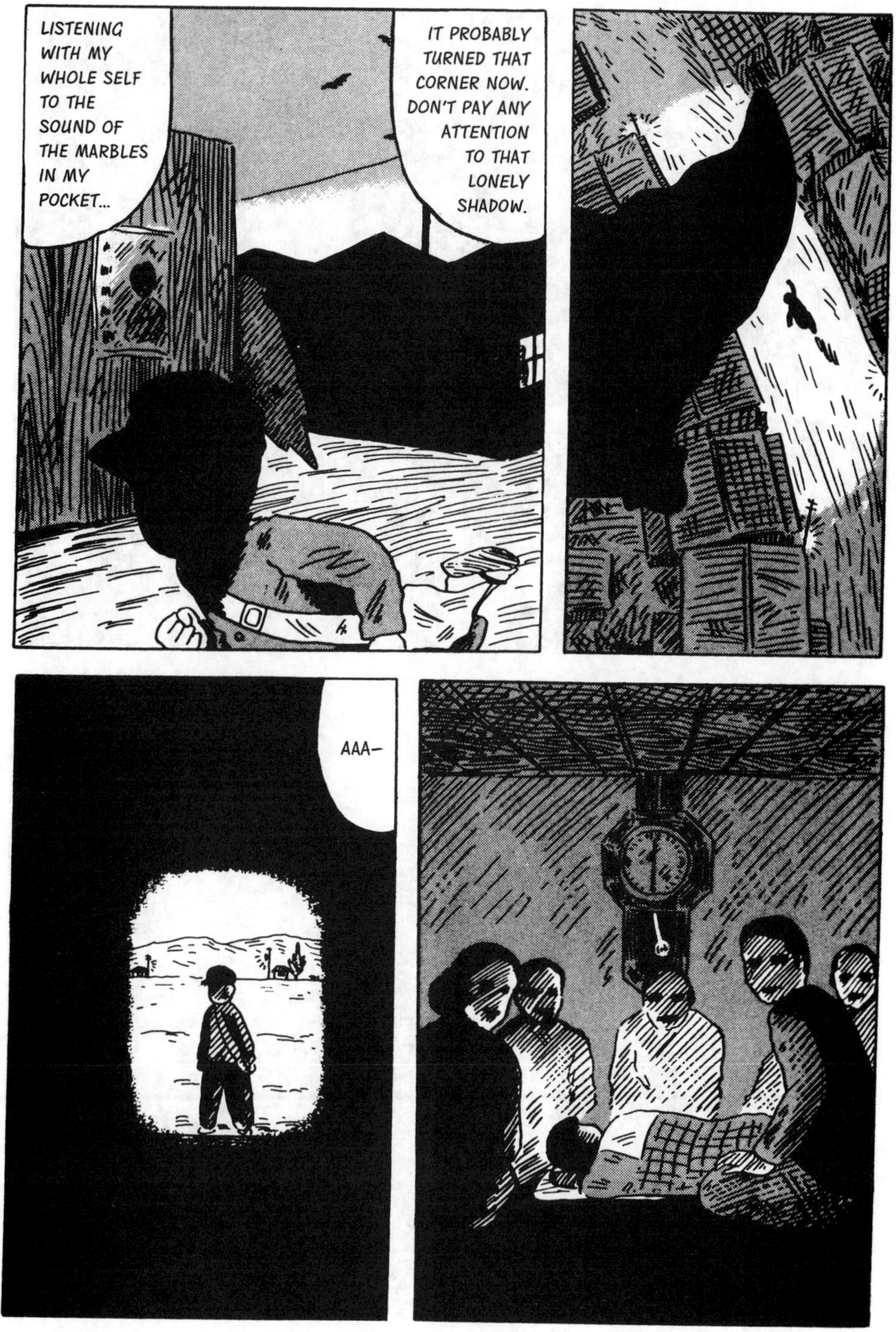
LISTENING WITH MY WHOLE SELF TO THE SOUND OF THE MARBLES IN MY POCKET...
IT PROBABLY TURNED THAT CORNER NOW. DON'T PAY ANY ATTENTION TO THAT LONELY SHADOW.
AAA–

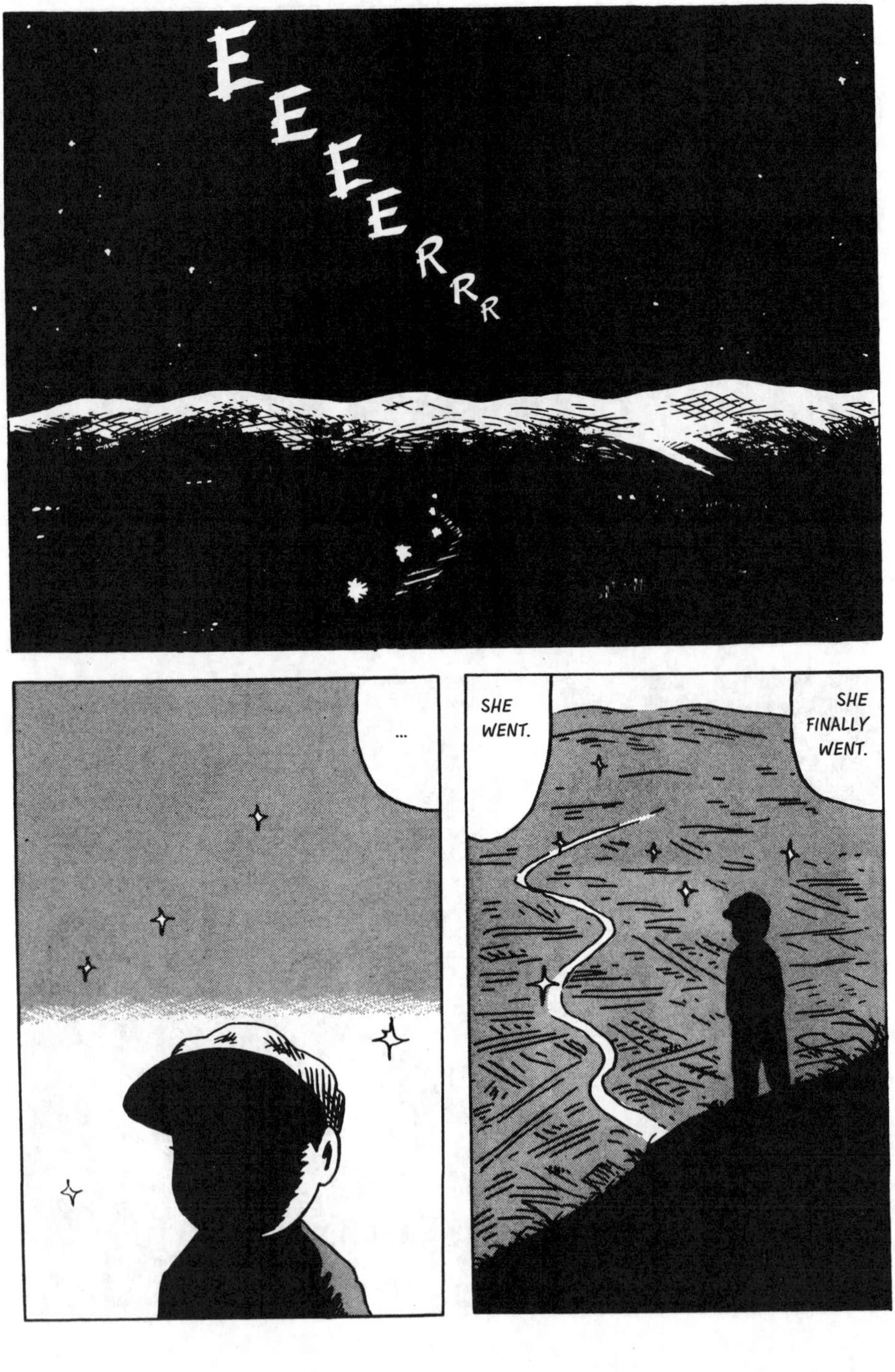
EEEERRR
...
SHE WENT.
SHE FINALLY WENT.

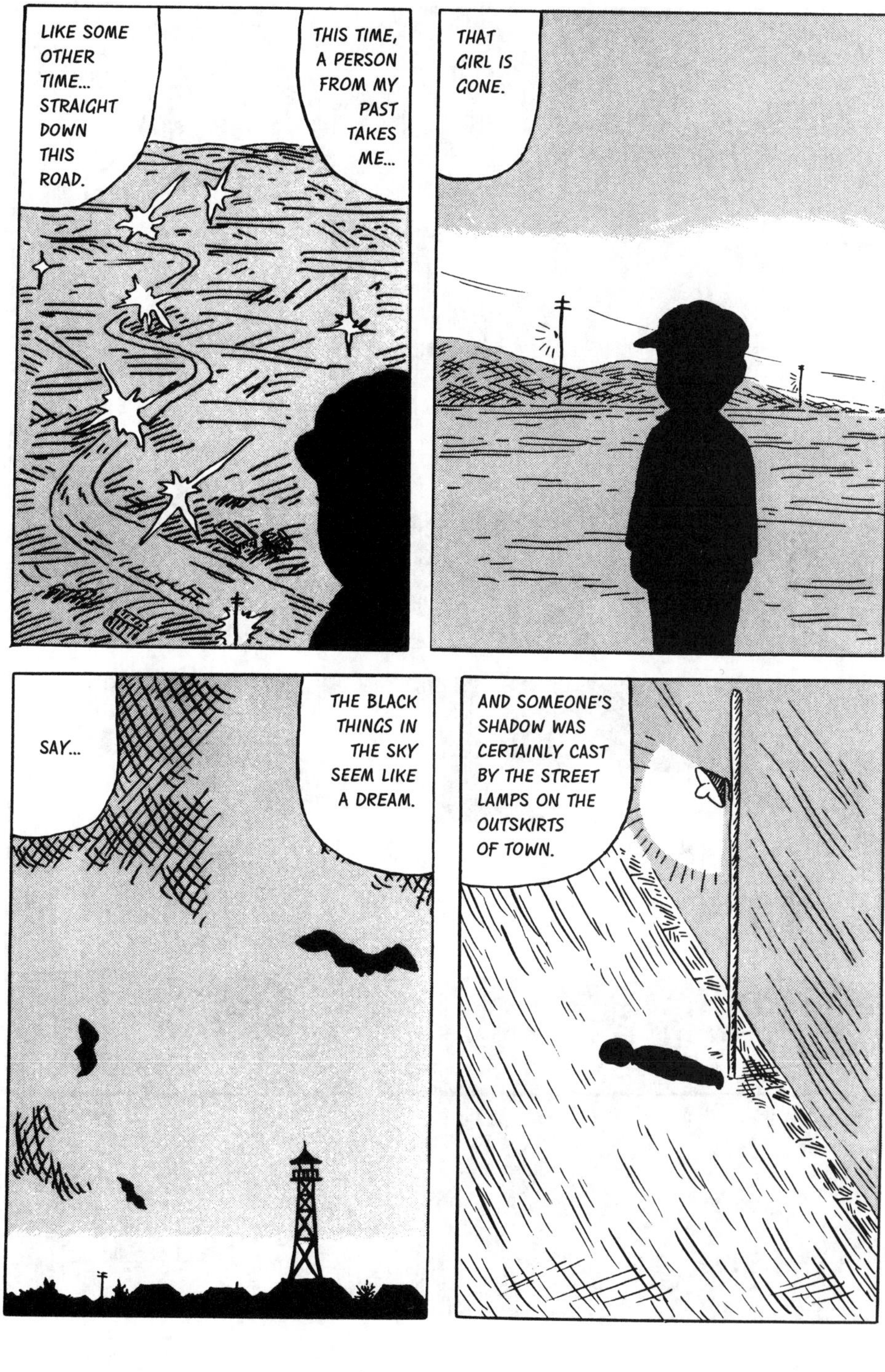
LIKE SOME OTHER TIME... STRAIGHT DOWN THIS ROAD.
THIS TIME, A PERSON FROM MY PAST TAKES ME...
THAT GIRL IS GONE.
SAY...
THE BLACK THINGS IN THE SKY SEEM LIKE A DREAM.
AND SOMEONE'S SHADOW WAS CERTAINLY CAST BY THE STREET LAMPS ON THE OUTSKIRTS OF TOWN.

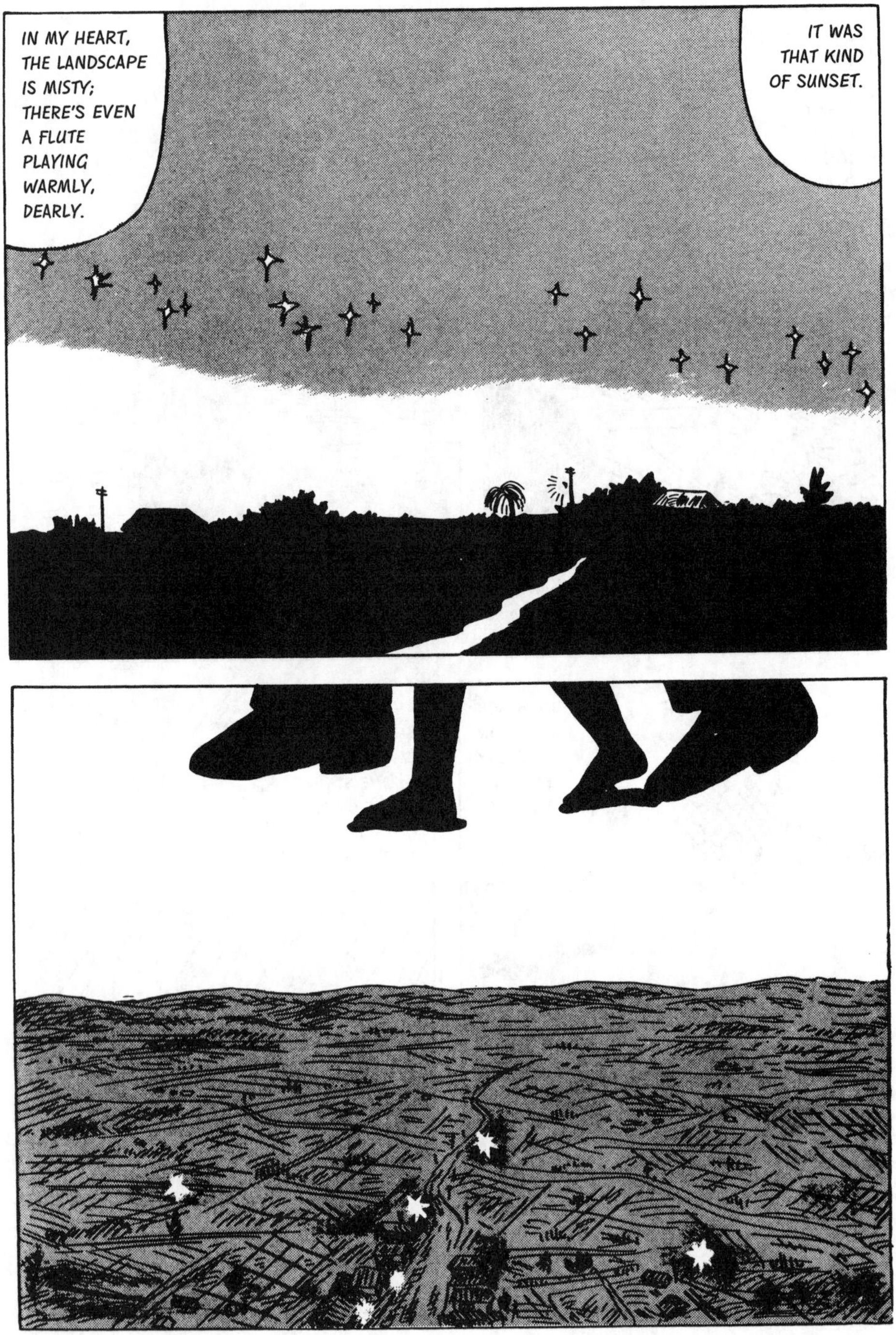
IN MY HEART, THE LANDSCAPE IS MISTY; THERE'S EVEN A FLUTE PLAYING WARMLY, DEARLY.
IT WAS THAT KIND OF SUNSET.

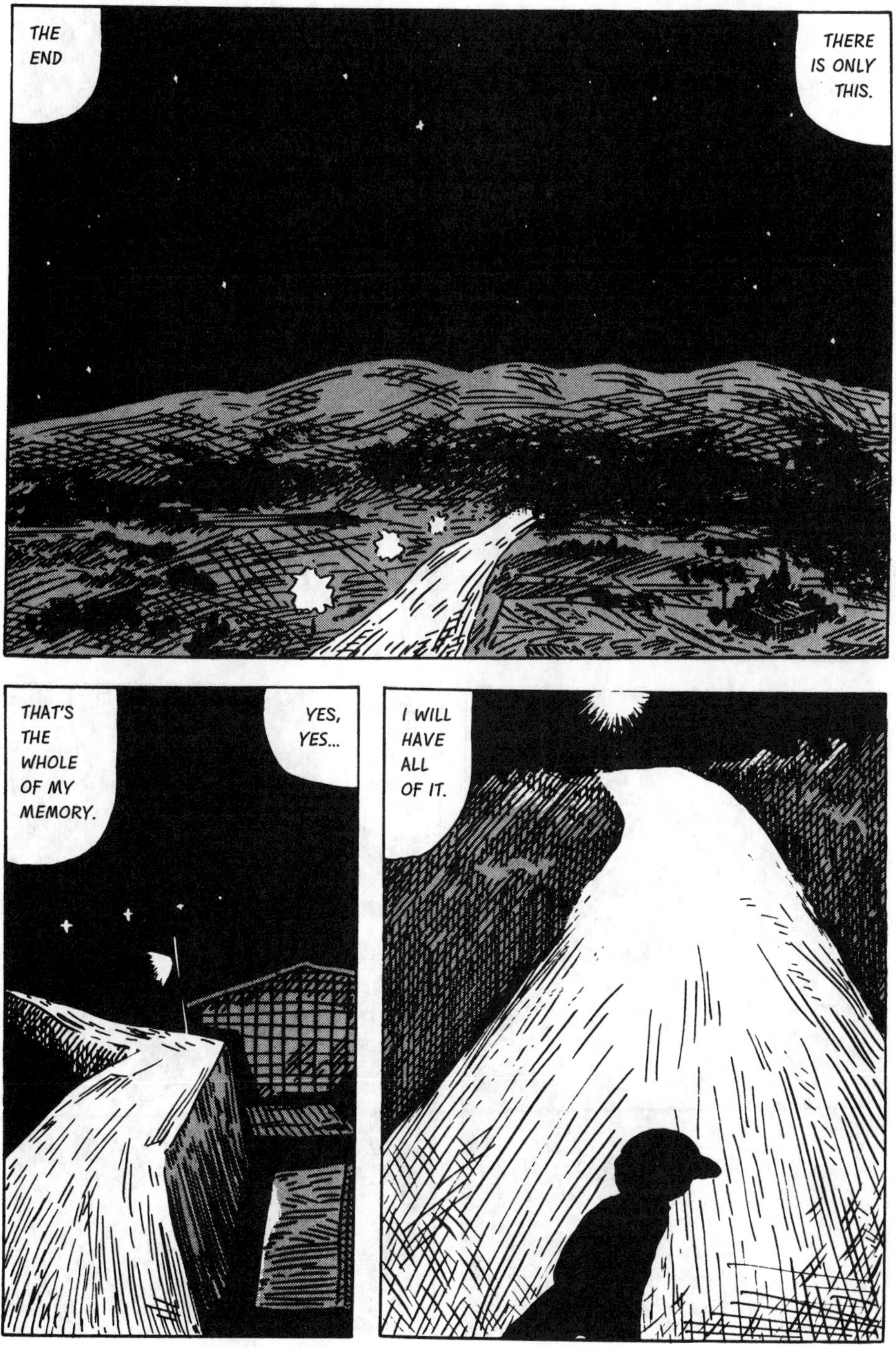
THE END
THERE IS ONLY THIS.
THAT'S THE WHOLE OF MY MEMORY.
YES, YES...
I WILL HAVE ALL OF IT.

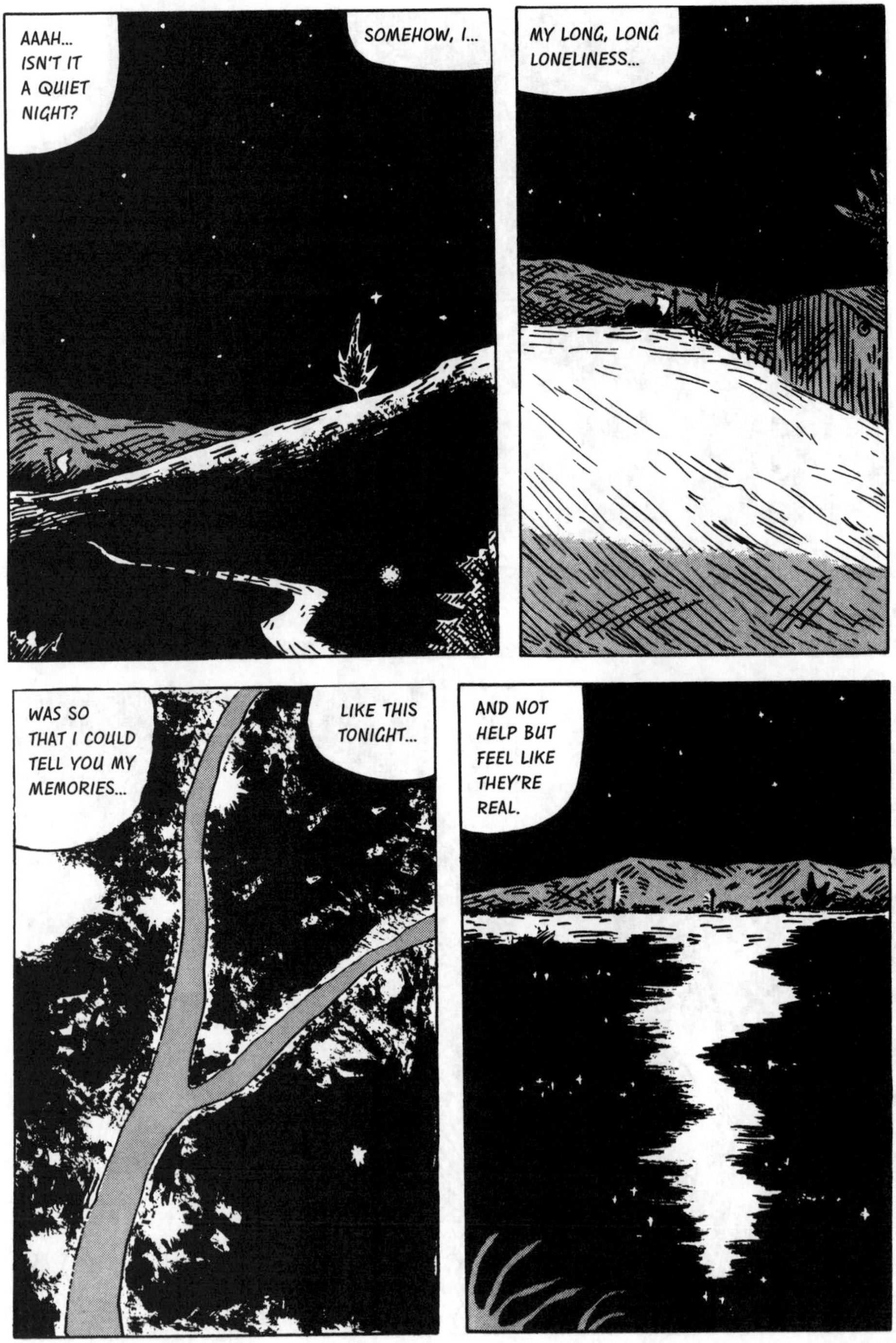
AAAH... ISN'T IT A QUIET NIGHT?
SOMEHOW, I...
MY LONG, LONG LONELINESS...
WAS SO THAT I COULD TELL YOU MY MEMORIES...
LIKE THIS TONIGHT...
AND NOT HELP BUT FEEL LIKE THEY'RE REAL.

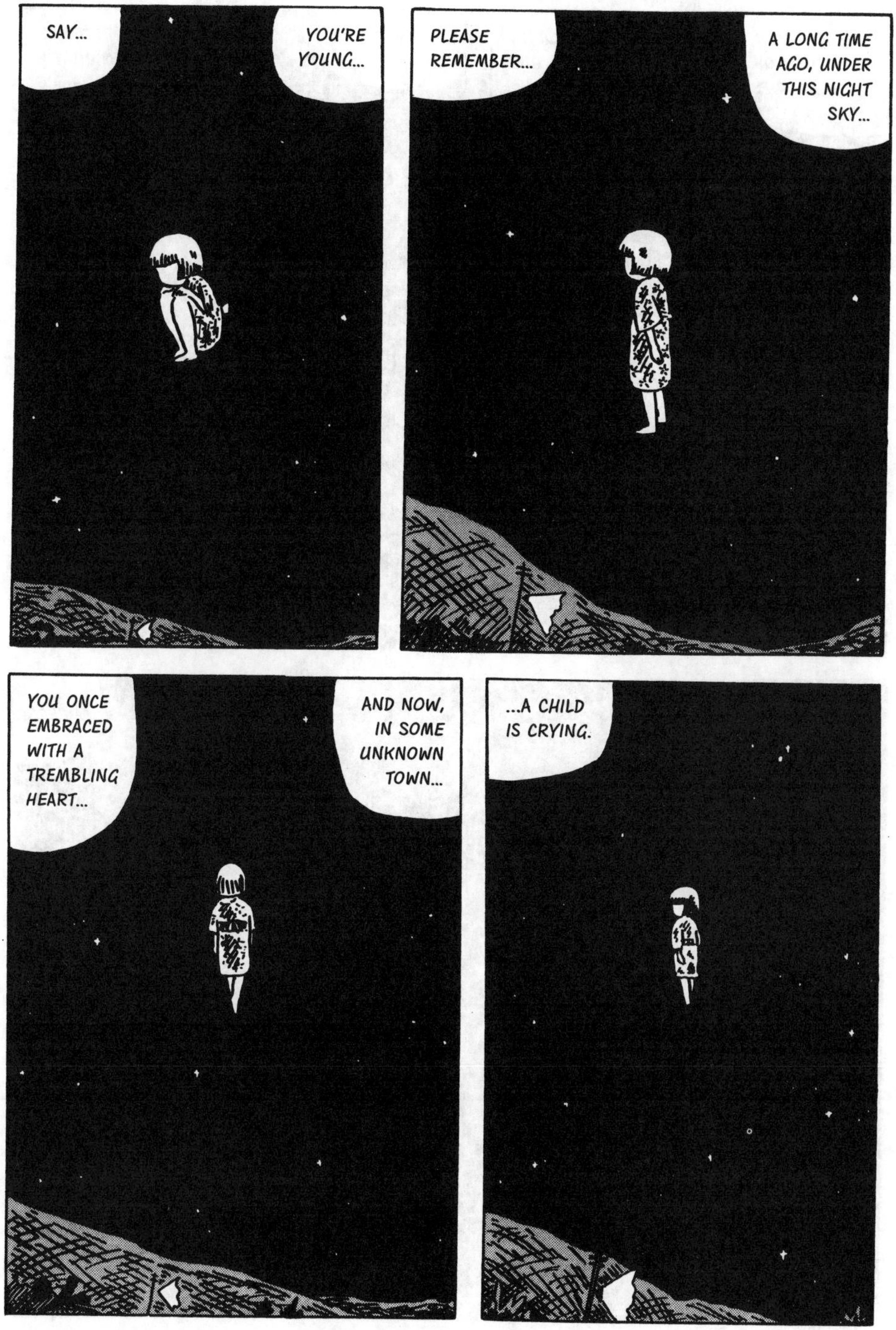
SAY...
YOU'RE YOUNG...
PLEASE REMEMBER...
A LONG TIME AGO, UNDER THIS NIGHT SKY...
YOU ONCE EMBRACED WITH A TREMBLING HEART...
AND NOW, IN SOME UNKNOWN TOWN...
...A CHILD IS CRYING.

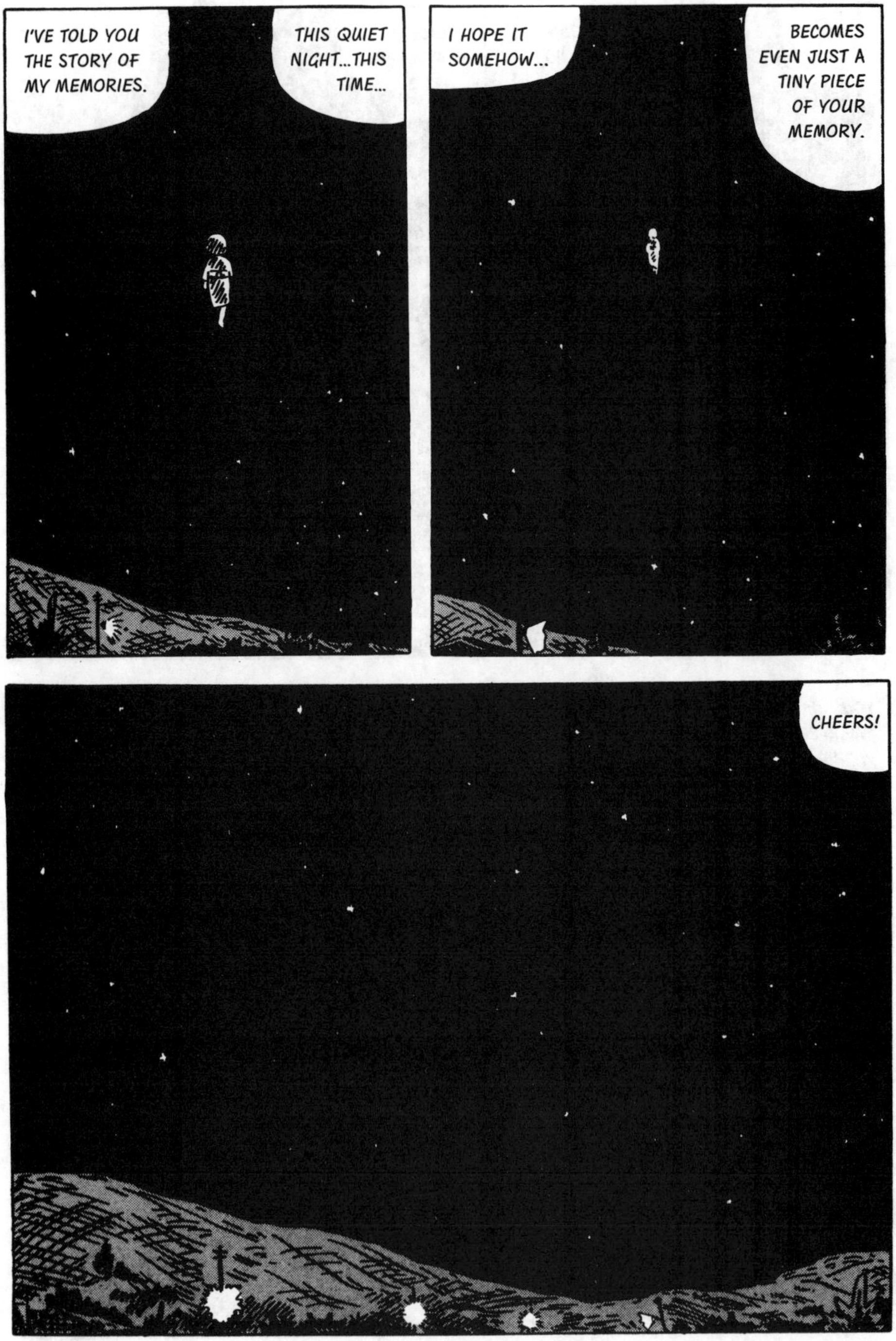
I'VE TOLD YOU THE STORY OF MY MEMORIES.
THIS QUIET NIGHT...THIS TIME...
I HOPE IT SOMEHOW...
BECOMES EVEN JUST A TINY PIECE OF YOUR MEMORY.
CHEERS!

WORLD
COLORED
PANTS

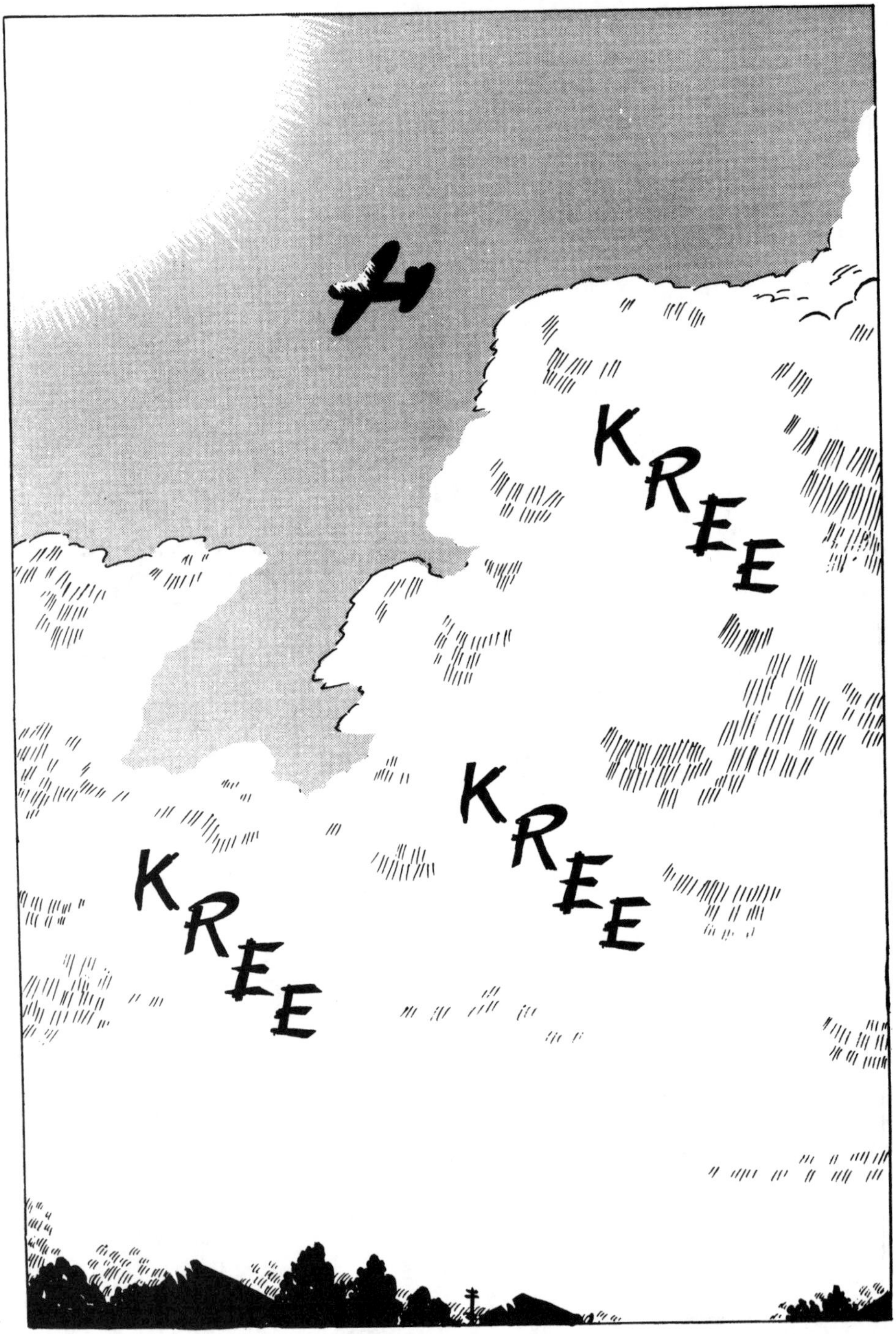
KREE
KREE
KREE

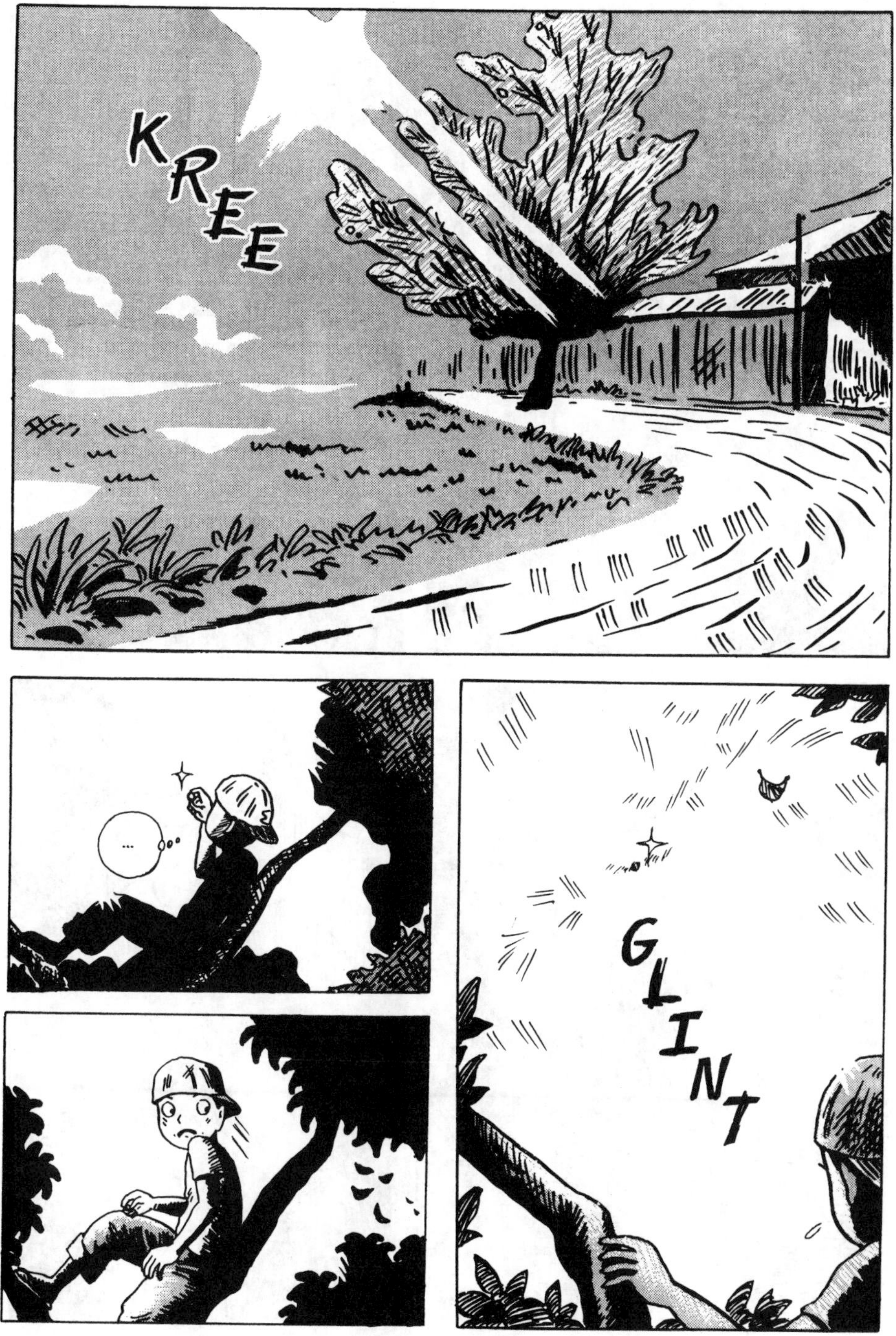
KREE
...
GLINT

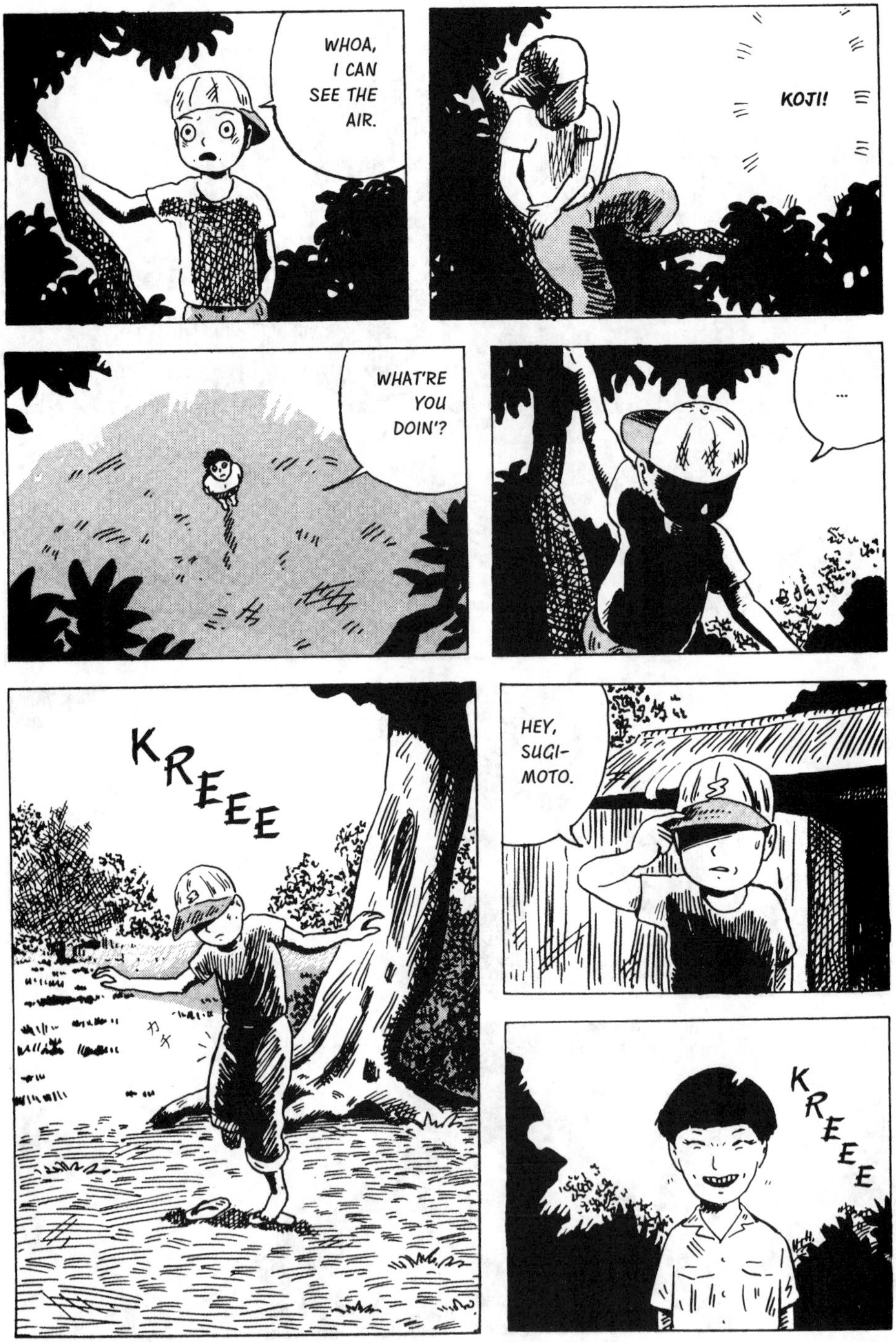
WHOA, I CAN SEE THE AIR.
KOJI!
WHAT'RE YOU DOIN'?
...
KREEEE
HEY, SUGI-MOTO.
KREEEE

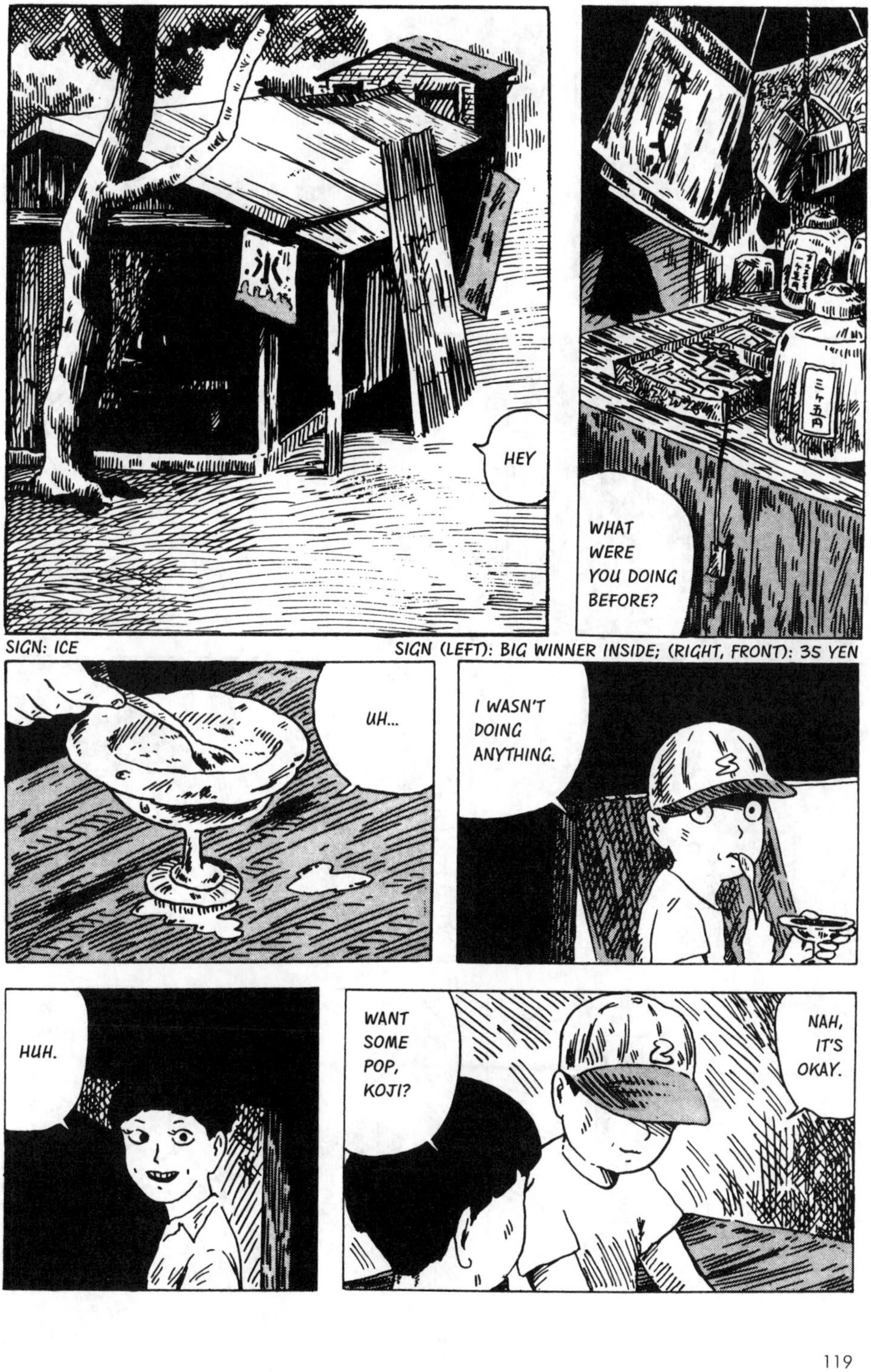
HEY
WHAT WERE YOU DOING BEFORE?
SIGN: ICE
SIGN (LEFT): BIG WINNER INSIDE; (RIGHT, FRONT): 35 YEN
UH...
I WASN'T DOING ANYTHING.
HUH.
WANT SOME POP, KOJI?
NAH, IT'S OKAY.

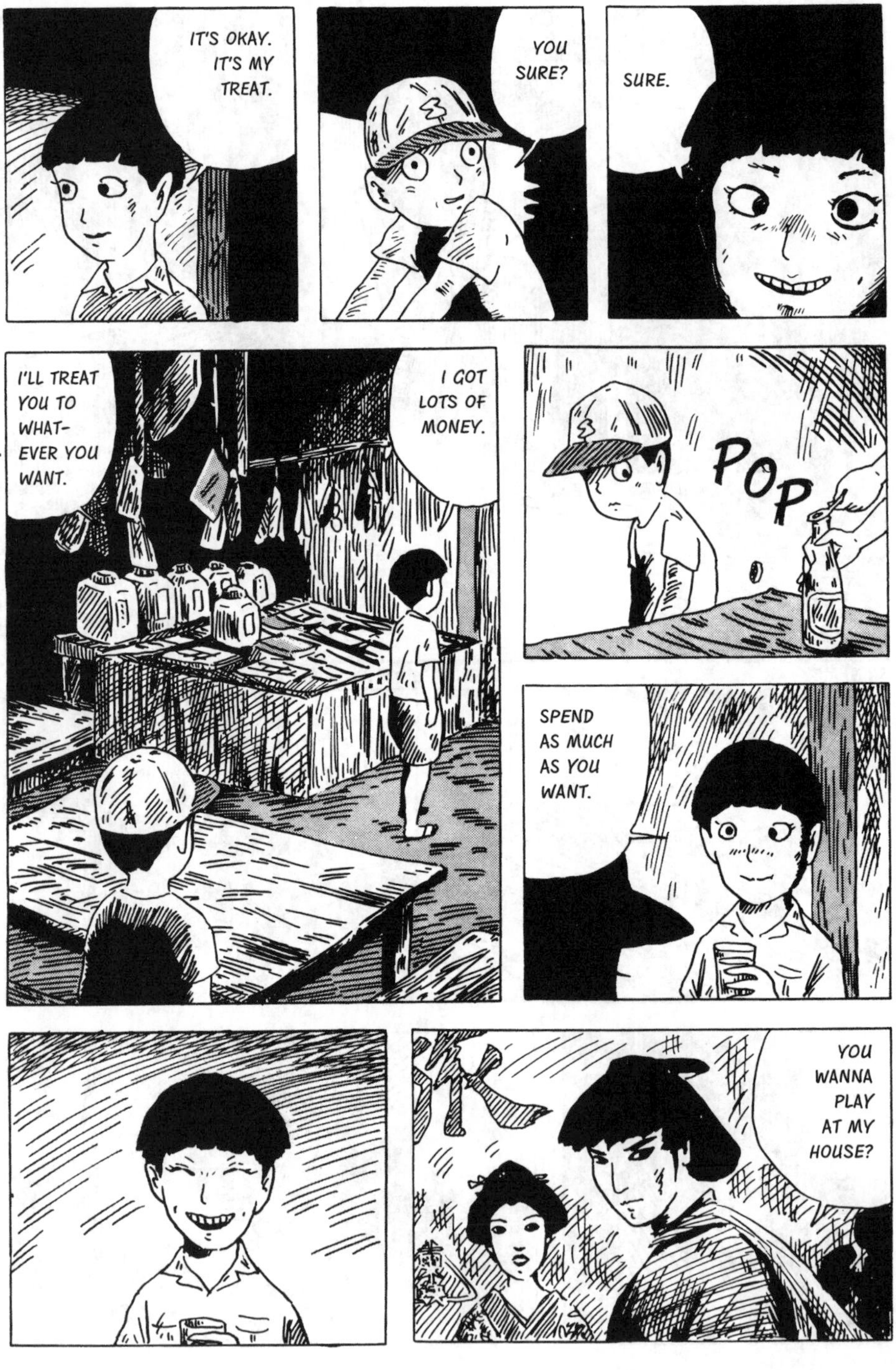
IT'S OKAY. IT'S MY TREAT.
YOU SURE?
SURE.
I'LL TREAT YOU TO WHAT-EVER YOU WANT.
I GOT LOTS OF MONEY.
POP
SPEND AS MUCH AS YOU WANT.
YOU WANNA PLAY AT MY HOUSE?

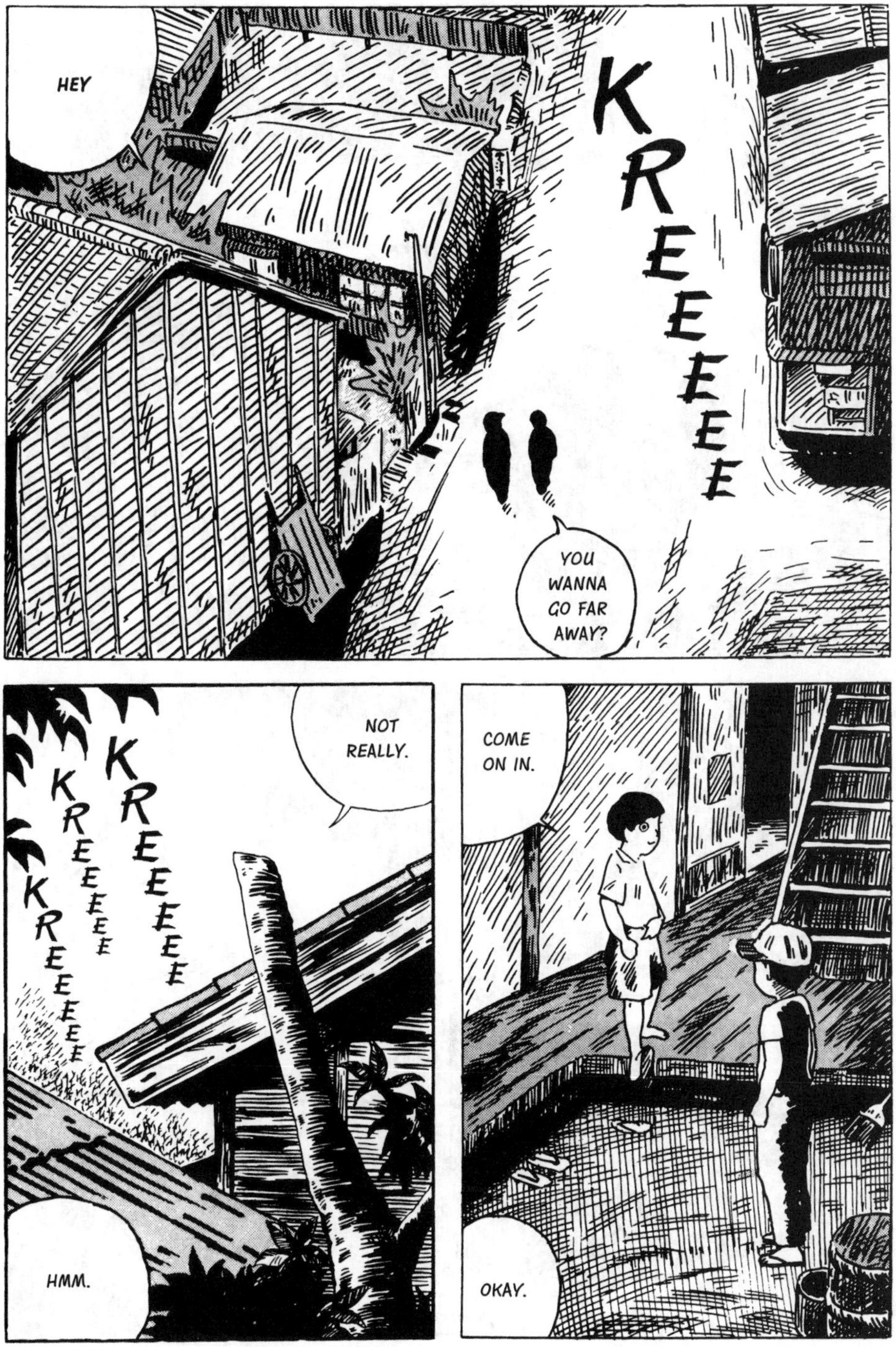
HEY
KREEEEE
YOU WANNA GO FAR AWAY?
NOT REALLY.
KREEEEE
KREEEEE
KREEEEE
HMM.
COME ON IN.
OKAY.

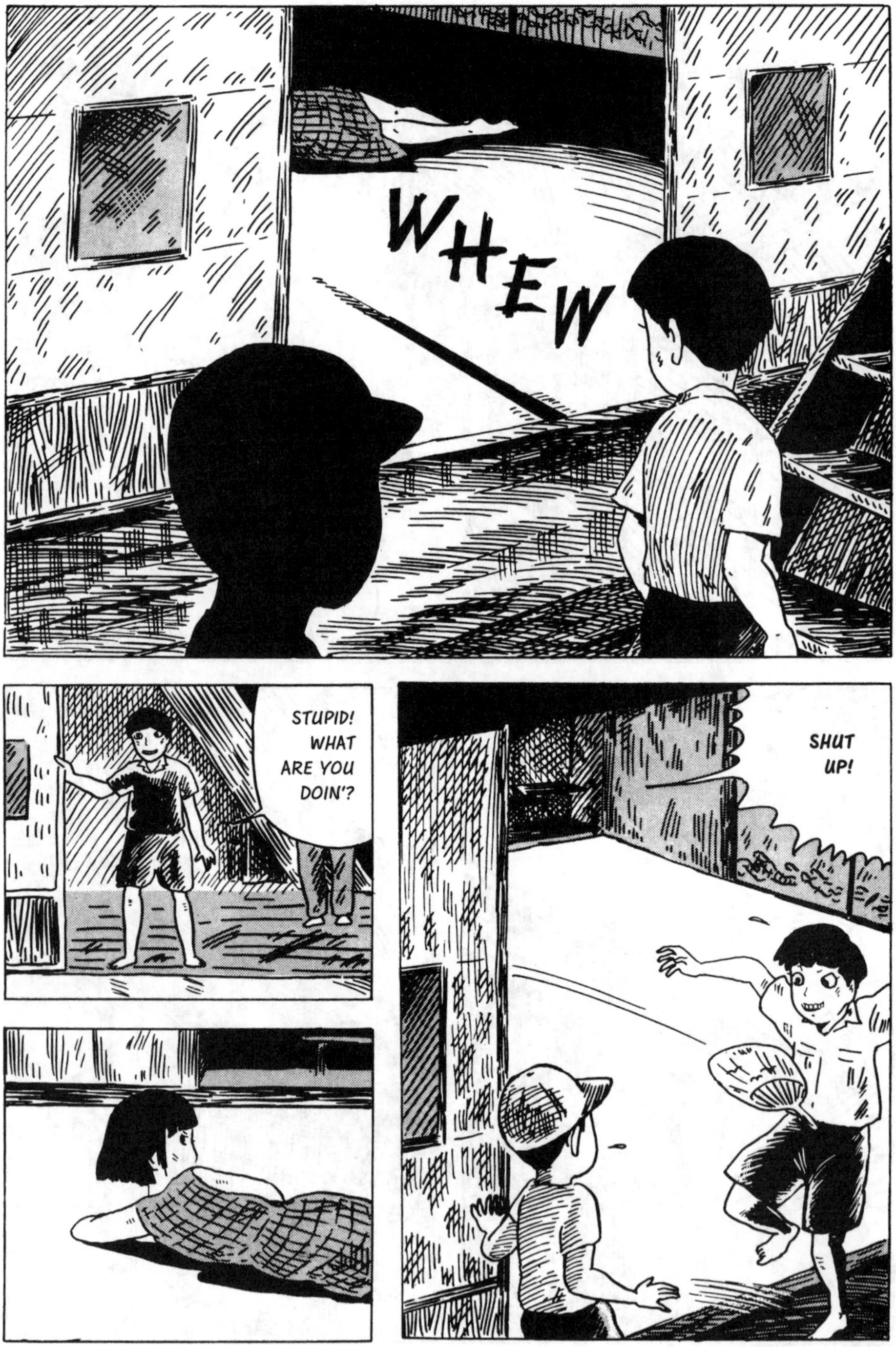
WHEW
STUPID! WHAT ARE YOU DOIN'?
SHUT UP!

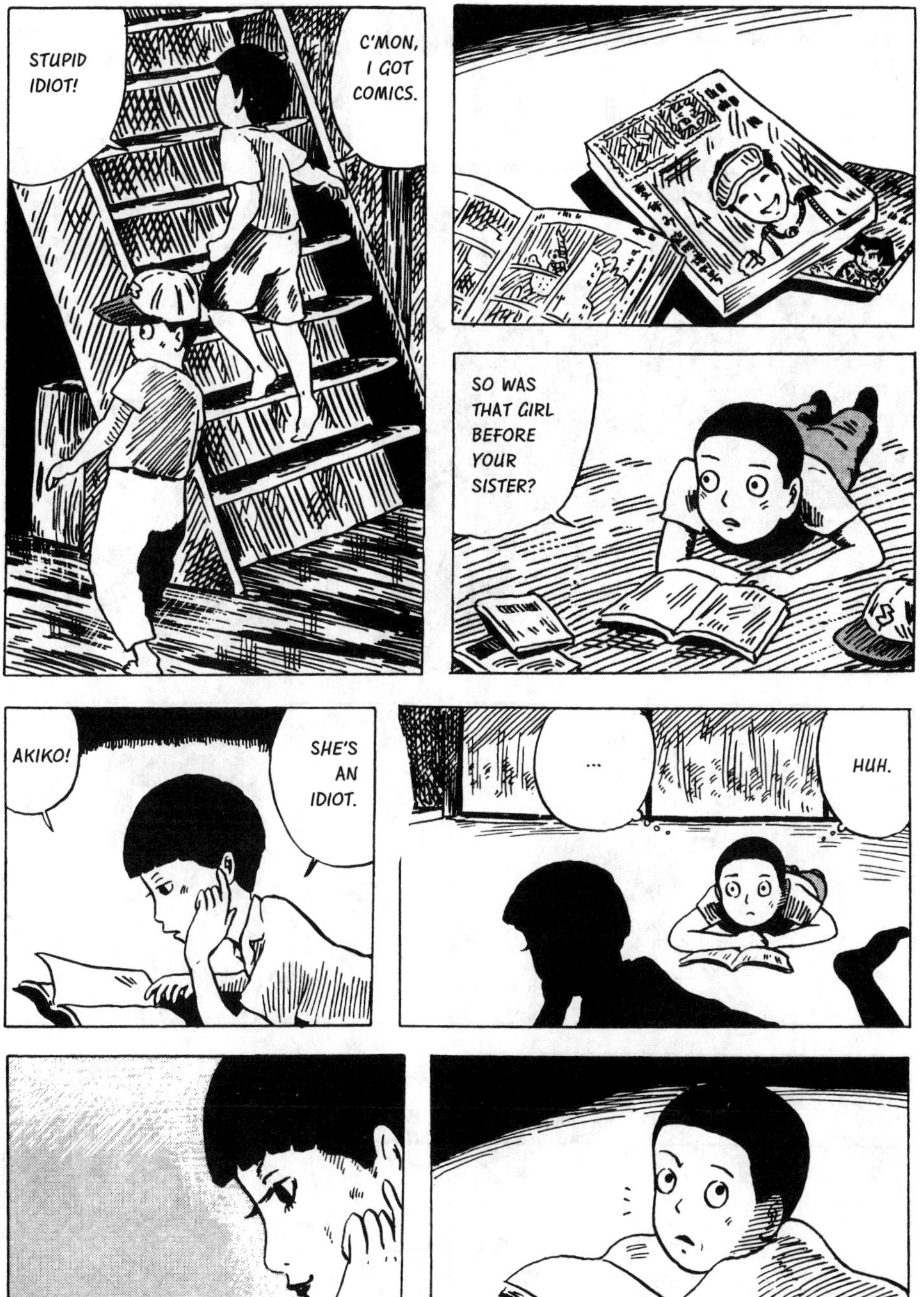
STUPID IDIOT!
C'MON, I GOT COMICS.
SO WAS THAT GIRL BEFORE YOUR SISTER?
AKIKO!
SHE'S AN IDIOT.
...
HUH.

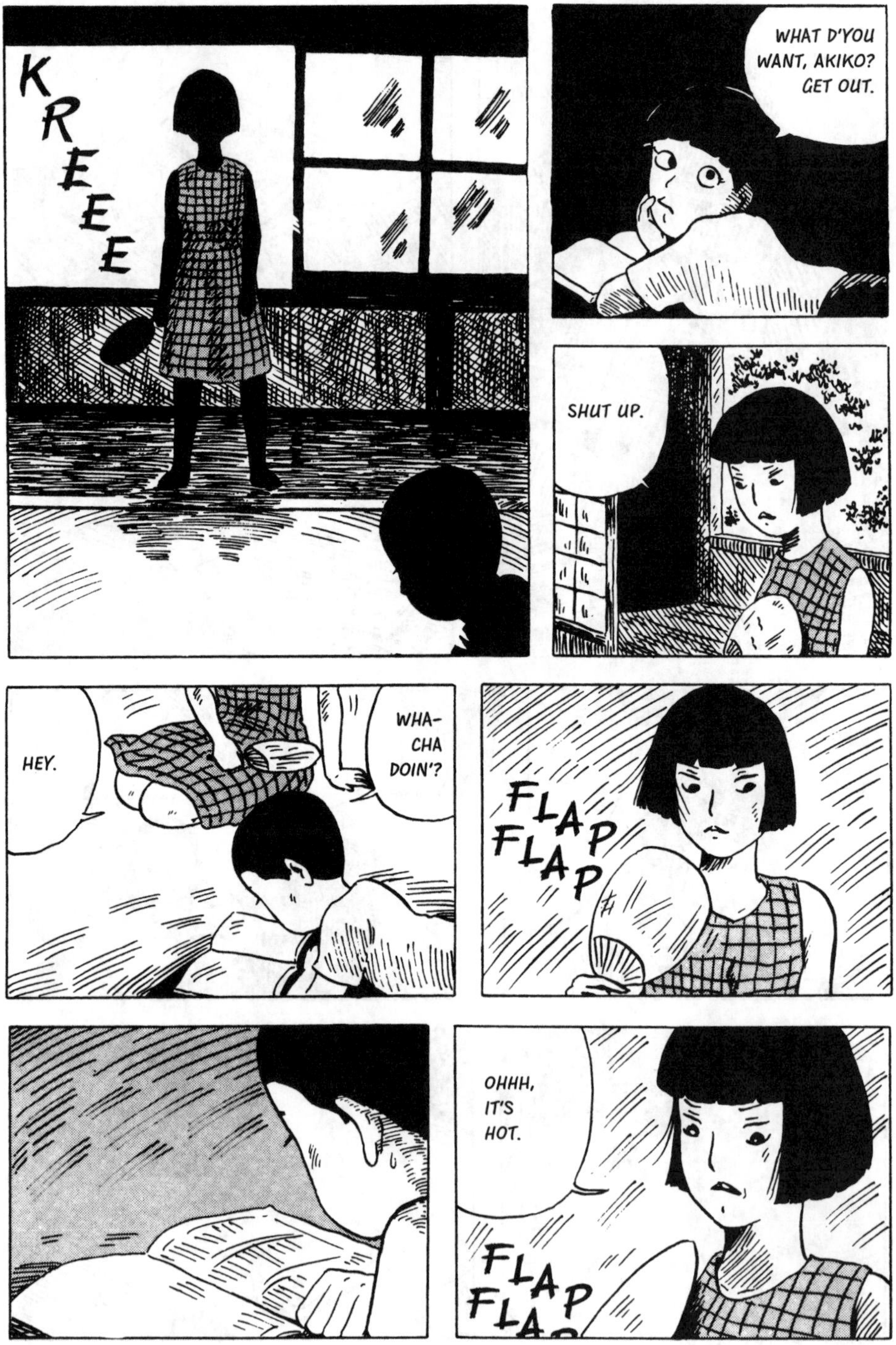
KREEE
WHAT D'YOU WANT, AKIKO? GET OUT.
SHUT UP.
HEY.
WHA-CHA DOIN'?
FLAP FLAP
OHHH, IT'S HOT.
FLAP FLAP

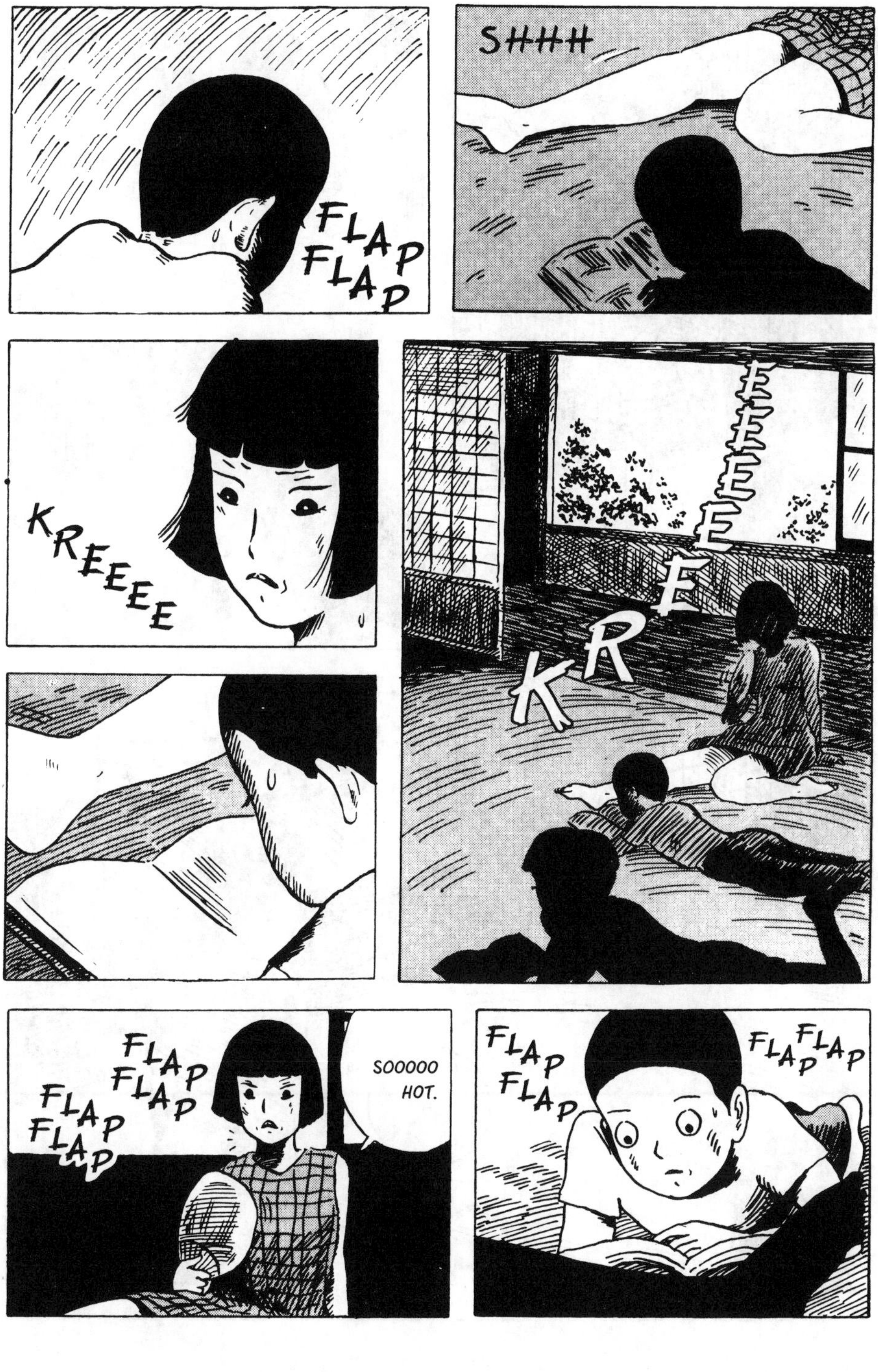
FLAP
FLAP
SHHH
KREEEEE
KREEEEEE
FLAP
FLAP
FLAP
FLAP
SOOOOO HOT.
FLAP
FLAP
FLAP
FLAP

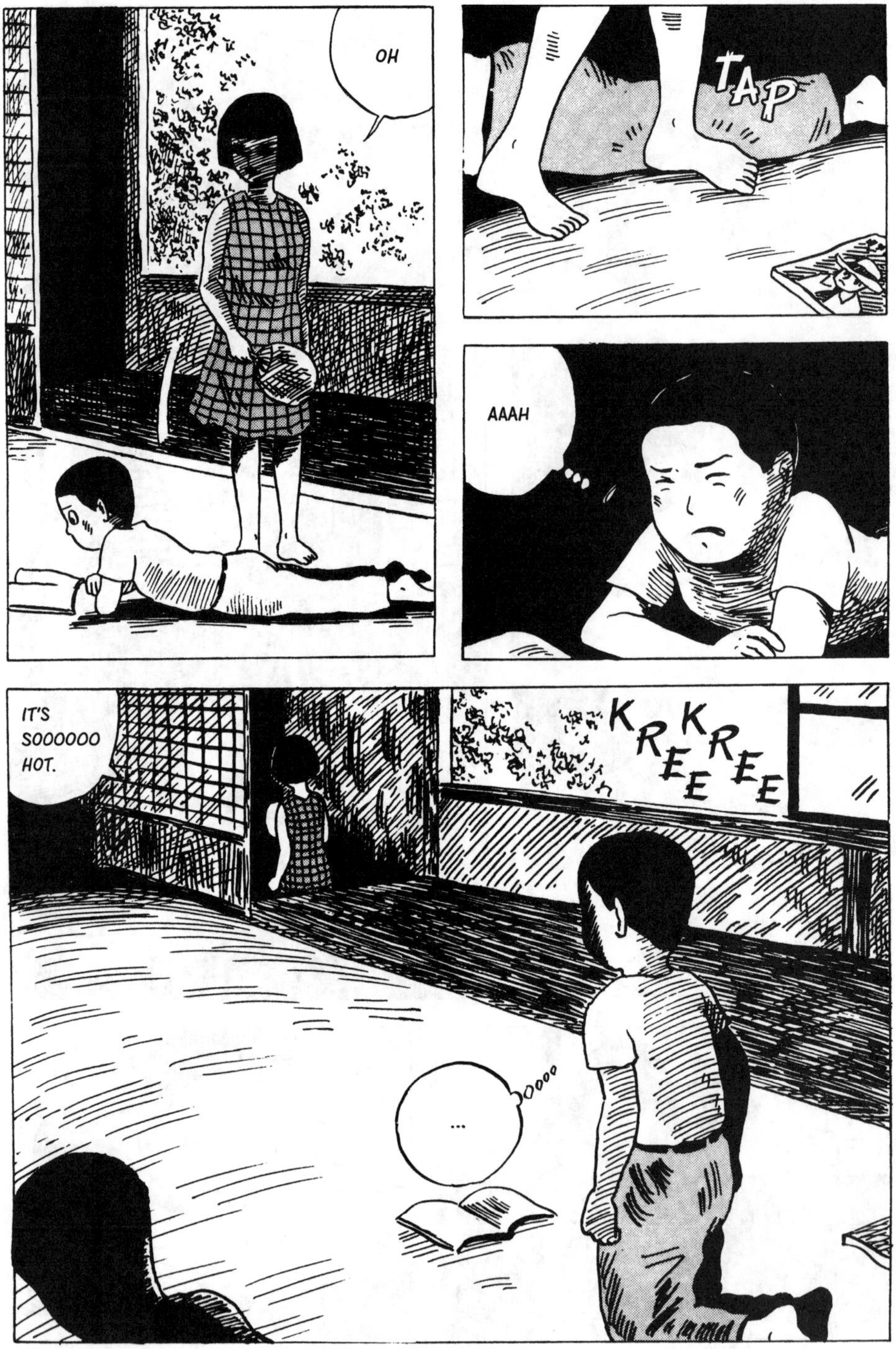
OH
TAP
AAAH
IT'S SOOOOOO HOT.
KRKREEKREE
...

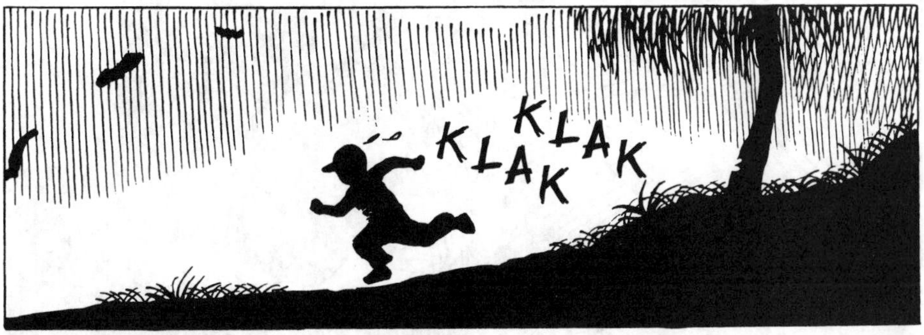
KLAK
KLAK
KLAK

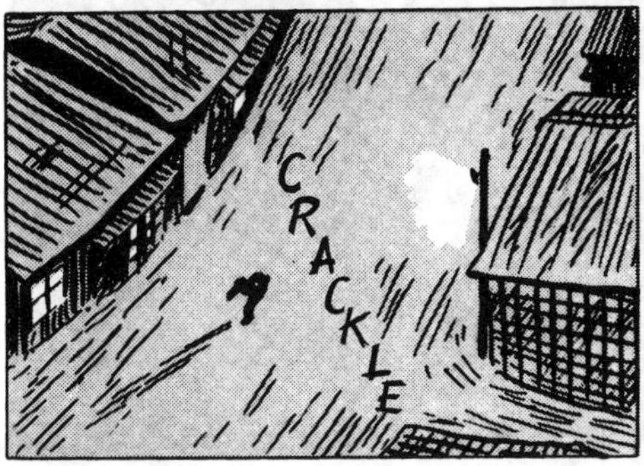
CRACKLE

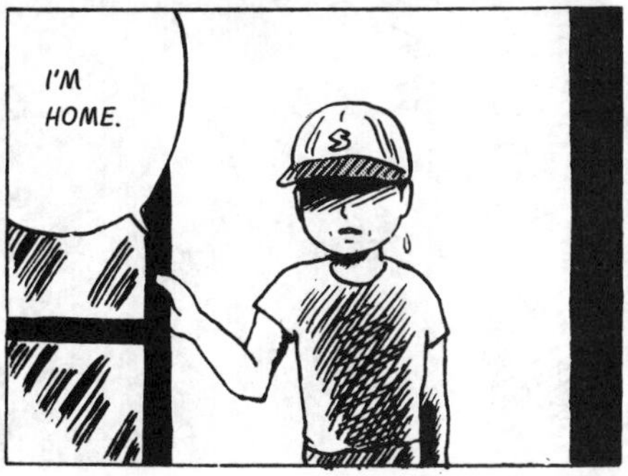
I'M HOME.

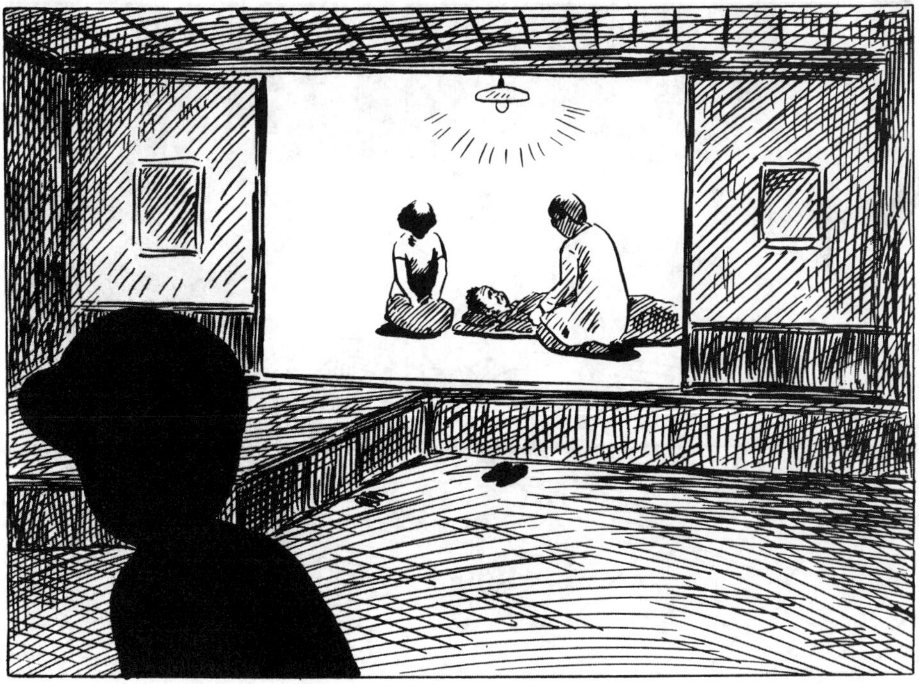

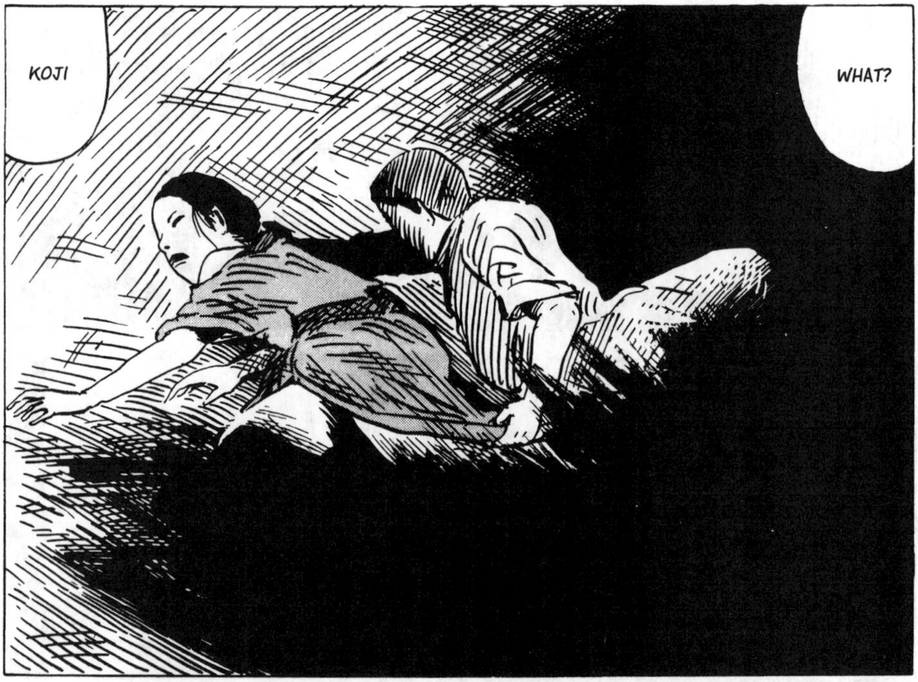
KOJI
WHAT?
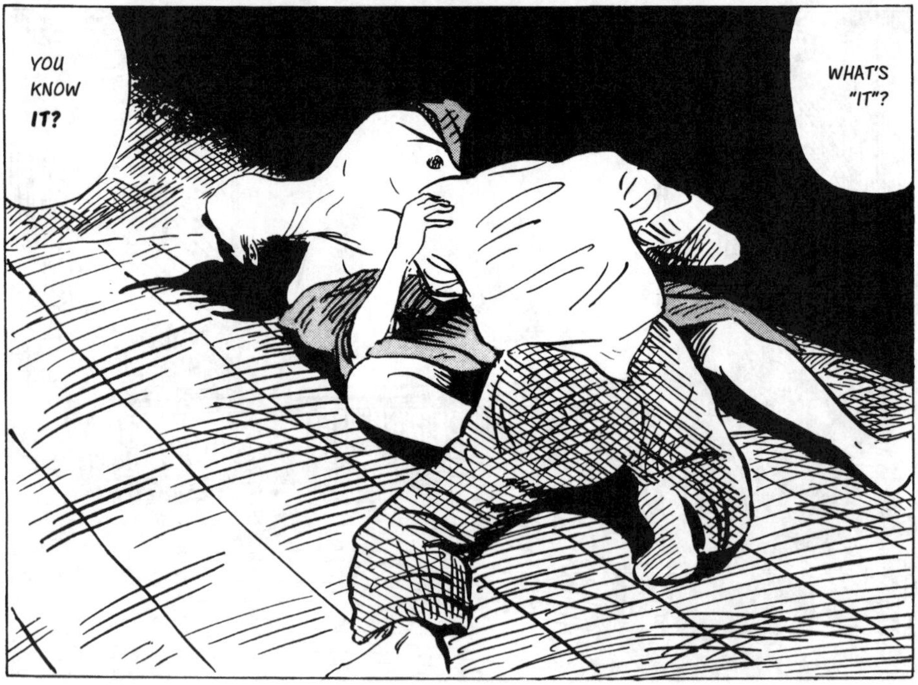
YOU KNOW IT?
WHAT'S "IT"?

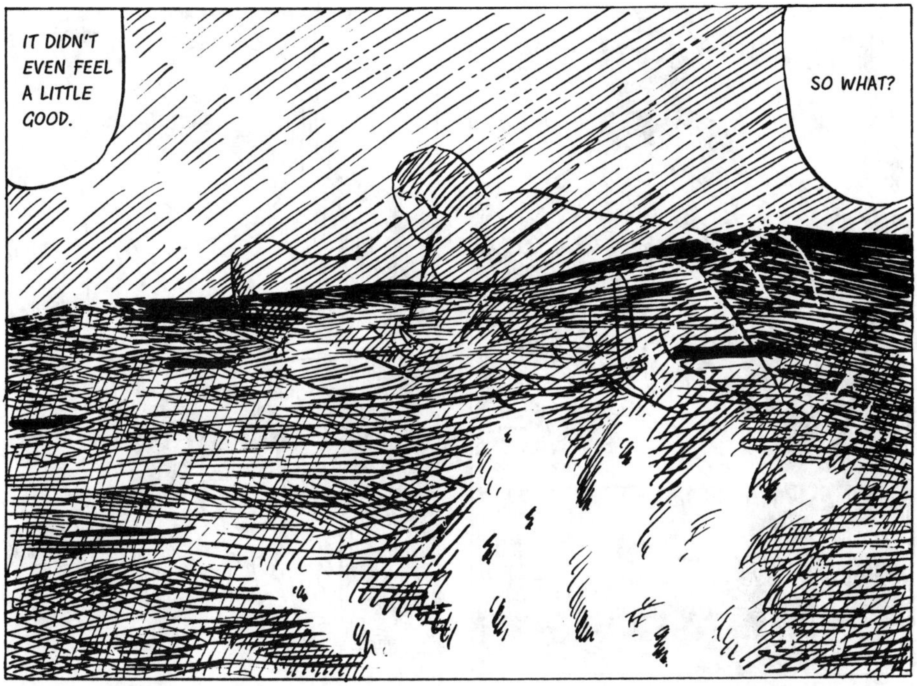
IT DIDN'T EVEN FEEL A LITTLE GOOD.
SO WHAT?

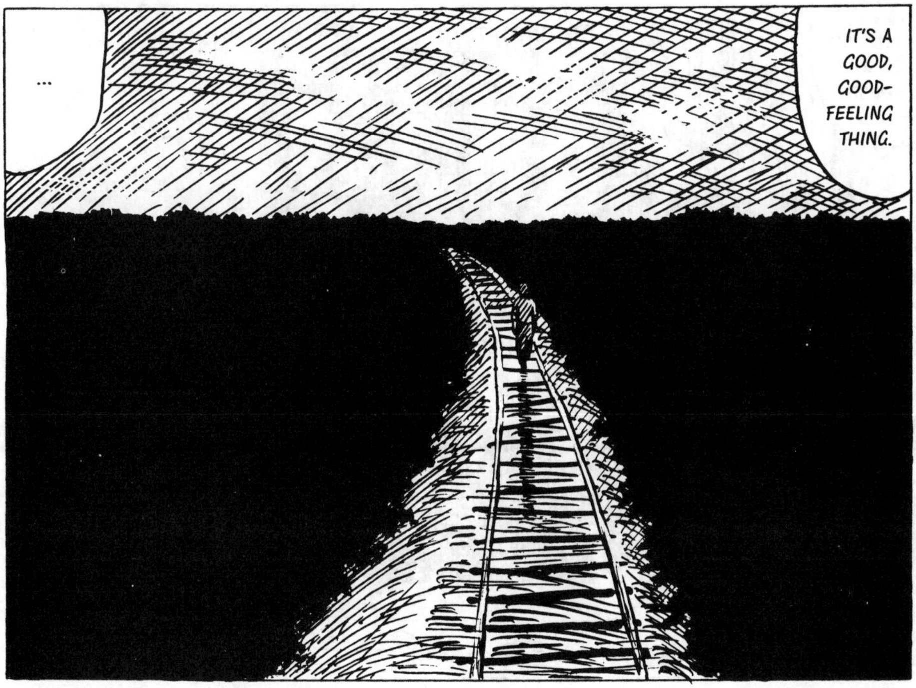
...
IT'S A GOOD, GOOD-FEELING THING.

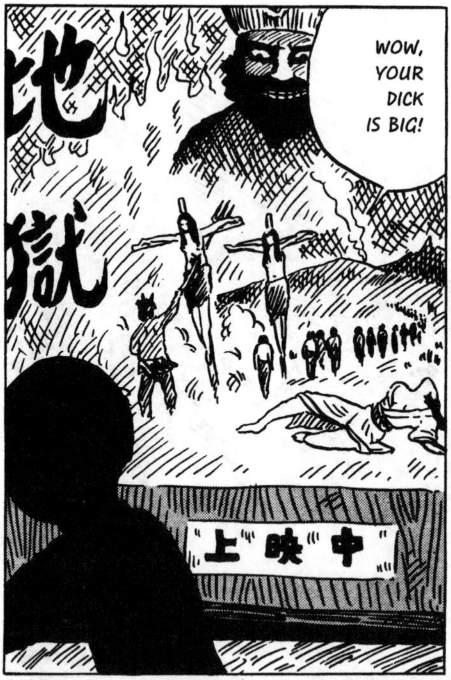
WOW, YOUR DICK IS BIG!
上映中
POSTER: HELL; NOW PLAYING

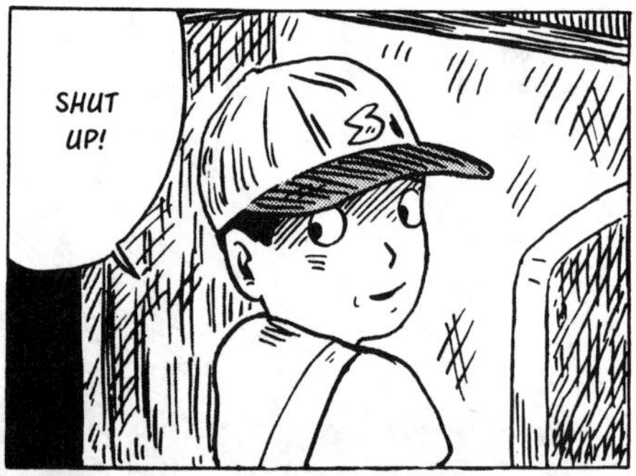
SHUT UP!

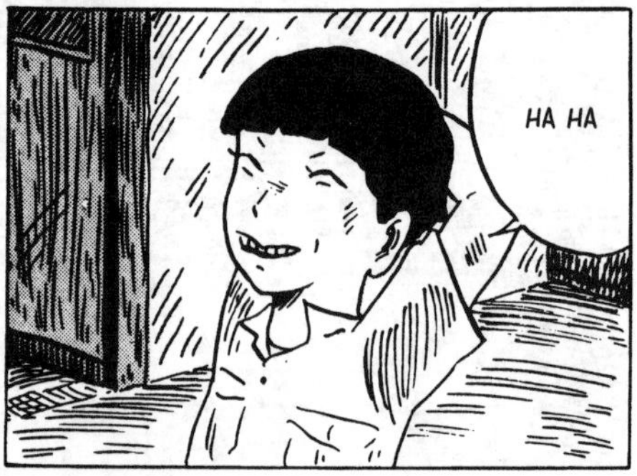
HA HA

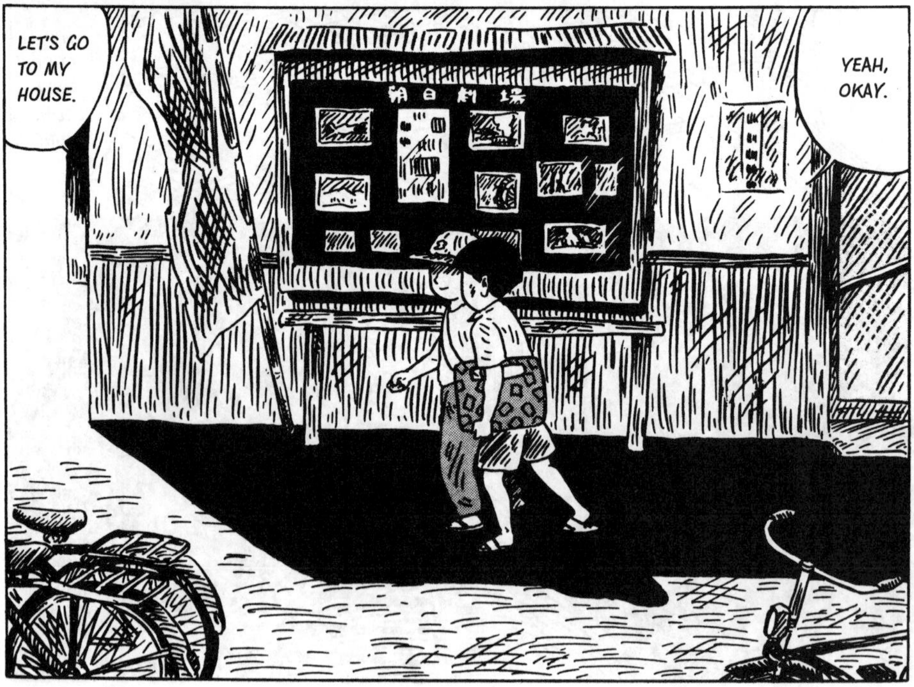
LET'S GO TO MY HOUSE.
YEAH, OKAY.

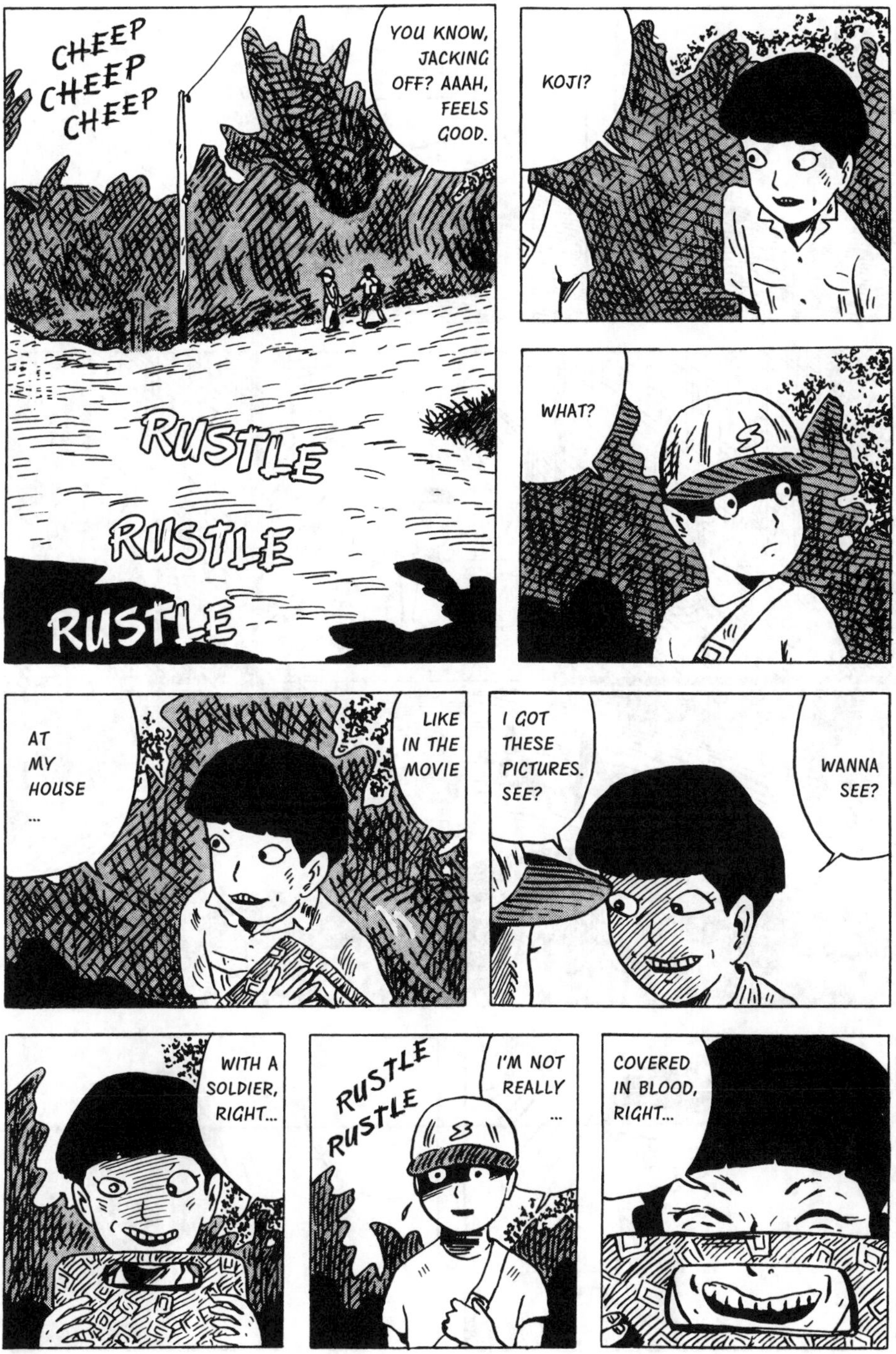
CHEEP CHEEP CHEEP
YOU KNOW, JACKING OFF? AAAH, FEELS GOOD.
RUSTLE
RUSTLE
RUSTLE
KOJI?
WHAT?
AT MY HOUSE ...
LIKE IN THE MOVIE
I GOT THESE PICTURES. SEE?
WANNA SEE?
WITH A SOLDIER, RIGHT...
RUSTLE RUSTLE
I'M NOT REALLY ...
COVERED IN BLOOD, RIGHT...

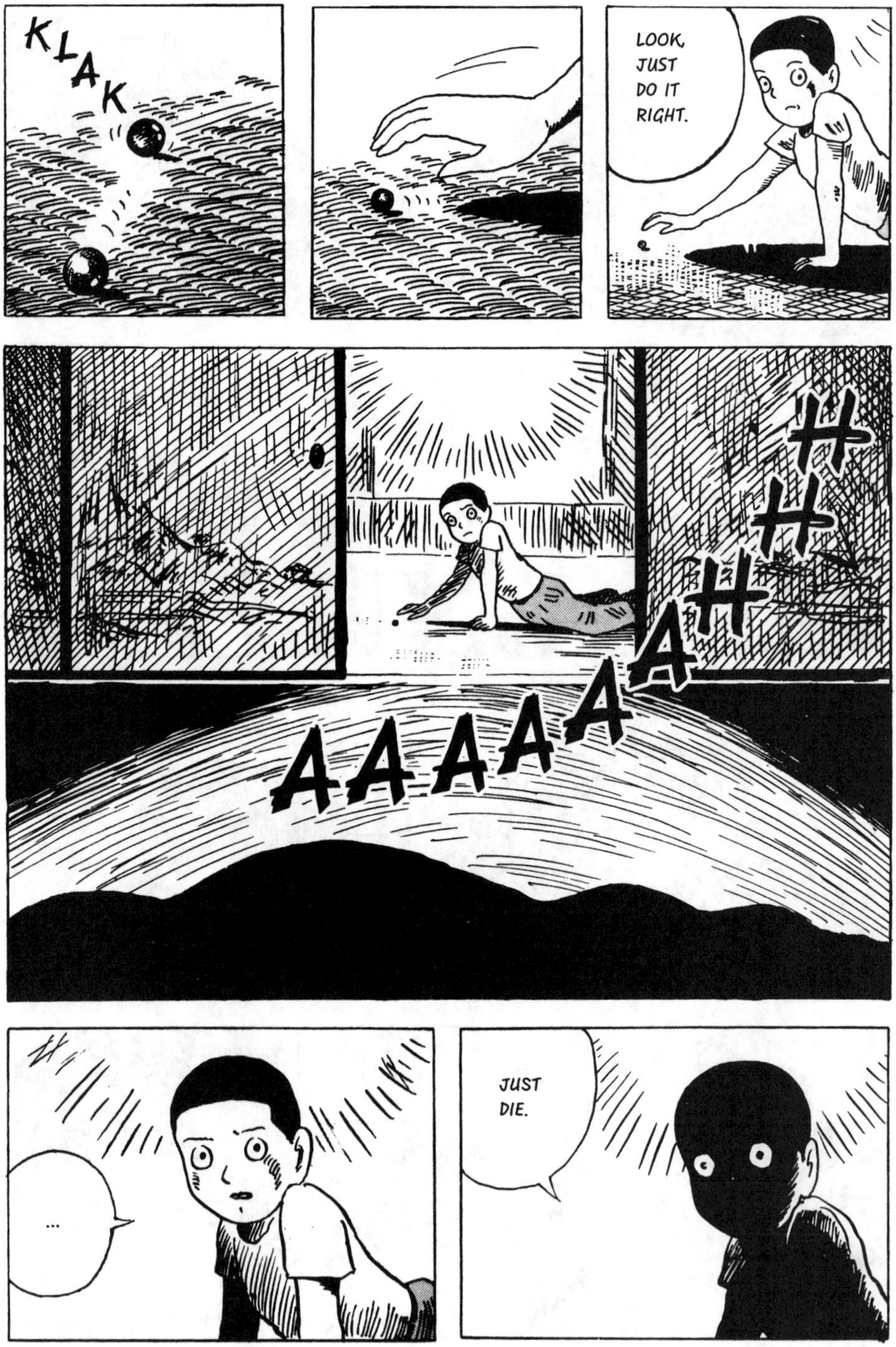
KLAK
LOOK, JUST DO IT RIGHT.
AAAAAAAHHHH
...
JUST DIE.

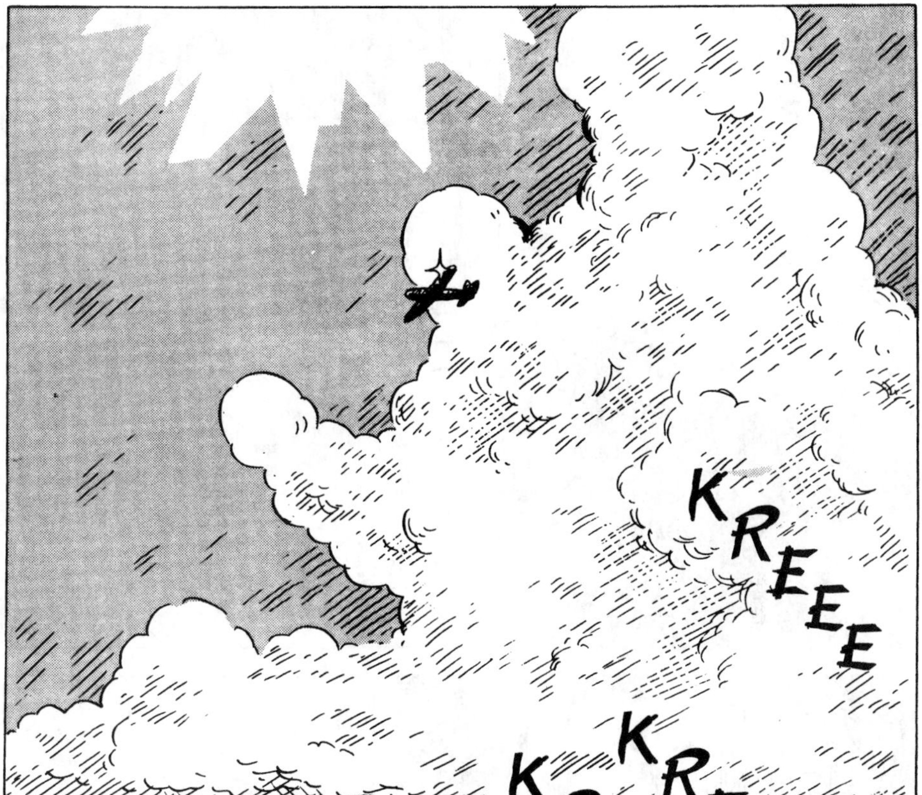
KREEEE
KREEEE
KREEE
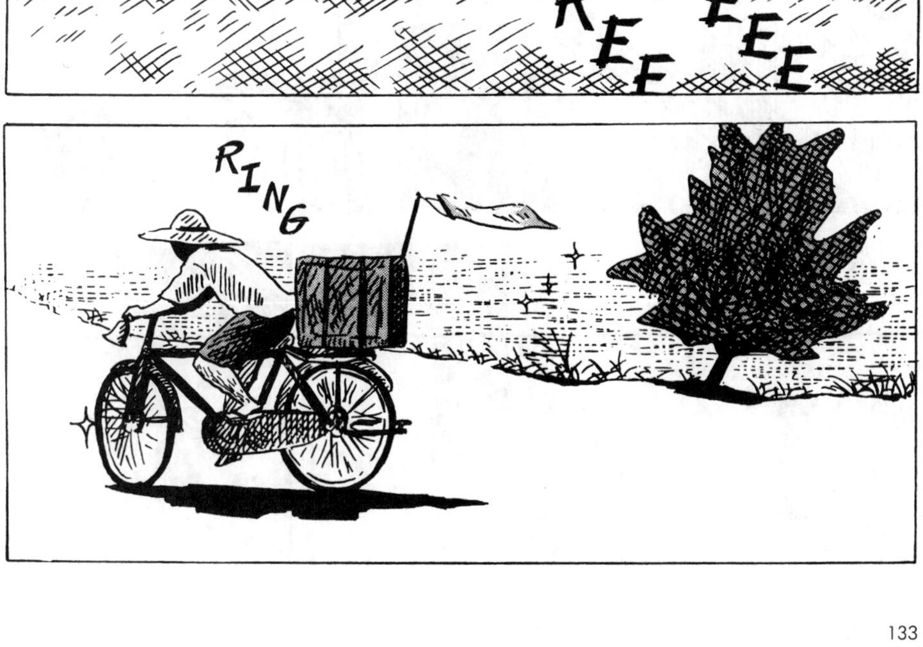
RING

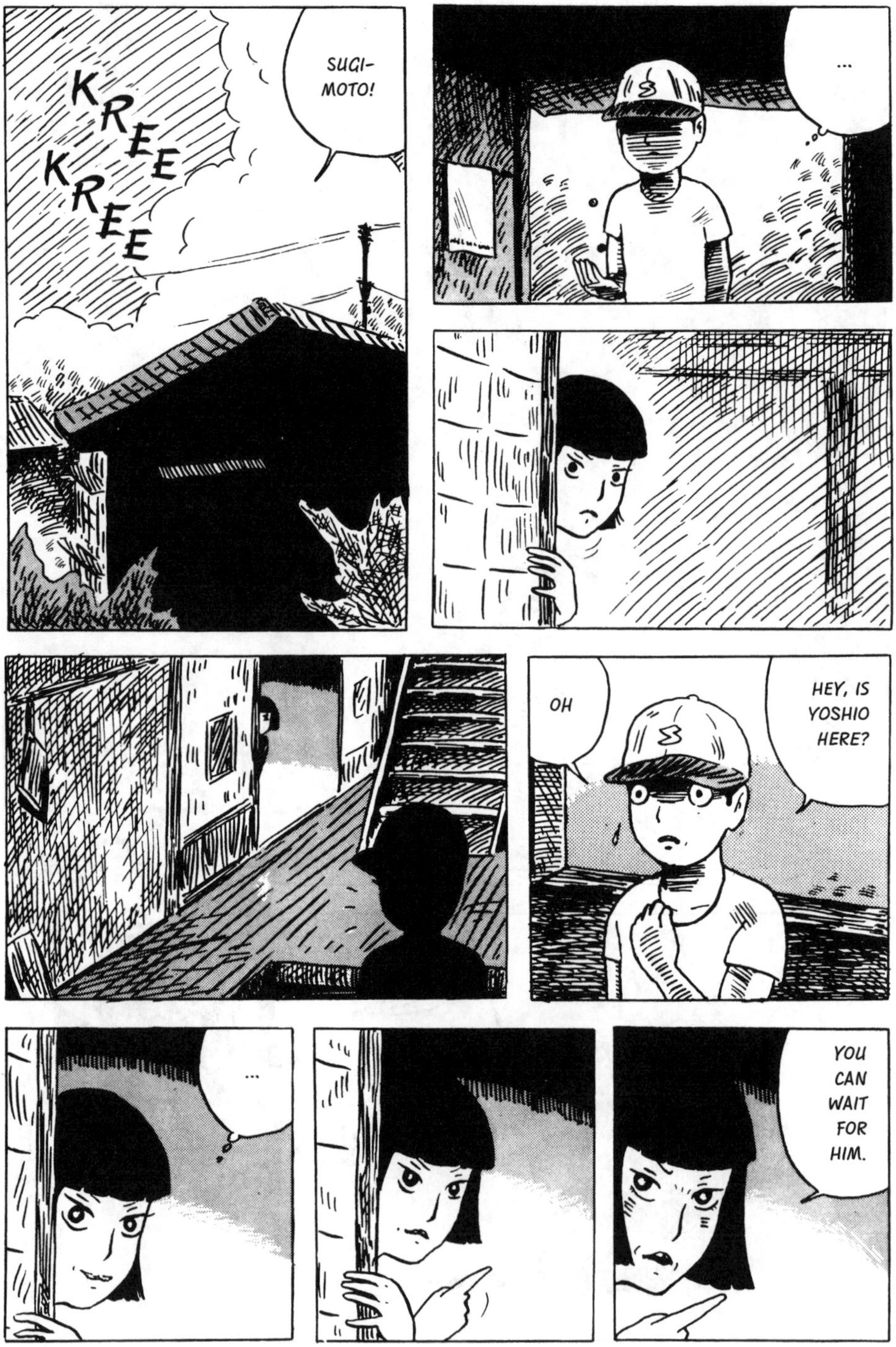
KREE KREE
SUGI-MOTO!
...
OH
HEY, IS YOSHIO HERE?
...
YOU CAN WAIT FOR HIM.

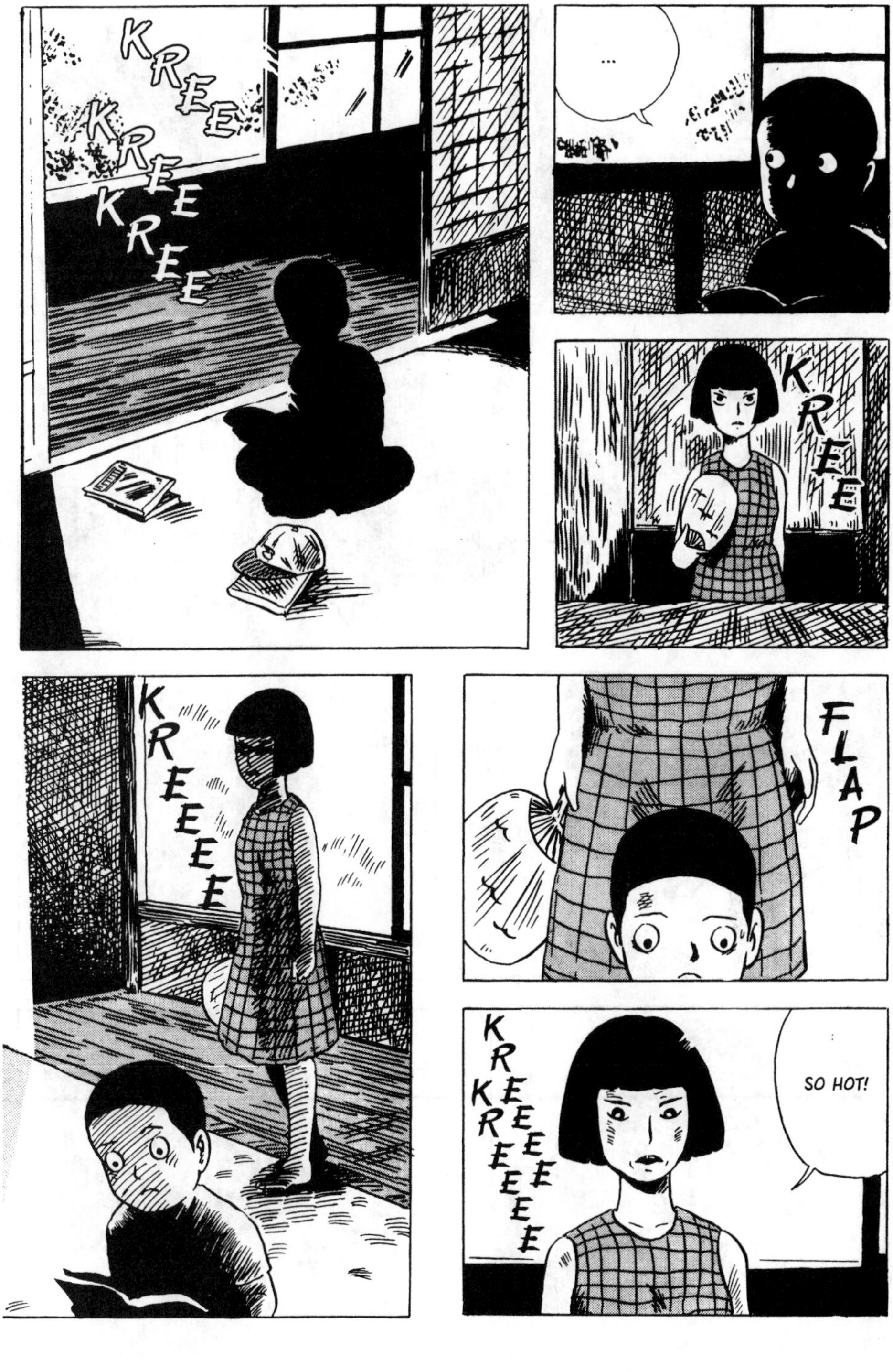
KREE
KREE
KREE
...
KREE
KREEEEE
FLAP
KREEEE
KREEEEE
SO HOT!

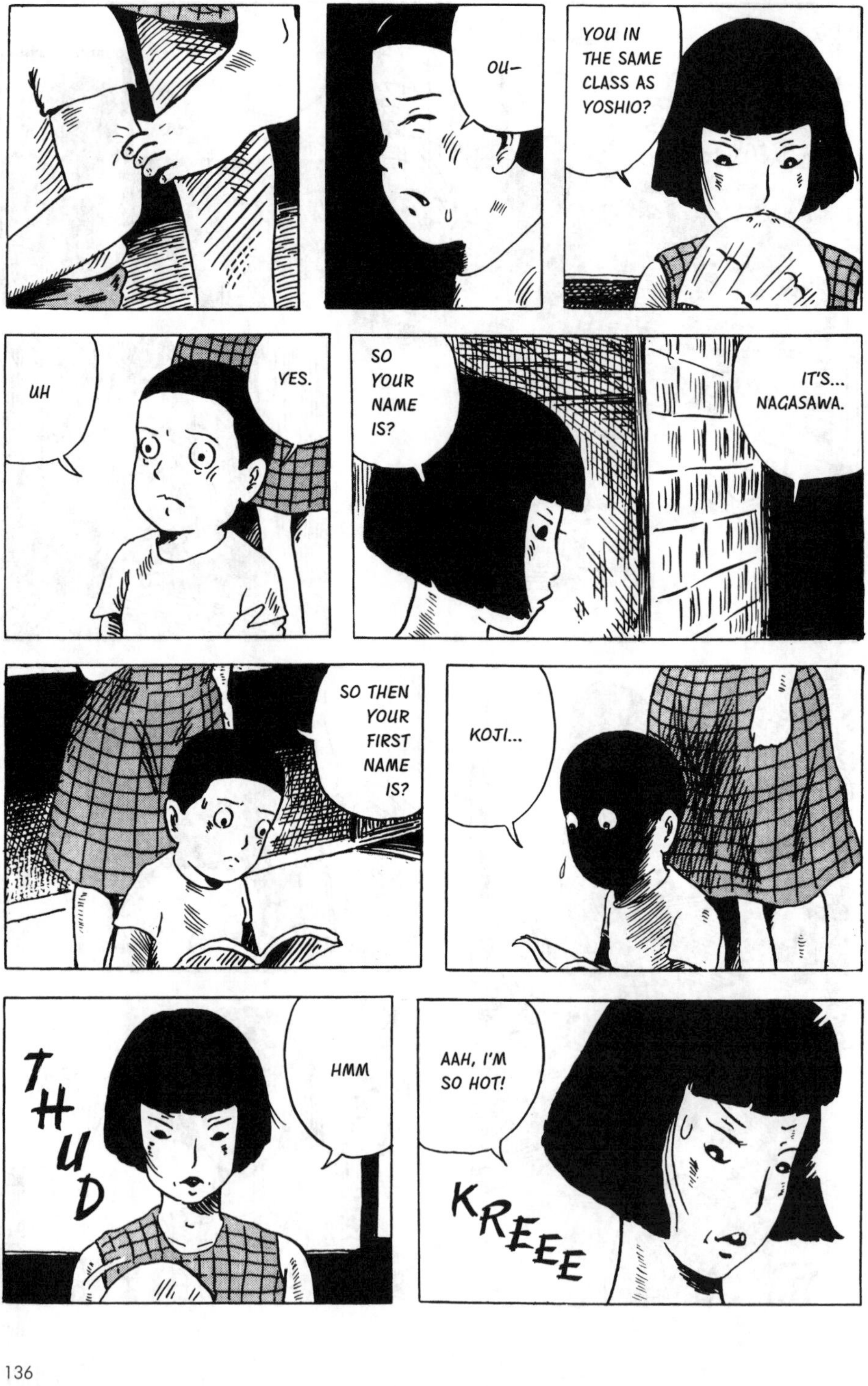
OU-
YOU IN THE SAME CLASS AS YOSHIO?
UH
YES.
SO YOUR NAME IS?
IT'S... NAGASAWA.
SO THEN YOUR FIRST NAME IS?
KOJI...
HMM
THUD
AAH, I'M SO HOT!
KREEE

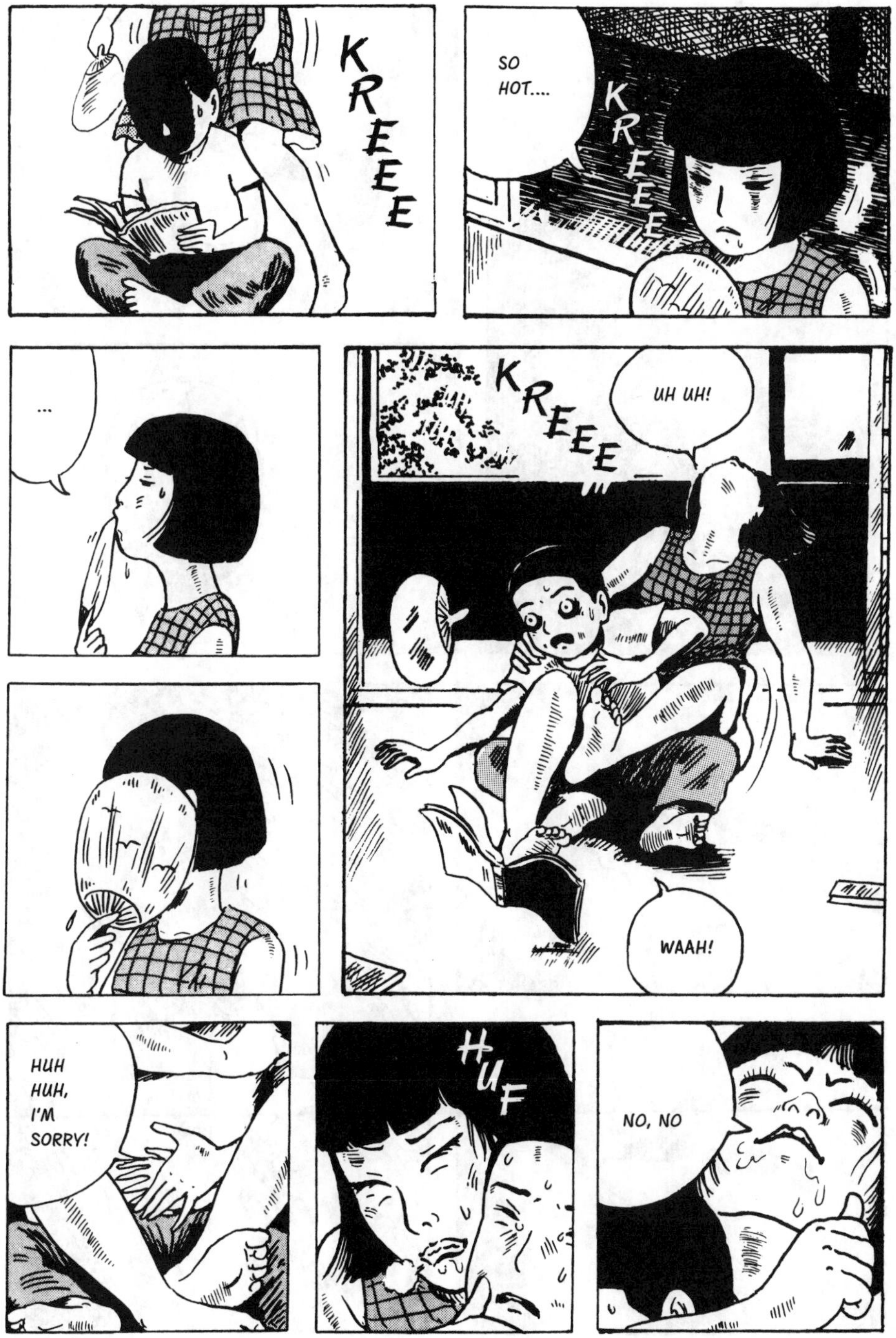
KREEE
SO HOT....
KREEE
...
KREEE
UH UH!
WAAH!
HUH HUH, I'M SORRY!
HUF
NO, NO

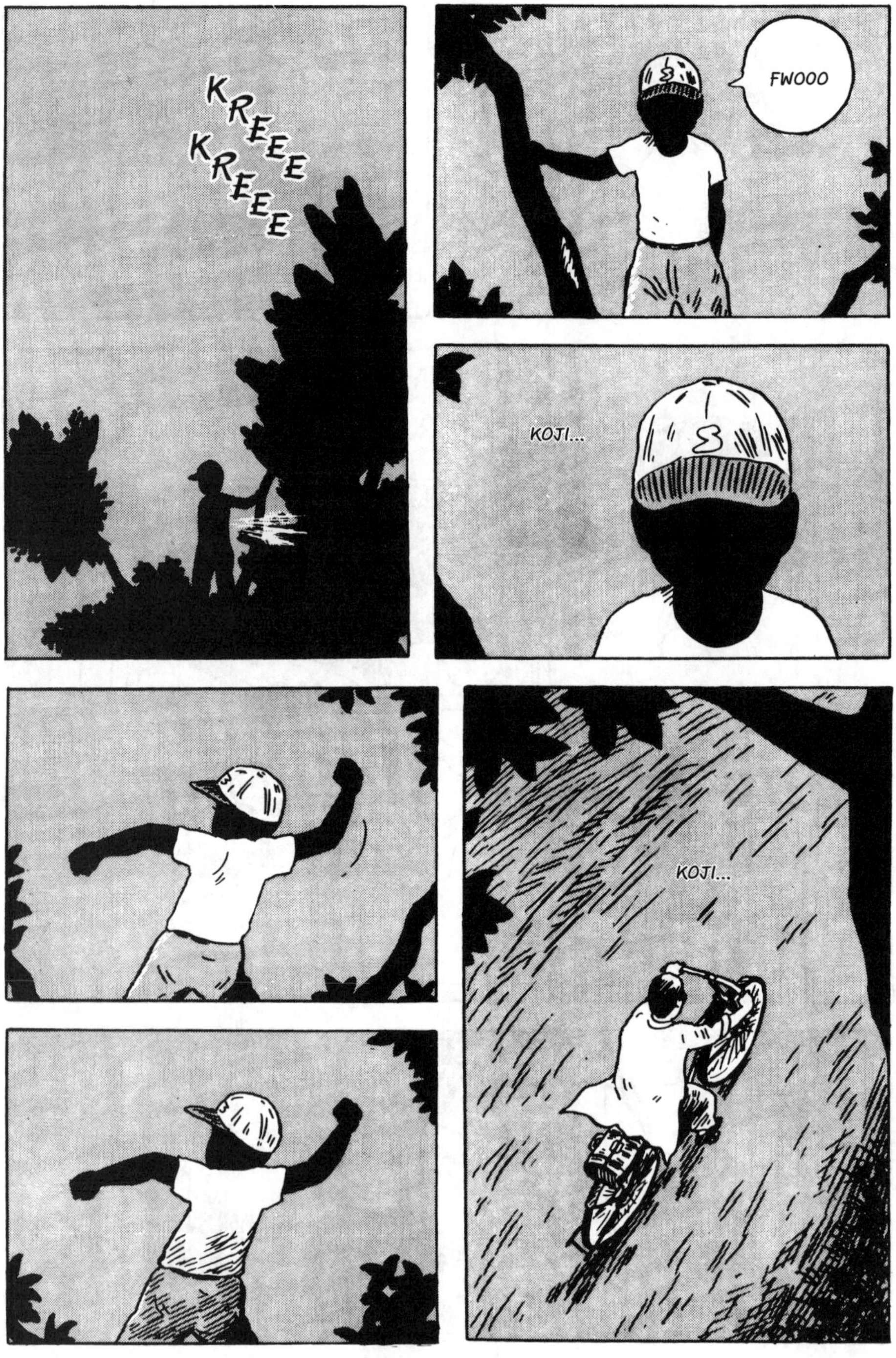
KREEE
KREEE
FWOOO
KOJI...
KOJI...

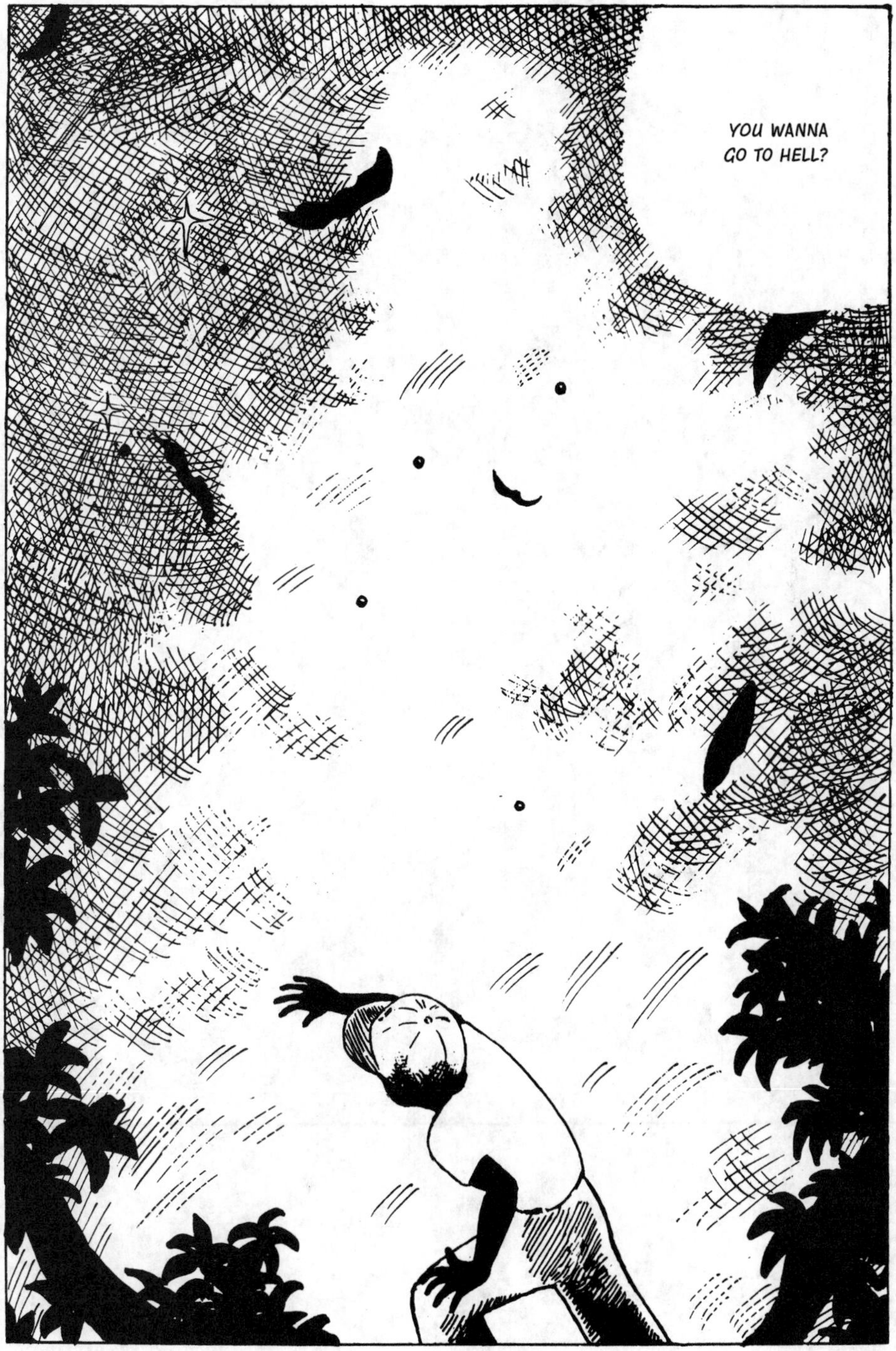
YOU WANNA
GO TO HELL?

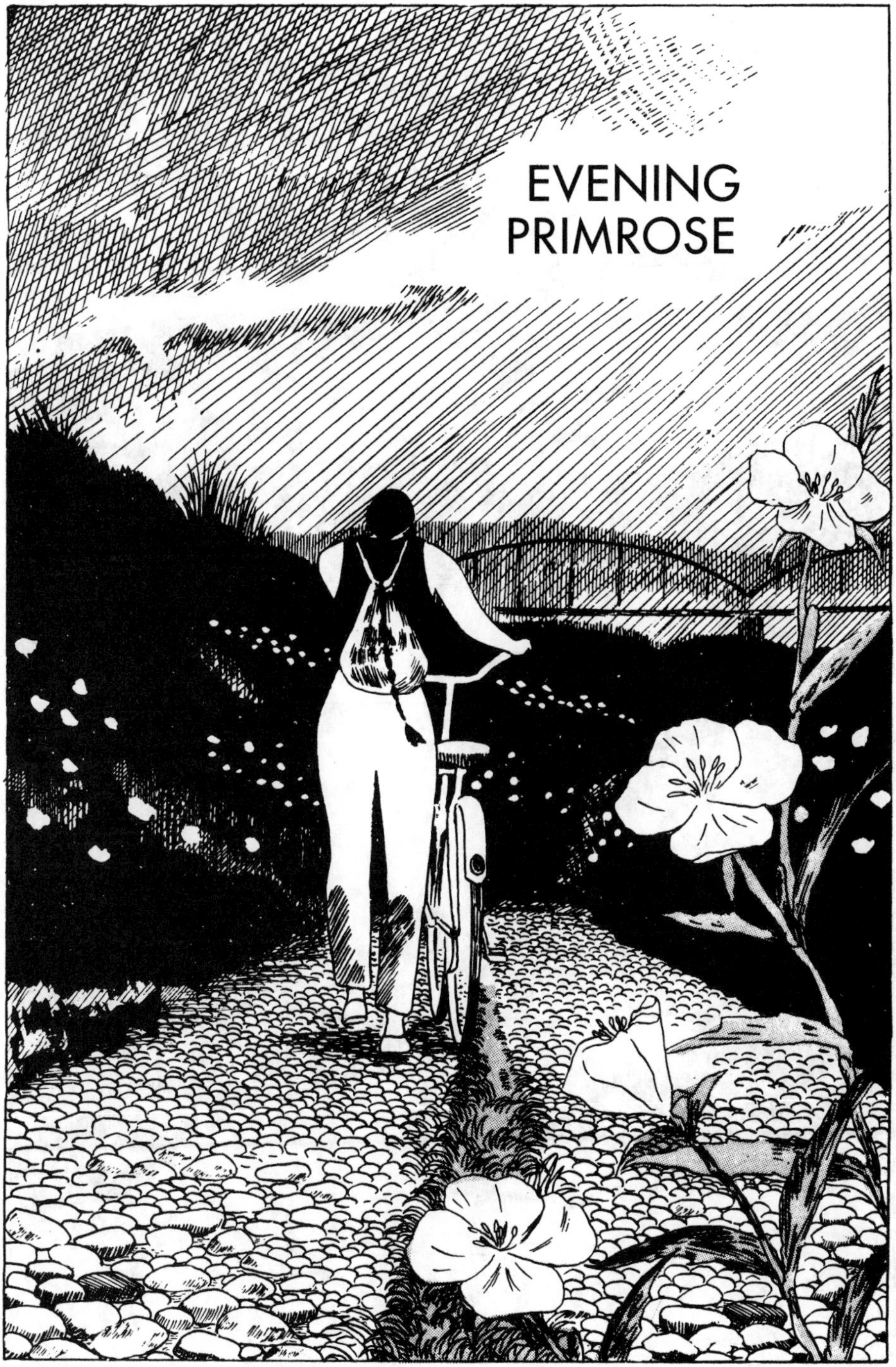
EVENING
PRIMROSE

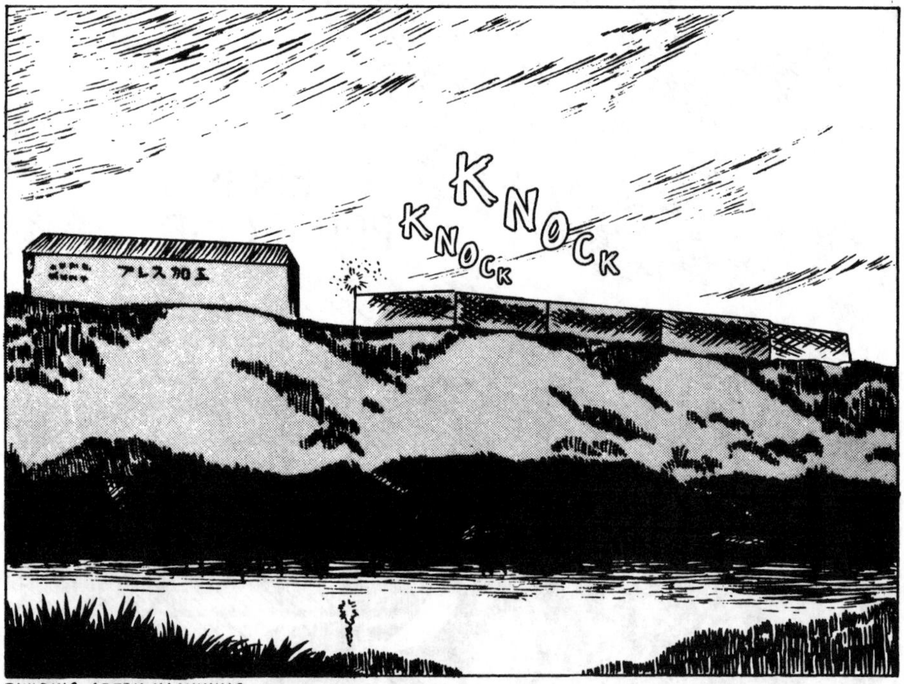
アレス加工
KNOCK
KNOCK
KNOCK
KNOCK
BUILDING: ARESU MACHINING

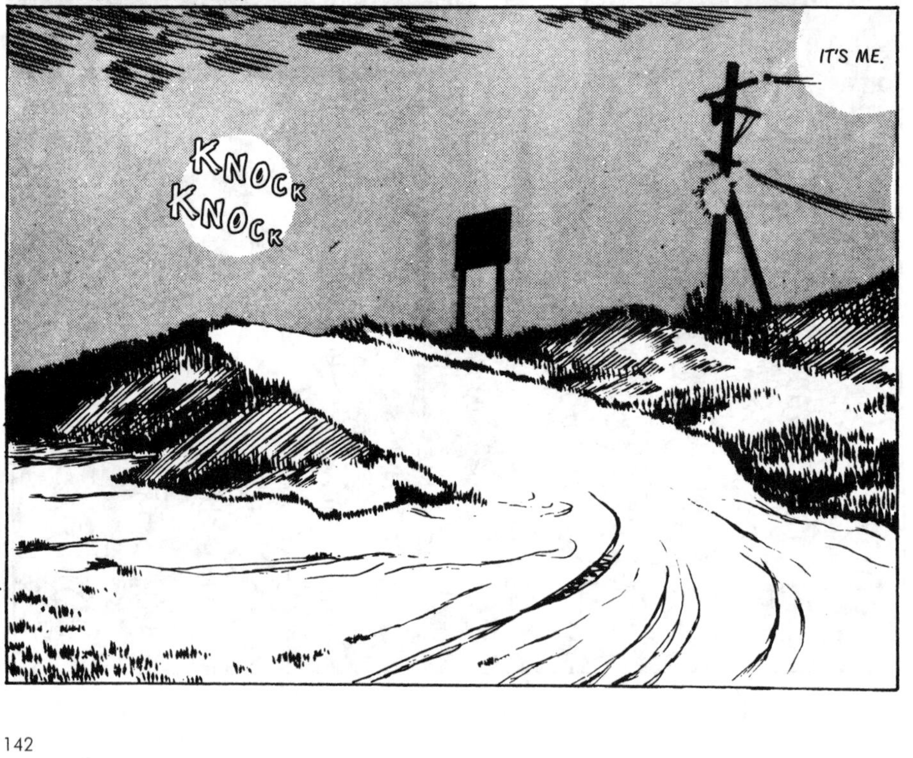
KNOCK
KNOCK
IT'S ME.

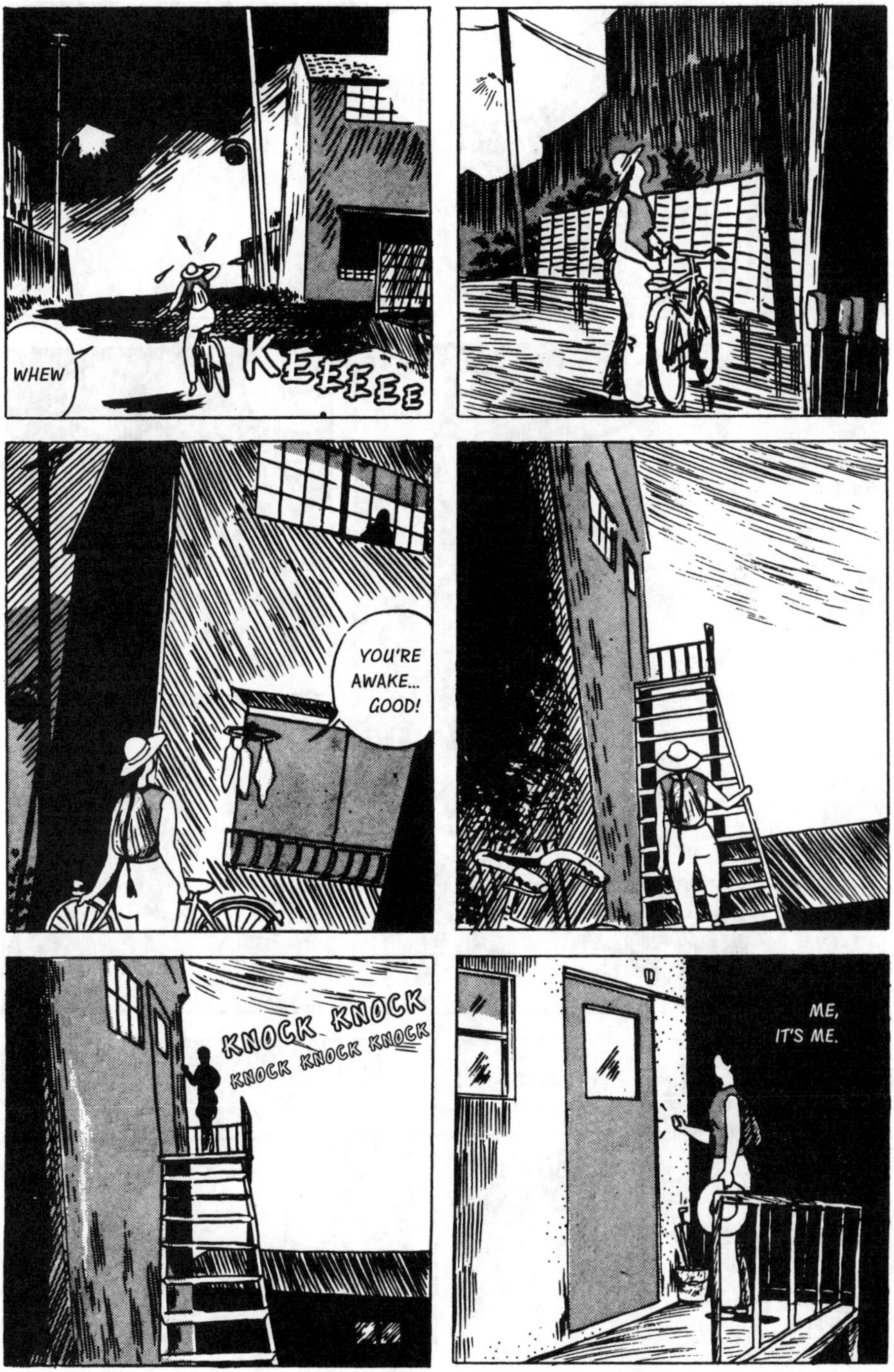
WHEW
KEEEEEE
YOU'RE AWAKE... GOOD!
KNOCK KNOCK
KNOCK KNOCK KNOCK
ME, IT'S ME.

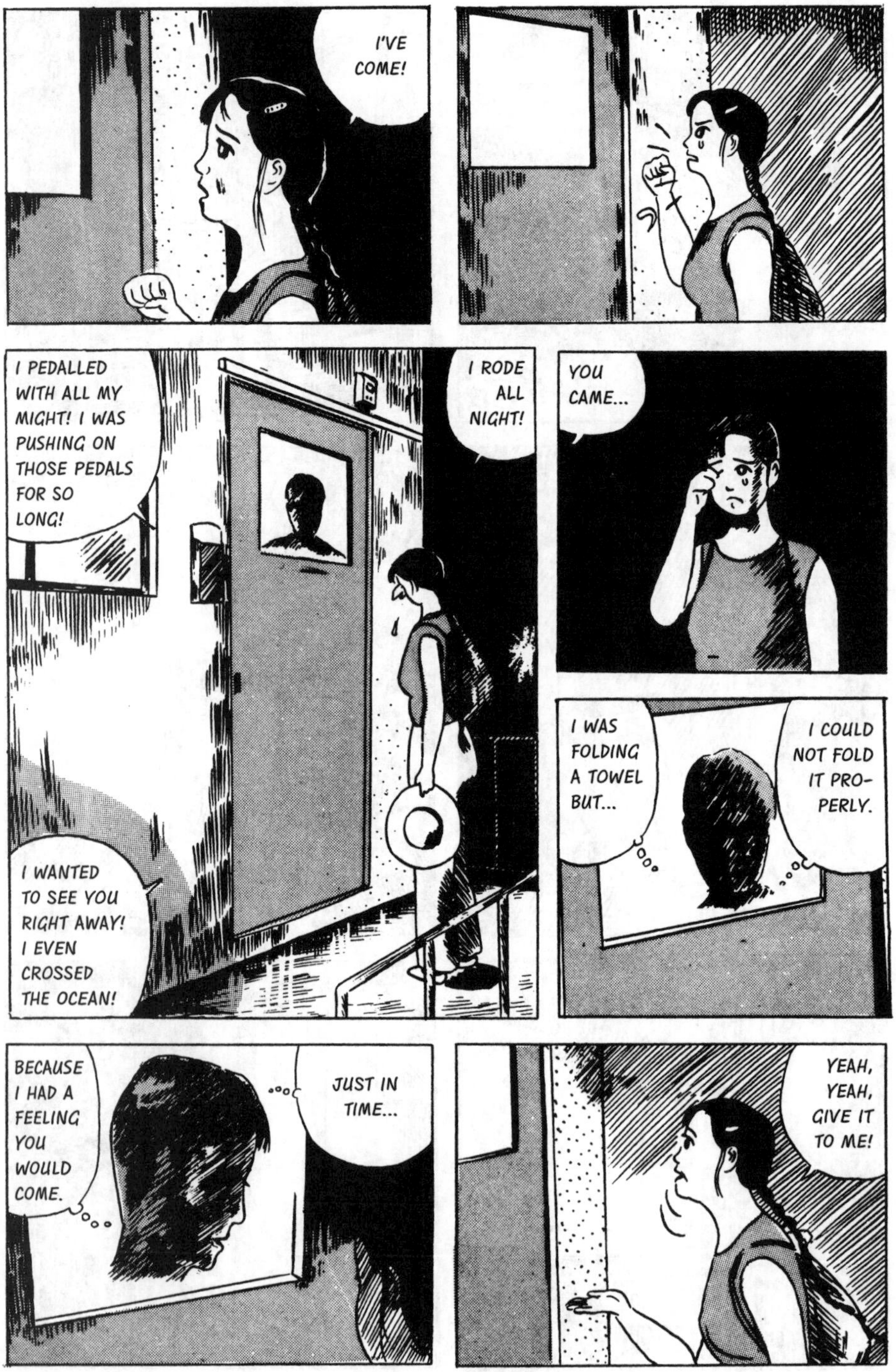
I'VE COME!
I PEDALLED WITH ALL MY MIGHT! I WAS PUSHING ON THOSE PEDALS FOR SO LONG!
I RODE ALL NIGHT!
I WANTED TO SEE YOU RIGHT AWAY! I EVEN CROSSED THE OCEAN!
YOU CAME...
I WAS FOLDING A TOWEL BUT...
I COULD NOT FOLD IT PRO-PERLY.
BECAUSE I HAD A FEELING YOU WOULD COME.
JUST IN TIME...
YEAH, YEAH, GIVE IT TO ME!

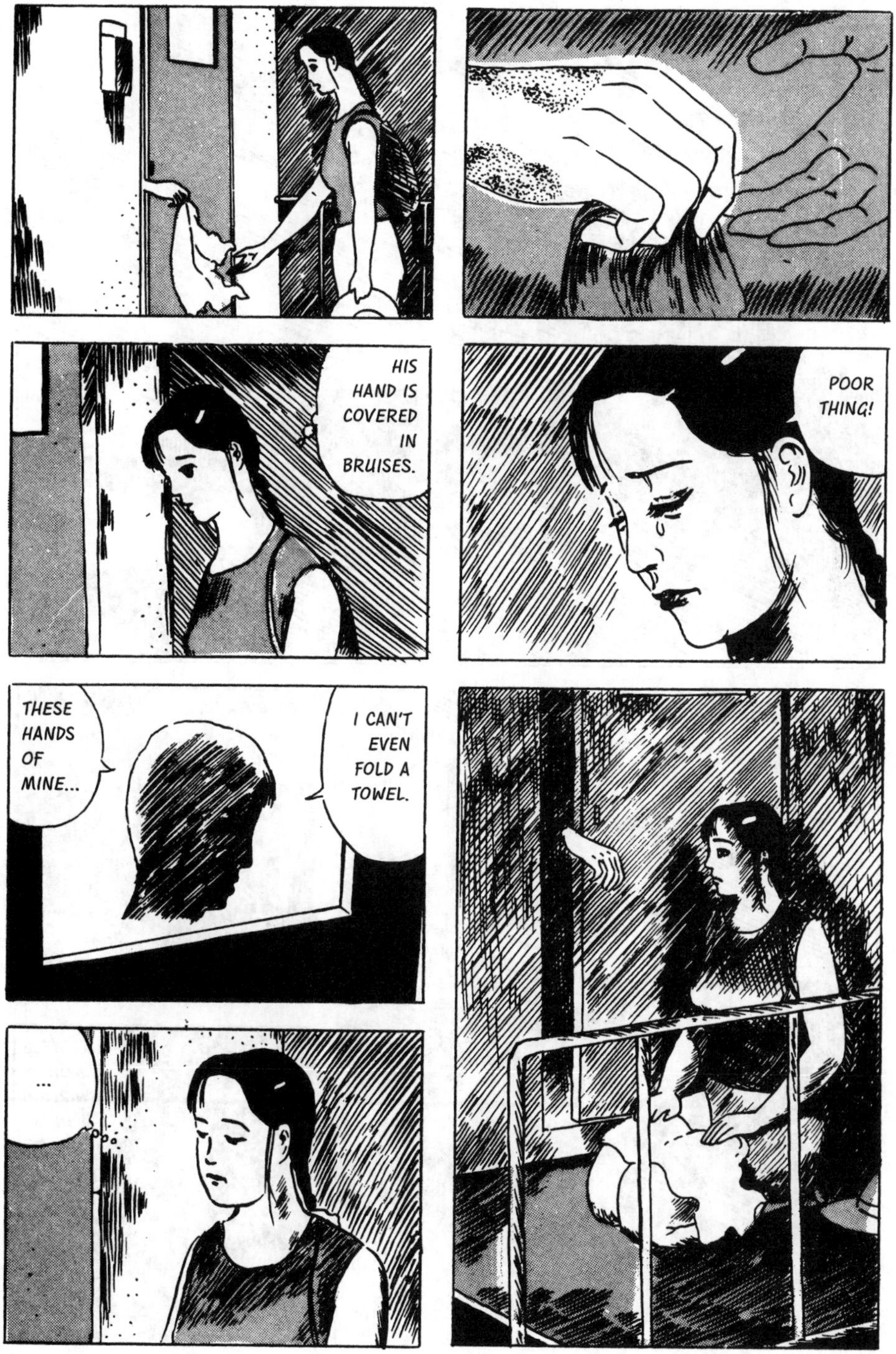
HIS HAND IS COVERED IN BRUISES.
POOR THING!
THESE HANDS OF MINE...
I CAN'T EVEN FOLD A TOWEL.
...

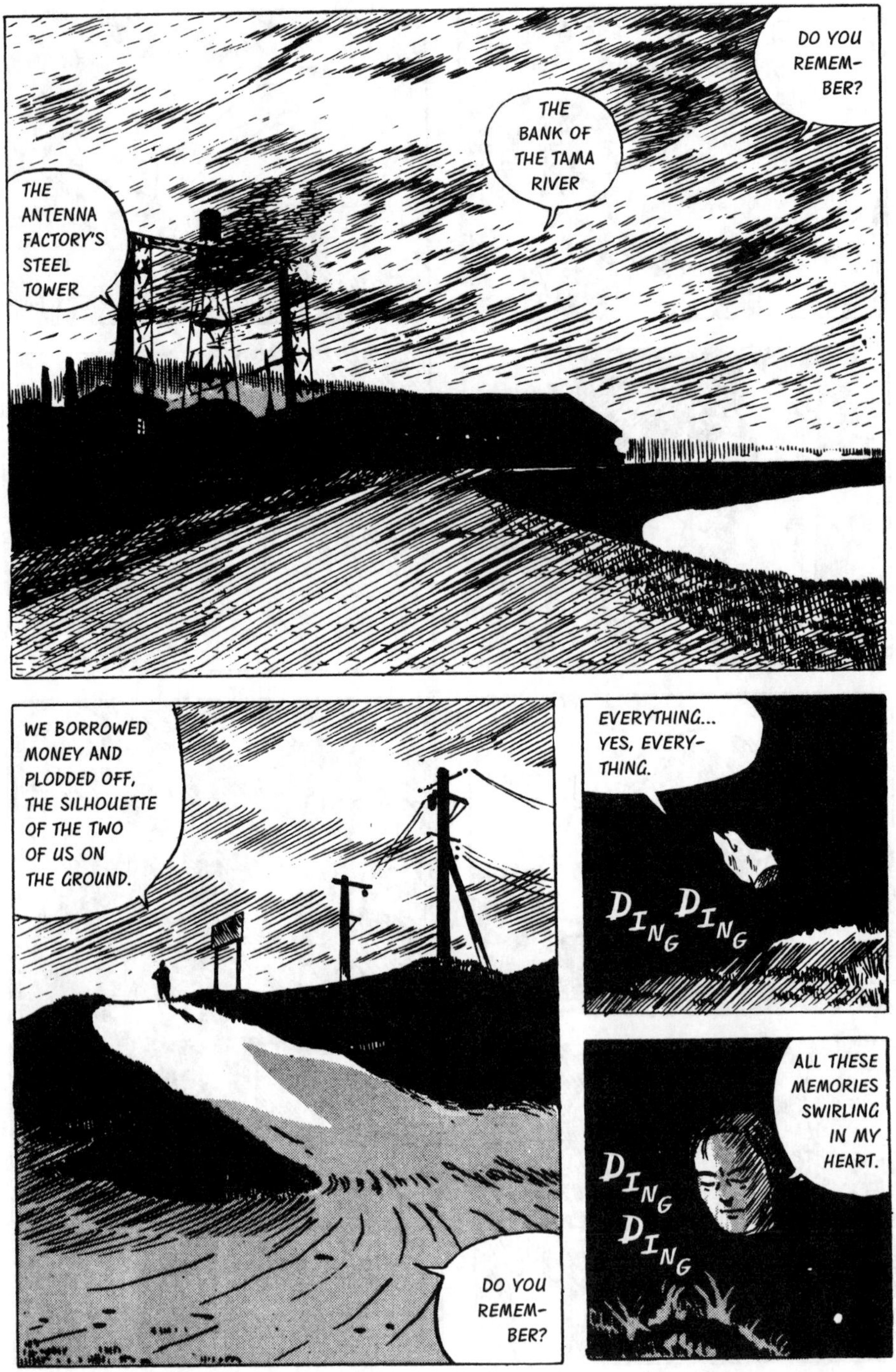
THE ANTENNA FACTORY'S STEEL TOWER
THE BANK OF THE TAMA RIVER
DO YOU REMEMBER?
WE BORROWED MONEY AND PLODDED OFF, THE SILHOUETTE OF THE TWO OF US ON THE GROUND.
DO YOU REMEMBER?
EVERYTHING... YES, EVERYTHING.
DING DING
ALL THESE MEMORIES SWIRLING IN MY HEART.
DING DING

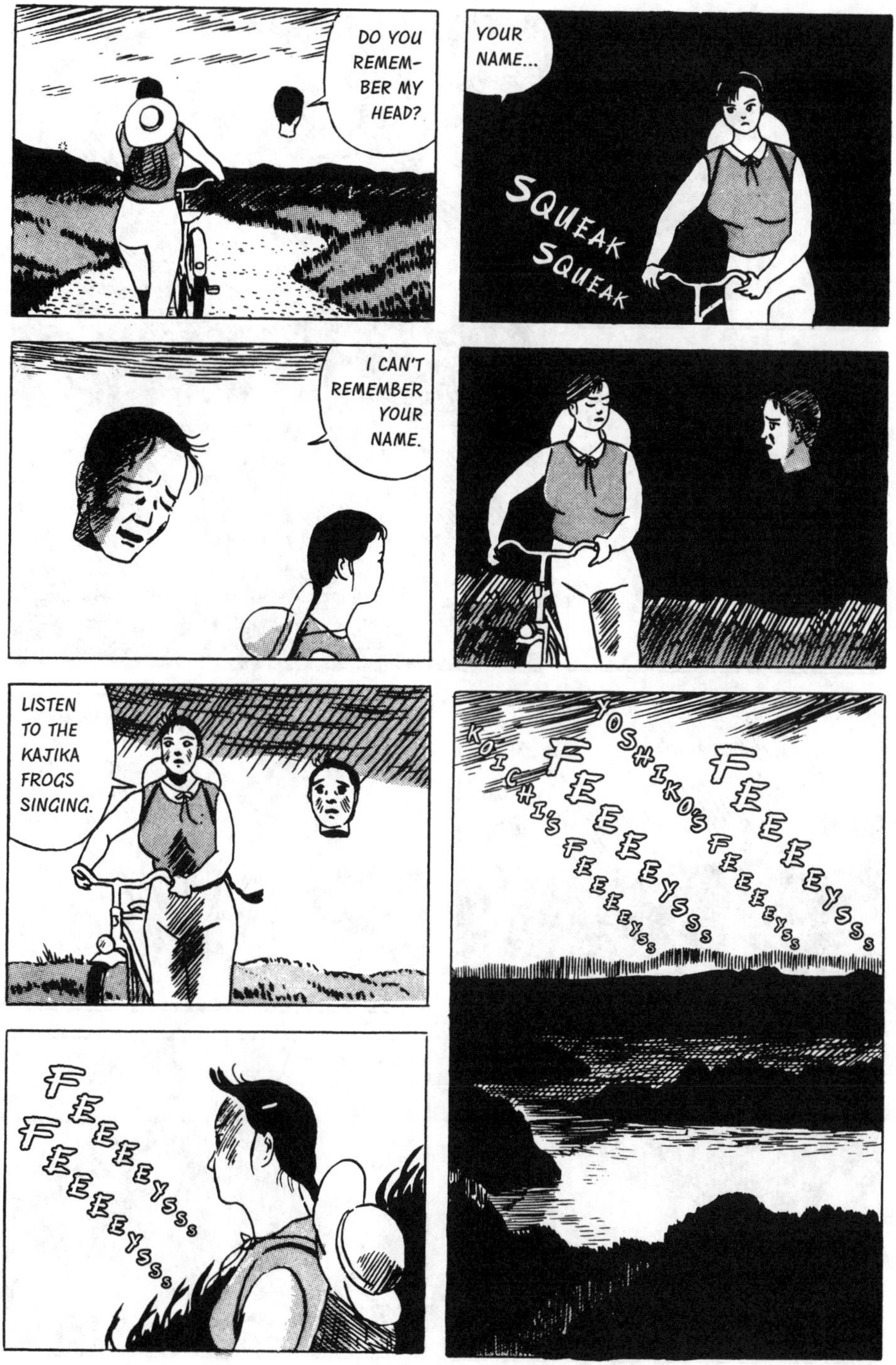
DO YOU REMEMBER MY HEAD?
YOUR NAME...
SQUEAK SQUEAK
I CAN'T REMEMBER YOUR NAME.
LISTEN TO THE KAJIKA FROGS SINGING.
FEEEEYSSS
FEEEEYSSS
FEEEEYSSS
KOICHI'S FEEEEYSS
YOSHIKO'S FEEEEYSS
FEEEEYSSS

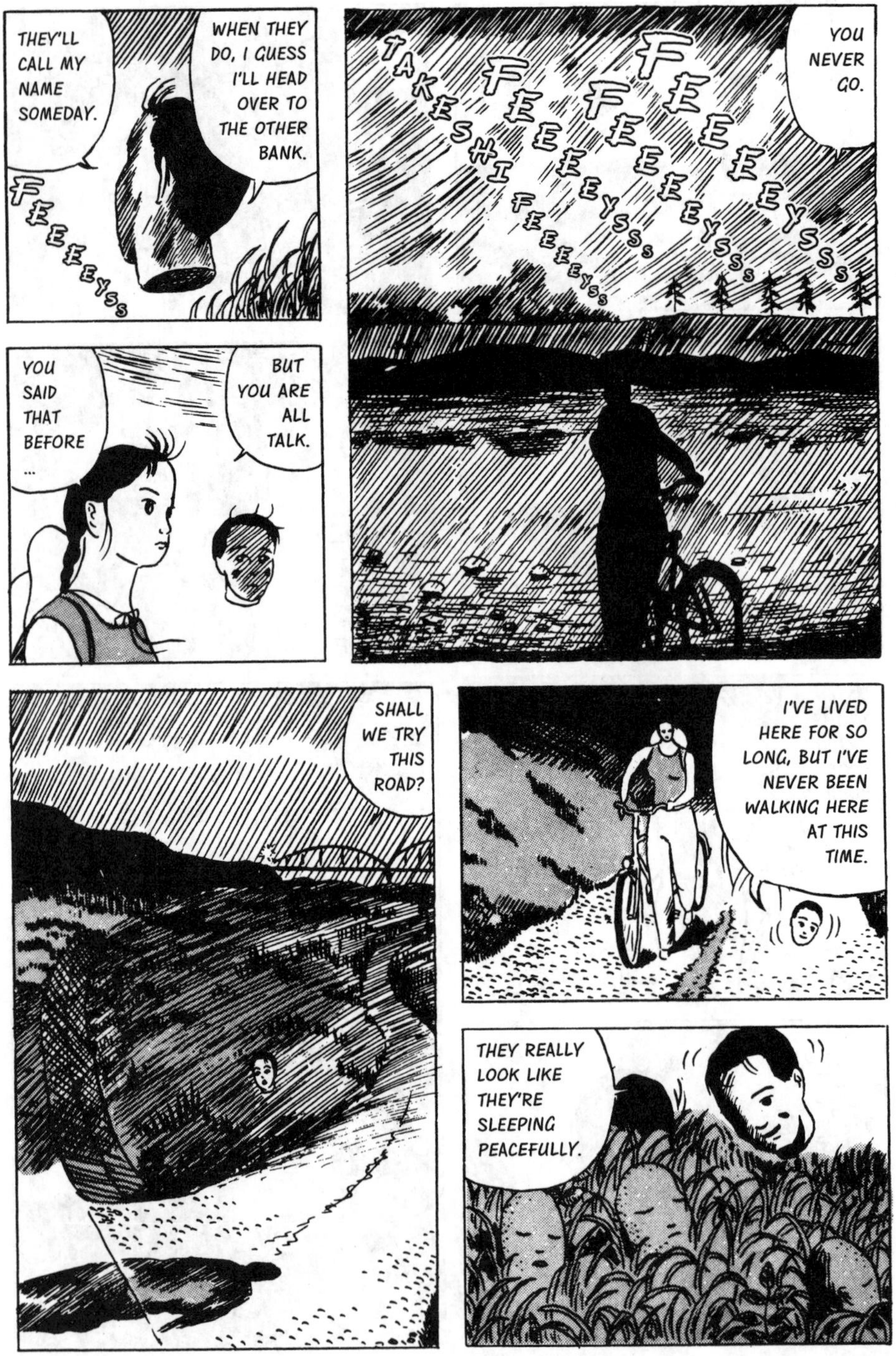
THEY'LL CALL MY NAME SOMEDAY.
WHEN THEY DO, I GUESS I'LL HEAD OVER TO THE OTHER BANK.
FEEEEYSS
YOU SAID THAT BEFORE ...
BUT YOU ARE ALL TALK.
TAKESHI FEEEEYSS
FEEEEEYSSS
FEEEEEEYSSS
YOU NEVER GO.
SHALL WE TRY THIS ROAD?
I'VE LIVED HERE FOR SO LONG, BUT I'VE NEVER BEEN WALKING HERE AT THIS TIME.
THEY REALLY LOOK LIKE THEY'RE SLEEPING PEACEFULLY.

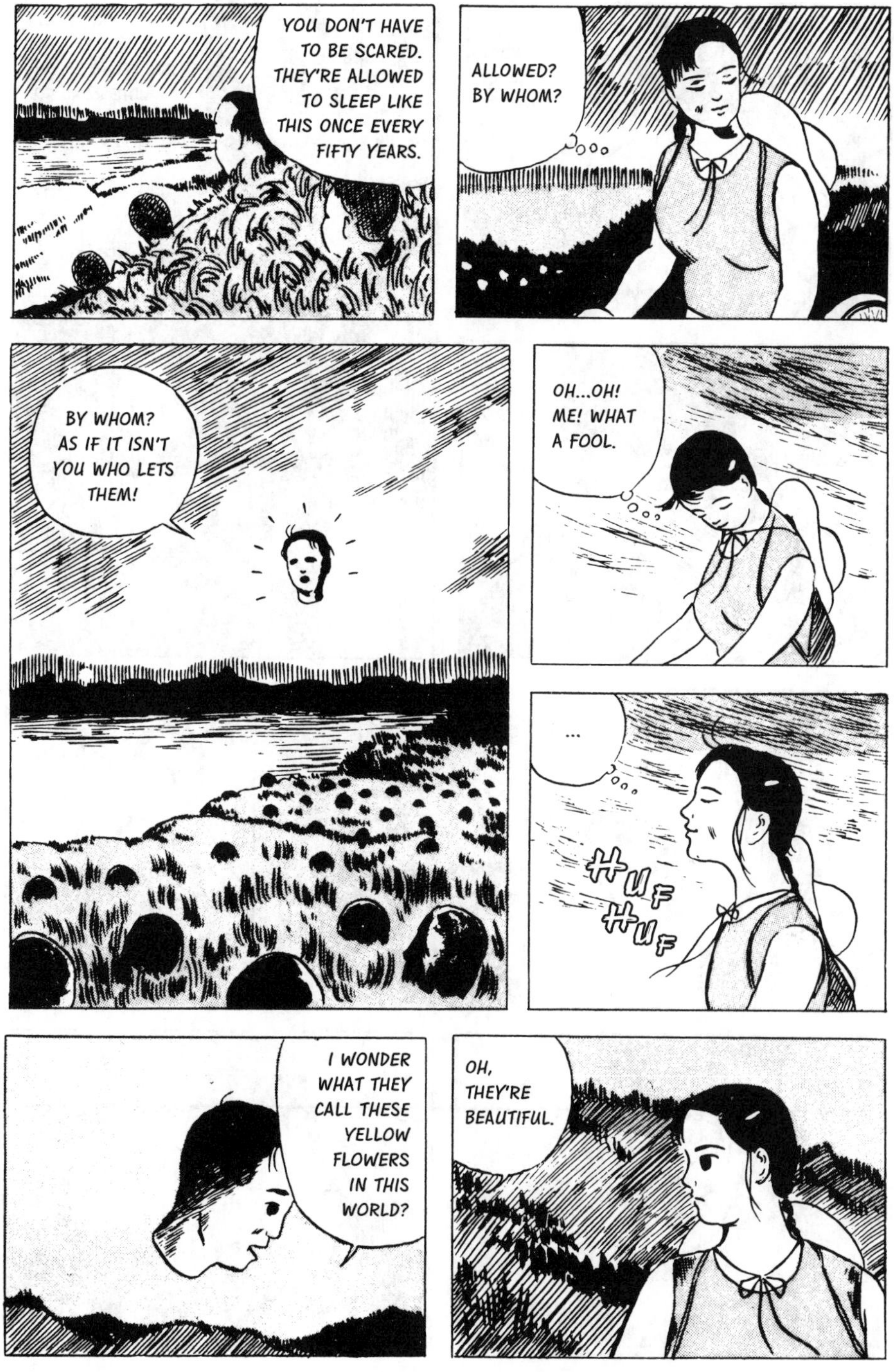
YOU DON'T HAVE TO BE SCARED. THEY'RE ALLOWED TO SLEEP LIKE THIS ONCE EVERY FIFTY YEARS.
ALLOWED? BY WHOM?
BY WHOM? AS IF IT ISN'T YOU WHO LETS THEM!
OH...OH! ME! WHAT A FOOL.
...
HUF HUF
I WONDER WHAT THEY CALL THESE YELLOW FLOWERS IN THIS WORLD?
OH, THEY'RE BEAUTIFUL.

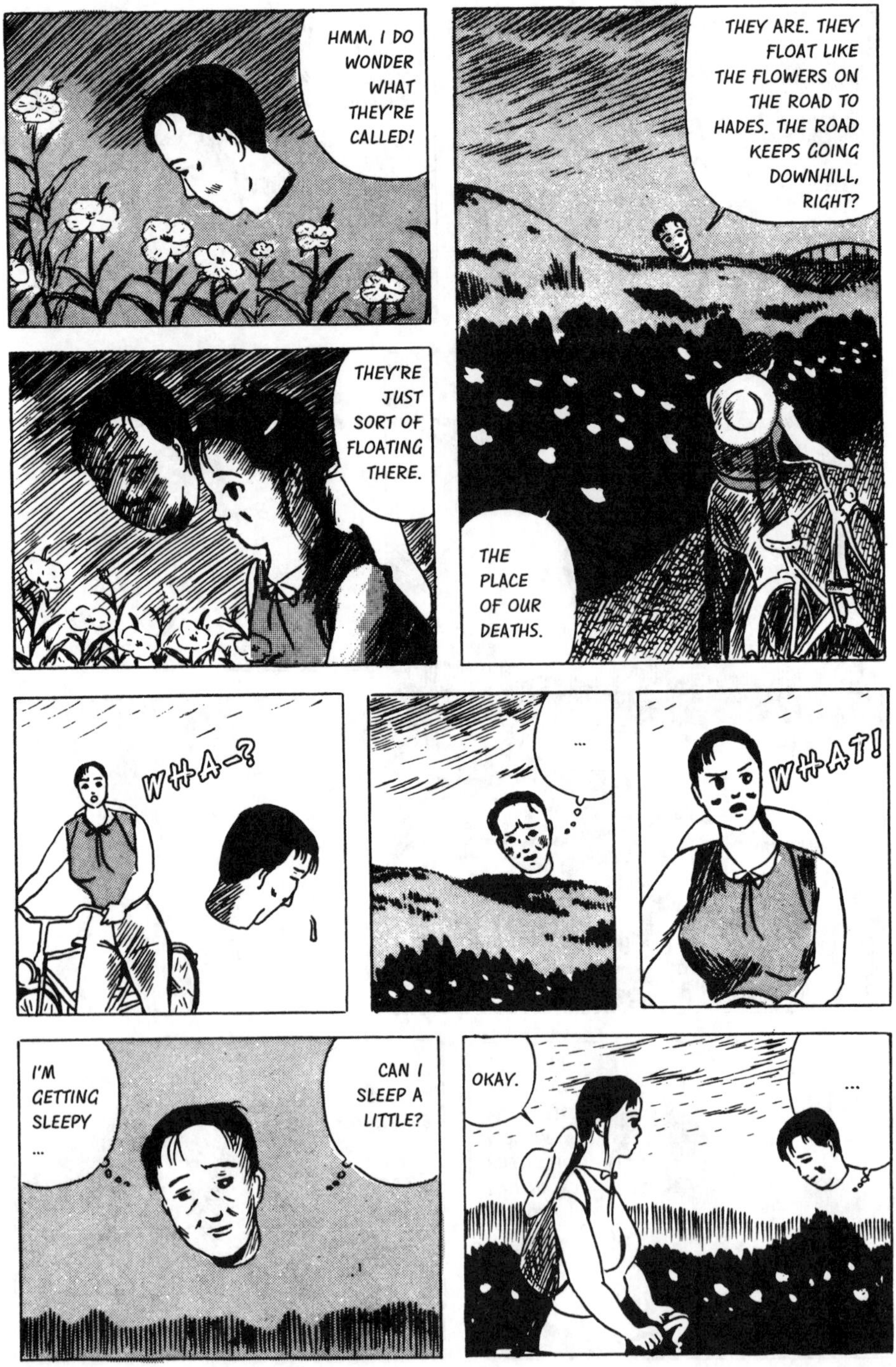
HMM, I DO WONDER WHAT THEY'RE CALLED!
THEY ARE. THEY FLOAT LIKE THE FLOWERS ON THE ROAD TO HADES. THE ROAD KEEPS GOING DOWNHILL, RIGHT?
THEY'RE JUST SORT OF FLOATING THERE.
THE PLACE OF OUR DEATHS.
WHA-?
...
WHAT!
I'M GETTING SLEEPY ...
CAN I SLEEP A LITTLE?
OKAY.
...

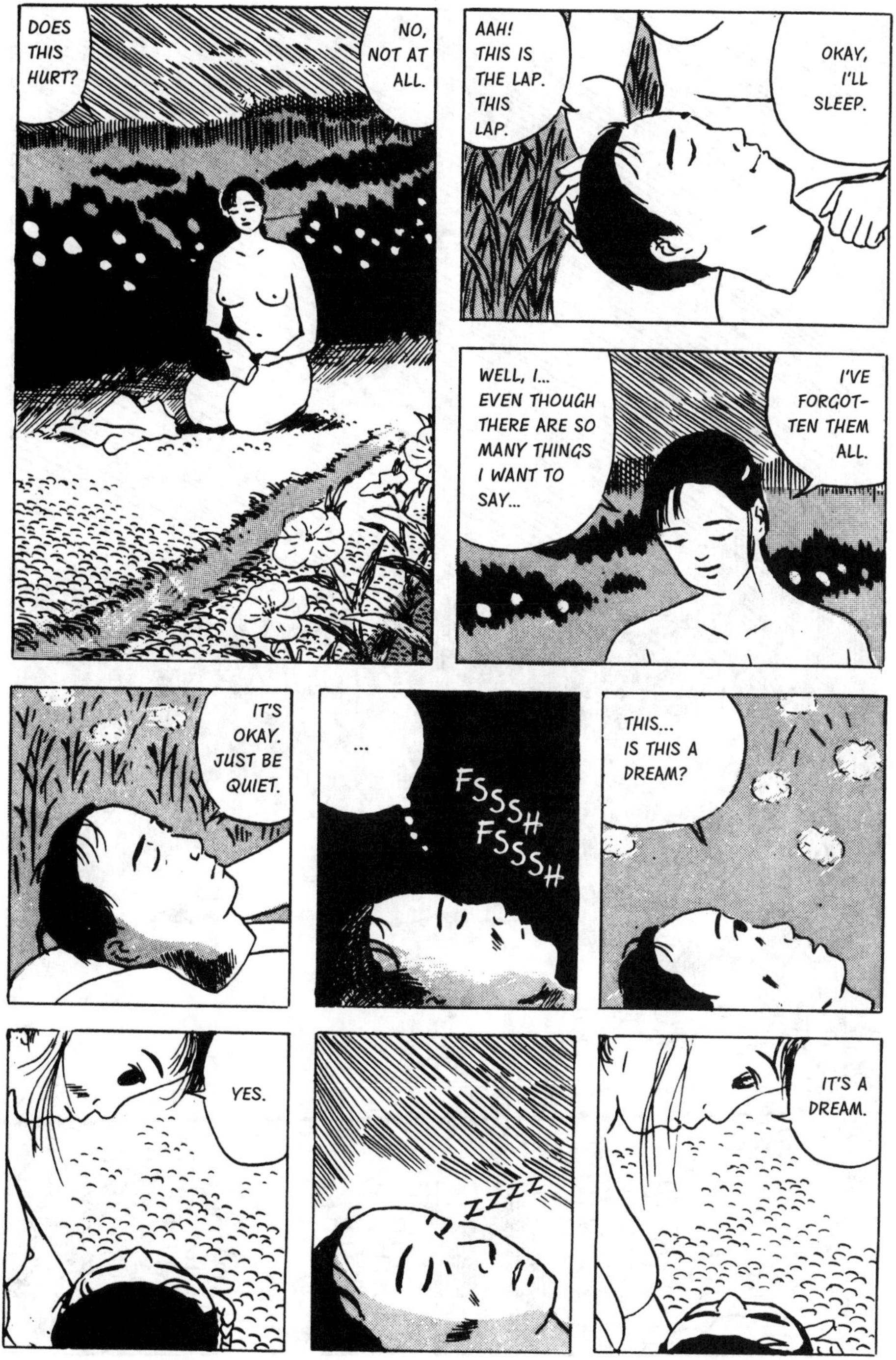
DOES THIS HURT?
NO, NOT AT ALL.
AAH! THIS IS THE LAP. THIS LAP.
OKAY, I'LL SLEEP.
WELL, I... EVEN THOUGH THERE ARE SO MANY THINGS I WANT TO SAY...
I'VE FORGOTTEN THEM ALL.
IT'S OKAY. JUST BE QUIET.
...
FSSSH FSSSH
THIS... IS THIS A DREAM?
YES.
ZZZZ
IT'S A DREAM.

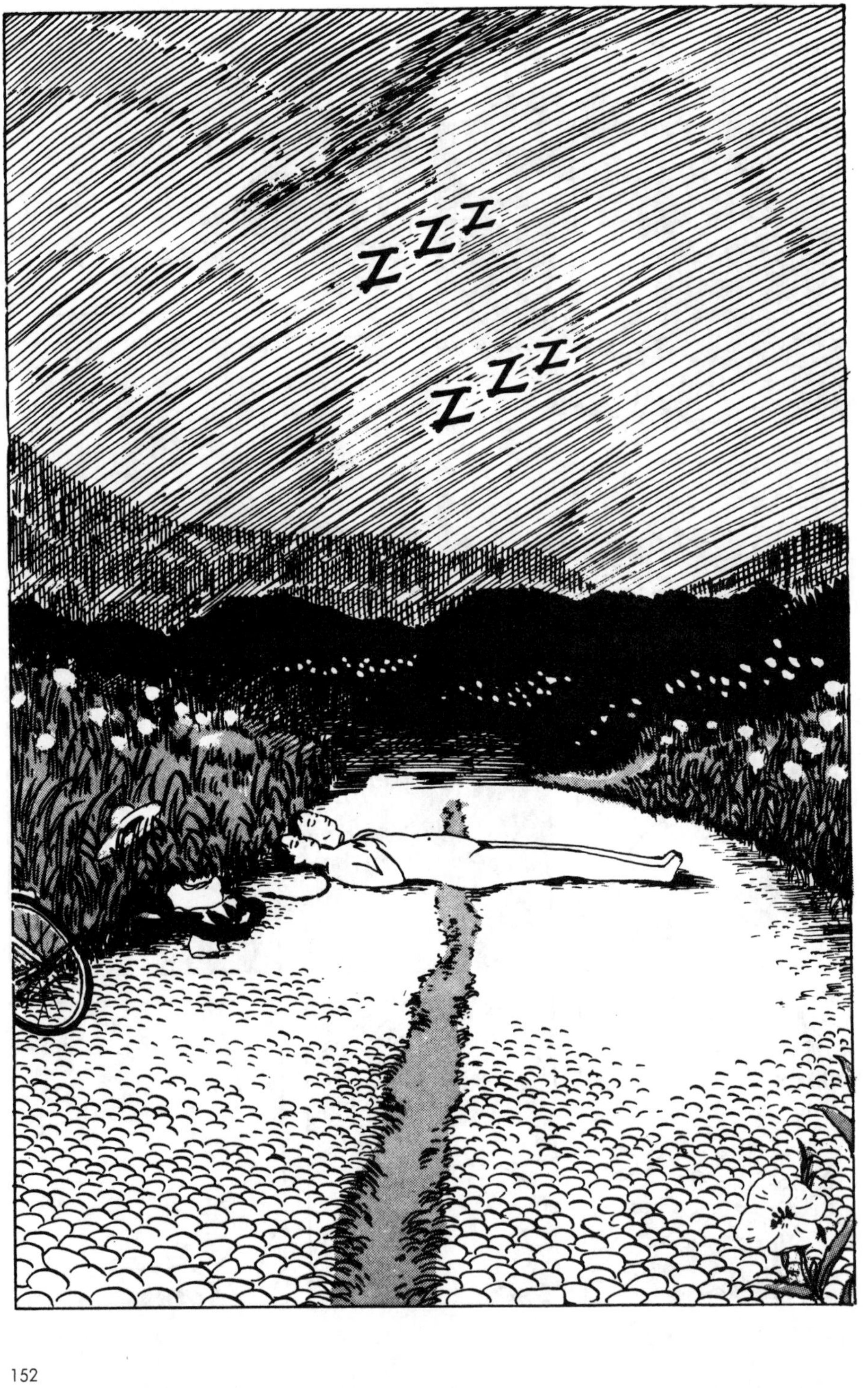
ZZZ
ZZZ

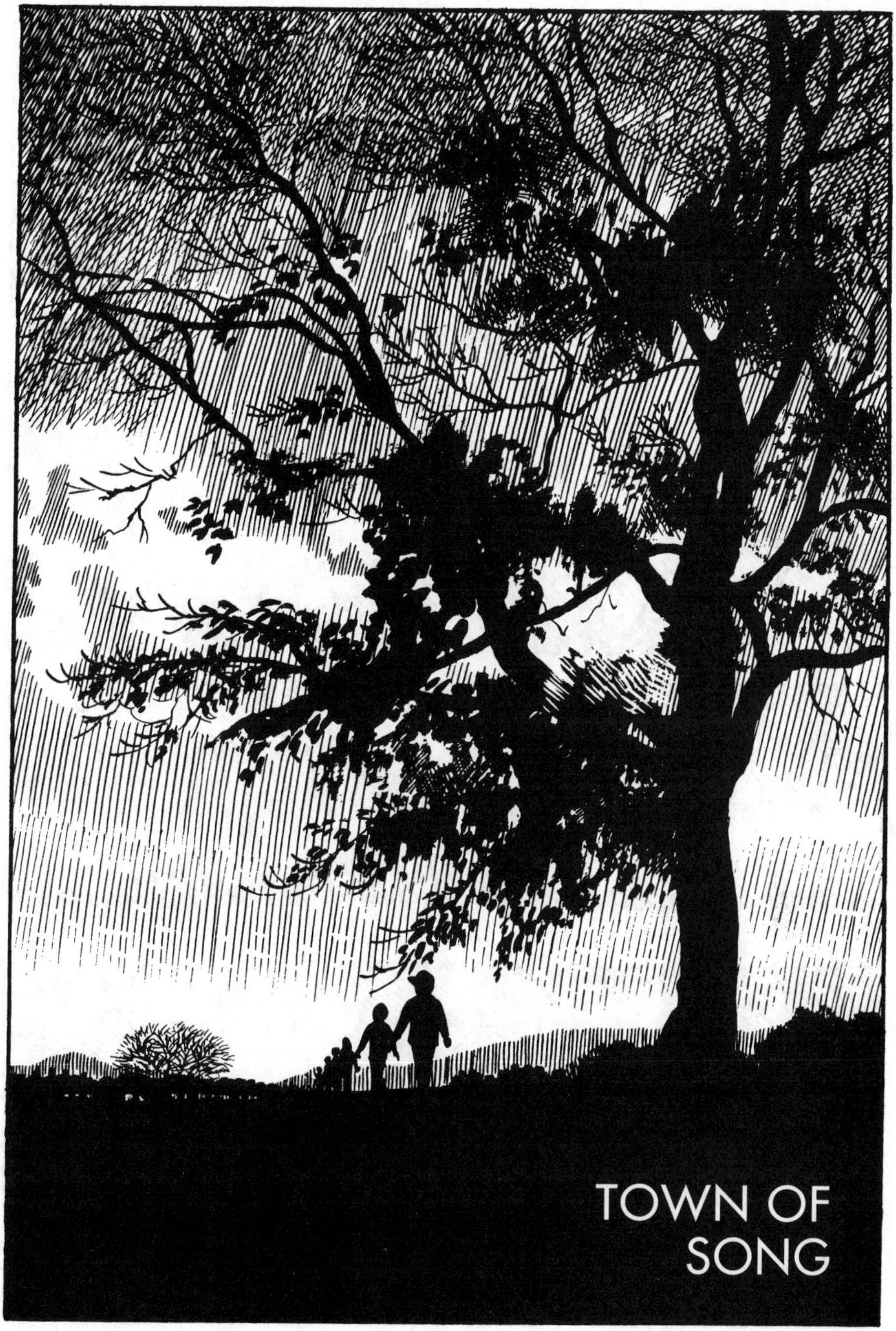
TOWN OF
SONG

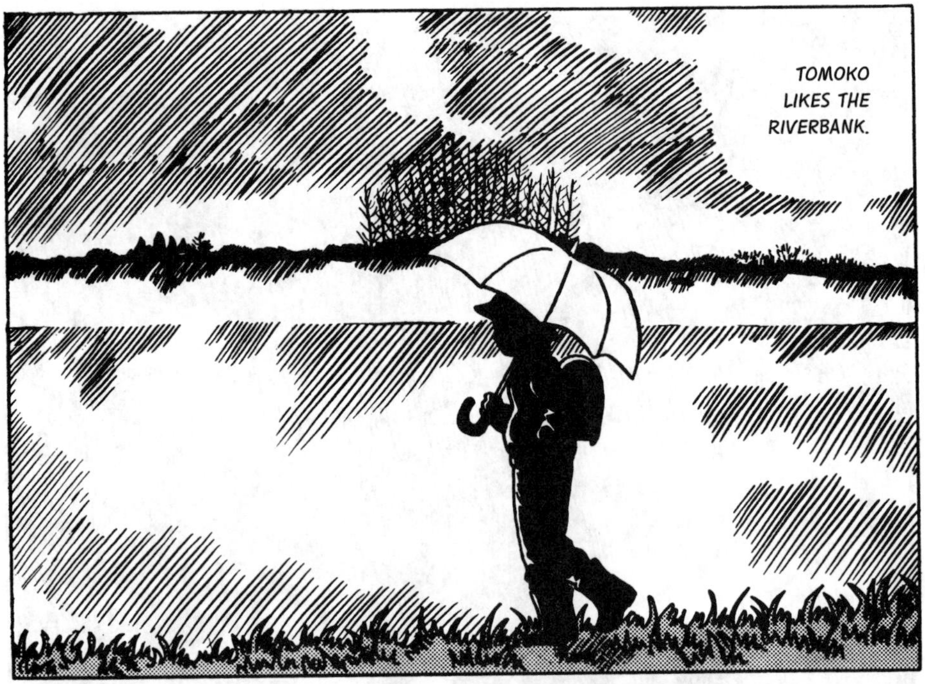
TOMOKO
LIKES THE
RIVERBANK.

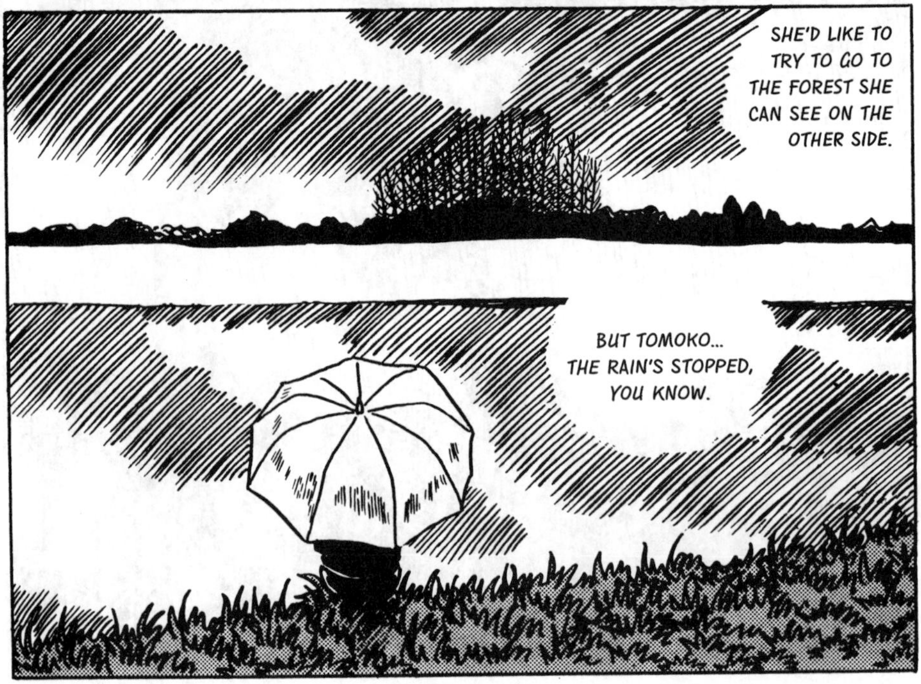
SHE'D LIKE TO
TRY TO GO TO
THE FOREST SHE
CAN SEE ON THE
OTHER SIDE.
BUT TOMOKO...
THE RAIN'S STOPPED,
YOU KNOW.

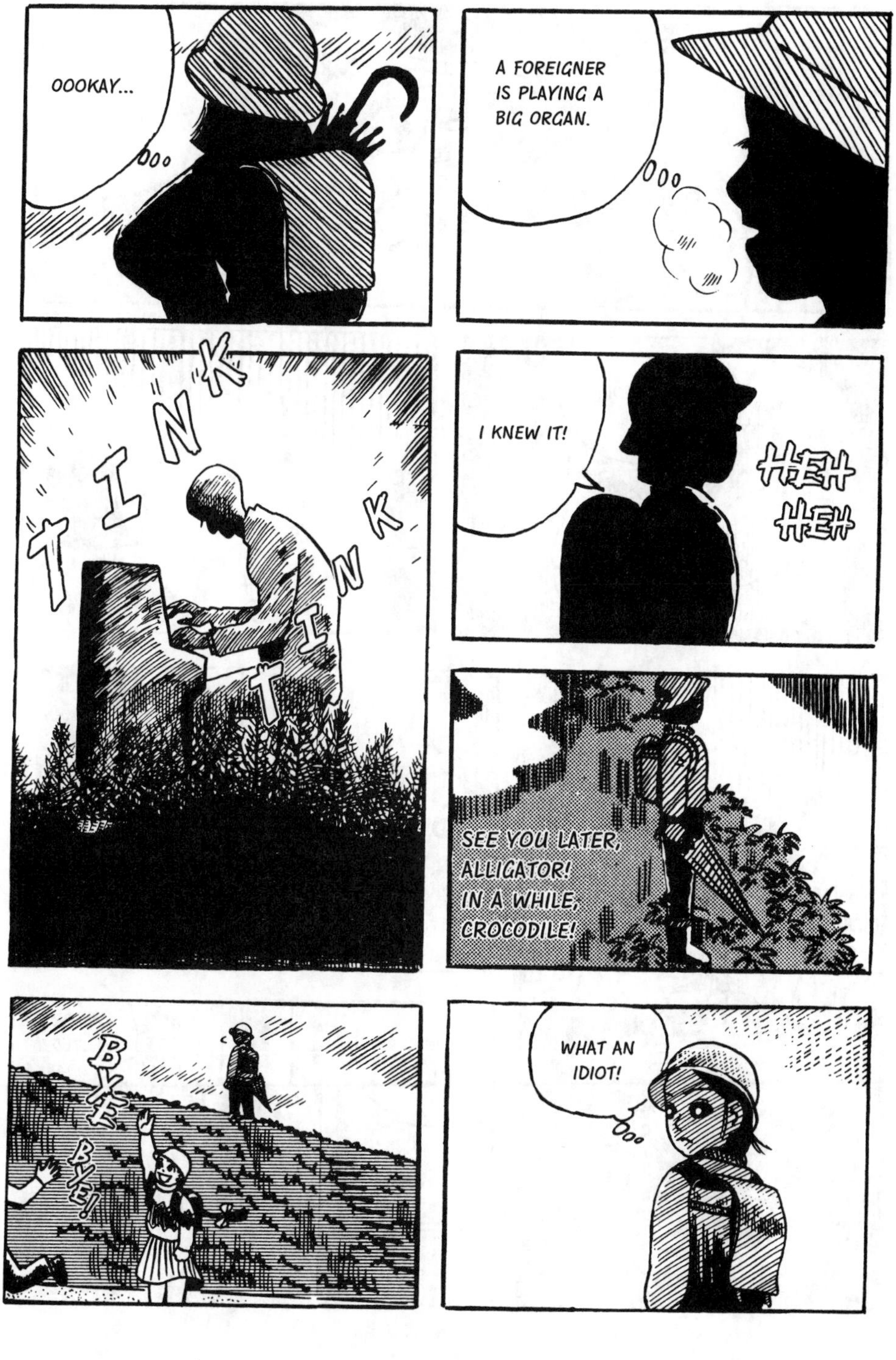
OOOKAY...
A FOREIGNER IS PLAYING A BIG ORGAN.
TINK
TINK
I KNEW IT!
HEH HEH
SEE YOU LATER, ALLIGATOR! IN A WHILE, CROCODILE!
BYE
BYE!
WHAT AN IDIOT!

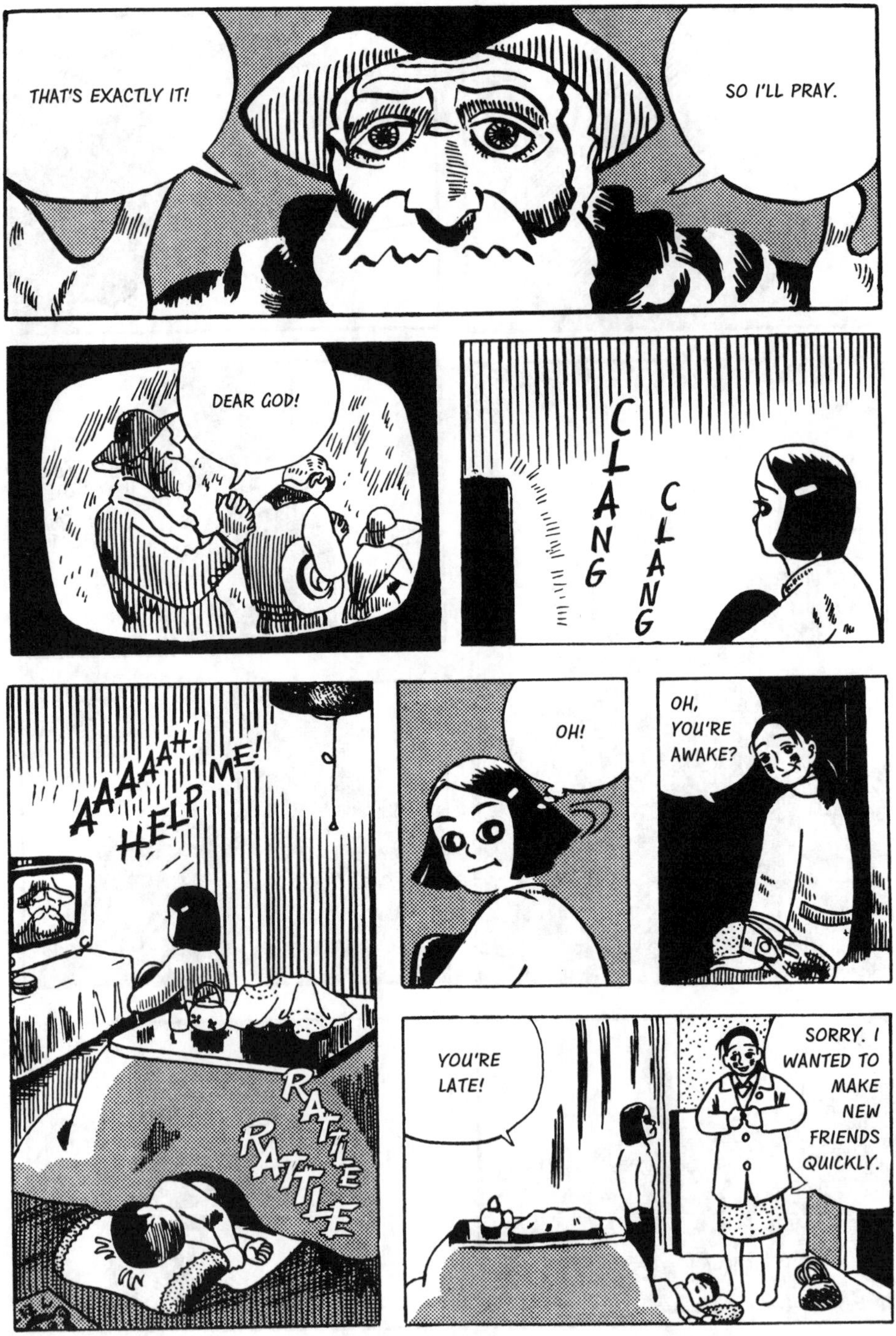
THAT'S EXACTLY IT!
SO I'LL PRAY.
DEAR GOD!
CLANG
CLANG
AAAAAH!
HELP ME!
RATTLE
RATTLE
OH!
OH, YOU'RE AWAKE?
YOU'RE LATE!
SORRY. I WANTED TO MAKE NEW FRIENDS QUICKLY.

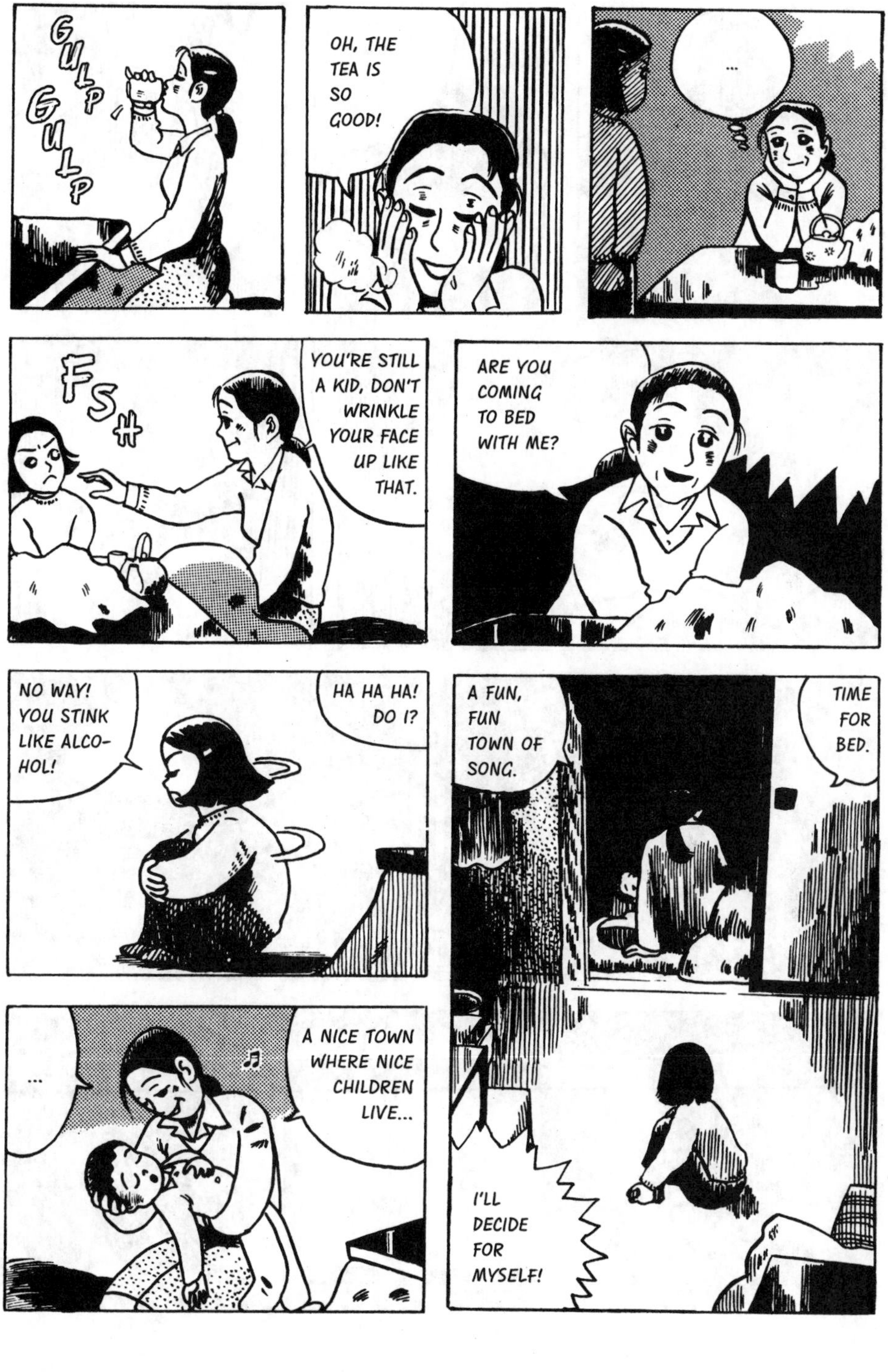
GULP GULP
OH, THE TEA IS SO GOOD!
...
FSH
YOU'RE STILL A KID, DON'T WRINKLE YOUR FACE UP LIKE THAT.
ARE YOU COMING TO BED WITH ME?
NO WAY! YOU STINK LIKE ALCO-HOL!
HA HA HA! DO I?
...
A NICE TOWN WHERE NICE CHILDREN LIVE...
A FUN, FUN TOWN OF SONG.
TIME FOR BED.
I'LL DECIDE FOR MYSELF!

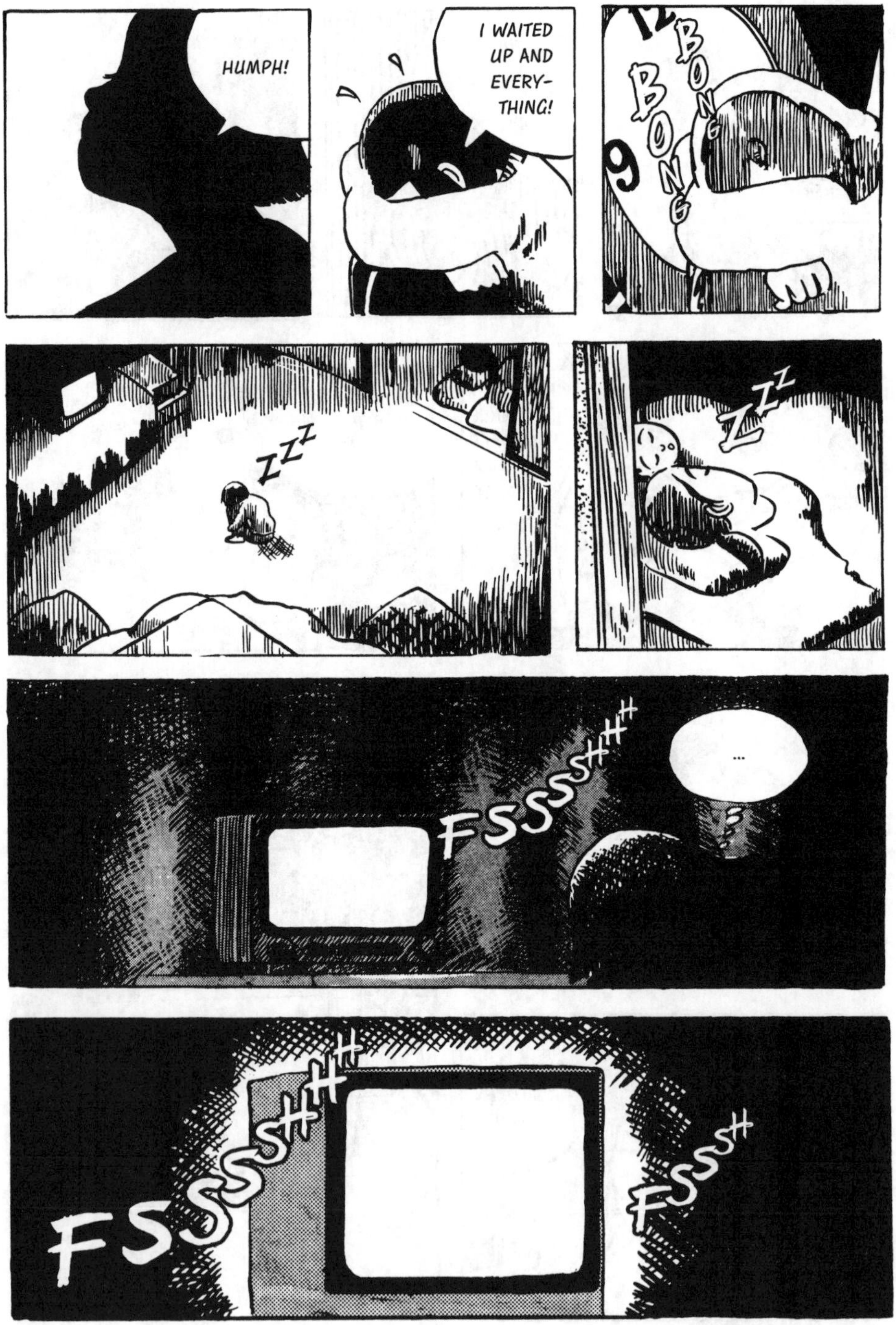
HUMPH!
I WAITED UP AND EVERY-THING!
BONG
BONG
ZZZ
ZZZ
FSSSSHHH
...
FSSSSHHH
FSSSH

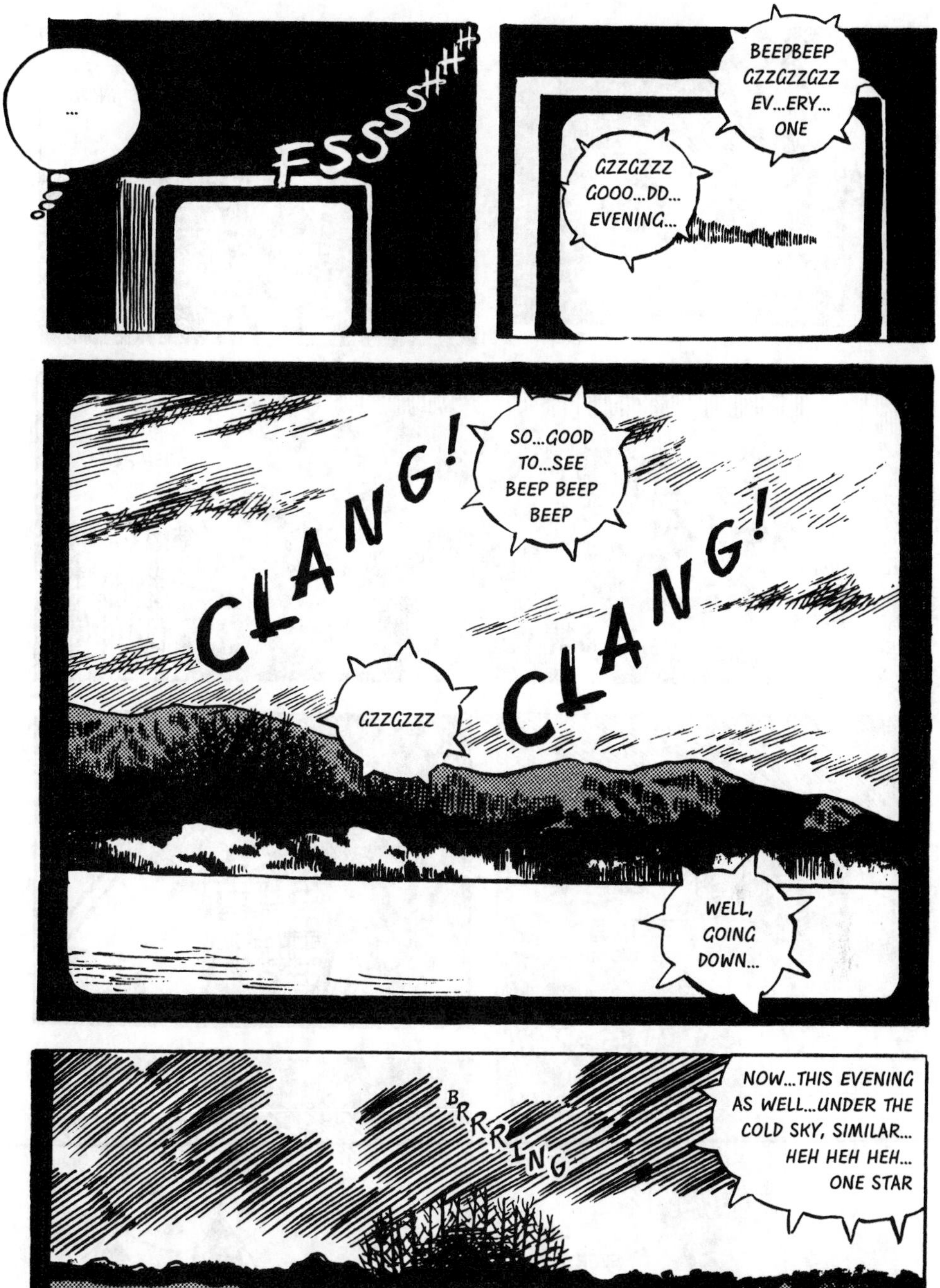
...
FSSSSHHH
BEEPBEEP GZZGZZGZZ EV...ERY... ONE
GZZGZZZ GOOO...DD... EVENING...
CLANG!
SO...GOOD TO...SEE BEEP BEEP BEEP
CLANG!
GZZGZZZ
WELL, GOING DOWN...
BRRRING
NOW...THIS EVENING AS WELL...UNDER THE COLD SKY, SIMILAR... HEH HEH HEH... ONE STAR

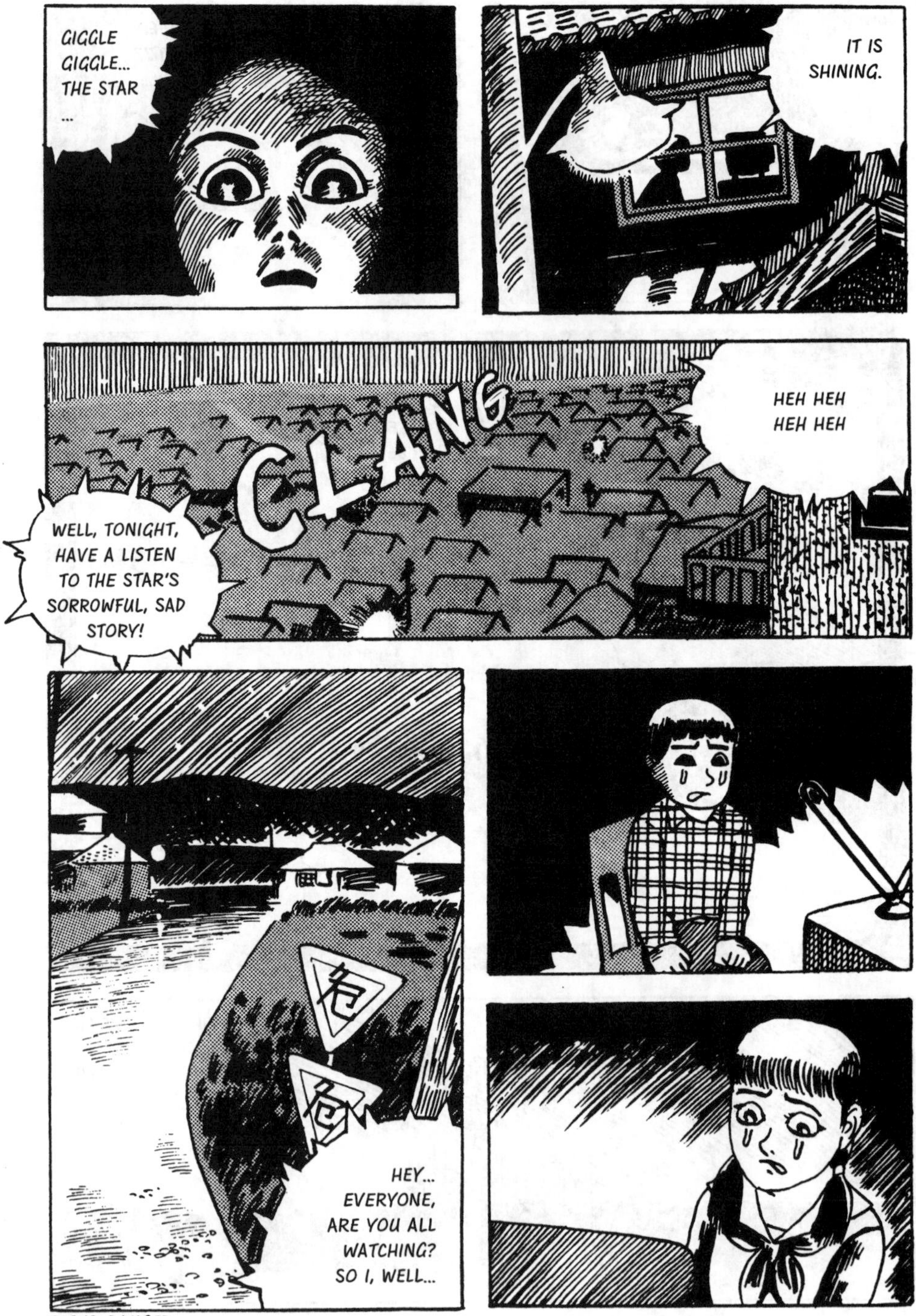
GIGGLE GIGGLE... THE STAR ...
IT IS SHINING.
CLANG
HEH HEH HEH HEH
WELL, TONIGHT, HAVE A LISTEN TO THE STAR'S SORROWFUL, SAD STORY!
危
危
HEY... EVERYONE, ARE YOU ALL WATCHING? SO I, WELL...
SIGNS: DANGER

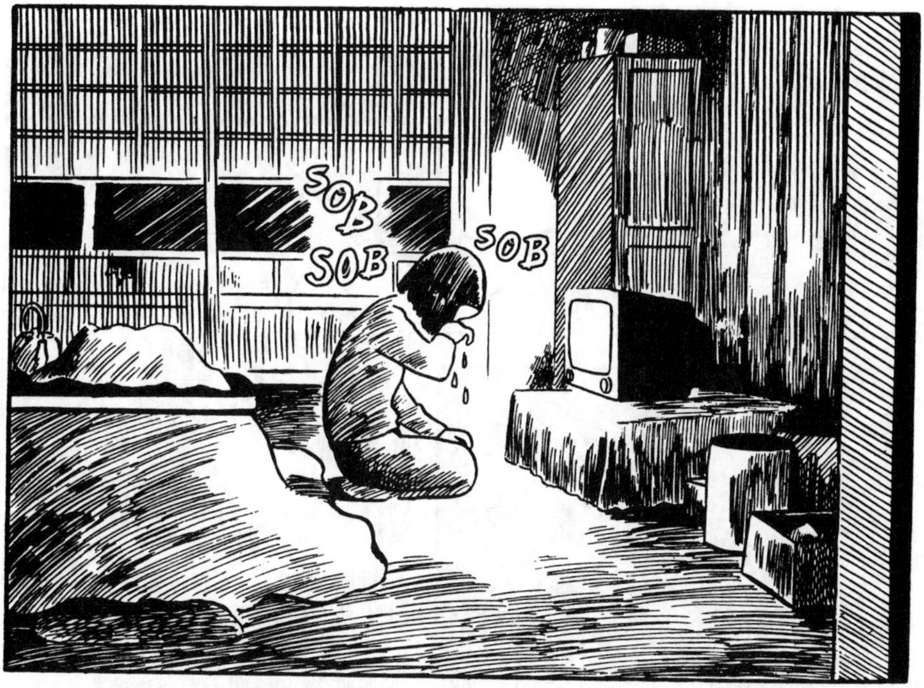
SOB
SOB
SOB

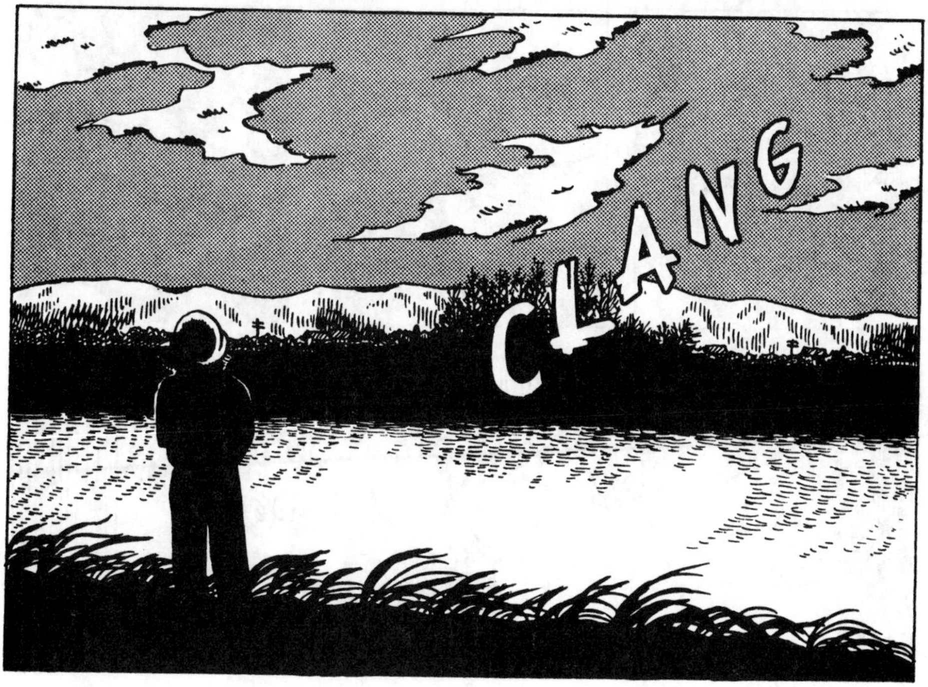
CLANG

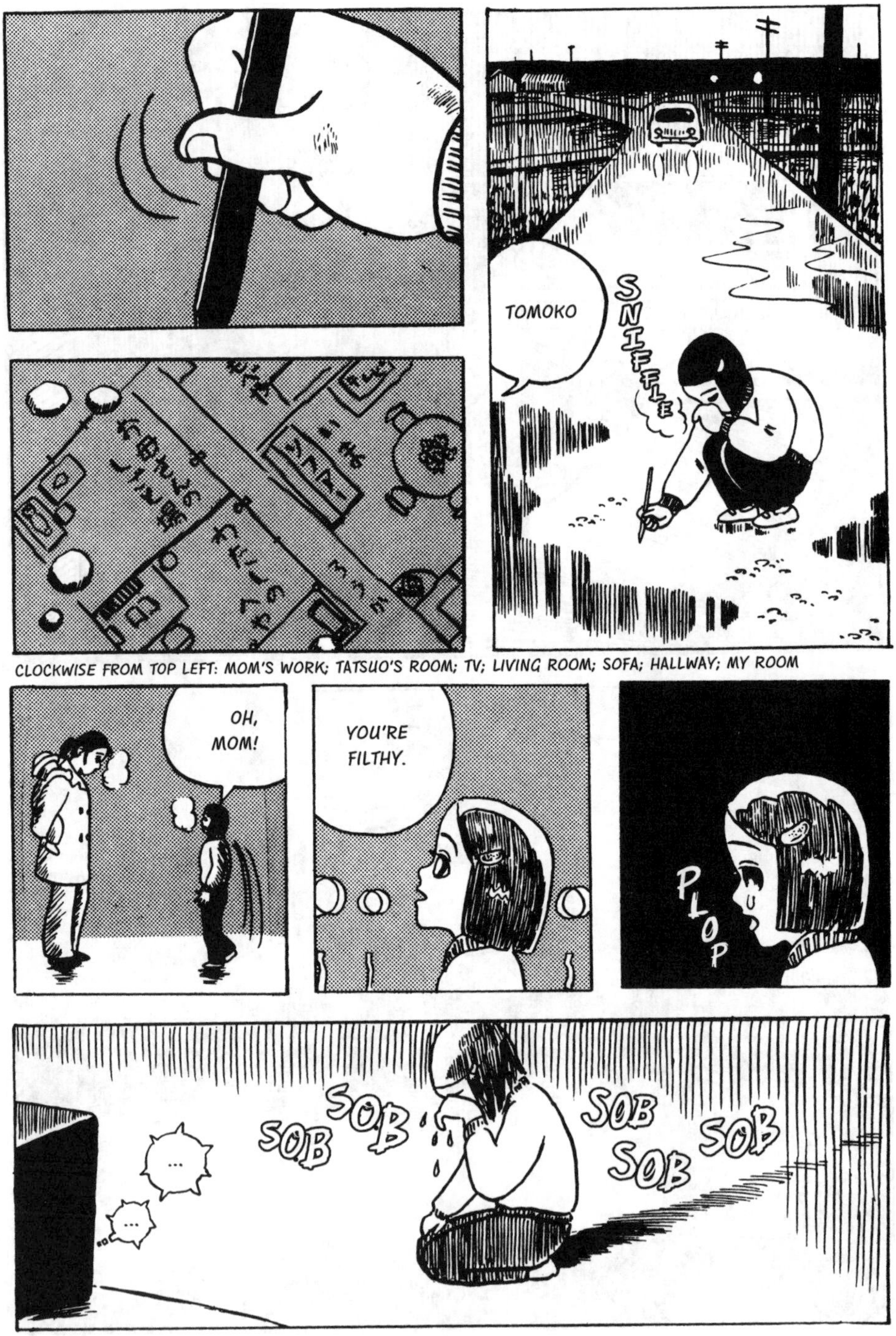
TOMOKO
SNIFFLE
CLOCKWISE FROM TOP LEFT: MOM'S WORK; TATSUO'S ROOM; TV; LIVING ROOM; SOFA; HALLWAY; MY ROOM
OH, MOM!
YOU'RE FILTHY.
PLOP
SOB SOB
SOB SOB SOB
...
...

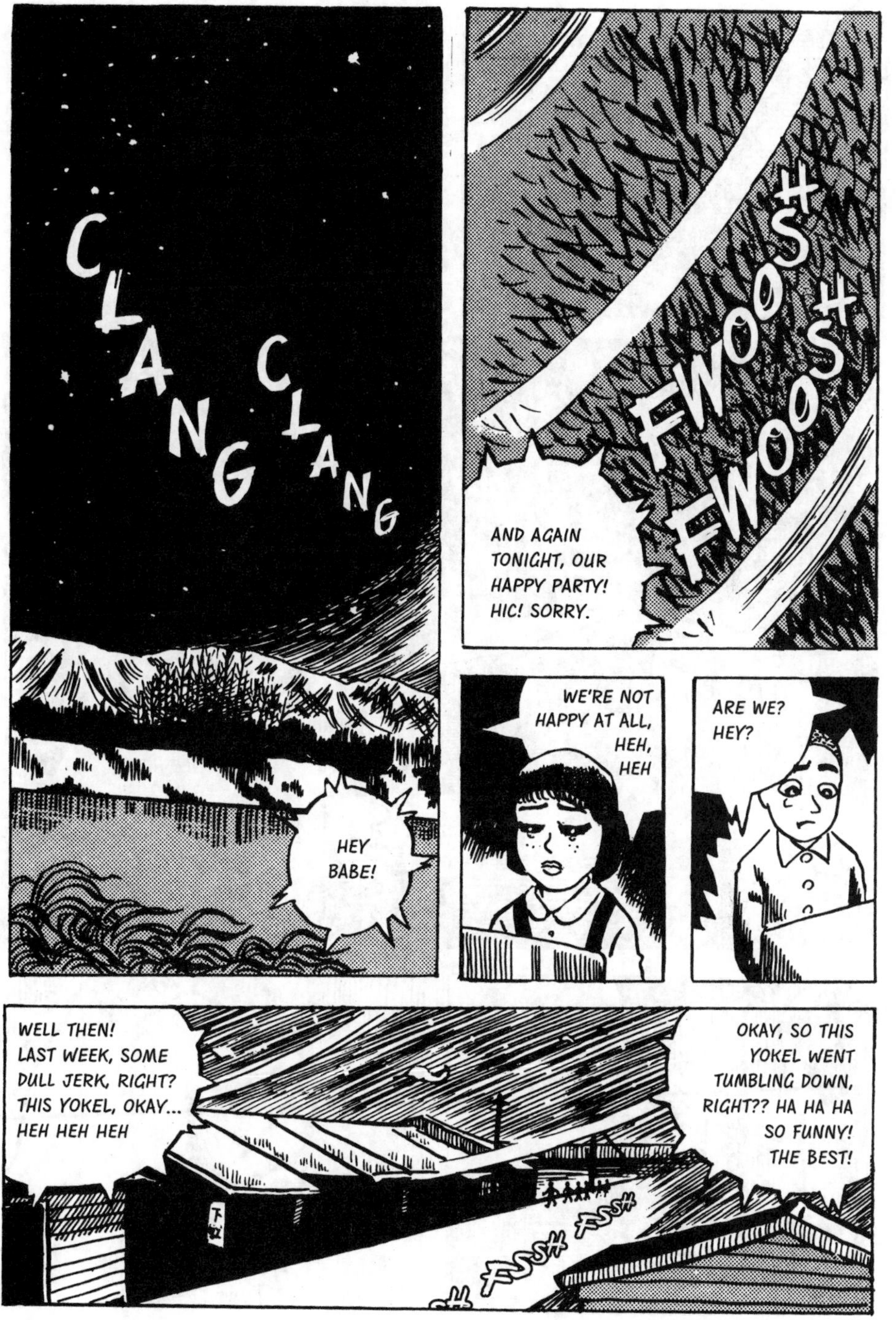
CLANG CLANG
HEY BABE!
FWOOSH FWOOSH
AND AGAIN TONIGHT, OUR HAPPY PARTY! HIC! SORRY.
WE'RE NOT HAPPY AT ALL, HEH, HEH
ARE WE? HEY?
WELL THEN! LAST WEEK, SOME DULL JERK, RIGHT? THIS YOKEL, OKAY... HEH HEH HEH
OKAY, SO THIS YOKEL WENT TUMBLING DOWN, RIGHT?? HA HA HA SO FUNNY! THE BEST!
FSSH FSSH

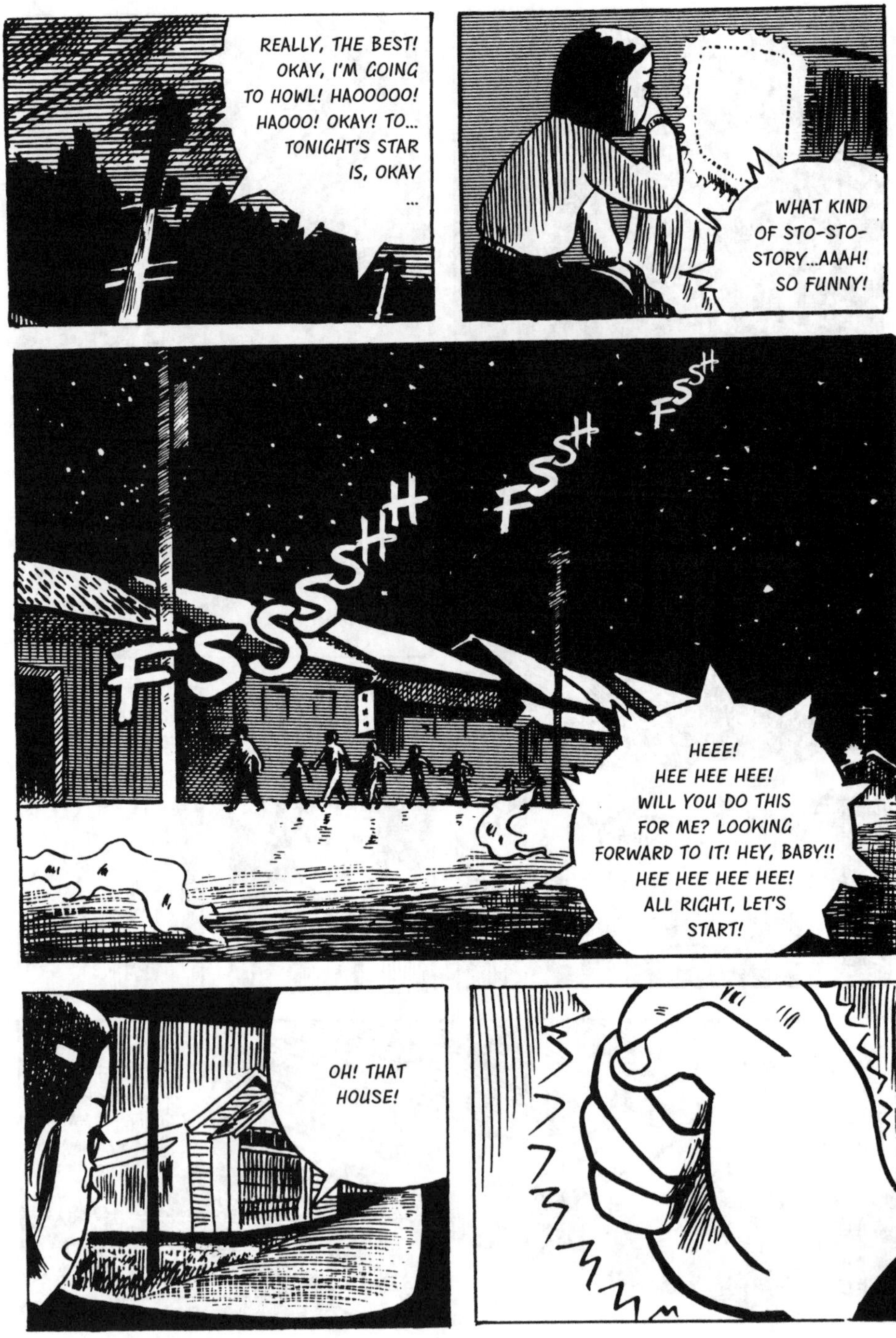
REALLY, THE BEST! OKAY, I'M GOING TO HOWL! HAOOOOO! HAOOO! OKAY! TO... TONIGHT'S STAR IS, OKAY ...
WHAT KIND OF STO-STO-STORY...AAAH! SO FUNNY!
FSSSSSHH FSSH FSSH
HEEE! HEE HEE HEE! WILL YOU DO THIS FOR ME? LOOKING FORWARD TO IT! HEY, BABY!! HEE HEE HEE HEE! ALL RIGHT, LET'S START!
OH! THAT HOUSE!

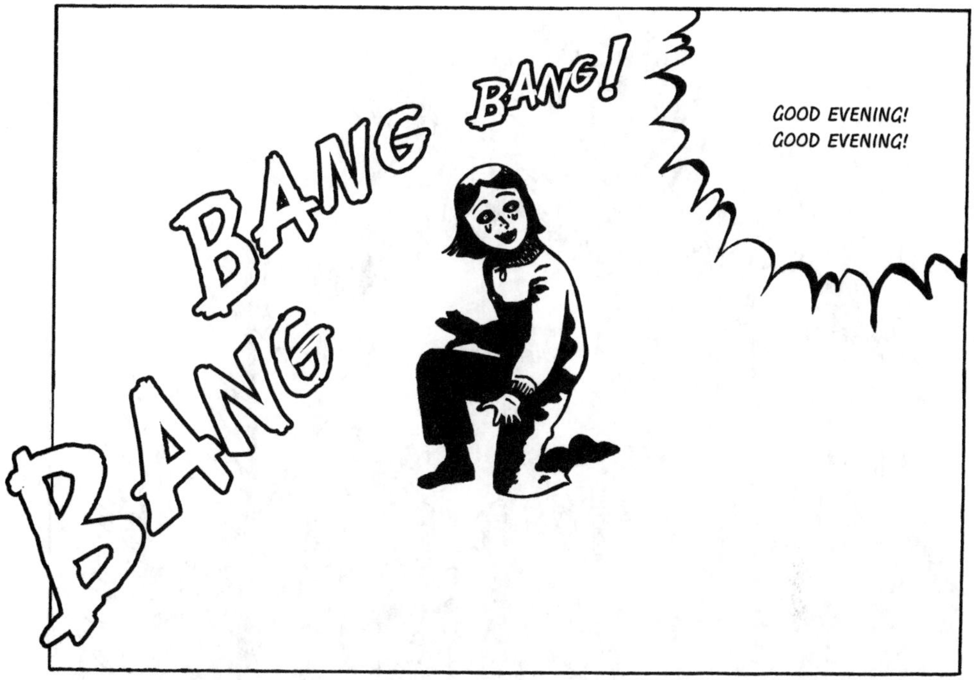
BANG BANG BANG!
GOOD EVENING!
GOOD EVENING!
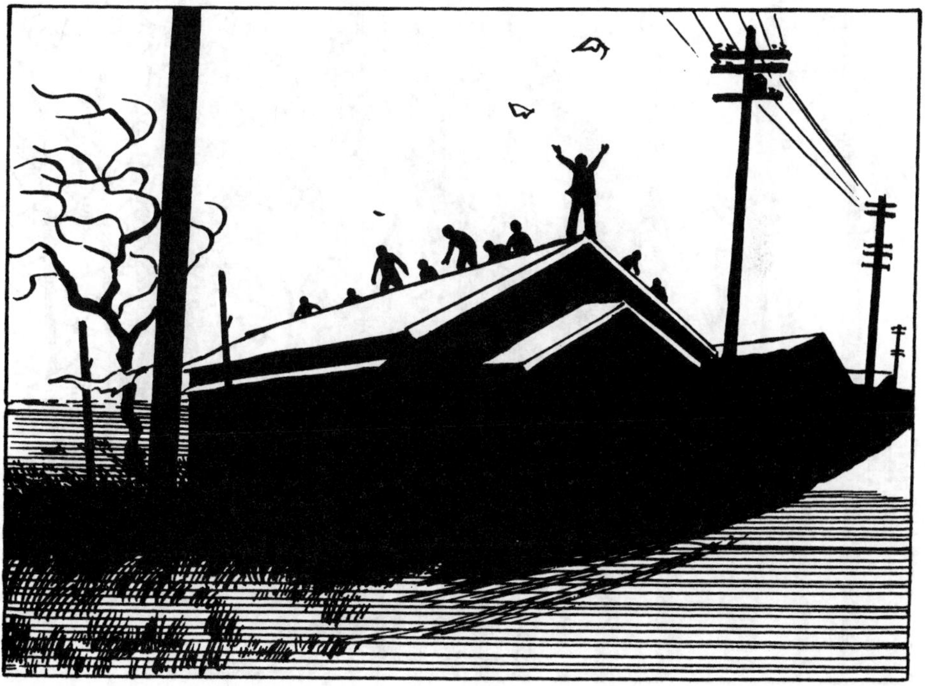

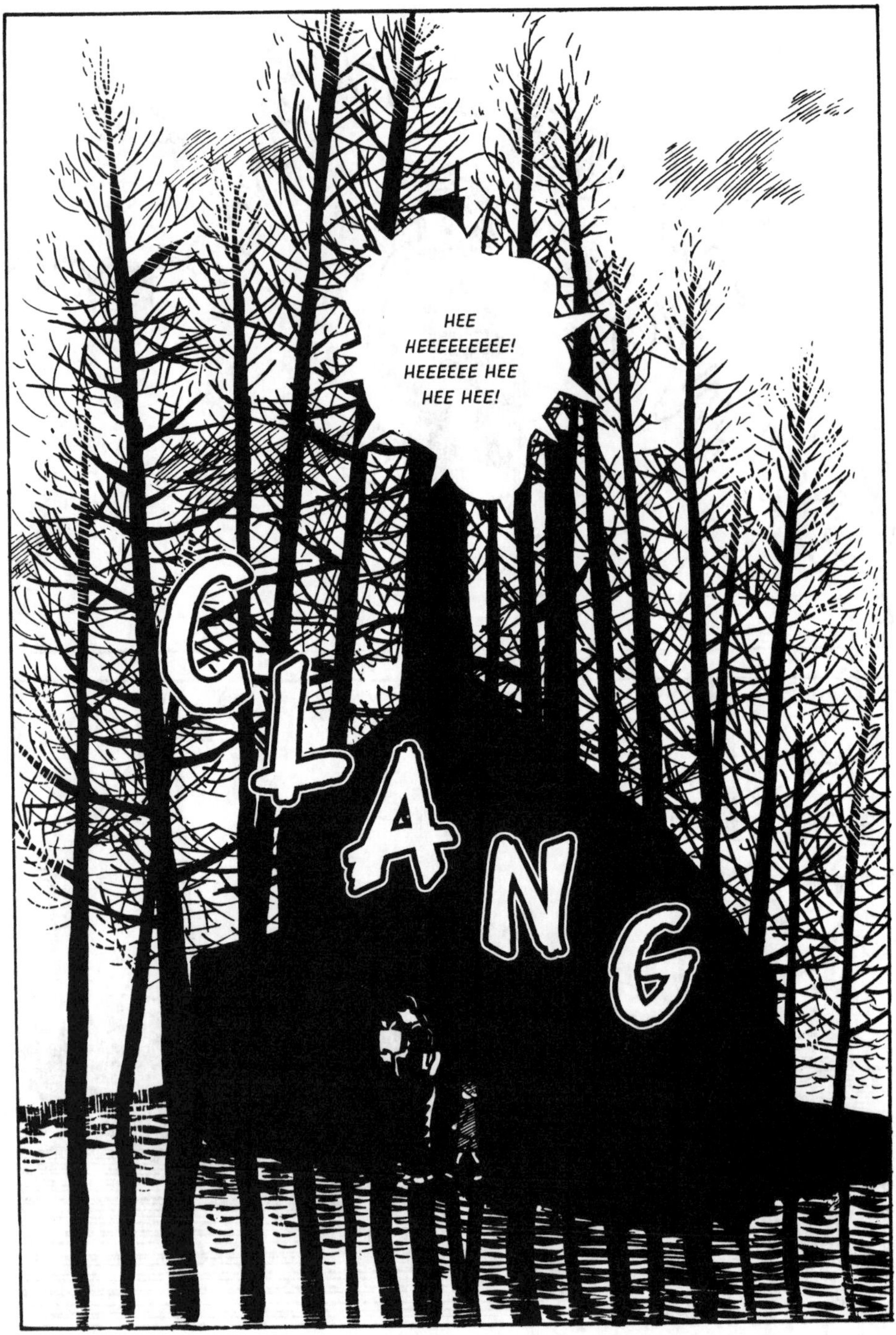
HEE HEEEEEEEEE! HEEEEEE HEE HEE HEE!
CLANG

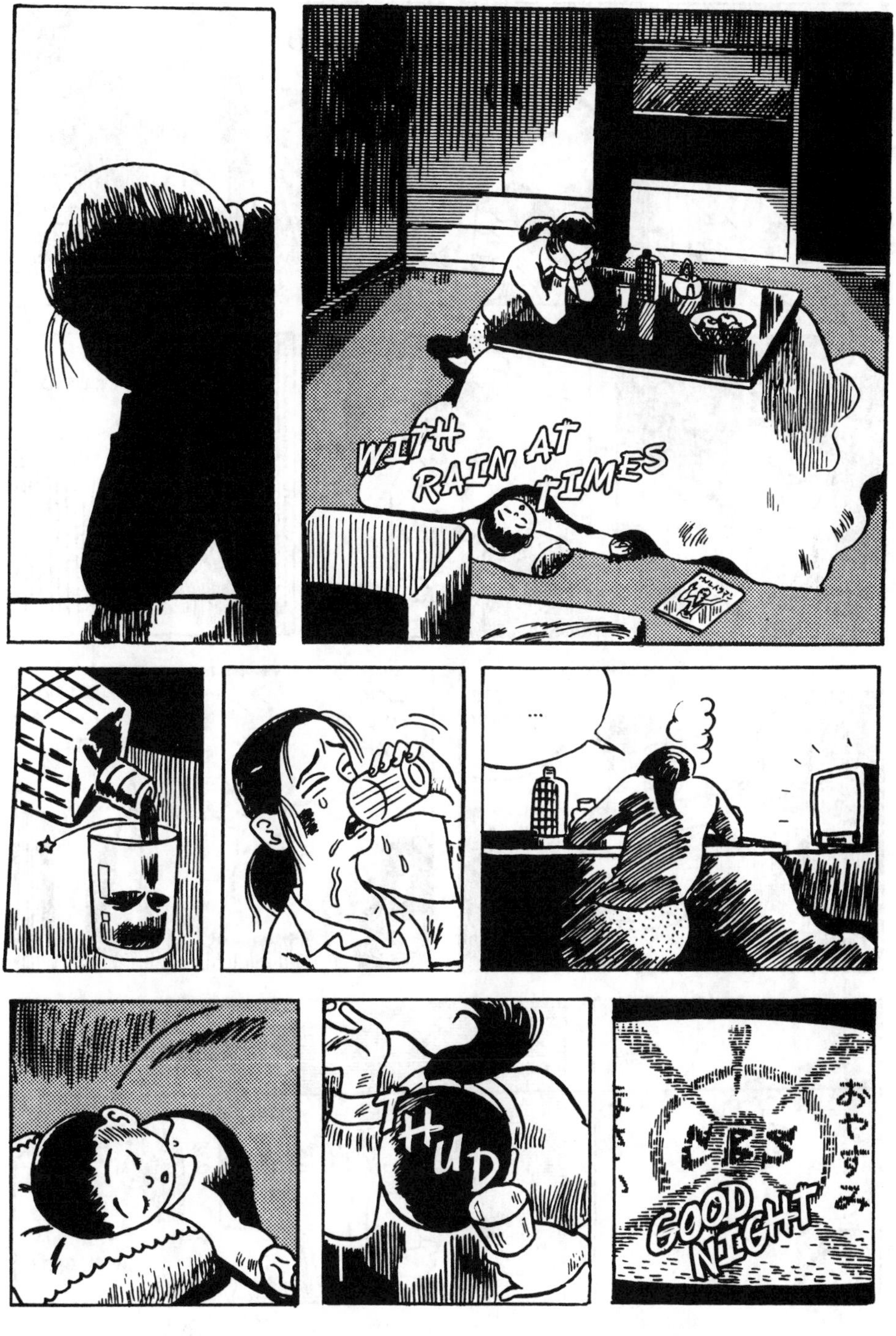
WITH RAIN AT TIMES
...
THUD
CBS
おやすみ
GOOD NIGHT

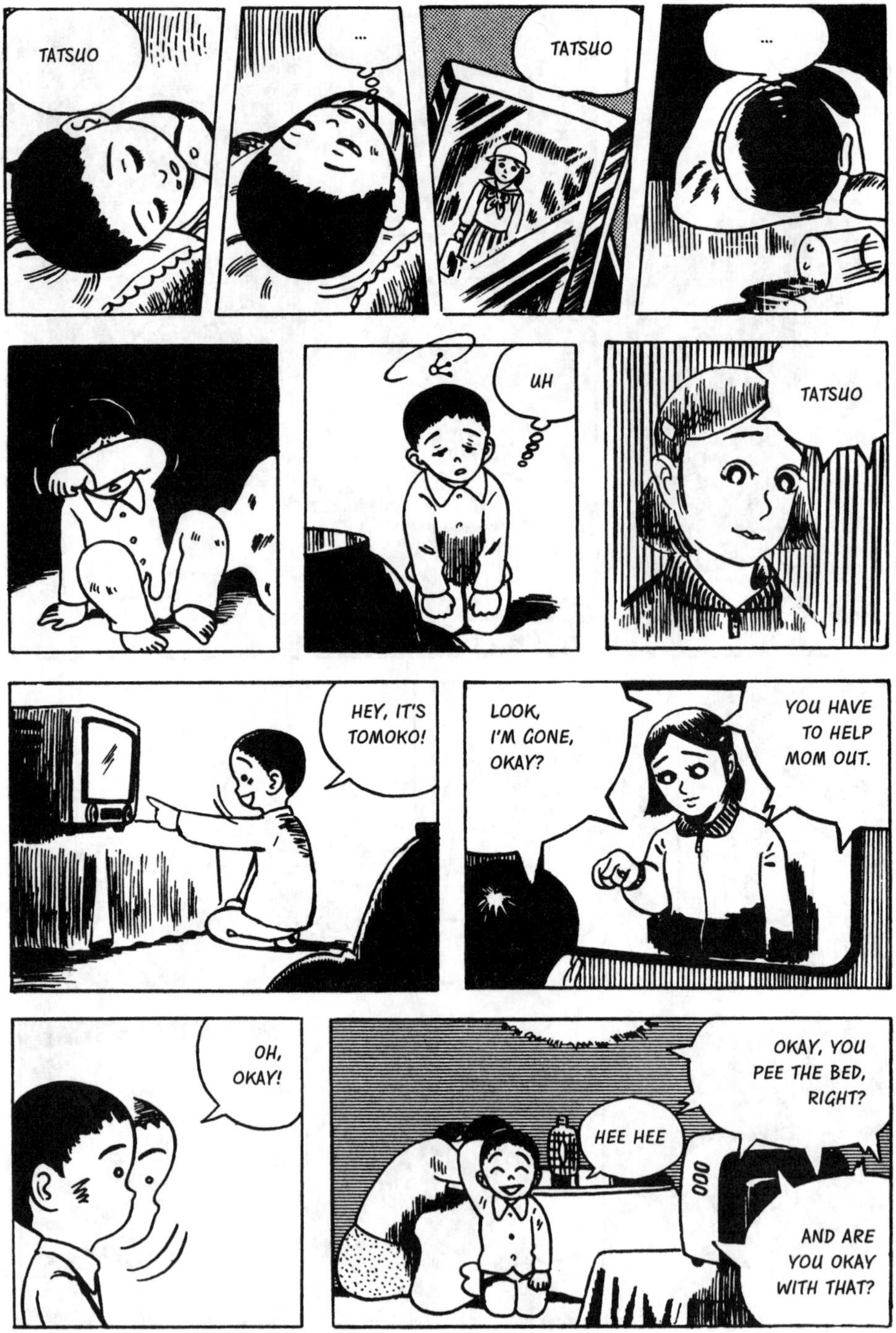
TATSUO
...
TATSUO
...
UH
TATSUO
HEY, IT'S TOMOKO!
LOOK, I'M GONE, OKAY?
YOU HAVE TO HELP MOM OUT.
OH, OKAY!
OKAY, YOU PEE THE BED, RIGHT?
HEE HEE
AND ARE YOU OKAY WITH THAT?

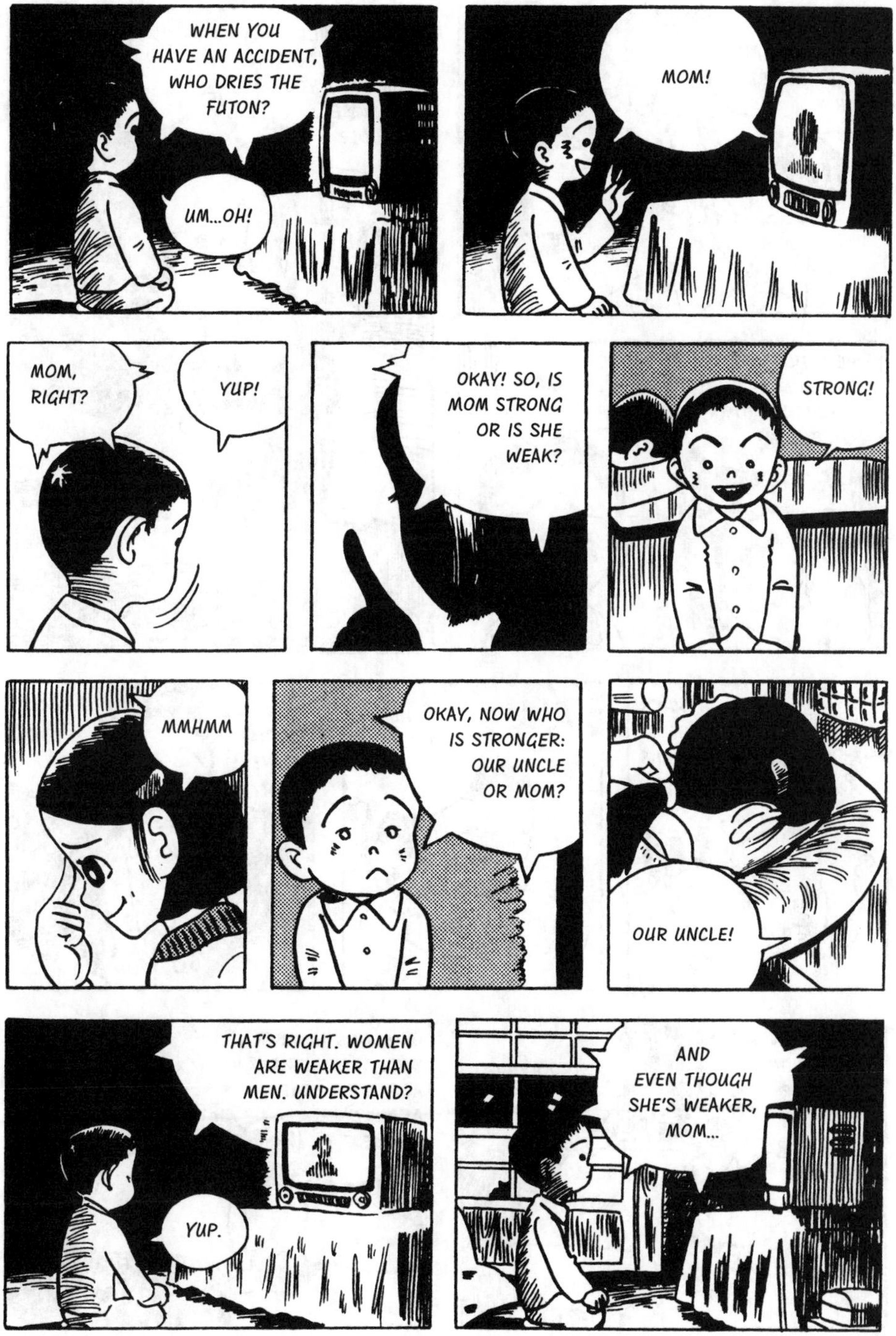
WHEN YOU HAVE AN ACCIDENT, WHO DRIES THE FUTON?
UM...OH!
MOM!
MOM, RIGHT?
YUP!
OKAY! SO, IS MOM STRONG OR IS SHE WEAK?
STRONG!
MMHMM
OKAY, NOW WHO IS STRONGER: OUR UNCLE OR MOM?
OUR UNCLE!
THAT'S RIGHT. WOMEN ARE WEAKER THAN MEN. UNDERSTAND?
YUP.
AND EVEN THOUGH SHE'S WEAKER, MOM...

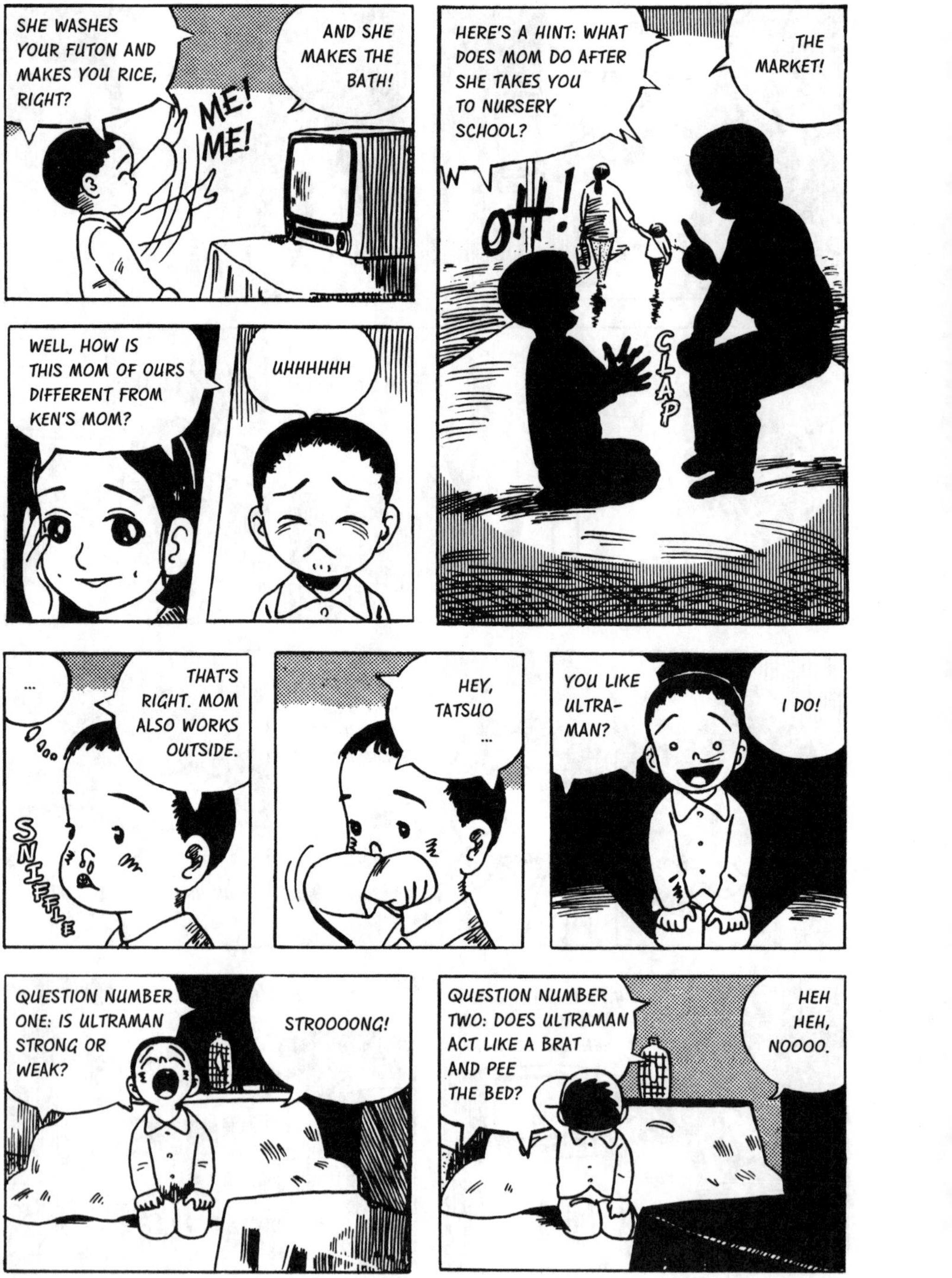

SHE WASHES YOUR FUTON AND MAKES YOU RICE, RIGHT?
ME! ME!
AND SHE MAKES THE BATH!
WELL, HOW IS THIS MOM OF OURS DIFFERENT FROM KEN'S MOM?
UHHHHHH
HERE'S A HINT: WHAT DOES MOM DO AFTER SHE TAKES YOU TO NURSERY SCHOOL?
THE MARKET!
OH!
CLAP
...
THAT'S RIGHT. MOM ALSO WORKS OUTSIDE.
SNIFFLE
HEY, TATSUO ...
YOU LIKE ULTRA-MAN?
I DO!
QUESTION NUMBER ONE: IS ULTRAMAN STRONG OR WEAK?
STROOOONG!
QUESTION NUMBER TWO: DOES ULTRAMAN ACT LIKE A BRAT AND PEE THE BED?
HEH HEH, NOOOO.

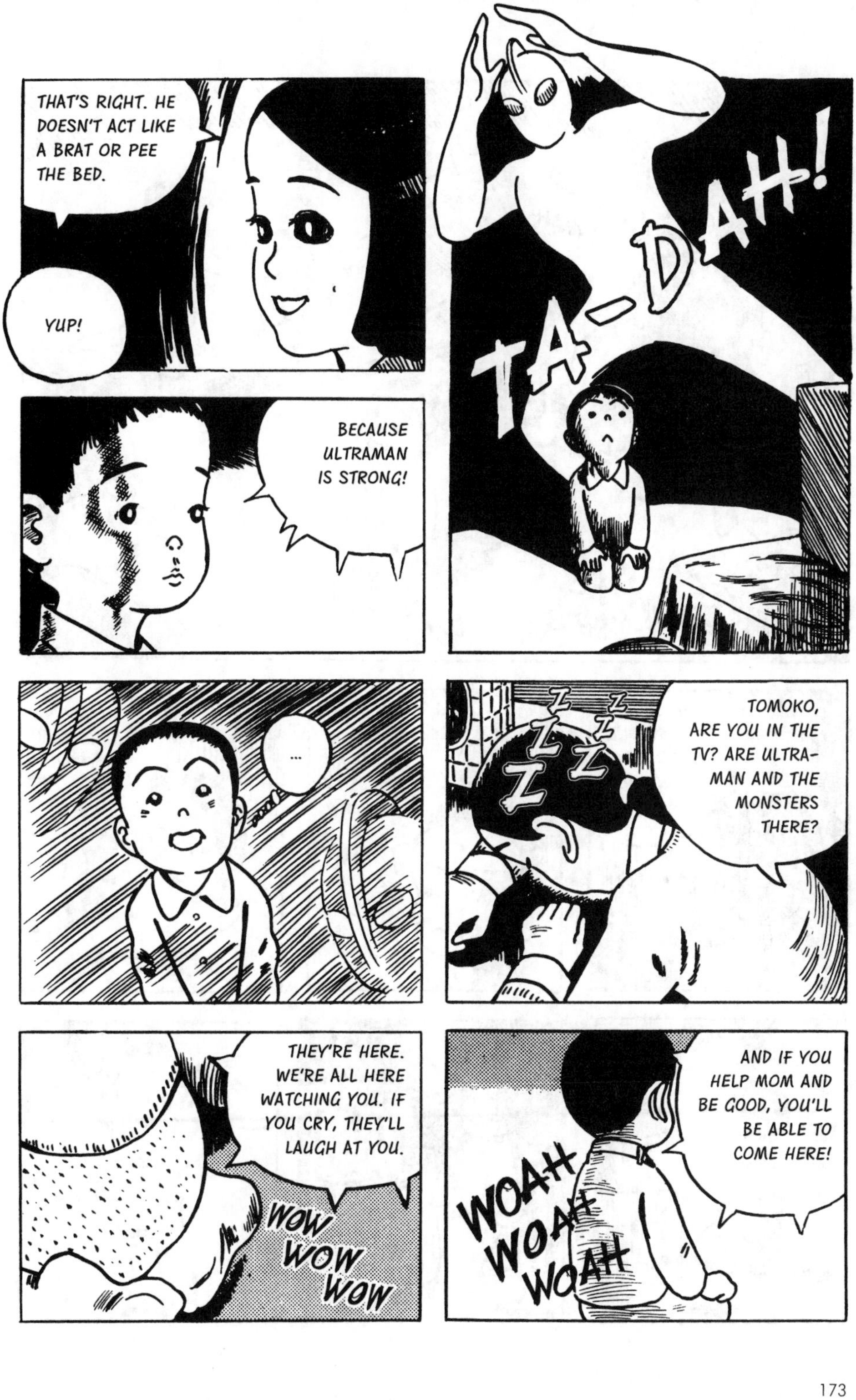
THAT'S RIGHT. HE DOESN'T ACT LIKE A BRAT OR PEE THE BED.
YUP!
TA-DAH!
BECAUSE ULTRAMAN IS STRONG!
...
TOMOKO, ARE YOU IN THE TV? ARE ULTRA-MAN AND THE MONSTERS THERE?
THEY'RE HERE. WE'RE ALL HERE WATCHING YOU. IF YOU CRY, THEY'LL LAUGH AT YOU.
WOW WOW WOW
AND IF YOU HELP MOM AND BE GOOD, YOU'LL BE ABLE TO COME HERE!
WOAH WOAH WOAH

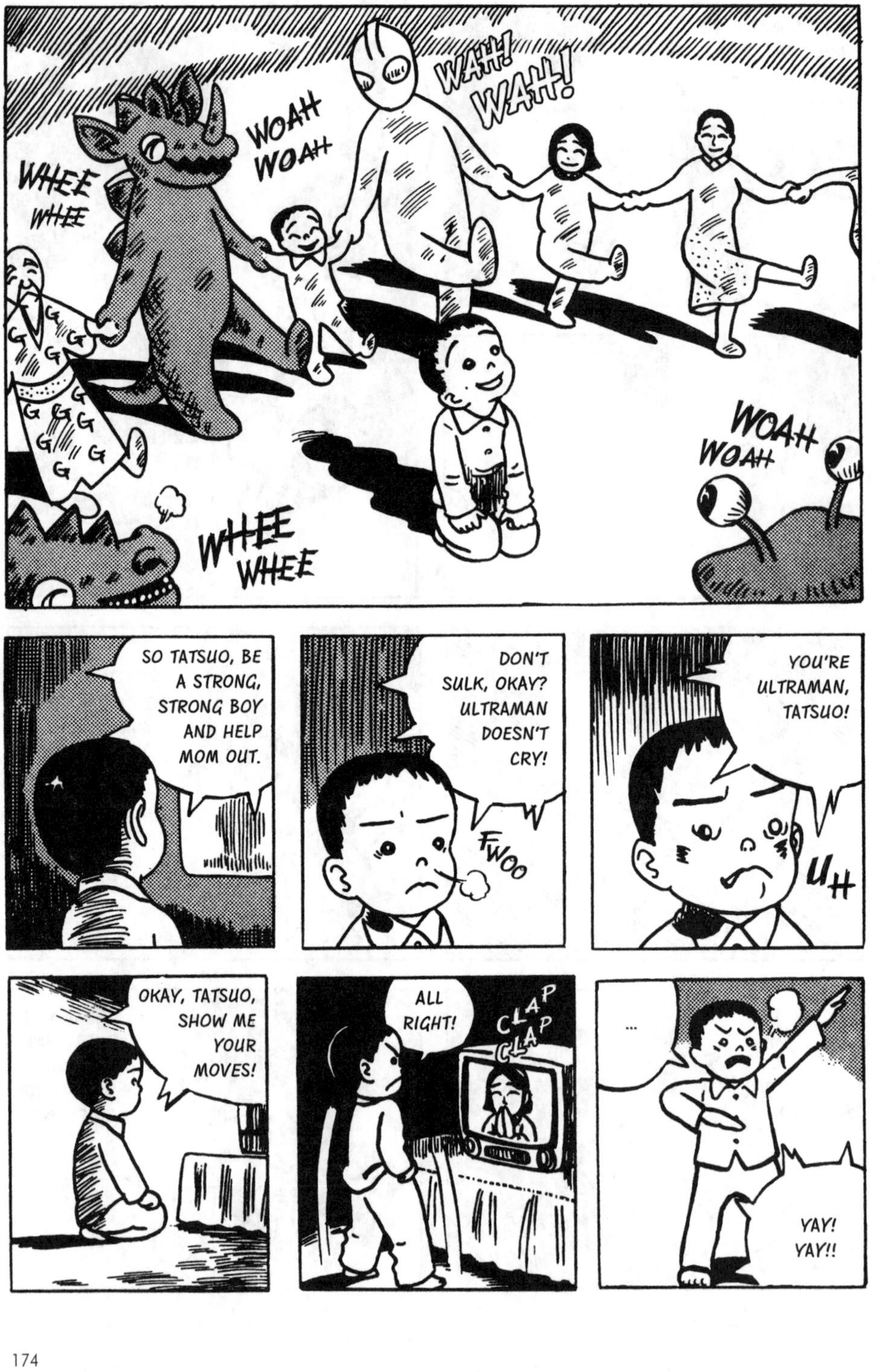
WHEE WHEE
WOAH WOAH
WAH! WAH!
WHEE WHEE
WOAH WOAH
SO TATSUO, BE A STRONG, STRONG BOY AND HELP MOM OUT.
DON'T SULK, OKAY? ULTRAMAN DOESN'T CRY!
FWOO
YOU'RE ULTRAMAN, TATSUO!
UH
OKAY, TATSUO, SHOW ME YOUR MOVES!
ALL RIGHT!
CLAP CLAP CLAP
...
YAY! YAY!!

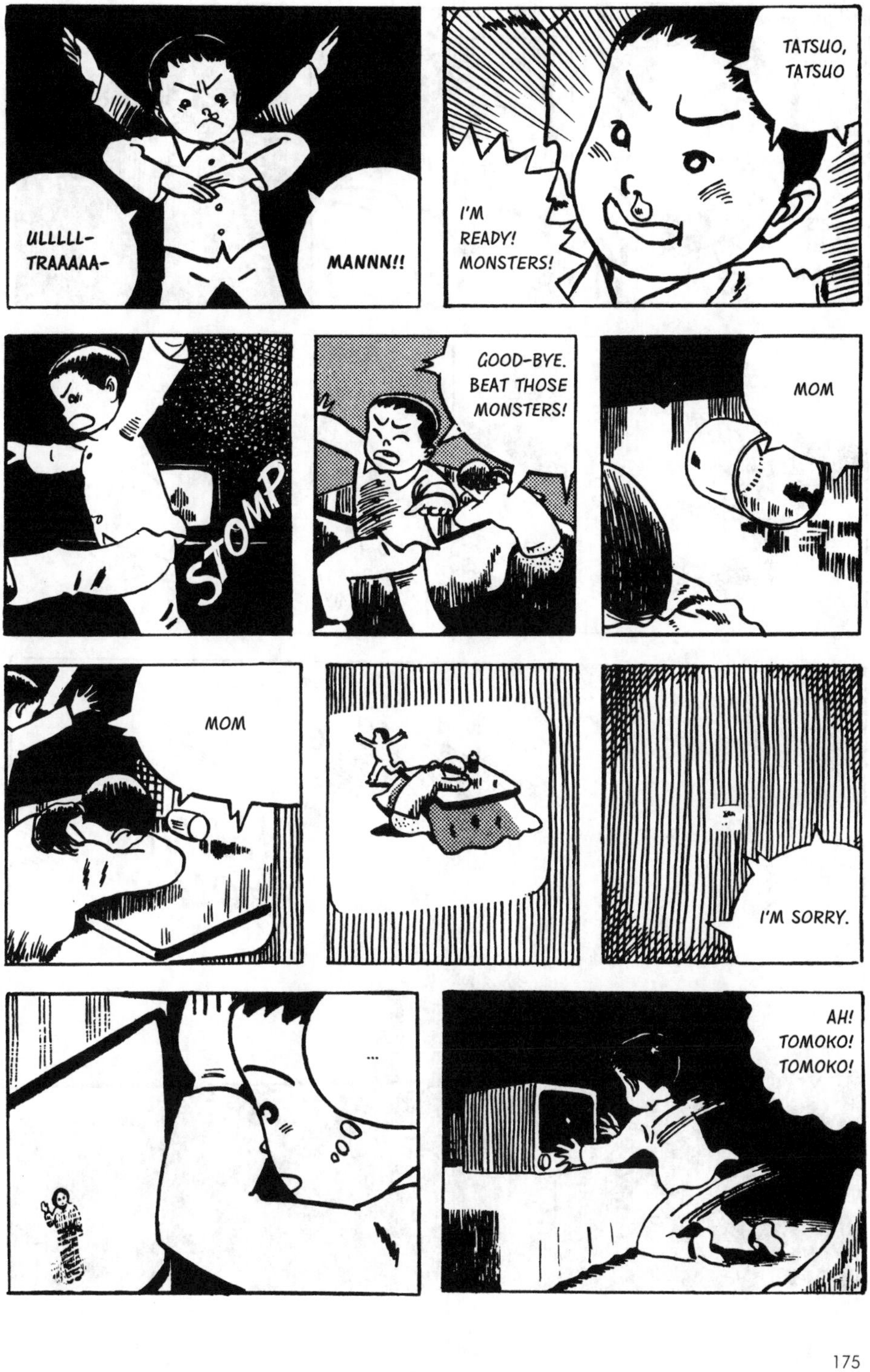
ULLLLL-
TRAAAAA-
MANNN!!
TATSUO, TATSUO
I'M READY! MONSTERS!
STOMP
GOOD-BYE. BEAT THOSE MONSTERS!
MOM
MOM
I'M SORRY.
...
AH! TOMOKO! TOMOKO!

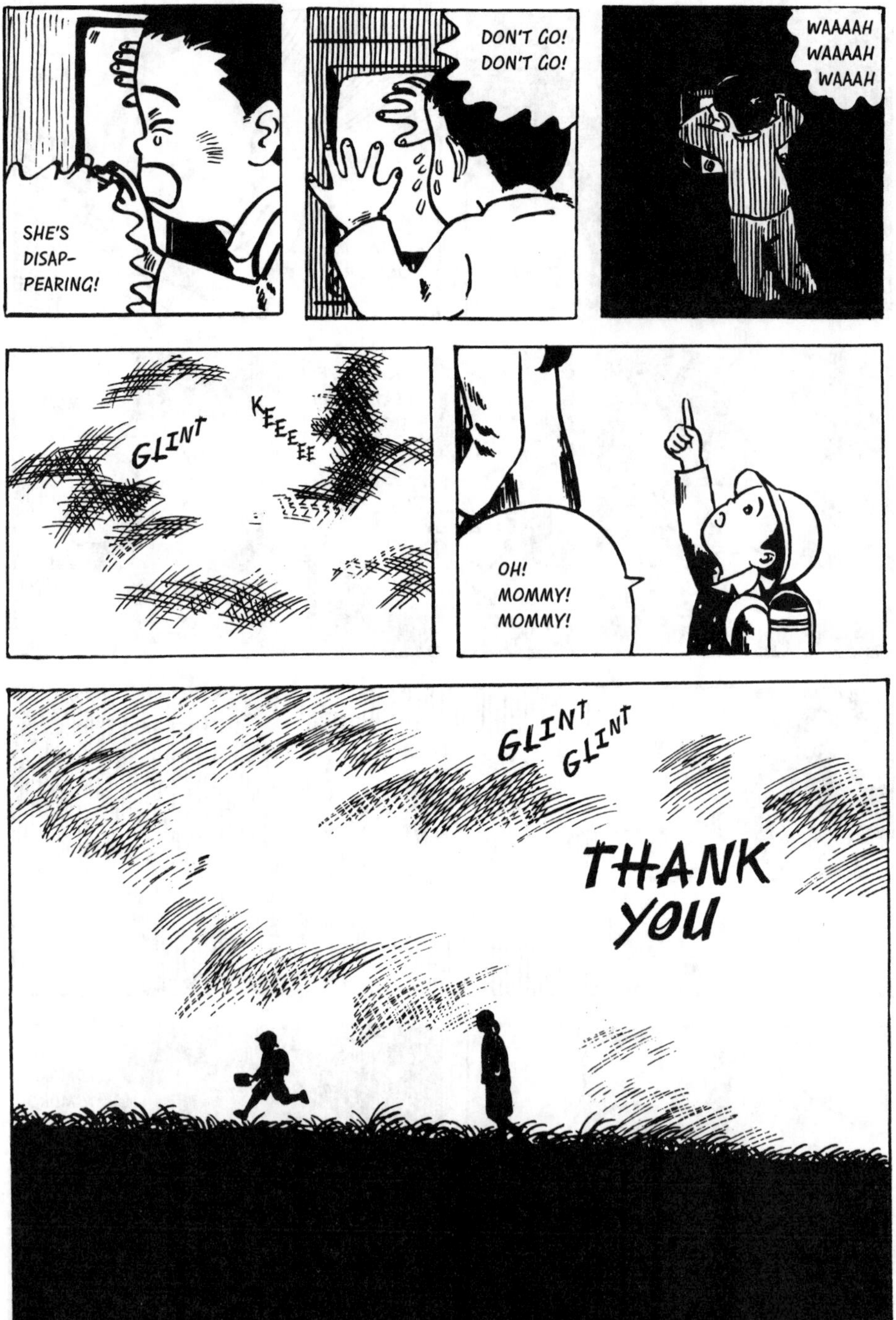
SHE'S DISAP-PEARING!
DON'T GO! DON'T GO!
WAAAAH WAAAAH WAAAH
GLINT
KEEEEE
OH! MOMMY! MOMMY!
GLINT GLINT
THANK YOU

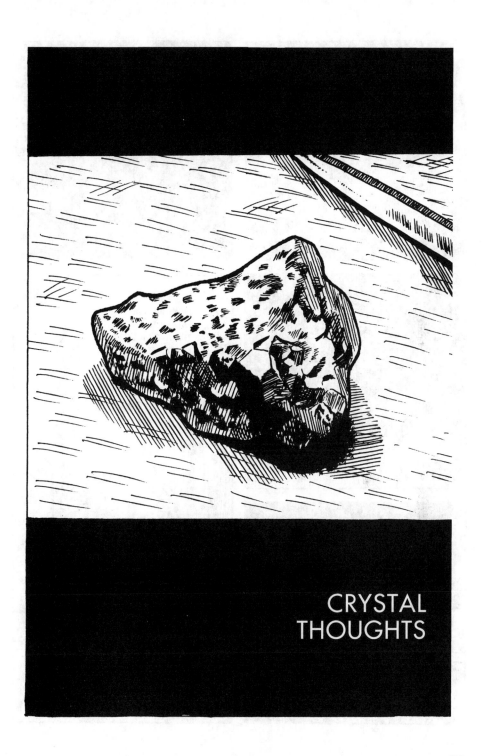

CRYSTAL
THOUGHTS

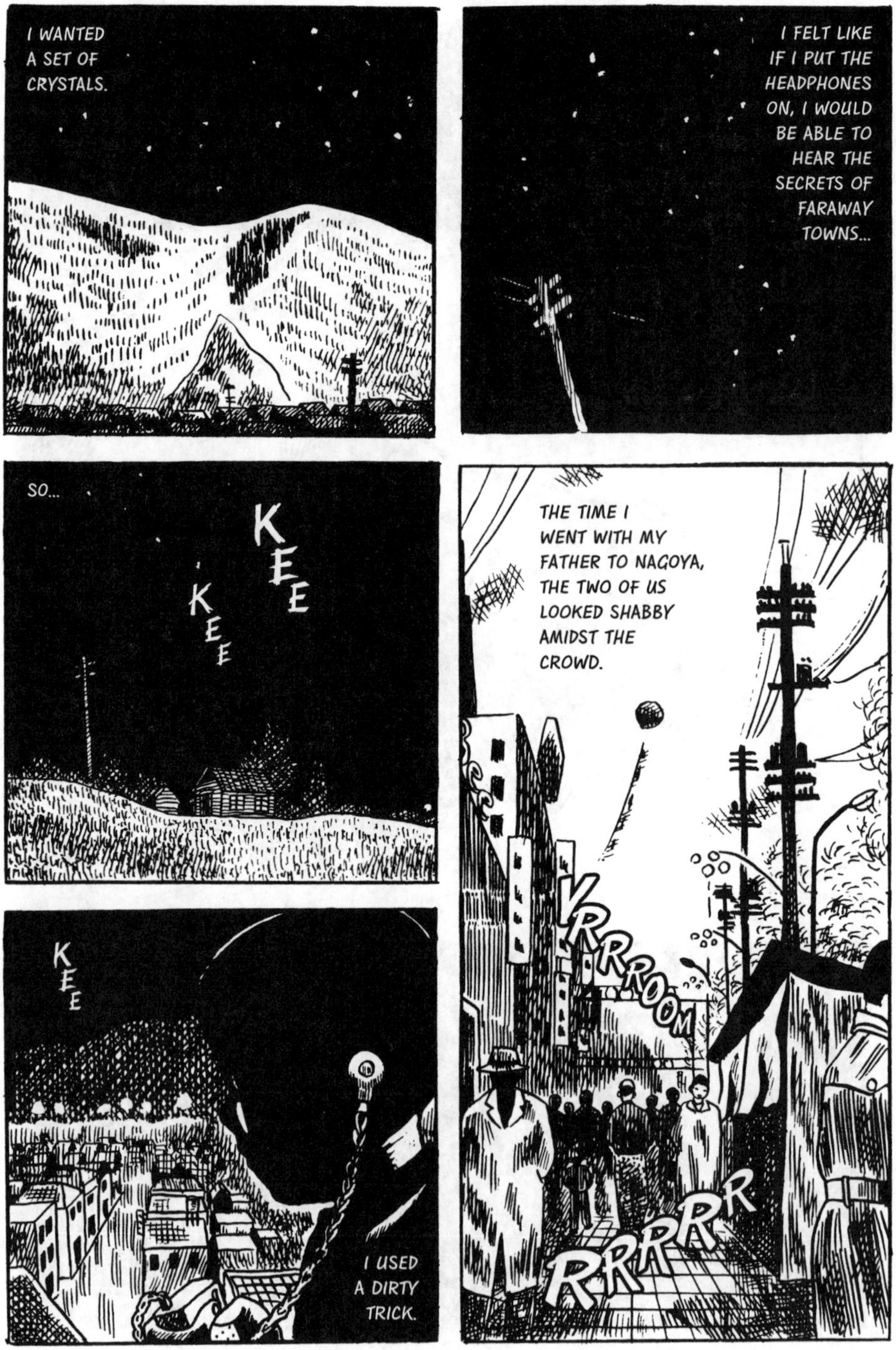
I WANTED A SET OF CRYSTALS.
I FELT LIKE IF I PUT THE HEADPHONES ON, I WOULD BE ABLE TO HEAR THE SECRETS OF FARAWAY TOWNS...
SO...
KEE
KEE
KEE
I USED A DIRTY TRICK.
THE TIME I WENT WITH MY FATHER TO NAGOYA, THE TWO OF US LOOKED SHABBY AMIDST THE CROWD.
VRRROOM
RRRRRR

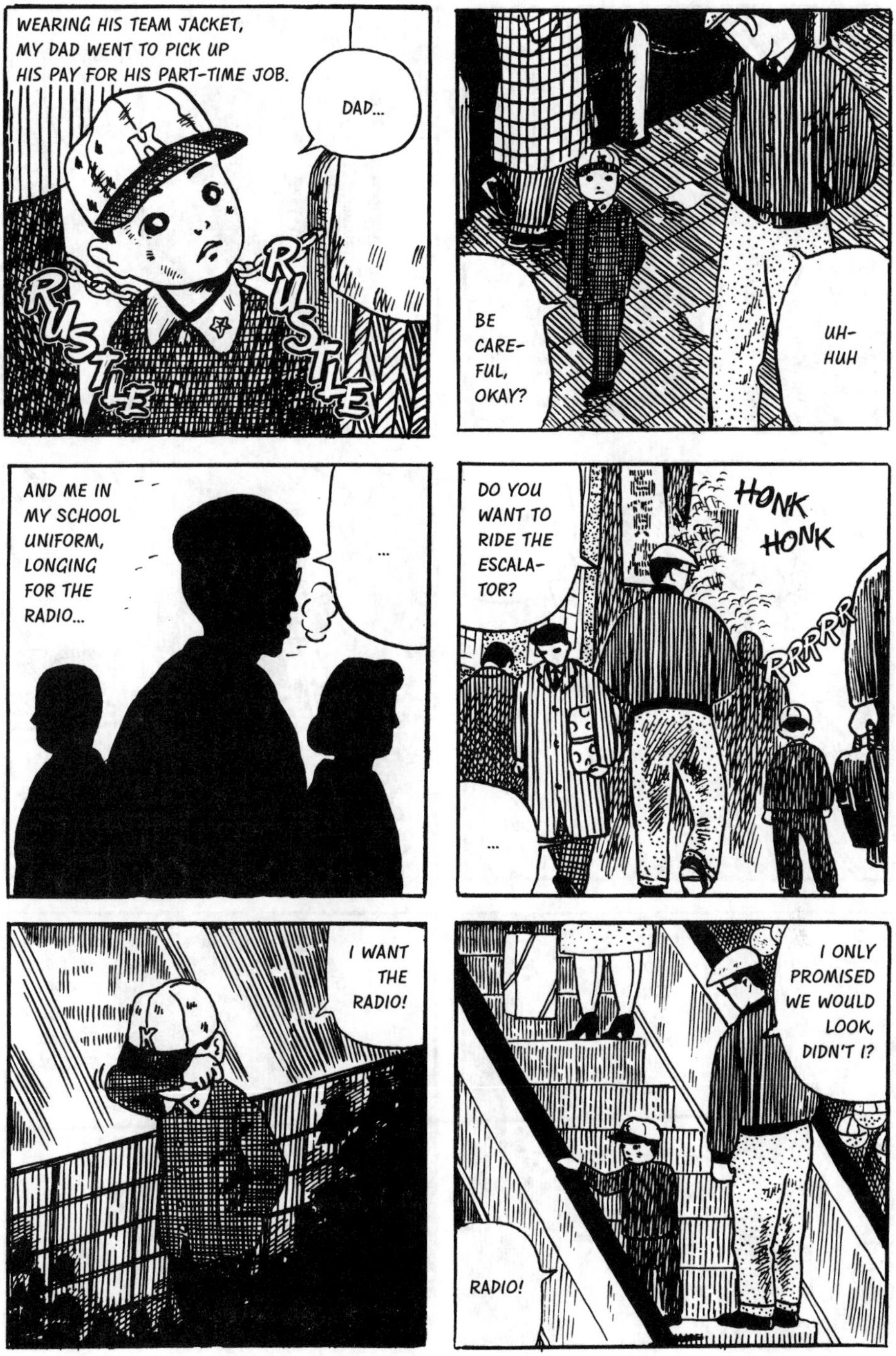
WEARING HIS TEAM JACKET, MY DAD WENT TO PICK UP HIS PAY FOR HIS PART-TIME JOB.
DAD...
RUSTLE
RUSTLE
BE CARE-FUL, OKAY?
UH-HUH
AND ME IN MY SCHOOL UNIFORM, LONGING FOR THE RADIO...
...
DO YOU WANT TO RIDE THE ESCALA-TOR?
HONK HONK
RRRRRR
...
I WANT THE RADIO!
I ONLY PROMISED WE WOULD LOOK, DIDN'T I?
RADIO!

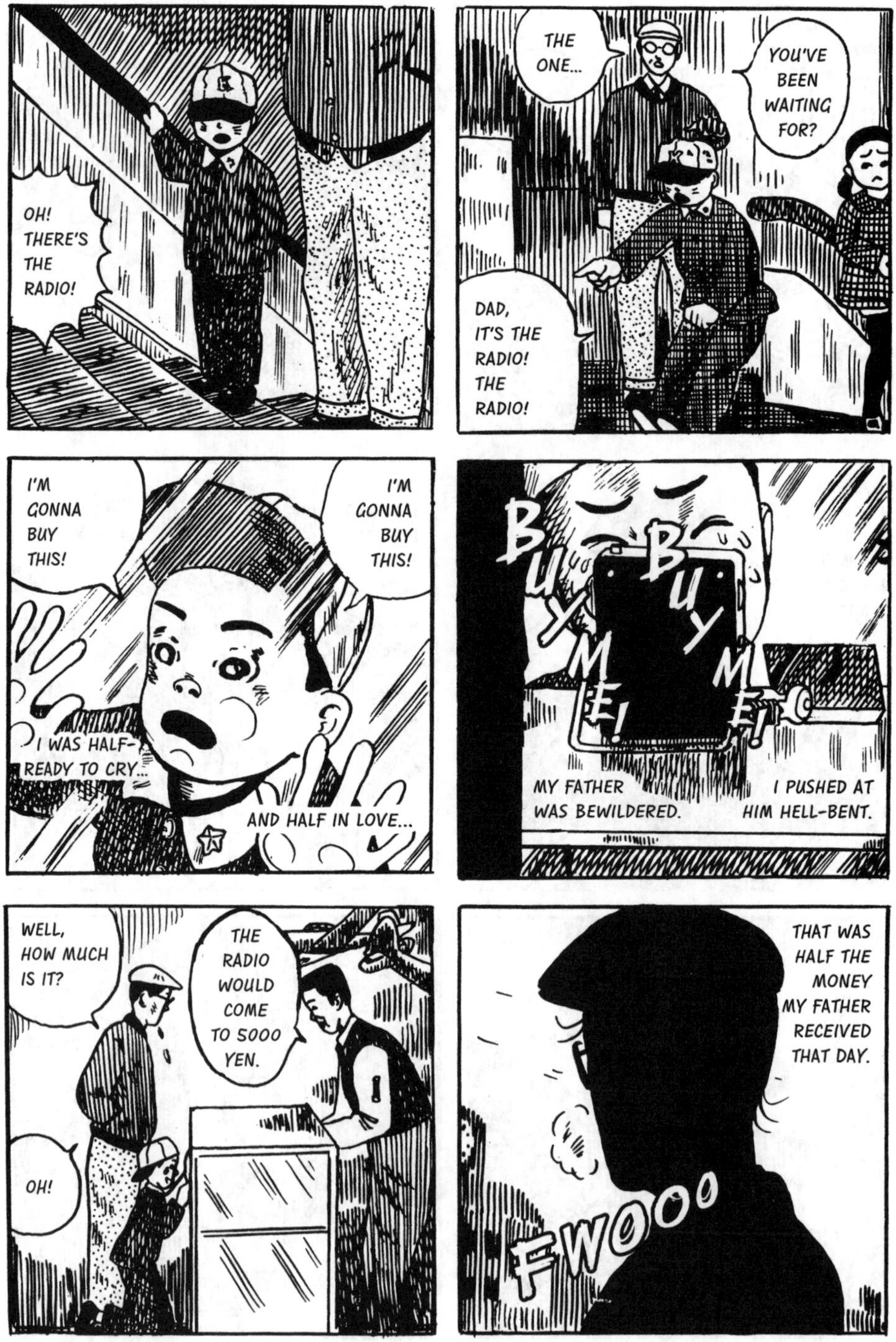
OH! THERE'S THE RADIO!
THE ONE...
YOU'VE BEEN WAITING FOR?
DAD, IT'S THE RADIO! THE RADIO!
I'M GONNA BUY THIS!
I'M GONNA BUY THIS!
I WAS HALF-READY TO CRY...
AND HALF IN LOVE...
BUY ME!
BUY ME!
MY FATHER WAS BEWILDERED.
I PUSHED AT HIM HELL-BENT.
WELL, HOW MUCH IS IT?
THE RADIO WOULD COME TO 5000 YEN.
OH!
THAT WAS HALF THE MONEY MY FATHER RECEIVED THAT DAY.
FWOOO

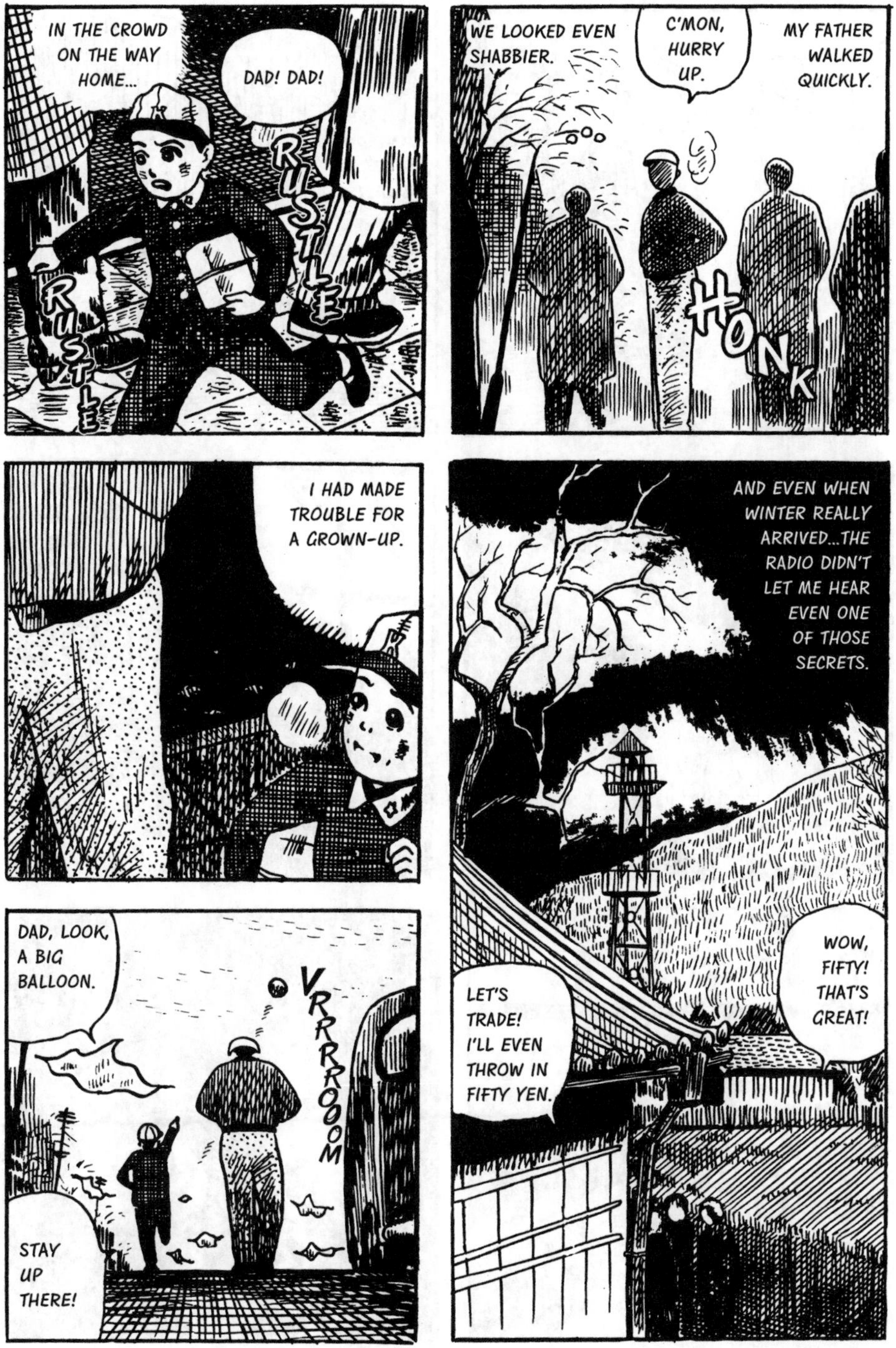
IN THE CROWD ON THE WAY HOME...
DAD! DAD!
RUSTLE
RUSTLE
WE LOOKED EVEN SHABBIER.
C'MON, HURRY UP.
MY FATHER WALKED QUICKLY.
HONK
I HAD MADE TROUBLE FOR A GROWN-UP.
DAD, LOOK, A BIG BALLOON.
VRRRROOOOM
STAY UP THERE!
AND EVEN WHEN WINTER REALLY ARRIVED...THE RADIO DIDN'T LET ME HEAR EVEN ONE OF THOSE SECRETS.
WOW, FIFTY! THAT'S GREAT!
LET'S TRADE! I'LL EVEN THROW IN FIFTY YEN.

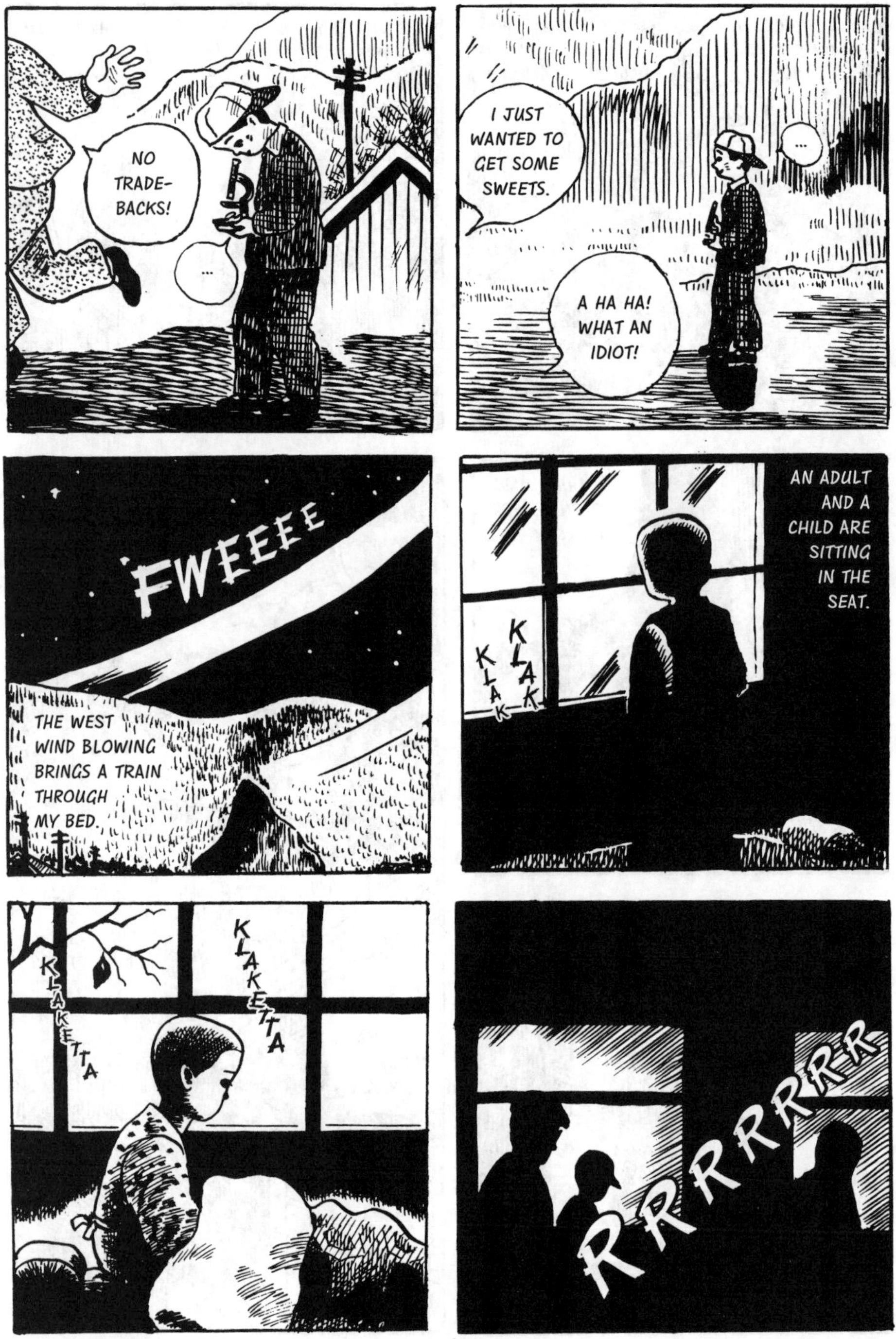
NO TRADE-BACKS!
...
I JUST WANTED TO GET SOME SWEETS.
...
A HA HA! WHAT AN IDIOT!
FWEEEE
THE WEST WIND BLOWING BRINGS A TRAIN THROUGH MY BED.
AN ADULT AND A CHILD ARE SITTING IN THE SEAT.
KLAK KLAK
KLAKETTA KLAKETTA
RRRRRRRR

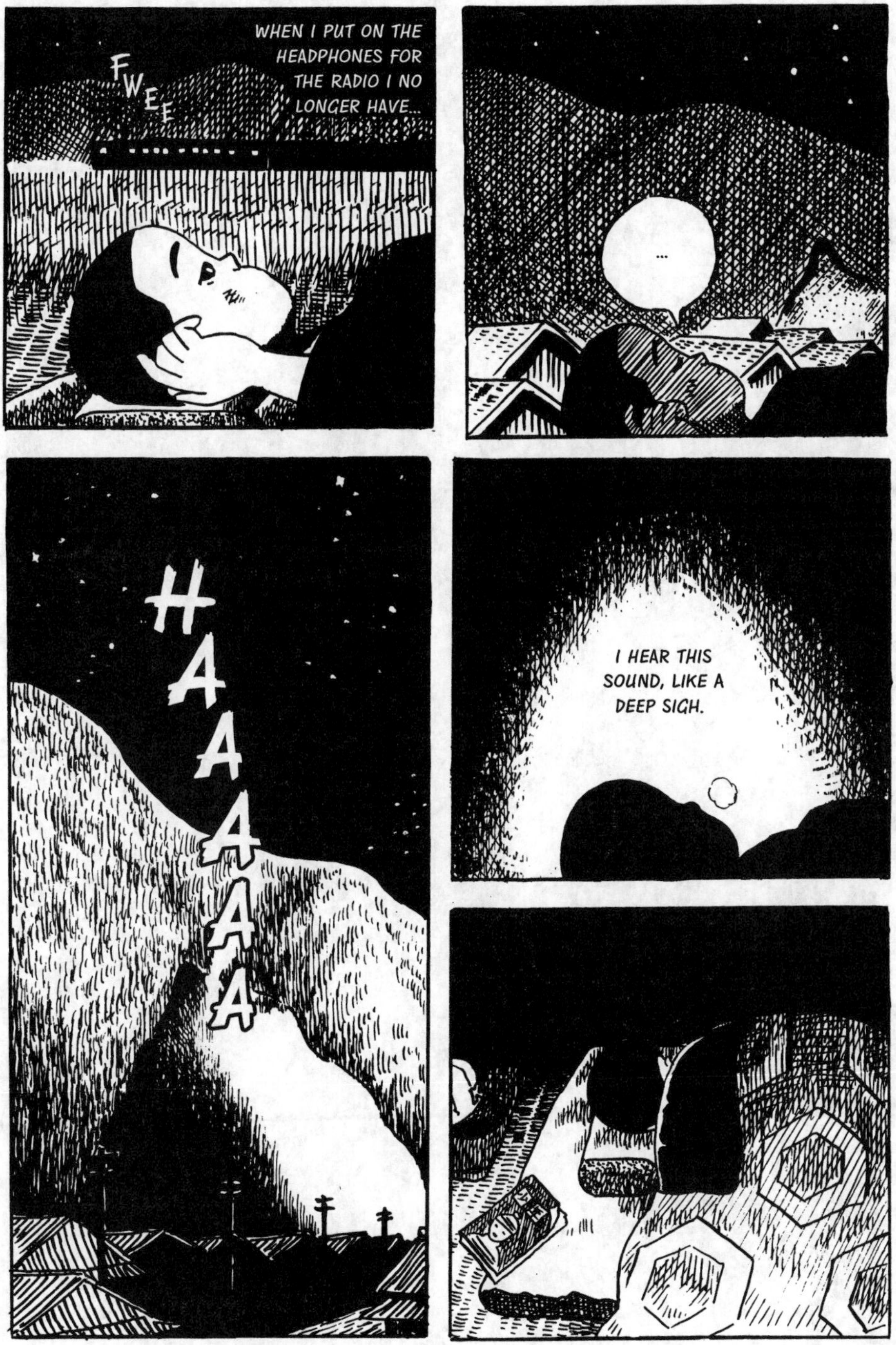
WHEN I PUT ON THE HEADPHONES FOR THE RADIO I NO LONGER HAVE...
FWEE
...
HAAAAAAA
I HEAR THIS SOUND, LIKE A DEEP SIGH.

MOUNTAIN
TOWN

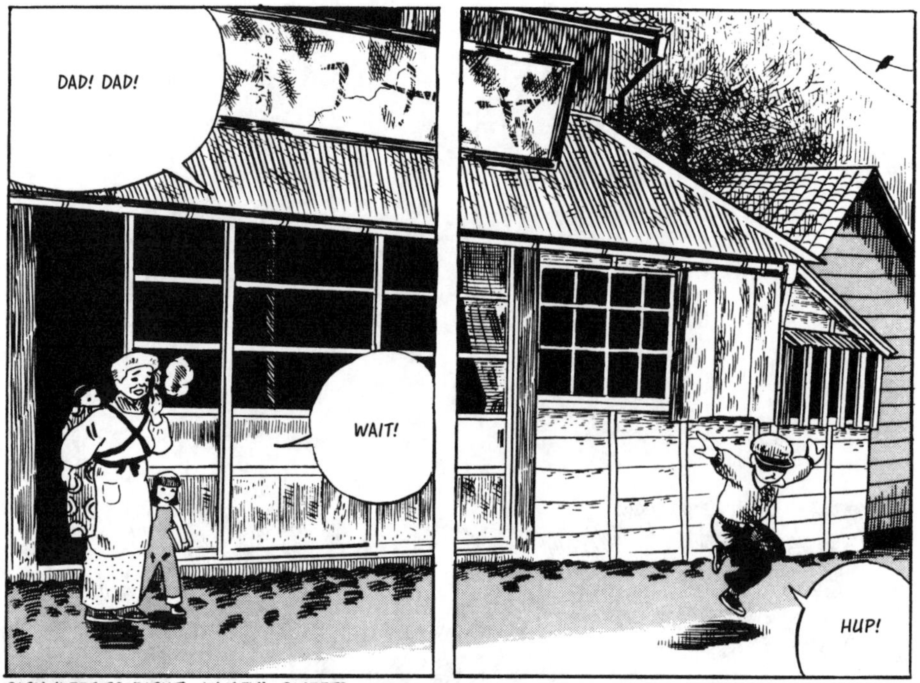
DAD! DAD!
WAIT!
HUP!

SIGN (LEFT TO RIGHT): KAMEYA; SWEETS

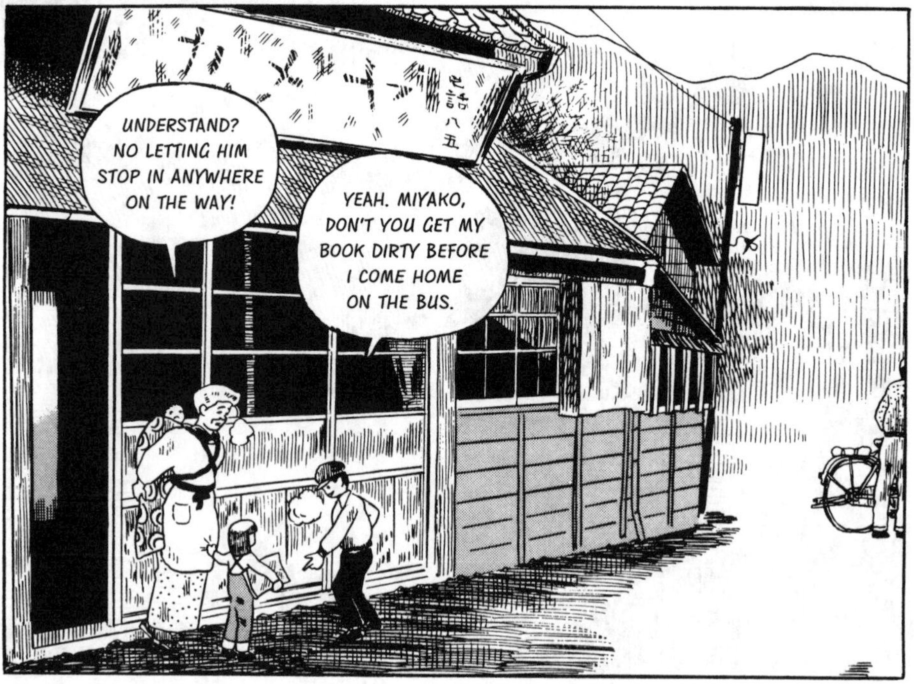
UNDERSTAND? NO LETTING HIM STOP IN ANYWHERE ON THE WAY!
YEAH. MIYAKO, DON'T YOU GET MY BOOK DIRTY BEFORE I COME HOME ON THE BUS.

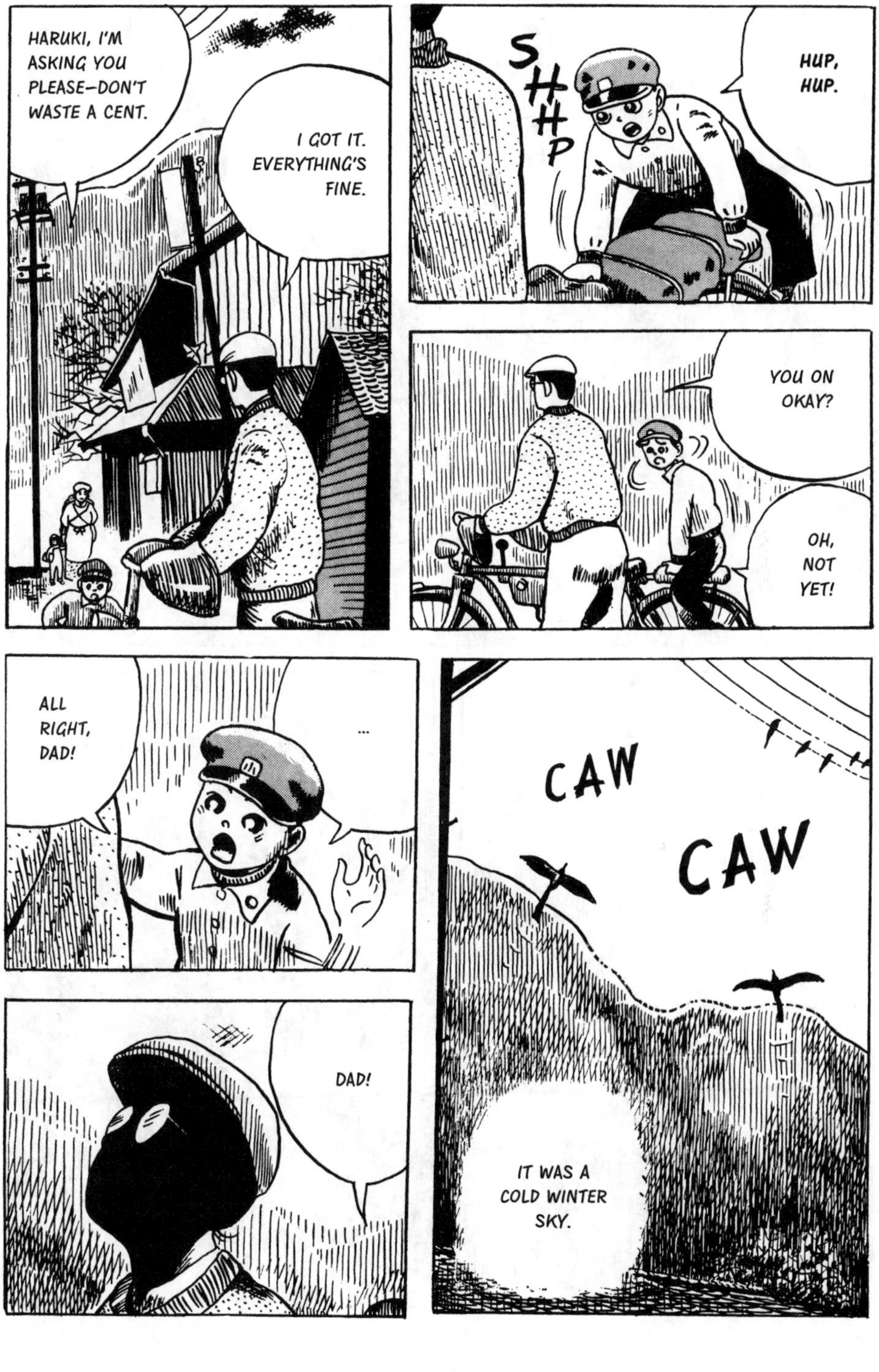
HARUKI, I'M ASKING YOU PLEASE—DON'T WASTE A CENT.
I GOT IT. EVERYTHING'S FINE.
SHHP
HUP, HUP.
YOU ON OKAY?
OH, NOT YET!
ALL RIGHT, DAD!
...
DAD!
CAW
CAW
IT WAS A COLD WINTER SKY.

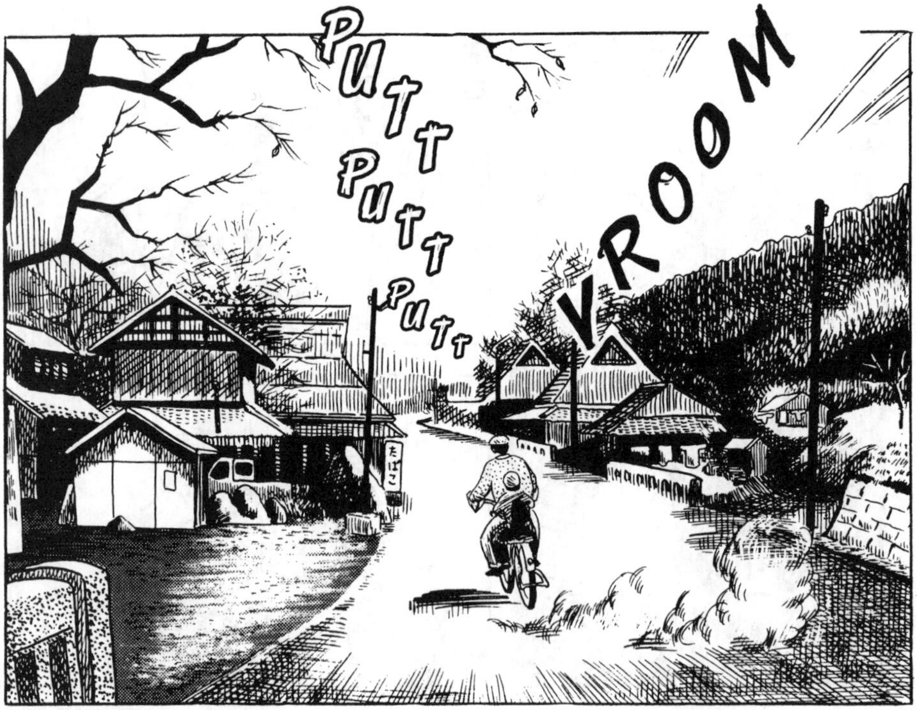
PUTT
PUTT
PUTT
VROOM
たばこ
SIGN: CIGARETTES

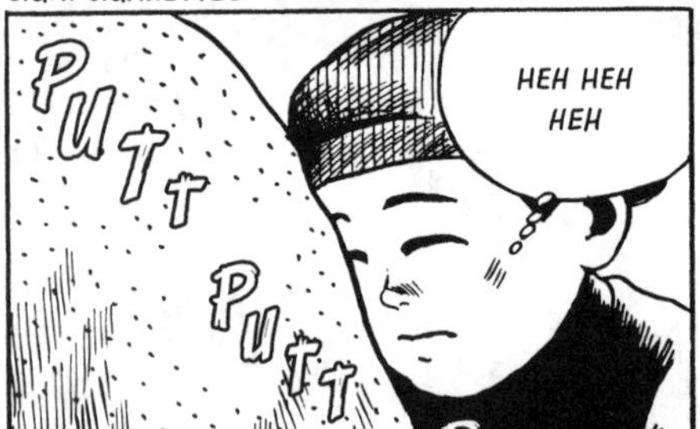
HEH HEH HEH
PUTT
PUTT
PUTT

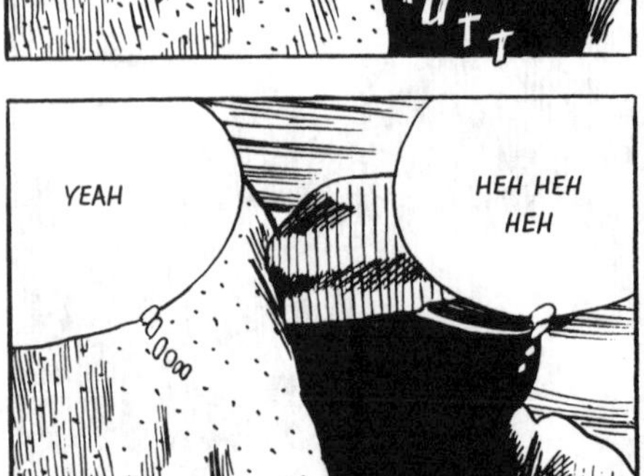
YEAH
HEH HEH HEH

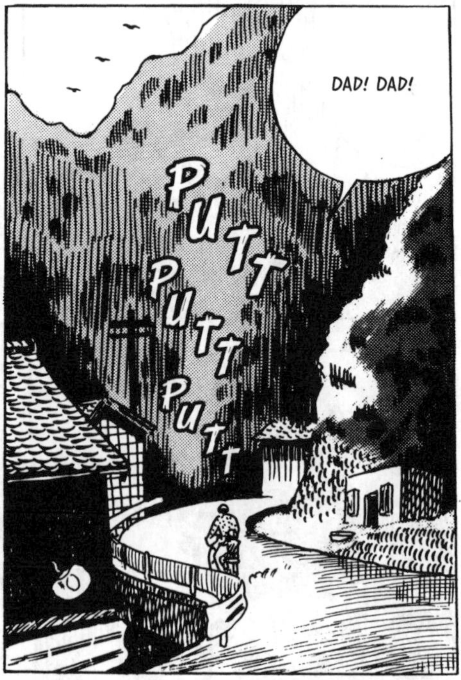
DAD! DAD!
PUTT
PUTT
PUTT

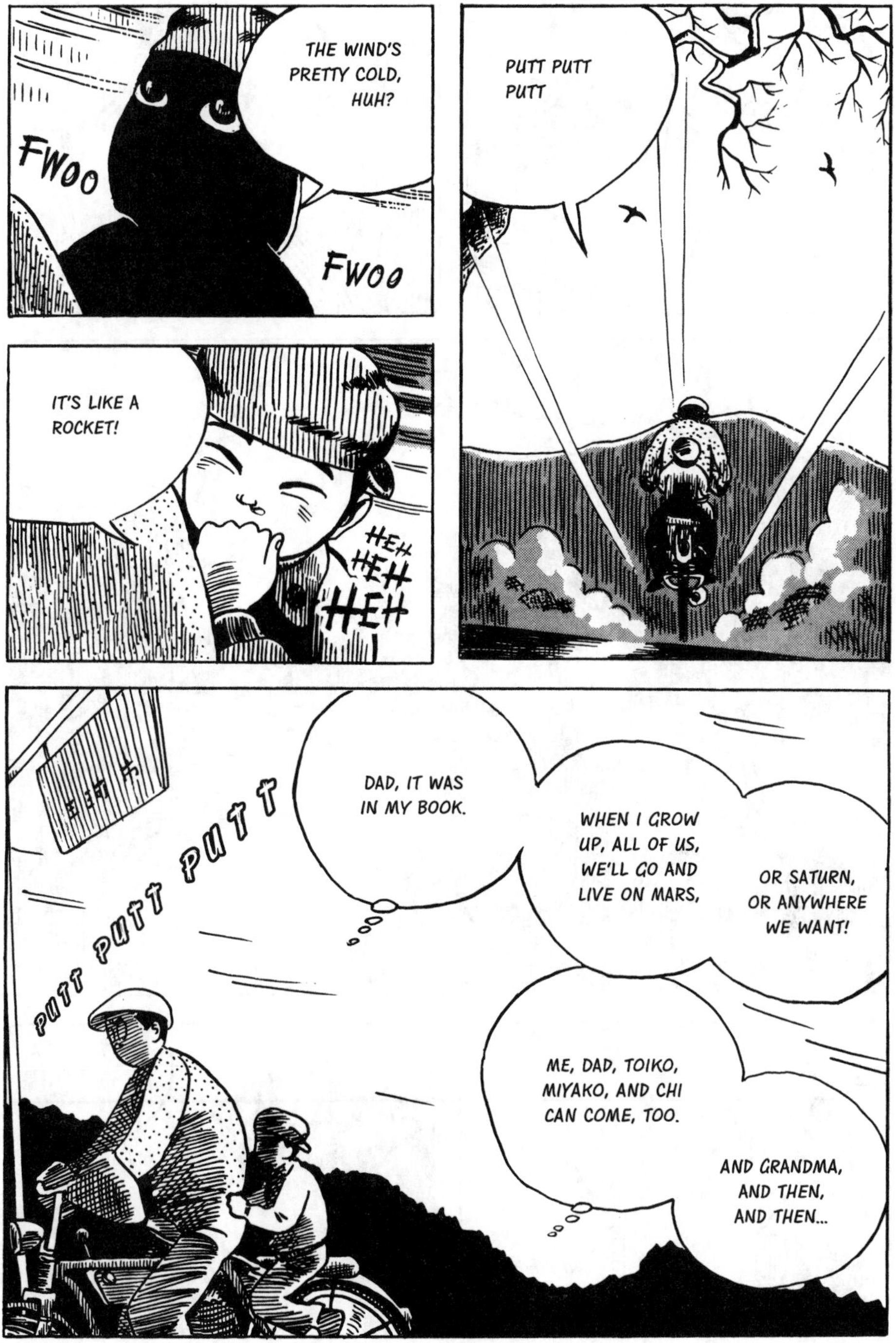
THE WIND'S PRETTY COLD, HUH?
FWOO
FWOO
IT'S LIKE A ROCKET!
HEH HEH HEH
PUTT PUTT PUTT
PUTT PUTT PUTT
DAD, IT WAS IN MY BOOK.
WHEN I GROW UP, ALL OF US, WE'LL GO AND LIVE ON MARS,
OR SATURN, OR ANYWHERE WE WANT!
ME, DAD, TOIKO, MIYAKO, AND CHI CAN COME, TOO.
AND GRANDMA, AND THEN, AND THEN...

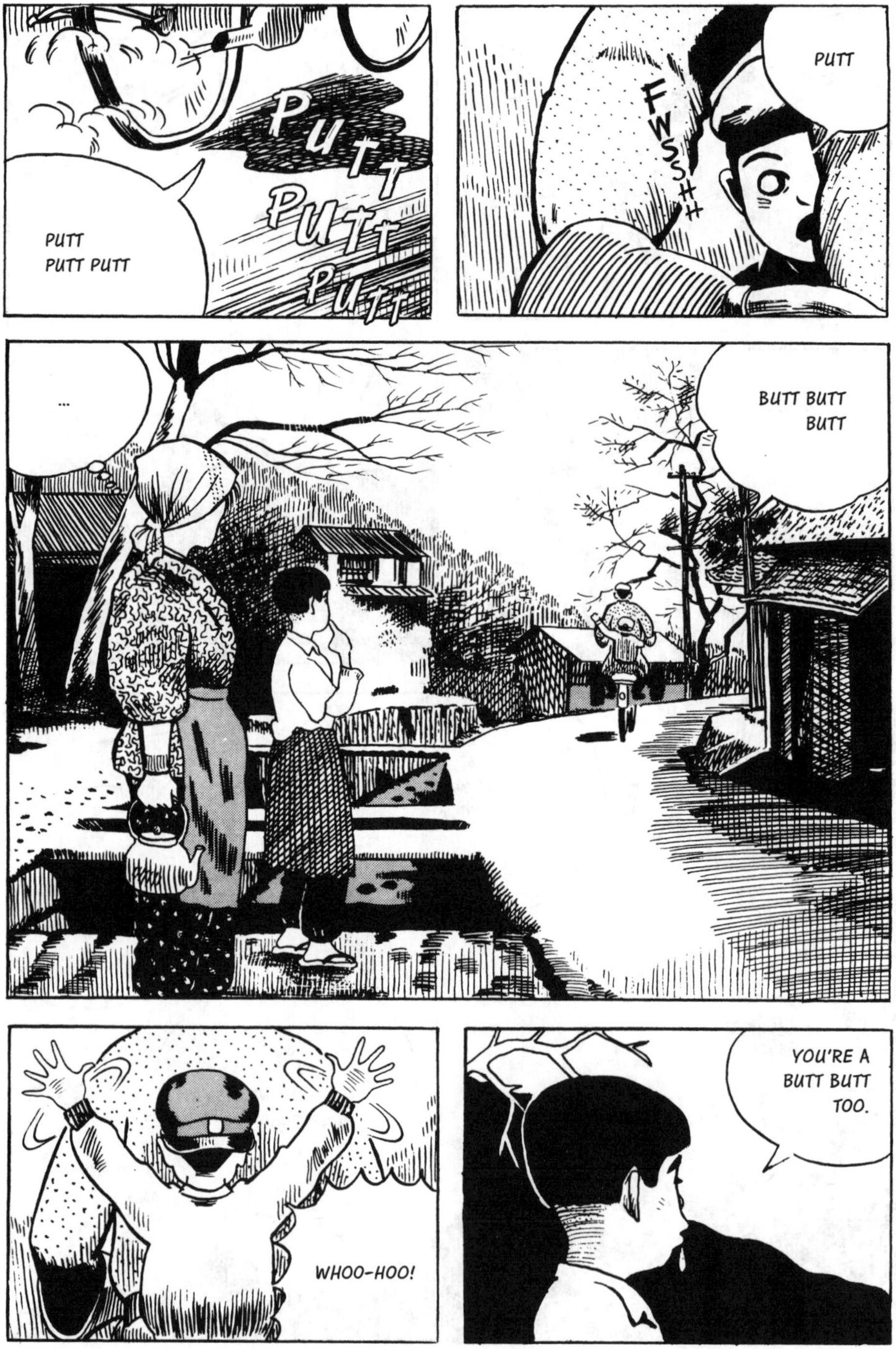
PUTT
PUTT PUTT PUTT
PUTT
PUTT
PUTT
PUTT
PUTT
FWSSHH
...
BUTT BUTT BUTT
WHOO-HOO!
YOU'RE A BUTT BUTT TOO.

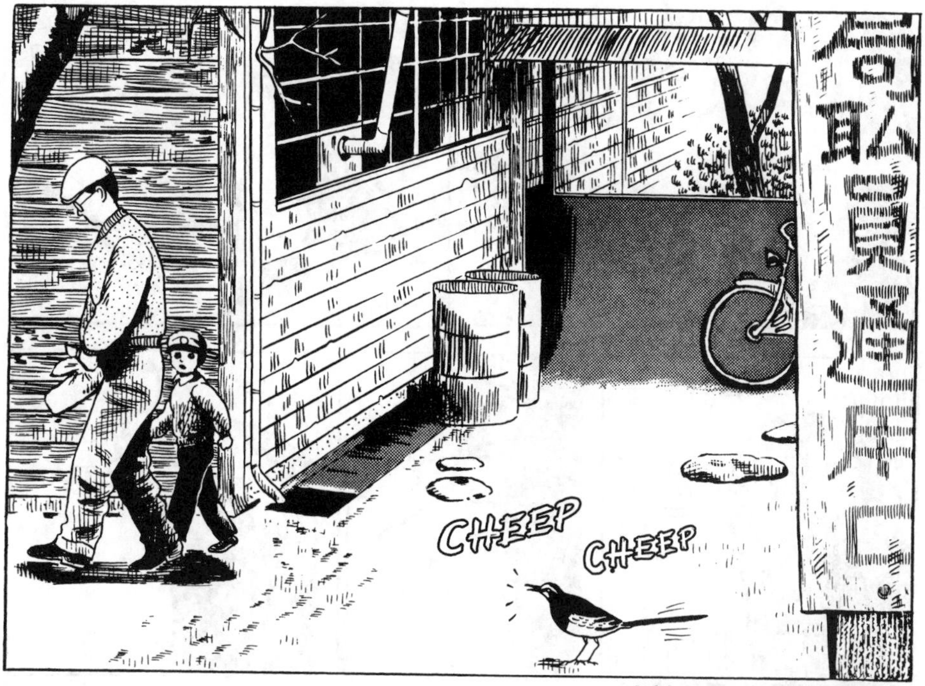
CHEEP
CHEEP

SIGN: OFFICE SERVICE ENTRANCE

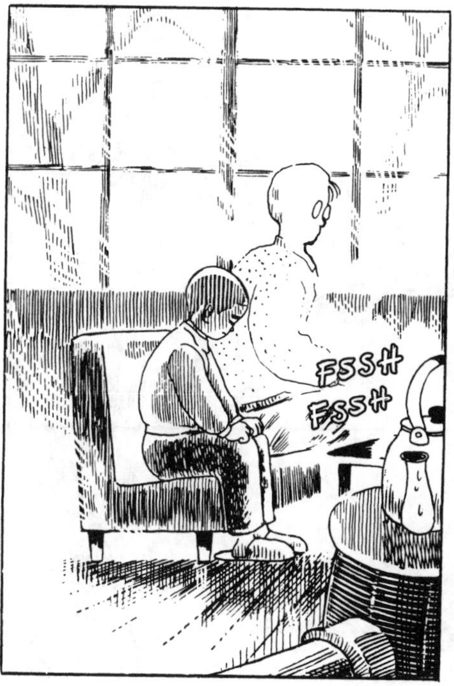
FSSH
FSSH

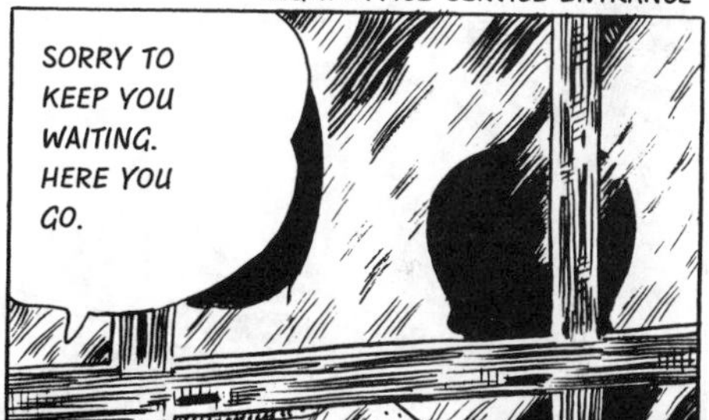
SORRY TO KEEP YOU WAITING. HERE YOU GO.

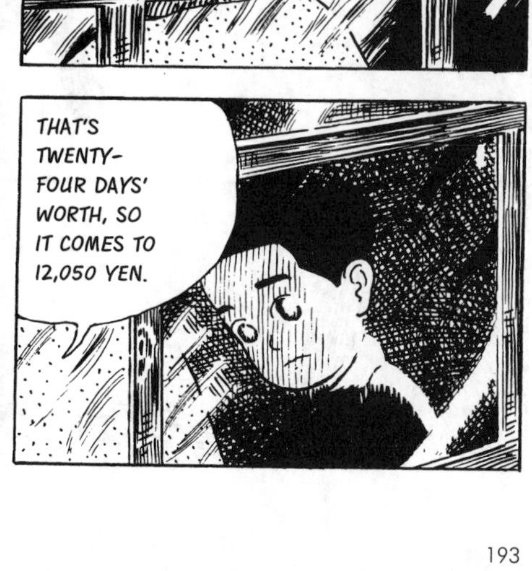
THAT'S TWENTY-FOUR DAYS' WORTH, SO IT COMES TO 12,050 YEN.

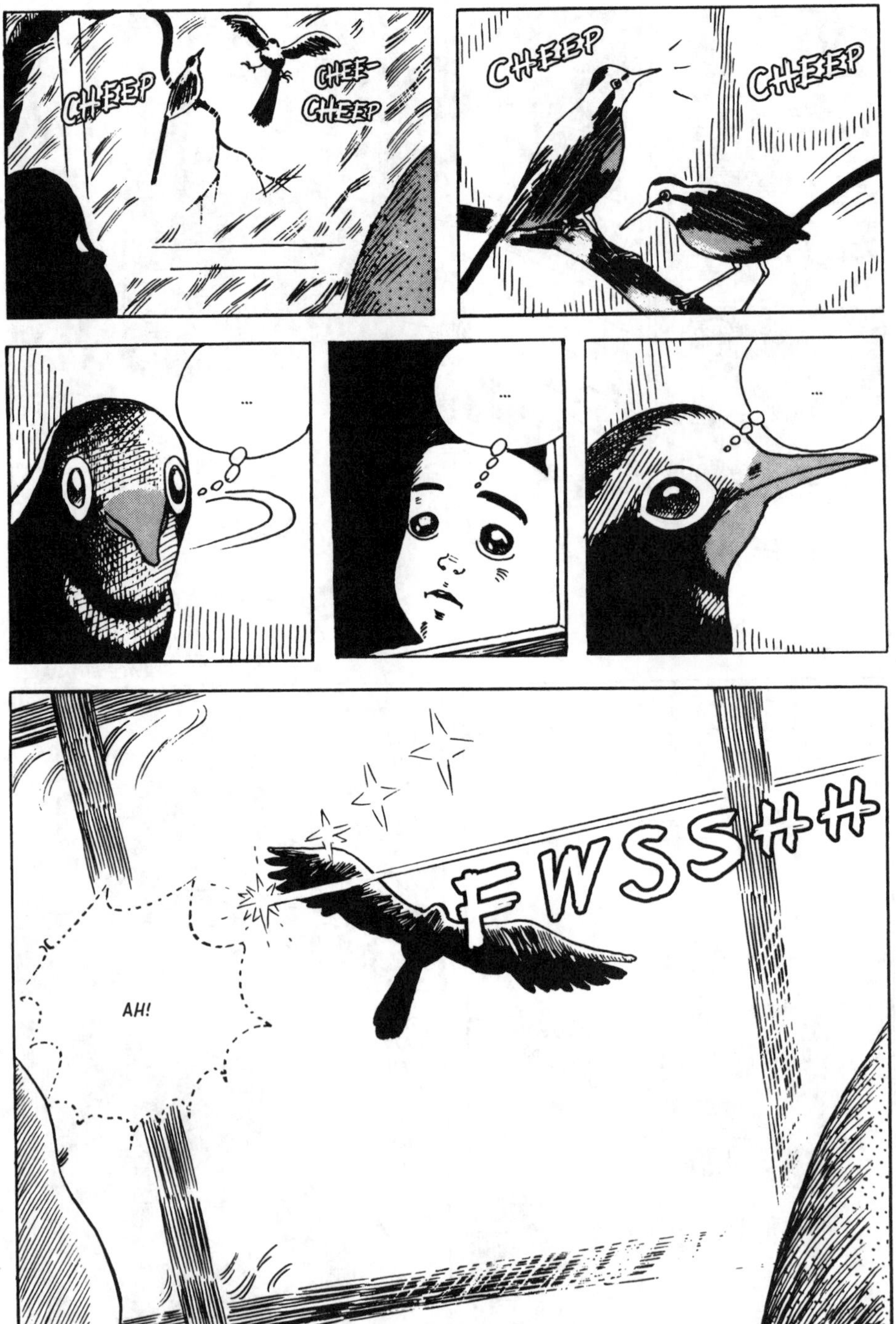
CHEEP
CHEE-CHEEP
CHEEP
CHEEP
...
...
...
FWSSHH
AH!

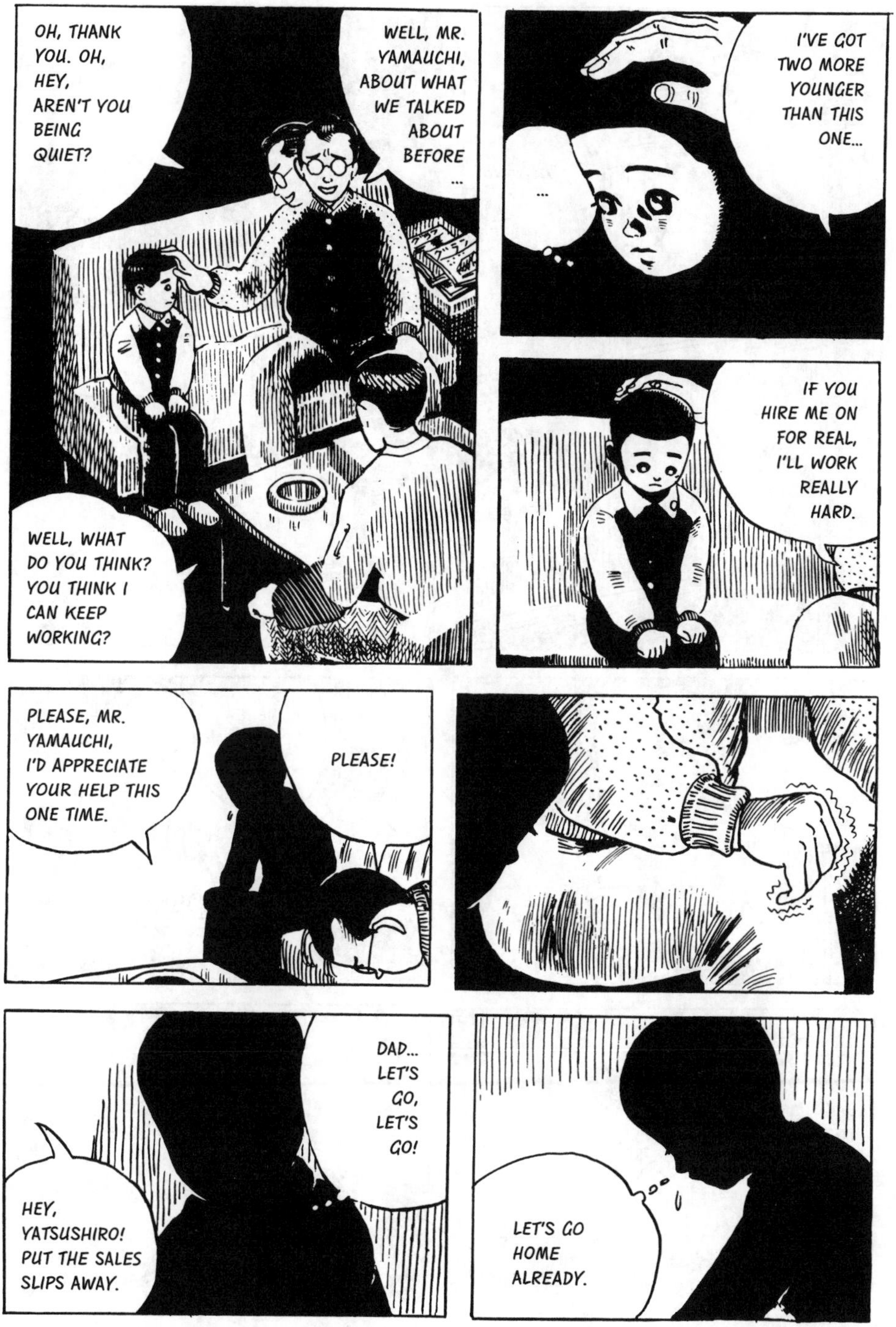
OH, THANK YOU. OH, HEY, AREN'T YOU BEING QUIET?
WELL, MR. YAMAUCHI, ABOUT WHAT WE TALKED ABOUT BEFORE ...
WELL, WHAT DO YOU THINK? YOU THINK I CAN KEEP WORKING?
I'VE GOT TWO MORE YOUNGER THAN THIS ONE...
...
IF YOU HIRE ME ON FOR REAL, I'LL WORK REALLY HARD.
PLEASE, MR. YAMAUCHI, I'D APPRECIATE YOUR HELP THIS ONE TIME.
PLEASE!
DAD... LET'S GO, LET'S GO!
HEY, YATSUSHIRO! PUT THE SALES SLIPS AWAY.
LET'S GO HOME ALREADY.

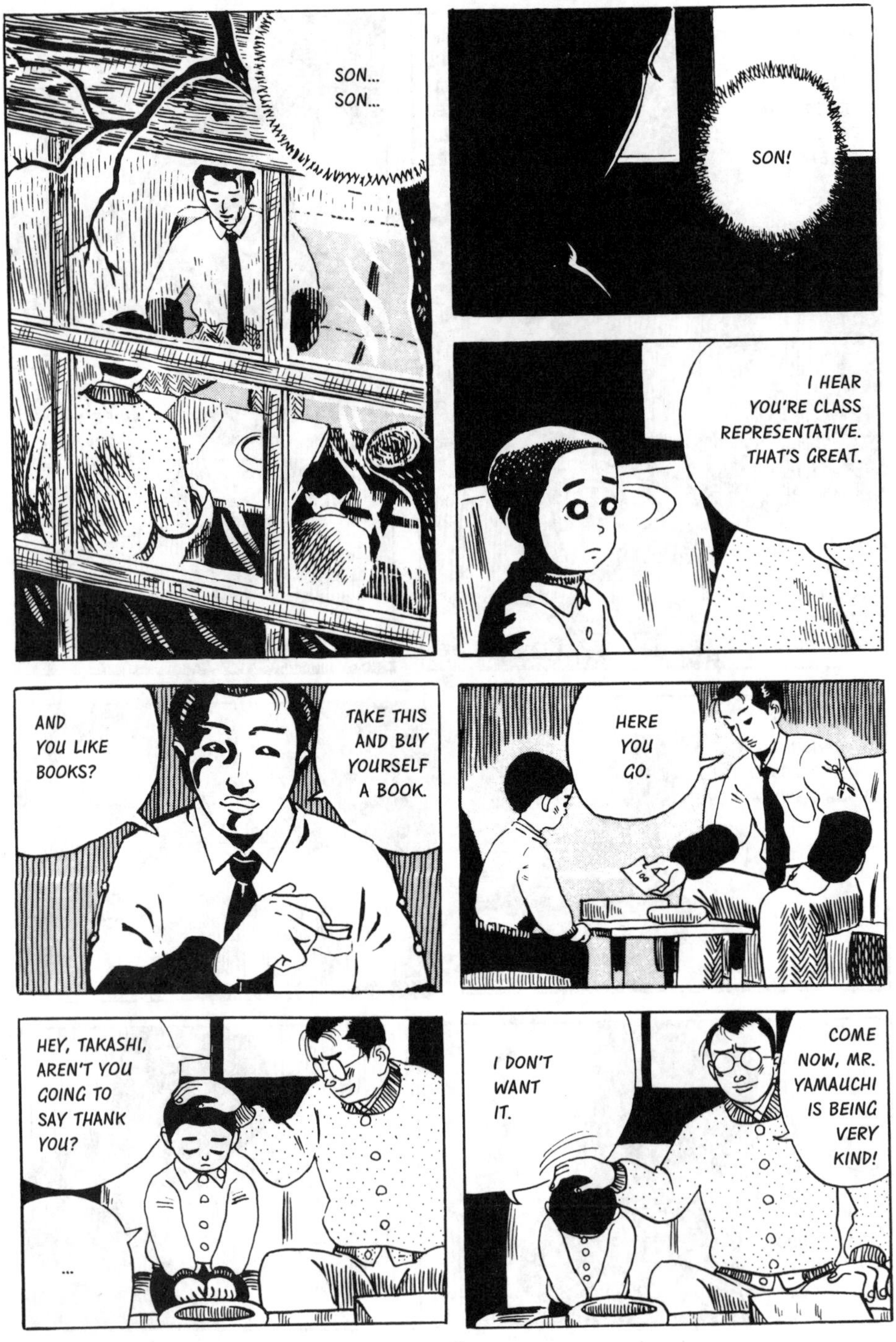
SON...
SON...
SON!
I HEAR YOU'RE CLASS REPRESENTATIVE. THAT'S GREAT.
AND YOU LIKE BOOKS?
TAKE THIS AND BUY YOURSELF A BOOK.
HERE YOU GO.
100
HEY, TAKASHI, AREN'T YOU GOING TO SAY THANK YOU?
...
I DON'T WANT IT.
COME NOW, MR. YAMAUCHI IS BEING VERY KIND!

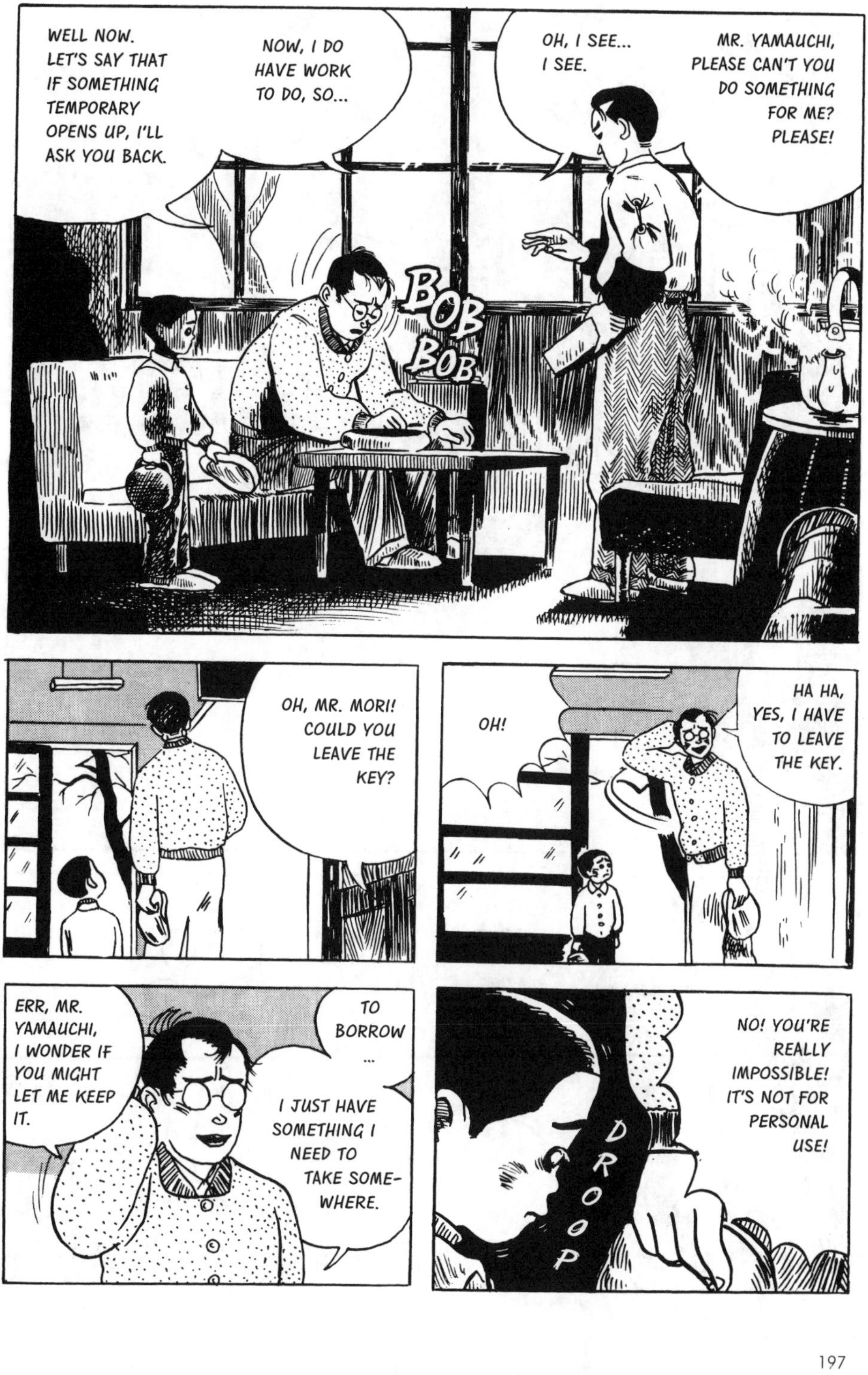
WELL NOW. LET'S SAY THAT IF SOMETHING TEMPORARY OPENS UP, I'LL ASK YOU BACK.
NOW, I DO HAVE WORK TO DO, SO...
OH, I SEE... I SEE.
MR. YAMAUCHI, PLEASE CAN'T YOU DO SOMETHING FOR ME? PLEASE!
BOB BOB
OH, MR. MORI! COULD YOU LEAVE THE KEY?
OH!
HA HA, YES, I HAVE TO LEAVE THE KEY.
ERR, MR. YAMAUCHI, I WONDER IF YOU MIGHT LET ME KEEP IT.
TO BORROW ...
I JUST HAVE SOMETHING I NEED TO TAKE SOME-WHERE.
NO! YOU'RE REALLY IMPOSSIBLE! IT'S NOT FOR PERSONAL USE!
DROOP

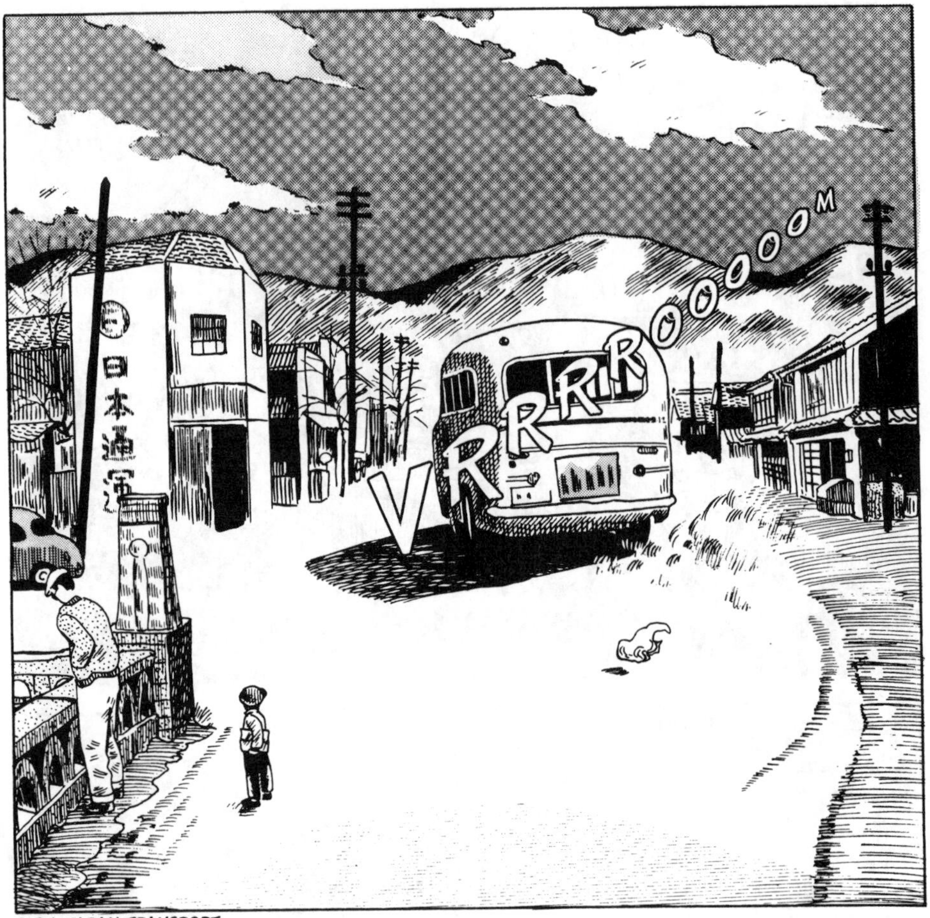
日本通運
VRRRRROOOOOM
SIGN: JAPAN TRANSPORT

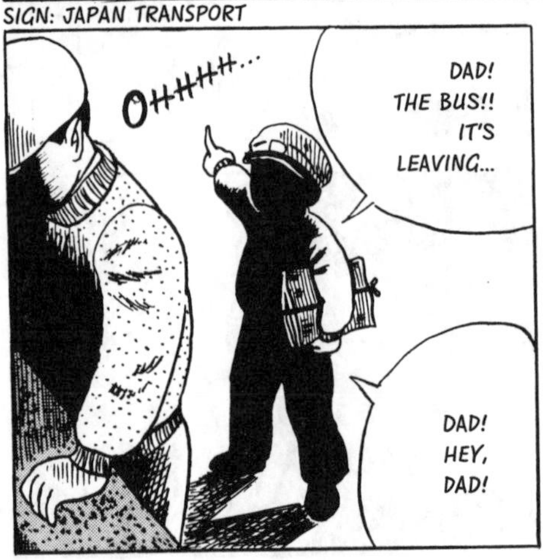
OHHHH...
DAD! THE BUS!! IT'S LEAVING...
DAD! HEY, DAD!

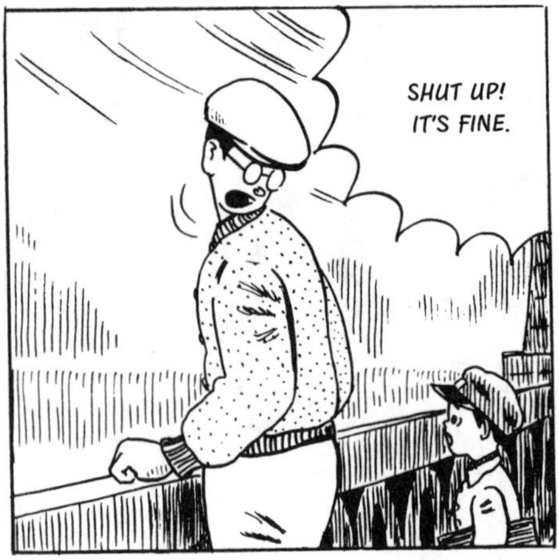
SHUT UP! IT'S FINE.

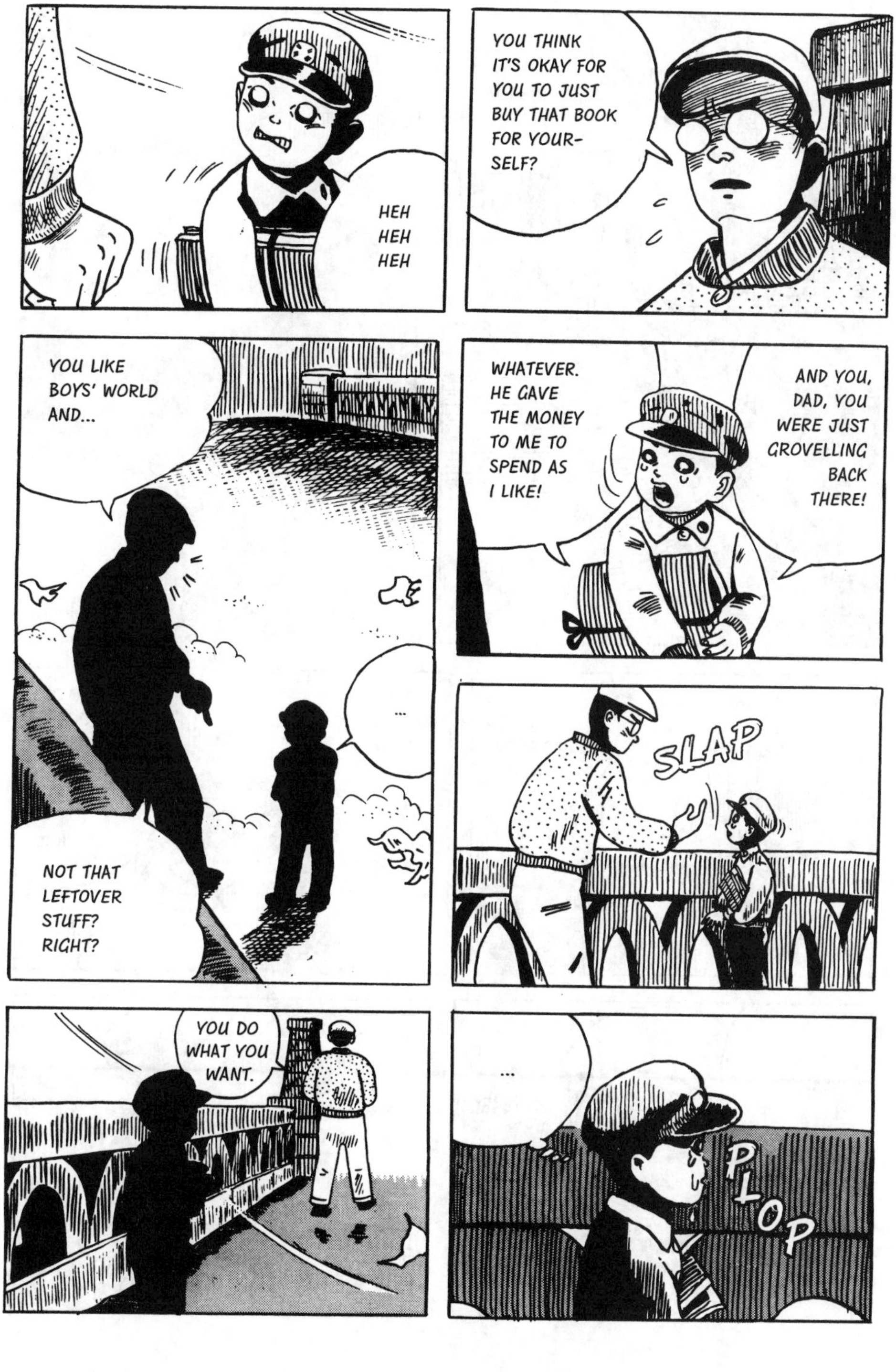
HEH HEH HEH
YOU THINK IT'S OKAY FOR YOU TO JUST BUY THAT BOOK FOR YOUR-SELF?
YOU LIKE BOYS' WORLD AND...
NOT THAT LEFTOVER STUFF? RIGHT?
...
WHATEVER. HE GAVE THE MONEY TO ME TO SPEND AS I LIKE!
AND YOU, DAD, YOU WERE JUST GROVELLING BACK THERE!
SLAP
YOU DO WHAT YOU WANT.
...
PLOP

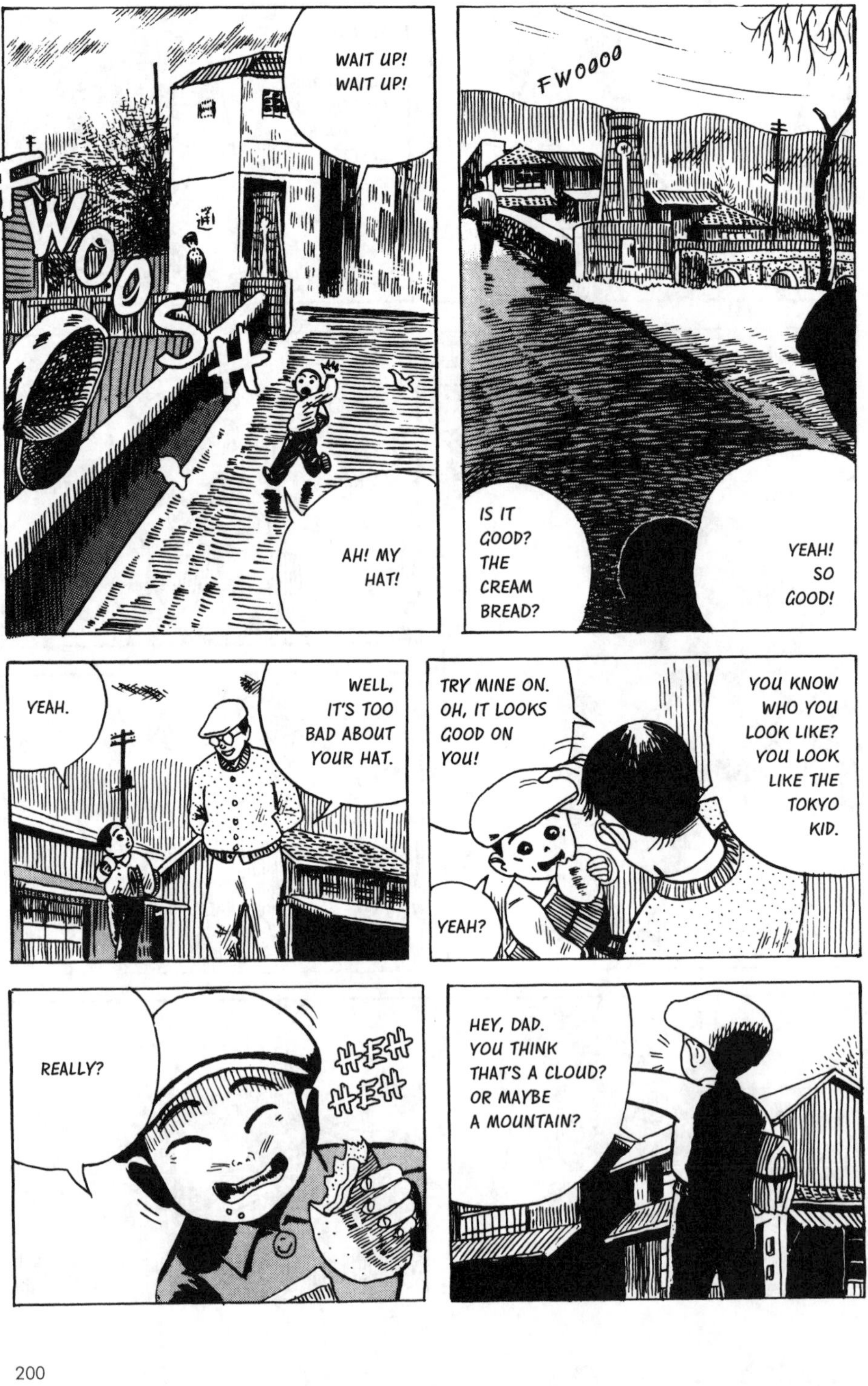
WAIT UP! WAIT UP!
FWOOSH
AH! MY HAT!
FWOOOO
IS IT GOOD? THE CREAM BREAD?
YEAH! SO GOOD!
YEAH.
WELL, IT'S TOO BAD ABOUT YOUR HAT.
TRY MINE ON. OH, IT LOOKS GOOD ON YOU!
YOU KNOW WHO YOU LOOK LIKE? YOU LOOK LIKE THE TOKYO KID.
YEAH?
REALLY?
HEH HEH
HEY, DAD. YOU THINK THAT'S A CLOUD? OR MAYBE A MOUNTAIN?

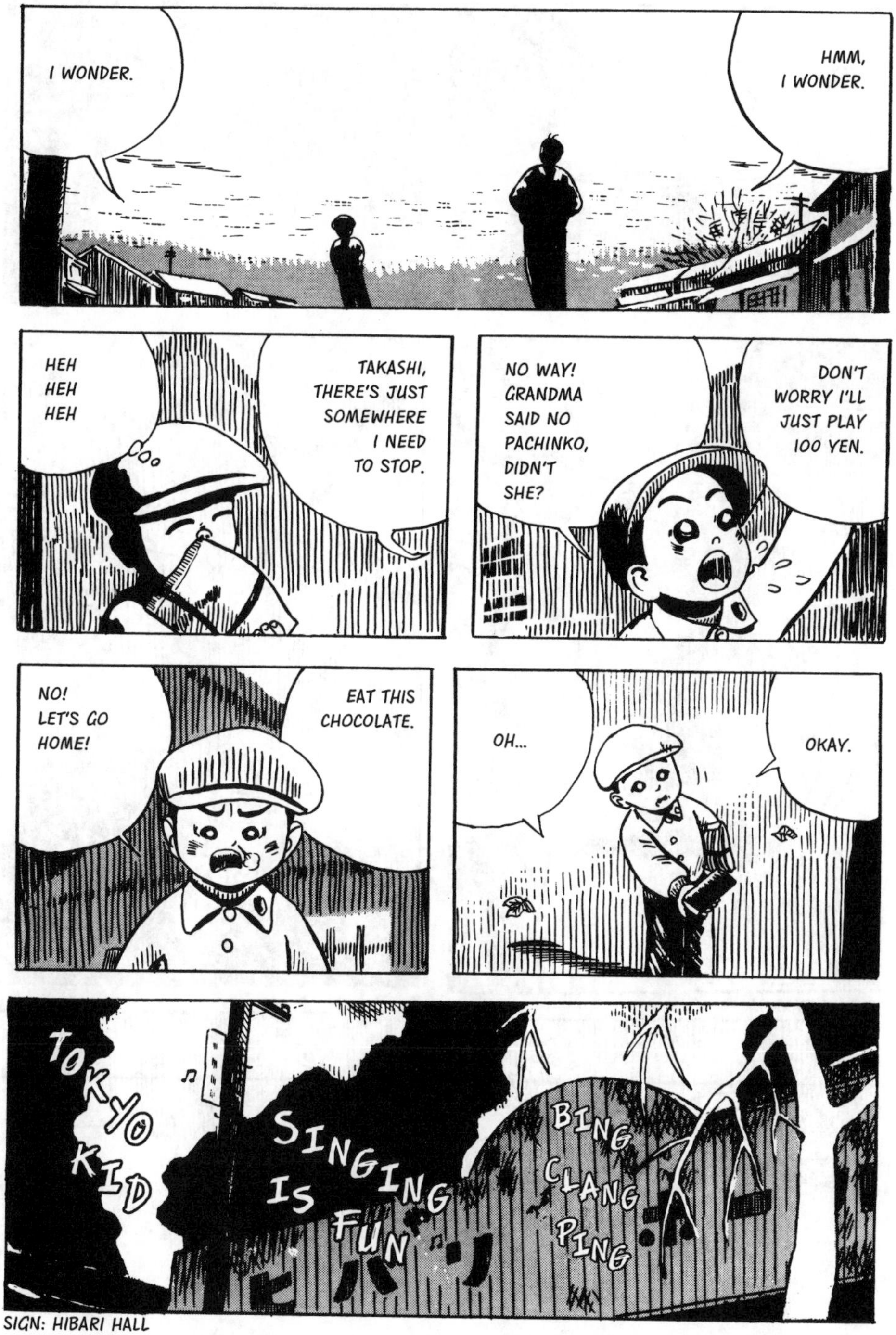
I WONDER.
HMM, I WONDER.
HEH HEH HEH
TAKASHI, THERE'S JUST SOMEWHERE I NEED TO STOP.
NO WAY! GRANDMA SAID NO PACHINKO, DIDN'T SHE?
DON'T WORRY I'LL JUST PLAY 100 YEN.
NO! LET'S GO HOME!
EAT THIS CHOCOLATE.
OH...
OKAY.
TOKYO KID
SINGING IS FUN
BING CLANG PING
SIGN: HIBARI HALL

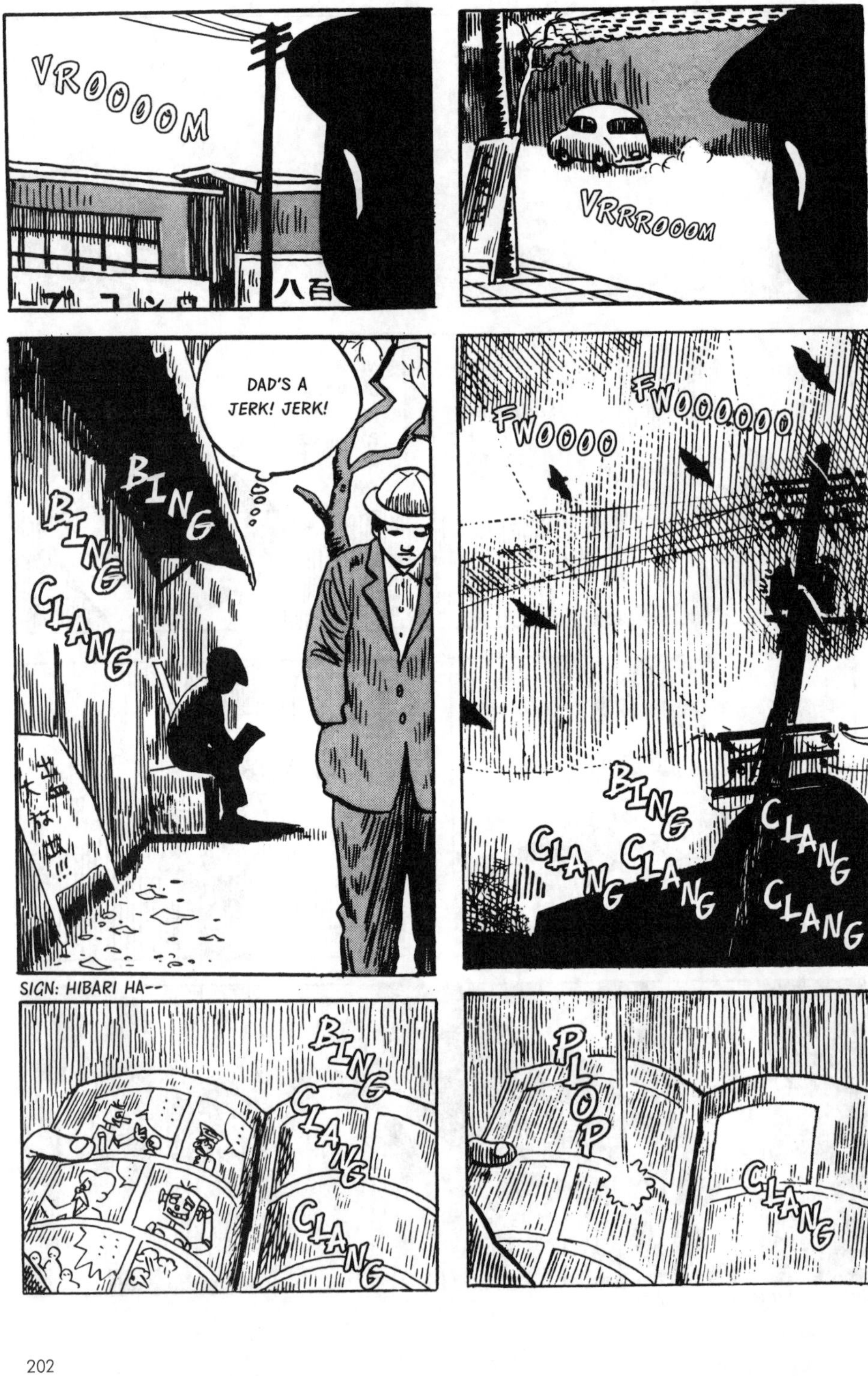
VROOOOM
VRRRROOOM
DAD'S A JERK! JERK!
BING BING CLANG CLANG
SIGN: HIBARI HA--
FWOOOO
FWOOOOOOO
BING CLANG CLANG CLANG CLANG
BING CLANG CLANG CLANG
PLOP
CLANG

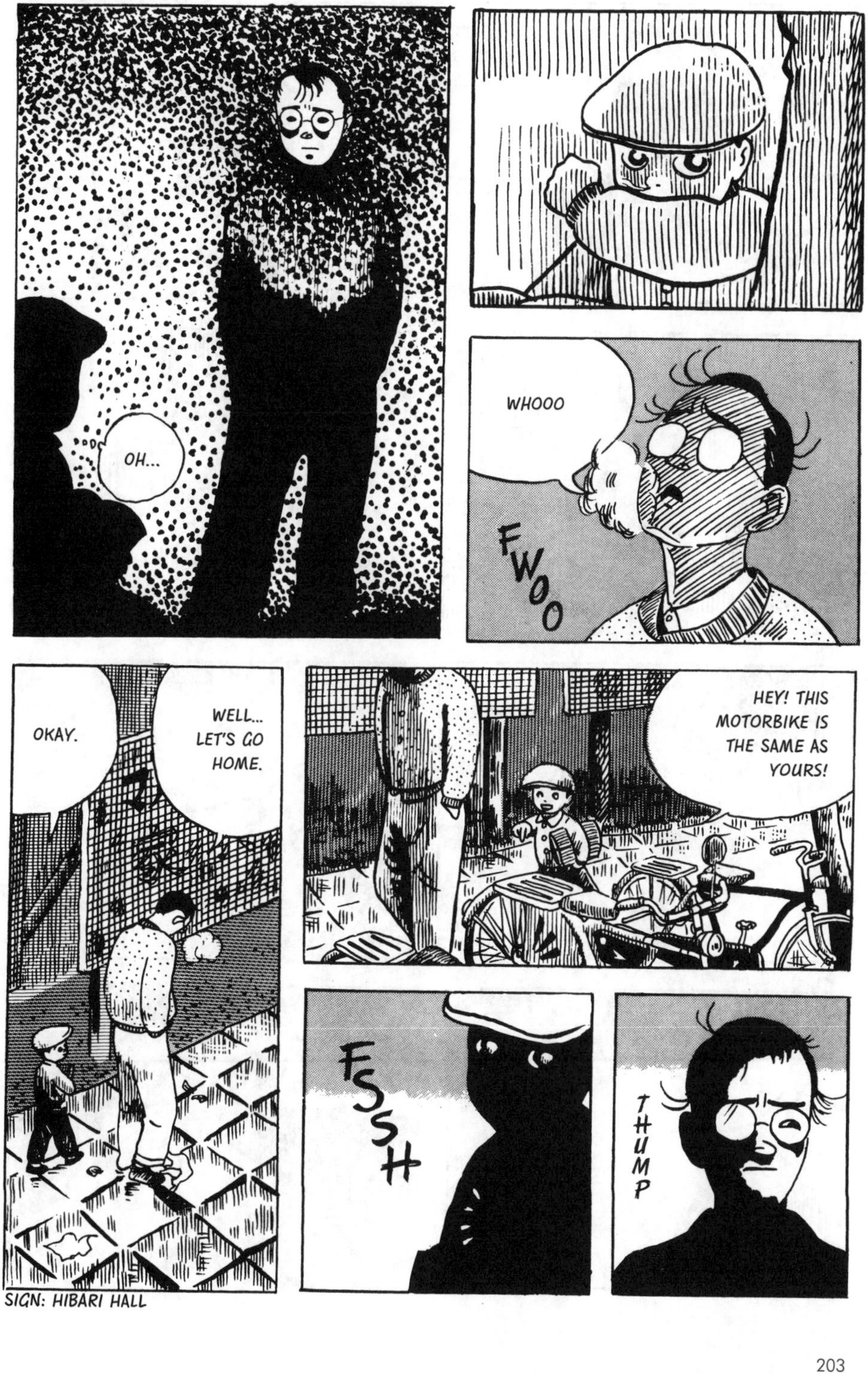
OH...
WHOOO
FWOOO
OKAY.
WELL... LET'S GO HOME.
HEY! THIS MOTORBIKE IS THE SAME AS YOURS!
FSSH
THUMP
SIGN: HIBARI HALL

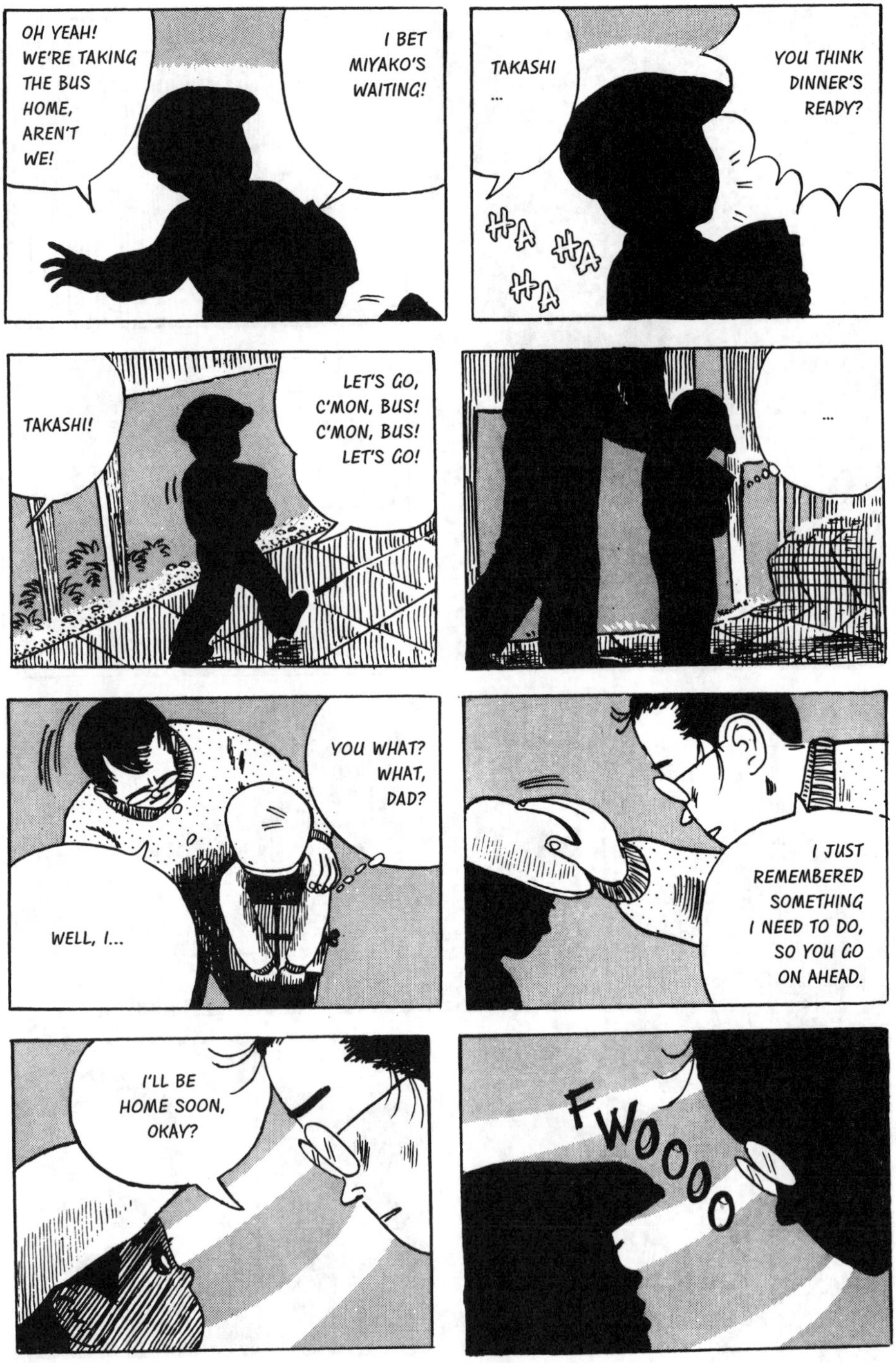
OH YEAH! WE'RE TAKING THE BUS HOME, AREN'T WE!
I BET MIYAKO'S WAITING!
TAKASHI ...
YOU THINK DINNER'S READY?
HA HA HA
TAKASHI!
LET'S GO, C'MON, BUS! C'MON, BUS! LET'S GO!
...
YOU WHAT? WHAT, DAD?
WELL, I...
I JUST REMEMBERED SOMETHING I NEED TO DO, SO YOU GO ON AHEAD.
I'LL BE HOME SOON, OKAY?
FWOOOO

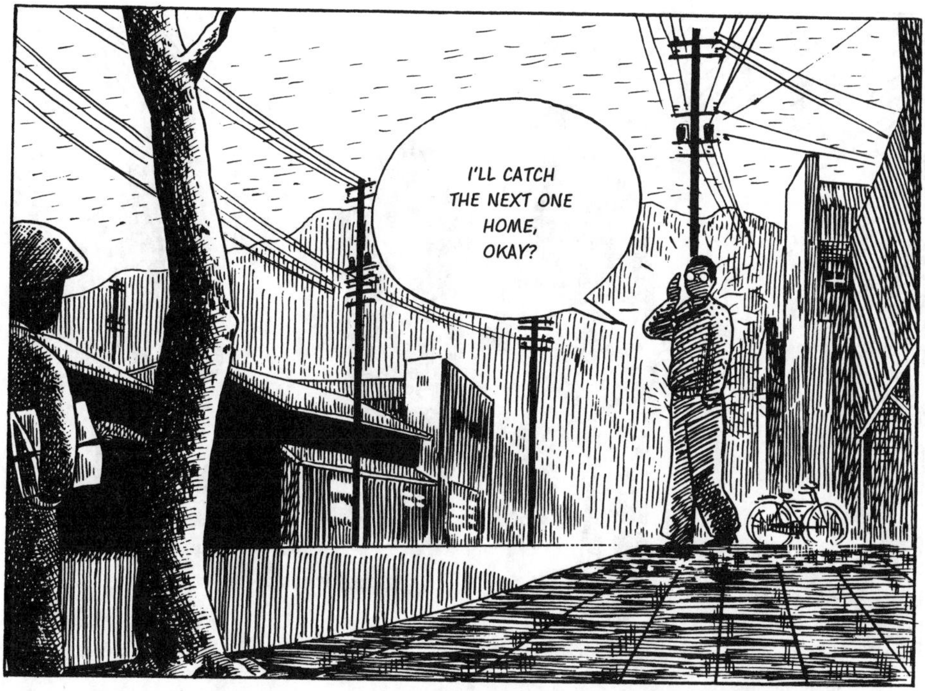
I'LL CATCH THE NEXT ONE HOME, OKAY?

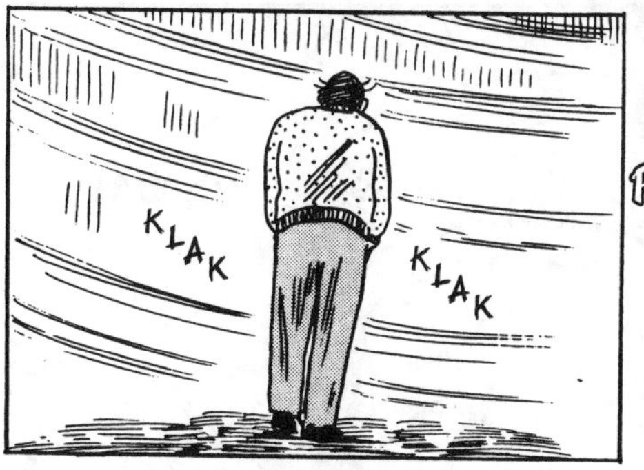
KLAK
KLAK

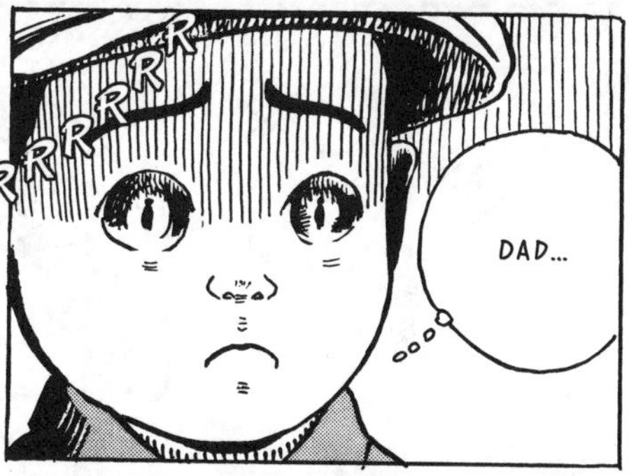
RRRRRRR
DAD...

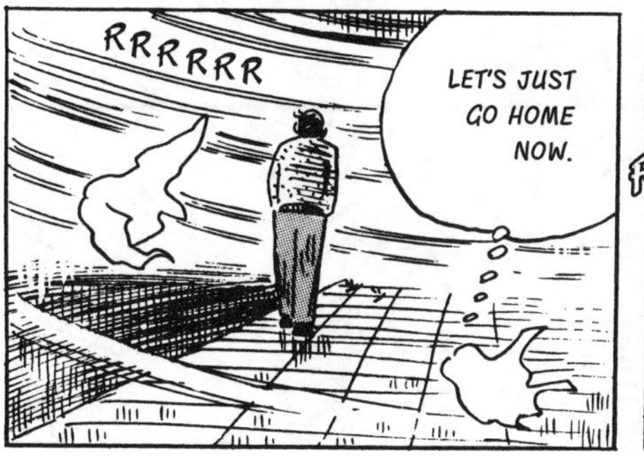
RRRRRR
LET'S JUST GO HOME NOW.

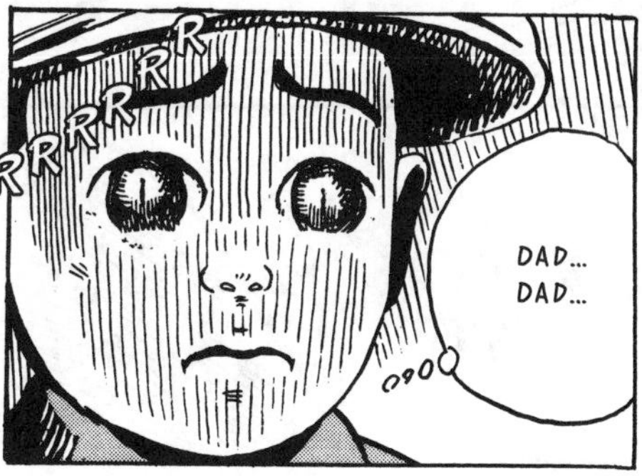
RRRRRRR
DAD... DAD...

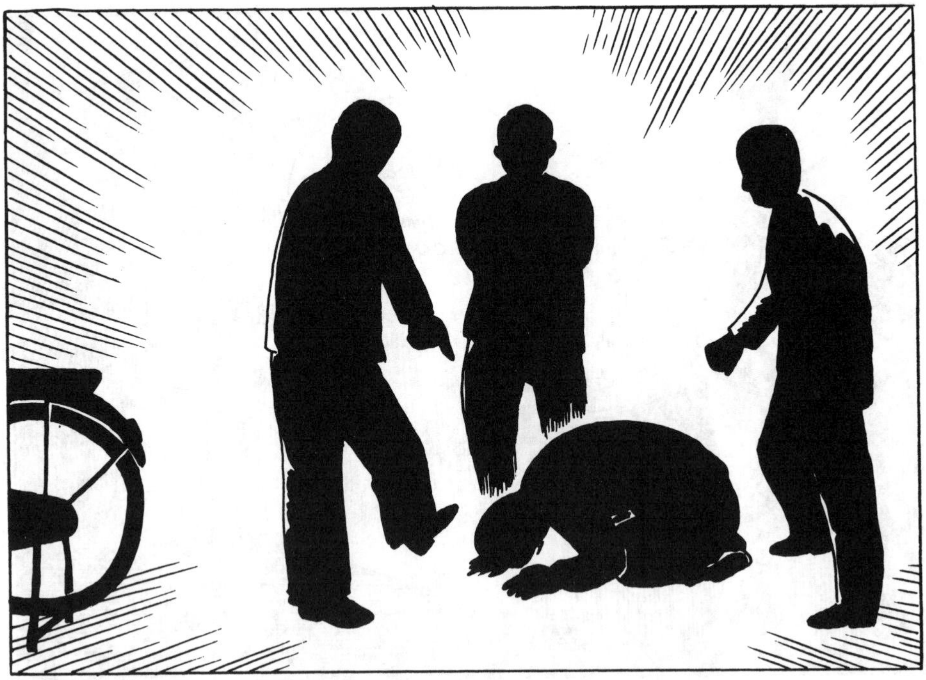

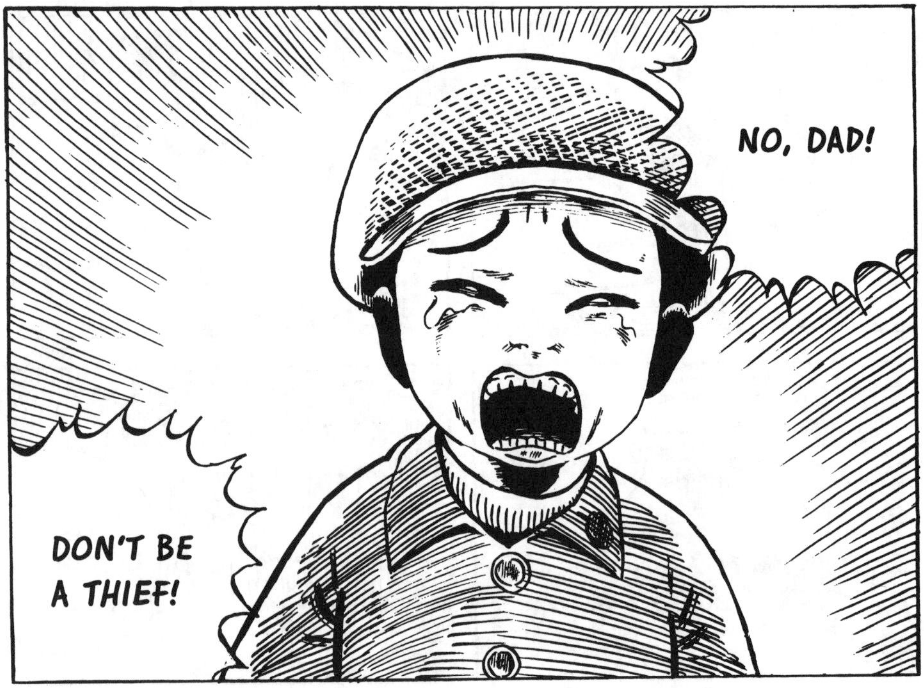
NO, DAD!
DON'T BE
A THIEF!

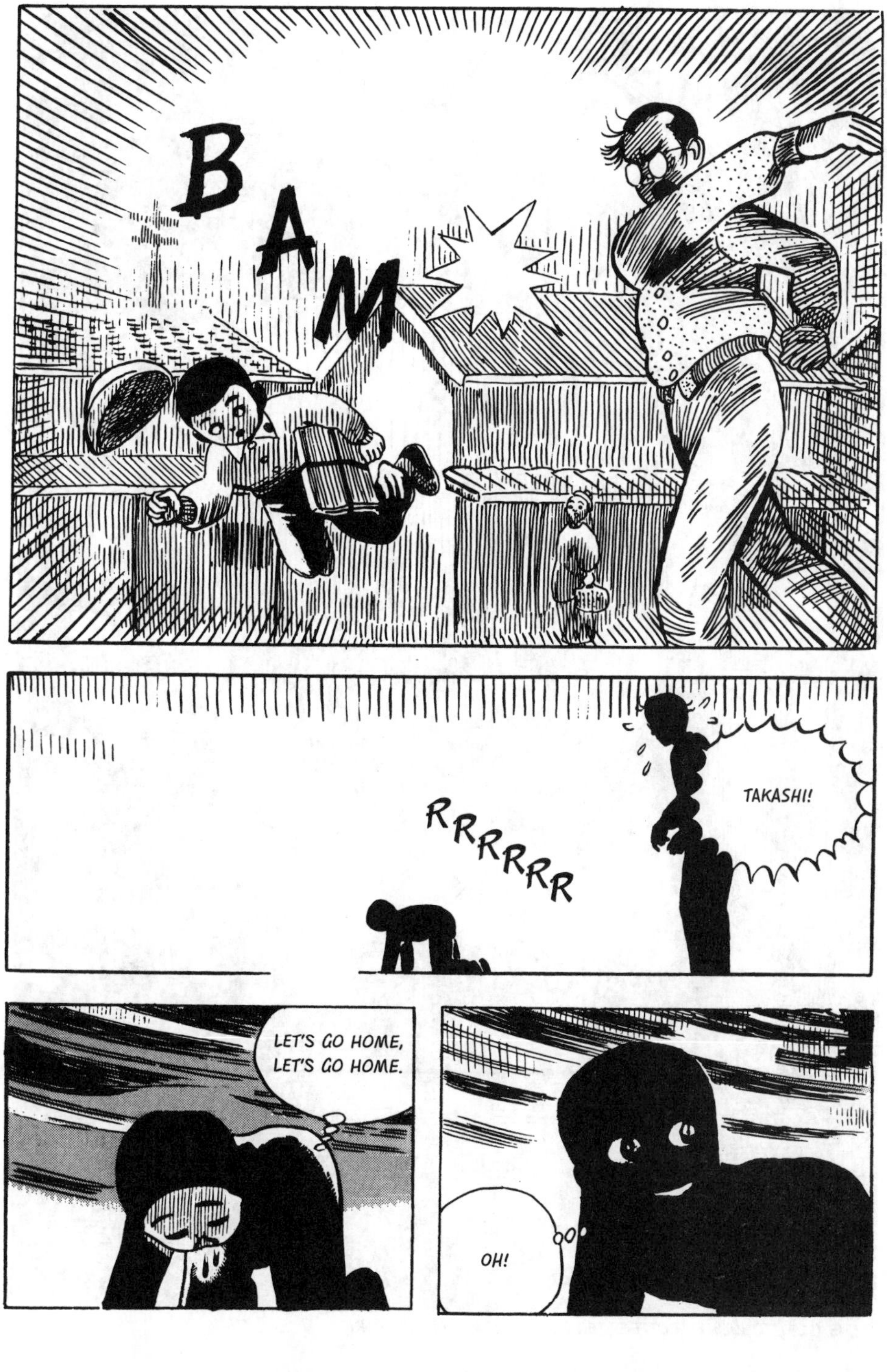
BAM
RRRRRRR
TAKASHI!
LET'S GO HOME, LET'S GO HOME.
OH!

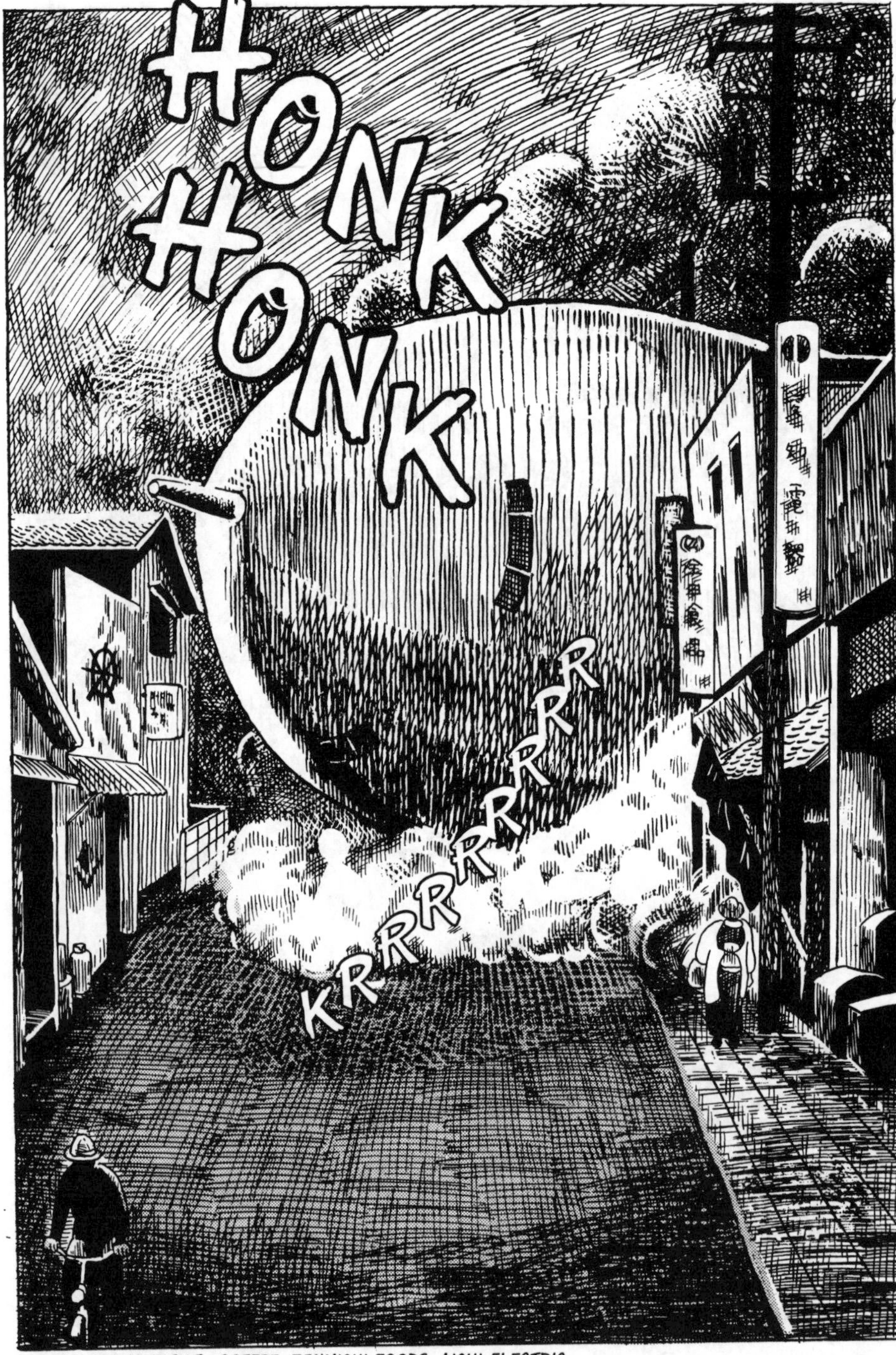
HONK HONK
KRRRRRRRRRRR
SIGNS (LEFT TO RIGHT): COFFEE; ZENNICHI FOODS; AICHI ELECTRIC

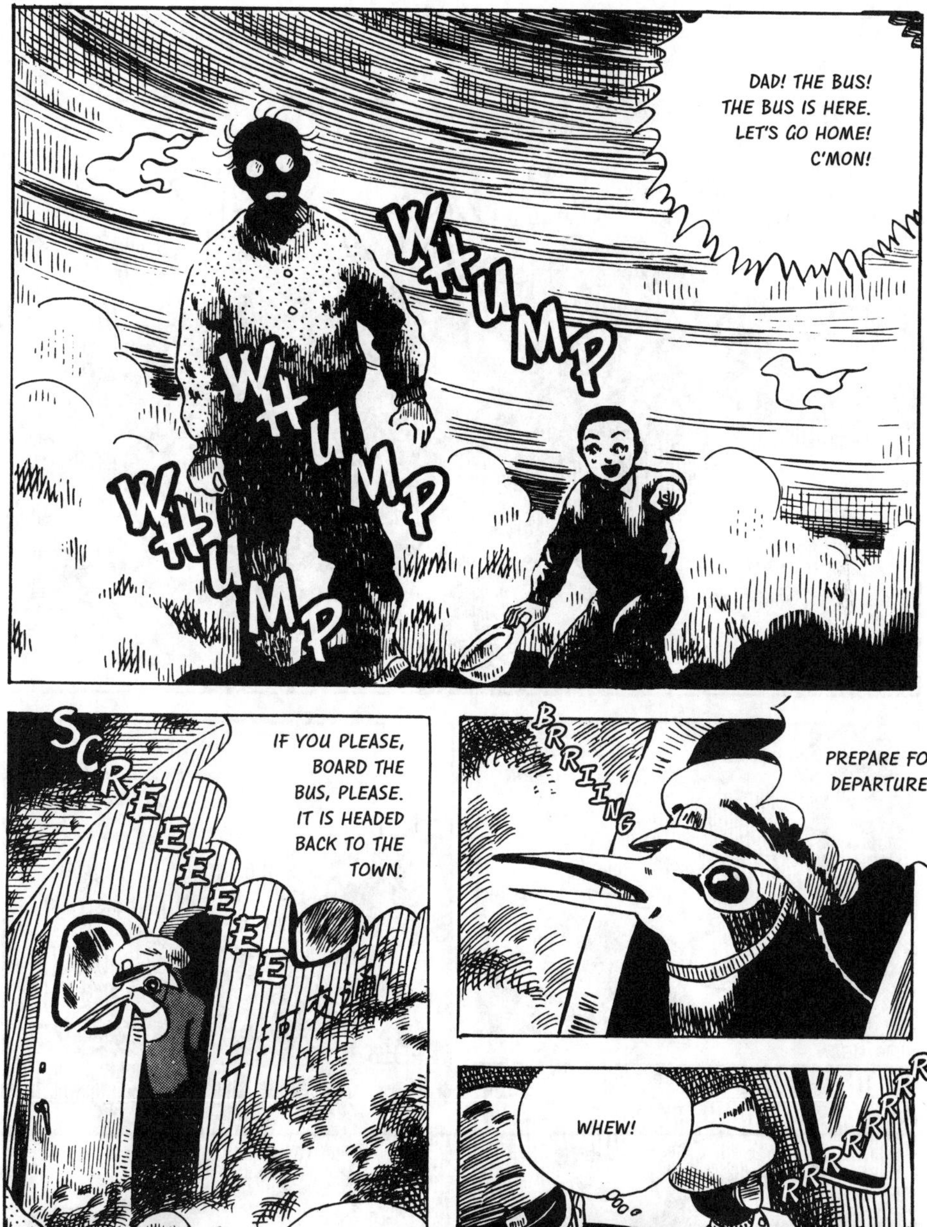
DAD! THE BUS! THE BUS IS HERE. LET'S GO HOME! C'MON!
WHUMP
WHUMP
WHUMP
SCREEEEEEEEE
IF YOU PLEASE, BOARD THE BUS, PLEASE. IT IS HEADED BACK TO THE TOWN.
HURRY! HURRY UP, DAD!
BRRIING
PREPARE FOR DEPARTURE!
WHEW!
RRRRRRRRR
BUS: MIKAWA TRANSIT

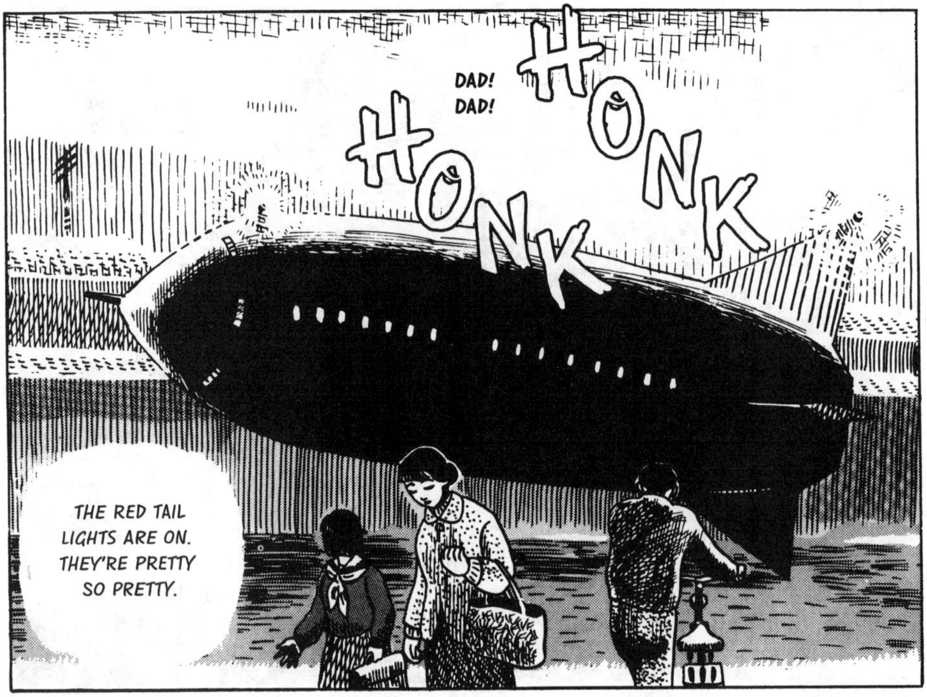
DAD!
DAD!
HONK
HONK
THE RED TAIL LIGHTS ARE ON. THEY'RE PRETTY SO PRETTY.

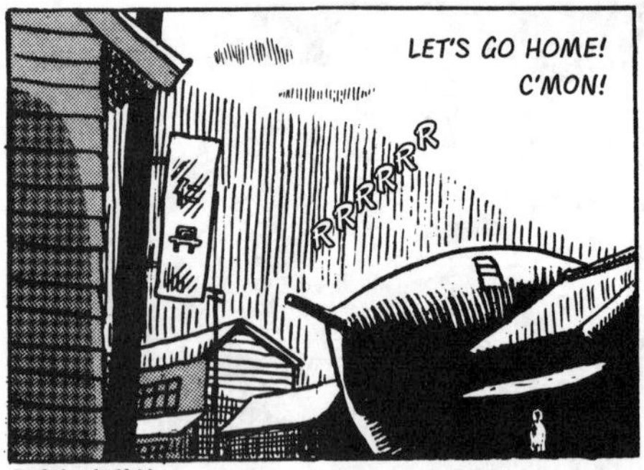
LET'S GO HOME! C'MON!
RRRRRR

SIGN: NITAN

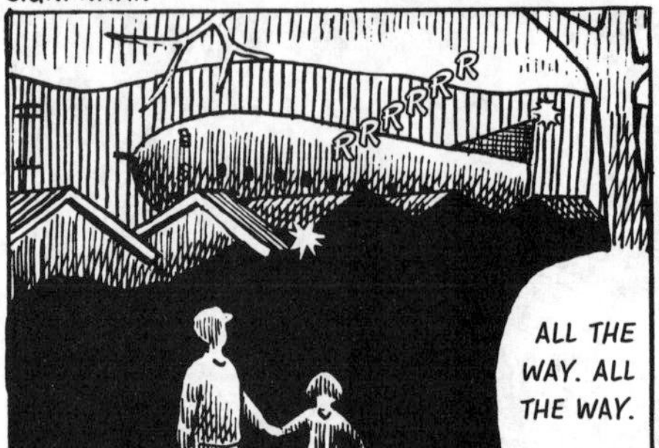
RRRRRR
ALL THE WAY. ALL THE WAY.

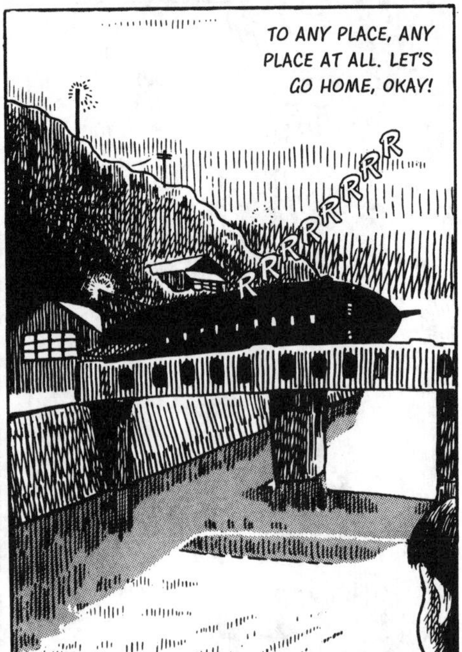
TO ANY PLACE, ANY PLACE AT ALL. LET'S GO HOME, OKAY!
RRRRRRRRR

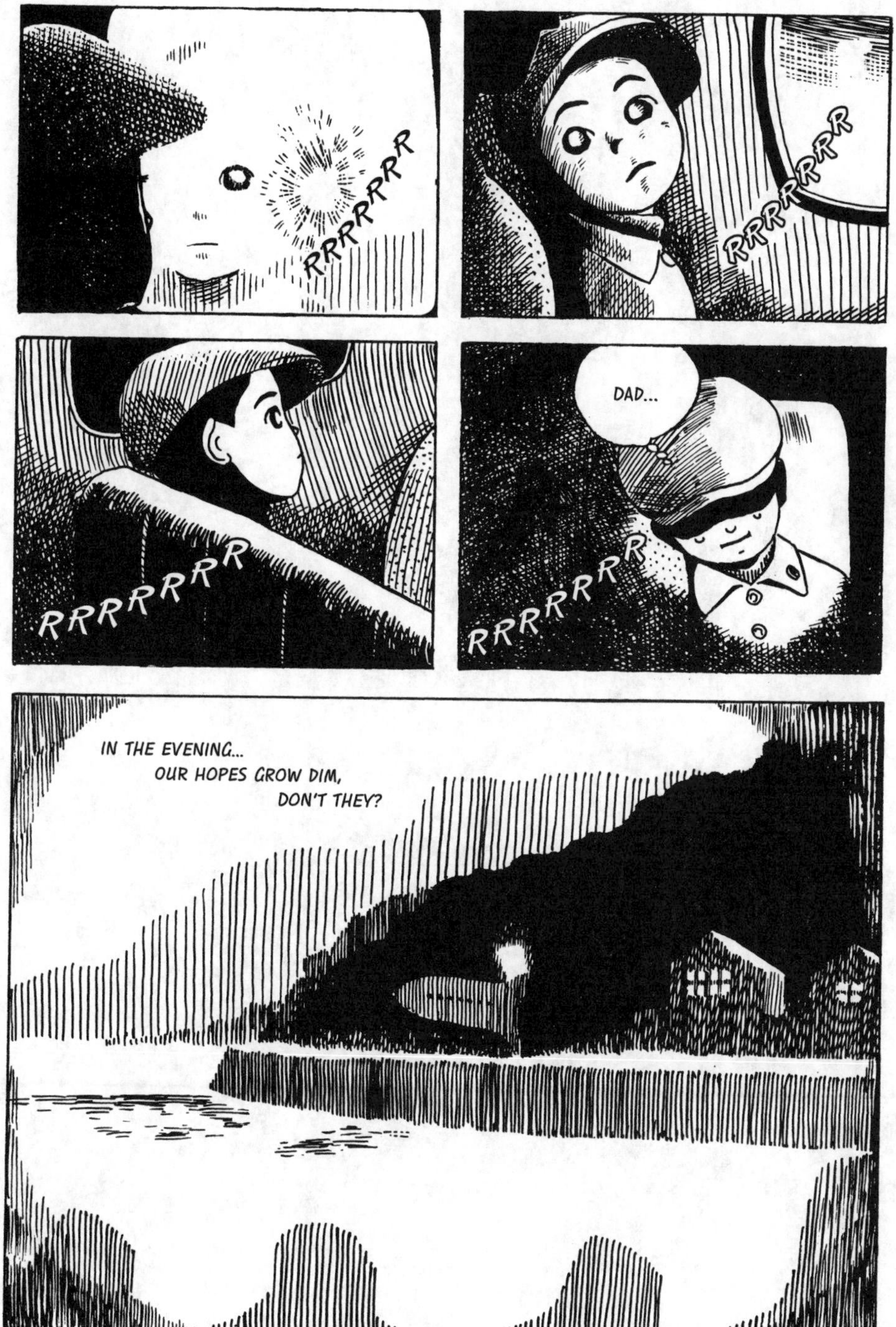
RRRRRRRR
RRRRRRRR
RRRRRRRR
DAD...
RRRRRRRR
IN THE EVENING... OUR HOPES GROW DIM, DON'T THEY?

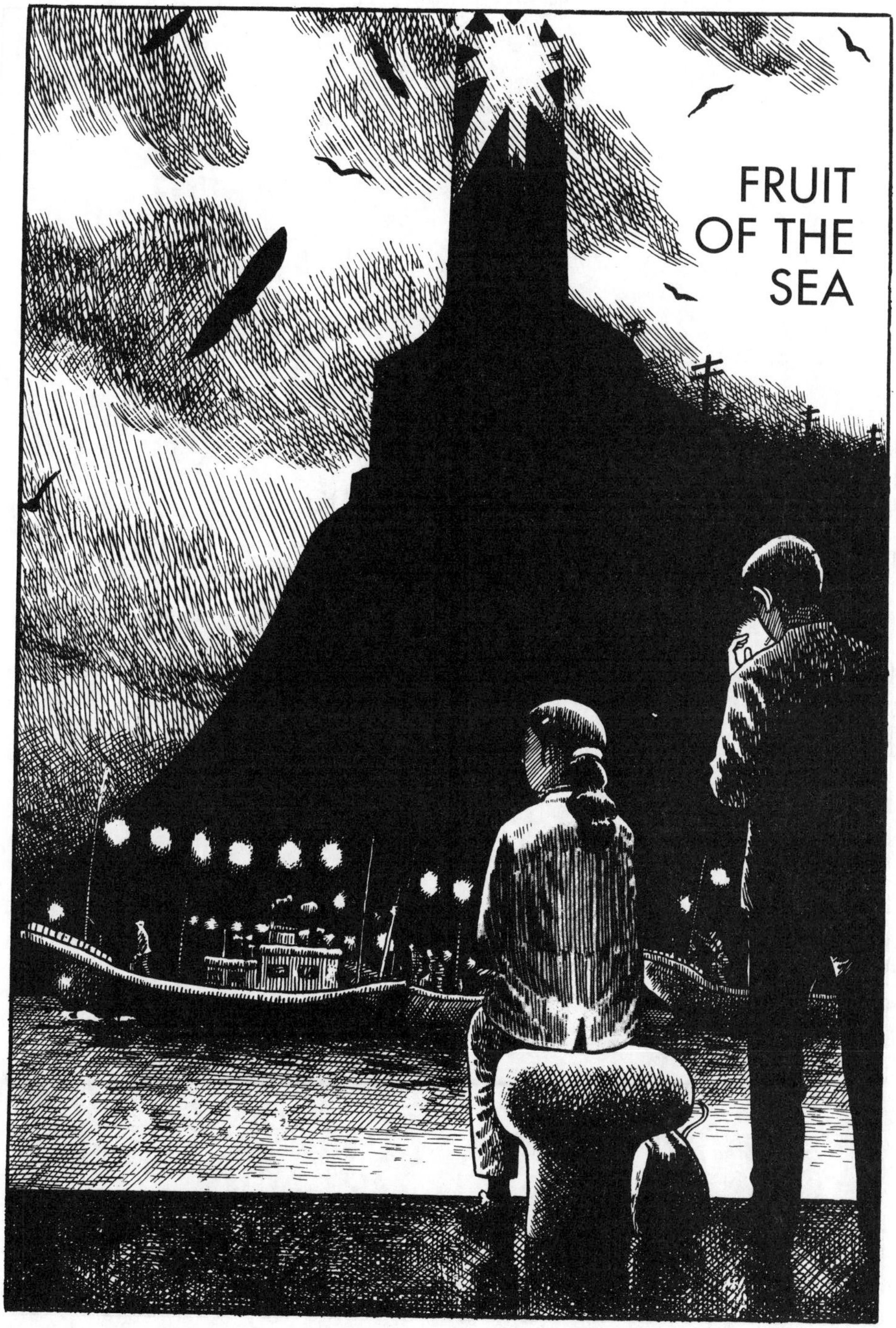
FRUIT
OF THE
SEA

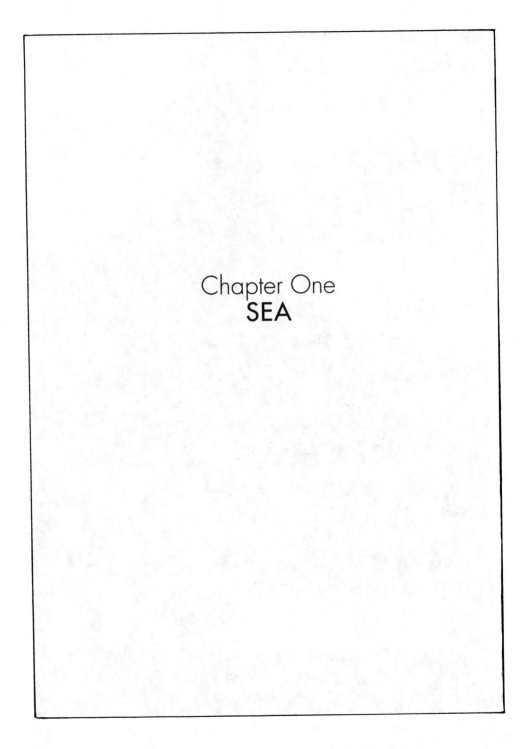

Chapter One
SEA

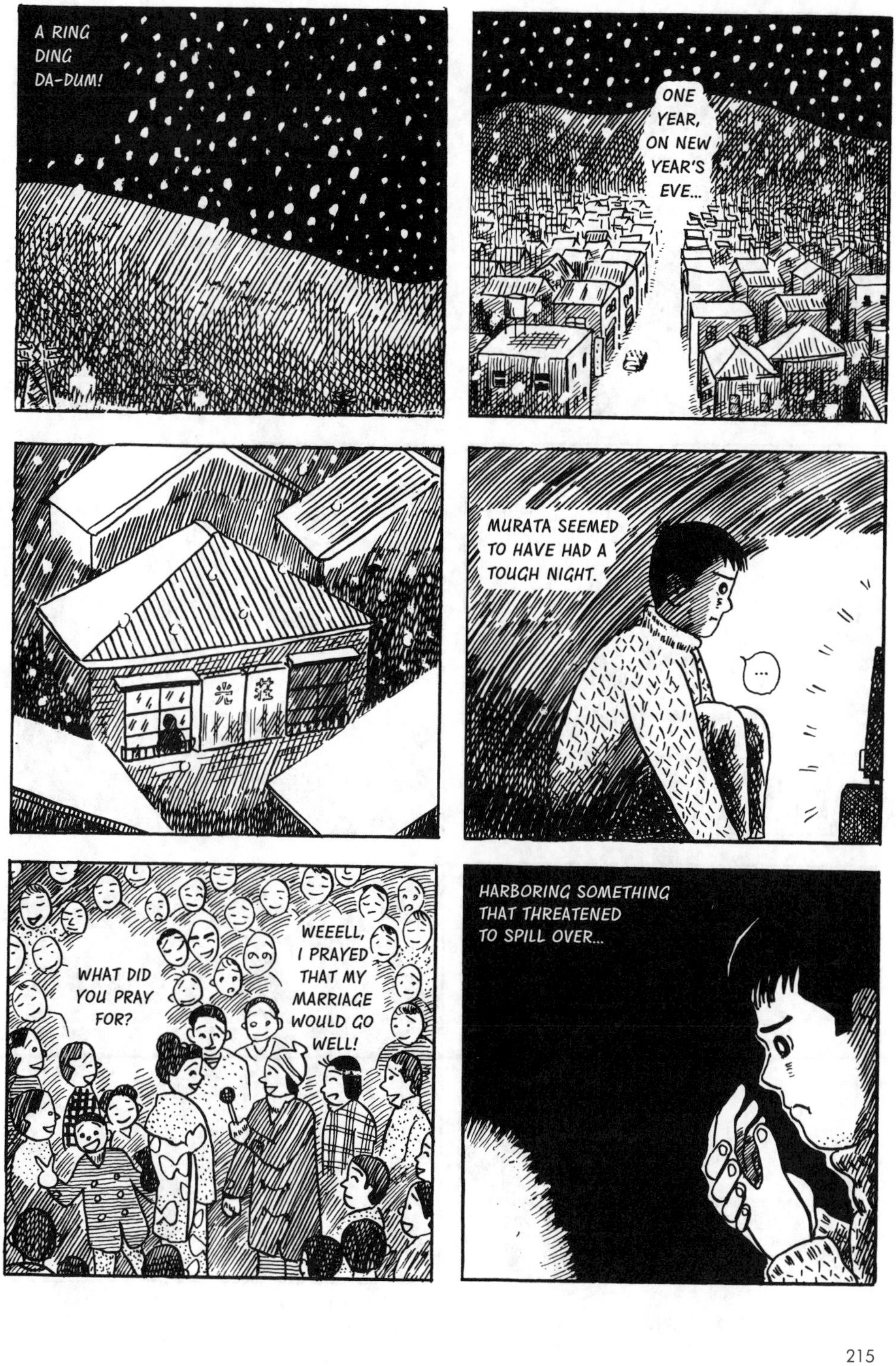
A RING DING DA-DUM!
ONE YEAR, ON NEW YEAR'S EVE...
MURATA SEEMED TO HAVE HAD A TOUGH NIGHT.
...
WHAT DID YOU PRAY FOR?
WEEELL, I PRAYED THAT MY MARRIAGE WOULD GO WELL!
HARBORING SOMETHING THAT THREATENED TO SPILL OVER...

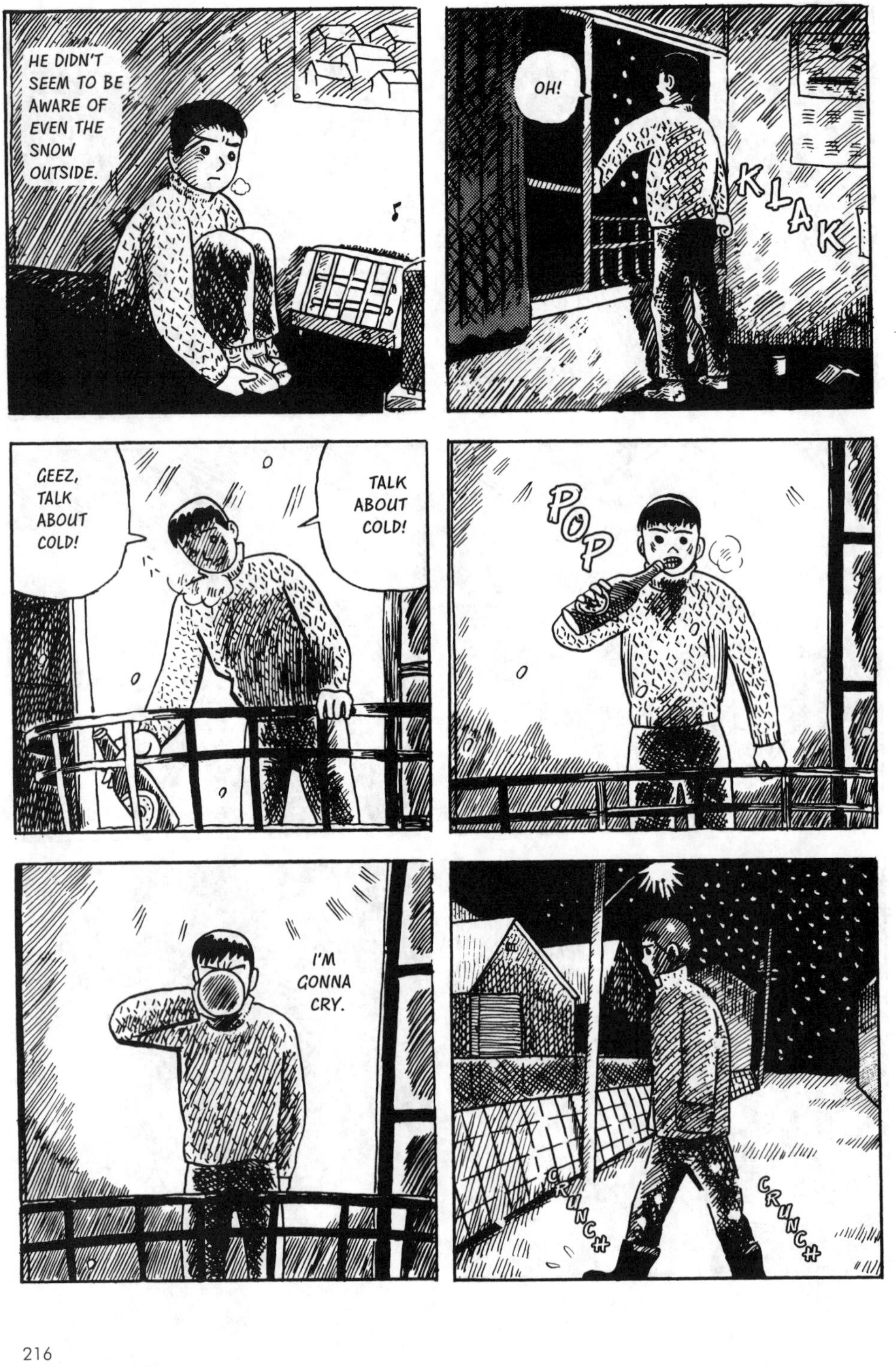
HE DIDN'T SEEM TO BE AWARE OF EVEN THE SNOW OUTSIDE.
OH!
KLAK
GEEZ, TALK ABOUT COLD!
TALK ABOUT COLD!
POP
I'M GONNA CRY.
CRUNCH
CRUNCH

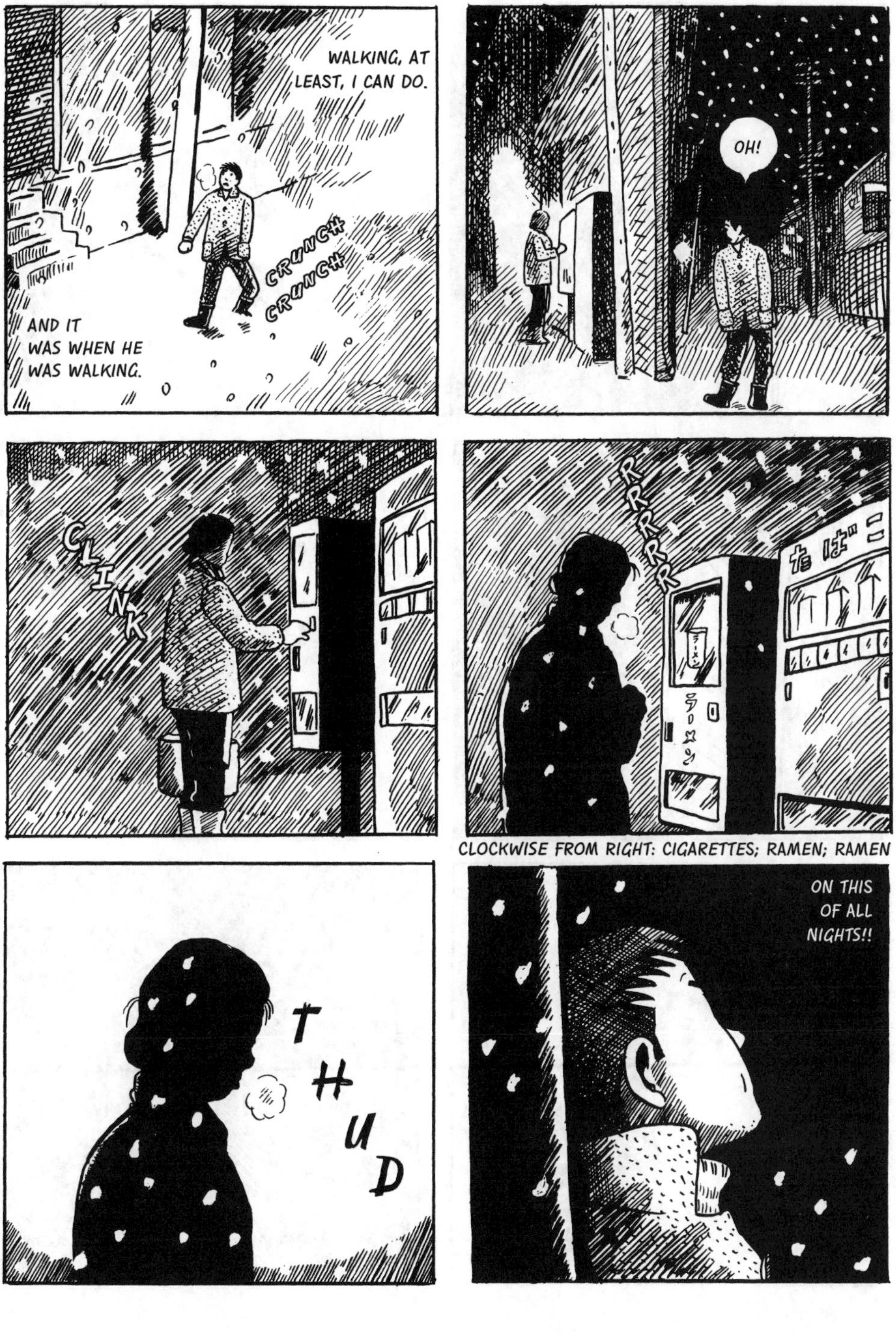
WALKING, AT LEAST, I CAN DO.
CRUNCH CRUNCH
AND IT WAS WHEN HE WAS WALKING.
OH!
CLINK
RRRRR
たばこ
CLOCKWISE FROM RIGHT: CIGARETTES; RAMEN; RAMEN
THUD
ON THIS OF ALL NIGHTS!!

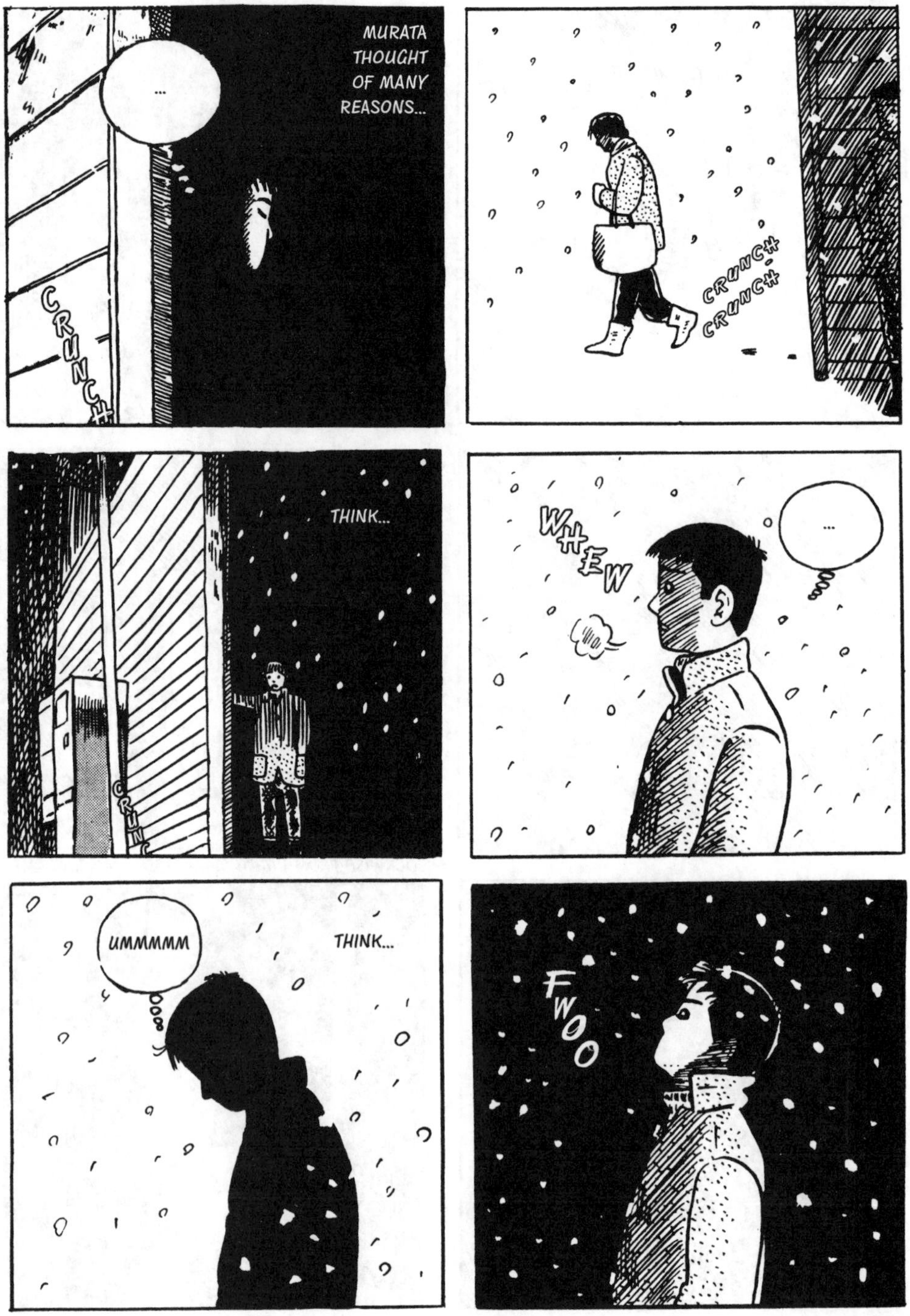
...
MURATA THOUGHT OF MANY REASONS...
CRUNCH
CRUNCH CRUNCH
THINK...
WHEW
...
UMMMMM
THINK...
FWOO

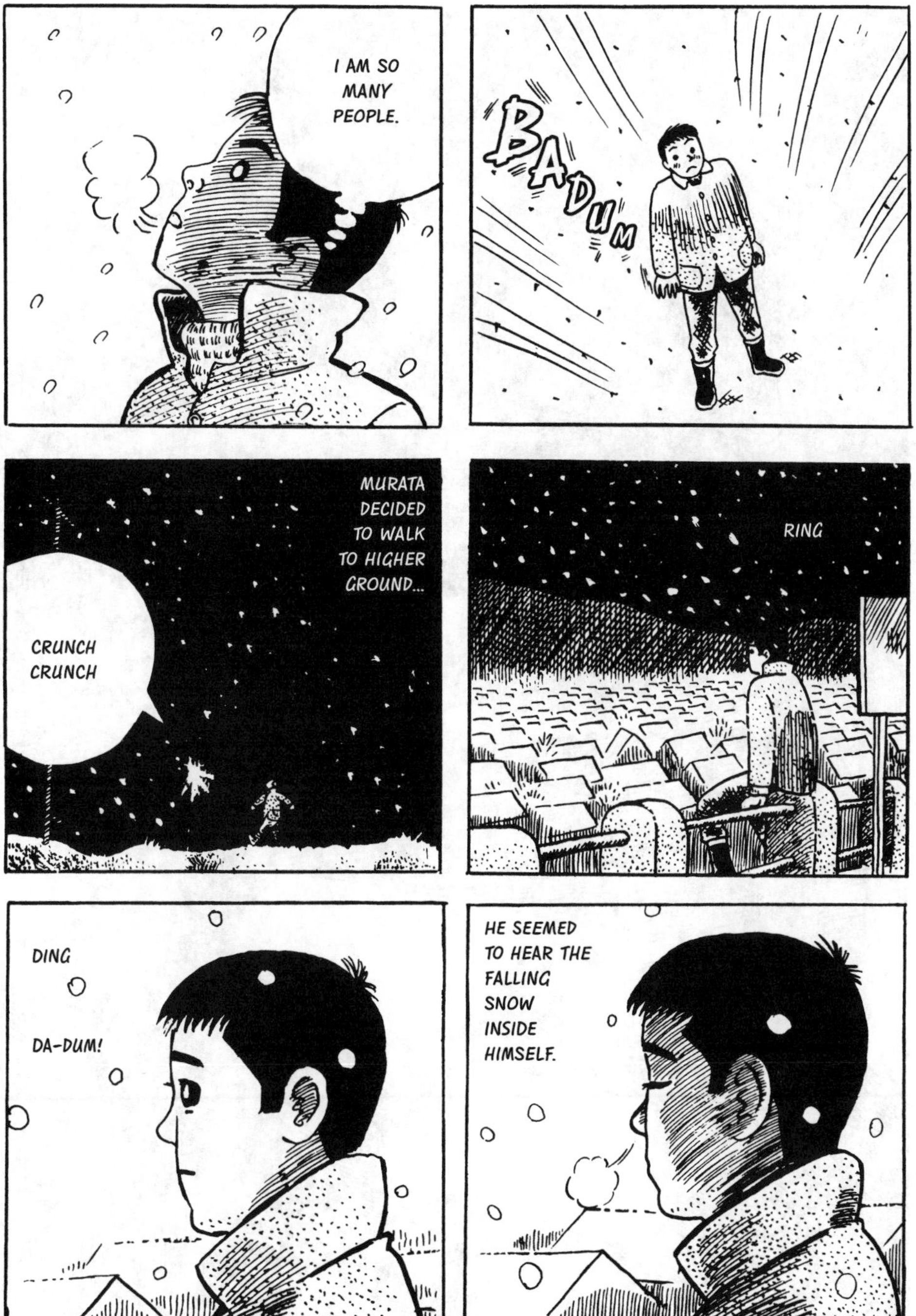
I AM SO MANY PEOPLE.
BADUM
MURATA DECIDED TO WALK TO HIGHER GROUND...
CRUNCH CRUNCH
RING
DING
DA-DUM!
HE SEEMED TO HEAR THE FALLING SNOW INSIDE HIMSELF.

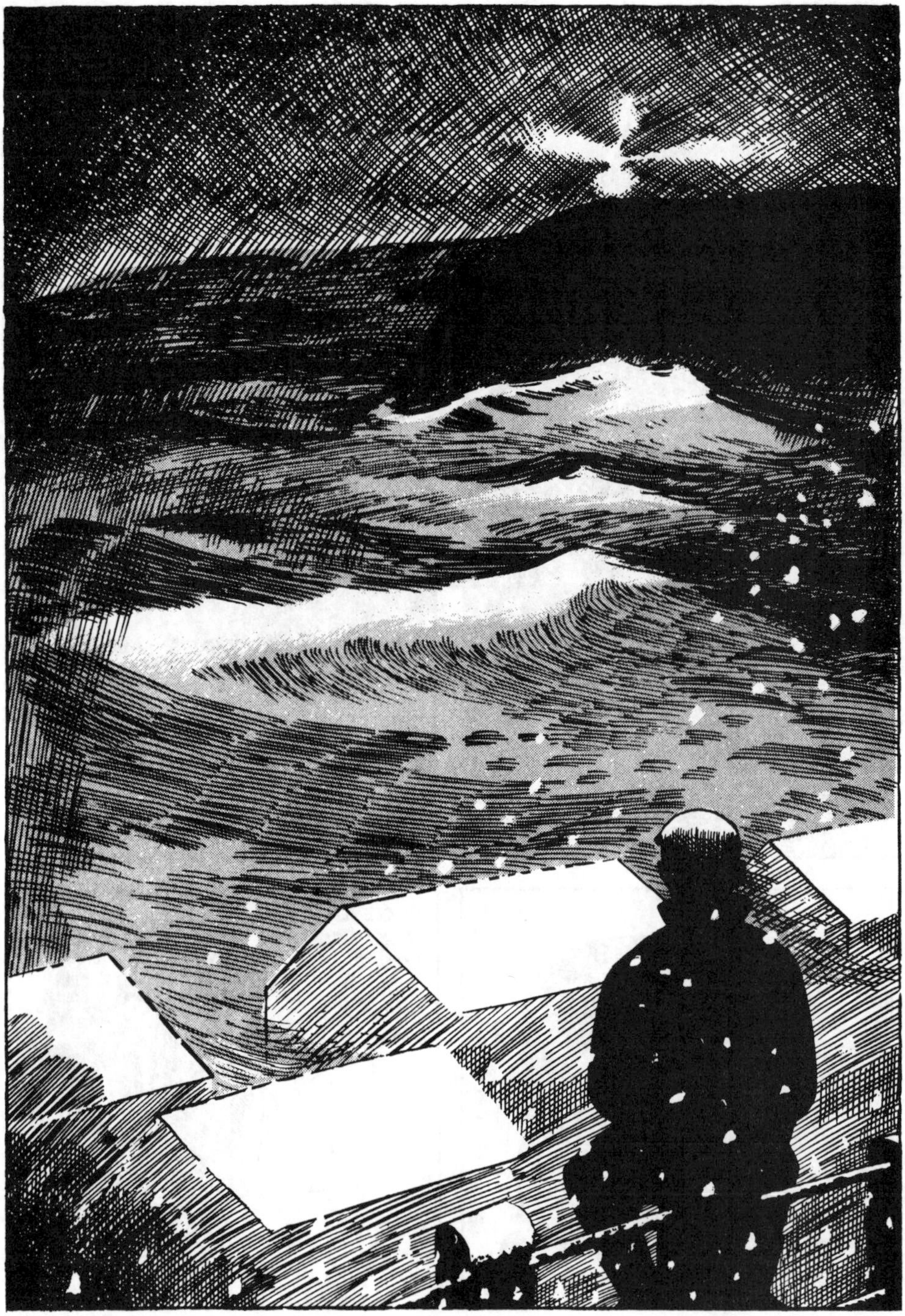

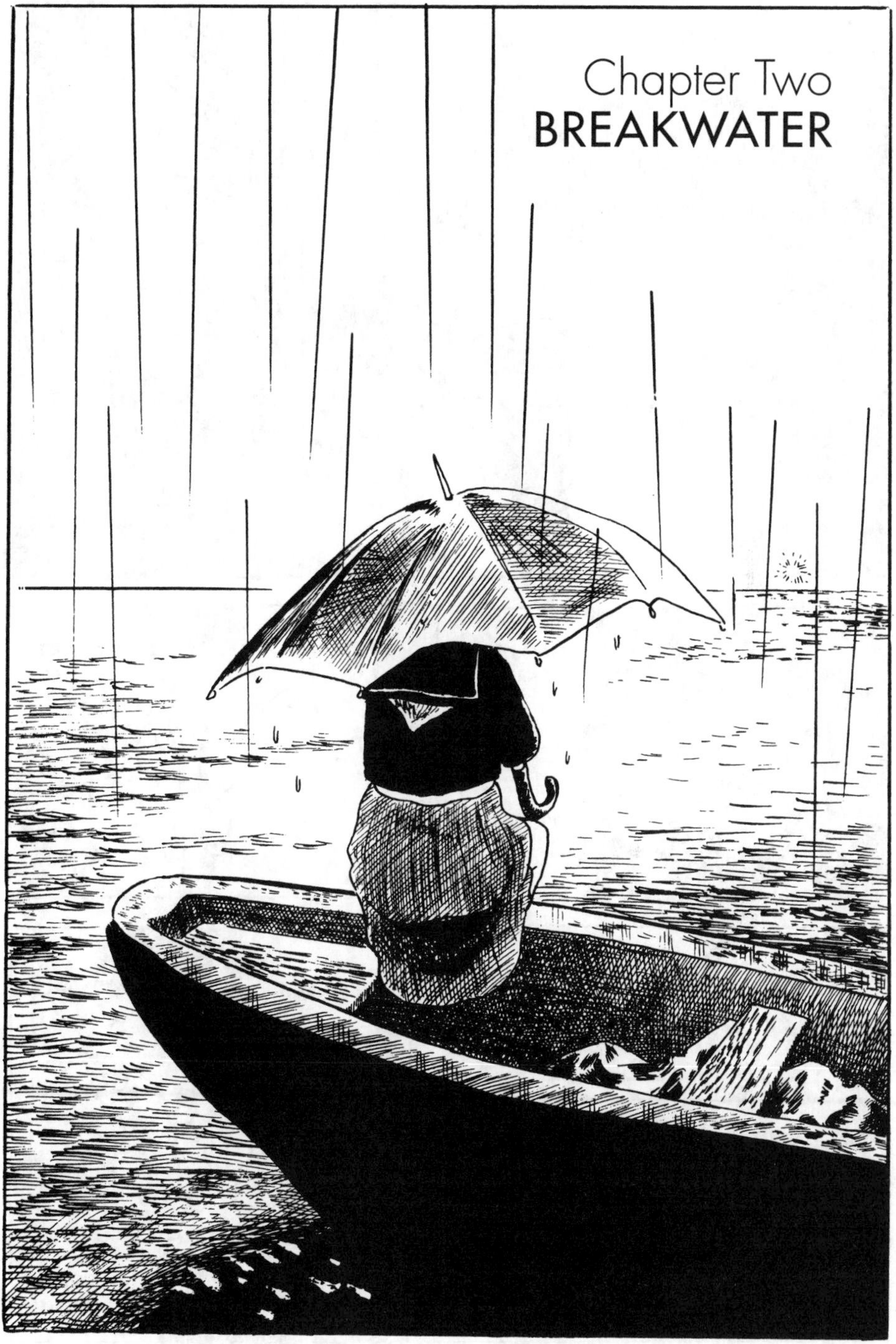
Chapter Two
BREAKWATER

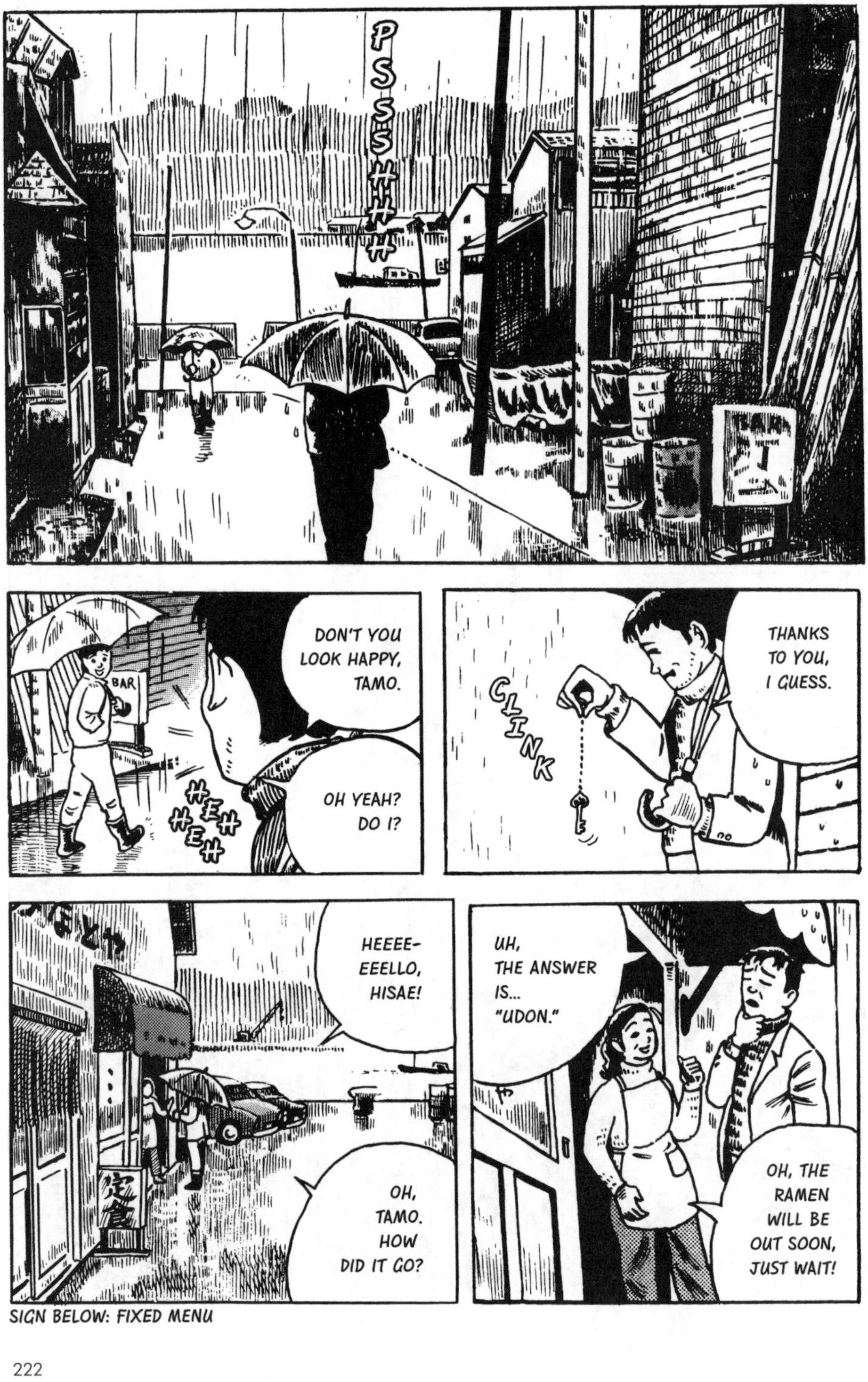
PSSSHHHH
DON'T YOU LOOK HAPPY, TAMO.
BAR
HEH HEH HEH
OH YEAH? DO I?
CLINK
THANKS TO YOU, I GUESS.
HEEEE-EEELLO, HISAE!
OH, TAMO. HOW DID IT GO?
UH, THE ANSWER IS... "UDON."
OH, THE RAMEN WILL BE OUT SOON, JUST WAIT!

SIGN BELOW: FIXED MENU

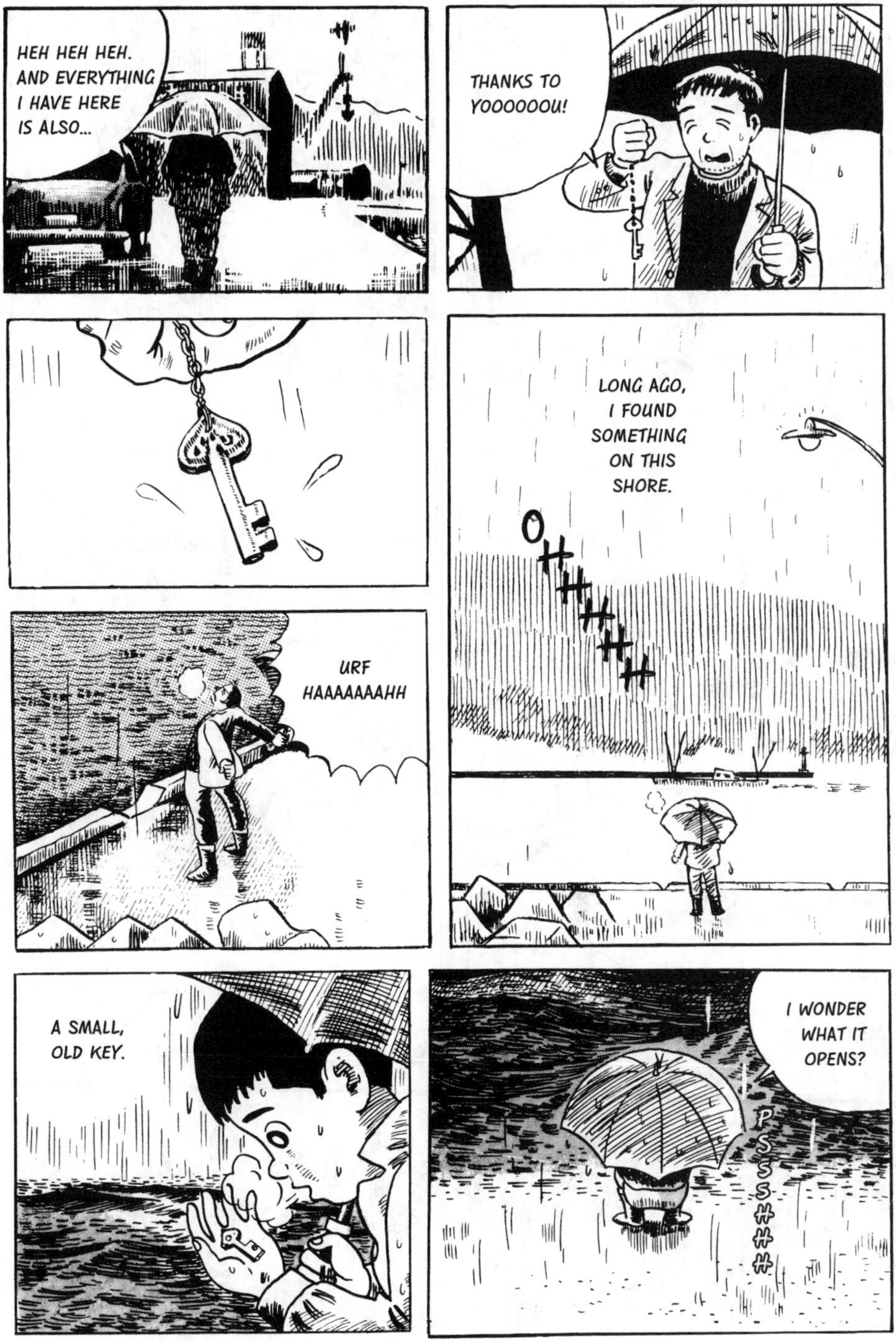
HEH HEH HEH. AND EVERYTHING I HAVE HERE IS ALSO...
THANKS TO YOOOOOOU!
LONG AGO, I FOUND SOMETHING ON THIS SHORE.
OHHHHHHH
URF HAAAAAAAHH
A SMALL, OLD KEY.
I WONDER WHAT IT OPENS?
PSSSHHH

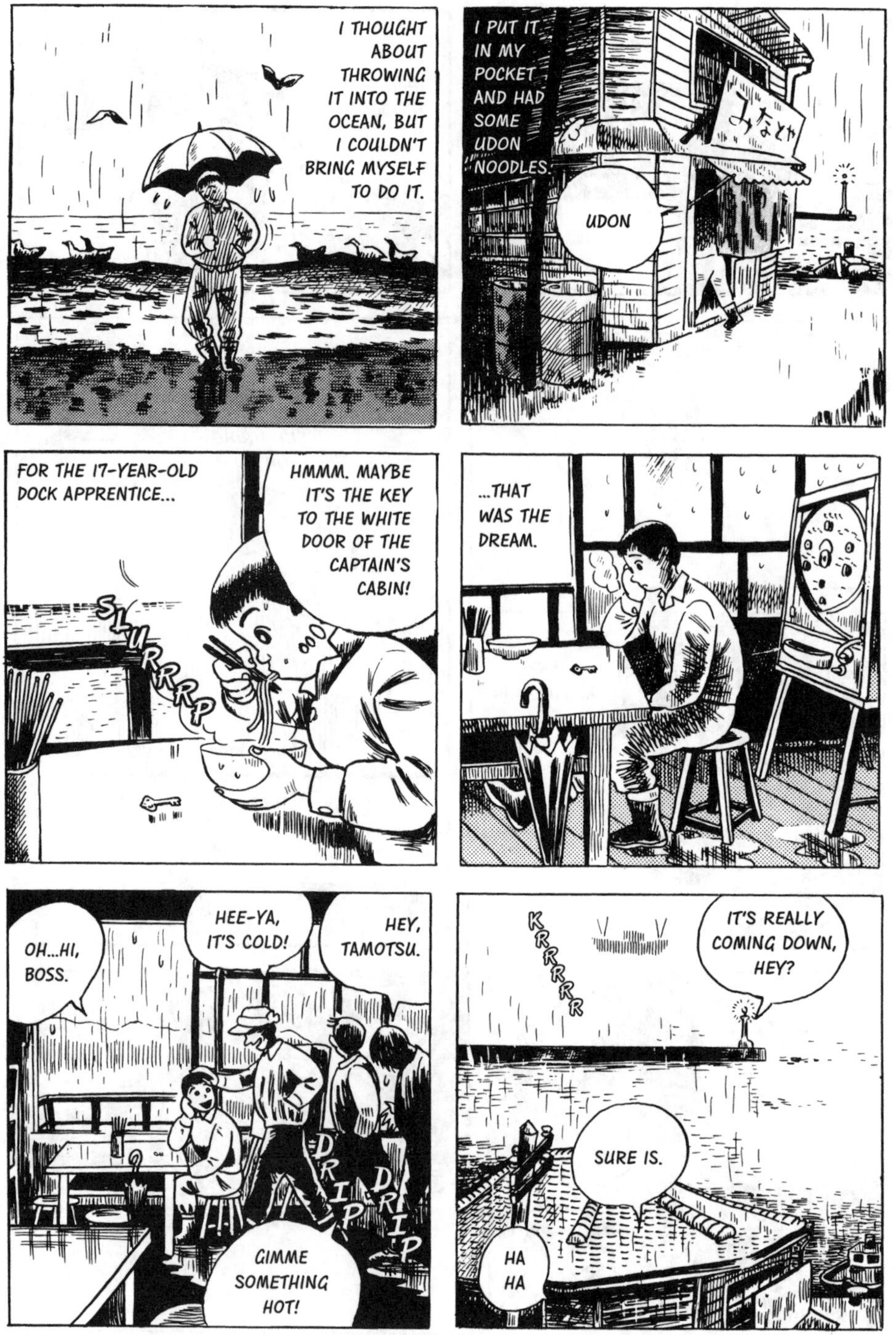
I THOUGHT ABOUT THROWING IT INTO THE OCEAN, BUT I COULDN'T BRING MYSELF TO DO IT.
I PUT IT IN MY POCKET AND HAD SOME UDON NOODLES.
みなとや
UDON
FOR THE 17-YEAR-OLD DOCK APPRENTICE...
HMMM. MAYBE IT'S THE KEY TO THE WHITE DOOR OF THE CAPTAIN'S CABIN!
SLURRRRP
...THAT WAS THE DREAM.
OH...HI, BOSS.
HEE-YA, IT'S COLD!
HEY, TAMOTSU.
DRIP
DRIP
GIMME SOMETHING HOT!
KRRRRRR
IT'S REALLY COMING DOWN, HEY?
SURE IS.
HA HA

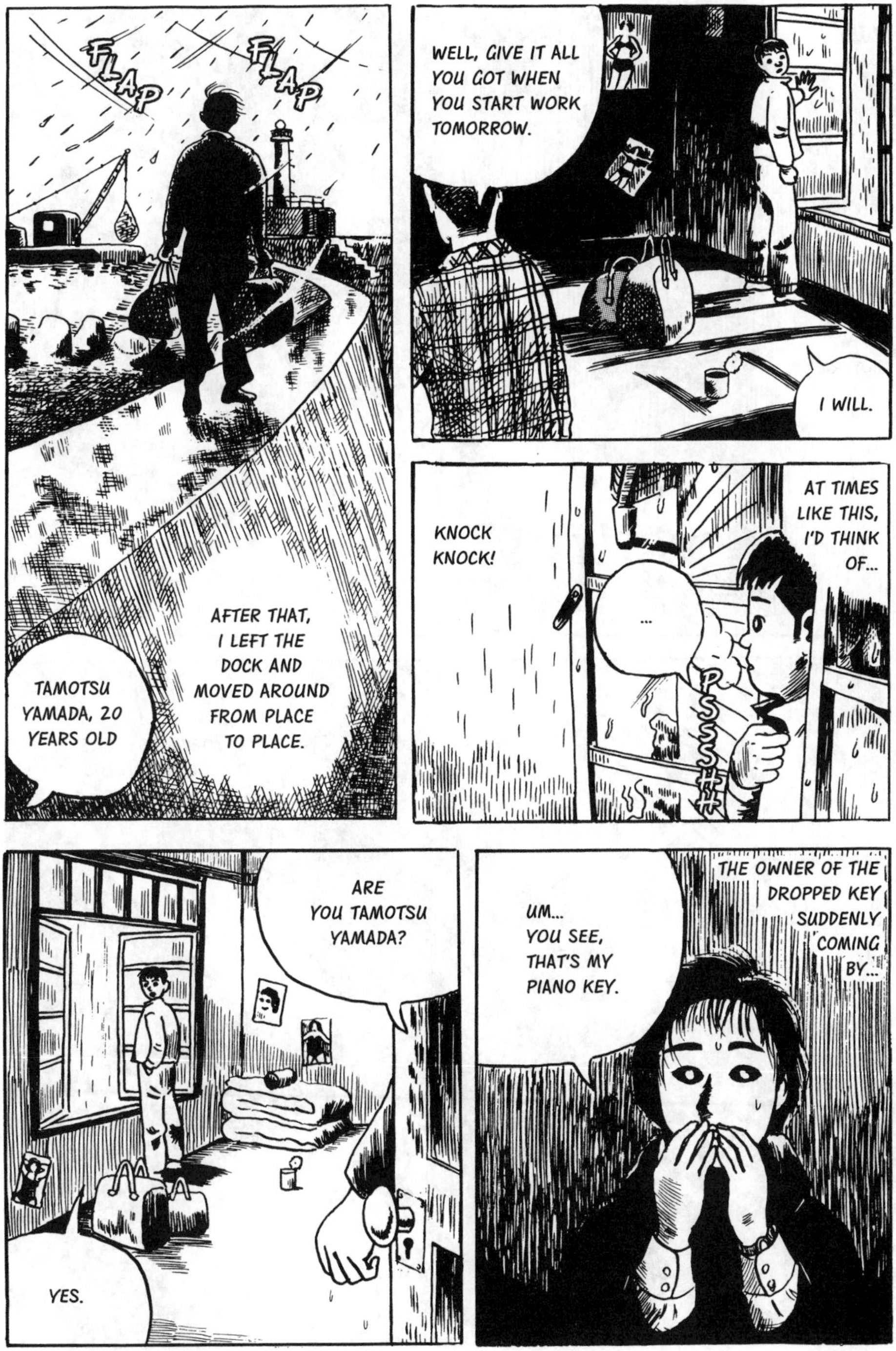
FLAP
FLAP
TAMOTSU YAMADA, 20 YEARS OLD
AFTER THAT, I LEFT THE DOCK AND MOVED AROUND FROM PLACE TO PLACE.
WELL, GIVE IT ALL YOU GOT WHEN YOU START WORK TOMORROW.
I WILL.
KNOCK KNOCK!
...
AT TIMES LIKE THIS, I'D THINK OF...
PSSSHH
ARE YOU TAMOTSU YAMADA?
YES.
THE OWNER OF THE DROPPED KEY SUDDENLY COMING BY...
UM... YOU SEE, THAT'S MY PIANO KEY.

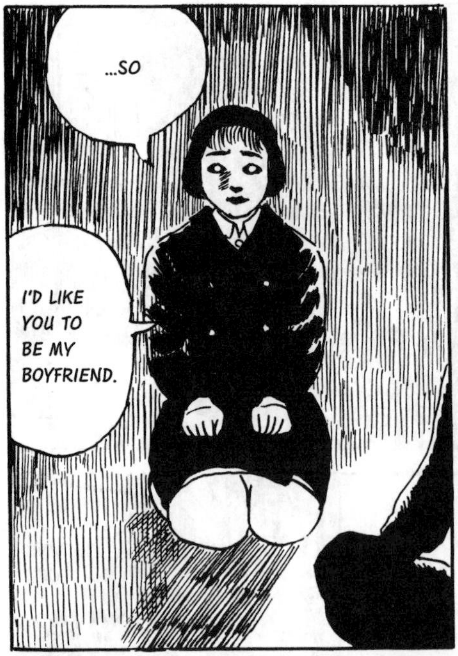
...SO
I'D LIKE YOU TO BE MY BOYFRIEND.

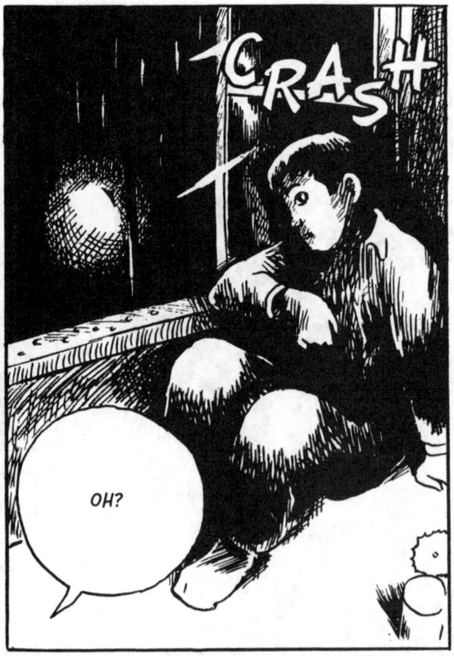
CRASH
OH?

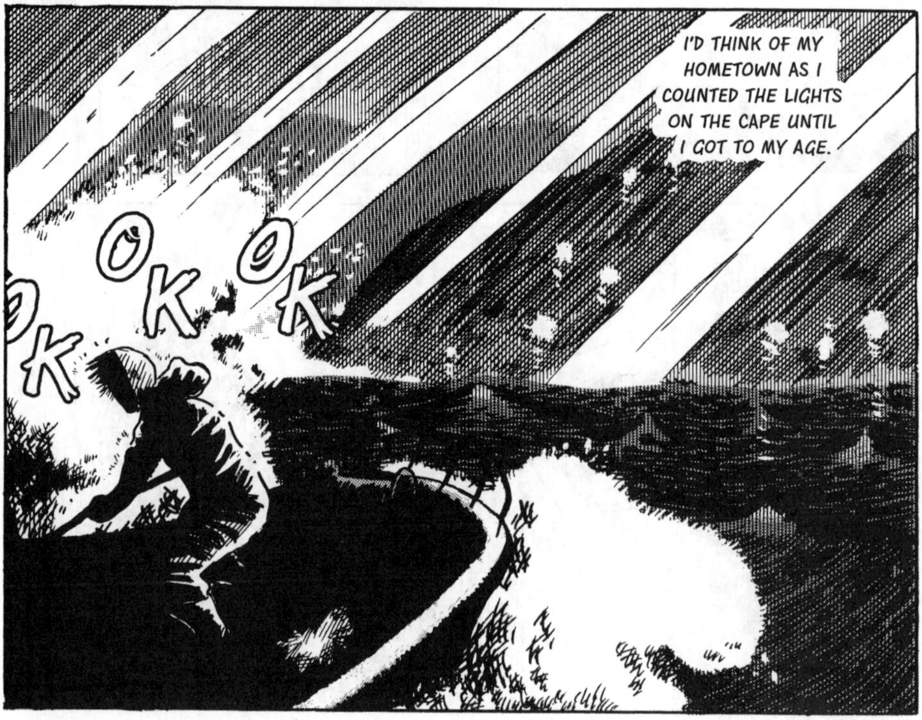
I'D THINK OF MY HOMETOWN AS I COUNTED THE LIGHTS ON THE CAPE UNTIL I GOT TO MY AGE.
OK OK

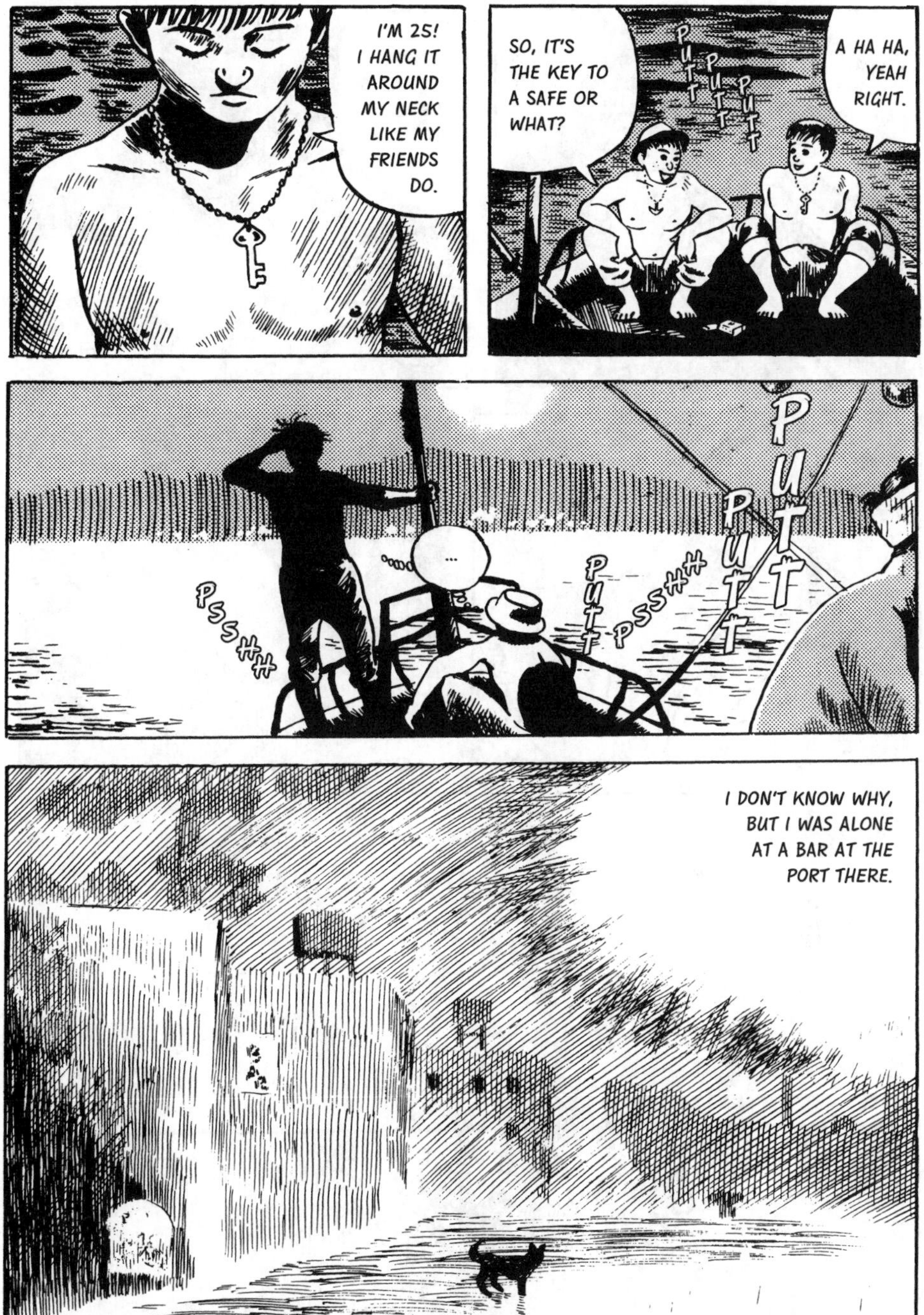
I'M 25! I HANG IT AROUND MY NECK LIKE MY FRIENDS DO.
SO, IT'S THE KEY TO A SAFE OR WHAT?
PUTT PUTT PUTT
A HA HA, YEAH RIGHT.
PSSHH
...
PUTT
PSSHH
PUTT
PUTT
I DON'T KNOW WHY, BUT I WAS ALONE AT A BAR AT THE PORT THERE.

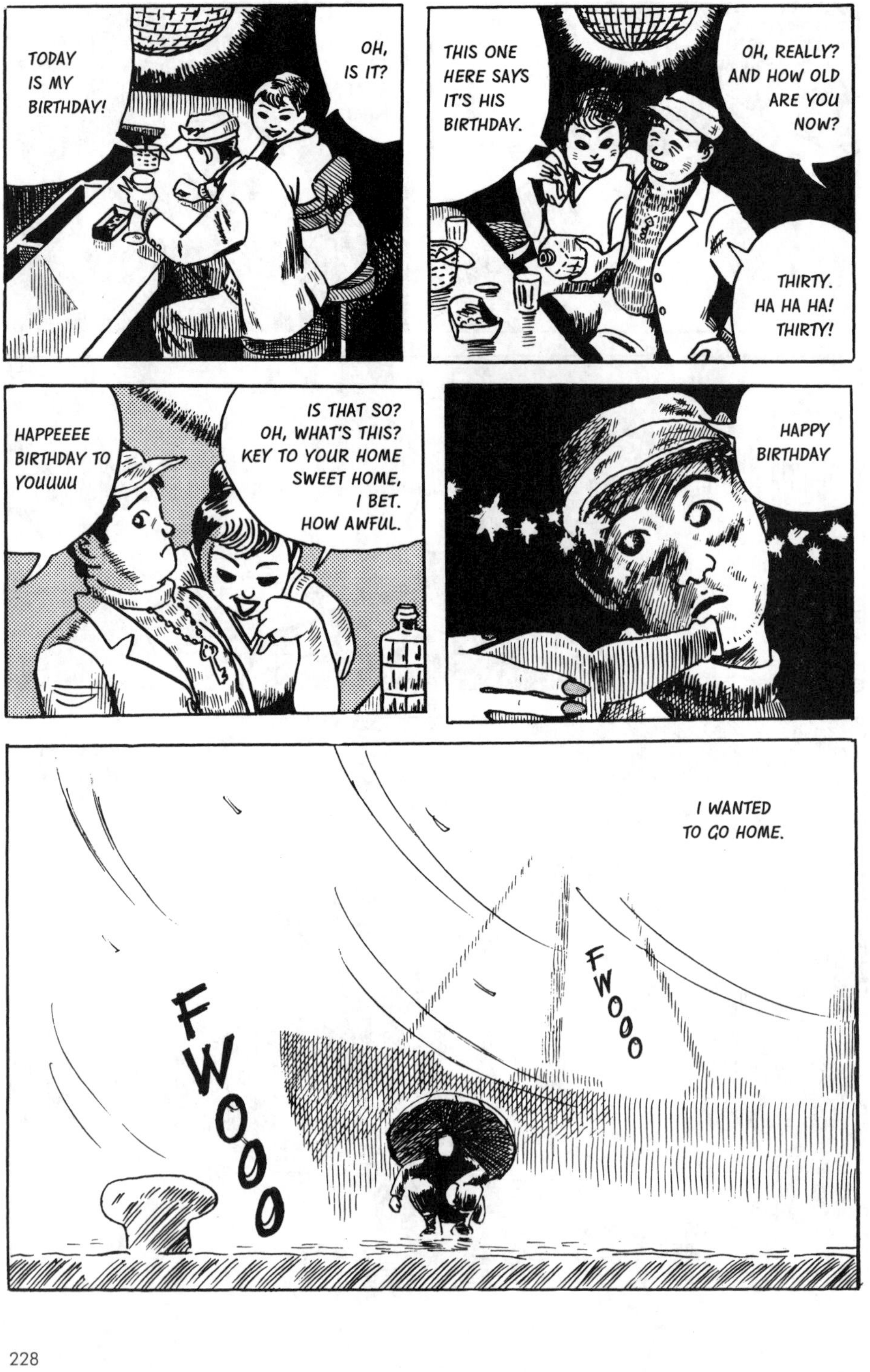
TODAY IS MY BIRTHDAY!
OH, IS IT?
THIS ONE HERE SAYS IT'S HIS BIRTHDAY.
OH, REALLY? AND HOW OLD ARE YOU NOW?
THIRTY. HA HA HA! THIRTY!
HAPPEEEE BIRTHDAY TO YOUUUU
IS THAT SO? OH, WHAT'S THIS? KEY TO YOUR HOME SWEET HOME, I BET. HOW AWFUL.
HAPPY BIRTHDAY
I WANTED TO GO HOME.
FWOOO
FWOOO

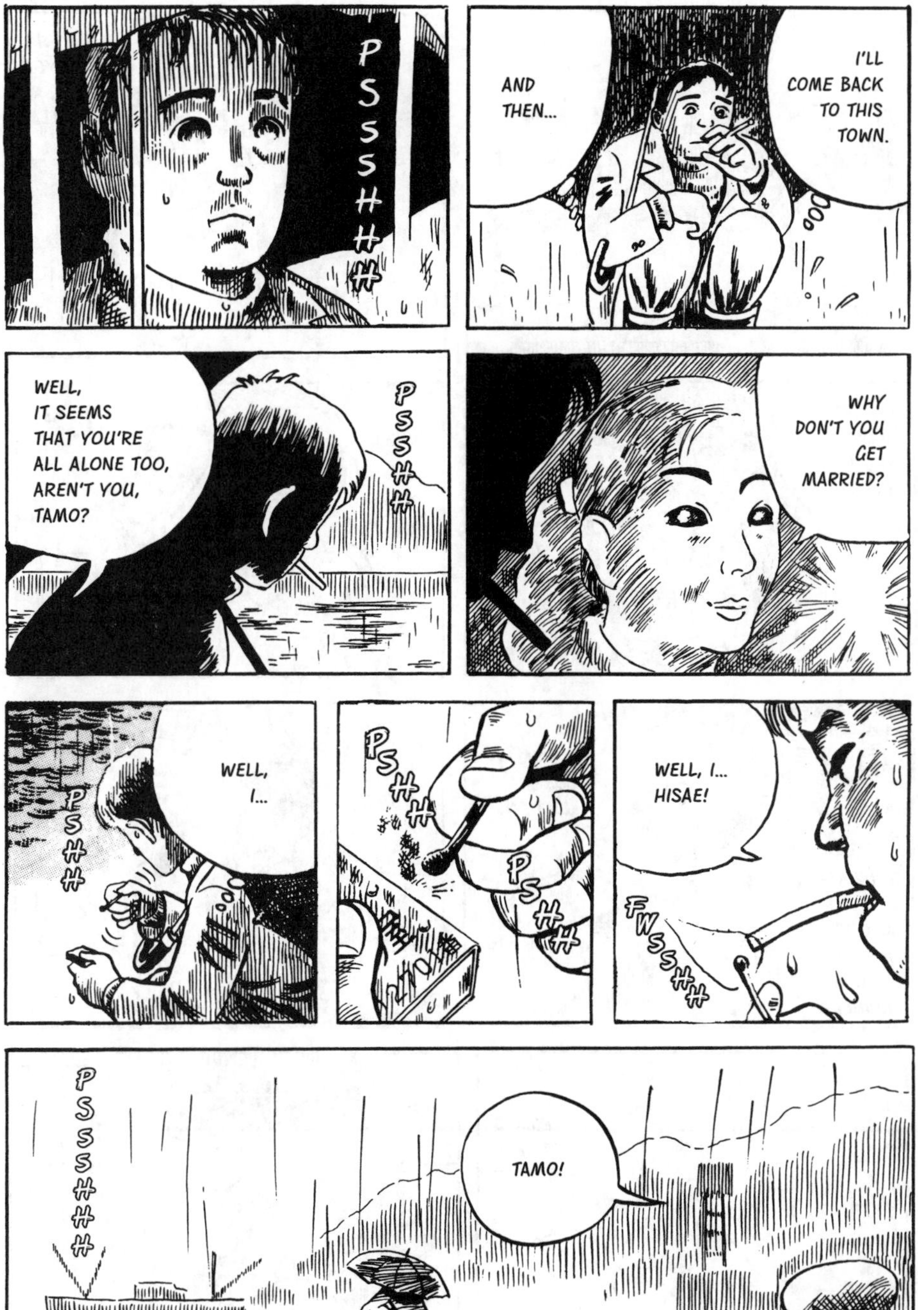
PSSSHHH
AND THEN...
I'LL COME BACK TO THIS TOWN.
WELL, IT SEEMS THAT YOU'RE ALL ALONE TOO, AREN'T YOU, TAMO?
PSSHH
WHY DON'T YOU GET MARRIED?
WELL, I...
PSHH
PSHH
PSHH
WELL, I... HISAE!
FWSSHH
PSSSHHH
TAMO!

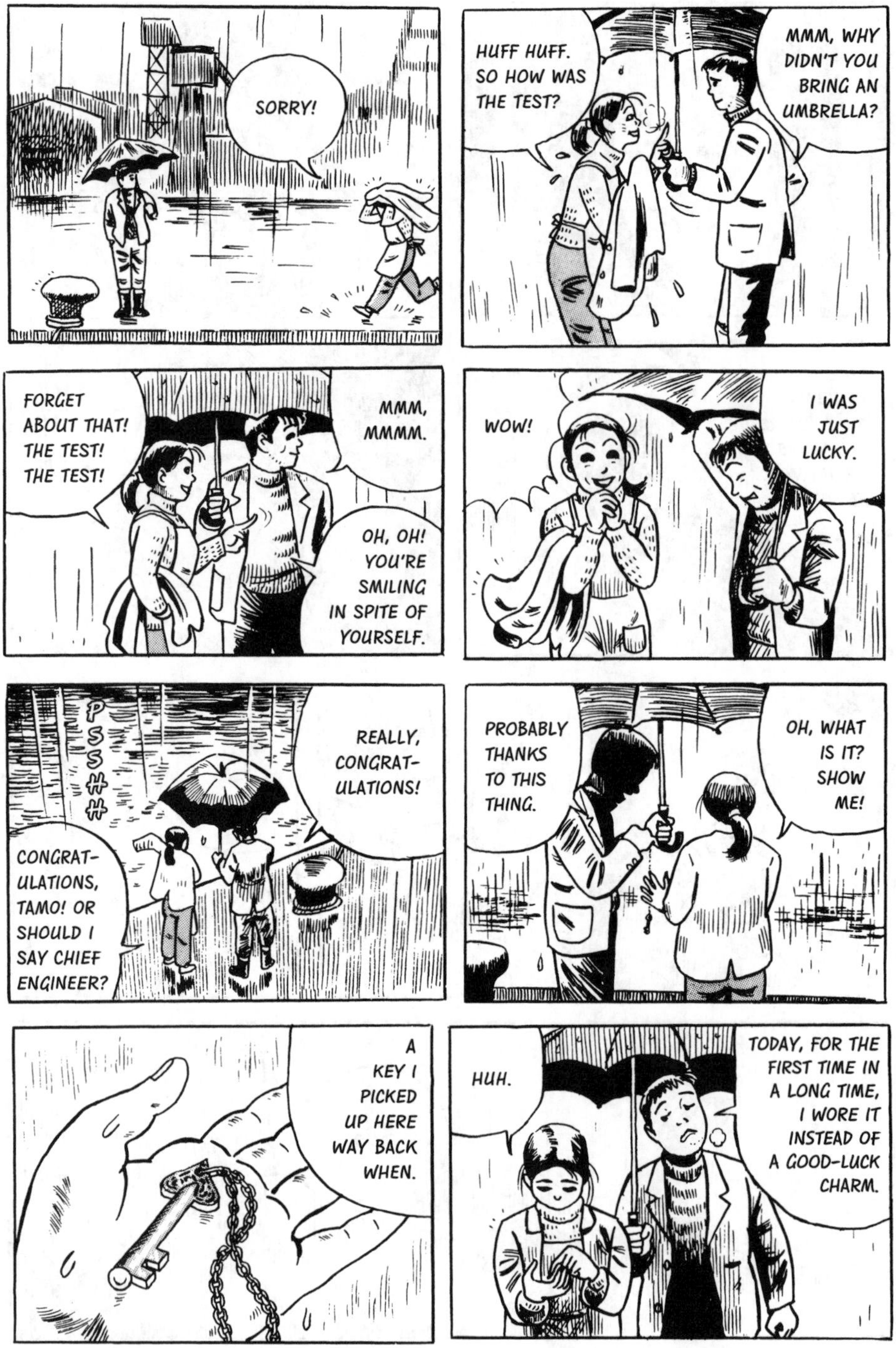
SORRY!
HUFF HUFF. SO HOW WAS THE TEST?
MMM, WHY DIDN'T YOU BRING AN UMBRELLA?
FORGET ABOUT THAT! THE TEST! THE TEST!
MMM, MMMM.
OH, OH! YOU'RE SMILING IN SPITE OF YOURSELF.
WOW!
I WAS JUST LUCKY.
PSSHHH
REALLY, CONGRAT-ULATIONS!
CONGRAT-ULATIONS, TAMO! OR SHOULD I SAY CHIEF ENGINEER?
PROBABLY THANKS TO THIS THING.
OH, WHAT IS IT? SHOW ME!
A KEY I PICKED UP HERE WAY BACK WHEN.
HUH.
TODAY, FOR THE FIRST TIME IN A LONG TIME, I WORE IT INSTEAD OF A GOOD-LUCK CHARM.

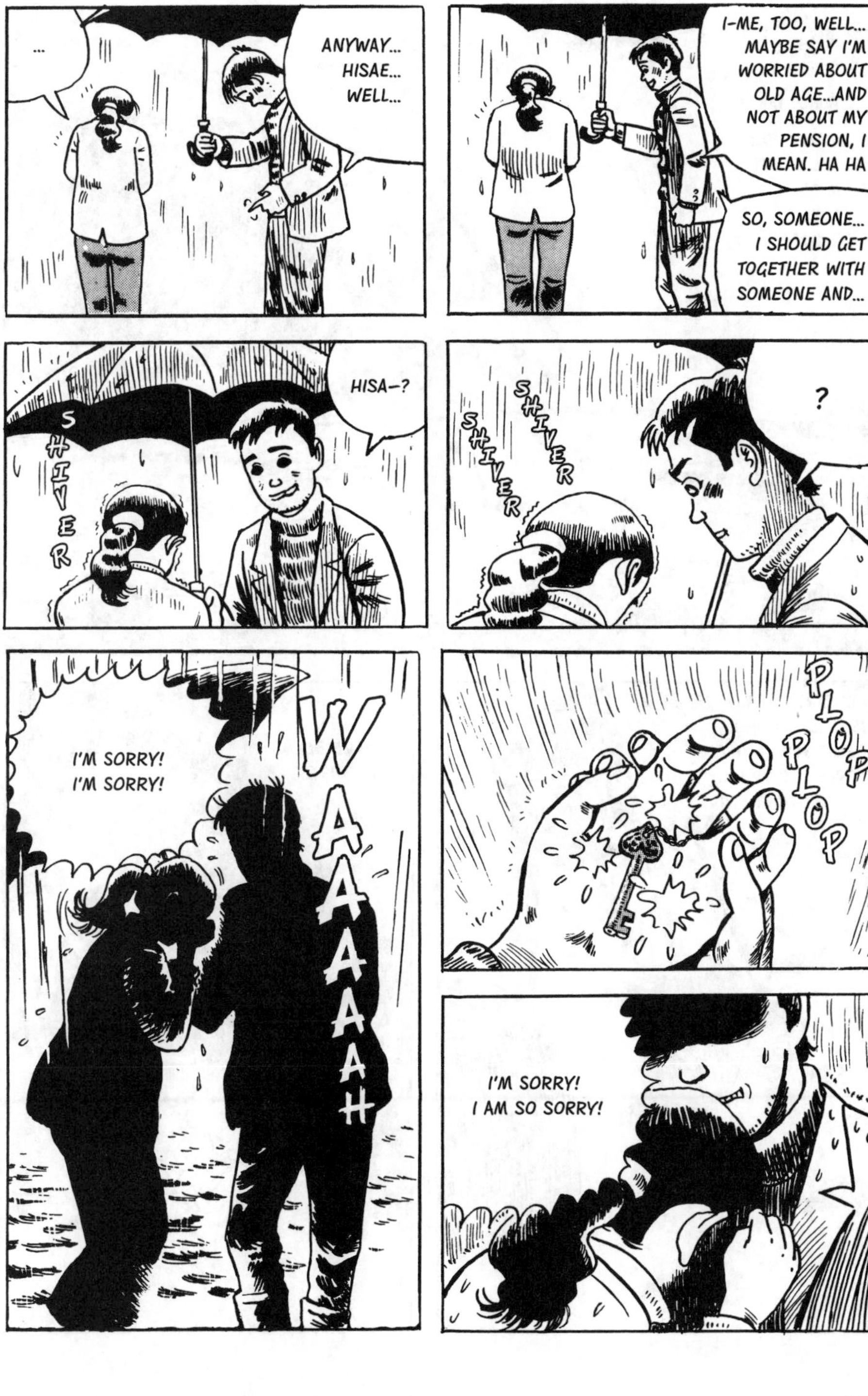
...
ANYWAY... HISAE... WELL...
I-ME, TOO, WELL... MAYBE SAY I'M WORRIED ABOUT OLD AGE...AND NOT ABOUT MY PENSION, I MEAN. HA HA
SO, SOMEONE... I SHOULD GET TOGETHER WITH SOMEONE AND...
HISA—?
SHIVER
SHIVER
SHIVER
?
I'M SORRY! I'M SORRY!
WAAAAAH
PLOP PLOP PLOP
I'M SORRY! I AM SO SORRY!

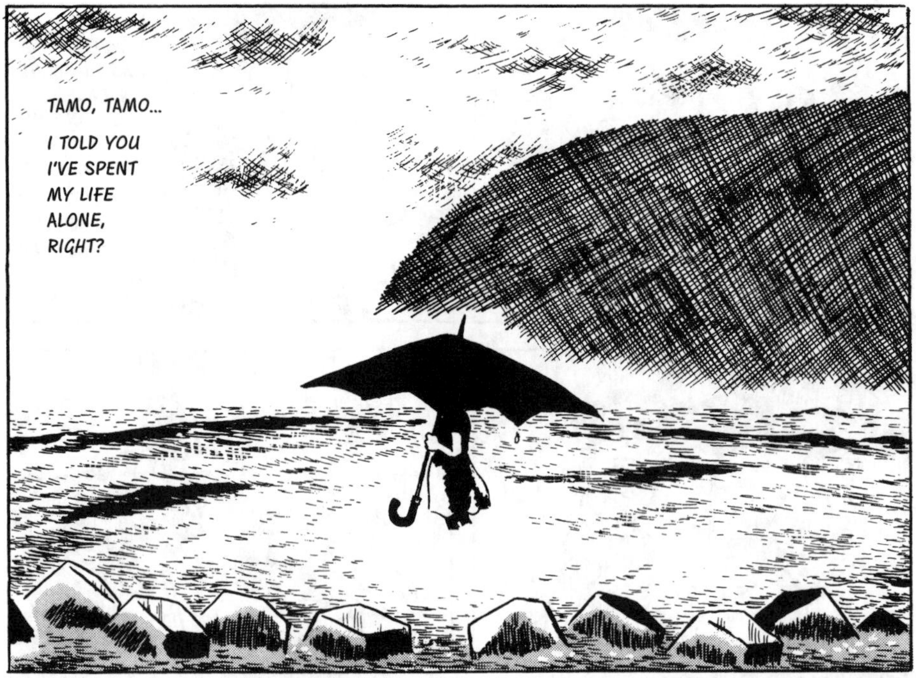
TAMO, TAMO...
I TOLD YOU I'VE SPENT MY LIFE ALONE, RIGHT?

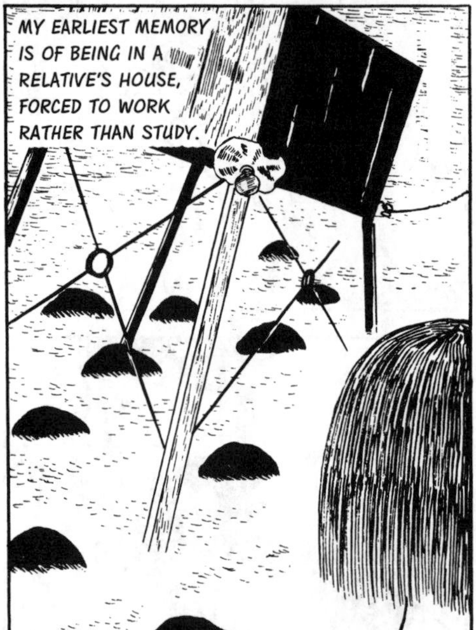
MY EARLIEST MEMORY IS OF BEING IN A RELATIVE'S HOUSE, FORCED TO WORK RATHER THAN STUDY.

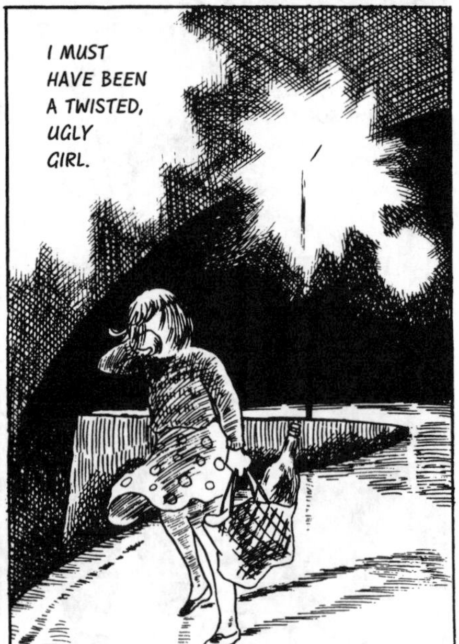
I MUST HAVE BEEN A TWISTED, UGLY GIRL.

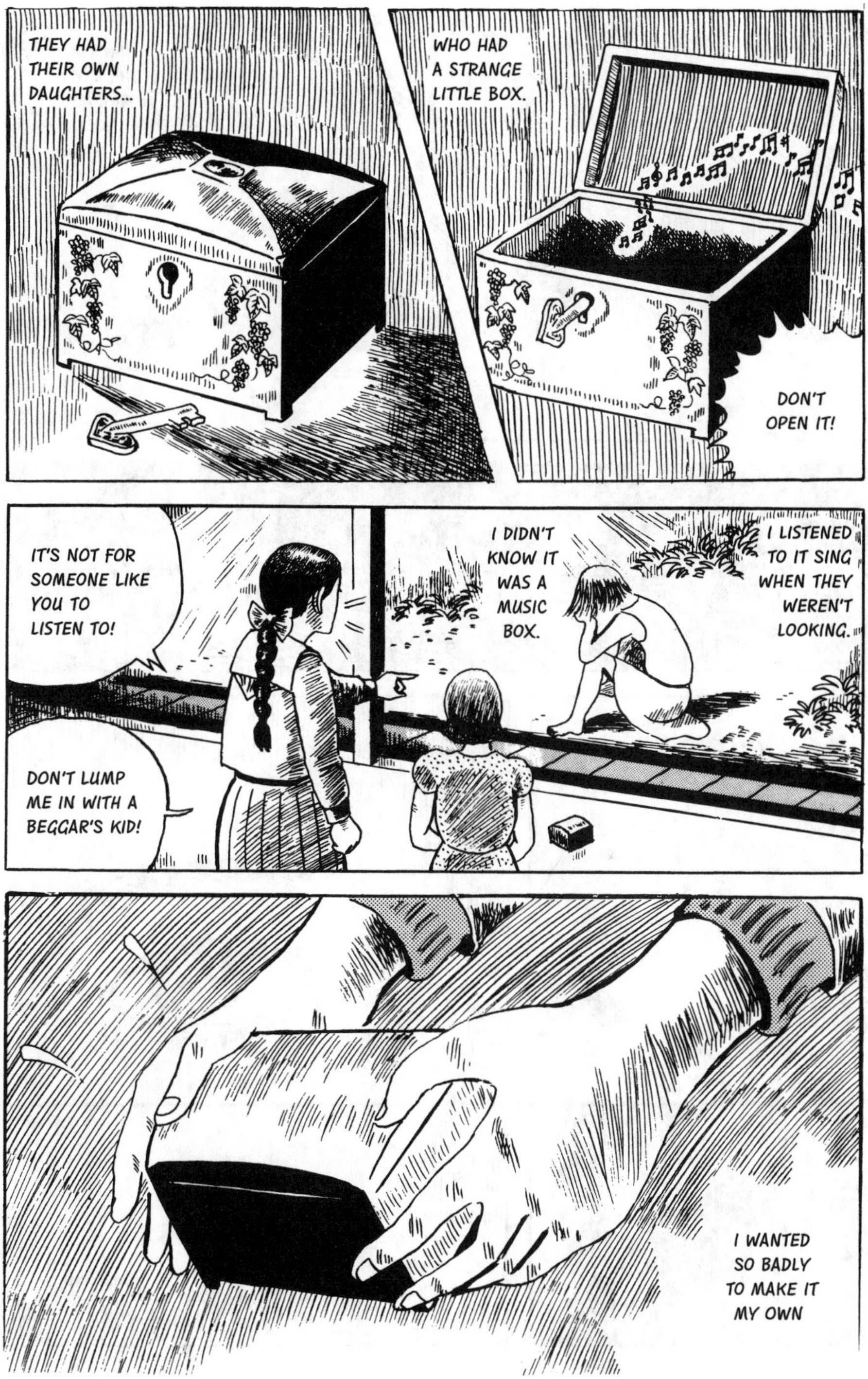
THEY HAD THEIR OWN DAUGHTERS...
WHO HAD A STRANGE LITTLE BOX.
DON'T OPEN IT!
IT'S NOT FOR SOMEONE LIKE YOU TO LISTEN TO!
DON'T LUMP ME IN WITH A BEGGAR'S KID!
I DIDN'T KNOW IT WAS A MUSIC BOX.
I LISTENED TO IT SING WHEN THEY WEREN'T LOOKING.
I WANTED SO BADLY TO MAKE IT MY OWN

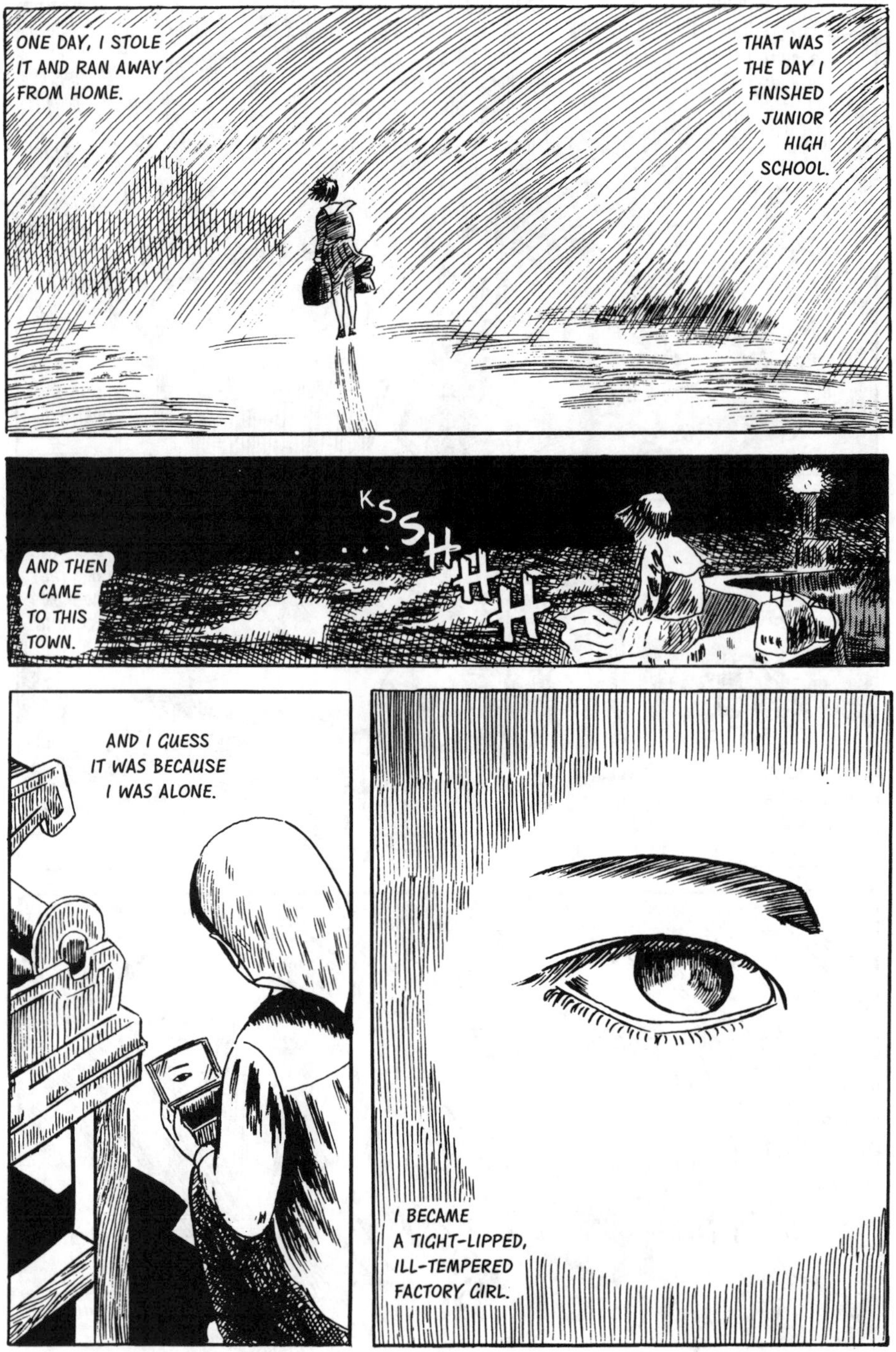
ONE DAY, I STOLE IT AND RAN AWAY FROM HOME.
THAT WAS THE DAY I FINISHED JUNIOR HIGH SCHOOL.
AND THEN I CAME TO THIS TOWN.
KSSHHHH
AND I GUESS IT WAS BECAUSE I WAS ALONE.
I BECAME A TIGHT-LIPPED, ILL-TEMPERED FACTORY GIRL.

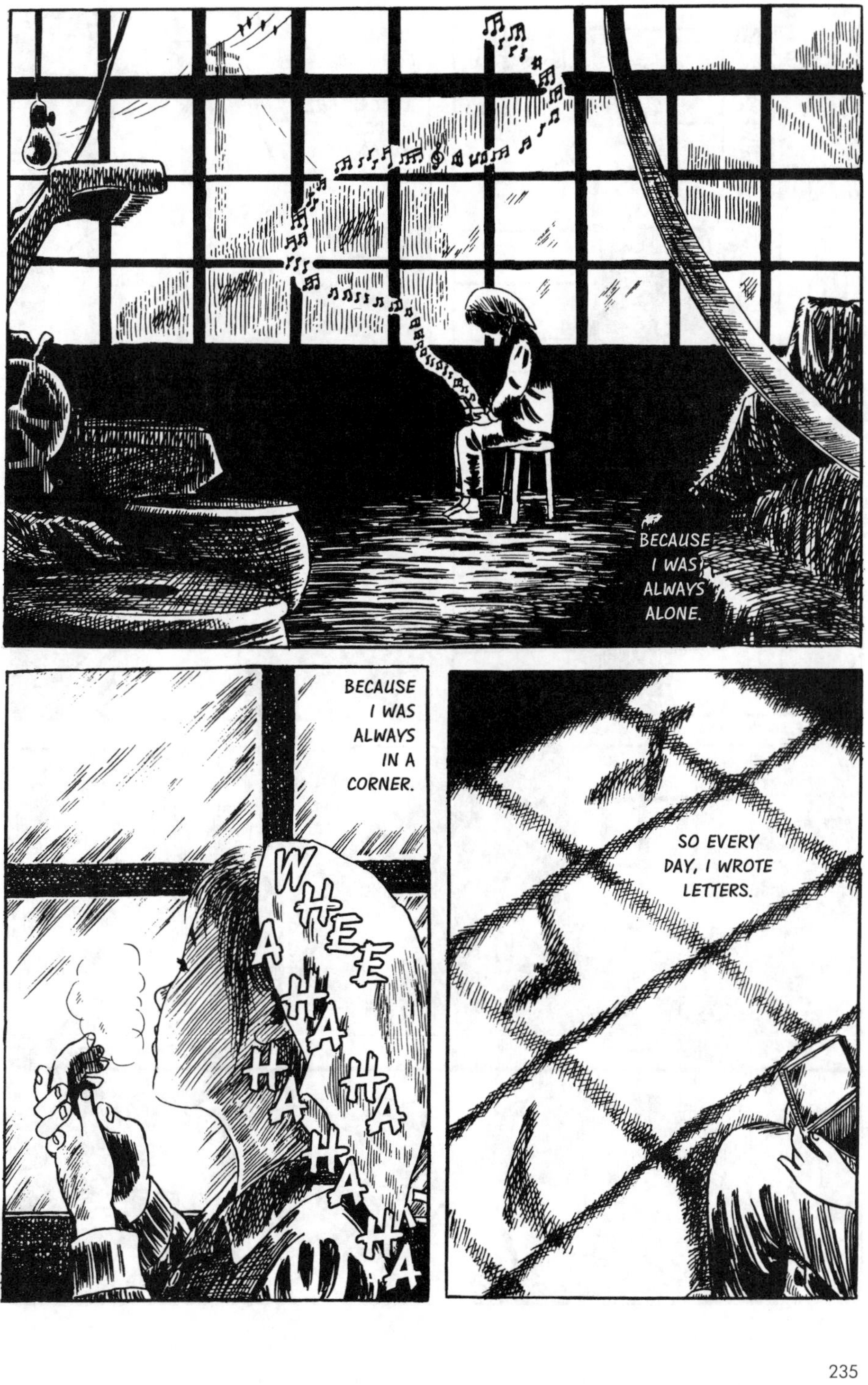
BECAUSE I WAS ALWAYS ALONE.
BECAUSE I WAS ALWAYS IN A CORNER.
WHEEE
AHAHAHAHAHAHAHAHA
SO EVERY DAY, I WROTE LETTERS.

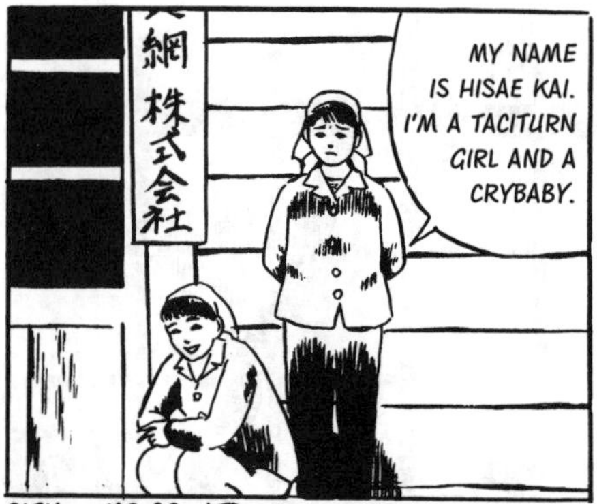
網株式会社
MY NAME IS HISAE KAI. I'M A TACITURN GIRL AND A CRYBABY.

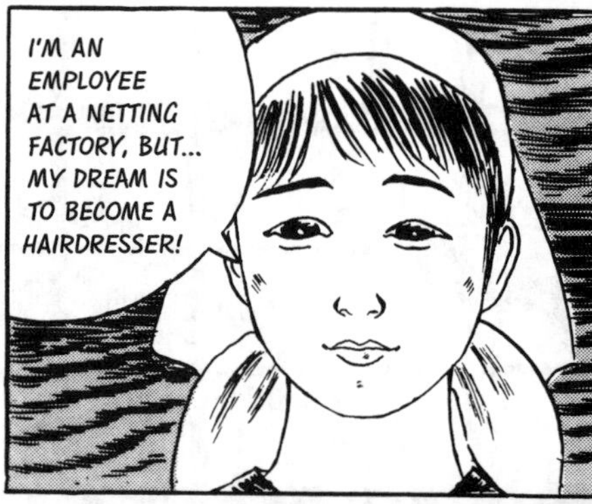
I'M AN EMPLOYEE AT A NETTING FACTORY, BUT... MY DREAM IS TO BECOME A HAIRDRESSER!

SIGN: --MO CO., LTD.

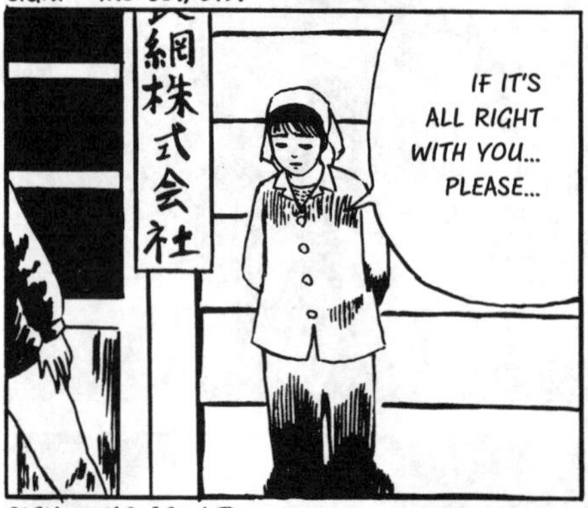
網株式会社
IF IT'S ALL RIGHT WITH YOU... PLEASE...

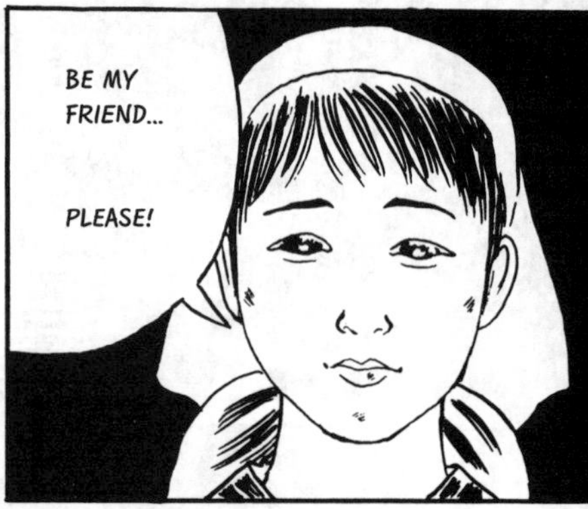
BE MY FRIEND...
PLEASE!

SIGN: --MO CO., LTD.

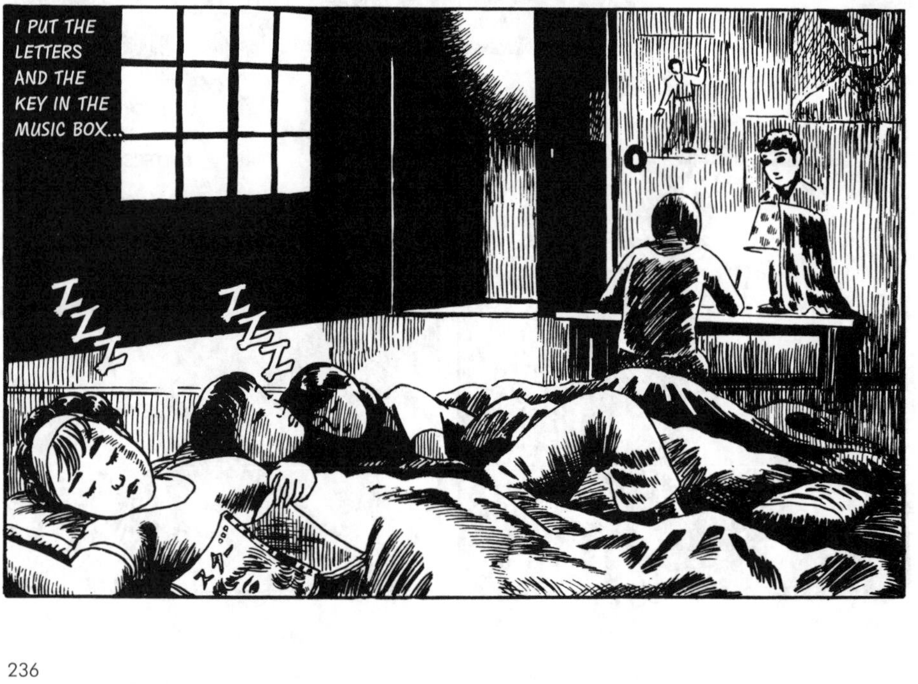
I PUT THE LETTERS AND THE KEY IN THE MUSIC BOX...
ZZZ
ZZZ

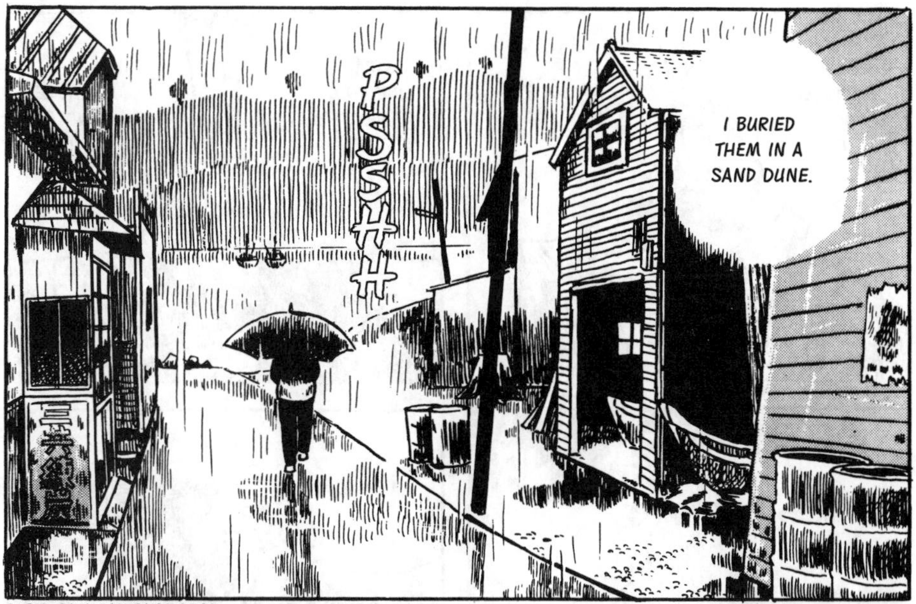
PSSHH
I BURIED THEM IN A SAND DUNE.

SIGN: SANKYO CHARCOAL

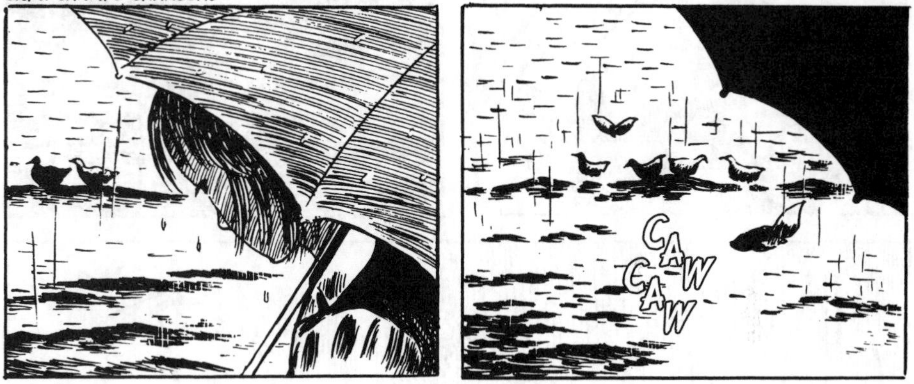
CAW CAW

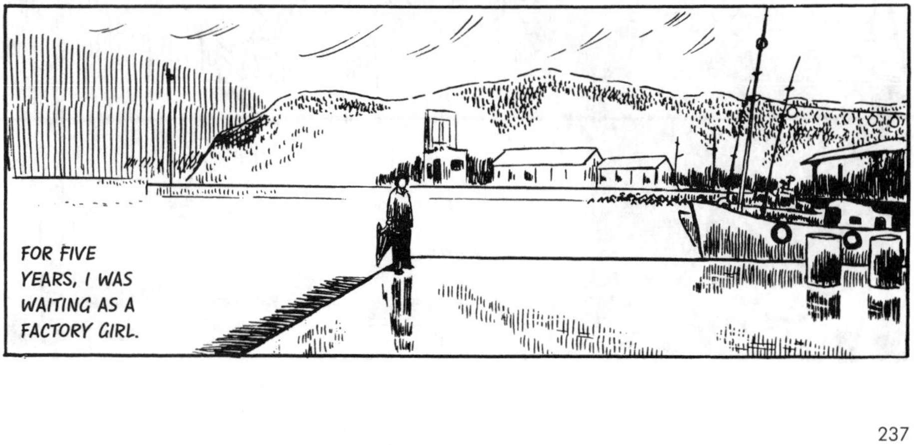
FOR FIVE YEARS, I WAS WAITING AS A FACTORY GIRL.

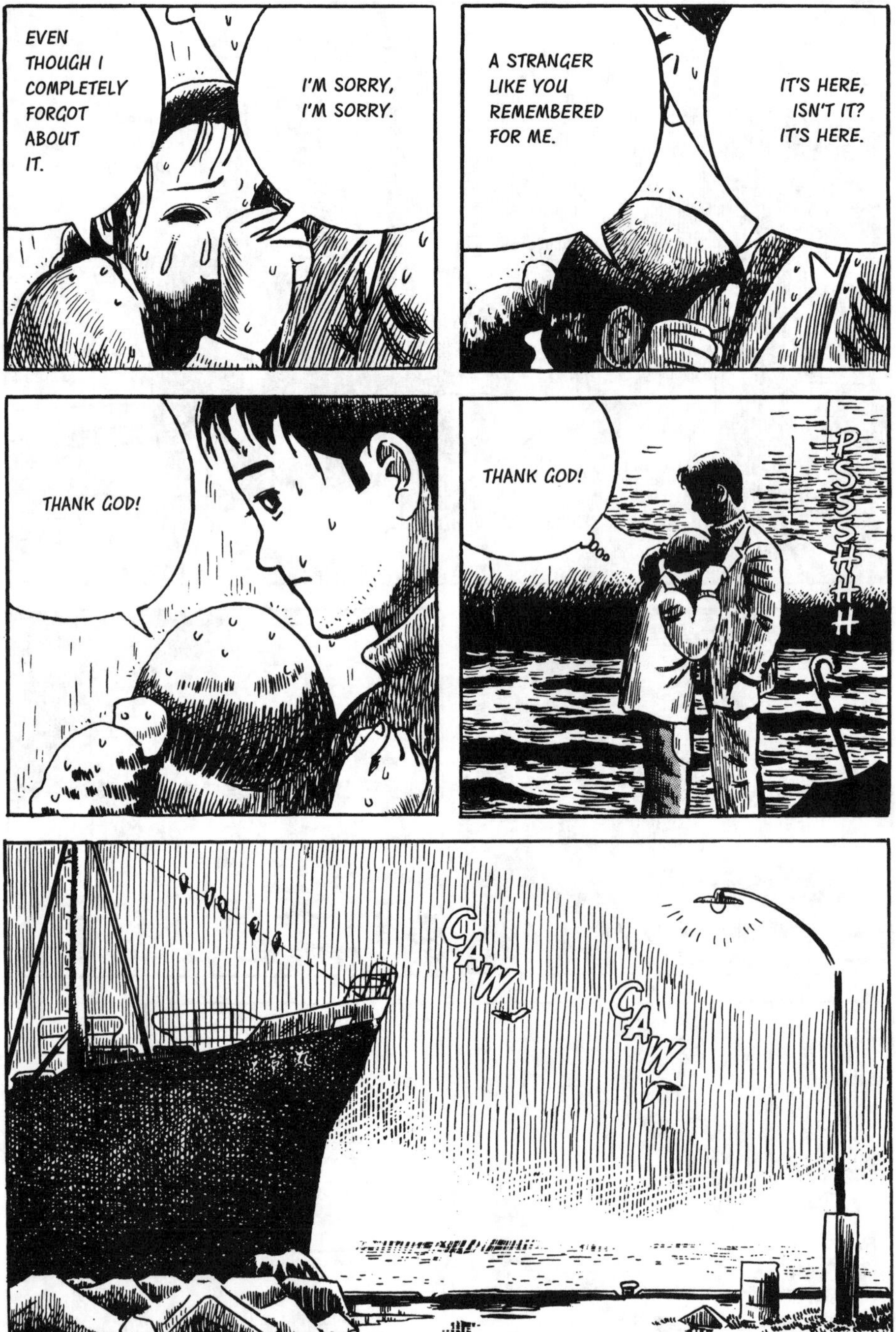
EVEN THOUGH I COMPLETELY FORGOT ABOUT IT.
I'M SORRY, I'M SORRY.
A STRANGER LIKE YOU REMEMBERED FOR ME.
IT'S HERE, ISN'T IT? IT'S HERE.
THANK GOD!
THANK GOD!
PSSSHHH
CAW
CAW
CAW

Chapter Three
WATERWAY

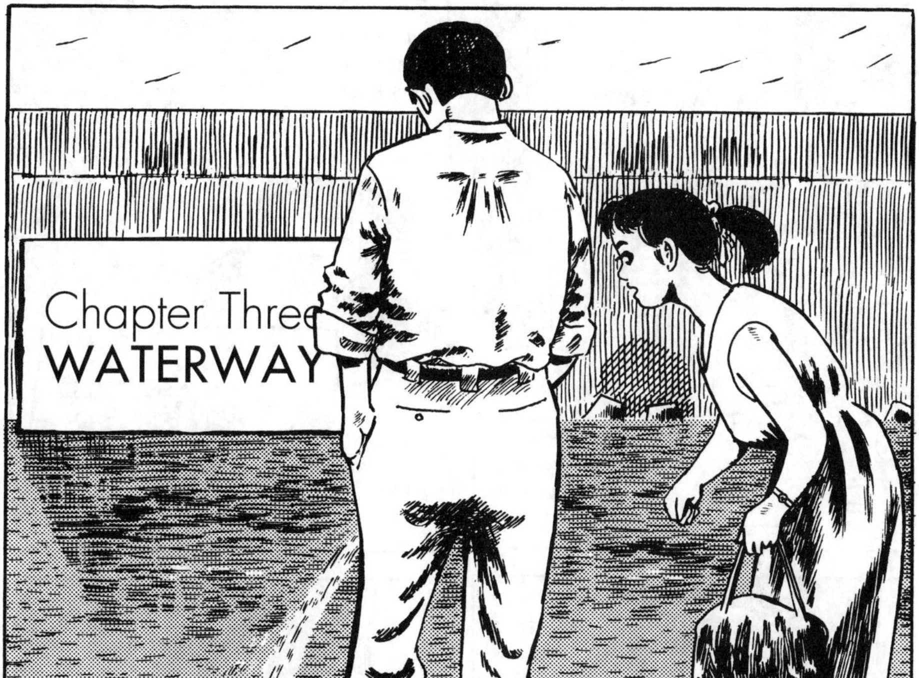

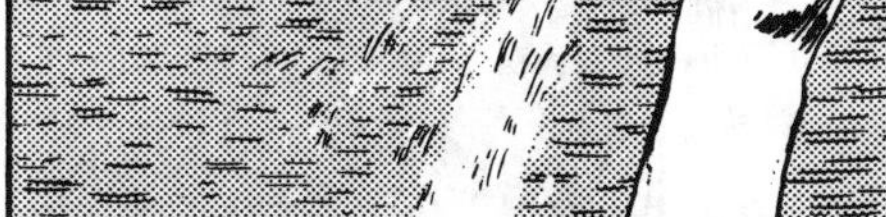
WOW! AMAZING!

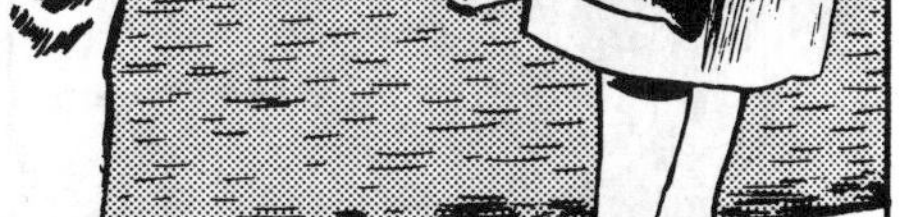
THIS IS GREAT, HUH? WE HAVE TO THANK MY MOTHER. HEY, HOW ABOUT YOU WRITE A STORY ABOUT PEARS?

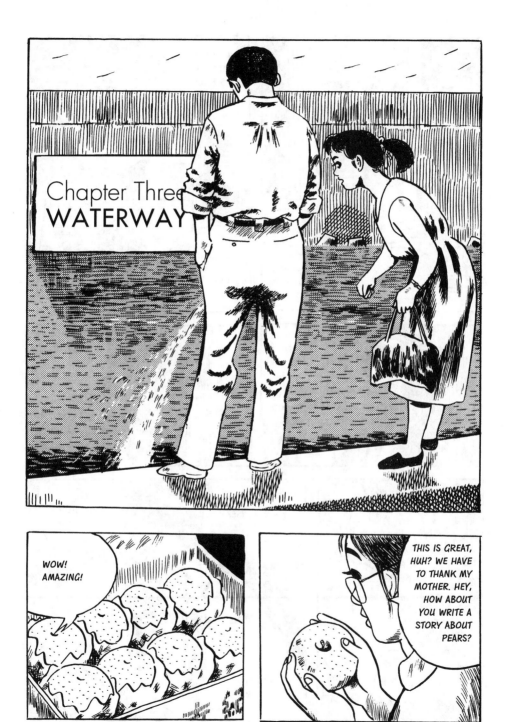

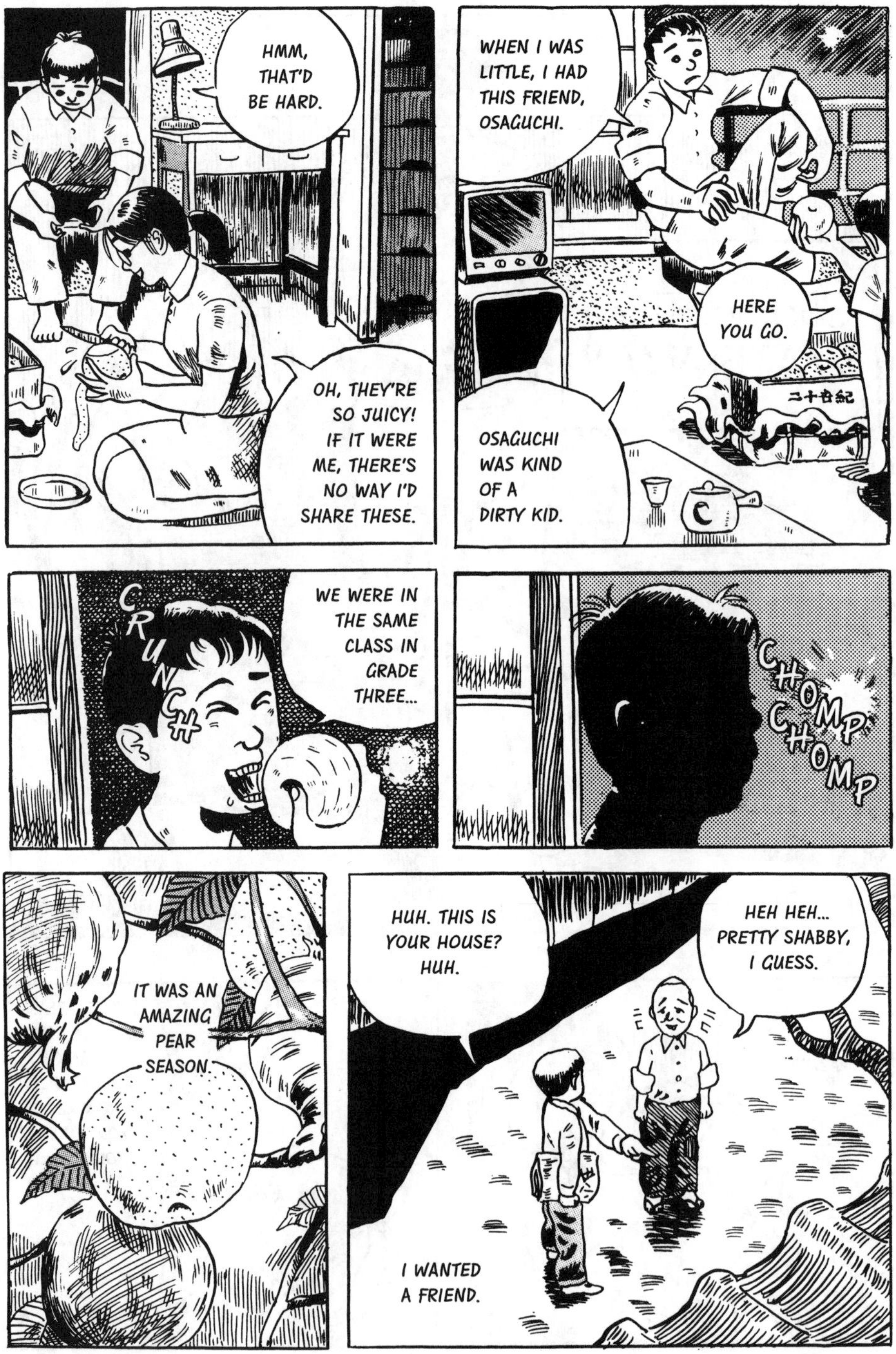
HMM, THAT'D BE HARD.
OH, THEY'RE SO JUICY! IF IT WERE ME, THERE'S NO WAY I'D SHARE THESE.
WHEN I WAS LITTLE, I HAD THIS FRIEND, OSAGUCHI.
HERE YOU GO.
二十世紀
OSAGUCHI WAS KIND OF A DIRTY KID.
CRUNCH
WE WERE IN THE SAME CLASS IN GRADE THREE...
CHOMP CHOMP
IT WAS AN AMAZING PEAR SEASON.
HUH. THIS IS YOUR HOUSE? HUH.
HEH HEH... PRETTY SHABBY, I GUESS.
I WANTED A FRIEND.

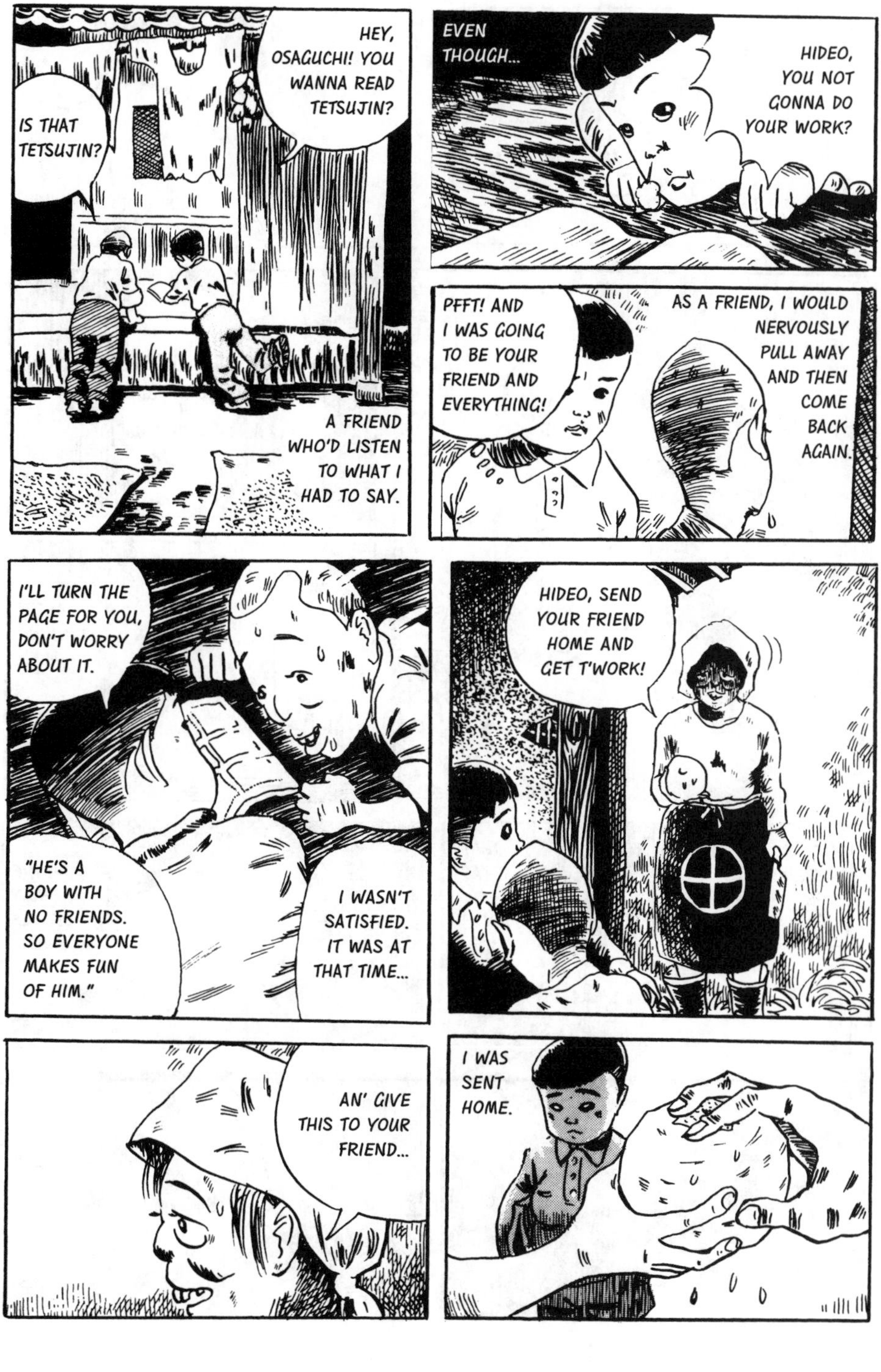
IS THAT TETSUJIN?
HEY, OSAGUCHI! YOU WANNA READ TETSUJIN?
A FRIEND WHO'D LISTEN TO WHAT I HAD TO SAY.
EVEN THOUGH...
HIDEO, YOU NOT GONNA DO YOUR WORK?
PFFT! AND I WAS GOING TO BE YOUR FRIEND AND EVERYTHING!
AS A FRIEND, I WOULD NERVOUSLY PULL AWAY AND THEN COME BACK AGAIN.
I'LL TURN THE PAGE FOR YOU, DON'T WORRY ABOUT IT.
"HE'S A BOY WITH NO FRIENDS. SO EVERYONE MAKES FUN OF HIM."
I WASN'T SATISFIED. IT WAS AT THAT TIME...
HIDEO, SEND YOUR FRIEND HOME AND GET T'WORK!
AN' GIVE THIS TO YOUR FRIEND...
I WAS SENT HOME.

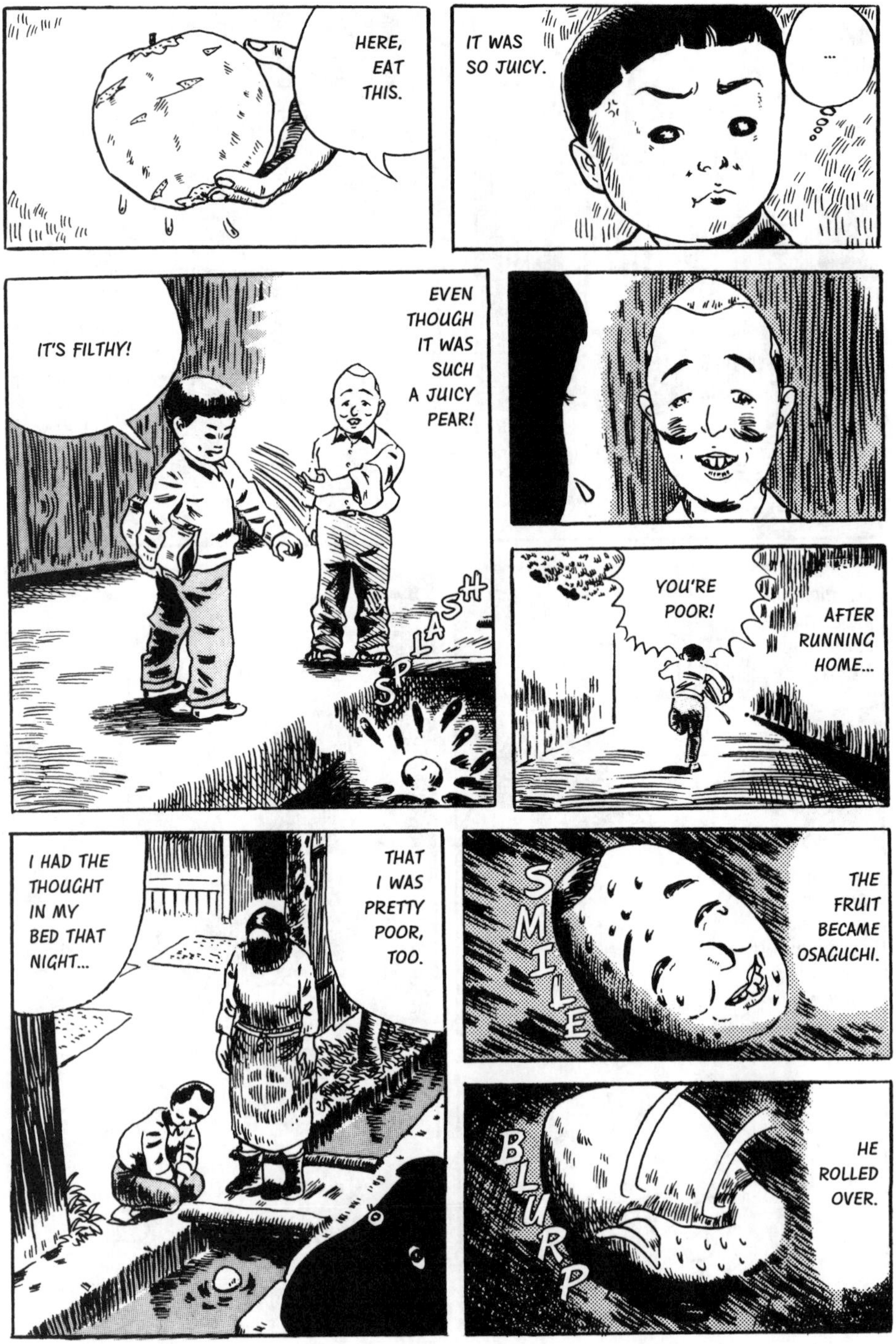
HERE, EAT THIS.
IT WAS SO JUICY.
...
IT'S FILTHY!
EVEN THOUGH IT WAS SUCH A JUICY PEAR!
SPLASH
YOU'RE POOR!
AFTER RUNNING HOME...
I HAD THE THOUGHT IN MY BED THAT NIGHT...
THAT I WAS PRETTY POOR, TOO.
SMILE
THE FRUIT BECAME OSAGUCHI.
BLURP
HE ROLLED OVER.

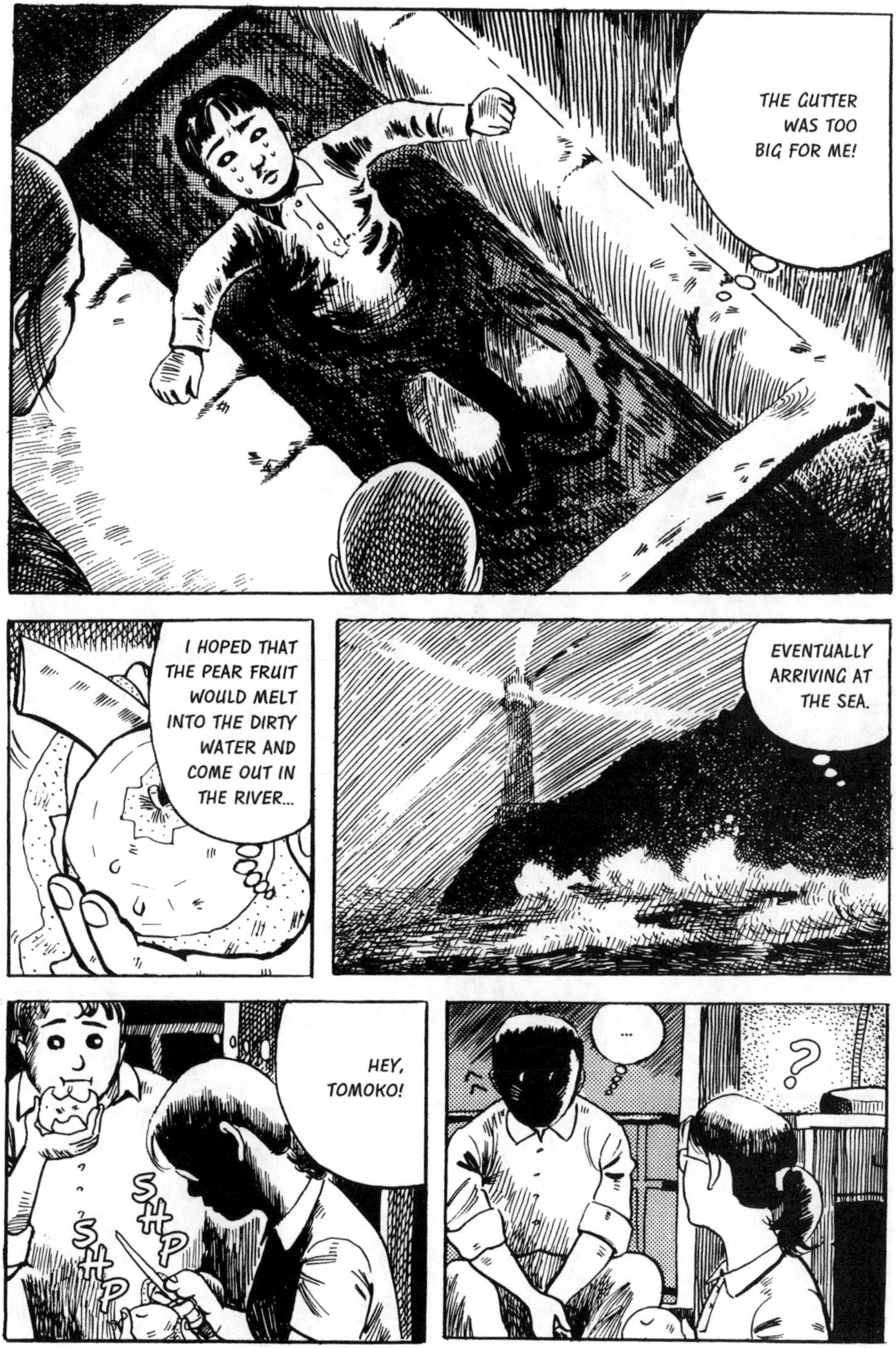
THE GUTTER WAS TOO BIG FOR ME!
I HOPED THAT THE PEAR FRUIT WOULD MELT INTO THE DIRTY WATER AND COME OUT IN THE RIVER...
EVENTUALLY ARRIVING AT THE SEA.
HEY, TOMOKO!
SHP SHP SHP
...
?

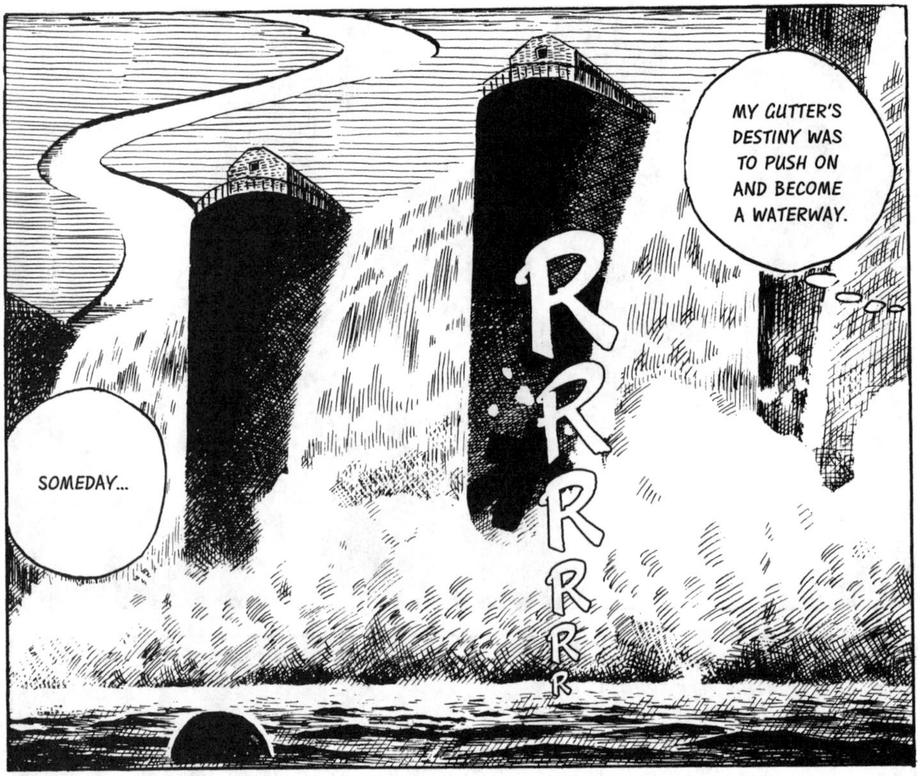
MY GUTTER'S DESTINY WAS TO PUSH ON AND BECOME A WATERWAY.
SOMEDAY...
RRRRRR
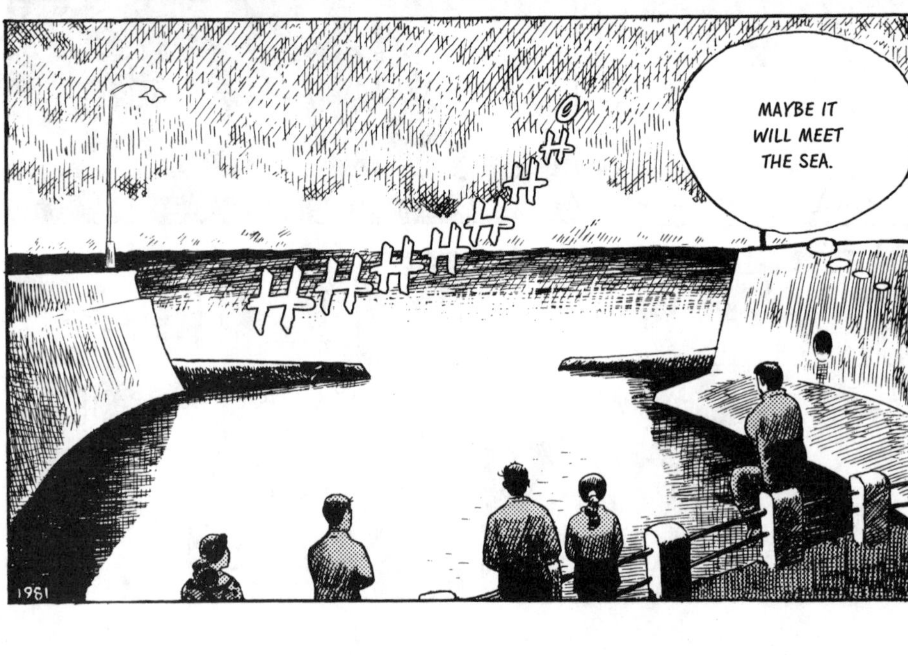
MAYBE IT WILL MEET THE SEA.
HHHHHHHO
1981

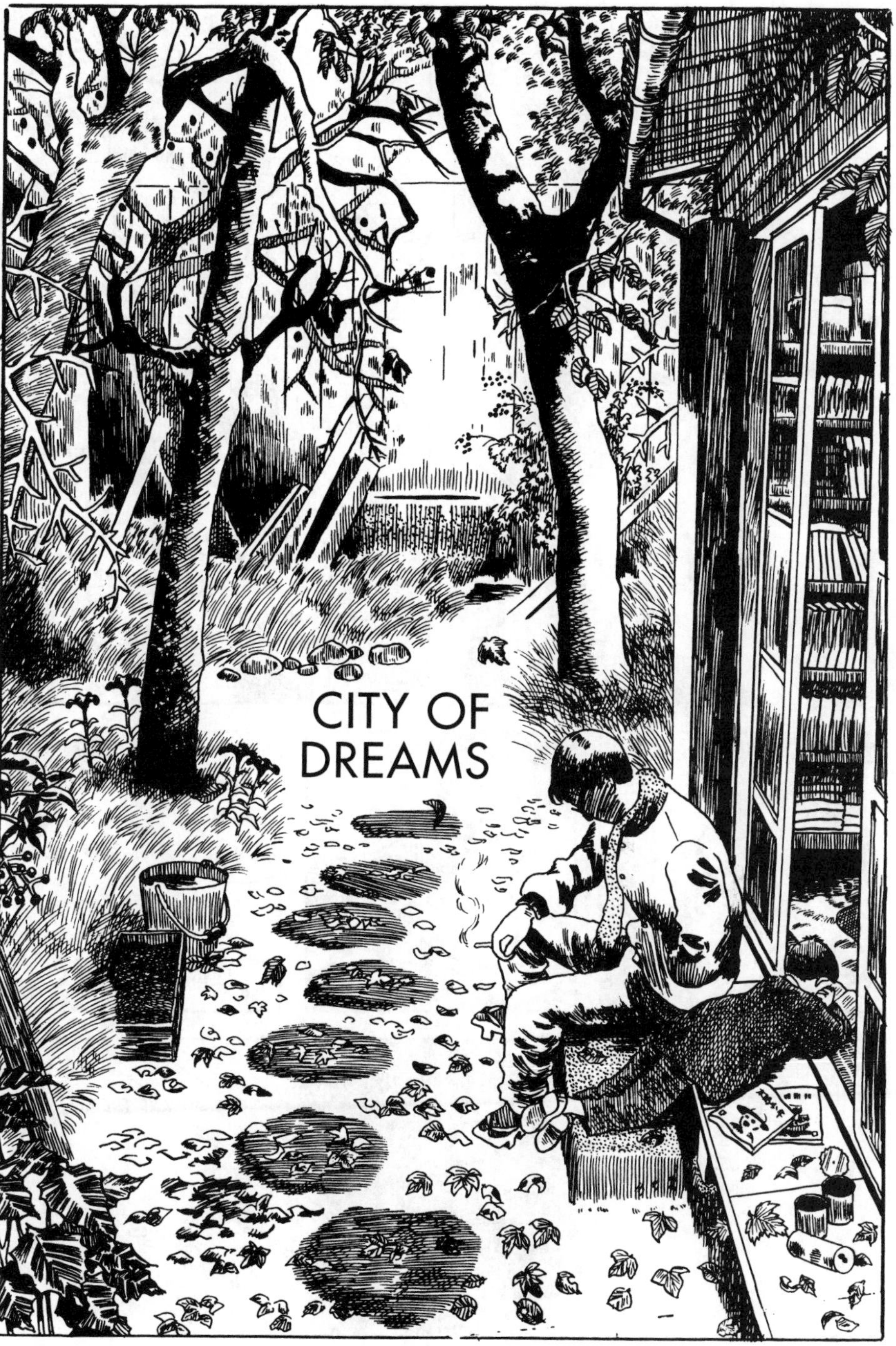
CITY OF
DREAMS

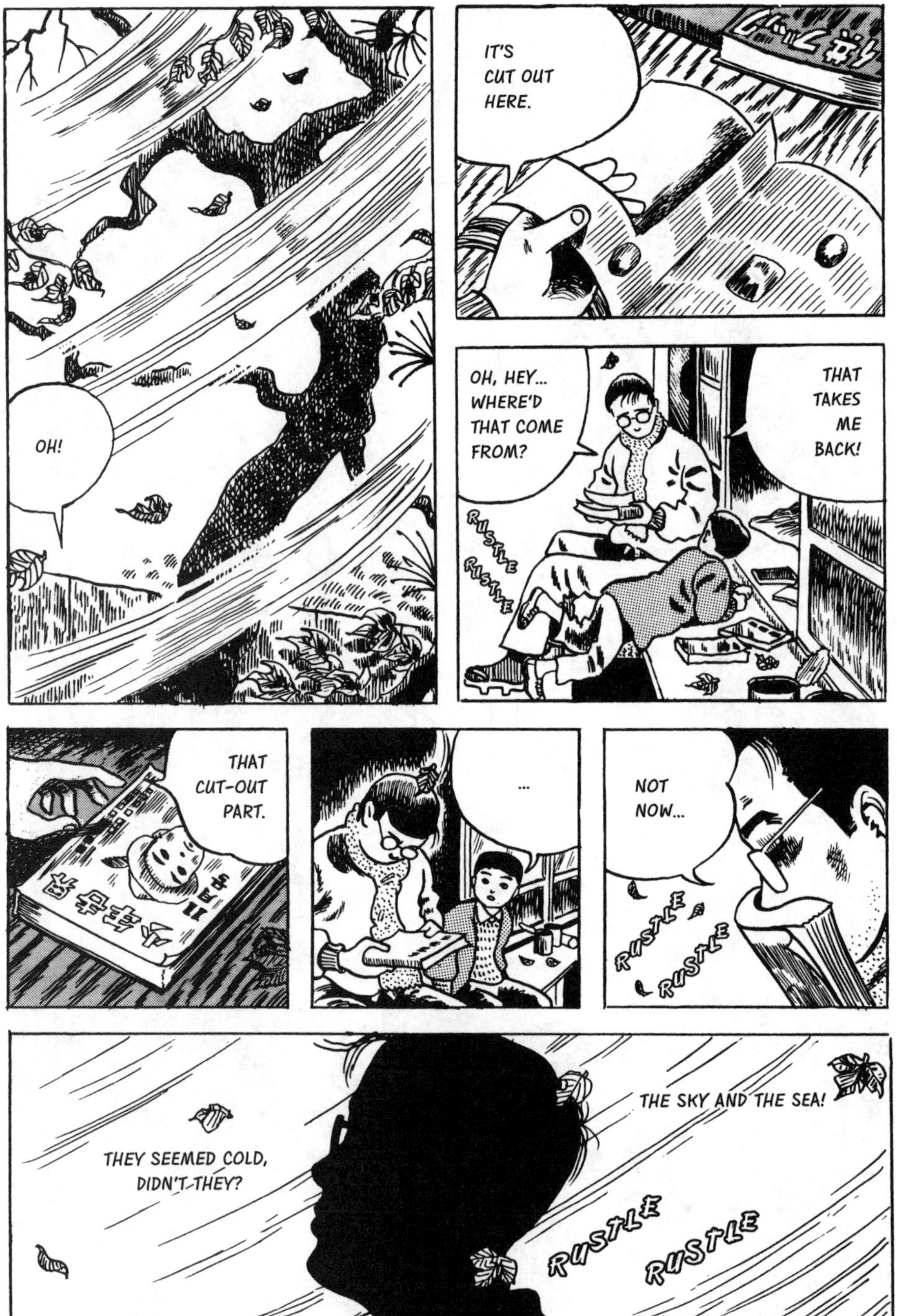
OH!
IT'S CUT OUT HERE.
OH, HEY... WHERE'D THAT COME FROM?
THAT TAKES ME BACK!
RUSTLE RUSTLE
THAT CUT-OUT PART.
...
NOT NOW...
RUSTLE RUSTLE
THEY SEEMED COLD, DIDN'T THEY?
THE SKY AND THE SEA!
RUSTLE RUSTLE

IN THOSE TIMES, RECESSION WAS IN THE AIR THROUGHOUT THE COUNTRY.

THE FIRE OF WAR THAT HAD SPREAD TO THE PENINSULA...

BROUGHT PROFIT TO THE COUNTRY, BUT...

THERE WERE SOME, LIKE THE CHILD'S FATHER...

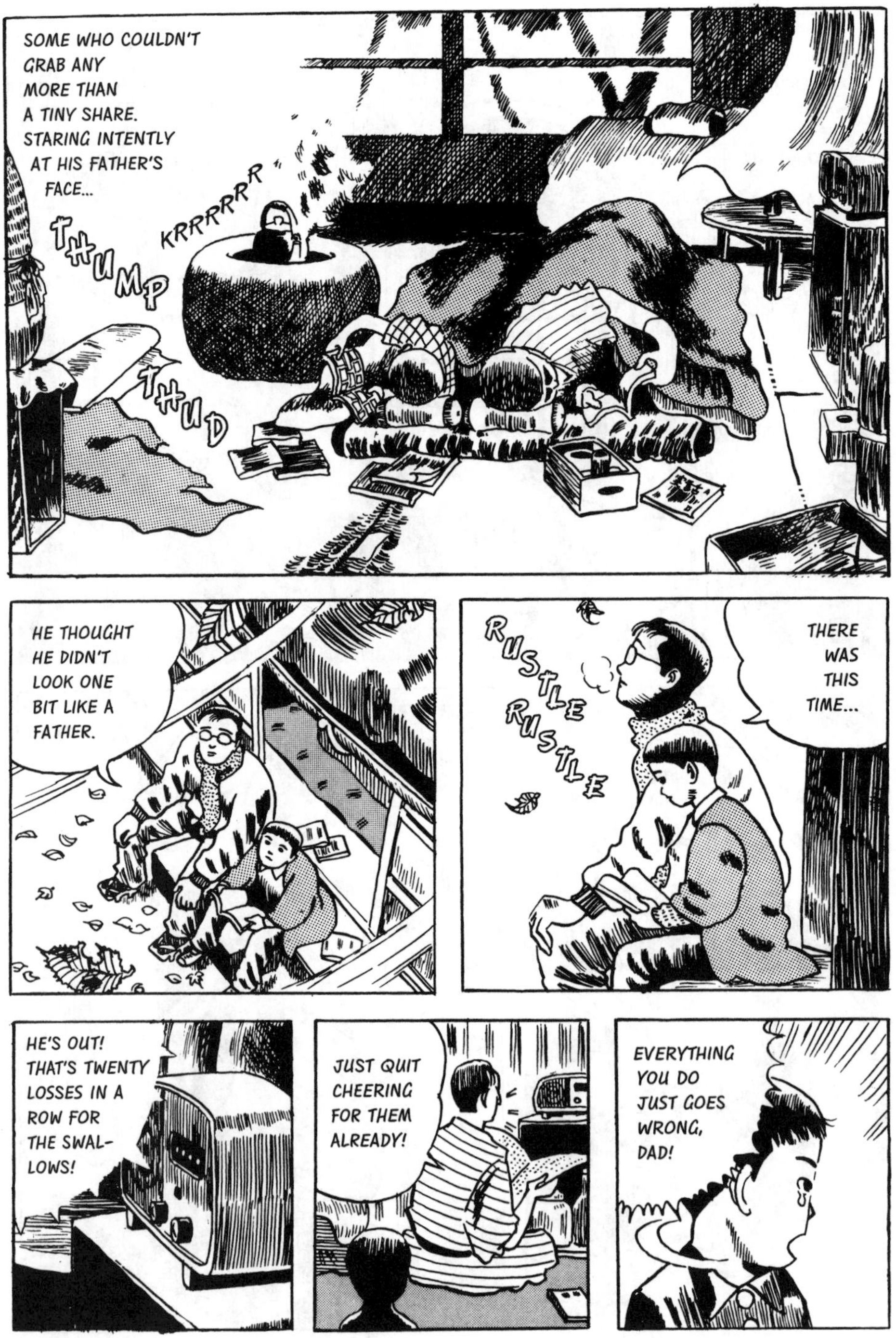
SOME WHO COULDN'T GRAB ANY MORE THAN A TINY SHARE. STARING INTENTLY AT HIS FATHER'S FACE...
THUMP
KRRRRRR
THUD
HE THOUGHT HE DIDN'T LOOK ONE BIT LIKE A FATHER.
RUSTLE RUSTLE
THERE WAS THIS TIME...
HE'S OUT! THAT'S TWENTY LOSSES IN A ROW FOR THE SWAL-LOWS!
JUST QUIT CHEERING FOR THEM ALREADY!
EVERYTHING YOU DO JUST GOES WRONG, DAD!

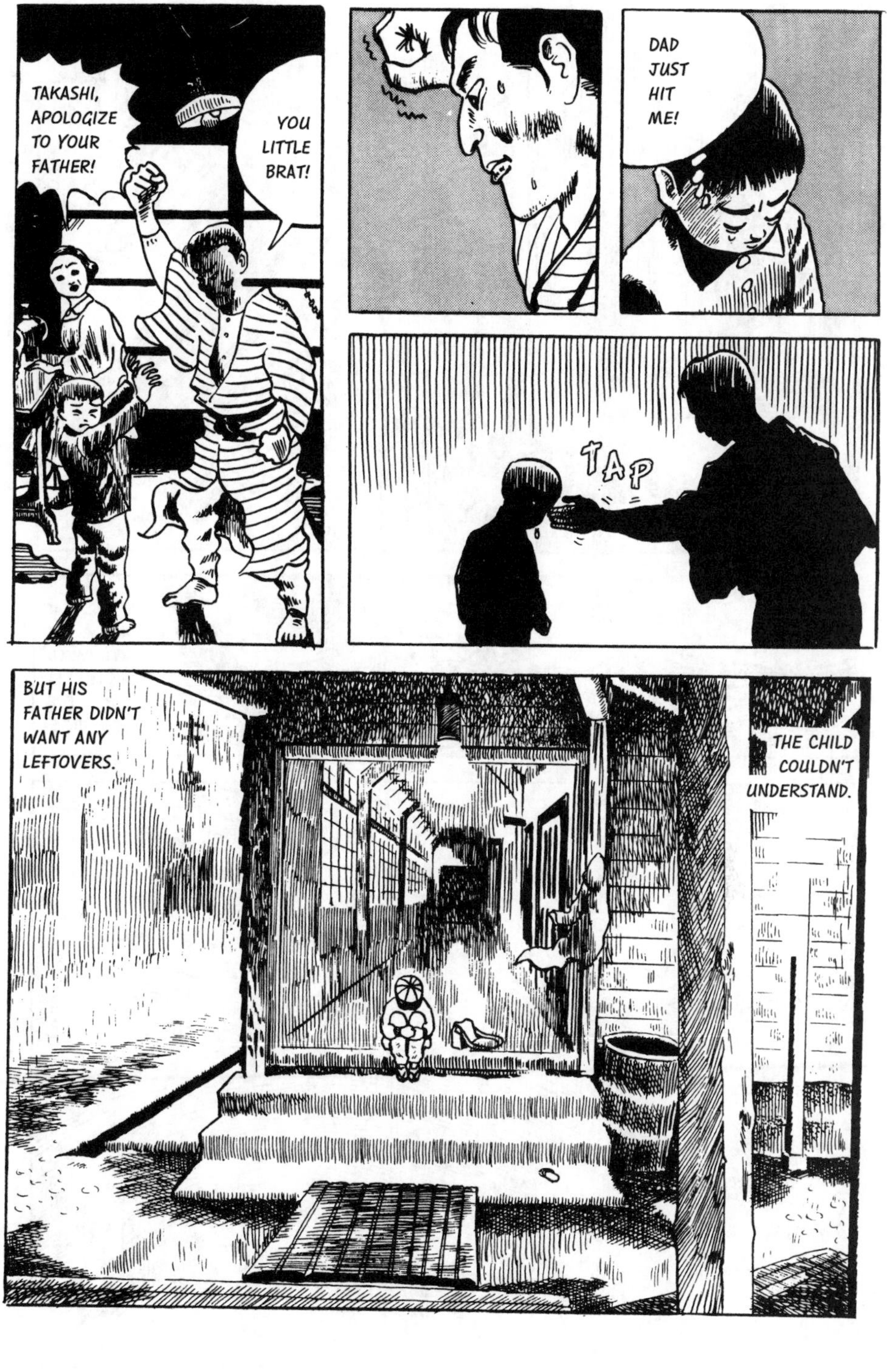
TAKASHI, APOLOGIZE TO YOUR FATHER!
YOU LITTLE BRAT!
DAD JUST HIT ME!
TAP
BUT HIS FATHER DIDN'T WANT ANY LEFTOVERS.
THE CHILD COULDN'T UNDERSTAND.

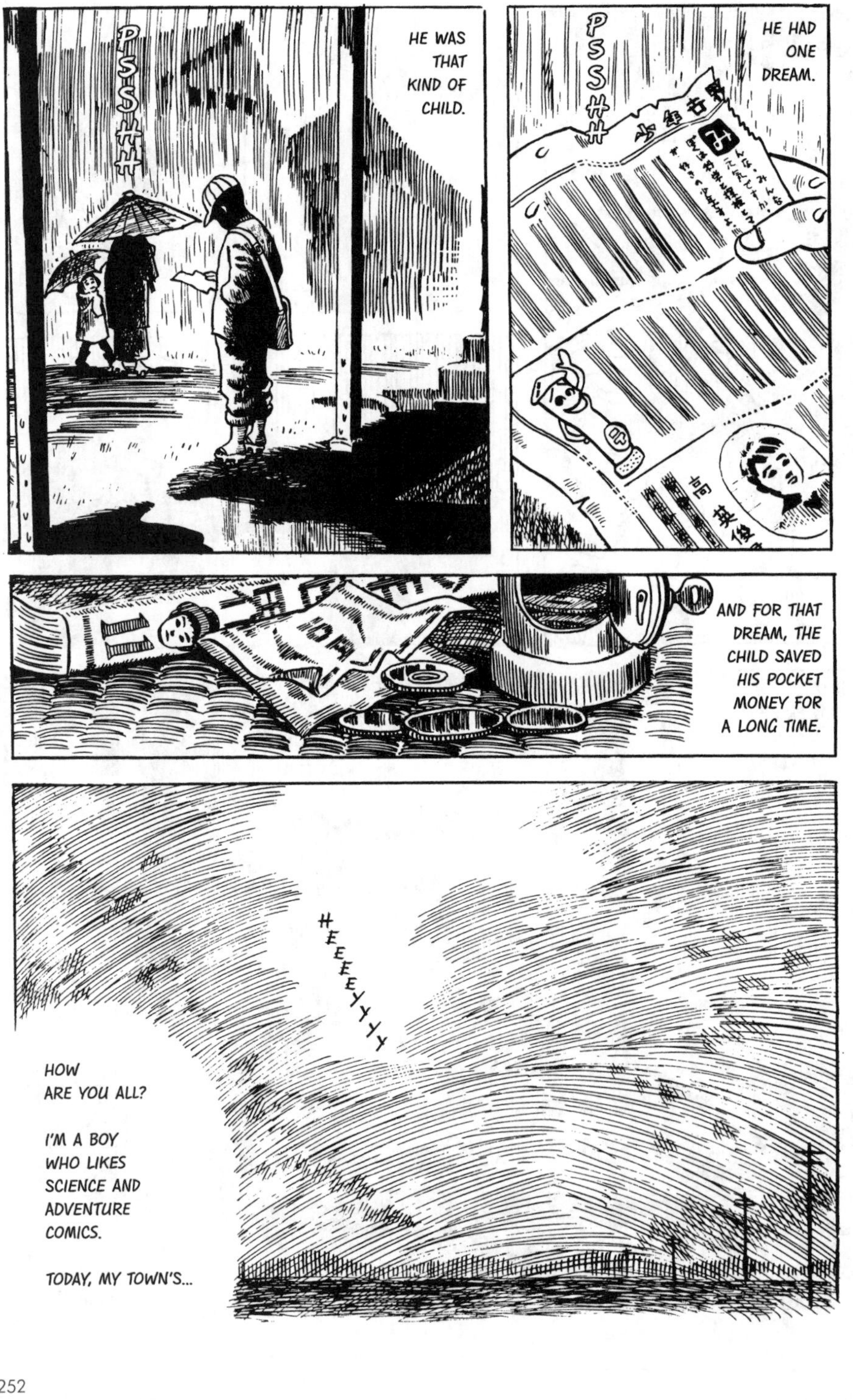
PSSHH
HE WAS THAT KIND OF CHILD.
PSSHH
HE HAD ONE DREAM.
AND FOR THAT DREAM, THE CHILD SAVED HIS POCKET MONEY FOR A LONG TIME.
HEEEEYYYY
HOW ARE YOU ALL?
I'M A BOY WHO LIKES SCIENCE AND ADVENTURE COMICS.
TODAY, MY TOWN'S...

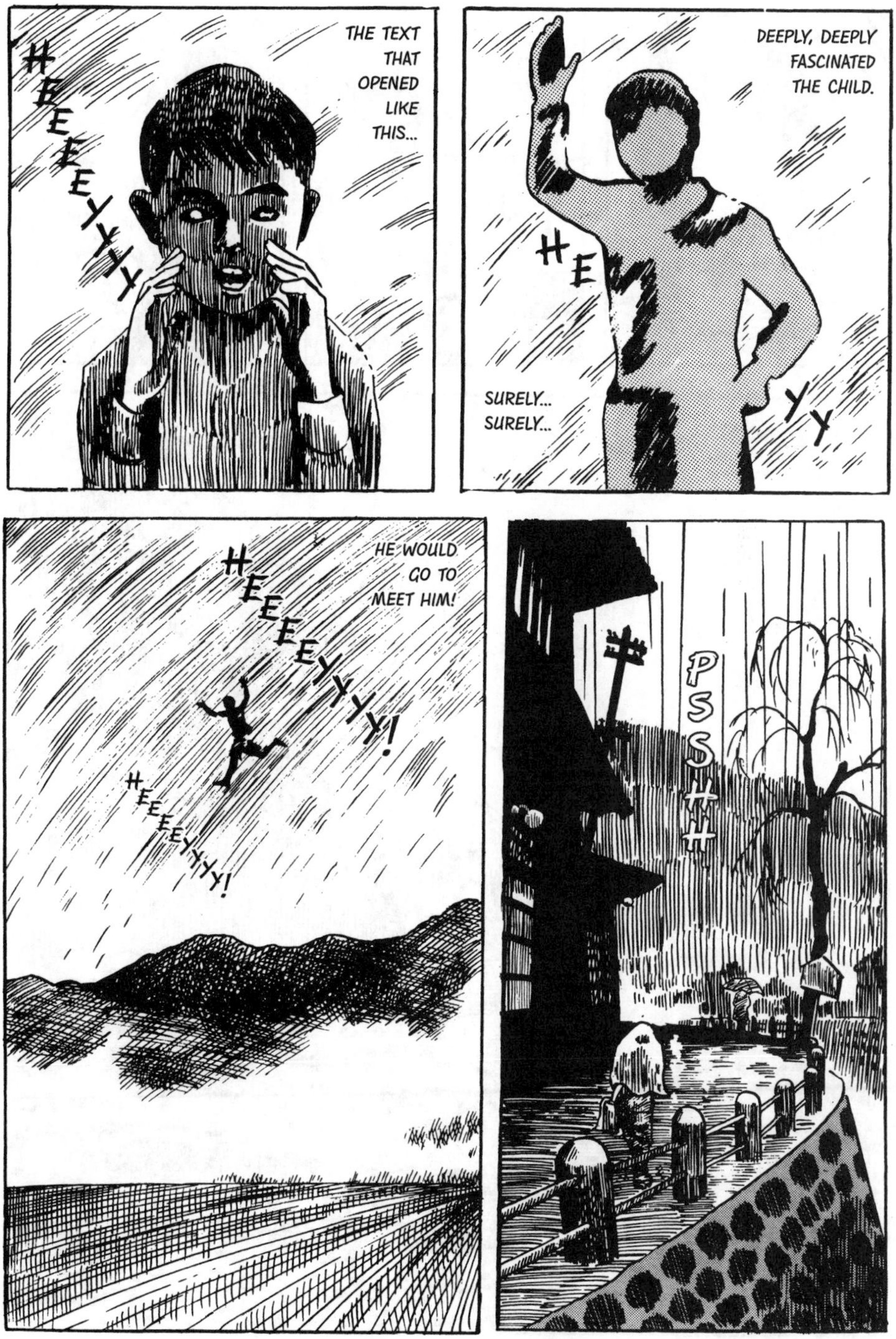
THE TEXT THAT OPENED LIKE THIS...
HEEEEYYYY
DEEPLY, DEEPLY FASCINATED THE CHILD.
HEYY
SURELY... SURELY...
HE WOULD GO TO MEET HIM!
HEEEEYYYYY!
HEEEEYYYY!
PSSHH

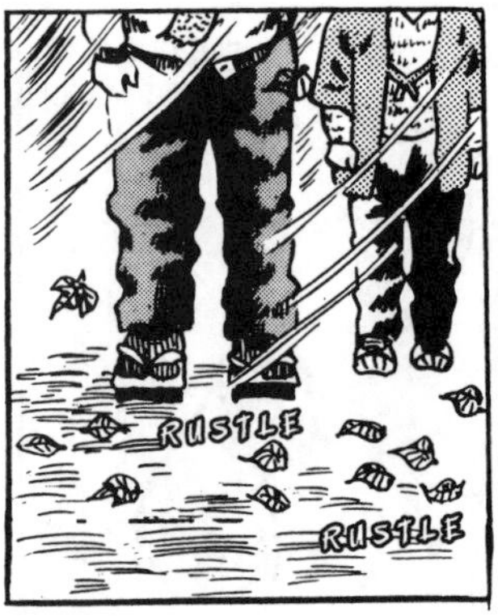
RUSTLE
RUSTLE
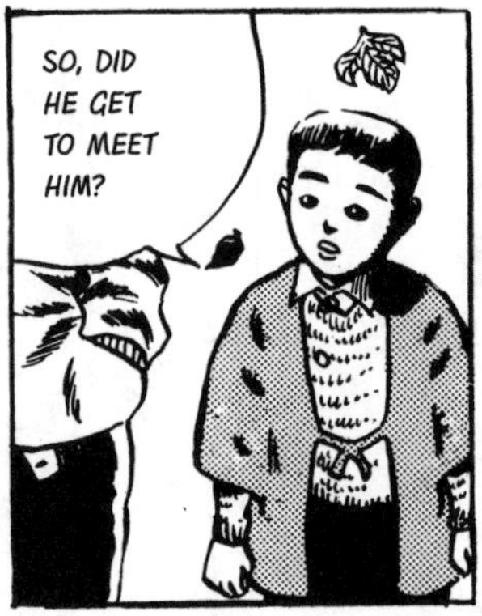
SO, DID HE GET TO MEET HIM?
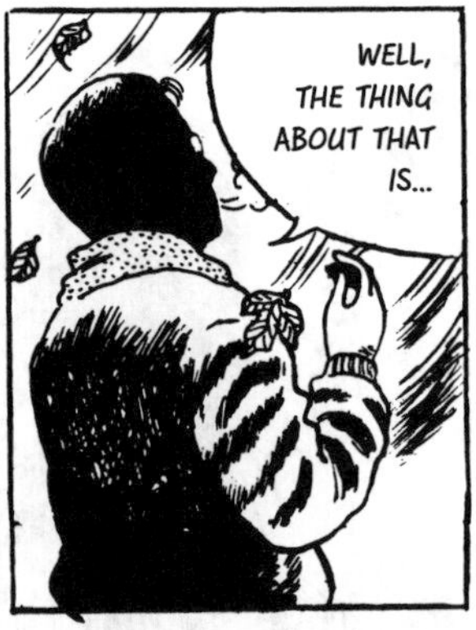
WELL, THE THING ABOUT THAT IS...
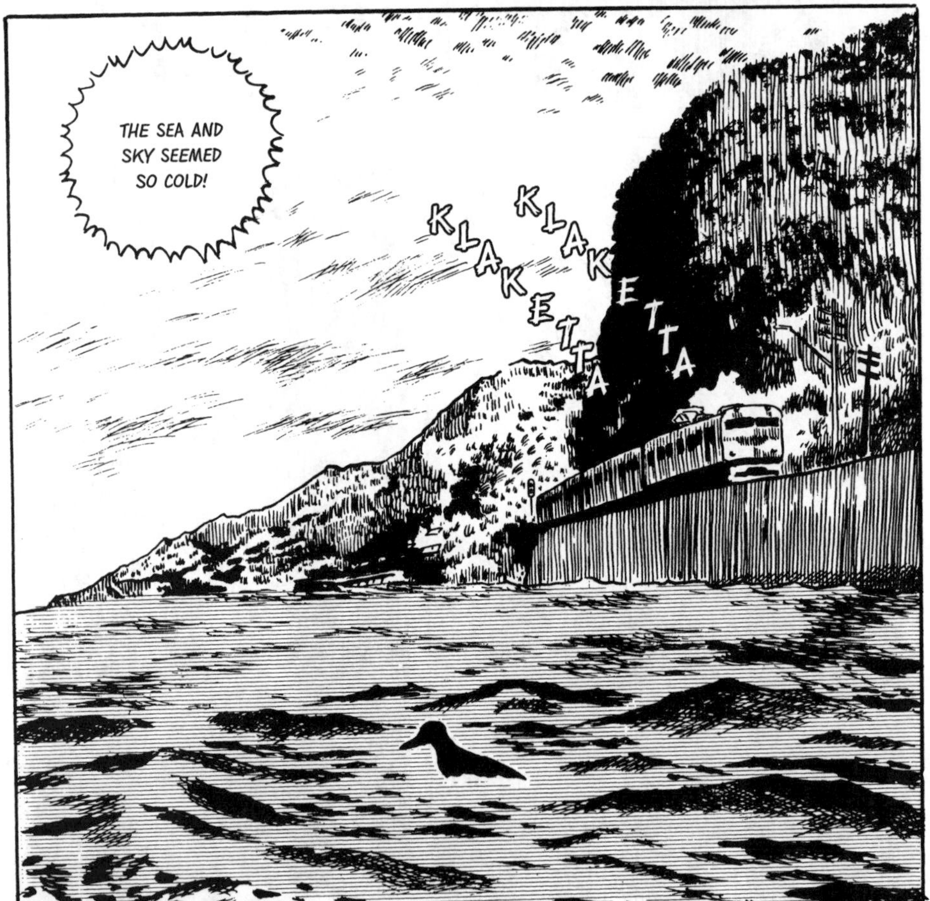
THE SEA AND SKY SEEMED SO COLD!
KLAKETTA
KLAKETTA

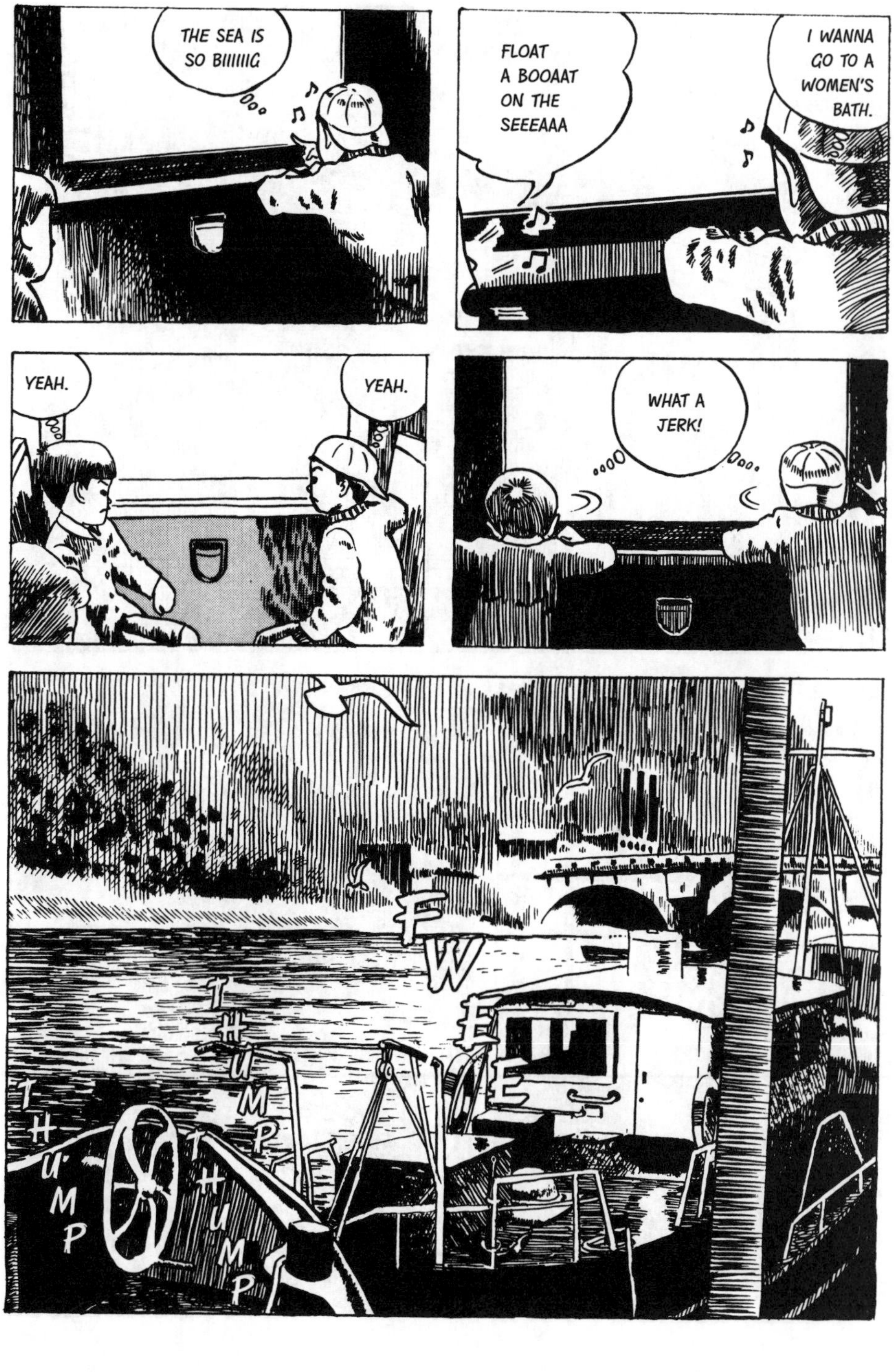
THE SEA IS SO BIIIIIG
FLOAT A BOOAAT ON THE SEEEAAA
I WANNA GO TO A WOMEN'S BATH.
YEAH.
YEAH.
WHAT A JERK!
FWEE
THUMP THUMP
THUMP THUMP

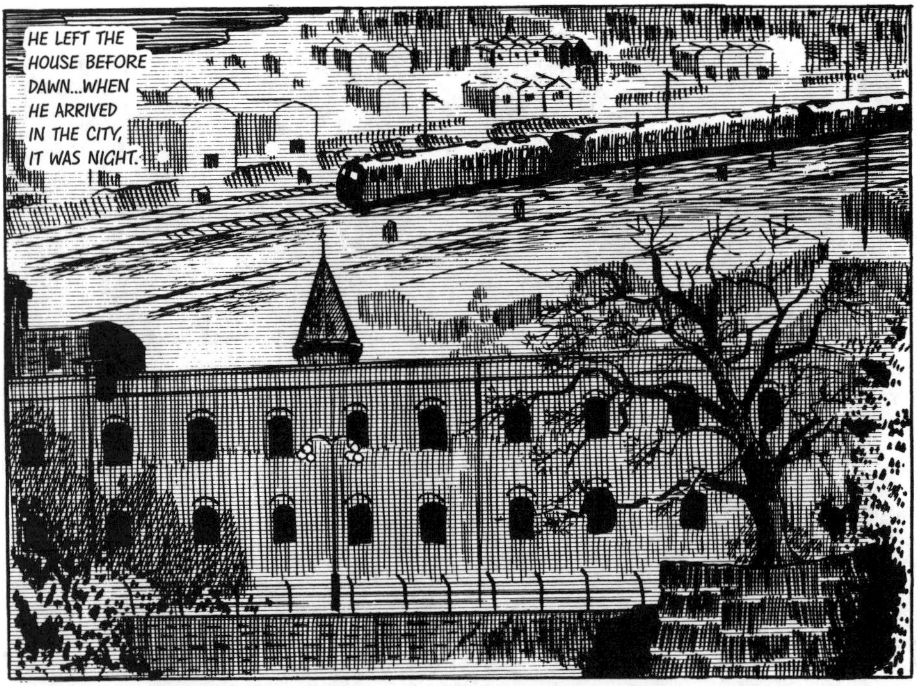
HE LEFT THE HOUSE BEFORE DAWN...WHEN HE ARRIVED IN THE CITY, IT WAS NIGHT.
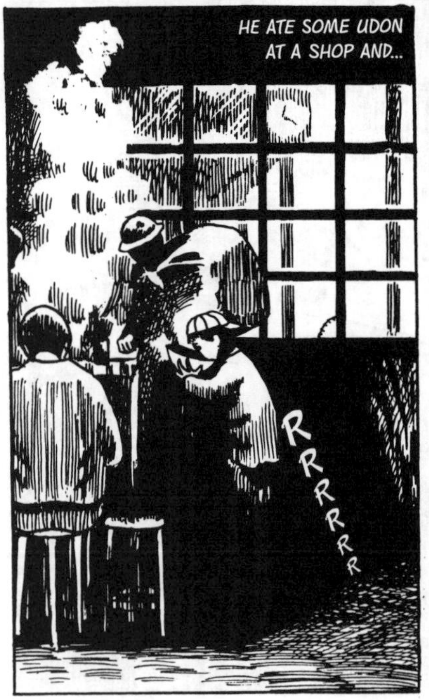
HE ATE SOME UDON AT A SHOP AND...
RRRRRR
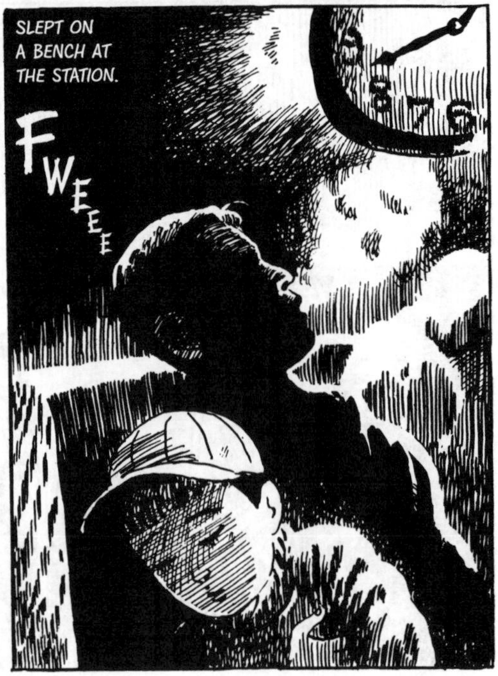
SLEPT ON A BENCH AT THE STATION.
FWEEE

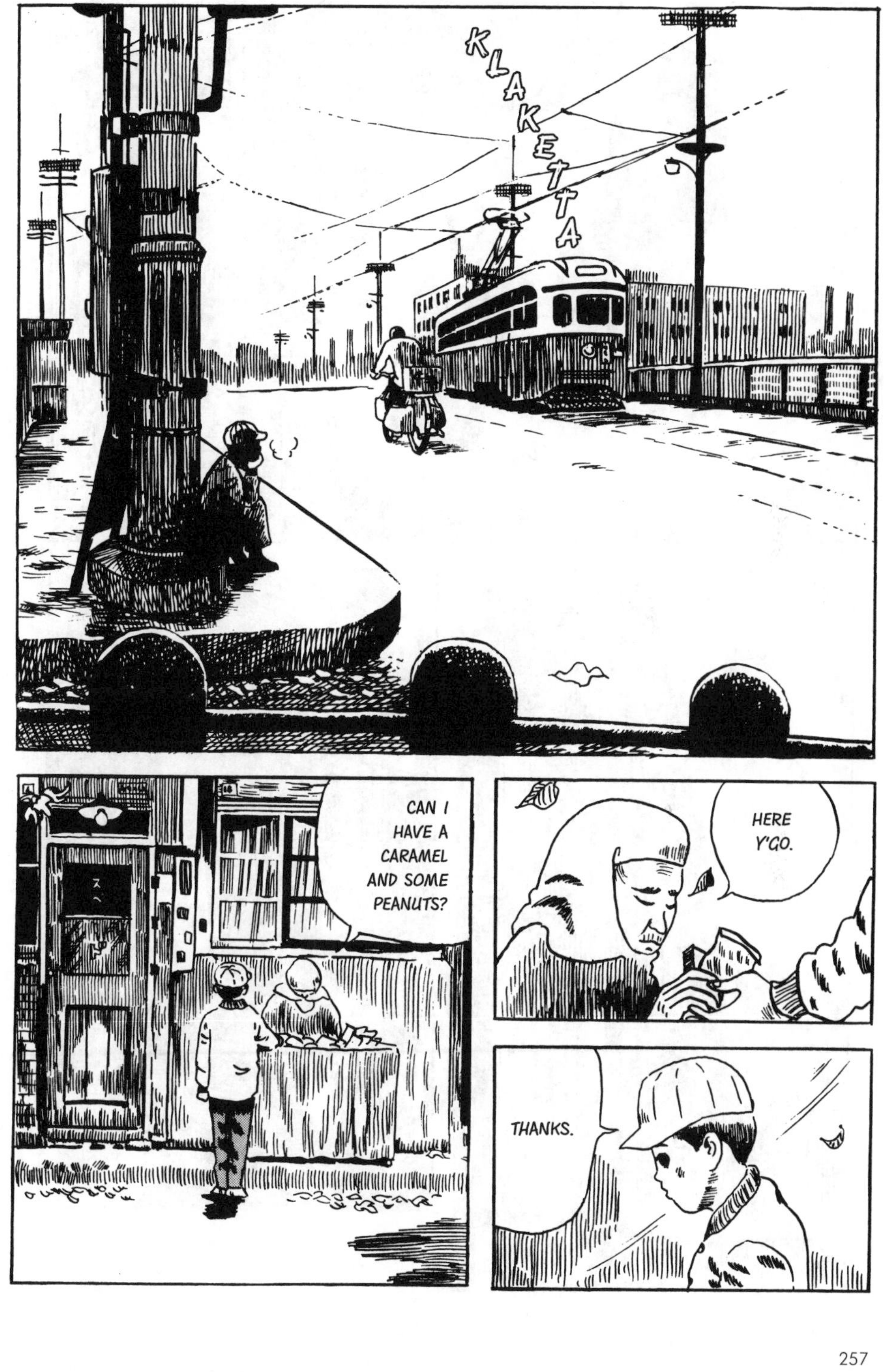
KLAKETTA
CAN I HAVE A CARAMEL AND SOME PEANUTS?
HERE Y'GO.
THANKS.

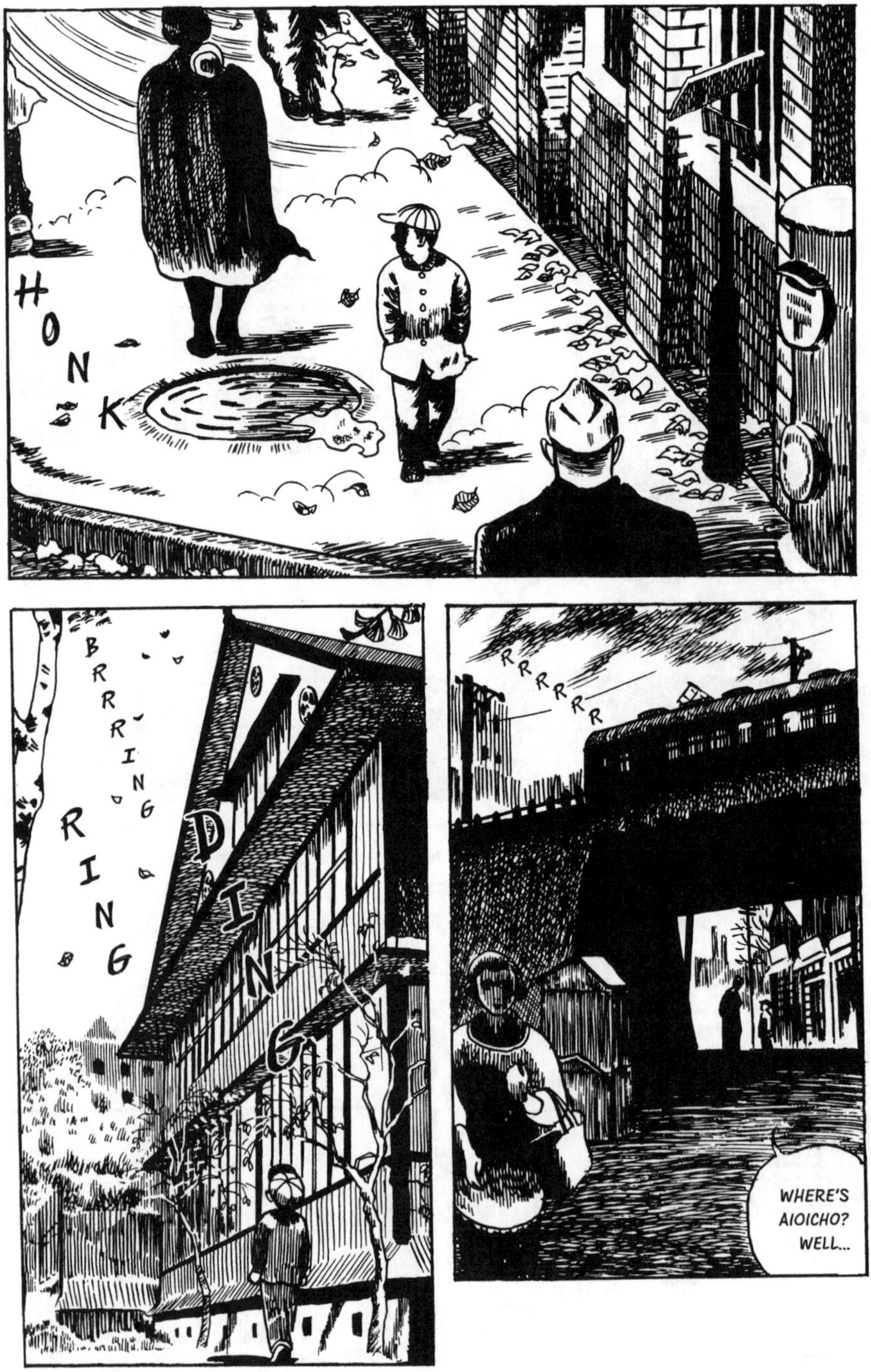
HONK
BRRRING
RING
DING
RRRRRR
WHERE'S AIOICHO? WELL...

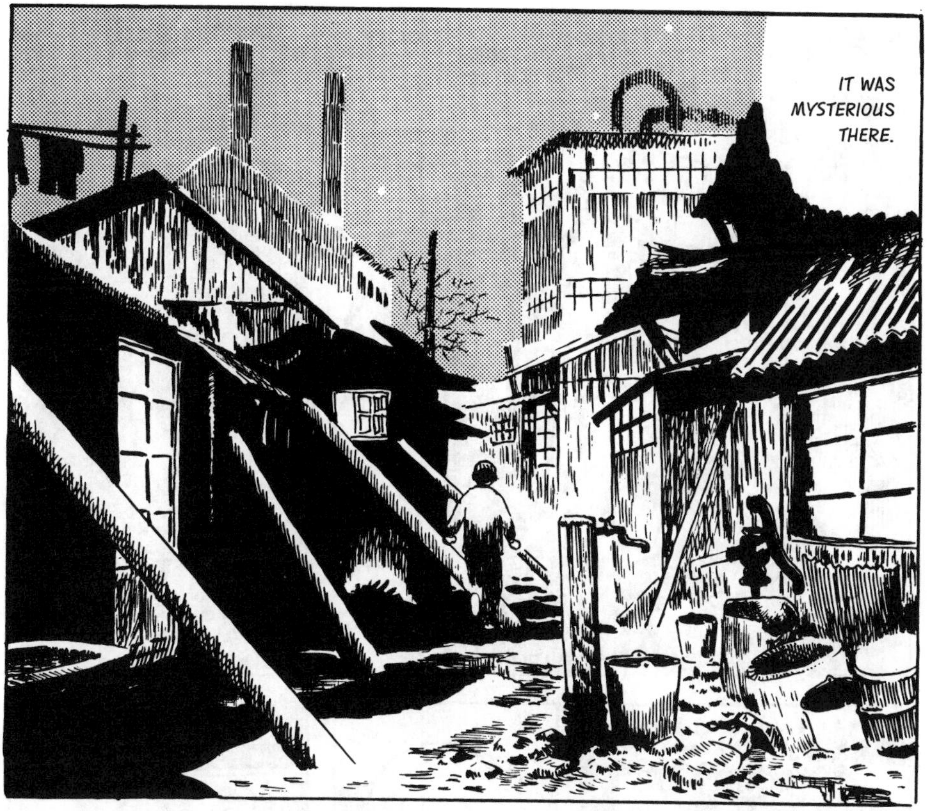
IT WAS
MYSTERIOUS
THERE.

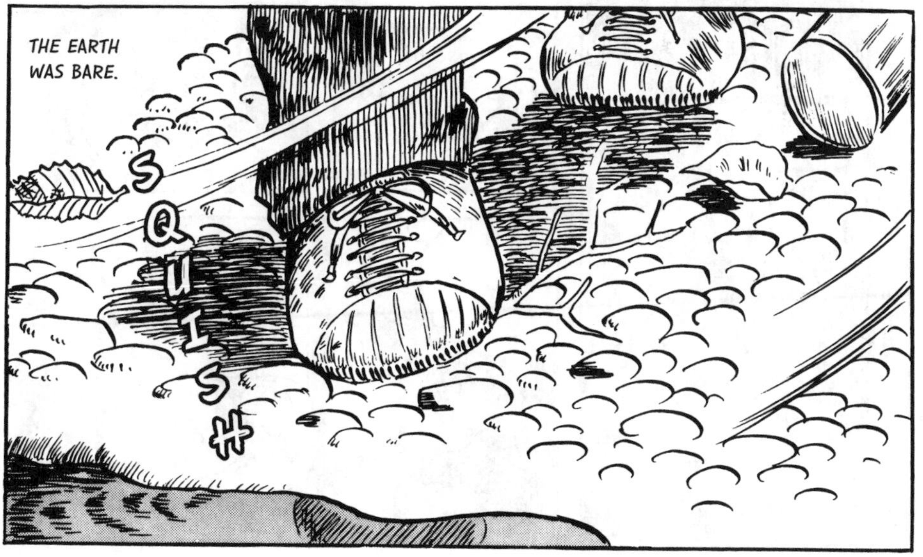
THE EARTH
WAS BARE.
SQUISH

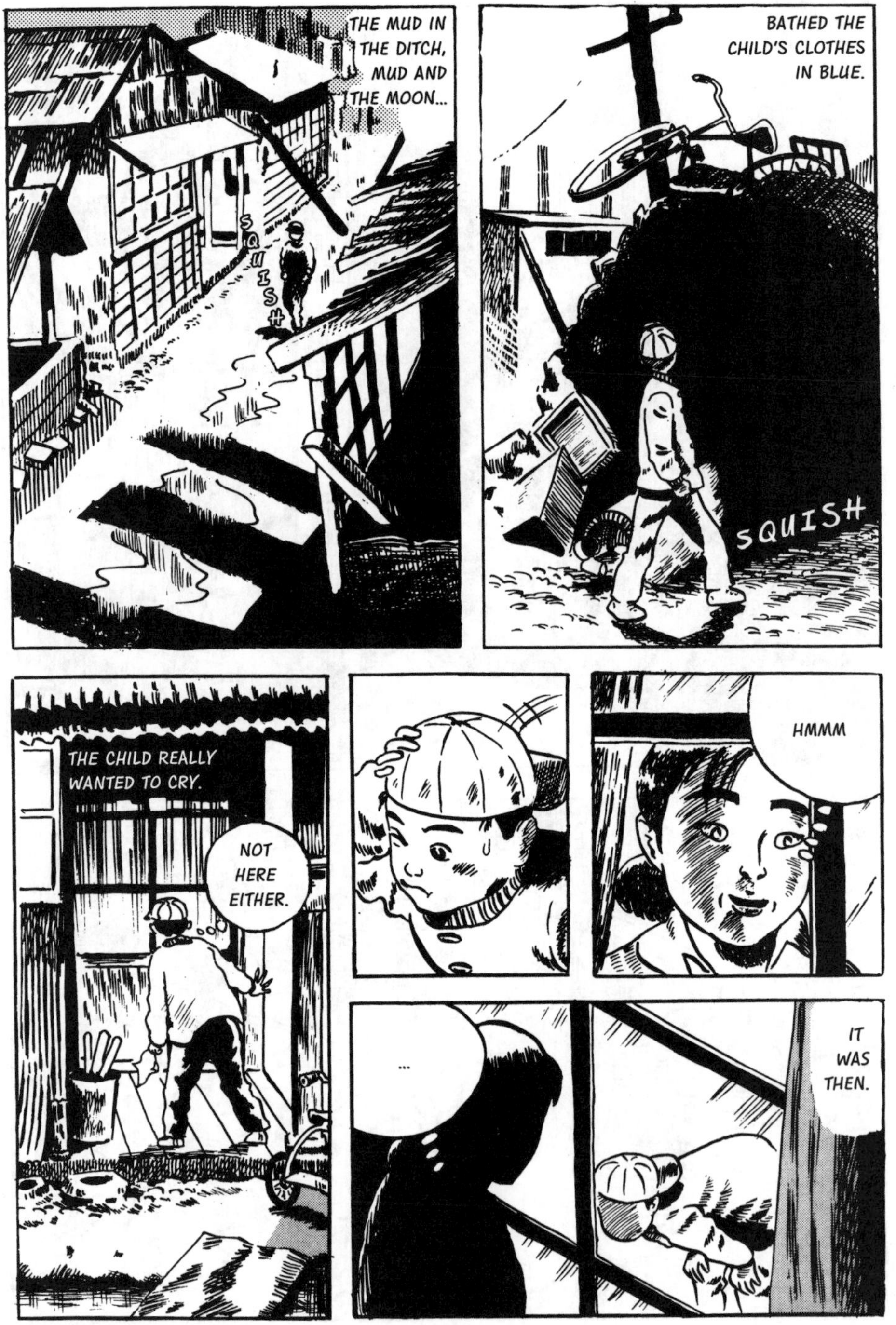
THE MUD IN THE DITCH, MUD AND THE MOON...
SQUISH
BATHED THE CHILD'S CLOTHES IN BLUE.
SQUISH
THE CHILD REALLY WANTED TO CRY.
NOT HERE EITHER.
HMMM
...
IT WAS THEN.

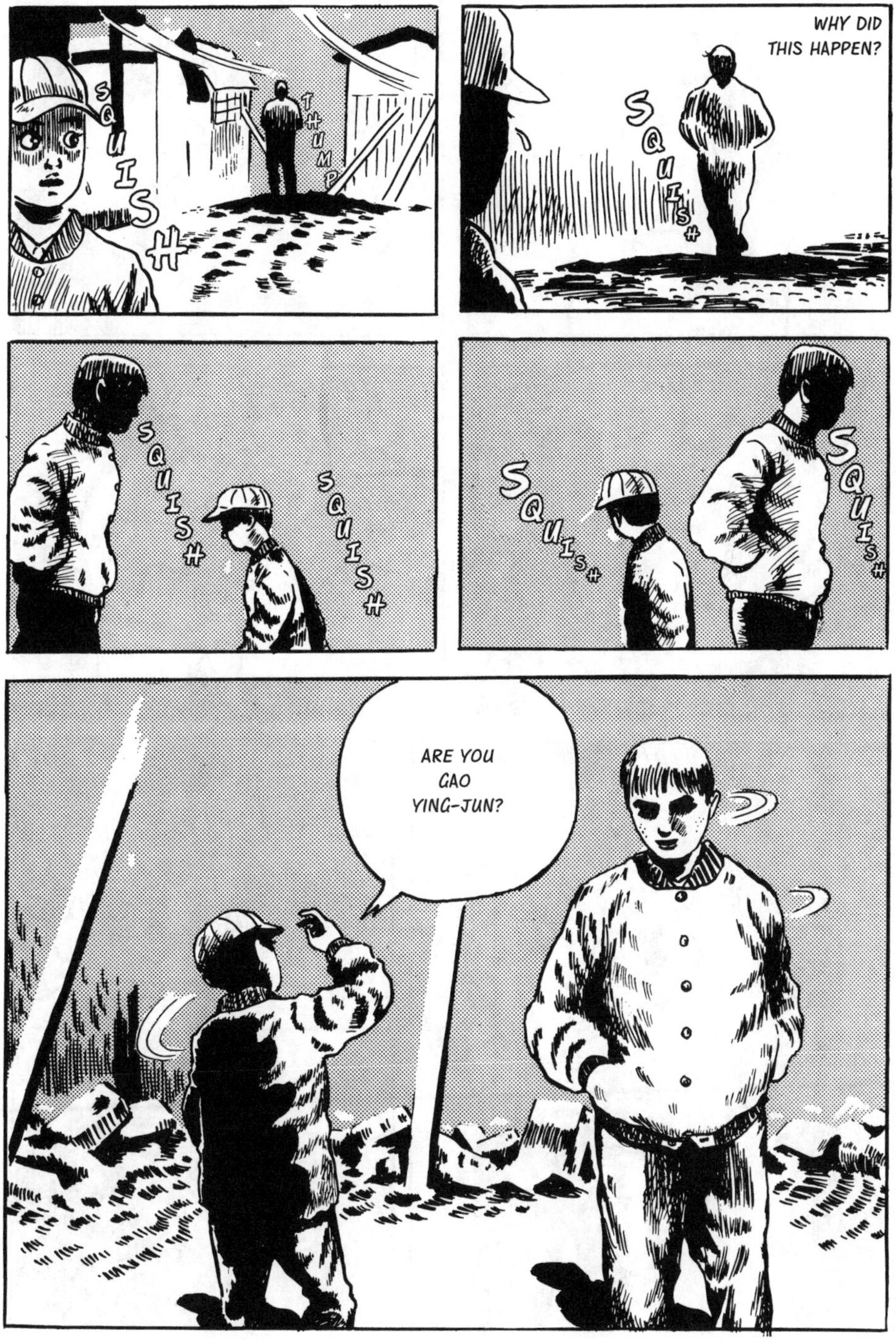
SQUISH
THUMP
WHY DID THIS HAPPEN?
SQUISH
SQUISH
SQUISH
SQUISH
SQUISH
ARE YOU GAO YING-JUN?

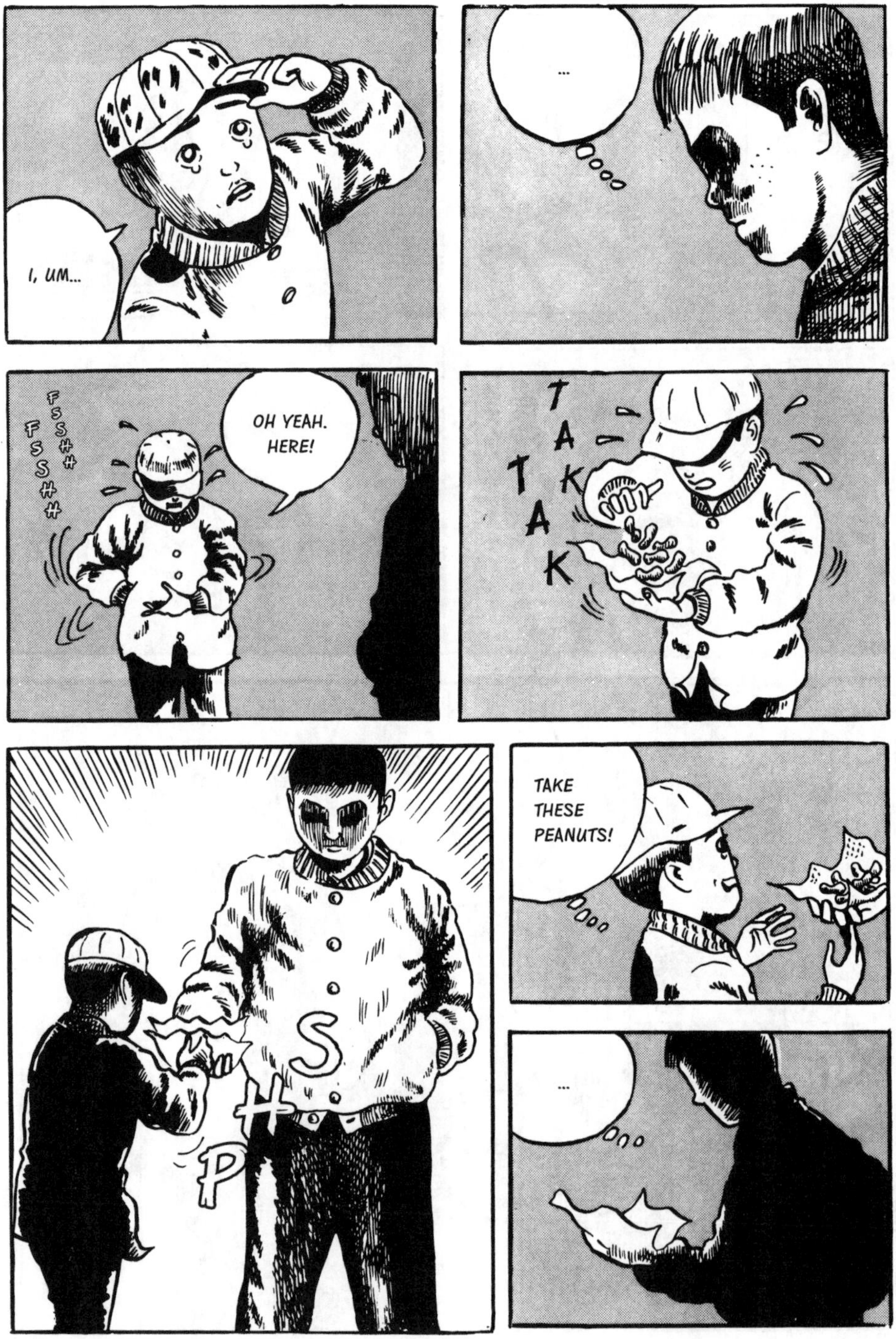
I, UM...
...
F S S H H
F S S H H
OH YEAH. HERE!
TAKTAK
S H P
TAKE THESE PEANUTS!
...

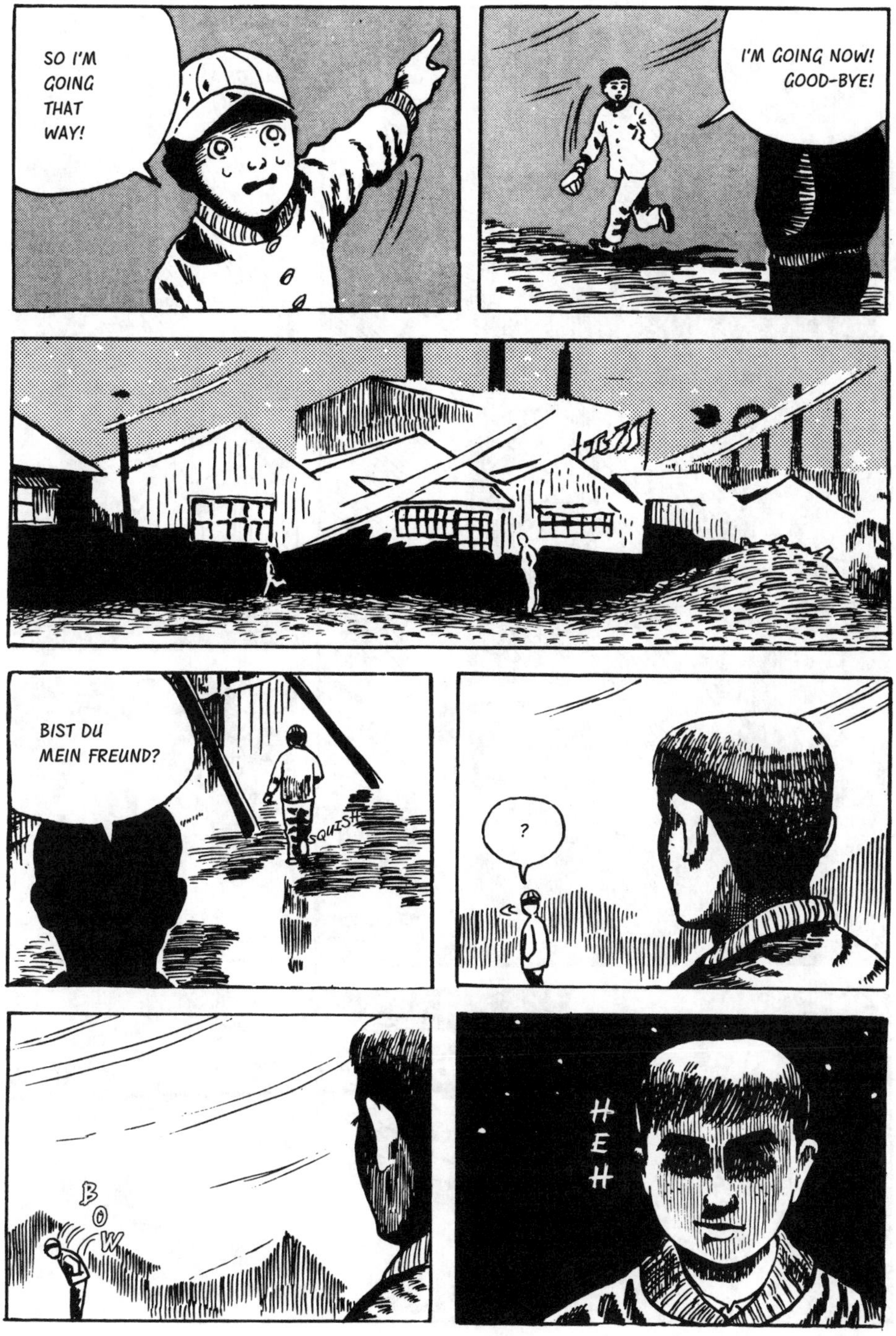
SO I'M GOING THAT WAY!
I'M GOING NOW! GOOD-BYE!
BIST DU MEIN FREUND?
SQUISH
?
BOW
HEH

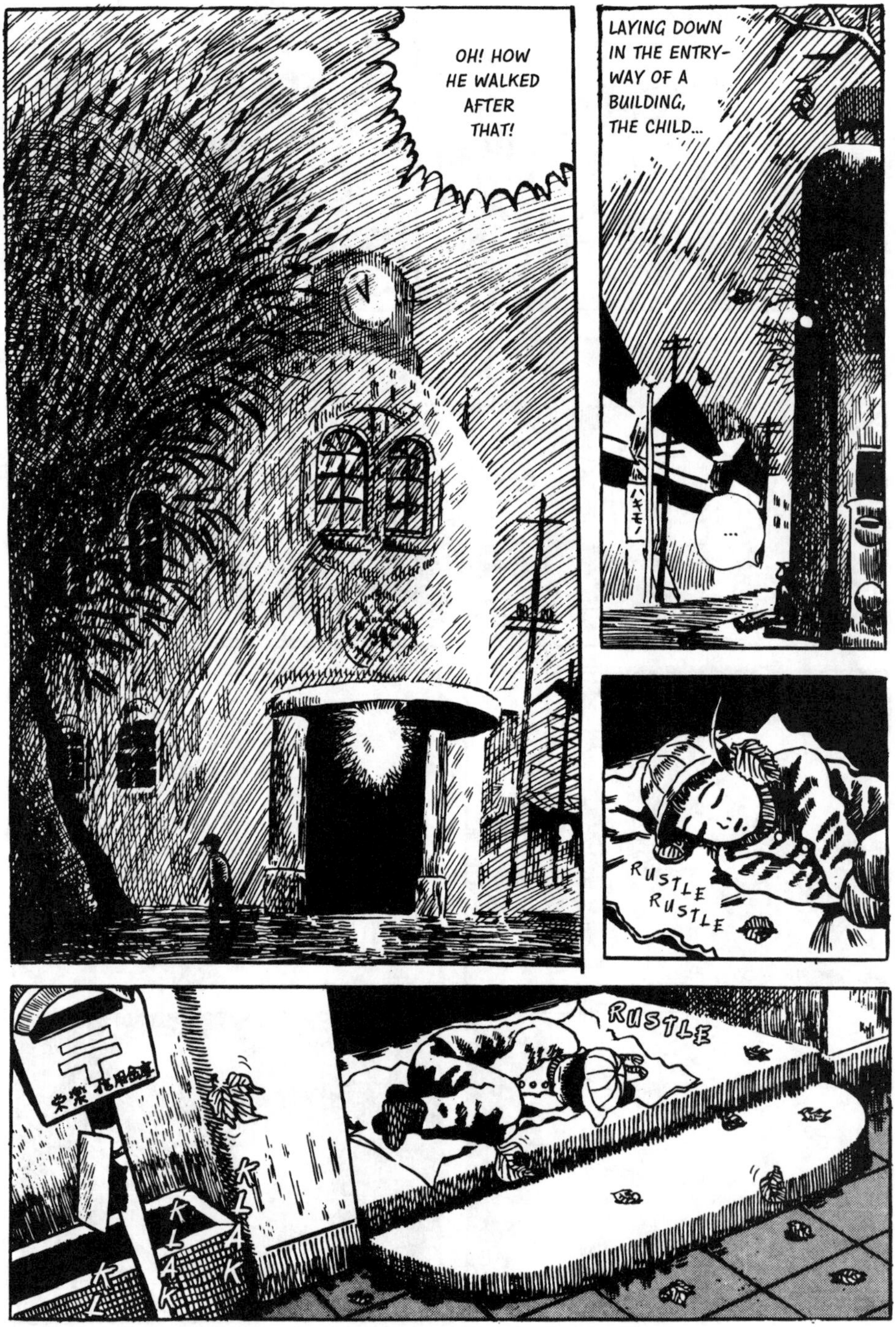
OH! HOW HE WALKED AFTER THAT!
LAYING DOWN IN THE ENTRY-WAY OF A BUILDING, THE CHILD...
ハキモノ
...
RUSTLE RUSTLE
RUSTLE
KLAK
KLAK
KL

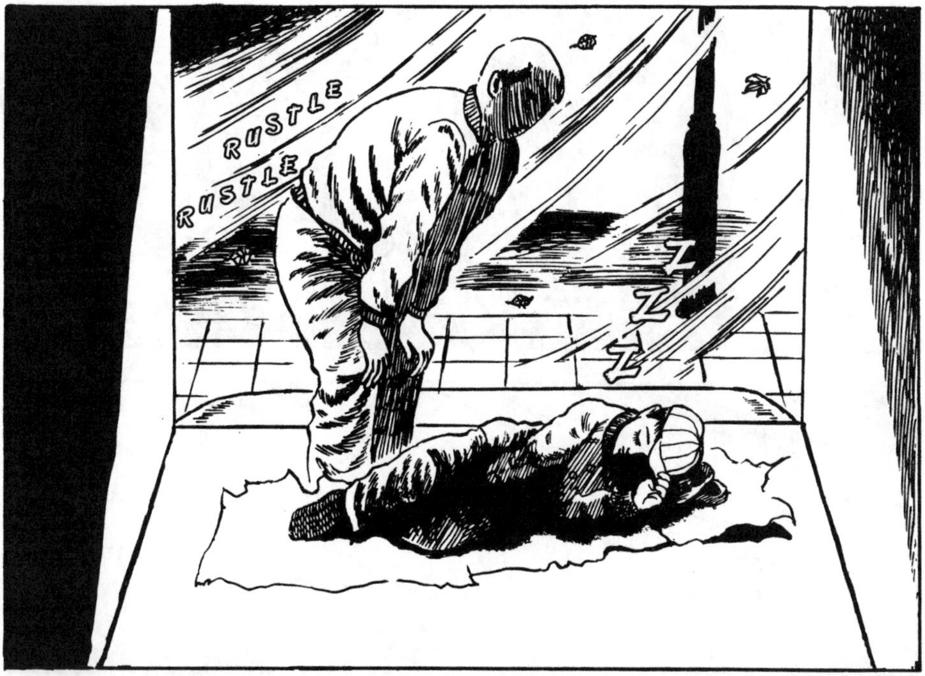
RUSTLE
RUSTLE
ZZZ
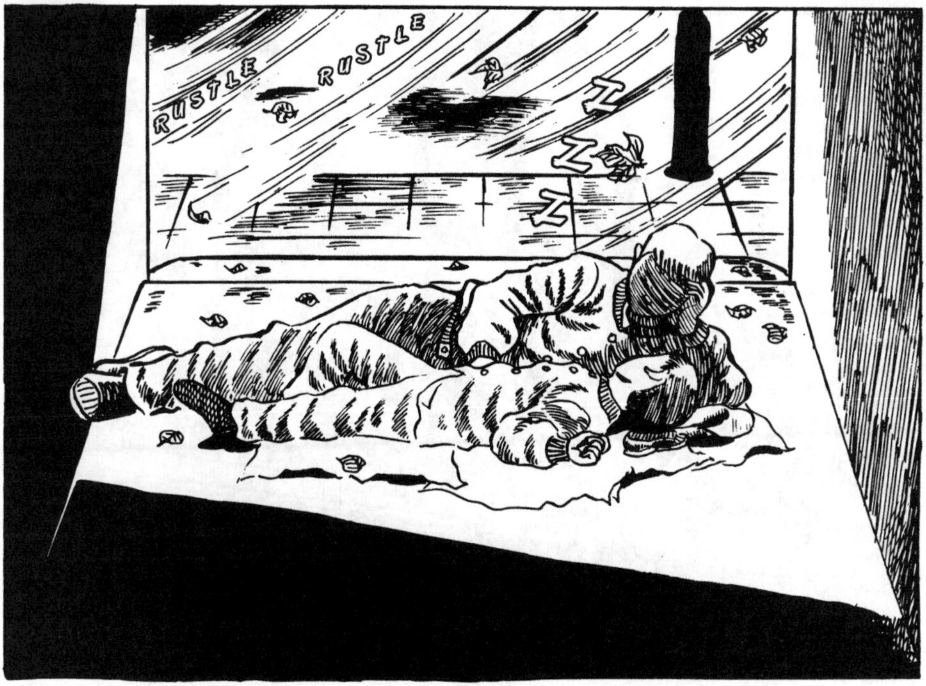
RUSTLE
RUSTLE
ZZZ

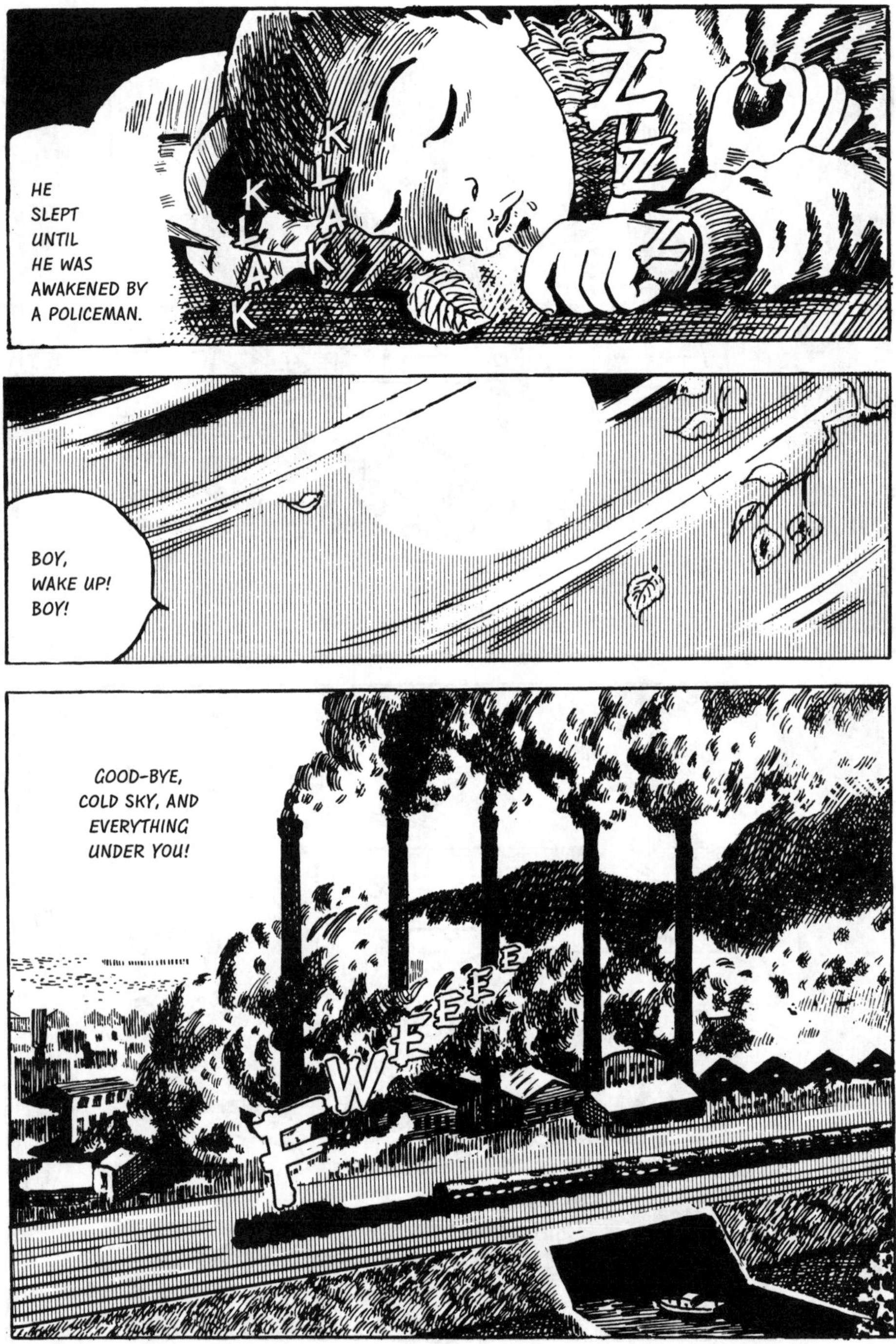
HE SLEPT UNTIL HE WAS AWAKENED BY A POLICEMAN.
KLAK
KLAK
ZZZ
BOY, WAKE UP! BOY!
GOOD-BYE, COLD SKY, AND EVERYTHING UNDER YOU!
FWEEEE

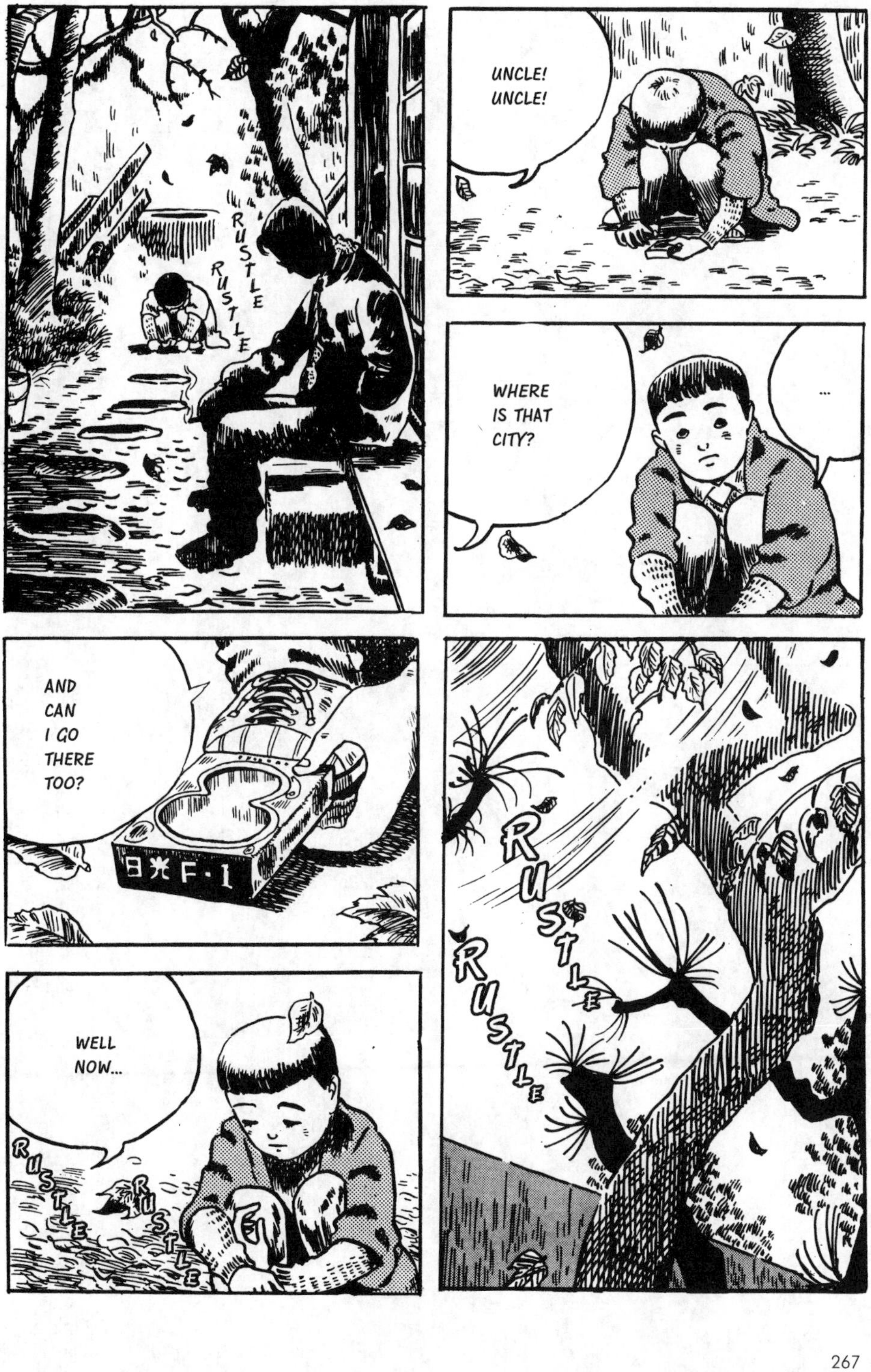
RUSTLE
RUSTLE
UNCLE!
UNCLE!
WHERE IS THAT CITY?
...
AND CAN I GO THERE TOO?
WELL NOW...
RUSTLE
RUSTLE
RUSTLE
RUSTLE

Oji Suzuki was born in 1949 in Nagoya, Japan. He moved to Tokyo in 1967 and within two years his first short stories were published in the avant-garde Japanese comics magazine *Garo*. Throughout the 1970s and 1980s, at least ten collections of his short stories were published. Suzuki has also produced short films and has written and drawn children's books.

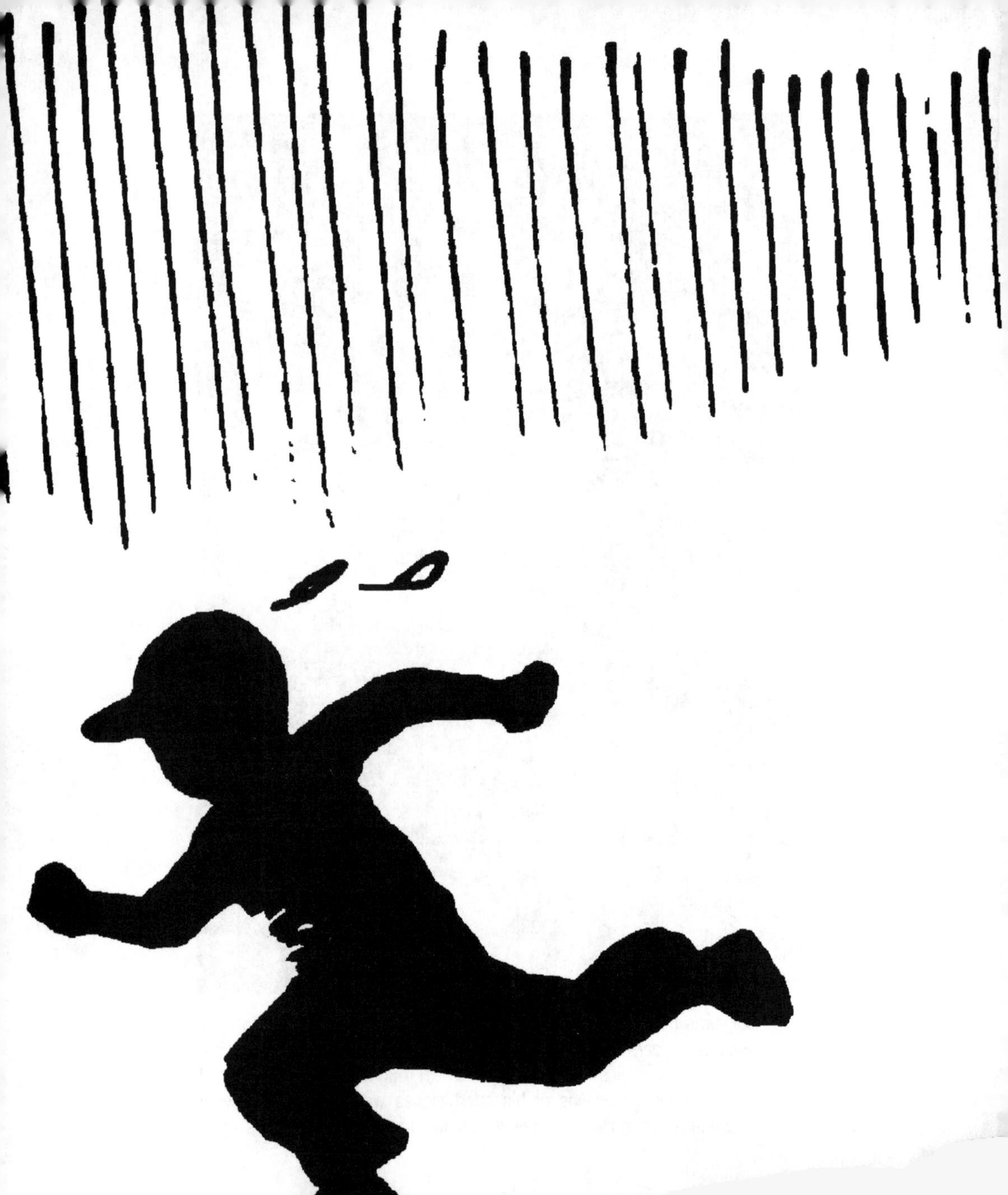

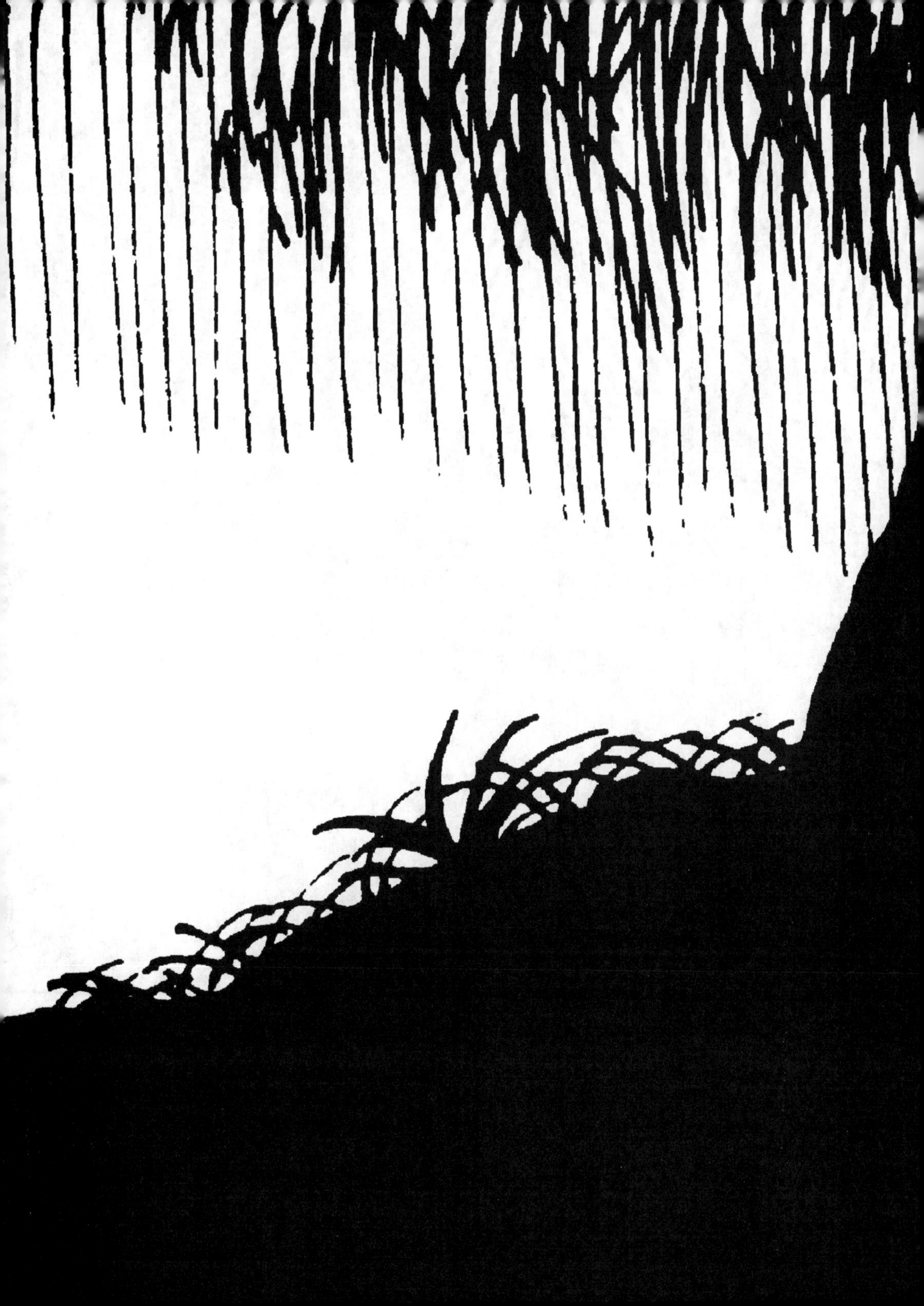

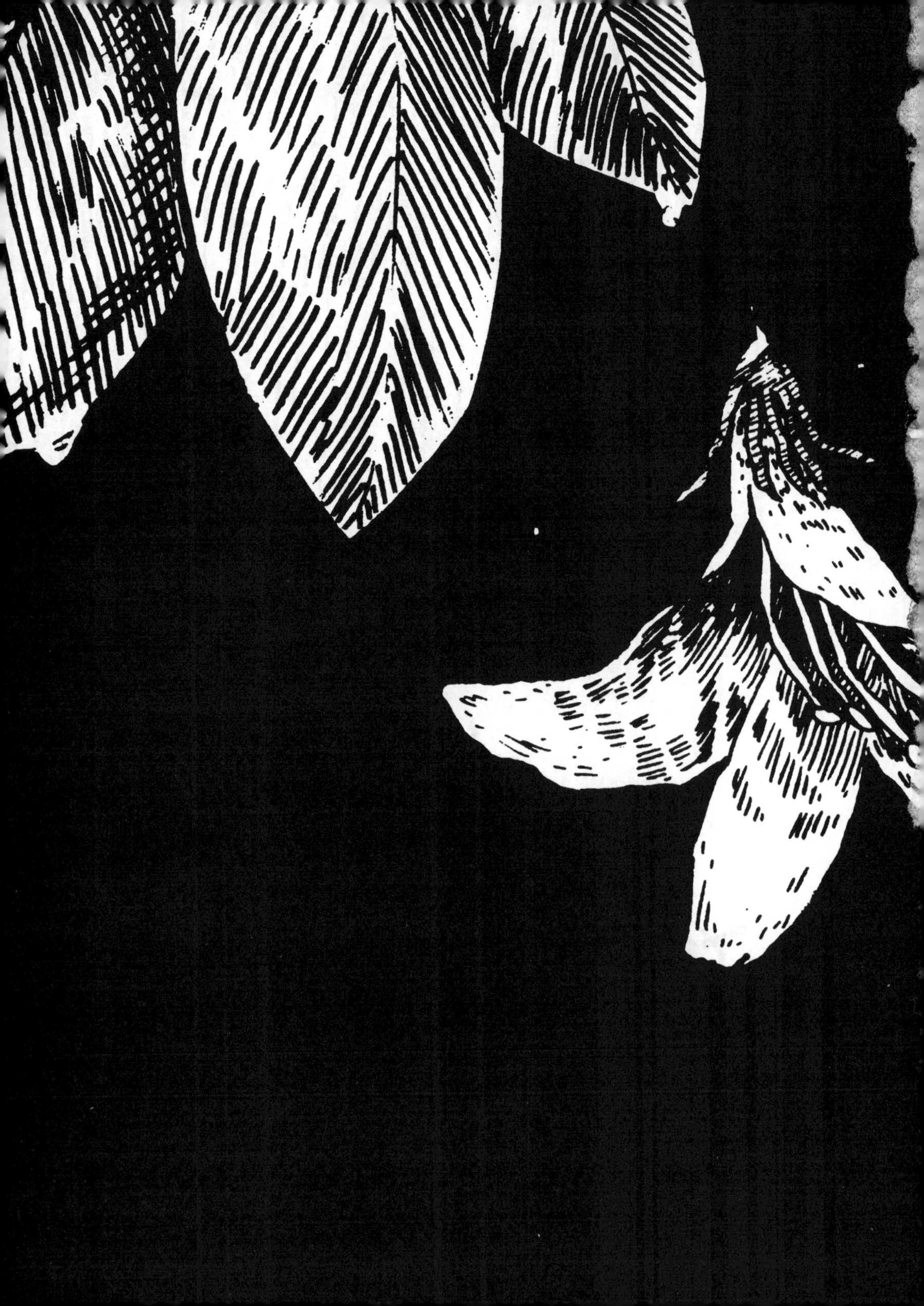

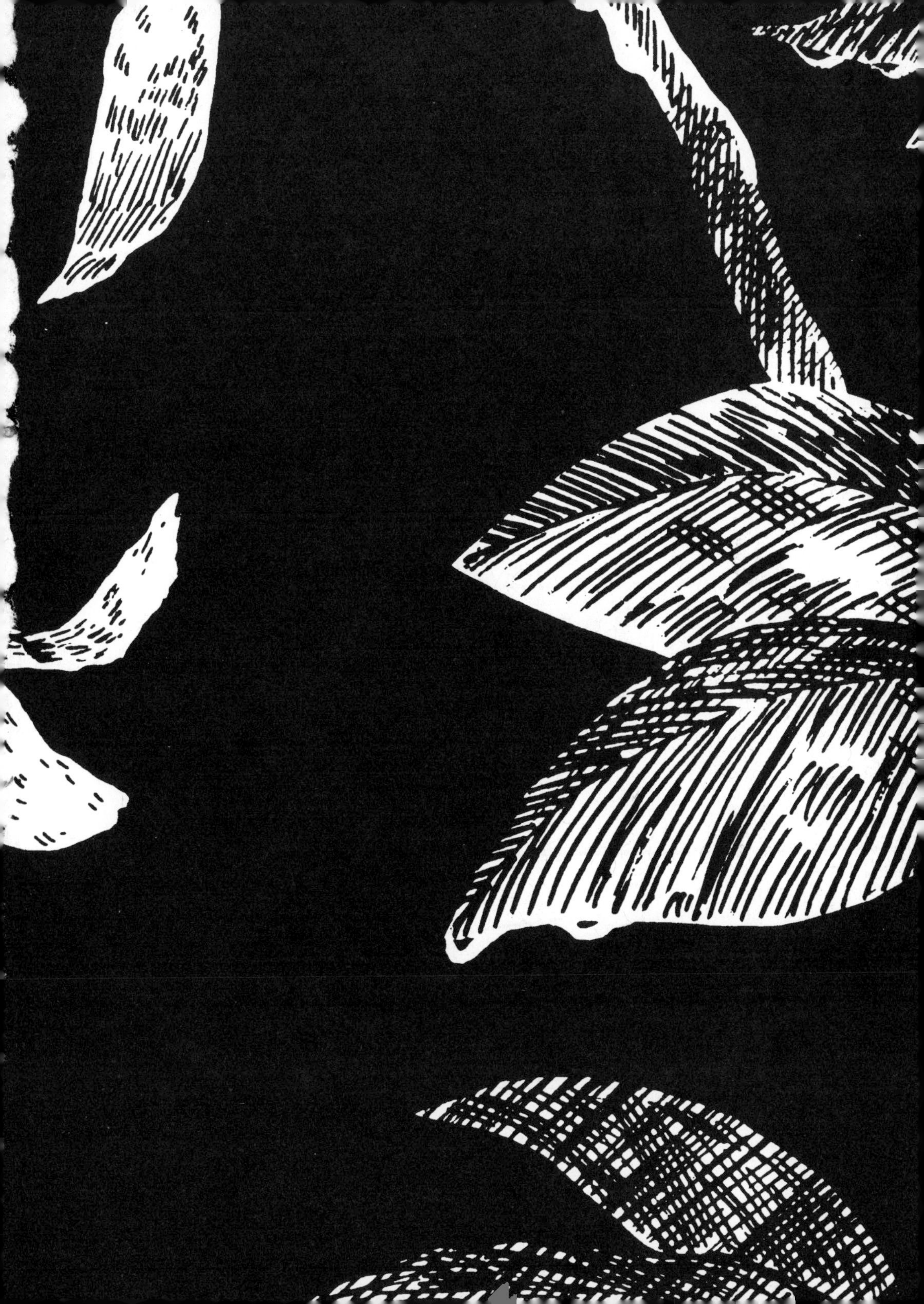

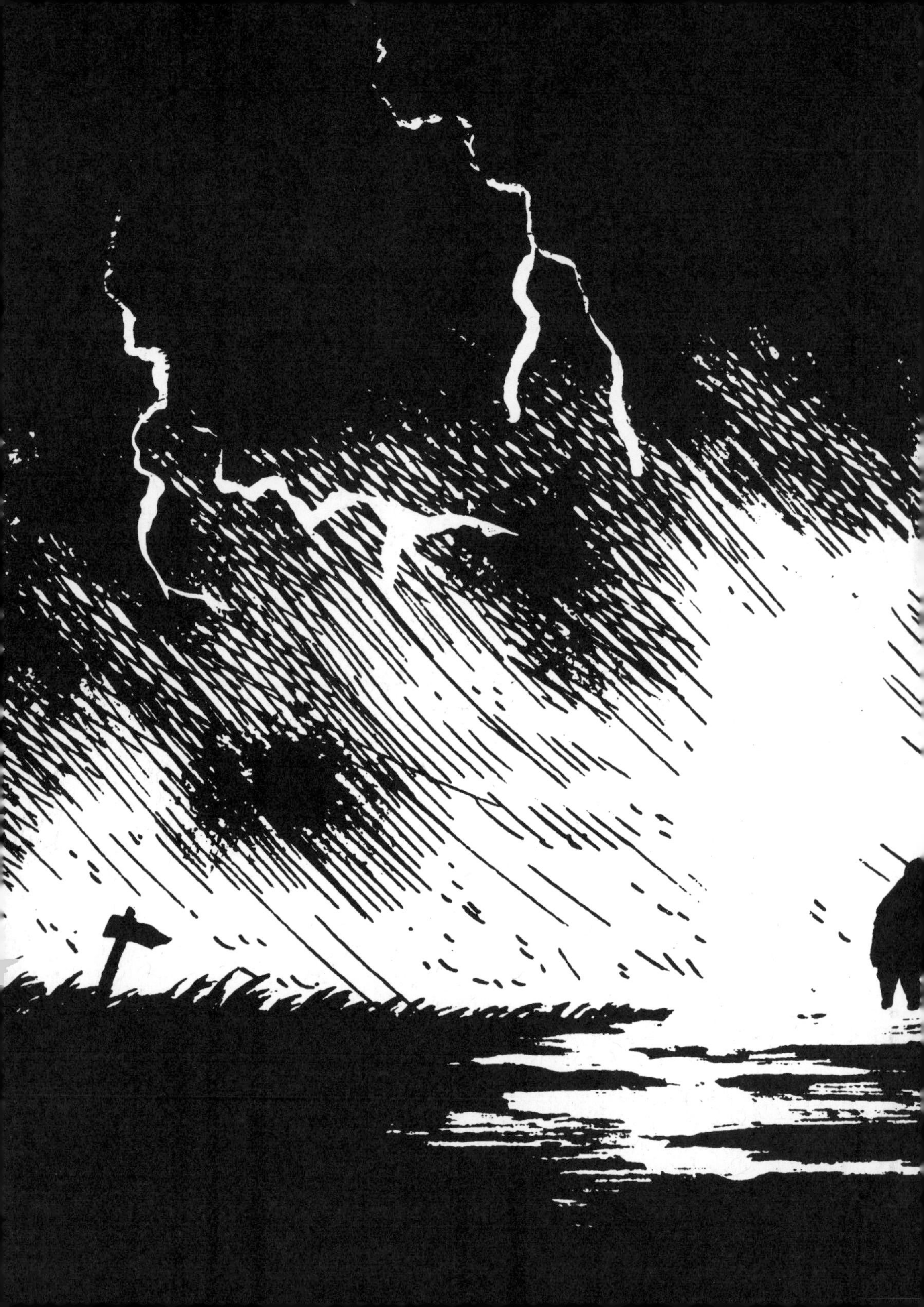